The Untold Forgotten Great Civilization of the People of Ham

Vansworth McKenzie

The Untold Forgotten Great Civilization of the People of Ham

ISBN: 978-1-956884-23-4
4th edition
ALL EDITING BY Vanworth McKenzie
Book Cover Design: Ramona (Cassey) Parker

Printed in the United States of America
Published by Imprint Productions Inc.
Finale Edition 2023

Contact

imprintproductionsinc@gmail.com / (678) 860 - 6237

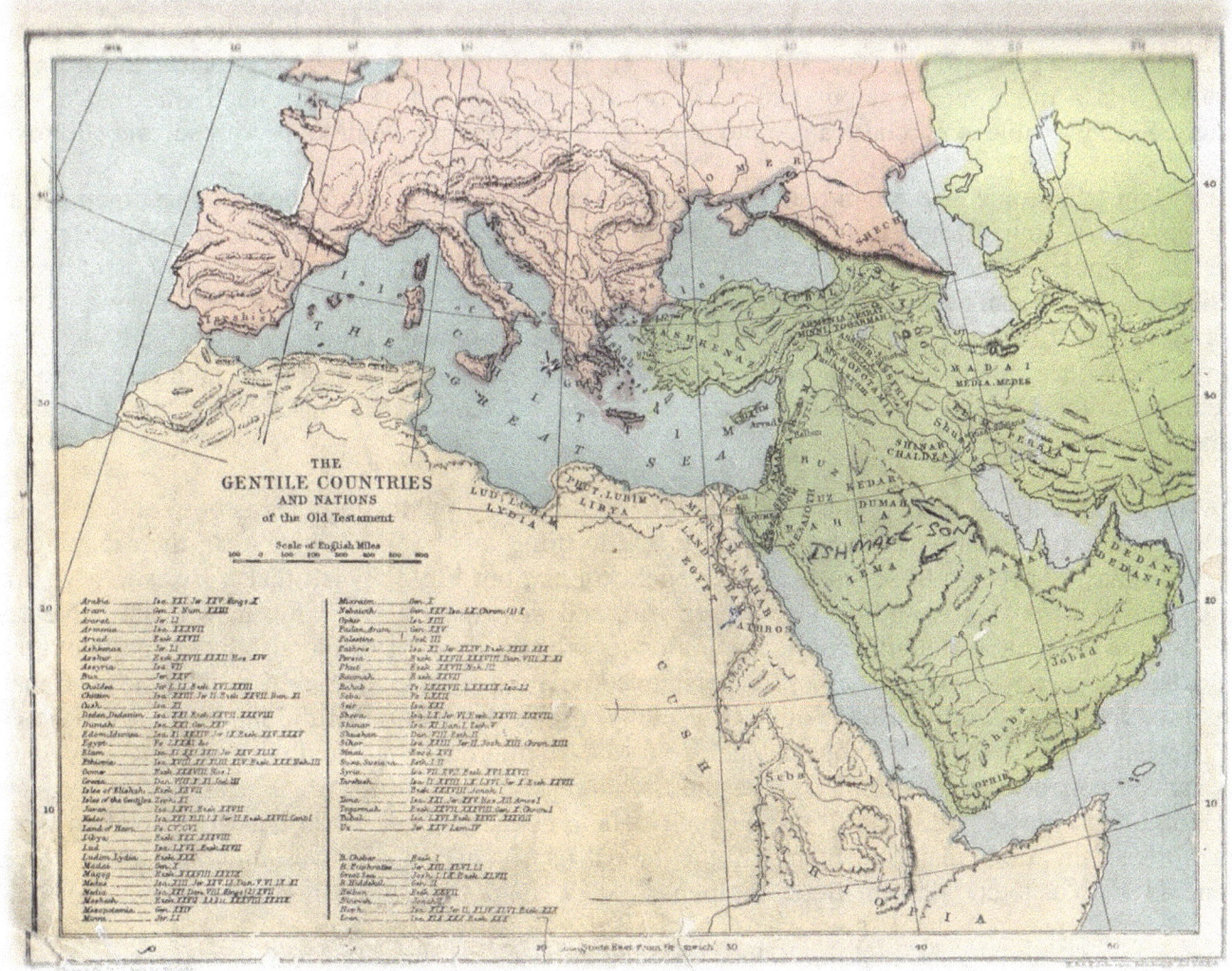

The Untold Forgotten Great Civilization of the People of Ham

I would like the readers of this book to know that this is a third revive version of the same book that came out in 2009. But due to the various errors that were made by the first publisher, and their editor, I have decided to try my best to try to straighten out the various mistakes they had made in the first edition, and to bring out the book new. This book was also published again, in 2019 by Author House publisher, but when I did received a copy of the book they had publish, and came across the amount of bad spelling, and allot of mistake they had made.

Plus they had left out the various pictures I had in the book, showing of the various people of Ham of the ancient world that gone by. So, I decided to cancel the publishing of the book with their company, and to look for another publisher, to publish the book again. I have also located another publisher I am presently working with, but after I had paid this new publisher $1700.00 as a down payment, and when I received a copy of the editing they were doing, for about three to four months, I was not satisfy with their editing. So, I decided to do the editing of the book myself, and to send back the book to the publisher, when I am finished with the editing. I do hope this publisher I am now working with, may do a better job in the publishing of the book, more than that of the other two publishers I did used before. Many Hamite's people who may read a copy of this book when it is published again, have no idea of the amount of pain, suffering, losing of money, and allot of aggravation I have been true, trying to bring out this third edition of this book to light, to benefit many Hamite's people, who might read a copy of this book. Various time working with Microsoft Office Word 365, and with other various software I was using to proofread and edit the book, where I would see the book just disappear from my sight, from my laptop, and also from my desktop computer before my very eyes. So it was just like Satan himself fighting against me, to prevent me from brining out this third edition of this book to light. It was a good thing, my daughter encourage me to purchase an Apple Mac computer to work on the book, because according to what I was told, it is a more safer computer to work on my document, more than that of the rest of the other computers. So, I was able to purchase an Apple Mack Air, I am presently using to proofread, and edit my book.

So, many Hamite's people who might read a copy of this book, do not have any idea of the amount of sabotage, and the amount of money I have lost, trying to bring out this book to light. This was to benefit the minds of many Hamite's people world wide, who do not have any knowledge of their great civilization, and history they, and their ancestors is coming from. This were way before colonialism, and slavery, and the many indoctrination we has a people of Ham, had receive from our Gentile European slavers master, and also from the Mohammedan Muslim people of what became known as the Saudi Arabia people of Ishmael. Who also had enslave many of their Hamite's captives, to become followers of Mohammed, and the worship of his god Allah, as a way of life for them to follow.

I also want to explain that many times I felt like giving up on the publishing of this book, because of all the aggravation, pain, and sorrows I have been true trying to bring this book to light. Also, the sabotage, and the amount of money I have lost trying to bring this book to light, but I told myself that if I was to give up on the publishing of this book, it would be very ungrateful, and disrespectful to Yahweh, who has given me this knowledge, and the enlightenment, and the inspiration to write this book. I would also like to point out that what is now called as the Middle East, is a part of Persia we know today as Iran, as well as the land of Canaan, and what is now known as North Africa. Which is a totally a false description of the land area, they the Gentiles people of what is now known as Europeans, named as the Middle East, Asia and what became known as North Aprica, by the conquest of the Romans. (See the Scripture Map of 1890), showing on the book cover of the Untold Forgotten Great Civilization of the people of Ham, of the ancient world that gone by. Showing of the ancient world of that time, that did began with the three sons of Noah, their wives, and their many descendants that came down to us today, after the flood of Noah.

So, there were no Middle East, or Middle Eastern people during the time of Noah, Shem, Ham, Japheth, and their many descendants who have populated the earth of the different people of today. Sad to say that many people of the so-call Middle East, of the land of Canaan, and what became known as North Africa, is a total washout people, that is mixed up with the blood of the Persians, Greeks, Romans, Turks, and with that of the rest of the Gentile family, who came from out of the breakup of the Roman Empire. They have establish, their empire of ruler ship, over the so-call Middle East, and what became known as North Africa, and they have also, left their many offspring's behind as the new natives of the land of Ham, and Canaan, many people see in the land area of today, as the new natives, of what they named as the Middle East, and the Middle Eastern people. So, this terminology as the Middle Eastern people, it is a false name, and a false identity of the geographical land area, they the Gentile people of Europe name as the Middle East, and the Middle Eastern people. I must also point out that there was no Middle East, or Middle Eastern people of the ancient world that gone by.

Acknowledgments

Thanks be to Yahweh for bringing all these hidden ancient histories of the knowledge of the people of Ham to light, true this book, the Untold Forgotten Great Civilization of the people of Ham, that many Hamite's people of today, and others have no knowledge of these histories, I have written about in this book. After working on this book for over thirty-five years, and going over it many times, making correction of what I have written. Also adding photographs from other history books I have read from, so from the reading of these books, I have gain much knowledge that I did not know anything of before. It did help me with the knowledge, and the understanding of the writing of this book. This is for many Hamite's people to come to a better knowledge of understanding, of the ancient world, of the people of Ham, and their history that gone by, that they do not know anything of. This is also from the internet, showing many Hamite's people who were the native of what became known as East Asia, by the Gentile Europe people. Also, many other places of that area, that the ordinary people of today have no knowledge of these facts, of the people of Ham living in these areas of the world, they name as the Middle East, and Asia of their conquest.

So, these natives Hamite people of the area, of what they now named as Asia, were the true natives of the area, way before the coming of the Gentile people of Europe, of their conquest of people, and their lands, that did become their colonies. Yet had it not been for the mercies, and kindness of Yahweh, in giving me this inspiration, zeal, and the enlightenment, of the knowledge of these true histories, so as to write this book. Of the knowledge of the ancient world that gone by, that did help to bring in the modern world, of the people of Europe of today. So, as to bring to light of this true knowledge, of the ancient world of the people of Ham, to the minds of many Hamite's people of today. Many of whom do not have any knowledge, and understanding of this true history I have written about that gone by. I have written about these things, so as to bring to light of knowledge, to many Hamite's people minds of today, many of whom do not have any knowledge of their history, I have written about in this book.

Yahweh as also put many things within my spirit, which did help me to proceed with the writing of this book, of light, and knowledge, otherwise, it would have never come into existence. The Scripture Map of 1890, showing on the book cover of the Untold Forgotten Great Civilization of the people of Ham, did show the land area of the ancient world, that was stated with the people of Ham, that did begin from the area of the Mediterranean, they the Gentile people of what is now known as European, name as the Middle East, and the Middle Eastern people. Also, what become known as North Aprica, which this name Aprica came from the Romans, when they were able to defeat the Carthaginian army of the people of Ham. That did become known as North Aprica, of their conquest, and ruler ship over the people of Ham, of the ancient world that gone by. This word Aprica later became known as North Africa, by the Angles, and Saxon Germanic people of Europe, who were under Roman captives of slavery, and colonialism. Who they also had gotten their education of reading, writing, and arithmetic from. Also from the Roman Catholic Church, that they did not know anything of before the conquest of   the   Romans. Later when these Angles and Saxon Germanic people became literate people, able to read and write for themselves, then they put an f into this Latin word Aprica, that became known as Africa, rather than the way the Romans had spell the word Aprica. The Scripture Map of 1890, also shows the different land areas of the various sons, and grandchildren of the people of Ham, who gave birth to what the people of Europe, did called as the Middle Eastern, and the Middle East, people. As well as what they called as the North African, East African, and what is now known as the South African people. Many of this information of these histories I have written about in this book, were not mentioned in the first edition of the book that came out in 2009, this is my reason for incorporating some of these books I have written before, into this new book, to benefit many of the readers of this new edition I am presently bringing out. To give one a good idea of how much Yahweh had me in mind of the writing of this book, I can remember sometime in the latter part of 1970, while I was working in the New Jersey area of Union, at an Auto body shop, l lost the job because they said I was too slow a worker.

The reason why they had considered me as a slow worker, it is because when I was working in London, I use to work on very expensive cars, and everything had to come out perfect. So, coming to work in the United States, where everything was quite different from the way it were in London, because many things in the United States is based upon mask production, and speed, to make more money, to get rich. So, because of the way I used to work in London, I could not keep any job for a long period of time, because they said I was too slow a worker. After I had lost the job in Union, while I was driving along a thought came into my mind, telling me to drive over the bridge I was passing by, and forget about life, and the disappointments that come with life. While this thought came into my mind, out of the blue, a little voice spoke to me, and said, "what about the book"? At the time when this little voice spoke with me, I had no intention of writing any book, I did not actually begin the writing this book until sometime in 1990. I must also point out that I did not have any foreknowledge of any of these histories I have written about in this book during the period. Please allow me to bring in my early childhood background into focus, I left school in Jamaica at the age of ten years old, because I did not have all the nice fine clothing to keep on going to school. Although I was a very bright student.

The way it was when I was growing up in Jamaica, as a little boy, going to school in the Kingston area of Jamaica, if one did not have all the nice closing, looking good going to school, many of the other children would not favor that other student very much. Who were looking kind a raggedy, going to school. Technically speaking, he or she would be discriminated against by the other children at the school, because he or she did not have all the nice closing to put on to go to school. Such it was in my case, when I was going to school in the Kingston area, barefooted, without any shoes, and did not have all the fine nice closing to put on going to school. So, I could not cope with that kind of mentality, and the kind of attitude, many of the other students had toward me at the time. So, I decided to drop out of school, rather than having to go true such bad experiences every day, I could not cope with. One must realize that many of the Hamite's people of the island of Jamaica, has a British slavery mentality, of who they see as the high class, and the low-class people.

Many of whom came from out of the slavery experience their ancestors before them went true, who were not able to left any form of wealth for their many off springs, after they did pass off from the seen of life. So, if a person did not have all the nice fine closing, looking good going to school, he or she would literally be scorn, and look down on as the lower-class people, and the ghetto people, they the other student detests. Although many of the other students themselves came from out of poor homes, but many of them were in better off position than myself. Many Hamite's people of Jamaica who had classified themselves to be educated people, because they had some form of reading, and writing skills, they had learn from their Gentile Europeans teachers, did not know anything about these histories I have written about in this book. Much of this knowledge of these histories I have written about, were written for the benefit of the Gentile people of Europe, because they were writing to each other, and they did not have us in mind and though at whatsoever.

This knowledge of these history were not available to many Hamite's people of Jamaica during those time when I was going to school during the early fifties. My reason for saying this is, one must realize that many of the history's books I have written from, were written from the 14th to the 19th hundreds, when many Hamite's people of that time were in slavery, and they were not permitted to go to school to learn to read, or to write in any of the Gentile people language of Europe, whom they were enslave by. I must also point out that, if any slaves of that time, were even given the chance to get any form of schooling, they were only schools, from a Gentile European standpoint, to see things from their way. This is according to what they wanted them to know, and to understand from their point a view only. By so doing, many Hamite's people way after slavery was abolish, to our present time, were only schools from a European stand point, for them to see themselves as educated people. From what little chance that were given to some of us, by our Gentile European slaver masters, for us to see ourselves as educated people, from what they wanted us to know. I must point out that according to the Webster's Collegiate Dictionary of the Fifth Edition, the dictionary explain that the word educated, do not mean in the way many people were thought in the various schooling system of the people of Europe, for their many captives to see themselves, as educated people.

This is according to what they wanted us to know, and to see things from their point a view as the educated people, from the little chance that were given to some of us, by our Gentile slave masters, for us to see things their way. So, according to the Webster's Collegiate Dictionary of the Fifth Edition, there it explained that the word educated, was taken from the Latin word educatus. This word educatus from the Latin people point a view, of the people of Rome, was to bring up a child, mentally, and morally, so as to cultivate, as a form of discipline, to take them true life, to respect other people. This word educated that were taken from this Latin word educatus, also mean to be able to read and write, to gain knowledge of the way we as people art to live our lives to please Yahweh from day to day. In taken knowledge from His Word the Scripture, that it may go well with us, if we were to choose to live, and go by His Word, the Scripture. While He allow us to keep on living here on this earth, before the final day of His wrath come, where everyone must give an account of themselves, before His judgment seat, and that of Yashua. So, this word educated is used very loosely in this European colonial world of today, of their schooling system for us their many captives people who were able to attend their institution to see things their way. This was for their many students who attend these institution to see themselves as educated people from the Gentile European people point a view, of what they want them to know. These institution of their schooling system, were design to make money, from their various students who were able to attend these institution. Otherwise, these students would not be there in there in the first place, because these institution were design to make money from their various students, who were able to attend these institution.

So, this word educated also mean to taking knowledge from the Word of Yahweh, of what become known as the Scripture, that it may go well with us, if we was to chose to do so. (There in Proverbs Chapter 1, and verse 7,) the verse went on to say, the fear of Yahweh is the beginning of knowledge, but foolish people despise this fear of the knowledge, wisdom, and instruction of Yahweh. It is also written in (Proverbs Chapter 3, and verse 1), where the Scripture mention, by saying, my son forget not my laws, but let your heart keep my commandments: for length of days, and long life, and peace, shall they add to you.

Also let not mercy and truth forsake you: bind them around your neck, and write them upon the table of your heart, so will you find favor, and good understanding in the sight of Yahweh, and man. It is also mentioned in (Proverbs Chapter 4, and verse 5), where the Scripture mention, get wisdom, get knowledge, and get understanding, and forget it not. Neither move away from the Words of Yahweh, for wisdom is the principal thing; therefore, get wisdom: and with all you're, getting, get understanding. It is also written in (Ecclesiastes Chapter 12, reading from verse 1), there the Scripture went on to say, remember now your Creator in the days of your youth, while the evil days come not, nor the ears draw near, when you shalt say I have no pleasure in them. So, the only way a man can remember his Creator, is to be able to read and write, and to taking knowledge from His Word the Scripture, which is the book of life, knowledge, wisdom, and death, which we all have to face, and answer to Yahweh, when that time come. When I was growing up in Jamaica in the fifties, all the books that were used in the school systems, were sent from Britain, or if it was made in Jamaica, it was made, and design under the British system, of their ruler ship, for us to learn what they want us to know, and to understand exclusively from their point of view only.

I could remember when I was going to school in Jamaica; there was a book that were taught in my class, that were called as 'The Royal Radiant Reader. In this book, there is a story I can remember go like this, dickery dickery duck, the mouse run up the clock, the little dog laugh to see such a fun, and the dish ran away with the spoon, and the cow jump over the moon. This is the kind of slavery mentality nonsense they had thought to many of us Hamite's people of Jamaica, of those days, to see ourselves as educated people, all from their concept, as a form of their education for us people to go by. Of what they want us to know, and to see ourselves as educated people. So, all the various history books of today, whether it is the dictionaries, Encyclopaedia's, the Scriptures, and the Scripture Map of 1890, it was made, and design only, for the Gentile people of Europe benefit. Because they did not have us in mind and thoughts whatsoever. They were only writing to each other, of what they, and their forefathers had done to many nations of people, who came under their captivity of colonialism, and slavery. Also of their conquest of the world, of people, and their lands to get rich, which has made them to become rich people of today from slave labor, and their conquest of people, and their lands.

I would also like to point out that what they the Gentile people of Europe call as science and technology; did not begin with the people of Europe as how they has been teaching us their many captives to believe, and to see things to be so. So, what they name as science, and technology was started with the people of Ham, of the so-call Middle East, of the land of Canaan, and what became known as North Aprica by the Romans conquest. So, the impression they the people of Europe gave to us their many captive, is that what they name as science, and technology, were started with the people of Europe. This they has been teaching to many of us their captives, to believe, who came under their captivity, of slavery, and colonialism, that reading, writing, and arithmetic, that were known as craft, and skills by the people of Ham, came from them. These early crafts, and skills, that many of the people of Ham had develop, was from the early beginning of the human family, which did become known in the modern world of the Gentile people of Europe, as science, and technology. Yet many Hamite's people of today, who see themselves as educated people, according to what many of us their captive's people were thought to believe. Because some of us their many captives were able to attend this European schooling system, for them to learn what they wanted them to know, and for them to see themselves as educated people. So, from this little opportunity that were given to some of us Hamite's people of today, to learn to read, and write, it was many years after slavery was abolish. It was also, from a Gentile European point of view, of what they want us to know, and to see things from their point of view.

So, many Hamite's people, who were able to attend the various schooling system of the Gentile people of Europe, were only thoughts to understand things from their point of view, and no more than that. So, form this little chance of education that many Hamite's people may had received, it have help many of us, their captives, to be able to exist in their established modern world of today, that came under their colonial conquest, and ruler ship. So, as to be able to find employment, to pay rent, buy food, pay taxes, with other bills, to be able to exist in their modern colonial world, of today. So, many Hamite's people of today, who see themselves as educated people, it was from the little chance that were given to some of us, by our Gentile colonial teachers, for us to see, and to know things from their perspectives. Of what they see as right or wrong, from what they want us to know, and to believe from their philosophies.

So, from this little chance that were given to some of us, their many captives people of their schooling system, of what became known as their educational system, of the people of Europe, that many of us Hamite's people may had received. It did depend on what countries of Europe, we were enslaved, and ruled by. According to 'A Short History of the West Indies, there it explain about the island of Haiti, of how Toussaint L'Ouverture, and later Dessalines, who were former slaves, lead the uprising for their freedom from their French slave masters, which did lead to self-rule in 1804. Yet slavery were still in process for many Hamite's people, in many parts of their New World, Europe, and also in the land of Ham after 1804. According to A Short History of the West Indies' page 156, there it mentioned that the Act of the abolishment of the slave trade was put into force, on January 1st of 1808, by the British people. Also, in 1827, another Deceleration was passed by the British Government making the slave trade business, a crime of piracy punishable by death. Although Great Britain at the time were one of the biggest slave suppliers, along with the Dutch, Portuguese, Spanish, and the French. Due to the fact that they the British, was able to conquer three quarters of the world land mass from the other Gentile colonial powers of Europe, during their colonial period. They the British, become the colonial ruler of three-quarter of the world population of people, and their lands, that become their colonial empire.

Which gave them the title as Great Britain, because they were able to conquer three quarter of the world land mass, from the other Gentile European colonial rulers, and conquerors. According to A Shot History of the West Indies 'there it also mention that Denmark abolished their slave trade in 1804, this act was followed by Sweden in 1813, the Dutch in 1814, France in 1818, and the Spanish in 1820 did abolish their slave trade. Yet slavery did continue in many parts of the Gentile People New World, Europe, and also in the land of Ham itself, after the decoration was sign by the British to end the slave trade. Cuba was importing slave up to the time of 1865, and the country of Brazil that is rule, and were conquered, by the Portuguese, slavery continue even longer, before many Hamite's people were given some form of freedom by their Portuguese slave masters.

According to volume 6 of the Encyclopaedia Britannica, there it explained that the slavery plantation system of Jamaica collapsed with the abolishment of slavery in 1830, by the British. Yet many Hamite's people of Jamaica at the time, following up to the 1830, were still in some form of slavery, struggling to make ends meet from the little pennies they may had received, as wages from their former slave masters, who became their new bosses. I could remember when I was growing up in the fifties, in the Kingston area of Jamaica, there were many domestically workers, who used to work for five Shilling per week, in the British money system, and they had to pay room rent from out of this little five Shilling per week. So, as to have some where to rest their heads. Even from the time of the 1920th, leading up to the 1950, many Hamite's people were discriminated against, in the areas of schooling, and employment. So, many Hamite's people of Jamaica who had seen themselves as free people, were only poor struggling people. Trying to exist in the Gentile People of Europe New World of their system, of their exploitation they had established true slavery, and colonialism to get rich. So, from day to day, from an economical stand point of pressure, they put on many of us, their free slave people of today, who became their citizens, so as to bring in extra revenue into their system of exploitation.

By paying taxes, police tickets, paying rent, with all sorts of court fees, for them to make money from their many free slaves captive's people, who became their citizens. I must say that I am very glad, I did not have the ability, of their schooling, to attend any of their college, or any of their university, of their higher learning, of the Gentile people of Europe schooling system. That came down from the slavery system, to our present time, because f I did, probably today I would have been a strong believer in the evolution theory of Charles Darwin. Also, a believer of Mother Nature, of what they the Gentile People of Europe, has been teaching to the world of people, who came under their colonial captivity of slavery, to believe in this idolatry belief of Mother Nature, who they say created this or that. Also, of what they the scientist say, and their philosophies of their teaching as facts, with that of what the archeologist says, more than what is written, and taught in the Scripture of truth. Which is the book of life, and death that many of the so-call educated people of today, do not believe in what is written in the Scripture, because of the teaching they did received from these men, who see themselves as men of knowledge.

Who know how this or that came about, as how many of them profess to be of today, because the Scripture teaching do not blend with that of the scientists, and with that of the archeologist, of the ways they see things. So, from their vain modern philosophies, of one million, or ten million years ago, this was, and that was, when none of these men were around in one, or ten million years ago, to know what was. But they only came up with these teaching of theirs, to deceive many people who came under the captivity of the Gentile family, of what became known as Europe for them to see things their way. Many of whom see themselves as the wise men of today, who many people look up to these men of knowledge, who know how this or that came about 10 million, or one billion years ago. I must point out that the Word of Yahweh is what became known as the Scripture, and it were only given to the children of Israel, as a guideline of education for them to live by. This was for them to live, and to walk in the fare, and knowledge of Yahweh, to save them from the destruction, and the wrath of Yahweh of Himself. This was also to save them from idolatry worship, of devilism, and which craft, that were, so common in what became known as the Middle East, and North Africa, of those days. So, what became known as Christianity, was spread around the world by way of these Gentile people, and their conquest of people, and their lands of slavery, to get rich. They the Gentile people of Europe, has brainwash many of us their many captives, to believe in what, they put a label on, that became known as Christianity, of Roman Catholicism.

This was from the Roman Catholic Church, where many of their teaching, and belief came down from, which were of paganism, and idolatry worship to their many gods, and goddess. So, the Way of the teaching of Yashua became known as Christianity, by the Gentile people of Europe, in the city of Antioch, of the Turkey area of Europe, with their deception, to conquer many people, and their lands to get rich. This teaching, and knowledge of the Scripture, did not come from the people of Europe, but this teaching of the Scripture, came from Yahweh to Yashua, and his Apostles, of the children of Israel. This was to teach other believers, how they must live their lives, to please Yahweh, and Yashua, who is our King and Master.

This Christianity teaching of the Gentile people of Europe, were to control the world of people, who came under their captivity, with corruption, immorality, and their philosophy of what they think life should be like. As how it is in our modern colonial world, of today, by the Gentile people of Europe, of their conquest of people, and their lands to get rich. The fact is this, the Scripture that become known as the Bible, were only given to the ancient children of Israel, when Yahweh take them by the hands, to lead them from out of the land of Mizraim, that become known as Egypt, by the hand of Moses. Yahweh also gave them His Commandment, His name, and His Laws that were known as the Scroll, that later become known as the Scripture, which mean writings, for them to live by, that it may go well with them, if were to chose to live by His Words. This writing of the Scripture later became known as the Bible, by the Greeks, translators of Europe, which meant, a book. So, the reason why they the Gentile people of Europe were given the opportunity to translate the Scripture, that became known as the Bible. It is, because as it so written, in (Isaiah Chapter 60), and verse 3, that the Gentile people of what is now known as Europeans people, were going to come to the light of the knowledge, and the writing of the children of Israel. So, this is the reason why the Scripture that, became known as the Bible, were translated by the various Gentile translators of Europe. This was to fulfill the prophecy that was mentioned. So, it is because the word of Yahweh must come to pass, as our Lord Yashua mentioned, that the prophecy of the Scripture cannot be broken. So, whatever Yahweh had said, it is seal, and down away with, and no man can take from what Yahweh as said, unless of course, Yahweh change His own mind, which He sell dem do.

So, when these Gentile European translators was expose to the writing of the Scripture of the children of Israel, as it was so prophesy, then they came up with their Cannon laws of deceptions of their rules, and regulation, to their many church members. Also, of their many mistakes by the Ecclesiastic bishops, and Popes, that did become known as Christianity, to the minds of their many conquered people. Who came under their captivity of ruler ship, to see things their way. So, if one should read the Scripture in it totality, one would see that all the various deity's, of the people of Europe were translated as gods, with a common g. All these dates of the people of Europe was given names by their worshipers of that time.
But the name of Yahweh was only known by the children of Israel, because of the faith of Abraham, who is the father of the Israelites people. Who also were a friend of Yahweh, to whom Yahweh reveals Himself to only, because Abraham did obey His voice, and please Him well. Yet they the Israelites people of Jacob, were given many privileges, and chances, in comparison to many of the early Hamite's kingdoms of the area, whom Yahweh had destroyed, because He was not please of their doings, and wickedness, of idolatry worship, and that of which craft that Yahweh were not please of. Many Hamite's people, and their kingdoms were also destroyed for the children of Israel, and for other Abrahamic seeds. Moreover, no one can question the authority, and the doings of Yahweh, of how they see it, whether it is right, or wrong in their eyes. Because Yahweh is the boss of life, and He do what pleases Him, and that is the reality of life, whether we like it or not. They the Israelites people of Jacob, and the Gentile people, along with many of the people of Shem, of what is known today as Asia. Were given the opportunities to take over from where the Hamite's people, and their kingdoms left off, that were destroyed. That did add to the advancement of the Gentile people, and that of the Asiatic people of Shem, of the so-call Asia. So, from these destroyed kingdoms, and civilization of the people of Ham, gave birth to many modern technology, and civilization of today, that they the Gentile people of Europe, and the Asiatic people call as science, and technology. Which did come from the people of Ham, that were known to them as craft, and skills. From this craft, and skills of writing, reading, and arithmetic of the people of Ham, gave birth to the writing of the Scripture, by the children of Israel. That did become known as the Old, and New Covenant part of the Scripture, because they the children of Isreal mothers, came from among the many grand daughters of the people of Ham, who they were living around, in the so-call Middle East, and what became known as North Africa.

This writing of the Scripture, were by the prophets, and that of the apostles of Yashua, of the children of Israel. Also, this writing of the Apostles did become known as the New Testament by the the Gentile European people of Greece, and that of the Romans. Also, by other Gentile people of Europe, who came from out of the Greek, and Roman conquest. This writing of the New Covenant Law, were to serve as a guideline to other believers, of how they must live their lives to please Yahweh and Yashua.

This is from day to day, to save those who believe, and keep the commandment, of the New Covenant Law of Yahweh, from the wrath, and destruction of Yahweh that is to come on this world of today. This will come on all the UN Yahweh like people, who do not live their lives by the teaching of the Scripture, to please Yahweh, and our Lord Yashua. This Old Covenant Law, Yahweh did gave to the ancient children of Israel, were replace by the New Covenant Law, Yahweh did give to Yashua, to teach the people of Israel, those who did believe, from their sin, and death. Roman Catholicism of the Roman Catholic Church, has brought into the Scripture, that did become known as the Bible, their religious law (Canon) that was to govern their convert of Roman Catholicism., of their does, and don't. So this Law Cannon were to govern their many church members life, who were ruled, and govern by the Ecclesiastical body of the Popes, priests, and Bishops, of how they must live their lives to please the church, and to pay their tide, and offerings to the church. Roman Catholicism, from where the name 'Christianity' sprang from, that was previously known as 'the Way. Speaking of Yashua, who was the Way, to the people of Isreal to the Father, many of who did believe, from the wrath of Yahweh. So, these laws of Roman Catholicism did not come from the writing of the Scripture, that was only given to the ancient children of Israel only, for them to live their lives by, to please Yahweh. As a guide line that became today as religious church doctrines, by the Roman Catholic Church, of the people of Europe.

Yet many Hamite's people of Jamaica, who had seen themselves as educated people, fom what they were thought by their Gentile European teachers, have no knowledge of these ancient histories of the people of Ham I have written about in this book. This writing of mine, is to give enlightenment, and knowledge to many of Hamite's people minds of today. Many of whom are in total darkness, and ignorance of these knowledge, and history I have written about in this book. It was a good thing I went to live in London, and went to night school there, because I were a lover of the reading of the Scripture, and various other history books, I came across, to gain knowledge from, what I have read. It did instill in me the desire to share these findings of mine, in my own words, so as to benefit many of the people of Ham worldwide, of today. As, well as other people at large, who do not have any idea of this knowledge, of this history I have written about in this book.

When I was growing up in London, I was always searching the Scripture, to gain some knowledge of understanding, of where we as a people of Ham came from. Before slavery, and colonialism was imposed on us as a people, that have cost us not to know who we are, and where we are coming from. Yet, when I was attending night school in London, which I did not spend allot of years going to this night school where I was attending, and I did not graduate from of this night school in London. I must also point out that I did not have any foreknowledge of these histories, I have written about in this book, while I was attending night school in London. Matter of fact, I dough it very much, if any of those teachers at the night school where I was attending, had any knowledge of these histories I have written about in this book. All of my awareness, and enlightenment of the writing of this book, I have done, was from the Scripture, the Encyclopaedia's, and other histories books that were written for the benefits of the Gentile people of Europe alone. Because they were writing to each other, and they did not have us in thought, and mind whatsoever, because they did not thought we as a people had any civilizations, and history. This knowledge of enlightenment I came to, fell from off their tables into my hands, of the doing of the Gentile people, along with their forefather's doings, from the fourteen to the eighteen hundred, and beyond. That has brought riches, and glory to the people of Europe, from slave labor, and from their conquest of people lands to get rich.

So, from these histories 'books of theirs, it has help me to write this book, and to gain the knowledge that I have come to. Also, this knowledge of the writing this book came from my many experiences living in different Gentile countries of Europe, as well as living in their captured lands, of what become known as the United

States, living for over fifty years. It has helped me to sit down, and to observe the laws, and the regulations, and the various doings of these Gentile people of the United States, toward many of their Hamite's captives, who became their citizens, and pray. Also, to that of many other people, who came under the captivity of the Gentile people of Europe, of their colonies. I have engrafted some of these observations of the doing of these Gentile European conquerors, of what became known as the United States, over their many captives, who become their citizens, and pray of their ruler ship. Still for all, I did not have any fore knowledge of these histories I have written about in this book, until the various dreams I had, before I went to the Kingdom Hall of Jehovah Witness.

Also, after I left from attending the Kingdom Hall of Jehovah Witness, I had a dream telling me, that a new congregation were formed, and I became an elder, that I have mentioned in what I have call as my own testimony, of my experiences of attending the Jehovah Witness Kingdom Hall, in page 456 of this book, the Untold Forgotten Great Civilization of the people of Ham. So, after this dream I had, after leaving the Jehovah Witness Kingdom Hall, I began to write about twenty books or so. But many of these books I have written, is not publish as yet, because it would take a lot of money I do not have, to pay to different ones to proof read, and edit for me, and also to have these books to be published. This is the reason, why I have incorporated some of these books I have written, into this new update version of this same book, of 2009, I am presently working, on to benefit many people who might read a copy of this book. I would have loved to publish the rest of these other books I have written, but again, I do not have the money to do so, and I do not know if I will live long enough to acquire enough resources to bring out the rest of these additional books. Informative histories, such as the wars like people of Greece, who become known as the Greek people of Japheth, and the complete history about the Romans. The Hamite's people who are living in the island that become known as Jamaica, also the history of the island of Barbados, and the Spanish Era, by way of Columbus of 1492.

The Spanish, and the Portuguese who had the New World all to themselves, for over one hundred years, before the coming of the other Gentile pirates of Europe, who came, and fourth the Spanish, and stole colonies from the Spanish, they did established, as their colonies of the New World. Also, a book that is called the Hamite's people who are living in what become known as the United States, and a book that is called the Persians. Many of these histories I written about, were referenced taken from 'History of the West Indian People, book 2. Also, from 'A Short History of the West Indies, 'by JH Parry, Philip Sherlock, and Anthony Maingot, and from various volumes of the 'Encyclopaedia Britannica '1986 edition.

I would like to point out that my purpose of writing this book, is to give enlightenment to the minds of many Hamite's people, many of whom do not have any knowledge of their great civilization, and history, we and our ancestors is coming from. I have written about these ancient kingdoms of the people of Ham that gone by, so as to give enlightenment to the minds of many Hamite's people of today. Many of whom do not have any knowledge of these ancient kingdoms of the people of Ham, I have written a bout in this book that gone by. This is because many of these histories I have written about, is mentioned in the Old Covenant part of the Scripture, that is also showing, and mentioned on the Scripture Map of 1890. That many Hamite's people of today have no knowledge, or understanding of these histories I have written about. Many of these histories were hidden from us, Hamite's people, and the world at large, who do not have the understand of the reading of the Scripture. Many of whom also, many do not have the Scripture Map as I do, showing of the land of Ham, and his descendants of the ancient world, of that time, after the flood of Noah, and his sons. I am very glad, and thankful to Yahweh, that I am now able to write about many of these things, in my own words, so as to bring much knowledge, and understanding to the minds of many Hamite's people worldwide. This is of their grate pass, and history, they have no knowledge of. Many of whom feel very sorry for themselves, of who they are, because of the slavery, and the colonial mentality teaching, many of us had received from our Gentile European slave masters. This was for us as a people, to see ourself having no civilization, and no history.

Also, we as a people have no knowledge of our history, apart from what they the Gentile European people as been teaching us to believed, and to see things from their own concept. So, from the various false names, false history, and false identities they have given to many of us Hamite's people to go by. It has caused many Hamite's people of today, to feel deeply sorrowful of who they are, and many of whom have try their best, to run away from themselves, and to look like that of other people. Mainly the Gentile people of Europe, because many Hamite's people are a shame of who they are, because they have no knowledge of who they are, and where they are coming from.

I do hope to awaken many of them about their great past, and history that we as a people of Ham we are coming from, before slavery, and colonialism was imposed on many of us, as a people. That have cause us as a people not to know who we are, and where we are coming from. This is a part of the fulfillment of the prophecy of the Scripture, that is mention in (Luke Chapter 12, and verse 2, to verse 3), where Yashua said, for there is nothing covered that shall not be revealed, neither hid, that shall not be made known. Therefore, whatsoever he, which mean you, have spoken in the dark, shall be heard in the light. Also, whatsoever you have spoken in the ear, in the closets shall be proclaim, or to be make known upon the house top. My reason for mentioning this prophecy of the Scripture, that Yashua had spoken about, it is because they the Gentile people of Europe, have tried their absolute best, to keep us Hamite's people down in darkness. Also, in ignorance, for many centuries, not knowing all these things I have written about in this book. Although they the Gentile people of Europe, have written about many of these things themselves, and have full knowledge of these things, I have written about in this book. My reason for saying this, it is because, they the people of Europe, have translate the Scripture, that become known as the Bible, and also, the Encyclopaedias, and their various dictionaries, and have full knowledge of these histories I have written about in this book. Yet they have set out themselves to distort the history, to suite themselves, by teaching their false history of lies, as true history. They have also, corrupt many people mines of the world, who came under their colonial captivity with lies, and false history, that came from out of their own mind set. So, we as a people of Ham of today, have no knowledge, of who we are, and where we are coming from, before they had taken many of our ancestors as slave, from the land of Ham, and give us their offspring's who around today, their many false identities, and false histories, for us as a people to go by.

Also, various flags from the various slave ports, countries, and islands, where many of us were born, and raised in these lands, so as to see ourselves belonging to these places, as our native's lands. Though they have tried their absolute best, to suppress this light of knowledge of enlightenment from the minds of the people of Ham worldwide, yet Yahweh who sees in darkness, has allowed this light of knowledge to shine true these pages of this book. To benefit many of the people of Ham, who are around today.

Many of whom do not have any knowledge, of who they are, and of the great civilization we as a people are coming from as a people. Yet Yahweh as allow this light of knowledge to shine true, this written history book of mine, the Untold Forgotten Great Civilization of the people of Ham to give enlightenment to the minds of many of the people of Ham, and the world over.

The picture above were taken from Dictionary of the Bible, page 143, showing men, and women of ancient Mizraim, who became known as the Egyptians people.

The picture to the left was taken from Dictionary of the Biblc, showing a former king of ancient Mizraim, and a picture of Imotep, who is consider by the Gentile family to be the father of medicine, and what become known as doctors of today. This word doctor, was taken from the word physician, that were use by the people of Ham in the time of the ancient world. This crafts and skills, is what they the Gentile people of today, teach as medical science of technology, as if to say they were the ones, who have brought about this craft, and knowledge, that is now known as doctors, medicine, and the word science of technology, as if to say they were the ones, who have brought about this craX, and knowledge, that is now known as doctors, medicine, and the word science of today.

The picture to the left was also taken from Dictionary of the Bible, showing a palace of ancient Babylon, that was one of the former kingdoms of Nimrod, who himself was the lost son of Cush, and Cush was the first son of Ham, according to (Genesis Chapter 10, and verse 6).

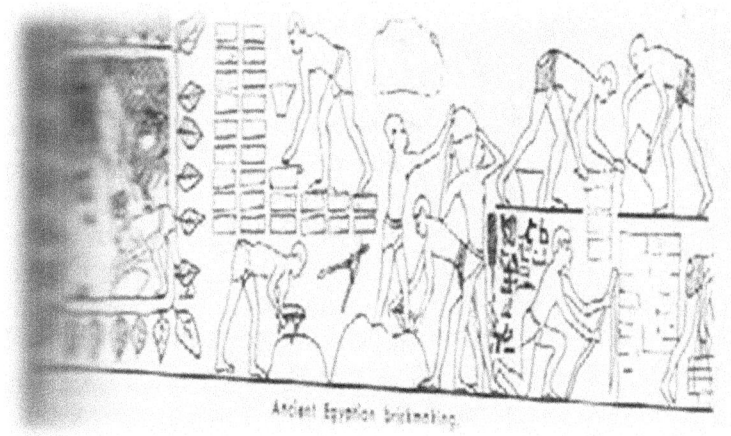

Ancient Egyptian brickmaking.

The picture above, was taken from Dictionary of the Bible, page 107, showing the people of Mizraim, who became known as Egyptian people, making bricks, and laying bricks. This knowledge, and craft of the making of bricks, and the laying bricks, were first started by the people of Mizraim, and also, by many other Hamite's tribes of the area, of what is now known as a part of the so-call Middle East, and of what became known as Europe. Also to the rest of people of the world, who came under the colonial conquest, and slavery of the Gentile people of Europe.

The picture to the left is showing furniture of ancient Mizraim, that became known as the land of the Egyptians people. That were in various people living quarters of that time, of the early civilization of mankind. This picture, was also taken from Dictionary of the Bible, written by John L. McKenzie, who himself is from the Gentile European people background, from the land of what become known as Europe. This picture, with other pictures, that is showing in Dictionary of the Bible, along with other pictures, and statues that are in the various museum, of the people of Europe, throughout their conquered world. Showing of these great craft, and skills that came from the land of Ham, and his people, that many people of today do not have any knowledge of these things, but the Gentile people of Japheth do have knowledge of these things. This is also of the great civilization of the people of Mizraim, the Assyrian, the people of Haran, that is now known as Iraq. The Babylon, the Philistines, with other great civilization, and kingdoms of the people of Ham, of the so-call Middle East, and what is now known as North Africa, that is gone by, that we as a people of Ham of today's, have no knowledge of these things.

But they the Gentile people of Europe, do have knowledge of these things, but they have try their very best, to hide these things from us, their many conquered people. This is the reason why they have these things showing in their various museums throughout the world, and also, in their various history books. Showing these things they had capture from us, the people of Ham, during their conquest of the world that came under their colonial control.

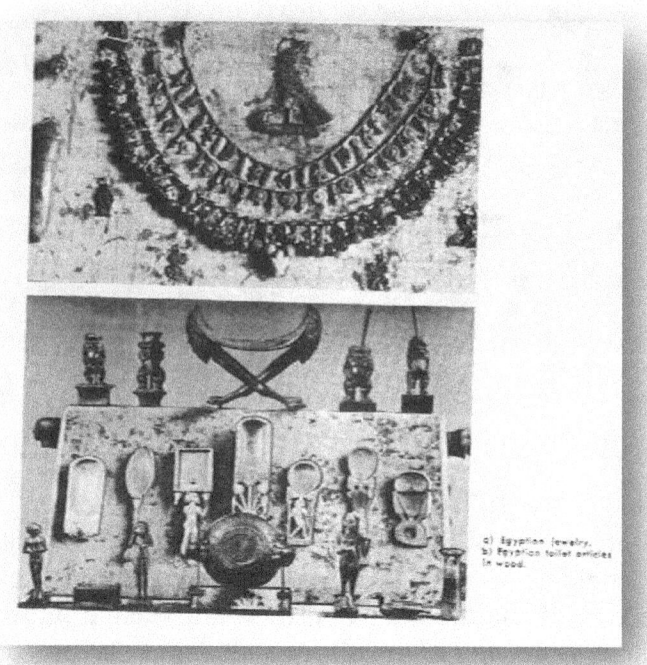

a) Egyptian jewelry.
b) Egyptian toilet articles in wood.

The picture with its jewelry is showing of the jewelry of the land of ancient Mizraim, that become known as Egypt, which were taken from Dictionary of the Bible. This art of the making of jewelry, was started way before all the modern art, of the making of jewelry, came down to the people of Europe. They had copy this art of the making of jewelry, from the people of Ham, and it became a big part of their modern technology, of the making of jewelry, of today. This picture was also taken from Dictionary of the Bible.

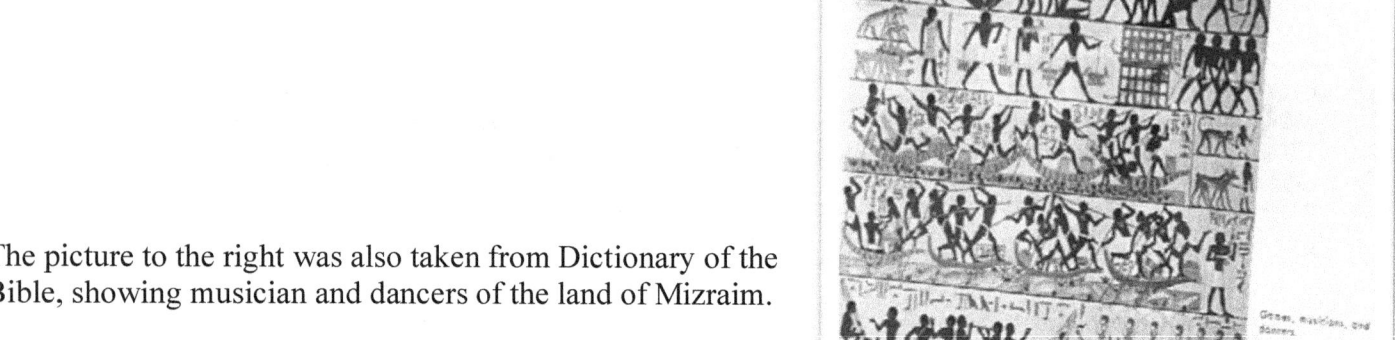

The picture to the right was also taken from Dictionary of the Bible, showing musician and dancers of the land of Mizraim.

The picture TO Left was also taken from A Political History of Tropical Africa, page 13, showing a ship of Queen, Hatshepsut's of ancient Mizraim going to a place in the land of Ham, that was known as Punt. I came to this knowledge about the land of Punt, from watching You Tube, that they say this land area of what was known as Punt, is located in the land area that is now known as Somalia.

The picture statue to left is that of Tutankhamen, who was a Pharaoh of his time of ancient Mizraim, that become known as Egypt. This picture was taken from a book called The Complete Tutankhamen, of the king tomb of his royal treasure, that was discover by Lord Carnarvon, and Howard Carter in 1922. This book is by Nicholas Reeves, and Thames & Husdson, showing of these treasures of the king.

This also another picture of King Tutankhamun of ancient Mizraim that was taken for the book, The Complete Tutankhamun.

This is also another picture of the statue of King Tutankhamen of Mizraim that became known as land of Egypt, by the Gentile Greek conquest, of Alexander the Great, and his Greek settlers, over the land of Ham, and Mizraim.

This picture to the right was also taken from the book, The Complete Tutankhamun, of his burial chamber, page 160 of the king playing what is known today as draft.

This picture to the left was also taken from the burial chamber of Tutankhamun, showing of the art, and skills and treasure of the people of Mizraim of that ancient time of the human family, that is gone by.

This also another picture, that was taken from the burial chamber of Tutankhamun, by Howard Carter, and Lord Carnarvon, when they had open the thumb of Tutankhamun.

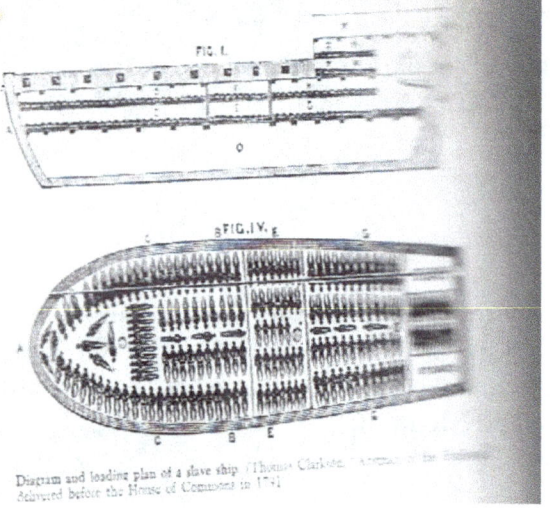

The picture to the left was also taken from A Political History of Tropical Africa, page 148, showing a slave ship that were used by the Portuguese, and other Gentile powers of what became known as European. This were to transport Hamite's slaves, who were taken as captives from the land of Ham, to wheresoever they were to be sold to the high bidder, for the right price.

The picture above was also taken from A Political History of Tropical Africa, page 11, sowing a king of the land of Cush, that become known as the land of Sudan. This knowledge I came to, is by comparing the world map of today, with that of the Scripture Map of 1890, showing the land of Cush.

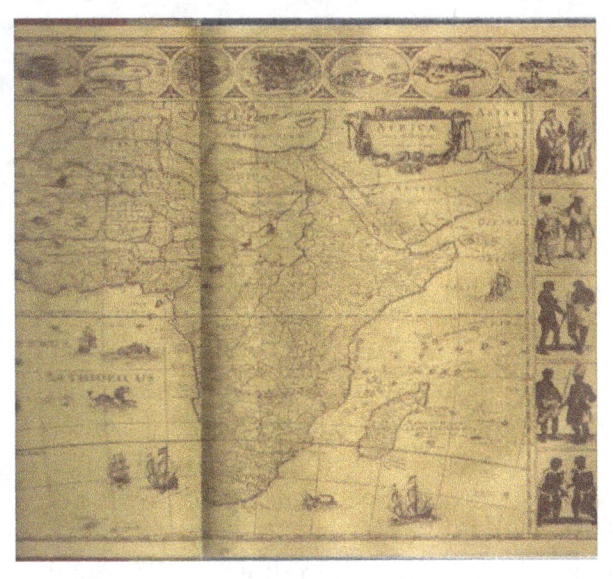

This map to the left was also taken from the book tile, A Political History of Tropical Africa, that were taken from the Grooten Atlas of 1648. Showing what they the Gentile people had called as Tropical Africa. This was during the conquest of the Portuguese, and other Gentile powers of Europe, of their conquest, and the enslavement of the people of Ham to be their empire, and their colonies. This land description was started from the Mediterranean, to the so call Middle East, all the way to what is known today as South Africa. This book was written by Robert I. Rotberg, and was publishes by Harcourt and Brace, & World.

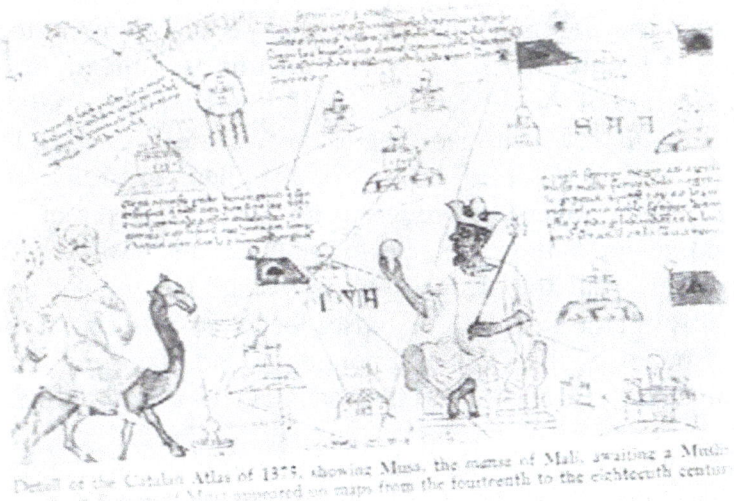

Detail of the Catalan Atlas of 1375, showing Musa, the mansa of Mali, awaiting a Mud[...] Mansa appeared on maps from the fourteenth to the eighteenth centur[...]

The picture above were taken from A Political History of Tropical Africa, showing the ancient kingdom of Mali, that were conquered and it is now ruled by the Gentile people of what become known as France.

Battles between Ethiopian Christian warriors and turbaned Muslims: in one case a Muslim, who is always seen only in profile, has evidently discarded a matchlock. F[...] in early eighteenth-century man[...]

The picture to left was taken from A Political History of Tropical Africa, showing the Ethiopian Christians, and their Muslim counterpart fighting over religious wars, that were impose on them by their Gentile colonial conquers, who dad see themselves as Christians, and Christians countries of Europe. This was also, by the Mohammedans who become known as the Muslim people, spreading their philosophy and their doctoring's of Islam, to their conquered people minds, who did became a part of their colonies of captive's people.

These philosophies of what they had call as Christianity, and Islam religious doctoring to their various captives, having them fighting among themselves over these religious doctoring that was impose on them by their conquerors, to see things their way. Which these religious belief of theirs have nothing to do with the true worshipers of Yahweh. For a true worshiper of Yahweh must be obedient to the teaching of the Scripture of truth. Which is the Laws and Commandment of Yahweh to all believers for them to lives their lives by. Especially the New Covenant part of the Scripture that was establish by Yashua before his death. This New Covenant Law was given to the Apostles of Yashua to write as the New Covent part of the Scripture, which is based upon peace and love, among all the people of Yahweh of His creation. Yashua gave these doctrines of teaching to his Apostles to write, to benefit other believers, who will apply these things to their daily lives. This was to please Yahweh, and to become a part of the family of Yahweh true Yashua His Son, in the new order of things to come. (According to Matthew Chapter 5, and verse 5), there the Scripture mention that blessed are the meek, which mean peaceable one, for they shall inherit the earth. Living under Yahweh new Kingdom order of things that is to come, where there shall be peace and tranquility. Not like how it is in this Satan tannic ruler ship that came down from the colonial slavery system of the people of Europe. So, for a person, who called themselves a follower of Yashua, that become known as Christianity by the Roman Catholic Church. They cannot be of war, fighting and killing other people, thinking to themselves that they are following the teaching of Yashua. Who are the true servant, and true worshipers of Yahweh. But they are only fooling themselves, because they are of the servant of Satan the devil, and his fallen angels, who are known in the Scripture as the demon, doing their wills. According to the Webster's Collage Dictionary, there it explained that the word meek mean mild temper humbleThis is what is called dived and conquer, they have families and friends fighting among themselves over these religious doctoring of men that were pass on down the line to them by the various colonial conquers, to their subjects, to see things their way. For them to whole on to as true gospel, because they do not have any real knowledge of the Laws and Commands of Yahweh, that became known as the Scripture, to please Yahweh and Yashua. Otherwise, they would not be fighting and killing each other, over these religious laws, and belief of their colonial conquers, and slave masters that they called as Christianity and Islam, by Mohammed and his followers to his god Allah, as a way of life for them to follow.

 I must also point out that this is the exact thing that that is taking place all over the land of Ham of today, where various families are fighting, and killing each other, some claim to be Muslim, and others claim to be Christians. These religious doctrines that these people were given to hold on to, has nothing to do with the true worshipers of Yahweh. Those who are following the teaching and the law of Yashua, he gave to his Apostles to teach other believers. To followers throughout their lives, to please him and his Father Yahweh. This teaching of Yashua is now call as the New Testament part of the Scripture that Yahweh gave to Yashua to establish before his sacrificial death. This New Covenant part of the Scripture became known as the New Testament by the Greeks and the Roman translators of the Scripture, and this was for all believers to follow, and to apply to their daily lives, to please Yahweh, and Yashua, as the people of Yahweh.

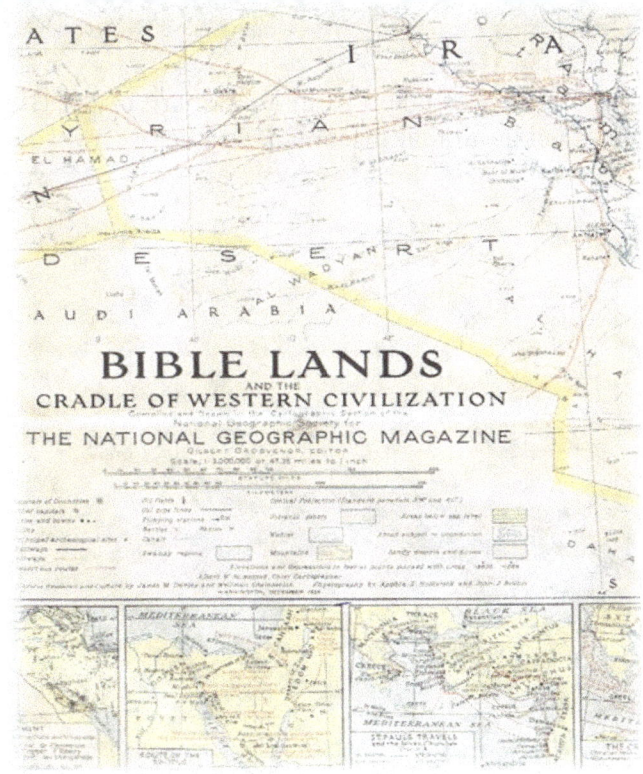

The map above was taking from the National Geographic Magazine that was taken from the Encyclopaedia Britannica, showing what they the Gentile people of Europe did call as the Bible land. This Bible land was the cradle of Western civilization, that the National Geographic Magazine called as the Bible lands.

Which were the various land area of the descendants of the people of Ham that the Gentile people of Europe call as the Middle East. Also of what become known as North Aprica by the Latin Romans, and North Africa by the Angles and Saxon Germanic people. The word Western civilization simple mean, the beginning of the Gentile people civilization, that originally came from the people of Ham, that was spread to Eastern and Western Europe by the Greeks, and by the Romans. Who also had conquered many parts of Europe that became a part of their empire, that they did pass on much of their knowledge they themselves did received from the various kingdoms of the people of Ham. This was before many of these kingdoms of the people of Ham were destroyed by

The type of beard worn by the Assyrians and

Yahweh, for their deeds that did not, please Him.

The picture above was taken from Dictionary of the Bible, showing the bearded head of an Assyrians king, who was also one of the kingdoms of Nimrod, before the kingdom of Assyria were destroyed by Yahweh, because He was not pleased with the kingdom of Assyria, and their doings.

The picture to the right was taken from Dictionary of the Bible, showing people of Mizraim making bread, and bear.

The picture to the right was taken from Dictionary of the Bible, showing of the people of Mizraim making bread.

This carving picture to the left was taken from a Political History of Tropical Africa, showing the Oba Kingdom of Benin, of what became known as Nigeria.

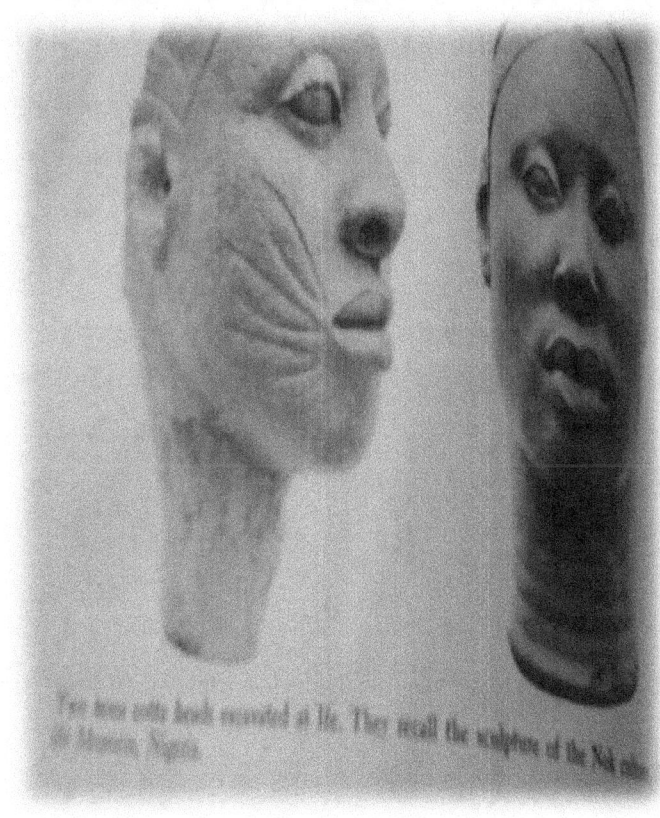

The sculpture picture above was also taken from A Political History of Tropical Africa, that was taken from the Museum of Nigeria, showing of the Nok people culture that become known as Nigeria of today.

This is a bronze head carving that was also taken form A Political History of Tropical Africa, showing of the craft and skills of the ancient kingdom of Benin, that was also taken from the Primitive Museum of New York.

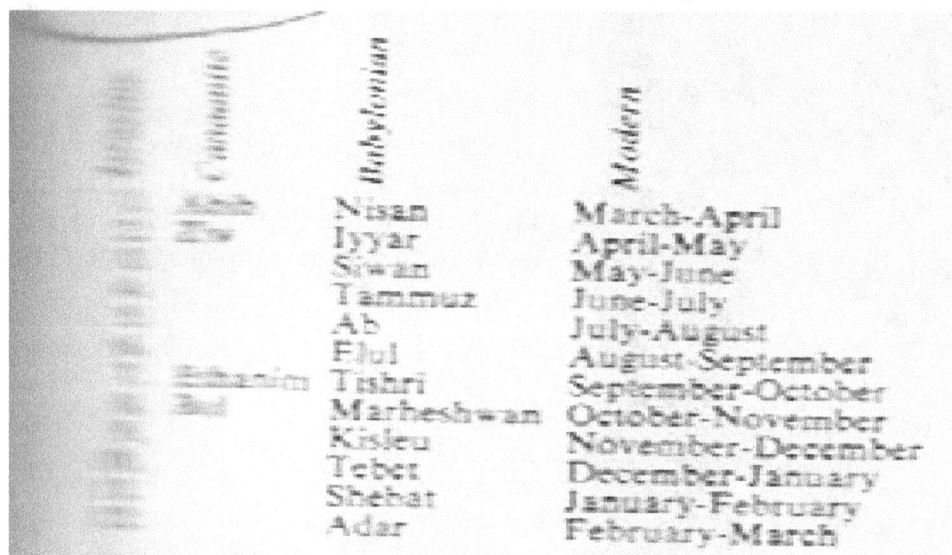

	Canaanite	Babylonian	Modern
	Abib	Nisan	March-April
	Ziv	Iyyar	April-May
		Siwan	May-June
		Tammuz	June-July
		Ab	July-August
		Elul	August-September
	Ethanim	Tishri	September-October
	Bul	Marheshwan	October-November
		Kisleu	November-December
		Tebet	December-January
		Shebat	January-February
		Adar	February-March

The picture writing above was taken from Dictionary of the Bible, showing the Babylon calendar that the ancient children of Israel had as their months of the year. Along with some Canaanite months that became a part of the Hebrew months of the years.

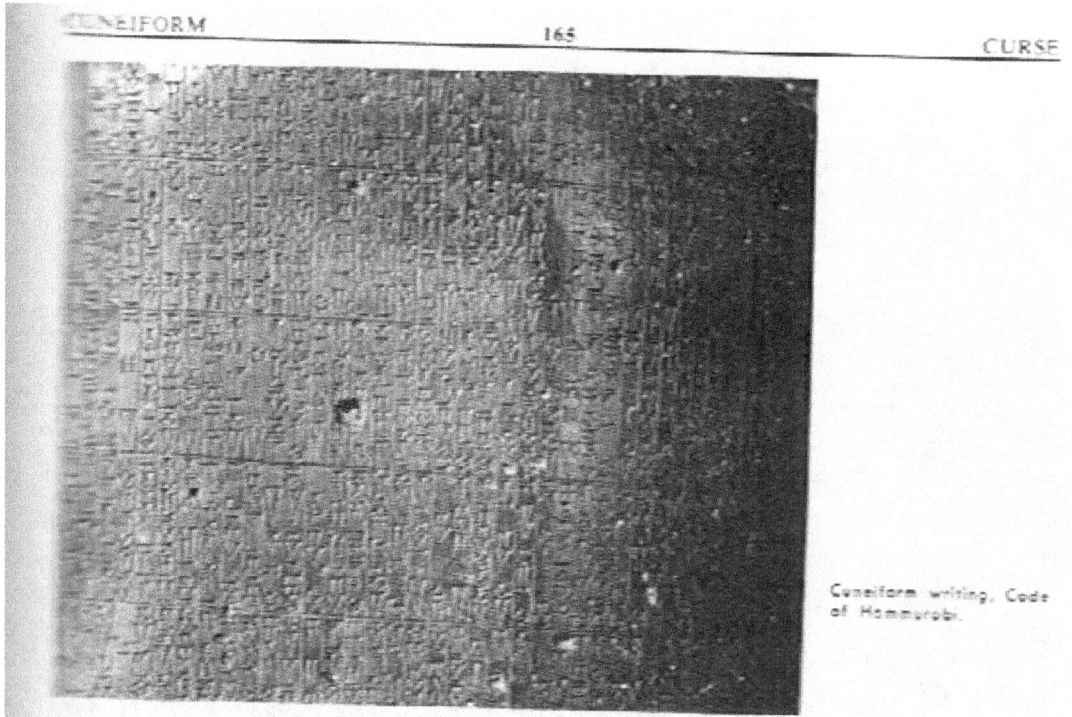

Cuneiform writing, Code of Hammurabi.

The picture writing above is showing of the Assyrian, and the Hethites Canaanites Cuneiform writing that was taken from Dictionary of the Bible. This writing did become a part of the Persian empire of writing, because these kingdoms of the people of Ham, were conquered by the Persian, and became a part of the Persian empire.

The pictures above are a picture of myself.

The picture above is also a picture of myself.

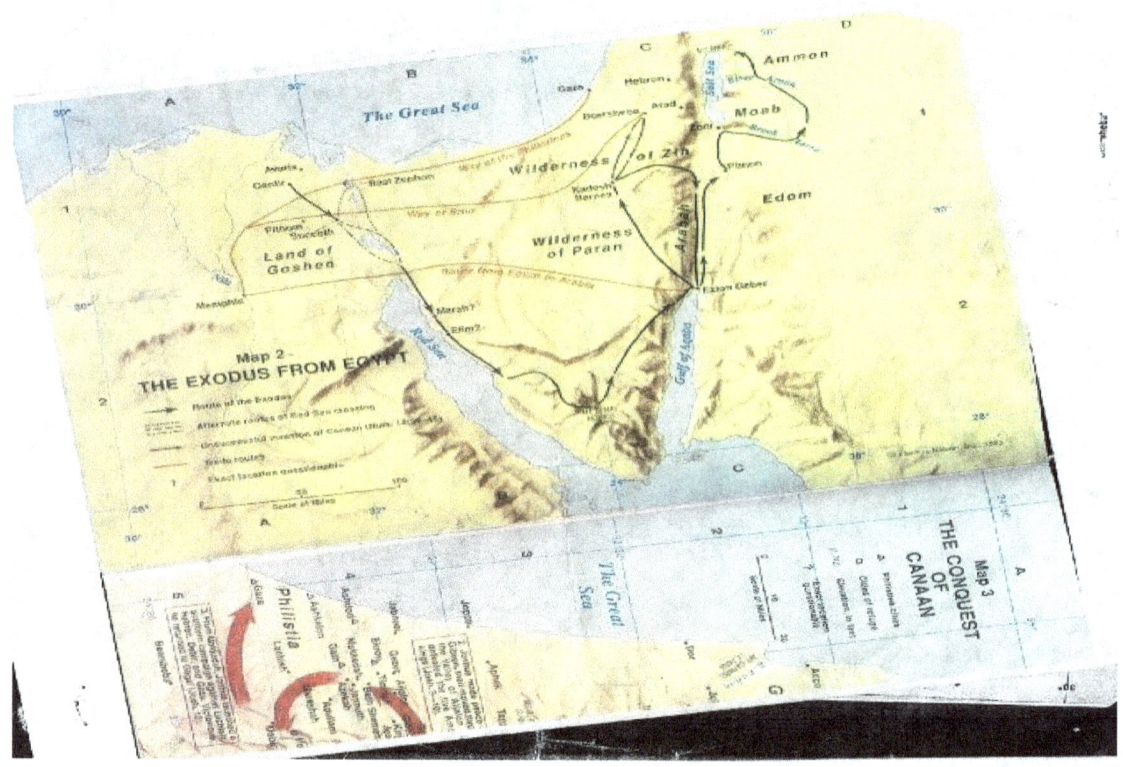

The map above was taken from the Scripture Map of 1890. Showing the land of Goshen, where the children of Israel was living in the land of Mizraim, now known as Egypt.

Contents

Chapter 1 - Africa, Lies and Truth

From the knowledge of (Genesis Chapter 10, and verse 6, to verse 20), and the Scripture Map of 1890, showing the land of Ham and his descendants, I came to the knowledge that from these sons, and grandsons of the people of Ham, came forth what is known today as a part of the so-call Middle Eastern people, and the so-call African people. I would also like to point out that what is now called as a part of the Middle East, by the Gentile people of Europe, is the land of Canaan, with the land area of his two sons, who were known as Sidon, or Zidon, with his brother Heath, and their many descendants. But the name Sidon, it is a Greek, and Latin name that was given to the land of Zidon by the conquests of the Greeks, meaning Alexander, the Great and his Greek settlers, who had settled in the land of Zidon. These sons of Canaan had their kingdoms from the land of Zidon, now known as the land of Syria, stretching all the way to the land of Mizraim, known today as Egypt. Also, to Jordan, Lebanon, and to the city of Tire, with their many descendants of Zion, and his brother Heth. This was way before many of these Hamite's people and their kingdom's was destroyed by Yahweh, for their evil deeds that did not please Him well. Also for the children of Israel, and for other Abrahamic seeds. This land of Canaan did also consist of the many other various kingdoms of the many grandchildren of the people of Ham, who also had their kingdoms there in the land of Canaan, known today as a part of the so-call Middle East. What was called as North Aprica by the Romans, is now known as North Africa, by the Angles and Saxon Germanic people, which was the land area of Ham, and his sons, and grandchildren's that did surround his land area, that they now called as the African people, and the so-call Middle Eastern people. East of the land of Canaan is the land of Elam, which was known before as Persia, where Shem and his off springs had settled after the flood of Noah. Also, after the confusion of the language of the people, who were building the Tower of Babel to reach up to heaven.

This land area of Shem also became known as a part of the so-call Middle East of today, by the Gentile people of Europe, who named this land area as the Middle East, which was the land of Persia, now call as Iran, after the conquest of Alexander the Great, and his army of Macedonia, of the Gentile land of Europe.

What is now called as Asia, is the land area of Persia, that included India, Pakistan, China, and Afghanistan, which is now called as Asia, who are the many descendants of the people of Shem, before the name Asia came about by the Gentile people, of what become known as Europeans people. This land of the people of Shem, was also called as the people from the East, during Scripture time. One can check out (Genesis Chapter 10, and verse 30), under the descendants of Shem, where the Scripture speak of their dwelling place, that was from Mesha, as you goest unto Sephar, which were a mounting area of the East. According to (Genesis Chapter 10, and verse 22), there the Scripture explained that Elam was the first son of Shem, and his land area become known as Elam, and later the land of Elam became known as Persia. Persia later became known as Iran, after the conquest of Alexander the Great, who had conquered from what became known as East Africa, North Africa, the so-call Middle East, to Persia, and what became known as India. Looking at the Scripture Map of 1890, showing the land of Elam, and Persia where Cyrus the Great came from, that is now known as Iran. Which is also called as a part of the so-called Middle East, that was so named by these Gentile people, of what became known as the European's people of Europe. According to (Genesis Chapter 10, and verse 22), Shem had five sons, and these was the names of his sons, Elam, Asshur, Arphaxad, Lud and Aram. Sad to say that it is extremely hard for a person of today to trace out the land area that was named after the five sons of Shem, and their off springs. This is because the name of the land area of the ancient world was changed by various conquerors, who had conquered the land, and changed its names to suit themselves. The same is true for the land of Ham, and the land of Canaan, it is extremely hard for many people of today to trace out the land description that was name after Ham, his sons, and grandchildren's. Because of colonial conquest, and the names of these land area was changed to suit the conquerors desire. North of the land of Canaan is the Gentile land of what become known as Europe. The land of Europe is also called in the book of Jeremiah Chapter 6, and verse 22, as the people of the north, who a very wicked and cruel people, who have no mercy, and this land area is also close to the so-called Middle East.

These people are the various descendants of the last son of Noah, who were known as Japheth, of the people of Europe. So, north of the land of Canaan, that is now known is Isreal, is the people who become known as the people of Europe, which this name Europe came from Greek mythology.

My reason for using the word so-call Middle East, it is because all the various names mentioned above, are false colonial names, that was given by various colonial conquerors to deceive many people of today. Many of whom were educated by the Gentile people of Europe to see things their way, according to what they want them to know, and to understand from their point a view. Mainly, we the people of Ham, who are in total darkness and ignorance, as far as this knowledge of history and awareness is concerned. This fact also goes for the Mohammedans Muslim people of Ishmael, of what become known as the Saudi Arabian people. Many of whom had conquered, and enslave many of their captives to the belief, and the worship of their god Allah, by the Koran, and the sword, to become follower of Mohammed, and the worship of his god Allah. Who many people were taught to believe, that this god Allah, is that of Yahweh, the one God of the universe, which this religious worship of there, is of idolatry worship. Because all worship belongs to Yahweh only, true the name of His Son Yashua, who is our king, master, and High priest to Yahweh. Who also became the sacrificial lamb for the sins of the people of Israel, and for the rest of the people of the world. That true the sacrificial blood of Yashua, we can all be forgiven of our sins, we have committed agains Yahweh. Those people who believe, and follow the teaching of Yashua, will be saved from the wrath of Yahweh, and the destruction that is due to come upon all the people of this word. Those people who are not worshipers of Yahweh, and who are not following the New Covenant Law that was set up by Yasua, before his sacrificial death, will be destroyed from this planet earth. But those people who believe and flow the teaching of Yashua, will be called the people of his sheep's, and the people of Yahweh. First before I really get down into details about the Hamite's people great past, civilization, and history, I must give thanks and praise to Yahweh, for bringing all these history, and the knowledge of the people of Ham to light.

True the writing of this book, the Untold Forgotten Great Civilization of the people of Ham. Praise be to Yahweh to whom alone all praises, worship and thanks must be given to. Who, alone has our lives, and our future in his hands, through the name of His Son Yashua, who is our king, Lord and master. Which the name Yashua is Hebrew, who became known to many as Jesus and Christ, which the names Christ, and Jesus, is a Latin and a Greek name, that were given to Yashua by the Gentile people of who become known as European people. Thanks be to Yahweh for bringing all these hidden histories to light, through His Word the Scripture, and the Scripture Map of 1890. Yahweh has given me this light, of knowledge of the ancient world of the people of Ham, so as to benefit many of the people of Ham who may read a copy of this book , to gain knowledge from what is written there in. Also give parse and thanks to Yahweh for giving me the wisdom, knowledge, and the understanding of all these histories I have read and written about. That came from the various books of the European people writings, that came down into my hands, who were only writing to each other, of their doings, and of their ancestors doing, that has brought riches, and glory to the Gentile people of Europe. They did not have us in thought and mind whatsoever, because they did not want us as a people to come to this light of knowledge of the great civilization of the people of Ham, that we as a people are coming from that gone by. In which they have try their very best to suppress this history of the people of Ham, and only teach us, their many false history of lies, so as to brainwash us, for us to see and think things their way. Also, to keep us down in ignorant and darkness of these facts, and knowledge of the ancient world of the people of Ham that gone by. This truth of the ancient world of the people of Ham, that did shape the modern world of the people of Europe, that they teach as science, and technology. As if to say they were the ones who had brought about this craft, of knowledge and advancement, that they now name as science and technology, to bring glory to themselves. Many of my ancestor way before my time, were not fortunate to come to know about many of these histories I have written about in this book. Also, many of the present-day people of Ham of today, do not even have a clue of many of these ancient histories of the great civilization of the people of Ham I have written about that gone by. I have written about this great civilization of the people of Ham, so as to bring much light and knowledge to many of our Hamite's people minds of today. Many of whom are sleeping, and dreaming, and many of whom have no knowledge of who they are.

So, my chief reason for writing this book is to bring enlightenment to the minds of many Hamite's people of today, many of whom do not know of who they are, and where they and their ancestors is coming from. But many of whom who only go by the various false names, and false identities that were given to us as a people to go by, after they had stripped us of our history, and our identities, and has taken away all our lands, and belongings for themselves. They have also send our ancestors to their various conquered slave colonies, of their New World, of what became known as the Americas, and the West Indies.

So, we their off springs, who are around in today's time, were given different names, from the various slave colonies of the Gentile People New World, where our ancestors were taken as slaves, and leave us behind. They have given us these false names, as a deception, of these places, where we were born, and rase in, to see ourselves as natives of these lands, of their conquest, from the various natives. So, many Hamite's people who were born and raised in these slave colonies, were given different national flags, as a form of their identities for them to embrace, as their nationalities. Also, countries, and islands of the world, where many of us were born and raised in these lands, because of slavery and colonialism, to see ourself belonging to these places. It is a false deception to deceive many of whom do not know any better of who they are, and where they are coming from, because they do not have any knowledge, and the understanding of their pass history, I have written about in this book. Due to the fact that a man belongs to the land of his ancestors where he originated out of. The Scripture Map of 1890, that is showing on the book cover of the Untold Forgotten Great Civilization of the people of Ham, did show the various land area, of the sons, and grandchildren of the people of Ham, where we and our ancestors are coming from, that they the Gentile people of Europe name as Africa, and the so-call Middle East. Who were the true native of the land, long before Abraham, Lot and their many descendants came along, and who had children with the various native Hamite's women, who gave birth to their off springs in the land of Ham and Canaan. This was also before various foreigners of the Gentile people of Europe came along, and established their colonies in the land of Ham by way of conquest, and slavery.

According to a map I have in my possession, called The National Geographic Magazine, that came from the Encyclopaedia Britannica, showing of what was the known world of the ancient time, of the land area they the Gentile people of Europe called as the Bible land, which did belong to the various descendants of the people of Ham. This map went on to show the extended land area of what is now known as Saudi Arabia, which was the land area of Cush fourth son, who was known as Raamah. This information about the land of Raaamah, is according to Genesis Chapter 10, and verse 7, explaining about the land of Raamah. Apart of this land area of Raamah was given to Ishmael by his mother Hagar to settle on. So, Hagar the mother of Ishmael, was a native of the land of Ham, and Mizraim that became known as the land of Egypt, by the conquest of the Greek people of Europe.

Hagar also gave her son Ishmael a wife from among her own people of Mizraim, because at that time of Hagar and Ishmael, they were all one family of the people of Ham, living close together. This little land area of Ishmael that was given to him, was later name after his ninth son, who was know as Tema, that gave birth to the people who are known today as the Saudi Arabian, and the Muslim people, of the so-call Middle East. But many of the land area of what is now known as the land of the Saudi Arabian people, wore conquered Hamite's people lands they the Mohammedans had conquered, and have taken over as a part of their land of position. This land area of Raamah is near the Red Sea, and the land area that became known as Egypt. These Ishmaelite people have spread them selves out, by way of conquering their fellow Hamite's people's lands. They have also captured, and have enslaved many of their fellow Hamite's people, and have sold many of their Hamite's neighbors to the Gentile people of what is now known as European's people as their slaves. One can read (Genesis Chapter 25, and verse 15) where the Scripture mentions about Tema. My purpose for using the term extended land of what is now called as Saudi Arabia, it is because the map shows this land, and many of the lands that was conquered by the Mohammedans, who become known as the Muslim people. As the land of the Arab people, are now known as the Saudi Arabian people, which were indeed the Hamite's people, of the ancient world that gone by. I would also, like to point out that the name Arab, it is a false make up name that was given by the Gentile European conquerors of what become known as the European people. I say this, because according to the Webster's Collegiate Dictionary of the Fifth Edition, the word Arab came from Greeks to the Romans as Arab. when the Roman conquered and enslave many of these Germanic people, then the word Arab became known to the French people as Arabe, who the dictionary describes, and call as Arab people, and the Semitic people, of what is now known as the Saudi Arabian people.

I would also, like to explain that this name Semitic people, it is also a false makeup name, because there were no such a people during the early time of Noah, Ham, Abraham, and Jacob, who were known as the Semitic tribe of people, who became known as the Arabians 'people of today. According to the Webster's Collegiate Dictionary page 54, there the dictionary explained that the name Arab came from Greek to Latin, and later to the French people as Arabe. Who was a part of the various colonial conquers, and rulers of what became known as North Africa, and the so-call Middle East of today.

In the time of Jacob, these people of what is now known as the Saudi Arabians people, were only known as the Ishmaelite's people of Ishmael, because they came from out of the seed of Ishmael, and Ishmael was a son of Abraham, who came from the land of Babylon, of one of the kingdoms of Nimrod. Nimrod himself was the last son of Cush, according to (Genesis Chapter 10, and verse 8), and Cush himself was the first son of Ham. One can read (Genesis Chapter 16, starting from verse 1 to verse 11), to get the full understanding of the knowledge about Hagar and her son Ishmael. The Scriptural Map also shows the Canaanite land of Jordan, the Sinai area, and what is now known as Syria, and the land of Israel, of what the Romans did name as the land of Palestine, that gave birth to the word Palestine people. Which these people who are now call as the Palestine people, are the many descendants of the various colonial rulers, who had left their many descendants, and offspring behind as the new natives of this land area, now known as the so-call Middle East, and the Middle Eastern people. According to volume 25 of the Encyclopaedia Britannica, there it explained that the region of what the Roman did name as Palestine, was the eastern part of the Mediterranean area. Which did consist of what is now Israel, Jordan, and what is now known as Egypt, not for getting the land area of Carthage also. According to this same volume 25 of the Encyclopaedia Britannica, there it explained that the Romans also had call what become known as Syria as Palaestina, from the second century, in which Syria was also a Roman province. This provenience, of what is now known as Syria, was first conquered by the people of Greece, who had this land area as a part of their colony, before the time of the Romans. So, from what is written, one can clearly see that the name Palestine and the Palestinian people, it is a false make up name that was given by the time of the Romans. This was at the time of their conquest, and ruler ship over the land of Ham and Canaan, that became known as a part of the Middle East. The Red Sea is not too far away from the land that is known today as Egypt, where Ham himself was living, as a part of this Bible land, because according to (Genesis Chapter 78, and verse 51), there the verse spoke, of the tabernacle of Ham.

According to the Webster Colligate Dictionary, the word tabernacle mean a dwelling place where one live. So, what the Scripture is telling us, is that Ham used to live in the land area that became known as Mizraim, and and later became known as Egypt, by the Greek conquest. But as I have mention many time, that the name Egypt it is a Greek name, that was given to the land of Ham, during the time of the Greek ruler ship over the land of Ham, and Mizraim, and Mizraim was the second son of Ham. Also, (Psalm Chapter 106, and verse 22), where the Scripture spoke about the land of Ham, where Yahweh did wondrous works for the children of Isreal, when He parted the Red Sea, and let the children of Isreal walk true on dry land, when they left from out of the land of Mizraim to go and take over the land of the Canaanite people land. I must also point out that this map of the Scripture did not mention anything about the Canaanite land of what is now called as the land of Palestine, but I happen to know of these things from the reading of the Scripture, and the Scripture Map of 1890, showing the land of Ham and his descendants. Also, from this map of the Encyclopaedia Britannica, also showing the land of Ham and his people. This National Geographic Magazine of the Encyclopaedia Britannica went on to explained that this Bible land, was the cradle, or the beginning of Western Civilization. The word Western Civilization simply means, the Gentile European people civilization that originally came from out of the people of Ham. This also included the civilization of the ancient children of Israel, who acquired many of their earning, and education's from the people of Ham. Because many of the children of Israel mothers were Hamite's women, who gave birth to this nation of people, along with other Abrahamic seeds of the area. This Western Civilization of the people of Ham was spread to the Gentile land of what became known as the land of Europe by the Hethites, and the Phoenicians people, who w a ere a Canaanites people of Ham. Because Canaan was the last son of Ham, according to (Genesis Chapter 10, and verse 15). This civilization of the people of Ham did also include the people of Mizraim, the Babylonians, and the Assyrian people, of Nimrod, that was also a part of the Cushites family of the kingdom of Cush. Not for getting the Philistines people who also, were known as the Philistim people, according to (Genesis Chapter 10, and verse 14). Who came from out of the family of Mizraim, and this this tribe of the people of Mizraim were living in the Garza strip of Ekron, Ashkelon, and Ashdod of what is now known as a part of the so-call Middle East.

These people also gave light of knowledge to the Gentile people of what became knows Europe, because according to the Encyclopaedia Britannica, many of the writings of the Gentile people of what become known as the European people, came from the Canaanites, the people of Mizraim and also so the Babylonians people of Nimrod. According to (Genesis Chapter 20, and verse 9, to verse 15), there the Scripture explain that Abimelech who was one of the kings of the Philistines people, who were a ruler of a city that was known as Gerar, where Abraham and Isaac were living, before the death of Abraham and Isaac.

Also (Genesis Chapter 26, starting from verse 1 to verse 16), there the Scripture clearly mentions that this city of Gerar is where Abraham and Isaac was living, which were a Philistine city). So, many times, looking at the Gentile European people television program, they often show these people looking like the people of Europe. This was to deceive many people of the world of today, who do not have any knowledge of who these people were. This was to make them to believed that these people were from the Gentile European people background, known today as European's people, of what became known as Europe. This information about these Philistines people, who were livening in the area that I have mention, was also taken from the book of (Zephaniah, Chapter 2 starting from verse 4 to verse 6). This Western Civilization of the people of Ham were also spread into the Gentile New World of what become known as the Americas. Which consists of what is now known as South America, Central America, and North America. (North America is now called as Canada, and the United States) Mexico, also including what became known as the West Indies of the Caribbean. This also Including wheresoever these Gentile people of Europe people went and conquered, and enslaved, and colonized in the name of Christianity, and set up their system of ruler ship to suit themselves. This was by using what became known as the Bible, and what became known as Christianity as a part of their tools, to conquered, and to enslaved many people to get rich. This they have spread around the world by way of their conquest, and domination over the lives of their many captives, and victims. I would like to point out that, the English language, and many of the language of what become known as the European language, came from Latin and Greek, that in turn came from the Phoenicians, Hethites, Babylon, the Assyrian, and the people of Mizraim, of what is now known as the Egyptian people of Ham.

In turn the people of Greece who became known as the Greek people, get their literacy of reading, writing and arithmetic from the Canaanites Phoenicians. This was also from the Hethites people of Canaan, and from the people of Mizraim, now known as the Egyptians people, and also, the Babylon, and the Assyrian people of Nimrod. According to volume 5 of the Encyclopaedia Britannica, there it explained that the Greek alphabetical writing system came from the Canaanites Phoenicians, Hethites, and from the people of Mizraim, now known as the Egyptians people. Which is the ancestor of all the writings that came down to what is known today as the land of Europe.

Also, according to Dictionary of the Bible written by John McKenzie, who himself is of a European background, there, he mentioned that the alphabetical writing system of Hebrew and Greek came from the Phoenicians people. Who Dictionary of the Bible describe as Semitic people, when there were no such a people who were known as the Semitic people of the ancient world. So, this name Semitic, it is a false makeup given name to fool the crowed of people of today, who do not know any better, about where these name came from. Because they do not have the knowledge, or the understanding of where these names came from. So, they just simple accept these teaching of the people of Europe as truth, according to what they were taught to believe, a facts, from the various schooling system of the Gentile people of Europe. This is a typical example of how hypocritical, deceptive, devilish, and wicked these Gentile people of Japheth has been to the world of people at large, who came under their captivities. Also, that of the various Hamite's people whom they had taken, as their captives, as slave, and have brainwash them to believe in their false teaching of lies, and false history. My reason for making this kind of statement it is because, the Gentile people have given many false names and false identities to the various people of Ham, whom they had taken as their captives, slave, and colonies. When I first started to write this book of mine sometime in 1990, I came up with the idea of calling us the Hamite's people, because I acquired the knowledge from the reading of (Genesis Chapter 10, and verse 6, true to verse 20). Also, from the Scripture Map of 1890, showing the land of the people of Ham, and his descendants, who were the true natives of the land of the ancient world. I must also point out that the Scripture, and the Scripture Map both did not use these various words of mine, I have used to describe us as a people of Ham, but this was my own words and thoughts of describing us as a of people of Ham.

This was without realizing that the phrase of the word "Hamite's race of people" was already mentioned in the Webster's Collegiate Dictionary of 5th Edition. I also suppose it is also mentions in other dictionaries of writings of the Gentile family of Europe. Yet they the Gentile people of Europe had set out themselves to deceive us, in giving us these many false names, and false identities to suit themselves. Such as the name Black people, African people, Middle Eastern people, Palestinian people, Colored people, the West Indian people. Also, what they name as the Hispanic and the Latino people, and what they called as the Afro American people of the United States, of the Americas.

So, we the Hamite's people, and many other people of the world of today, who came under the captivity of the Gentile people of Europe, just accepted these lies and teaching of theirs, we go along with, because we know no any better. Plus, we as a people of today have no knowledge of our history of who we are, and where we are coming from. So, it is extremely easy for them to fool us, and to deceive us, as they have been doing for many centuries. I was reading the Webster Colligates Dictionary of the Fifth Edition one day, and I came across the word "Hallowed". Which the dictionary explained by saying that the word Hallowed came from the Anglo-Saxon dialect. So, I went to check out the meaning of this word, and by so doing, to my surprise I came across the term "Hamites race of people." The meaning the dictionary gave for this word is that the "Hamite's people came from out of seed of Ham, who were the second son of Noah. His descendants are known as the Hamite's race of people, who were chiefly the native of the land area they the Romans name as North Aprica. The dictionary went on to explained that the Hamite's people are a Caucasian race of people, who is characterized as tall statuses people, with dark skin and black hair, who are the native of what they now called as Africa. So, where did the name Africa came from? According to volume 13 of the Encyclopaedia Britannica, there it explained that the name Aprica, that became known as Africa, came about, when they the Romans were able to defeat the Carthaginian army, during the first Punic Wars of 264-241 BC. So, after the defeat, they the Roman set up a base in the northern part of the land of Ham that became known as Tunisia of North Aprica. Also, according to volume 10 of the Encyclopaedia page 555, there it explained that the name Africanus came from a Roman general by the name of Publius Cornelius Scipio.

Who name himself Africanus, after he was able to defeat the Carthaginians army of Hannibal at Zama, with his ally army of Prince Masinissa, of what is now known as the country of Morocco, and Algeria. So, the name Africa with an f, did not come from the Latin spelling of the word Aprica, as how the Romans did spell the name Aprica. But according to volume 13 of the Encyclopaedia, the name Africa with a f, came from the Anglo-Saxon Germanic people, when they were educated by the Roman, and the Roman Catholic Church. This education of the Angles and Saxon Germanic people gave birth to the dialect that became known as English, or the Angles language, as it were supposed to be called. Due to the fact that this dialect was taken from the name of the Angles and the Saxons people of West Germany, who had conquered the Bretons people, who became known as the British people, and the English people of today.

So, because of the conquest of the Angles, and Saxon people of Germany, the writings of the Encyclopaedia, and many of the writing of today, came from the Anglo-Saxon dialect, that become known as Middle English, and Old English language. This name English was also taken from the name of the Angles, and Saxon people of West Germany, when reading from volume 20 of the Encyclopaedia Britannica. There it explained that the name Algeria, and Morocco came from the French people of Europe, when they conquered what became known as Morocco and Algeria to be their colony of conquest, and had many of these people in bondage of slavery. I recently visited the country of Morocco, and I was surprise to see the mount of European looking people, who are living there in Morocco as a little Europe. That is rule and control by many French people, with that of other Gentile European people, who are there, and who see themself as the natives of the country that became known as Morocco. The funny thing about this story, when I walking down the street of Morocco, it was very difficult for me to see many of the original Hamite's natives people of what became known as the country of Morocco. Because many of these people have totally washout themselves into half bread European looking people of Morocco, with that of the European man blood runny through these half-bread people veins of the country of Morocco. Many of whom see themselves as French people, with that of other European people blood running through these half breed people vans of Morocco. Many of whom have things under their control, as a little European society. So, many of these halfbreed people of Morocco see themselves as European people of Morocco, because their are near in skin color to that of the Gentile people of Europe. They the Angles and Saxon people got their knowledge of reading, writing and arithmetic from the Roman, and the Roman Catholic Church, and also, from the Greeks. Intern they the Greeks got their education of reading, writing and arithmetic from the Phoenician of Canaan.

Also from Carthaginians alphabetical writing system, that they the Angles people put an E to, that became known as the English language of today, rather than an A for the name Angles. The conquest of the Romans over the Greeks was after the fall of the various Greek Hellenistic kingdoms, of the various generals of Alexander the Great, and their descendants of dynasty to the new power of Rome. Who were to come up after the Greeks ruler ship, and become strong, and conquered many people of Europe, and what became known as North Aprica, and of the so-call Middle East.

This statement is according to the prophecy of (Daniel Chapter 2, and Daniel Chapter 7, verse 7), of the various beasts of power who were to come up and take over power of the earth, after the fall of Babylon to Persia. So, when reading from volume 7 of the Encyclopaedia, there it explained that the land area of what is now known as Algeria, and Morocco, were known during Roman time as the land of Numidia, which was also close to the land area of Carthage. Also when reading from (Genesis Chapter 10, and verse 13), there the Scripture explained that Mizraim, who became known as the Egyptian people, begat Ludim, who was the first son for Mizraim. So, when looking at the Scripture Map of 1890, showing the land of what is now known as Morocco and Algeria, where the land area of Carthage was also located. So, the land of Ludim is the land area that became known as Morocco, Algeria, and the land of Carthage also. So, this land of Ludim is near to the land area of the third son of Ham, who was known as Phut, but the land of Phut became known as the country of Libya of today. The Encyclopaedia explained that when the Romans conquered the northern part of the land of Ham, they called as North Aprica of their conquest, so the meaning of the name Aprica to the Romans, meant to them" a land that were sunny, without winter. Not like that of their Gentile land of Europe that have cold weather, and winter." So, this name Aprica was chiefly applied to the northern part of the continent of the people of Ham, that they the Gentile People, who are known today as the European people, regarded as the southern extension of the Gentile land of Europe. The Romans ruled the northern part of the continent, and called an area south of their settlement as Aprica, which eventually became known as the land of Africa, which were an area of a Berber tribe community, that was south of the land of Carthage.

The Encyclopaedia Britannica gave another explanation for the name Aprica, the explanation given for the name Aprica that become known as Africa, were given to a productive area of the land of Carthage that is now called as Tunisia, which meant to the Romans "Ears of Corn." According to the Encyclopaedia, the Arabic word for the name Africa is called as Ifriqiyah. Volume 13 of the Encyclopaedia Britannica explained that the Greeks before the Romans had called the northern part of the continent that came under their conquered ruler ship, as the land of Libya or Aprike. The words Aprike and Libya, simply meant to the Greeks "a land that was without cold and winter, not like that of their continent of Europe that have cold weather.

So, when the Romans came and conquered the land of Ham from the Greeks, they did not change the name Libya, but the name Libya was stuck to the land of Phut as the country of Libya. But Phut was the third son of Ham, and his land area, is still known today by its Greek name, as the country of Libya. According to Volume 3 of the Encyclopaedia page, there it explained that the land of Libya was also known as Cyrene or Cyrenaica by the Greeks. This was way before the coming of the Romans to the area they did name as Aprica, that is now known as North Africa. According to the Encyclopaedia, from about 631 BC, this land of Phut became known as Cyrene and Libya, because this land area were established as a Greek colony, by some Greek settlers who come from the island of Thera, which is in the Aegean Sea of Greece. Their leader, whose name were known as Battus, became the first king, who did establish a dynasty of the Battiads kingdom. This Greek ruler, ruled Cyrene or Libya for eight generations of his descendants, until their kingdoms were taken over by the Persians, and became a part of the Persian Empire. The kingdom of Mizraim was also conquered from the Persian, by Alexander the Great, and Alexander the Great later made one of his general, whose name was known as Ptolemy, to be the governor over the land of Mizraim. This was when he defeated the Persian army of Darius, so later when Alexander died, Ptolemy made himself king of Mizraim, that did became the Ptolemaic dynasty of Mizraim, Libya, Cyprus, a part of Syria, and a part of the Greek Turkey area of Europe, until the time of the Romans. Before the conquest of Alexander the Great, the land of Mizraim was under the power of the Persians, and the Persian was the ruling power over the northern part of the land of Ham, as well as what became known as East Africa. They the Persian also had ruler ship over the land of Canaan, and a part of the Gentile land of Europe, that were known as Asia Minor, of the Greek Turkey area of Europe. This was before the Greeks came, and take overpower from the Persian, as it were so prophesied in the book of Daniel. After the time of the Greeks and the Romans, then came the other Gentile people of Europe, who came from out of the brake up of the Roman Empire, and conquered the land area of the people of Ham, but they the Romans, did not change the name Libya, but the name Libya were left with its Greek name, as it is known as today, as the country of Libya. This Greek name was stuck to the land of Phut, who were the third son of Ham, and his land area is still known today as the country of Libya.

According to volume 8 of the Encyclopaedia Britannica, there it explain about the country that became known as Liberia, that were established during the administration of a United State president, by the name of James Monroe. So, from the name of Jame Monroe, give birth to the capital city of what became known as the country of Liberia, that got its name, by the American Colonization Society. This British colony of what become known as the United States, set up this settlement for the return of free slave from the Americas. Also from other part of their New World, where many of our ancestors were taken as slaves. This settlement of this town was established in 1822, that were known as Providence Island that was located at the mouth of the Mesurado River. According to volume 7 of the Encyclopaedia Britannica, there it explained that many free slaves came from what became known as North America. This was during the time of 1830-1887, who did make up this settlement of what became known as free town Liberia. This settlement was established as a home land for the return of free slave of the American Society, in 1816- 1821-1822, by Jehudi Ashmun, who was a Methodist minister, and who eventually became the director of the settlement of the colony, in 1824. So, this colony was given the named as Liberia, and its principal settlement did become known as Monrovia, which did take it name from James Monroe of the United States. According to this same volume 7 of the Encyclopaedia, Joseph Roberts of Liberia, who the Encyclopaedia describes as a nonwhite, referring to this false racial identity, as the so-call White man, and the so-cal Black man. So, this person of Liberia, who was not of a European descendants, was the first governor to declare Liberia independence in 1847. So, Joseph Roberts was also able to expand the borders of Liberia, and who also worked to end the illegal slave trade that was still taking place there, in the West African course. According to the Encyclopaedia, there was border disputes between the British, and the French for the control of the land area of Liberia. This border disputes lasted until 1892, when a treaty was established between the British and the French, and the French was able to control 2000 square mile of the land area of Liberia, as a part of their colony area. I must also, point out that I did not cover the full story about Liberia, and it's colonial rulers, fighting over the control of the wealth of the land area that did become known as Liberia, reading from volume 7 of the Encyclopaedia. The story of another part of the land of Ham that became known as Sierra Leone, that did became known as Freetown, according to volume 10 of the Encyclopaedia.

The Encyclopaedia explained that the land area of what did became known as Sierra Leone, was first vested by the Portuguese in 1495, on the modern site where they did build a fort that later became known as Freetown. During the 15th century Sierra Leone was visited regularly by various European powers, for slave and also for ivory. So, these European people as been killing off the elephants for a long time, and are still doing so today, by using various stupid native people to achieve their objective. The Encyclopaedia explained that, although the British did build a trading post along an area that was known as Bund, and York islands in the 17th century, but no officially European settlement was made in Sierra Leone, until 1787. This was after the abolishment of the slave trade by the British, on January 1st of 1830. Yet slavery did continue in many part of the Gentile European People, New World, Europe and in the land of Ham itself after 1830. According to what I have gathered reading from volume 10 of the Encyclopaedia, in 1787, a private establishment was set up for the return of free slave to resettle in what become known as Sierra Leone. This was after the British Government made the slave trade illegal, then they the British Government take over the area of Sierra Leone as a naval base for their operation against the slave traders. So the coastal area of Sierra Leone did become a British settlement, and a British colony. I must point out that I cannot say for sure how the name Sierra Leone came about, but I do believe the name came from the French.

I would also like to point out that all the modern names of the various countries of land of Ham, that one might see on the modern world map of today, were given by the various colonial conquerors. Who come in, and scrape up the land of Ham, and his people to be their colonies of position of their empire. I also want to explain about a video documentary I have purchase from Amazon, that is called White King, Red Rubber, Black Death of the Congo. This colony was conquered, and rule by a Belgium king, who was known King Leopold II Of Belgium, who put allot of pressure, and wickedness on the people of the Congo for them to bring in allot of rubber product to ship to Belgium, for him to become a rich man.

The picture is that of King Leopold II of Belgiu

This picture to the left is showing of a man from the Congo who is about to be shot, by one of King Leopold solders, to put pressure on the people of the Congo to bring in much rubber product to ship to Belgium of Europe.

This picture to the right is showing of the was cutoff in the Congo by the army of force the people of the Congo to produce trees, to send to Europe of Belgium, to into a rich country of Europe.

many people palms of hands that Leopold solders. This was to more rubber from the rubber make the country of Belgium

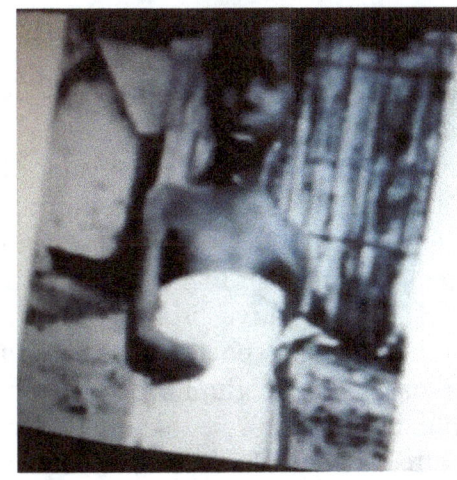

The picture to the left is showing of a Hamite man, whose two hands of his palm were cut off by the army of Leopold solders, to force the people of the Congo to produce more rubber, from the rubber tree.

This picture to the right that Is showing, of a little boy, whose palm of his hands were cut off by the solders of Leopold of the Congo, to force the people of the Congo to produce more rubber to ship to Belgium, so that Leopold can become a rich man.

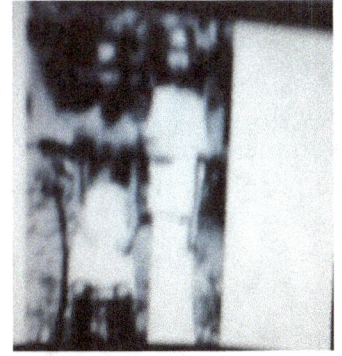

The picture to the left is showing a of lady, and a young boy, whose palm of their hands was cut off by Leopold solders. This was to force the people of the Congo to produce more rubber, to send to Belgium.

This is another picture, showing of a young boy, whose part of his hand, and foot was cut off, by the solders of Leopold. This was to force the natives to produce more rubber, from the rubber tress to send to Belgium. In this documentary of the Congo, they also show, many solders of Leopold who went about burning people homes, to force them to produce more rubber, to send to Europe.

In this same video documentary, they also show many pregnant women, and other women with children's, with rope tied around their neck, who was put into prison, with these ropes, and chains around their necks, to force their men, or their husbands to bring in more rubber, before they could be release back to their husbands. The funny thing about this story of Belgium, they were using various Hamite's men of the Congo in their army to burn, kill, and to cutoff many of their own people hands and foots. So, as to please the thirsts of their Belgium masters, without thinking of the destruction they were doing to their own people, and their own self. I also saw in this video of the Congo, many Hamite's solders, who tied their fellow Hamite's native brother's foot and hands, with their shirts off their backs. Their face down to the ground, and their backs expose, and they stretch them out beating them with whips, that was made from rhino hides, just to please their Belgium officers to show how loyal they were, to the army of Leopold. As I had mention before that many Hamite's people are suffering from colonial and slavery mentality, of stupidity, and ignorance that do affect many of our Hamite's people mine, and life, even till today. I must point out that this kind of citation would not happen if it was with the Gentile people of Europe. Also, with that of he Chinese people, and with that of many Indian people of what became known as Asia. They would join to gather, and fight against their oppressor, and slaver masters. Many of these foolish Hamite's men of the Congo was not as smart as their Hamite's slave brothers of the island that become known as Jamaica. Who had run away from the Spanish their slave masters, leaving them to fight against the British by themselves.

My reason for saying this is, during the 1600, when the British came to take away the island of Jamaica from the power of the Spanish. They the Spanish armed their Hamite's slaves with guns to fight on their behalf, against their brothers the British. But these Hamite's men was so smart, that when they received these guns, they took off up to the Cockpit Mounting of Jamaica, and leave the British, and the Spanish to fight among themselves. After these Hamite's men run away up to the mounting, they were given the name by the Spanish as the Maroons, which mean runaway slaves, according to the Webster's Dictionary.

According to this documentary, this story came to light, because of some British Missionary, as they saw themselves, who were there in the Congo, and who observe the cutlery of the army of Leopold men, pressuring the people of the Congo to produce more rubber, from the rubber tree to send to Europe. After the death of Leopold, the country of the Congo became an official colony of the Belgium Government, producing gold, diamond, rubber, and various other items to ship to Belgium, to make these Germanic people of the country of Belgium into a rich country of Europe.

This is the end of Africa lies and truth.

Before the Yehudahites and the Benjaminhites people who become known as the Jews, and Jewish people, in the dialect of the Anglo Saxon Germanic people, of West Germany that become known as the English language. Or the Angles, and Saxon dialect of Germany. According to (Joshua Chapter 10, and verse 3), there the Scripture explained that the Jebusite Canaanites tribe, and their king, who were known as Adonizedek, were the native of Jerusalem. This was before the Yehudahites, and the Benjaminhites tribe of the children of Israel came and take over their lands, Yahweh gave to them. This tribe became known as the tribe of Judah, by Roman, who took over the land area from the Greek, as a part of their colonial conquest of the so-call Middle East. So, the city of Jerusalem were given to the Yehudahites, and the Benjamites tribe of the people of Isreal, when they came from out of the land of Mizraim, now known as Egypt. At the time of conquest of the land Canaan by the people of Isreal, by the power of Yahwehs, when they came from out of the land of Mizraim, as how it is clearly explain in the Scripture of truth. (According to Joshua Chapter 10, starting from verse 1), there the Scripture explain that the Jebusite tribe of the Canaanite people, were the native of what is still known today as the city of Jerusalem. (According to Chapter 10) of the book of Joshua, it came to pass when Adonizedek king of Jerusalem heard how **Joshua** thad taken over the country of AI, and kill their king, with all the inhabitance who were there at the time. This place was known at the time of Joshua conquest as Bethel. (According to Joshua Chapter 8, and verse 17), there it explain that this city of Jericho which was in the Jordan area, of what they the Gentile people, name as the so-call Middle East. So, when Adonizedek heard that the Canaanite tribe, who was known as Gibeon, went and try to disguise themselves to the children of Isreal to be a people from a far away country, who went and made peace with Isreal, and become their servants. So, Adonizedek king of Jerusalem sent unto Hoham king of Hebron, and unto to Piram, king of Yarmouth, and also, to Japhia, king of Lachish, and unto Debir, king of Eglon, saying come up unto me, and help me that we may smite the country of Gibeon. Because they went and make peace with Joshua of the children of Isreal. So, according the book of Joshua, these five kings of the Canaanites, Amorites, and the king of Jerusalem went up to fight against the city of Gibeon, because they went and made peace with Isreal, and became their servants.

So the men of Gibeon sent message to Joshua for help, to fight against these kings, and Yahweh delivered these kings into the hands of Joshua. (Verse 11 of Joshua Chapter 10), went on to explained that Yahweh cast down great stones from heaven, which did slew many of these Canaanites, who were fleeing away from the army of Isreal. Because Yahweh were fighting on the behalf of Isreal, to destroy these mighty Canaanites, and their army from the land of Canaan, and to give the land to Isreal. One can read the complete Chapter of Joshua for themselves, to get a good understanding of the destruction of the Canaanites civilization by Yahweh. Also, that of the children of Isreal, because Yahweh was not pleased with many of the people of Canaan, and with that of many other Hamite's tribes of the area. So, this is the reason why many of these great civilization of the people of Ham are no longer around with us today. Because Yahweh did destroy many of these civilization of the people of Ham, in the early beginning of the human family after the flood of Noah. So, the land area of what is now known as a part of the Middle East, did belong to the Canaanites, and also that of the other Hamite's tribes, of the many grandchildren of the people of Ham, who was living there, and who had their kingdoms, in the land of Canaan. This was way before the land become known as the country of Isreal. This was also, way before many these people, and their kingdoms, was destroyed by Yahweh, for the children of Isreal, and also for other Abrahamic seeds, and for their own evil deeds that did not please Him well. So, many of these Canaanite people who might be around in today's time, are mixed up with the blood of Persians, Greeks, Romans, Turks, and with other Gentile people, who came from out of the brake up Roman Empire, and conquered, and had rule ship over the so-call Middle East, and what became known as North Aprica, that did become known as North Africa.

So, if any of these Canaanites tribes are still around in today time, they also have become a part of the Mohammedans Muslim family of people, because they were also conquered by Mohammed, and his followers, who were known as the Mohammedans, that become known as the Muslim people of today. The people of Ham land border line of that ancient world, according to what the Scripture Map of 1890 shows, was from what is now known as the Turkey area of Europe, to the Tigress, and the Euphrates River area. All the way to the land of Cush, and his descendants land area of what became known as East Africa, to what became known as the West and the South African course of the land of Ham.

This land of Cush is known today as Sudan, when compare the Scripture Map of 1890, with that of the word map of today, showing the land of Cush that became known as the land of Sudan, by the conquest of the Mohammedan Muslim people, of what became known as the Saudi Arabian people of Ishmael. This map of the Scripture, also show the various land area of the various sons of Cush, and his grandchildren, who were living very closely to the land area of their father Cush, as how it is clearly shown on the Scripture Map of 1890. Also, as how it is showing on the book cover of the Untold Forgotten Great Civilization of the people of Ham, of the so-call Middle East, and what became known as North Africa, as well as what became known as West Africa, to what became known as South Africa by the Dutch people of the Netherland of what is now known as Holland of Europe. So all the modern names of the various countries of the land of Ham, and the land of Canaan, many people know it as today, as the Middle East, and what become known as North Africa, are false colonial names, that was given by the various colonial conquerors. Who had control over the land and its people, as their subjects, pray and colonies. Due to the colonial conquest of the various kingdoms of the people Ham, it has cast many of the various tribes of the area, to push down into the inertia of the land of Ham, to set up their own little kingdoms. This was to avoid the colonial conquest of the Persian, Greek, Romans, and the Turks, who were at one time the colonial ruler of the northern part of the land of Ham, and Canaan, as their conquest. By so doing, many of the various tribes of the area, who did push down into the interior of the land of Ham, did lost the writing and mathematics skills their ancestors had developed before they came along, in what become known as North Africa, and the so-call Middle East. This time was way before the Mohammedans, and the Portuguese, penetrated deep into the inertia of the land of Ham, and conquered many of the various tribes, who were living there.

This conquest gave birth to the various colonial names of the various countries of the land of Ham, that is shown on the modern world maps of today, as many people know it as. As I had mentioned before that the Greeks, the Romans, and the Turks, did stick to the northern part of the land of Ham, of their conquest, who did not penetrate deep into the interior of the land of Ham, until the time of the Mohammedans, the Portuguese, and others European people who came from out of the brake up of the Roman Empire. They have penetrated deep into the interior and conquered many of the various tribes who were living there.

Due to the conquest by many of these conquerors, they have given many names to the various countries of the land of Ham, one sees on the modern world maps of today, so as to suit themselves. This was to deceive many people, of today, who do not know about the true history of the land area, of the people of Ham. So, these Gentile European colonial conquerors, had developed these maps of the world to suite themselves. This was also, to deceived other people who do not have any knowledge of the true history of the land area of the people of Ham, that did existed there in ancient time, before the Scripture was given to the children of Israel. When reading from (First King Chapter 10, and verse 22), the impression I got from the reading of this Chapter, it seems to me that the people of Tarshish, who become known as the Spanish and the Portuguese people, had a long history of dealing with the land of Ham, and his people, during those ancient time. My reason for making this kind of statement, it is because, when reading verse 22 of First King, Chapter 10, there it explain that the native of the land of Tarshish, who is known today as the Spanish and the Portuguese. With the native of King Hiram of the Canaanites kingdom, of what is known today as the country of Syria, with the city of Tire, and the city of Lebanon, went to the land of Sheba, known today as Yemen, to get gold from there, of the land of Ophir. According to the Scripture, this land of Ophir was located in the land of Sheba, as a land of gold, where these men were able to bring ivory, apes, gold, and precious stones, and peacocks for King Solomon at Jerusalem, as a present of gift to him. So when looking as the Scripture Map of 1890, there it show the lad of Ophir, that is in the land area of Sheba, near to the foot part of the land of Seba, known today as the land of Ethiopia. Also near to what is now known today as Saudi Arabia, which this land area, of Saudi Arabia, was the land, of Raamah, who were the fourth son of Cush, according to Genesis Chapter 10, and verse 7.

Also, when reading from volume 20 of the Encyclopaedia, there it explained about Dutch Guyana that became known as Suriname. The volume went on to explained that there was some African slaves of Suriname, who had run away from their Dutch slave masters, and set up their own little establishment in the jungle of what became known as Suriname. These runaway slaves became known as the Bush Negros to the Dutch, who had set up their own king, and carryon life just like when they was living in the Western part of the land of Ham, that become known as West Africa.

Many of these Hamite's runaway slaves, of what became known as Suriname, did adapt to their surroundings, and did adapt to many European cultures, of the Dutch, Spanish, Portuguese and the British. These adopted cultures was blended with that of their customary ways of life, from the part of the land of Ham they were taken from. Although they did lost many of their ancestor's civilizations that was first started from what become known as East Africa, to the North of the land of Ham, and to the land of Canaan, now known as the Middle East. My knowledge of understanding I came to about the land of Ham, and his descendants, that became known as the Middle Eastern people, and what became known as North Aprica by the Romans. It is by comparing the Scripture Map of 1890, with that of the world map of today, showing these lands areas of the people of Ham of the ancient world that gone by. Unfortunately, the world map of today only shows the land of Ham that is now known as Africa, as a much smaller land space, in comparison to the time when the Scripture was given to the children of Isreal, and the various Hamite's tribes, who were living there in the land of Ham at that time. Whose land area was of a bigger size, then what is shown on the modern map of today. When I saw the word Hamite's race of people in the Webster's Collegiate Dictionary, I was very surprised, because I thought to myself that the term "Hamite's people" was my own name of describing us as a people of Ham, because we as a people came from out of the seeds of Ham. Although they, the Gentile people have written about these things in their dictionaries, Encyclopaedias, the Scripture, and the Scripture Map, and knew of these things to be true. Yet they have set out themselves to deceive us as a people of Ham for many centuries.

Also, the world of other people at large, who came under the colonial captivity of the people of Europe, with their lies of false history. They had giving to us, all these many false names, and false identities to deceive us as a people, and the world of people at large. Who came under the colonial ruler ship of the people of Europe, to believe in all their lies, of false history, for us their many captives to see things their way. Despite all the wickedness, evilness, and the deceptiveness of these Gentile people of Europe, in trying to hide all these various histories from us as a people of Ham, and the world at large. Yahweh in His own time has brought out all these hidden histories to light, true the pages of this book, the Untold Forgotten Great Civilization of the people of Ham.

So, as to give many people of today this light of knowledge of truth, to shine forth in the minds of many people who might read a copy of this book, so as to come to a better knowledge of understanding, of the true history of the people of Ham of the ancient world that gone by. Due to this granting of Yahweh, I am now able to write about many of these things that are written in the Scripture, and in the Scripture Map of 1890, in my own words. So, as to benefit many Hamite's people of today, and other people of the world at large, who may read a copy of this book, to come to this light of true history of the people of Ham. Many of whom also came under the Gentile European conquered ruler ship of their world, of their their false histories, and lies of deception to get rich. So, many of these conquered people who came under the slavery colonial system of the people of Europe, do not have any knowledge, or understanding about this true history, of the people of Ham of the ancient world I have written about in this book. I am very thankful to Yahweh very much, for giving me this knowledge, wisdom and the enlightenment, and the understanding of all these things that were hidden from us Hamite's people, and the world at large. Who the Gentile people of Europe have tried their very best to keep us down in ignorance, and to destroyed us in many ways and means, because many of these histories I have written about, is mention in the Scripture, and is also showing on the Scripture Map of 1890. Also many of these things were hidden from us

Hamite's people, and the world at large, who do not have the understand, and the reading of the Scripture, many of whom do not have the Scripture Map as I do, showing the land of Ham, and his descendants.

I am extremely glad and thankful to Yahweh, that I am now able to write about these things in my own words, so as to bring much knowledge and understanding to the minds of the people of Ham, and the world of people at large. Because these Gentile people of Europe, had no idea, that we as a people of Ham would have ever come to this light of knowledge, and of awareness. Because they have been trying their very best to hide these things from us, and to keep us down in darkness and ignorant, of not knowing of these facts. But for us only to know, and to go by the various names, identities, and false history they have given to us as a people to go by. There is also an old saying that goes like this, you can fool some of the people some of the time, but you cannot fool all the people all the time.

The truth of the Scripture will all ways prevail, because it is the Word and the power of Yahweh, and no man can stop the truth, and the power of Yahweh from coming to light. When I was growing up in Jamaica, and went to live in London of Britain, I always heard the expression that what became known as Africa, is the Dark Continent. In my mind, I thought the reason why these Gentile people of Britain call what they name as the Dark Continent, it is because many people south of the Sahara Desert are of dark skin complexion. Not realizing that the reason why these Gentile people of Britain call what they name as Africa, as the Dark Continent, it is because they have been teaching the world of people, who came under their slavery colonial captivity, that the people they name as African's people had no civilization. According to their belief, they have been teaching to many people, who came under their captivity, is that they the African people did not invent anything, as did the Greeks, and the Romans, with other people of Europe and Asia, who had invented many things to benefit the needs of the human family. So, In their eyes and mind set, they see the people who they name as the African people, to be an uncivilized backward people, they called as savages and bush people. This is the reason why they have always showed on their Hollywood movies, and in their television programs, the various tribes of what they called African people, Running around with painted faces, and spars that they name as bush men and savages. I must point out that even the various spars, many of these people had made, who they called as bush men and savages. They had made from out of iron, just goes to show of the crafts, and skills these people had, way before the coming of these Gentile people of Europe.

Who came and take away their lands, and take many of them as their captives and slaves, to their conquered New World, of the Americas and the West Indies to become rich people, true Christianity, and the cross of Roman Catholicism. They the Gentile people of Europe, wanted to give to the people of the world the idea, who watches their movies and television programs, that these people who they call as African's people, are a backward people, who had no learning. This is what they have been teaching to the world of people who came under the colonization of the Gentile people of Japheth, to believe in their lies of false history. From what I have written from the Scripture, the Scripture Map of 1890, and even from the National Geographic Magazine of the Encyclopaedia Britannica, that was written by these same Gentile people of Britain.

One can see how much lies, and deception these Gentile people of Japheth have been deceiving the world of people, who came under their captivity, with false teaching of history, of lies. So, in reality many of the people of Japheth, of what become known as the European people, are like Satan the devil himself, who has been deceiving the world of people, who did came under their captivity with lies. False history, and with all sort of corruption of immorality, that is against the very Laws, and the Commandments of Yahweh for a person to live their lives by. Volume 20 of the Encyclopaedia Britannica explained that the conquest of the Romans, gave them the opportunity to dominate the people whom they had conquered and enslaved. This were to help to civilize many of these people, who did came under the colonial control, and ruler ship of the Romans. This statement the Encyclopaedia made about the Romans civilizing many nations of people who did came under their captivity, I am quite sure the Encyclopaedia had in mind of the various tribes, and nations of Europe, who did came under the ruler ship of the Roman. Which did help to civilize many of these people of Western and Eastern Europe, who did came under Roman captivity of slavery, and colonialism. So, I am quite sure the

Encyclopaedia could not be speaking about the Hamite's people of Ham, of the so-called Middle East, and what they the Gentile European people name as North Africa. Who themselves gave civilization of light to the Greeks, and the Romans, that did eventually spread throughout Eastern and Western Europe. According to volume 20 of the Encyclopaedia, there it explained that the Phoenician alphabetical writing system was copy by the Greeks, so the Greeks also did take over the alphabetical writing system of the Canaanites Phoenician people to be their own alphabetical writing system.

This writing system of the Phoenician people, did become the alphabetical writing system of the Greeks, that eventually gave literacy to the Romans, also to other people of Western and Eastern Europe. This civilization of the people of Ham gave birth of literacy to the Greeks and Romans, which did came from the Turkey area of Europe, that eventually spread to what became known as the Roman world of Eastern and Western Europe. The Romans got their civilization from the Greeks, and the Etruscans people, of what is now known as Italy, as volume 10 and volume 20 of the Encyclopaedia clearly points out.

The Greeks also got many of their knowledge and skills from the Canaanites Phoenician, the Hethites, the people of Carthage, and from the people of Mizraim, who become known as the Egyptians people. Also, from the Assyrian, and the Babylon's people of Nimrod, who was the last son of Cush. Also, from a people who were known as the Minoans of the island of Create. These people of Crete, may have also came from the people of Mizraim, because the Island of Crete is not too far away from the land of Mizraim, and it is not too far from the area of Greece. So, these people of the island of Crete could have originally came from out of the people of Mizraim. I say this, because when I was living in London during the sixties, there were many people who came to London from the island of Cyprus, and many of these people had tight curly hair. Just like that of many people from the land of Ham, now known as the African people, and the so-call Black people, who have tight curly hair. So, the island of Crete is very near to the island of Cyprus, so it is a good possibility that the people of Crete could have also came from out of the people of Mizraim. Which they the Gentile people of Europe says that the Greeks also got their learning from these people of Crete. According to Dictionary of the Bible, written by John L. McKenzie, who himself is from the Gentile European family, there the page begun to explain about the Alphabetical writing system in the form of picture words that became known as Hieroglyph. But Dictionary of the Bible did not break it down as to say, it was the people of Ham, who gave birth to this picture form of writing, that did become known as the Hieroglyph. But instead, they used other various names to describe these people I have already explained who these people were, because I have gotten this knowledge from the reading of the Scripture, and the Scripture Map of 1890, showing these land areas of the people of Ham.

This picture writing begun with the people of Mizraim, the Hethites people of Canaan, the Phoenicians people of Zion of Canaan, the Assyrian people, and what is now known as Iraq, and Babylon, of these kingdoms of Nimrod. From what I have read from Dictionary of the Bible, and also from the Encyclopaedia, this Cuneiform Akkadian writings came from the various kingdoms of Nimrod, such as Assyria, Haran that became known as Iraq, and the kingdom of Babylon, that they the Gentile people of Europe called as the Semitic, and Aramaic writing, and the Armenian people of the so-call Middle East.

I must also point out that the Gentile people of what become known as the European's people, as always created, and invented many artificial names, they give to the various people of Ham of the area, Have mention above. This was to suite themselves, and to deceived others people, who do not have much knowledge, and understanding of who these people were, I have mention. This was also to deceive, and to cause confusion, and ignorance to many Hamite's people minds of today, who do not have any knowledge of who these people were, and where they came from, because many of those ancient kingdoms of the people of Ham were destroyed by Yahweh, because of the children of Israel, and for other Abrahamic seeds. More over Yahweh were not pleased with many of the doings of those ancient kingdoms of the people of Ham that gone by. These people were sons and grandchildren of the people of Ham, that these Gentile people of Europe name as the Semitic people, Middle Eastern people, Palestinian, and Palestine people, and the Arab people. Although many of these people of the so-call Middle East, are a washout people, with that of the blood of many people of Europe who they classified as the Middle Eastern people, Arab people, Semitic people, and the Palestine people. Yet these names I have mention above, are a totally false identity, and false names, because there were no Semitic people, Palestinian, and Arab people of the so-call Middle East, during the time of Noah, Shem, Ham, Nimrod, Abraham, and Jacob, of that periods of time, of the ancient world.

According to this Dictionary of the Bible, from the Semitic alphabetical writings script of Ahiram of Byblos, which were a Canaanite city of Lebanon, which according to them was about 1000 BC. So, from this writing of Byblos gave literacy of writing to the people of Greece, who become known as the Greek people, during the time of the 9th century BC. According to this same Dictionary of the Bible, before the adoption of the Canaanites writing by the people of Greece, from the 9th century, there were no Greek inscription of writing then that from about the 8th to the 9th century BC. In which this Greek inscription was a copy of the Phoenicians Canaanites alphabet writing system, they the Greek took to themselves, and it become their alphabet form of writing system, that did spread to the rest of the Gentile land of Europe. Dictionary of the Bible went on to explained that the Greek alphabetical writing system was later taken over by the Latin writing of the Romans.

Which this Canaanite writing, is the ancestors of all the modern writings of today, except for those writings that directly came from the Semitic writing system of the Canaanite Phoenician people. According to this same Dictionary of the Bible, page 23, there it explained that the square characters of the modern Hebrew writings, which did appear in the Dead Sea Scrolls, which came about from the 2nd century BC, to the 5th or 4th century BC. Which were in many ways, and form identical with that of the inscription of the Canaanites Phoenician writings. Dictionary of the Bible went on to explained that from the foreign rulers of what became known as the Middle East, of the great powers of Babylon, Assyria, and Sidon, which supposed to be known as Zidon, and this land of Zidon is what became known as the land of Syria of today. Also, the Canaanite city of Byblos of Lebanon, the city Tyre, and the cities of Ashkelon, which were cities of the Canaanites, and of the Philistine people. Also, the city of Jerusalem of the Jebusites of the Canaanites people. Also Gezer, Lachish, Megiddo, and many other cities of what is now called as Middle East, are the important document of history that did shed light of knowledge to the West. Which is speaking of Western, and Eastern Europe. Dictionary of the Bible went on to explained, that the Hebrew writing also came from the Canaanites family of people. I must say that I am not surprised to come to know of this knowledge of history, because Abraham who is the forefather of the Hebrew people, was a Cushites man from the country of Babylon. This was by his mother side of people, which was one of the kingdoms of Nimrod, where Abraham was born and raise, until when Yahweh told him to leave from Babylon.

This was for Abraham to go were the Canaanite people was mostly living, so as to take over their lands Yahweh had given to him, and his seed after him. As I have also mention many times that the children of Israel mothers, were from the granddaughters of the people of Ham. Who they were living around in the so-call Middle East, and what became known as North Africa, that gave birth to this nation of people. So, from these mothers, and granddaughters of the people of Ham, gave birth to this nation of people who become known as the Israelites people of Jacob, who they were living around in the so-call Middle East, and what became known as North Africa. As I had mention many times, that Nimrod himself was the last son of Cush, and all these Hamite' people of that time, use to live very close together as neighbors, in what became known as the so-call Middle East, and what is now known as North Africa.

This time was way before all the various kingdoms of the people of Ham was destroyed by Yahweh. Also before the land of Ham were conquered by so many different colonial conquerors, and their many kingdoms were destroyed, or taken over by other people. According to this Dictionary of the Bible, the Aramaic writing and language did become the center of the Persian Empire. So, what this information is telling me, is that the writing of what became known as the Indian writing, the Chinese writing script, originally came from the Hieroglyph writing of the people of Mizraim. Also, from the Phoenicians, Hethites, Assyrians, the Babylonians, and from other Hamite's kingdoms, of what they the Gentile European people called as the Middle Eastern people, that eventually spread to Asia of the people of Shem. Dictionary of the Bible, went on to explained that the early

46

Israelites months of the year, came from the Canaanites names of their months, they the children of Israel did adopt as their months of the year, they were first using, before they went into captivity into Babylon. These months of the year that the children of Isreal were first using, before they were taken as captive in Babylon, is also mentioned in the Old Covenant part of the Scripture, such as Ziw, Ethannim and Bul. According to this Dictionary of the Bible, during the time of the Israelites exile in Babylon, in the time of (587 BC), the Babylonian name of the months was also adopted by the children of Israel, while they were in captivity in Babylon.

So, the name of the Babylonian names of the months they the children of Israel did adopt to, were known as Nisan, which is now correspond to March and April. Iyyar, which is now correspond to April and May. Siwan, which is now correspond to May to June. Tammuz, which is correspond to June and July. AB, which is now correspond to July and August. Elul, that is correspond with August to September. Tishri, which is now correspond with September and October. Marheshwan is correspond to October and November. Kisleu, which is now correspond to November and December. Tebet, which is now correspond with December to January, Shebat that is connected to January and February. Adar that is correspond to February and March. According to some printed document I did receive, while I was attending plumbing school, at the Essex Vocational Technical Institute, in the Newark area of New Jersey, that is called the Plumbing History, beginning and beyond.

There in page 11 of these printed documents; it is stated that from the time of AD 455 to AD 1400, this was after the breakup of the Roman Empire, ruling over Western Europe. This brake up of the Empire ruling over the Western Europe, was brought about by a Germanic tribe who were known as the Visigoths. Also by a Germanic tribe who were known as the Vandal, and by the Huns, who were a Chinese looking people, of what become known as Asia. According to what I have read from volume 20 of the Encyclopaedia, this time is what they the Gentiles people of Europe did call as The Dark Ages, or Medieval Europe. Their reason for using the word Dark Ages, it was because of the Roman Empire, that did brought light of knowledge, of learning to the people of Western, and Eastern Europe. Who were in total darkness of ignorance, of reading, writing and arithmetic for themselves. It was not until the time of the Greeks, and the Romans conquest, ruling over Western and Eastern Europe, that gave light of knowledge, of reading, writing and arithmetic to the people of Western, and Eastern Europe. Due to this light of knowledge that came from the Greeks, and the Romans, gave light to the rest of the people of Europe, to become literate people, able to read and write for themselves. This is the reason why the word classical, and classic is used in the Webster Colligate Dictionary of the Fifth Edition, of what became known as the English language. It is, because the word classical came from the word classic, which meant during Greek and Roman time of their ruler ship, over the Gentile land that became known as Europe, and other part of the known world of that ancient time. During this Dark Ages of what they had call as Medieval Europe, many people of Europe used to throw their chamber pots of human waste into the streets, because they did not know any better. Due to their ignorance, caused diseases after diseases to break out in Europe, that they did call as a plague, that did destroyed more than one-quarter of the population of Europe.

This plumbing history document clearly mention that the sanitary plumbing system, as we know it as today, was first started in the land of Mizraim that become known as Egypt. I also want to point out that the people of Mizraim started the making of bricks long before the Romans, and the Greeks, who they the Gentile people of Europe say, it was the Greeks and the Roman who had started the civilization of the world, according to their lies of false history. This knowledge of the making of bricks eventually spread to the Gentile land of Europe, that they now showed many time on their television, and on their history channel, how to make bricks, and lay bricks.

As if to say they were the people who has started this craft, and skills of the laying of bricks, and the making of bricks. So, I am quite sure the Encyclopaedia could not be speaking about many of the people of Ham, who gave birth of light of knowledge and civilization to the world of people, and Europe. Many of whom were later conquered by the Greeks, Romans, and by the rest of the Gentile family of Europe, when they became a strong nation of people to deal with. This downfall of the various kingdoms of the people of Ham, was according to the various prophecies of (Daniel Chapter 2, and Daniel Chapter 7), that I have mentioned before, that had been full field upon the various kingdoms of the people of Ham, of the ancient world that gone by. This fulfillment of these prophecies have brought our downfall, of the ancient world of the people of Ham of the ancient world that gone by. When I went to live in London in the sixties, many of the people was so backward, that the fish and chips shops would serve their customers fish and chips in newspaper. Many times I had protested to different fish and chips shops, that I did not want my fish and chips in newspaper, because it is unsanitary to serve food in newspapers. But to the people of Britain, it meant nothing all, because that were apart of their way of life, and custom. I consider serving fish and chips in newspaper to be very dirty, and unsanitary to serve food in, but again, it did not meant anything to the people of Britain. Different times I have seen people buy bread in Britain that was not covered with paper, but it were just left wide naked, as when it comes from out of the baker's oven. They would just put it under their arm, or in a baby push chair, that they call as a pram. Or they would just put it down anywhere, and it did not meant anything to them at all. In my mind I had considered that to be very filthy, and dirty, to serve food in.

But to the people of Britain it meant notting all, because that were a part of their lifestyle and culture. One time I did complained to a shopkeeper about putting bread rolls unwrapped in sack bags, that we people in Jamaica called as crocus bags. This crocus bag is what people would put their harvests from the field in, but this shopkeeper told me that Britain is cold, so there are no germs there in Brian, like that of Jamaica. But because Jamaica is hot, so there are germs there. From I have been lived in Jamaica until I was about fourteen to fifteen years old, and went to live in Britain, I have never seen any Hamite's people of Jamaica, buy unwrapped bred and put it under their arm.

It would have considered by the Hamite's people of Jamaica, to be very unsanitary, and dirty. If an inspector of Jamaica was to see a bread truck, with bread unwrapped, with the door left wide open, for flies, and other insects to crawl on. They would see to it, that all those breads were dump and put in the garbage. Yet, these are the same people who have the audacity of telling us, how civilized they are, and how uncivilized we are.

The Arawak's, and the Caribs people with other natives tribes of the so-call New World, of the Gentile European people capture land, of what become known as the Americas, were the of the natives of these land area. Also what did become known as the West Indies, by way of Columbus, that later became known as the Caribbean, by these same Gentile European people of Europe. These native's people were the first slaves for the Gentile people of Europe, of their captured lands. This also did in clouded the Incas, Azteca's, Mayans with other various natives, who the people of Europe did called as the Indian people of their New World. Later the remainders of these people, who had survive from their slavery, and brutality, was given the name as the Latino's, and the Hispanic people, of their captured lands. These different tribes of the Eskimo's people, with other Asiatic Chinese, Indian looking people, who had cross over from Asia to Greenland, to Alaska. To what became known as Canada, and what became known as the United States, of America, which were a part of the various natives lands, they the Gentile people call as their New World. This is because of many of these natives people, did become a part of their victims, of slavery, and many of these tribe of people were slater off their land by the Spanish, and other European conquerors. These people were the first slaves for the people of Europe, of their captured New World, of the Americas, and the West Indies, whom they the Gentile people of Europe, have try their very best, to keep this knowledge of history from the world of other people, who came under their captivity's as secret, to keep under the carpet.

They the Gentile people of Europe, only teach the world of other people who came under the European family captivities, that we the Hamite's people, who they name as the Negroes, Black people, and African people were their first, and only slaves, who were brought over from the land of Ham, of what is now known as Africa, to served them as their captives. I must point out that these Gentile people of Europe, did not bother to teach the world of other people, who came under their captivities, that these native's people were their first slaves, who they were praying upon for slave laborer, and to take away their lands to gain wealth.

This knowledge of understanding I came to, about the land area of what became known as Asia, Greenland, to the Americas, and the West Indies, it is by looking at the world Atlas, showing the land of Greenland that is in the Arctic area of the world. Greenland is not too far away from what is now known as Alaska, and Canada, who were various Eskimos, and Mohegans tribe people of Asia, who used to live in these land area of the world, before the coming of these Gentile European people of Europe. This land of Greenland was conquered by the Danish Germanic people of Europe, to be a part of their colonies. This land area of Greenland, to what become known as Alaska, did belong to the various Eskimos, Indian, Chinese looking people, who were given different names, to please these Gentile European people of Europe, of their capture lands. Such as the people who they named as Red Indians, and the Mohegans who used to live from what is now known as Canada to Boston Massachusetts, to what became known as New York. So, the name South America, were known before as the land of Guiana by the Arawak's people, who were part of the various natives, that meant to them, land of water. So, were the island the Arawak's people did name as Cuba, that meant to them land of water as well. Also, the island the Arawak's people did name as Haiti, that also did meant to them land of water as well. This land of Haiti were later rename by Columbus as Hispaniola, which meant to Columbus little Spain, because this island of Haiti did remind him very much of the land area of Spain. The Arawak's people also were the owner of the island they did named as Xaymaca, that meant to them land of water as well, but when Columbus came in 1494, to take away the island from the Arawak's people, he named the island as Saint Jago.

In 1665, Oliver Cromwell who were the Prime Minister of Britain at the time, he sent out Admiral Penn, and General Venables, to go and take away the island of Haiti from the power of the Spanish, who were the ruler of the island at the time. However, the British got chase off from the island of Haiti by the Spanish, so on their way back to Britain, they stop off at the island of Xaymaca to have a try in taking away this island from the power of the Spanish. The British was successful in their conquest of the island of Xaymaca from the power of the

Spanish. After the conquest of the island, they name the island as Jamaica, that did take it is name from the Arawak's name of Xaymaca.

The island of Trinidad did also belong to the Arawak's people, before the coming of the Spanish, and the British, who came to the island, to take away the island from the Arawaks people, according to the reading of History of The West Indian People, book 2. I must also mention that the island of what became known as the Bahamas, and the land area of what became known as Florida did belong to the Arawak's people. This was before the coming of these Gentile European people, who came and take away these people lands to gain wealth. Later when the Spanish take over from Columbus, and Americas Vespucci, who were working for the Spanish, then a part of the land area of Guiana became known as Brazil by the conquest of the Portuguese. This land area of Guiana also takes on various Spanish names, such as Panama, Colombia, Venezuela, Paraguay, Argentina, Chile, Bolivia, with other various Spanish names. One see on the various world map of today, that were develop by these same Gentile European people of Europe, to please themselves, and to deceive others people. This was also to fool the crowd of people of today, who do not have any knowledge about the history of these land areas of the Guianas. So, a part of the land area of Guiana, was also conquered from the power of the Spanish, by other various European colonial pirates. Such as the Dutch, who named a part of the land area of Guiana, of their conquest, as Dutch Guyana, that did become known as Suriname. The French pirates did also captured a part of the land area of Guiana from the power of the Spanish, and name the land as French Guyana. The British also captured a part of the land area of Guiana from the power of the Spanish, and they named the land area as British Guyana. The Spanish also did have Mexico, Texas, California, and Florida, and what did become known as the United States, that did become known as North America, with the land area of what did become known as Canada.

Looking at the World Atlas, showing the land of Mexico, Guatemala, Honduras, Nicaragua, with the land area of Costa Rica, that is now known as Central America. Which were the lands area of the Aztec and Mayans, that was taken away by the Spanish, and become a part of their territory's. Later the Dutch pirates, and the French pirates, and the British pirates forth the Spanish and take away a part of their New World, that did become known as North America, speaking of what is now known as the United States, Mexico and what is now known as Canada.

According to volume 8 of the Encyclopaedia Britannica, there it explained that the Mohegans, and a tribe who were known as the Munsee, were the natives of what is now known as Canada, and what become known as New York. The Encyclopaedia explained that New York was first settled by the Dutch, as their colony, that they did name as New Amsterdam in 1625. Later came the British pirates, and forth the Dutch, and take away control of New Amsterdam from the power of the Dutch in 1664, and they the British name the place as New York. So, later the British pirates, and the French pirates forth among themselves, and take over control of what become known as Canada, as a part of their colony of control. They the British take one part of the land area they name as Ontario, under their control of ruler ship. The French take over ruler ship of the other part of the land area, they did name as Quebec, to be under French control. After these European powers, fourth among themselves, and kill off the Mohegans, with other various natives 'tribes who were living in the land area. Then they made a movie that were called last of the Mohegans, because many of these people were no longer around in life. There was also the Aztecs and the Mayans of what is now known as Mexico, many of these people who did not get slater off, or who were not enslave to death, were given a new identity. Such as the Latino and the Hispanic race of people, by the Gentile people of what become known as the United States of America. Many of these people, are now known as the Mexican, and the Hispanic, and the Latino people, who are a mixture of the blood of the Spanish, with that of other European conquerors of their New World. Many of these Aztecs and Mayans people of today, who see themselves as the Spanish people, because they speak the Spanish language of Spain, who were their conquerors, and former slave masters of their conquered lands.

Many of these people do not have any knowledge of who they are, and where they and their ancestors is coming from. Because many of these people history are lost, and they were brainwash by the people of Europe to see themselves in whatever new names they the Gentile British settlers of what became known as the American, gave to them to see themselves as such. These different tribes of the area were the natives of what became known as Mexican, to what is now known as Honduras of Central America. Also, according to volume 2 of the Encyclopaedia, there it explained that before the European settlement of what become known as California, the language of the area was consists of various tribal natives.

 Such as the Na-Dene, the Hokan, Penuttian, the Aztec Tanoan, and mnany of the Aztec Tanoan is now known as a part of the Mexicans people, that is also consist of the many former Spanish settlers, who were the conquerors of the land. I just thought by bring out this little information about this place, would give some enlightenment of the history of this place of the so call New World, that did become known as California. These natives were living in this part of the world, before the coming of these Gentile European people, who came and enslave, and slather off many of these people from their lands, to gain wealth. According to a book, called A Short History of the West Indies, there it explains that before the conquest of Mexico by Cortes in 1519-1521, the population of these Aztecs and Mayans was estimated to be about 25 million or more. But after the brutality of force labor of slavery by the Spanish, brought the population of these people, to a mere 1 million, or a few thousands living sole of these people. In comparison to the millions, they were before the coming of the Spanish, and also that of other Gentile people of Europe, who came and take away their lands, to become rich people. Also, diseases that were brought over from Europe, by the Spanish, Portuguese, and other European people, had taken it toll on many of these natives people lives. Cortes sailed from the island of Cuba with a small army of about 600 men, 11 war ships, and 16 horses to go and captured the land of the Aztecs and the Mayans. Due to the capture of Mexico and Peru brought the Spanish an immense wealth of gold, silver, and copper.

 This cost a steady flow of the Spanish settlers to left from Hispaniola, Cuba, and Europe, to go and settle on the mainland that became known as South, and Central America. Because of the wealth that could be found on the mainland, that become known as the Americans. The wealth of Mexico was right on time, because the gold they had found in the island of Hispaniola, and Cuba was running out. The abundance of wealth found on the mainland, cost many Spanish settlers to lose interest in many of the smaller islands of the West Indies, because there was not much gold there to be found, like that of the mainland of what become known as the Americas. Although much Spanish settlement was made on the mainland, yet there were still small Spanish settlement that were made on Hispaniola, Cuba, Jamaica, and Puerto Rico. Many other parts of the West Indies were only useful to the Spanish for ships coming from Spain, and going to the mainland of the Americas, and to return back to Spain with their new-found wealth from their captured land of their New World.

A Short History of the West Indies explained that the Spanish settlement on the island of Puerto Rico, was in 1512, but before the Spanish settlement on the island, there were a group of Caribs who did lived on the island, before the Spanish came and take away their island. Also, they the Caribs resisted the Spanish settlement of Puerto Rico, and others part of their settlement, more than that of the Arawak's people of the island of Hispaniola, and in other places of their New World. Many people of today need to realize that this part of the world that is now known as the Americas, and the West Indies, did not belong to the people of Europe. Until the time of their conquest, by way of Columbus, and Amerigo Vespucci, for the people of Spain. This is also true for the other European pirates, who left from Europe to come and capture a part of the land area of the New World from the power of the Spanish. To be their colony of their mother country, were they came from. When I was living in the country of Denmark during the sixties, I take notice that there were quite allot of Chinese looking people who were living there in Denmark. These Chinese looking people were the natives of Greenland, that was conquered by the Danish people, and it is now ruled and govern by the Danish Germanic people of Denmark. According to the book, A Short History of the West Indies, written by JH Parry Philip Sherlock, and Anthony Maingot of the Fourth Edition, there the book explained that the name Caribbean came from the Spanish. Because they saw sign that many of the Caribs people were cannibals. Whether this story is true or not, one cannot say for sure, because in the eyes of the people of Europe, many of the people who they had conquered, were consider to them to be cannibals, and savages.

Because many of these people land were not develop as Europe, so according to this information from A Short History of the West Indies, the name Caribbean Islands, which simply mean savages, speaking of the Caribs people, who they say were cannibals and savages. Although many of the islands, and many other parts of what became known as the South American course, were in habited by the piece full Arawak's people. According to book I of the History of the West Indian People, the Spanish enslaved many of the Arawak's, and the Caribs people to death, where many of these people were dying off like flies, and many times, they would throw the dead bodies of these people, to the dogs for them to feast upon, because they were dying off in such great numbers.

Due to the fact that they could not cope with the pressure of slavery that was force on them, by these Gentile Spanish people of Europe. After the Spanish and the Portuguese, enslaved and brutalized, and caused the reduction of these people population to become a mere few thousand, or a million. In comparison to the population they were, before the coming of the Spanish, and other Gentile's people of Europe. Who came to their world as strangers, and enslaved them, and take way heir land to gain wealth. The way many of the Spanish settlers saw it on the island of Hispaniola, which was the first large settlement of the Spanish in their New World. The shortage of labor to work on their plantation's fields, the settlers solved the problem by subjecting many of the natives to force labor of slavery. The Spanish settlers, many of whom were Roman Catholic believers, believed to themselves that the conquest of these natives people was necessary to Christianize them to the belief of Roman Catholicism, of the Roman Catholic Church, that became known as Christianity. The Spanish settlers economy was heavily depended on force labor of slavery of these natives, to bring in much wealth into their established system. According to a proper gander statement that was made in the book, A Short History of the West Indies, there it explains that the Spanish conquest and settlement of the West Indies, and of the Americas was based upon spiritual, as well as the military might of their swordsmanship of their conquests, over these people, and their lands. (The principal opposition to the rule of their swordsmen ship, was the soldiers of the church, meaning the Roman Catholic Church). This was of their hypocritical of what they had called as Roman Catholic Christianity of deception, to the mind of their many captives.

Yet the way they saw it, it was necessary to keep the various tribal natives under bondage of force labor of slavery, because the Spanish settlers 'economy was heavily based upon the slave labor of these people, to bring in much wealth into their established system of conquest. It is also mention in the same book that was quoted, that many of the Arawak's people of the Bahamas use to commit suicide, rather than subject themselves to slavery of the Spanish. This book also mentions that one of the things many of the Spanish settlers use to do, so as to eradicate many of these people from life, were to drive their animals true their cultivation, so as to stave many of these people to death. Yet, these are the same so-call wicked Christian people, who had the nerves to called themselves follower of Yashua.

Who become known as Jesus and Christ, in the Greek and Latin language of the Romans. These so-call Christians people, had nothing to do with the true followers of Yashua. Like that of many of his Apostles, of the children of Israel, who were Yehudahites, and the Benjamites followers of Yeshua, who he was sent to by Yahweh. Many of these Spanish settlers who went to the West Indies, went there with the intentions to look for gold, silver, and pearl to get rich quickly, without having to do any kind of hard work. Also, Pizarro Francisco went and conquered the kingdom of Peru from Incas people, in 1533, that did also brought a lot of gold and other treasures from the conquest of the Incas to the Spanish kingdom of Spain. This was by him using what become known as Christianity of the Roman Catholic Church, as a front to conquer these people. Pizarro left from the island of Cuba, and went true what become known as Panama, to go and conquer the kingdom of Inker people of Peru. While he was near the Incas city of Cajamarca, he sent out a priest with the Bible, for him to go to the ruler of the Inca people, and for this ruler to accept Christianity, and Charles V of Spain to be their sovereign ruler. Atahuallpa, who was the ruler of the Inca people, flatly refused this religious philosophy of the Spanish Catholic Church believers, and he also did not entertain the idea of accepting Charles V as his sovereign ruler for he and his people, to be their master. One of the reasons why Atahuallpa may have thrown down the Bible that the Spanish Catholic priest did presented to him to accept as Christianity, it was because at the time the Bible was written in the Spanish language, a language Atahuallpa and his people could not read and understand.

It was not written in their language, until they were conquered, and converted by the Spanish to Christianity. Then the Spanish language become the language of many of these natives people, as their own language. Due to Atahuallpa rejection of what they had presented to him as Christianity, and for him to accept Charles V as their new ruler. After the priest by the name of Valverde, reported back to Pizarro of the rejection of Atahuallpa, Pizarro gave the order to attack the Incas. Many of these people, were cut down in the battle, and Atahuallpa was seized by Pizarro and his men. One of the demands Pizarro made to the Inca ruler, for his freedom, was that he must have a lot of gold and silver to be brought to him, for his release. After Atahuallpa submitted to his wishes for gold and silver to be brought to him, Pizarro came up with some fabricated charges he put against Atahuallpa.

After gold and silver was brought to Pizarro, Pizarro had him strangled to death, in August of 1533. After the death of Atahuallpa, the kingdom of Peru became that of Spain, and its rulers. Between the conquest of Mexico, Peru, with other countries of the Americas, brought the Spanish an immense welt, of gold and other treasures. Much of the information about Cortes was taken from volume 3 of the Encyclopaedia Britannica. Also, about Pizarro Francisco was taken from volume 9, of the Encyclopaedia Britannica. After the Spanish made themselves rich from the blood, sweat and tears of the many natives people of their New World, finally many of the Spanish settlers who become lawyers, priests, and aristocrats from the blood of these people. Many of their conscience started to bother many of them, to seek freedom, and justice for many of these people who were on the verge of becoming extinct. Because of slavery, and the brutality from the Spanish, and from the Portuguese, that was force on these people, they could not endure and cope with. In 1511, a complaint of opposition was started against the exploitation and slavery of these natives by a Catholic priest, whose name was known as Fray Antonio de Montesinos. Montesinos started his campaign of freedom for the natives of Santo Domingo, which did caused many of his fellow Spanish settlers' conscience to bother some of them, to seek freedom for these people, from the Crown of Spain. Montesinos was sent to Spain by some of his Spanish settlers of Santo Domingo. This was to seek better treatment for many of these natives, against many of his fellow Spanish plantation settlers. Whose livelihood and wealth was based upon the abusement, and the slave labor of these people. Finally, in 1512, a law was passed by Spain, that the natives was free men, and they were no longer slaves, and they were to be converted to Christianity by peaceful means, and not by force, and they was to put to work.

After the Spanish Government of Spain used and abuse these native people to gain wealth, they finally came to the reality that these people was fellow human bean like themselves, and they must be given their freedom. Spain finally came to the conclusion that the natives had rights like everyone else, and the enslavement of these people was forbidden by their laws from that standpoint onward. I must point out that reading from the book, A Short History of the West Indies, although the Spain had passed the law of freedom for these people, yet they were not free.

Many of them was still in bondage by many Spanish settlers of their New World, because the freedom law of Spain were ignored by many Spanish settlers of their settlement. Many of the locals who were in sympathy with the condition of these people, they had to appeal to Spain to get a closer supervision, and protection for the natives against many of their fellow Spanish settlers, who was abusing these people. This closer control of supervision was achieved by the Spanish Government, appointing paid salary governors, to replace that of the self-appointed Governors, and investors of their wickedness. The Crown of Spain also appointed judges who had to answer to Spain, and although law was passed to give these people their liberty, many of them was still denied freedom from many of these Spanish settlers. Another crusade for the right and life of these natives people, was made by one Bartolome de Las Casas, whose protest were made in Hispaniola. He continued his plea for the freedom of these native throughout his life, and he demonstrated liberty for them to the Crown of Spain that they must pass stiffer laws forcing the Spanish settlers of their New World to comply with the law, in giving these people there freedom. In 1516, he himself was appointed protector of the interest of these people to the crown of Spain. The hard reality was recognized, that the Spanish settlers in Hispaniola, and on the other islands of the West Indies, as well as on the mainland could not survive without slave labor of the various natives to work on their plantation's fields. Gold minds, as well as houseboys, and house girls, as well as yard boys, and yard girls, and a slave substitutes slave labor force was needed to take the place of the various natives, who were given their freedom from the Crown of Spain.

The replacement slave for the Gentile People of their New World, who they had name as Indians, who were replace by the Hamite's people of Ham, who were brought over to the Gentile people New World, who they had called as the Negros, Black people, and the African people. So, the various natives of their New World were given their freedom in 1500, and 1600, and the Hamite's people were brought over to the New World, as the new replacement slaves to serve them. This knowledge I came to, was taken from the book, History of the West Indies. I would also like to point out that, had it not been for the mercy and kindness of Yahweh, who is watching from above, who has prevented these Gentile people of Europe from destroying all the Hamite's people whom they had taken as their captives and slave. Otherwise there would not have been any of us dark skin Hamite's people left alive today. We would have become an extinct people by now, and we would only read about from the various European story books, they would tell from their own point of view, of who they think we were as a people. Many of us who would have survived from their brutality, would look more like the Mulattos people, that became known today as the Colored people, and the Hispanics and the Latinos people, because many of these people have more of the Gentile European man blood running through their veins. Many of whom are closer in skin color to that of the people of Europe, then many of us darker skin Hamite's people. No wonder many of the Gentile people of the land of what become known as Europe, were known as the barbarian's people, because many of the time they would invade and slaughter off other European tribes of their villages, who they wanted to take over, and control their lands. The reason for many of their invasion was because the invading tribes wanted to become the dominant ruler of the land, and to have control of the wealth of the village, or countries of their conquests.

So, this replacement slave labor was solved by the Portuguese, because, they did already started slavery in the land of Ham from the 1400, and they saw sign that the people of the land of Ham, were a much stronger set of people, more than many of the natives of their New World. Furthermore, from the Portuguese point of view, they the Hamite's people of the land of Ham, were a less primitive people, more than that of various natives of their New World, who were the first slave for these Gentile people, of their captured world.

Moreover, they the Hamite's people in the land of Ham, were more easier to adapt to their demands, and they could endure the hardship of slavery much better than many of the natives of their New World. So, in the eyes of the Portuguese people, with that of other European people, they the Hamite's people was a more stronger set of people. So, in other words, in the minds set of the Portuguese people, the Hamite's people make a better slave, then that of the natives who they had called as the Indians, of their New World. It was the Spanish priest, and the Spanish Government of Spain who had saved the Arawak's, Caribs, and other native tribes of their New World from total destruction from themselves. Plus the danger of many of these people becoming an extinct people. Many Spanish settlers of their New World, who had fought extremely hard for the freedom of many of the natives from slavery. Saw nothing wrong with the idea of the capturing, and the enslavement of many Hamite's people, who was rooted up, and shipped out from their homeland to serve them as the new replacement slaves. According to the book, A Short History of the West Indies, many Hamite's people who were captured, and uprooted from their homeland as slaves, many of them pine away and died. Matter of fact, it is also mentioned in the said book, that many of the slave ships that left from the land of Ham with their cargos of slaves, was like a floating tomb, because many of the slaves died on their way over to the New World of the Gentile people of Europe. The number of slaves who had died was in the millions, because their lives was worth nothing much but a dollar sign, or the pound sign of the British people money, or whatever form of money they were using during the slavery days.

It is also mentioned in the said book, that the have rigs slave life in the West Indies, and what become known as the Americas, was about nine years, because the way the slave masters saw it, they did not mind working them to death, because it was easier to replace slaves, then having the troubles of taking care of them. It is also stated in the said book that various slave masters mentioned, of how many slaves they had personally kill, as their personal pleasure of joy, of their thirst for shedding blood, and to commit wickedness of their evil deeds. This is because of the wicked and evil ways of the Gentile people of Europe, who love to shed blood, and to conquered other people and their lands to get rich. One must also realize that many of these books I have written from, they the Gentile people of Europe, were only writing to their own people, boasting of the things they and their ancestors, had done to many other people who become their captives, and slaves to get rich.

Now they are enjoying the wealth, and the fruit of their ancestor's deeds, by becoming rich people of their many conquests, and enslavement of many people to bring in much wealth into their system. These are the same people of today, who have set themselves up as judges, and lawyers, who many of the time we as a people have to go before them, in their court system to gain justice and freedom. These were the same people, who have been our murders, and destroyers for many centuries. No wonder the prison system of the United States, and in many other parts of their x slaver colonies, and islands of the world where many of our Hamite's people happen to find themselves, and called home. They have become the victims of their prison system, because it was design that way for them to fall into. Also for the people of Europe to get rich from their prison system, and from their court system. More over the prison system, and the court system of the Gentile European people, have become a big business, where the bond people make moneys to get a person free from their jails, or from their prisons system. The police force system gets paid, the lawyers, judges, and the probation officer, and the prison warden get paid to be a part of the prison system of the people of Europe. They make allot of money from their many free salve captives' people of today, going in and out of their prison system, so it as become a big business for them to make money from their many x slaves 'people who became their free slave citizens of today, going in and out of their prison system. They also used the court system as another form of business to bring in extra wealth, from many of their captive's citizens, because one must have to pays the court of their various fines, other wise they will go to prison for the rest of their lives. In, which many of their captive's citizens try their best to stay away from their court system, although it is very hard to do so, because the system was design to make money from their many free slave people of today, by way of the police, and their tickets. Also, by the court, of their many finds, they put upon their many free slave people who become their citizens, of their system. Which is a form of a business, to make more money for their citizens to get rich, from their many captives free slave people, of their system.

The slave labor of the Hamite's people was in such a big demand in their New World, and in some parts of the Gentile land of Europe, that it became a big business for the various nations of Europe to make wealth from various miners who wanted slave labor to work in their gold mines, and on their plantation fields.

So, in 1510, the Spanish government of Spain granted various agents in Seville licenses to ship out 250 of their Hamite's slaves they had there, to go and work in their gold mines they had in Hispaniola, now known as Haiti and Santo Domingo. A Short History of the West Indian People explained that the shipment of slaves to Spain, and Portugal did not turn out to be quite successful as they had hoped to be. So, when the settlers of their New World needed more slave laborers for the plantations field, because they had enslaved to death, or just slaughtered off many of the Arawak's people from the island of Hispaniola. Also, elsewhere of their New World, so when the settlers of Hispaniola appeal to King Charles for the need of more slave labor, King Charles V of Spain, who was the grandson of Ferdinand and Isabella, allowed the importation of 4,000 Hamite's slaves to be shipped to the island of Hispaniola. This was to take over from where the Arawak's people left off as the new slaves. So, by the time of the 16th century, most of the native Arawak's on the island of Haiti, or what did become known as Hispaniola by Columbus, had disappeared from off the island. So, it's either the Spanish had enslaved these people to death, or they were just slaughtered off the island, or had died off from various diseases that were brought over to the New World by these Gentile people of Europe. This was to infect the native, with these diseases, so that they would just die off, and they would to take away their lands of the New World for themselves, and to see themselves as the new natives. History of the West Indian People Book II, under the title of BARBADOS, that was called Little Britain of the West, or of the West Indies. This was because of the large numbers of British settlers, who had settled there on the island to establish the island as a British colony. The book mention that when the British capture the island of Barbados, and other various islands of the West Indies from the Spanish, many of the Arawak's and the Caribs people, were no longer living on these islands as before.

So, many of these people were either slather off by the Spanish, or they were enslaved to death. Volume 5 of the Encyclopaedia explained that the Spanish settlement on the Island of Haiti was very small in population, and they were mostly living near to the eastern part of the island that did become known as Santo Domingo. The slave trade was first started in the New World by the Portuguese, the Spanish, and later by the Dutch, French and by the British. So, in 1518, in order to stop the Portuguese, who were the big suppliers of captured slaves from the land of Ham, who were smuggling captured slaves into the New World for the rite price. The Spanish government had to grant special licenses to many Spanish slave traders to import slaves from the land of Ham to the West Indies, and the Americas, so as to make the slave trade business more competitive for everyone who were involved in the business, and not just for the Portuguese to make wealth from the slave business. The demand for the Hamite's slave labor in their various plantations, and gold mines, or whatever mine they had there in their New World, or in Europe. Became a high priority to the various slave dealers, that the Spanish government had to give special licenses to many subcontractors who had ships, to keep up with the supply of the Hamite's slaves labor. These licenses that were granted to various privateer's ship owners, were to fill the gap of the Hamite's slave labor market, that were in such a big demand for these Hamite's slave labor. Many of these dealers who had licenses, had to buy their slave supplies from the Portuguese merchants, because they the Portuguese started slavery first in the land of Ham, before the Spanish, Dutch, Belgium's, French and the British. The Portuguese started slavery in the land of Ham to support their sugar cane plantations, and other commodities they used to grew there in the land of Ham, they had learn from the various natives, of the land of Ham. These produce of the Portuguese would ship to Europe, to sell among themselves, to make big profits from slave labor. The Portuguese set up their trading post along what became known as the West African Coast, who were the first Gentile Europeans people to take many Hamite's slaves to ship to their New World of what they had named as Brazil. According to Volume 25 of the Encyclopaedia, a Portuguese man by the name of Pedro Alvares Cabral landed in the area that became known as Brazil, in April 22, of 1500, and he claim the land area in the name of Portugal.

By his conquest of what become known as Brazil, the Portuguese found diamonds and gold that brought an immense wealth to the Portuguese kingdom of Lisbon. From what I have read from reading Volume 25 of the Encyclopaedia, what become known as Portugal, became an independent state in the 12th century, because this place takes its name from Portus Cale. Which were an old Roman settlement, near the bank of the Douro River. The southern part of this Roman settlement was occupied by a Germanic Gaelic people, who were known as the Suebi people, who were living there in the time of 411 AD, that became known Portucale, or Porto. In AD 1139 Afonso Henriques take on the title as king, and he take over what became known as Lisbon, and his successor take over what became known as Alentejo, and Algarve from the Muslim occupation in 1252.

These Portuguese people went and capture the island of Madeira, and the island that became known as Azores in the 15th century, and made it a part of their settlement. A Political History of Tropical Africa explain that the Portuguese went to the land of Ham, with their ships, and with the cross of Christ to save souls for Christ, as they did put it. With their intention to rob and steal, and to murder in the name of Christianity to get rich. The Portuguese were the first Gentile European conquerors who came after the Greeks, Romans, and the Turks to penetrate deep into the interior of the heart of the land of Ham, they call as Africa. A Political History of Tropical Africa went on to explained that one of the reasons why the Portuguese was pushing their way deep into the interior of what they called as Africa. It was because they were looking for the rich kingdom of the Congo, and the kingdom of Ghana to scrape up the riches from the land, to take back to their Gentile land of Europe. This added to rivalry, greed, strive and conflict between the various Gentile countries of Europe fighting among themselves for world domination. Many of the times it would lead to various wars, and world wars among themselves fighting for colonial control of people and their lands, and the wealth that these lands produce. Portugal became a colony of Spain, and Phillip III setup a council to oversee the Portuguese colonial affairs that they had set up. According to Volume 6 of the Encyclopaedia Britannica, the Portuguese reached

India in 1497, by way of Vasco de Gama. Before the time of the Portuguese, it was the Greeks, and then the Romans, who had control over the riches of the land of Bharat that became known as India. Also, the land area that became known as Asia, that were under the Gentile European people control, which did became their colonies of position. According to Volume 25 of the Encyclopaedia Britannica, Spain rule Portugal from 1580, until they were able to get their independent from Spain in 1640. Phillip III setup this supervisory body with the Portuguese to oversee the Portuguese Trading House of India.

Philip III were also ruling over the kingdom of Portugal, when he setup this body to oversee the Portuguese colonial affairs of the land of Bharat, that became known as India. After the Portuguese got their independence from Spain they take back their colonial affairs of India's until they were forced out of India by the British. The British take over India from the Portuguese, and became the Lord of all India. Later they the British divided the land of Bharat that did become known as India, then they the British called one-part Bangladesh, Pakistan, and the other part of the land area, they name as India.

This was to cause conflict, confusion and division, and wars among the people who were living there, because indeed they were one family of the land area. These Gentile European people are like the cheaters, hyenas, lions, leopards, and the tigers of the land of Ham, and India. When the cheetah makes a kill, then come along the hyena, lion, or leopard to take away the kill, or some of the kill from the cheaters for themselves, because they are much stronger than the cheetah. It was the same way with the various Gentiles European colonial conquerors, fighting among themselves for the colonial control of people and their lands, to be their colonies of position to get rich. The Portuguese started their conquests after the Greeks, Romans, Turks, then came the Spanish, Dutch, French, and the British to fight and kill each other over the various conquered colonies of the Portuguese. These Gentile European colonial conquerors distinguish, and separate the Hamite's people who were living south of the Sahara as the so-called Black African nations. The other Hamite's nations who were livening in the northern part of the land of Ham, who are governed, and controlled by the Mohammedans, Muslim people of Ismael. They name these people as the Middle Eastern, and the Arab people, who shared the land area of the so-call Middle East, as the Middle Eastern people. After the fighting of wars between themselves that became known as world wars for greed, power, wealth, and control was over for a while. Then they would come together and form a peace treaty of laws to protect their stolen wealth from each other. The Spanish, Dutch, French, and the British came out on top, because, they were stronger than the Portuguese. The British came out at the very top, because they were like the lions, stronger than all.

This is why they the British got the name as Great Britain, because they were able to conquer three quarter of the world land mass from the other Gentile powers of Europe. During the time of their colonial conquest of people and their lands, to get rich, the Portuguese had their intentions to top the wealth of the people of the land they called as Africa, and the wealth of Asia, and to indulge in human cargoes of slaves. The first capture was the Canary Island in 1415, which is off the coast of Morocco that occurred. The Portuguese conquered a Moroccan seaport they named Ceuta. This conquest of this port, and town was important to the Portuguese people, because they wanted to gain inside knowledge from the people of Morocco about south of the Sahara Desert, they called as Black Africa. This was by the Portuguese, and with other Europeans people who came after the Portuguese to the land of Ham.

These Gentile European families, who came to the land of Ham, and conquered it, classified the Sudanese people, which was the land of Cush, to be the land of the so-call Negroes. What the Portuguese, with other Gentile European people, who came after the Portuguese, failed to realize, and understand, is that these same people who they separated, and called as the Black African nations. Were sons and daughters of the same people who were livening in the northern part of the land of Ham of ancient time, they now called as North Africa, and the so-call Middle Eastern people. The only difference is that they the Hamite's people from the Northern part of the land of Ham of ancient time, and what is now called as the Middle East, were of a darker shade of skin complexion. Before the conquest of the Persians, Greeks, Romans, Turks, also, with that of the other rest of the Gentile European families, who came from out of the brake up of the Roman Empire. Who now have control over the land of the so-call Middle East, and what became known as North Africa. They have added many of these original people into their melting pot people, producing different shades of colors of the area. One sees today in what became known as the so-call Middle East, and what became known as North Africa, with that of the Gentile European man blood running true these people vanes, that cost them to be in the complexion they are today. So, after the Portuguese conquered Morocco, they went on to conquer other places such as Cape Blanc, Grain Coast, Ivory Coast, gold Coast, and other places, of the area. Many of the names of these places I have mentioned, are modern colonial names that were given by their conquerors. The exploration of the Portuguese for colonial conquest was supported by King Joao I of Portugal, with that of many merchants, and ship owners, and by Prince Henrique of Portugal, who wanted to top the riches of Africa and India. The Portuguese claim they wanted to evangelize the heathens, as they did put it, meaning the people of Ham, and India with the good news of the cross of Christ, to save souls for Christ as they wanted people to believe.

These people were only interested to evangelizing the riches of the land of Ham and India, to take it over for themselves, with their guns, and their swords, and to take captives to work as slaves in their gold mines, plantations, or whatsoever minds they had there in the land of Ham, and India. The Portuguese were only using psychology and Christianity as a front to conquer the land, with its people. Also to quenches their thirst for gold, diamonds, and other raw material of the land of Ham to produce wealth.

With their evil deception of the crusading to save souls for Christ, as they wanted people to believe in their hypocritical form of Christianity, of robbing, stealing, and enslaving to become rich, and powerful people, by taking the life of their many captives, to gain wealth. As the Portuguese was going along conquering, they would sctup slave posts, for the capturing and buying of slaves to work in their sugar cane plantation they had established there in the land of Ham. The Portuguese also sent some of their captured slaves to a part of their captured New World that became known as Brazil. This was for them to work in their sugar cane, tobacco, and coffee plantations, they had there in the land of Brazil. Some of the slaves were also sent to Portugal, as their house boys, yard boys, as well as house girls, and yard girls, or whatever duties they were to perform in Europe. The Portuguese would also buy slaves from the people whom they named as the Arabs people, and from whatever sources they could get slave to buy. This strategy of diplomacy, was also used by the Spanish, Dutch, French, and later by the British, who came on the colonization, and the slavery bandwagon, using the Bible, and Christianity as their tools, to keep their captives under their control. One must realize that these Gentile families of Japheth are a very skill full people, when it comes down to using strategies, diplomacies, and psychologies, to conquer, and to control their victims. Who become their slave's population of conquered people, in different ways and means, that is also known as dived and conquer. These people was only using Christianity as a front to cover their wicked, greedy, and evil deeds. In my opinion, these Gentile European people, were only wolves in sheep clothing, in fact, I doubt it very much, if many of these Gentile people of Europe, really know the true meaning of what it means to become true worshippers of Yahweh.

Or what it meant to become true followers of Yashua, who were known as the Way in Isreal. This teaching of Yashua to his Apostles, became known as Christianity, by the Roman Catholic Church. This name Jesus was taken from Latin, and the Greek word Justus, and the name Christ, was also taken from the word Christos, that was taken from what was known in Israel as the Way. This was the teaching of Yashua to his Apostles, who were the true and faithful servants of Yashua, without any form of hypocrisy like that of the Gentile people of Europe, who had seen themselves as Christians, which mean followers of Christ, but not according to good dees.

These believers of the Apostles of Yashua, who were also called as those who follow of the Way, by many other Israelites, who did not believe on Yashua, that he was the Son of Yahweh, the one who was sent to them, the Israelite people of Jacob. Yeshua were sent by Yahweh to the people of Israel of Jacob whom Yahweh had taken them from out of the land of Mizraim, known as Egypt, to be His own personal people, to save them from their sins, and death. So, this is what true Christianity should mean, followers of Yashua, who become known in the Latin and Greek language as Jesus and Christ. Which were the Apostles, who were following the teaching of

Yashus, he gave to them his servants to apply to their daily lives, and to teach others, that did become known as the New Testament Law, to please Yahweh. This was for all believers to follow, and apply to their daily lies. This was also to save many who believe, and obey the teaching of Yashua from death and destruction by Yahweh. Yashua himself did not call himself a Christian nighter, but rather, he called himself as the Way to the Father, who was a person who were devoted to please his Father Yahweh, and his God. Who had sent him to earth to do His will, and to sacrifice his life for the sin of Israel, and for that of the other people of the world, as well. Yashua left these examples for his followers to follow, in their day to day lives, to please him and His Father Yahweh, that is written in the New Covenant part of the Scripture, by the Apostles his servants. This New Covenant Law, was for all believers to apply to their day to day lives, that they the Gentile people put a label on, they named as Christianity. With their many form of hypocrisies of deception, and false worship, to make money to get rich. The Apostles did not call themselves Christian's neither, who were the true followers of Yashua, but they the Apostles were called Christians, by the Gentile Catholic believers of Europe, in the Turkey city of Antioch, according to (Acts Chapter 11, and verse 26, and 27). Judging from these Gentile people actions of robbing, killing, lying, stealing, and deceiving people over the centuries, and calling themselves Christians.

It has given what became known as Christianity a bad taste, and a bad name in the minds of their many captives, who came under their colonial ruler ship of false teaching of deception, and lies to gain wealth. These Gentile Christian of Europe were only false followers of The Way, that became known as Christianity, in the city of Antioch of the Turkey area, by the teaching of the Apostle Paul. These Gentile people who had seen themselves as Christians, were only greedy, and wicked thieves, and oppressors.

Seeking to hide under the cloak of the followers of Yashua, but not in good deeds like that of the Apostles of Yashua, who were faithful to the word they did received from Yashua, without any form of hypocrisy, and cunningness to get rich. Like that of the people of Europe, who had profess to be Christian, but who were skimmers connivers, wicked, and greedy people, seeking after money to get rich. Yet Yashua point out in (Matthew Chapter 7, verse 16 and 18), that one shall know the tree by the kind of fruit it bare. So likewise in the same manner, one shall know the true followers of Yashua, by the things they say, do and teach. A Political History of Tropical Africa went on to explained that during this period, the Portuguese used to compete with the merchants of Castile Spain. Also, of Venice for spices, precious stones, and gold from the land of Ham and India. Since the Portuguese could obtain slaves, gold, and other raw materials in great quantities from the land of Ham and India. It naturally excited them, and encouraged them to push with more effort to raid for more slaves. According to A Political History of Tropical Africa, from 1443, the raiding for slaves by the Portuguese take on a new stage of importance. In the next year of 1444, six Caravels ships carrying the cross of the order of Christ, captured 235 Hamite's after a series of pitch battles. This battle took place between Castile Spain and Morocco, which made it a little bit more difficult for the Portuguese to get cheap labor to send to work in Portugal. Quite naturally the people of Portugal welcomed this new supply of slaves, who were captured to do household work, and other labors. The way the Portuguese saw it, no matter how honest they had tried to excuse their actions in the trafficking for slave labor, they justified it by saying that, it meant saving souls for Christ. The funny thing about this story, while they the Portuguese were shipping off many of the native Hamite's people to Brazil, and other places. They were in the meantime bringing their own Portuguese people over into the land of Ham, and India to colonize the land, so as to build up a colony of Portuguese European settlers, to take over the Hamate's people lands, and also in what become known as India, as the new natives.

They were bringing European settlers over into the land of Ham to build up a European community, to become the new natives of this land they had captured from the native Hamite's people, and also in the land of the Indian people of Shem. The Romans long before the Portuguese had done the same thing, when they conquer what became known as North Aprica, from the various natives who were living there.

Various Roman generals use to seek lands in what they had named as North Aprica, that did become known as North Africa, to settle their retried solders on. This was to build up a Roman Italian community. Many of these x solders had children with the local Hamite's women of the area, by so doing producing many shades of different people of the area, one sees today in what become known as North Africa, and what is now known as the Middle East, of their melting pot people. Alexander the Great did the same thing, when he capture what is now known as North, to the so-call Middle East, and what is now known as Asia. He married off ten thousands of his solders to the local natives women, and by so doing, producing many brown skin people of the area, with that of the European man blood flowing true these brown skin people veins. The same is true for the Portuguese, the Dutch, with other European people, who went to captured the land of Ham, they bread up many of these natives women, producing many brown skin people of the area. With that of the European man blood flowing true these brown skin people vines, that they the Dutch of what became known as South Africa named as the Colored people. While the Portuguese was raiding the interior of the land of Ham for slaves, that became known as Angola, they would take these Hamite's slaves they had captured, and march them to a place in Angola known as Luanda. There they would fatten them up, and wash them down with liquor, and rub them down with palm oil, so they would look attractive for their Gentile European purchasers. In these warehouses where these Hamite's captives were taken, the Portuguese merchants would train their captured Hamite's slaves for the plantation tasks they would later be expected to perform in Brazil. Finally, before these Hamite's slaves were embarked upon their voyage across the Atlantic Ocean, they were taken to a nearby church. Or to other convenient places, where they were baptized by a Parish Priest, in batches of a hundred at a time. The ceremony did not take very long, the Priest would say to each slave, "your name is Peter, yours is John, and your name is Frances," and so on.

Each slave was given a piece of paper with his name written on it, and a little salt was placed on each of their tongues, and holy water was sprinkled over the head of these Hamite's salves. A Negro interpreter would address them as follows, "look you people, you have already become children of God. You are going to the land of the Spanish and the Portuguese where you will learn things of the faith.

Do not eat dogs, rats, or horses, now go with a good will, and forget about where you are coming from. This information was taken from A Political History of Tropical Africa. The actions of these so-called Gentile Evangelizers, who claimed they came to the land of Ham to spread Christianity, and to win souls for Christ, under the banner of the cross, as a front to control their victims. To show wicked, evil and deceitfulness of these so-called Gentile European Evangelizers, to their many captives. As many of them did see themselves, as this Christian evangelizers, spreading the good News of the cross of Christ. They stole, enslaved, and killed to further their own interest of the diamonds, and the gold of the land, this is where their evangelizing spirit was, after the wealth of the land. Many people from the various villages of the land of Ham, did not have much knowledge, and understanding about the true worship of Yahweh, of His word, the Scripture of truth for themselves to live their lives by. So, as to to please, Him, in their day to day lives, like that of the people of Israel, who Yahweh gave His Laws, and His Commandment to, and to no other people. Because Yahweh had only deal with the children of Israel, as His own people, because of the faith of Abraham, who is the fore father of the people of Isreal. He also gave them His name, His Laws, and precepts for them to follow, and to keep though out all their generation, so as to please Him. Notice that they the children of Jacob, who become known as the children of Israel, were the only set of people who had the knowledge of Yahweh, of His Laws, His precepts, and His Commandment, that no other people were that fortunate to have and to know. These Laws Yahweh gave to them, was for them to live their lives by, that it might go well with them, if they were to do so. Yet in my opinion, many of the Hamite's people of their various villages in the land of Ham, had more Yahweh like qualities, and Yashua like qualities in their hearts, and mind, than many of these so-call Gentile European Evangelizers.

Who did see themselves as Christians, and Christian people of Europe, spreading the Good News of Yahweh Kingdom, like that of Yashua and his Apostles, who were faithful to the Word of Yahweh, in every sense of the word. Many of these so-call Christian's evangelizers who had seen themselves as Christians, followers of Yashua, as they did put it, were only hypocrites, and wicked people, who had the spirit of the devil, whom they claimed, they came to the land of Ham ,and India to spread Christianity among the heathen, as they did put it.

Many of these so-called Evangelizers were rapes, murders, thief's, pirates, and wicked and greedy people, who had no knowledge of Yahweh, and Yashua like qualities. But many of them were only skimmers, connivers, and thief seeking to hide under the cloak of Christianity, doing the will of their father Satan the devil. This practice of robbing, stealing, enslaving, and calling themselves Christians, saving souls for Christ, as they did put it. Did not help many of those Hamite's people, who were taken captive to Brazil to come to a better knowledge, and the understanding of the Word of Yahweh. Also, the teaching of Yashua, so as to help many of them to become a better people, living their lives to please Yahweh, and Yashua. But rather they did only gave them a misconception of truth, that they call as Christianity, of Roman Catholicism, of the Roman Catholic Church. This was of their own philosophy, and doctoring of what they see as right or wrong from their religious point of view. These religious philosophy of theirs, is mix-up with paganism, and idolatry worship of the Roman Catholic Church, that did not represent the true teaching, and the knowledge of the Word of Yahweh, to help their many captives to live a Yahweh lives. Yet, when Yashua was here on earth, he did not rob, steal, murder and, enslaved anyone to become rich and powerful from their blood, sweat, and tears, and for them to become followers of him, as did these Gentiles people of Europe, and also by the Mohammedans Muslim people of Ishmael did. Who are known today as the Saudi Arabian people, with their many captives, who became known as the Muslim people, in deceiving them to believe in their philosophy of their truth, that they call as the Koran, and Islam. The Portuguese had lied to many of these Hamite's people who were taken captive to Brazil, by way of this Negro interpreter, who they did used to translate their messages, to these various Hamite's captives. By telling them they were going to Brazil to learn things of their faith, as they did put it. So, when many of these people were taken to Brazil as slaves, to learn things of their faith, they were corrupted by these same Portuguese people beyond measure.

These were the same Christian people, who did present themselves to their many Hamite's captives, as an angel of light, but not in good deeds, in the eyes of Yahweh and Yashua, like that of the Apostles of Yashus, who were faithful to the teaching they did receive from Yashua. Their many captives people learned the ways of the Portuguese, with other various Gentile people of Europe, of their New World.

Many of whom become murders, lesbians, homosexuals, prostitutes, winos, drug addicts, thieves, and pickpockets, following the footsteps, and ways of their captors. The Portuguese named the land Brazil they had taken away from the native Arawak's, Caribs, and other tribes of the Eskimos people, who were living in the land area. Who Columbus and other Gentile people who came after Columbus, continued calling these people as Indians. From what I came to learn, and understand, the land of what became known as Brazil has the largest Hamite's population out side of the land of Ham, known today as Africa. Much more than the United States, and what become known as the Caribbean, by these same Gentile European people. Because they were taken there by the millions, although many of these Hamite's people of Brazil continue to melt out themselves into the Gentile European looking people, of their melting pot people, because many of them are suffering from slavery mentality, and inferiority complex, and stupidity, of not knowing who they are, and of the great civilization they and their ancestors is coming from, before slavery. According to A Short History of the West Indies, the slave population reached over 50 million, not counting those who had died along the way, or those who were not fit enough, or strong enough to be sold, but who were just slathered off or left to die. Before these Gentiles European people came to this parts of their New World, as they did called it, these natives people did not know anything about these corruptions of the Gentile people of Europe.

Nor did the people of Ham who were taken to this part of the world to learn things of their faith, as they did put it. As a matter of fact, wheresoever the Gentile people of Europe went and captured, and colonize in the name of Christianity, most of these places of their conquest, have always become full of violence, wickedness, corruption, and sexual immorality of all sort. Unfortunately, many of their captives people have copy the ways of these Gentile European people life stile, they left behind on the minds of their many captives people, for them follow, as a way of life. According to what I had read from A Political History of Tropical Africa, these Gentile Portuguese people, who had classified themselves to be Christian evangelist, would take red hot iron from the fire, and brand their names, or their company's names on each batch of the slaves they had in their possession. Their reason for doing so, was to keep an account of the slaves they owned.

Due to the fact that they did not want their slaves they own, to get mixed up with other slaves that was owned by other European people, who also had slaves. So, to avoid this confusion, each batch of slaves who were physically fit, and well enough to be sold to different European merchants. Or slaves they had for their own purposes, were branded on their chest or arm to show identify of ownership. Also, the sick, weak, and old were either killed, or left to die, or to be thrown overboard with chain, and big objects tied around their necks, so they would drown. Yet these are the same wicked people who had the audacity to call themselves followers of Yashua, that they name as Christianity. The Portuguese priests who did the baptizing of the various slaves, who were taken to Brazil as captives, was no priests of Yahweh, but they were priest of Satan the devil, doing his will. They were false priests, including all the priests of today who came from out of the Roman Catholic Church of paganism, and of idolatry worship. This was to their many gods, and goddesses, who were called as deities, which were infused into what become known as Christianity of Roman Catholicism, of the Roman Catholic Church.

The first priest Yahweh did choose and used, were during the time of Abraham, who were known as Melchisedec. Melchisedec was a king and a priest to Yahweh, and he was also a king of a district that were known as Salem, according to (Genesis Chapter 14, and verse 18). According Volume 10 of the Encyclopaedia, what were known as Salem, was a district of the land of Bharat that became known as India. The second priest Yahweh did choose to be a priest to Him, was Moses 'brother, whose name was known as Aaron. So, from the seed of Aaron, all the other priests Yahweh did used as His priest, was taken from the family line of Aaron. Aaron himself came from the tribe of Levi, from where Moses and Aaron came from, of the children of Israel, as it is so explained in the Scripture of truth. The last Priest Yahweh is using today, is after the New Covenant order, who is Yashua. Who Yahweh made King and High priest to Himself, after the order of Melchisedec. If anyone has any doubt about what I have said, that Yashua is our High Priest of today, they can turn to (Hebrew Chapter 7, and read from verse 17 to verse 28), to get a better knowledge, and understanding of what I have written, that Yashua is our High Priest of today. Also, the lower priests to Yahweh and to Yashua, is the Apostles class of people, who is called in the Scripture as the elect, and the little flock. The word elect that is mentioned in the Scripture, means chosen ones. This word elect is mentioned in various translations of the Scripture that became known as the Bible, by the Greeks and the Romans translate as the Saints. The word Saints came from out of the Roman Catholic Church for their many members to believe, and to see themselves as as the saints.

I would also like to point out to many of my Hamite's people, and others people, who have been brainwashed by the Gentile European family, in using the term or title of the word Saint, without having the full knowledge, and understanding from where this title or word came from. Like in the case of Saint Nicholas, and other Saints of the Roman Catholic Church, who they the Roman Catholic Church approve to be a Saint. This teaching, came from out of the Roman Catholicism of the Catholic Church, of paganism and of idolatry belief. This teaching of theirs, they have thought to many of their captives' people minds throughout the world, who came under their teaching of Roman Christianity, to see themselves as the Saints.

Which it is false doctrines, for their many captives to belief in, of their many church members for them to see themselves as the saints, because they are a good member of the church, and pay their tide to the church very regularly. So, from the viewpoint of Yahweh of things pertaining to Him, no man can give a man the title of a Saint, that was taken from the word elect, and chosen ones. Many of the Apostles of the children of Israel, and various prophets of Yahweh were the ones, who were classified as the chosen ones. Or the elect, that was translated as the Saints in many of the Bibles, and also by many of the various churches of Roman Catholicism. According to the Webster Colligate Dictionary of the Fifth Edition, there the dictionary explained that the word Saint came from the Latin language of the Romans. This word Saint was passed on down the line to the French, that become known in Old French dialect as Sanctus. This word Sanctus meant to be holy, which did apply to the various Roman Catholic priests, or bishops who were also known as the ecclesiastical body of the priest, and the Popes. Or a member of cretin religious body of the Catholic Churches, who had seen themselves as Holy people. I must also point out that to be a religious person, it doesn't not mean that he or she is a true worshiper of Yahweh. One who is following the teaching Yashua gave to his Apostles, that should have been known as the New Covenant Law. This New Covenant Law was translated as the New Testament Law, by the Greeks, and the Romans, that came down to the rest of the people of Europe, who came from out of the break up of the Roman Empire. This Law of the New Covenant, is what all believers should be following in their day to day lives, to please Yahweh and Yashua, as the people of Yahweh, doing His will.

That these believers may have right to the tree of life, that is mention in (Revelation Chapter, 22, and verse 2). According to the Webster Colligate Dictionary, the word ecclesiastical means the education of the monks, and priests who were also known as the clergies, of the Catholic church, religious organization of Rome. These priests were priests to whatever gods, or deities they had served and worship, as their gods, that became a part of the Roman Catholic Church religious organization that became known as Christianity. So technically speaking, the word Saints were taken from their pagan idolatry religious system, that become known today as Christianity, which did come from the various temple gods of the Gentile European people, to the worship of their many gods.

So, to be a religious church person mean nothing at all, unless of course this religious church person is a true devoted worshiper to Yahweh, one who is following the teaching of Yashua, he gave to his Apostles, for all believers to apply to their daily lives. So, as to please Yahweh and also Yashua, who is our Lord, master, and king, and high priest to Yahweh. If anyone has any doubt about what I have said, that the Apostles class is the lower priests to Yahweh, and to Yashua, they can turn to (Revelation Chapter 20, and read from verse 4, to verse 6) to get a better understanding of what I have written. There they will see that the Apostles class is known as the chosen ones, or the elects, who were given thrones to rule as kings and Priests with that of Yashua, who did not worship the beast, or its image. This image that is mention, is speaking of the political religious system that came from out of the last beast who was Rome. Which is speaking of the Roman religious system, who was the last beast, and their political system, that came down to the rest of the Gentile powers of Europe, who came from out of the brake up of the Roman Empire. There one will see in (Revelation Chapter 20) that this elect class of people were given the first resurrection from the dead to go to heaven. Which the heaven is the throne of Yahweh, where they will be with Yashua, ruling as king and priest to Yahweh and Yashua. This elect class as the Scripture clearly point out, will be priests to Yahweh, and to Yashua, which will be to a heavenly resurrection from the dead, because they will receive the first resurrection to go to heaven, as the heavenly class of people. This is the reason why it is mention in (Luke Chapter 12, and verse 32), where Yashua spoke to the Apostles by saying to them, fear not little flock, for it is your Father's good pleasure to give you the kingdom, and this kingdom will be a ruler ship over the earth. (John Chapter 10, and verse 16), there Yashua mention to his Apostles that he has other sheep's who were not of the fold of the Apostles class.

Which Yashua was speaking of the other believers of the world, who would later become believers on him true the writhing, and the teaching of his Apostles. These laws, of the teaching of Yashua, was later translated as the New Testament by the Greeks, and the Romans, and by other people of Europe. Also, this New Covenant Law is to all believers of today, in the keeping of the commandment Yashua he gave to his Apostles, to teach other believers for them to apply to their daily lives, to please him, and his Father Yahweh.

Yashua went on to say to his Apostles, them I must bring also, and they shall hear his voice; and they shall be one-fold and one shepherd over all the believers. Whether it would be that of the Apostles class, or that of the earthly class of the multitude of people who will come from out of the great tribulation that is to come. Yashua also mention at (John Chapter 5 and verse 28) that the time is coming when all the people who are in the grave, shall hear his voice, and they shall come back to life. Those people who did good things while they were alive before they died, will be resurrected back to life, to live in Yahweh earthly Kingdom that is to come. But those other people who will be resurrected back to life from the grave, who did not live their lives to please Yahweh and Yashus, while they were alive, but who did evil things while they were alive, will be resurrected back to life to face everlasting punishment of destruction for their deeds. The other believers who will be alive here on earth when Yashua return, who did live their lives in according to the teaching of the New Covenant Law. Yashua gave to this Apostles his servants, to teach other believers, they will enter into Yahweh earthly Kingdom that will be rule by Yashua, and his Apostles in the righteous new order of things is to come. But all the rest of the other peoples who will be alive here on earth when Yashua return, who did not live their lives to please Yahweh and Yashus, but who did evil things, will be destroyed from out of this earthly Kingdom of Yahweh and Yashua, that is to come. This is the reason why Yashua taught his disciples to pray for that kingdom of Yahweh to come, that is mention in (Matthew Chapter 6, verse 9, and 10). So, it will be just like when Yahweh destroyed the people in the flood of Noah days, only Noah and his family were the only set of righteous people, Yahweh did allow to come back to lived here on the earth. After He had destroyed all those wicked UN Yahweh like people, who did not, please Him well. It will be the same way in Yeshua second coming, but there will be more people save alive in Yashua second return. In comparison to the days of Noah, when he and his family was the only people save alive, and the rest of people of that time was destroyed from planet earth.

Although the various churches teach their church members, that all good people will be going to heaven to be with Yahweh and Yashua, this is not so according to the teaching of (Revelation Chapter 20, and Revelation Chapter 21, and verse 1). Where Yahweh mentioned that He is going to create a new heaven and a new earth where righteousness will dwell.

As it is so mentioned in (Revelation Chapter 20 and verse 6) that blessed and holy is he that will have part in the first resurrection of the dead back to life. On these little flocks of the Apostle class, the second death will have no power over them, because they will be priest to Yahweh and Yashua, and will reign with Yashua for a thousand years. This is speaking of the elect's class of his Apostles. So, there will be a heavenly class, and an earthy class of people in the new order of things to come, as the Scripture clearly teaches. So, it is not like what may people is thought in the various churches of today, that all good people will be going to heaven to be with Yashua and Yahweh. According to (Revelation Chapter 7, verse 9 and verse 14), in the coming destruction of this present world of the great tribulation, more people will be saved alive in comparison to the time of Noah. Verse (9 and verse 14 of Revelation Chapter 14) mention that there will be a great multitude of people which no man could number, out of all the nations, who come from out of great tribulation. Who has washed their robes in the blood of the lamb. This washing of the robe of these people, in the blood of Yashua, represents a believer faith and life in Yashua. In keeping to his commandment, he gave to his Apostles for other believers to fallow of the New Covenant Law, to please Yahweh and Yashua in their day to day lives. Furthermore, to prove my point that there will be a heavenly class, and an earthly class of people, according to (Matthew Chapter 5, and verse 5), there Yashua points out, by saying that blessed are the meek: for they shall in heart the earth. Also (Psalm Chapter 37, starting from verse 9 to verse 11), there the Scripture went on to say for evildoers shall be cut off: but those who wait upon the Lord Yahweh, they shall inherit the earth.

Verse 11 went on to say, but the meek shall inherit the earth; and shall delight themselves in abundance of peace. So, this statement Yashua mention, that is also express in Psalm, just goes to show to the various believers of today, who goes to the various churches. How much of the church false teaching they has listen to, and received from their pastors, that is of false teaching. This teaching of the various churches, and their pastors is not in harmony with the teaching of the Scripture of truth, that they teach to their many church members, that all righteous people will be going to heaven to be with Yashua and Yahweh. But this is a church religious doctrine, that came down from out of the Roman Catholic Church, and from out of the various Protestant churches, that they teach to their various members to believe in.

The word righteousness according to the Webster Colligate Dictionary of the Fifth Edition, mean right, wise, prudent, also doing what is right, in the eyes of Yahweh. Also fee from wrongdoing or sin, which according to the dictionary, this word came from the Angles and Saxon dialect that was spell as rihtwis. (Psalms Chapter 115 and verse 16), explained that the heavens belong to Yahweh, meaning that the heavens are the throne of Yahweh, but the earth, He gave to the children of men, to be their dwelling place. So, men were made for the earth and not for the heavens, which is the throne of Yahweh. So, for one to enter Yahweh into Yahweh new earthly system of things to come, one must live their lives righteously now, to please Yahweh in their day to day lives. Otherwise, there will be no chance to enter in to Yahweh new earthly paradise that is to come. I am quite certain from the stand point of the Scripture, these Catholic priests of the Portuguese who did baptize the various Hamite's slaves, and deceive them. By telling them they were going to Brazil to learn things of the faith, when they were no priests of Yahweh, so they would have to be priests of Satan the Devil, and his angels who are called as the demons in the Scripture. Or they must have been priests to the various idolatry gods of the Gentile land that became known as Europe. To show the hypocritical and deceitfulness of these wicked and greedy Gentile people, who had claimed they came with the cross of Christ to save souls for Christ, as they did put it. To spread what they did call as Christianity throughout their various colonies of the world, that became their subjects of properties, and their empires of today. What become known as Brazil, the United States, the West Indies, South and Central America, South Africa, Australia, with, many other parts of the world where these Gentile people went and conquered. That became their colonies, and empires of ruler ship, where many people were taken to be Christianize by them, to learn things of their faith as they did put it.

Many of these places have become full of all sorts of wickedness, prostitution, sodomy, that become known as homosexuals, lesbianism, murderers, with all sorts of deceitfulness, that were spread around the world by these Gentile European people throughout their colonial conquests to get rich. Who did see themselves as evangelizers, spreading the truth of Yahweh and Yashua to their many captives, who did came under their captives.

It is a known fact that wheresoever the Gentile people went and conquered throughout the world, in the name of Christianity, using the Bible, as a part of their tools to conquered. These places have always become full of violence, wickedness, and crookedness, because of these Gentile people, and their ways of life, and culture that strive upon exploitation, violence, and wickedness to get rich. Also, the creating of wars to sell their war weapons for conquest to get more wealth. There stealing, and killing, many of the time rubbed off on many of their captured people, and it also became a part of their captured people way of life, that many of them follow to get rich. Along with gambling, and sort of sexual immorality, as a way of life, that many of their captured people copy from these people. To show the wicked nature of these Gentile people of Europe, the Romans used to have the Gladiators to fight to their death, also, to throw many people in the Roman arena to be fed to the lions as a form of sport and laughter's. Many of whom were believers of what did become known as Roman Christianity of the Roman Catholic Church. Due to the violent nature of these Gentile people of Europe, this is the reason why they have invented boxing, and wrestling as a form of sport, and laughter, to make money to get rich. Also, to bring in much wealth into their system, because many of the time, they are the managers, and promoters of these boxers. This was all started by the Gentile people to make big profits from this sport of violence that many of them get their trill from, and become wealthy people from this sport of violence. They have always been able to turn people against each other, and called it a racial problem, when there was no racial problem before they came along, and turned people against each other. This is also true of what I have come to learn about India and their cast system. From what I have come to learn and understand, this cast system of India was set up by some early European conquerors.

Who had conquered the land, and brought about their religious cast system that they did establish, to these people, who they also classified as the Untouchable. Because they make sure that many of these darker skin people of India are the ones who they keep down, and who are the poorer ones, who do all their dirty works as the oppress people, and who has nothing. They have even convinced many of these dark skins people of India that they are unclean, and are worth less than the animals. But they of the lighter skin people of their caste system of India, which is a mixture of the Europe man blood running true the vanes of these lighter skin people of the high class people of India, as they see themselves.

Who they say, their gods put them in this passion to be rulers, and priests of their paganism of false worship of idolatry, of their cast system that they classified as truth. I must also point out that the first Gentile European people to have ruler ship over the land of Bharat that became known as India, was the Greeks, by way of the conquest of Alexander the Great. Then came the Romans, who defeated the Greeks, and take over the country of India. After the Greeks and the Romans, then it was the Portuguese who came and take over the land area of India, until they were push out by the British, who did become the over lord of all India. So many of the ways of life and cultures of the people of India came down from the people of Europe, who they were rule and govern by, and did accept many of their cultures and way of life. They have been oppressing many of these dark skin people of India with their philosophy of deceit, and lies that they force upon these people, to see themselves as a lesser human being to themselves, the conquerors. So, these Gentile people of Europe, must have been an agent of Satan the devil, who was sent to do his will. In costing disunity, confusion war and suffering among many of their conquered people, wheresoever they went out and conquer, in the name of Christianity. They have done so in their New World of what became known as the West Indies, the Americas, Australia, New Zealand, South Africa, and Southeast Asia. Or wheresoever these people went and conquered and set up their ruler ship of their empire over their various natives and captives of their lands. They have always seen themselves as Yahweh gift to the earth, and to the human family as a hole. Also, that every other people must pattern themselves after them, and to look like them, that they have brainwash many of their conquered people to see things this way.

Chapter 6 - The Capture of What Became as South Africa

According to A Political History of Tropical Africa, there it explained that what become known as South Africa, was first name as Cape of Storm by Bartolome Dias in 1487-1488 AD. Who was a Portuguese sea captain, who was seeking a sea route to go to the land of Bharat, that became known as the land of India. Bartolome Dias was on his way to what became know as Asia. But he got loss, and on his way back to Portugal he came across this vast land area he names as Cape of Storm. So, when he arrives back in Lisbon, King Joao of Portugal change the name of Cape of Storm, to the name of Cape of Good Hope. Volume 11 of the Encyclopaedia, explained that in 1652, a Dutchman by the name of Jan van Riebeeck, who was employed by the Dutch East India company, establish this colony that became known as South Africa, at the Cape of Good Hope. The reason for this establishment of this colony was to serve as a stopping point for their Dutch East India trading vessels, who were on their way to Asia, or what they had called as the East. These Dutch settlers of what became known as South Africa, who also became known as the Boors, and who later name themselves as the Afrikaners. These Dutch settlers who develop a dialect they called as Afrikaans language, that originally came from the early Dutch settlers, of their dialect. These Dutch settlers, of what became known as South Africa, who originally came from what is known as Holland, or the Netherlands.

These Dutch people who were a Germanic tribe of Europe, because when looking at a map showing in volume 20 of the Encyclopaedia, and compare this map with another map that is also showing in volume 20 of the Encyclopaedia. There it shows a map of Germany, with the land area of the Netherlands, that is near to the North Sea part of Germany. Also, looking at this map of the Encyclopaedia, showing the land of Germany, with the land area of the Saxon, that is very near to the land border of what is now known as the Netherlands, or Holland. So, according to what this map of the Encyclopaedia is showing, is that the Netherlands was known in the time of the Saxons, as the Friesland. This Friesland of what become known as Holland, is in the North Sea area near to what is known today as Germany.

This land area that is now known as the Netherlands, and Holland that is not too far away from Denmark, which is also another Germanic tribes who become known as the Danish people of Denmark. These Danish people were a part of the Viking Sea warrior of the Germanic barbarian people, of what became known as the European people. Who had conquer a large part of Europe, after the brake up of the Roman Empire ruling over Eastern, and the Western Europe. These Dutch settlers take over the land area they name as South Africa, from the various natives who were living there in the land that the Portuguese name as Cape of Good Hope. I came to this knowledge about these Dutch people, from reading various volume of the Encyclopaedia Britannica, explaining about who these people were. So, these people of the Netherlands were a Germanic tribe, according to what this map of the Encyclopaedia is showing, of the various tribes of Germanic people at the time of the Roman Empire, ruling over Europe. I must also mention that when reading from volume 20, and volume 18 of the Encyclopaedia Britannica, showing the area of Germany during Greek and Roman time. Germany was a much a bigger place before it was split up by the various warring factors of the Gentile land of what become known as Europe. These Dutch settlers take away the land area from the Portuguese who had named the land area of their colonial quest as Cape of Good Hope, that later became known as South Africa by these Dutch settlers. According to volume 27 of the Encyclopaedia Britannica, there it explain that, although the Portuguese had control over the Indies, and the African coastline, and also, what did became known as Angola, and Mozambique as a part of their colonial territory, they did not make any large settlement on what became known as South Africa.

During the 1500, South Africa was visited by the Dutch, and also by a British sea captain pirates, who were on their way to Asia, to control the spice trade, and what else they could steal to become the colony of their Motherland of Europe. Often time these Dutch pirates would pull a shore into what became known as South Africa, for water, and meat from the various natives. Volume 11 of the Encyclopaedia went on to explained that many of the early Dutch men interbreed with a native tribal women of the area, who were known as the San

Khoikhoi people. By so doing they create a set of half-breed people, who they had name as the Colored people. Or better put, as the melting pot of their Mulatto people.

With that of the Gentiles European man blood running trough these halfbreed people, veins who they name as the Colored people, of the Dutch and other European's settlers of what did become known as South Africa. According to a book that is called from Cape to Cairo, Rape of a Continent, that was written by Mark Strage, who is a Gentile European man. This book was published by A Helen and Kurt Wolff Book, Harcourt Brace, Jovanovich, Inc, 757 Third Avenue, New York, N.Y. 10017.

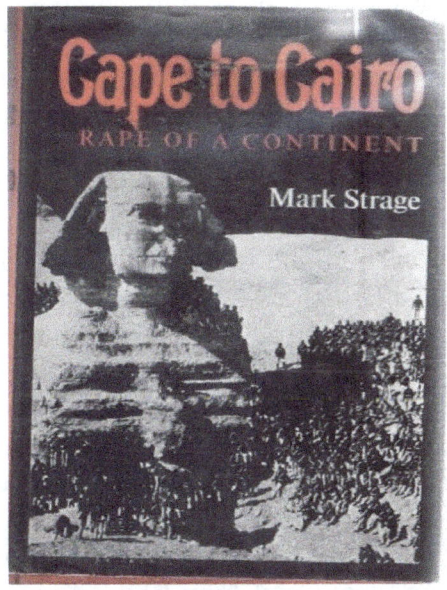

The picture of the book above, showing of the statue of the Sphinx, of what did became known as Egypt. That was taken from the book cover, Rape of a Continent, from Cape to Cairo, showing of this image. The meaning of the term from Cape to Cairo, it is because they the British did conquered from the other various Gentile European colonial conquerors, who were there before they came along. From Cape Town South Africa, to what become known as Cairo Egypt, as a part of their empire. The book went on to explained that the name South Africa came from the early Dutch settlers of the Dutch East India Company.

Who had sent out one of their employees by the name of Jan Van Riebeech in 1652, to setup a Dutch settlement in the area they did named as Table Bay, which is located at the northern end of the Cape Peninsula. The purpose of this Dutch settlement was to secure and control the sea area, which was very vital to their interest against other Gentile European shipping companies. Who was sailing from the Atlantic Ocean to the Indian Ocean of their conquest. This Germanic tribe who became known as the Dutch people, were seeking to protect their interest in this area of the East Indies. Also, to setup colony of the Cape area, and to scrape up the riches of the land of Ham to send to the Netherlands, or what became known as Holland. When I was living in Amsterdam in the sixties, I came to the knowledge that Amsterdam was called as the diamond capital of the world. The funny thing about this story, there are no diamonds in the soil of Holland to be found, so where these diamonds came from? The diamonds came from what become known as South Africa.

The picture above is showing of some Dutch men counting out their diamonds from what they had taken from a diamond mine that became known as Kimberly in South Africa. Where these Gentile settlers could scrape up gold, and diamonds like sand, to send to enrich Europe. The Dutch take over the conquest of South Africa from the Portuguese in 1600, and these Dutch begun to bring over their Dutch people, to settle down, and to colonize the land as a Dutch settlement, as did the Portuguese did before them in other colonies of what became known as Southern Africa. While they were colonizing the land, in the mean while, they were shipping off many of the natives Hamite's people from their lands to their overseas slave territories, to be sold for the right price. In this same book, it mentioned that the Dutch people used to take away the Hamite's people cattle of South Africa, and whatever they had, and afterwards they would ship them away. This situation continued until the French came and take away the colonial power of South Africa from the Dutch. The French

became the over Lord ruler of South Africa, along with that of the Dutch. Later came the British, who take over power of South Africa from the French, and the Dutch in 1775-1806. There was a fellow by the name of John Jourdain who was a merchant for the British East India Company, who arrived in South Africa on July 14, of 1608. He went to catch a fish, and he noticed that the fishes of South Africa were very big in size. He went on to say that he noticed that the soil of the land of South Africa was particularly good, if it were fertilized with manure, and in his opinion, the land would bear anything that was planted on it.

But in his mind, there was only one big problem, and that was the size of the native Hamite's population of South Africa. Twelve years later, six ships that was under the command of Andre Shilling, and Humphrey Fitzherbert, arrived at the Table Bay area. They were joined up with nine other Dutch vessels that were already there, waiting to scrape up the natives Hamite's people to ship them away as slaves, to be sold to their overseas merchants for the right price. These Dutch, and British people went on to ship off these native people from their lands to wheresoever part of their New World needed slaves 'labor to work on their plantations for the right price. After these people were shipped out from their native lands, two British captains climbed halfway up to the mountain top, and planted a flag of St. George, and they take over possessions of the land area, as far north as the next so called White settlement.

They name the land in the name of James I, who was then king of Britain at the time. In 1820, the first large group of British colonist, or settlers arrived in South Africa to establish it as a British colony. Their were about 5,000 of them, and their passage was paid for by a special fifty-thousand-pound parliamentary grant from Britain. They were settled on good lands that was cleared by the local natives. From this British settlement gave birth to a British man by the name of Cecil John Rhodes, who set out himself from what become known as South Africa, to scrape up as much land area as he could. By so doing, he chases off many of the native from off their lands, and establish a country, that was known as Rhodesia, that take its name from himself. Cecil John Rhodes did this because of all the wealth that could be found in these lands area, of what did become known as Southern Africa, and what become known as Rhodesia. According to the book, Rape of a Continent, because of the vast amount of gold, and diamond that could be found in the land area in what Cecil John Rhodes name as Rhodesia. He establishes a police force with guns to chase off the various natives from their lands. By so doing, they could scrape up the wealth of the land, and to form the next European settlement, that he names as Rhodesia, that was not too far away from what is now known as South Africa. There was also a land area in South Africa that was known as Kimberley, that had nothing but gold and diamond, so these Gentile European settlers, made themselves become rich and fat people, from the richness of the land that became known as Southern Africa, of Kimberley. Due to the abandon of gold, diamond and other precious wealth that they had found, in the land area, many of the local native Hamite's people who was left there to serve them, could not even walk, or bread properly in their own Yahweh given land. Because of these wicked, and greedy Gentile European predators, who think to themselves that the
world belongs to them alone.

The way they see it, when Yahweh was making this earth, He only had them in mind, so all of the other people of the world, are an intruder of their Yahweh given lands. After all this scraping up of the local native people, and their land, that made Cecil John Rhodes, and his comrades to become wealthy and fat men. From the riches they had found on these lands that they made themselves rulers over. Cecil John Rhodes died March 26th, 1902, at the age of 49-year-old. From what I have learned, the land of what was known as Rhodesia did receive back it original native name as Zimbabwe. Which was the former name of the kingdom that was there.
This was long before these Gentile European colonial settlers, came along and take over possession of the land area they name as South West Africa. I must also mention that I didn't cover the full story from the book, Cape to Cairo, Rape of a Continent, about the British in Southern Africa, with that of the other various Gentile European people, fighting among themselves for the control of the land of Ham, and his people to be under their colonial control, and to have the wealth of the land under their control.

The picture to the left is that of Cecil John Rhodes.

The picture to the right is showing of some Gentile European settlers of what did became known as Rhodesia, with their machine guns that were organize by Cecil John Rhodes to drive off the various natives from off their lands as policemen. These mob, and gangsters of their police men settlers, of the gold, and diamonds that could be found in the land area of Rhodesia, that they wanted to have control over. I also came to the knowledge, by watching YouTube, that some Dutch settlers of what become known as South Africa, have the audacity to say they are establishing a so-call White only city in South Africa, where there are no Blacks, or African people are not allowed, but European only. The funny thing about this story, it is because many of these foolish, and stupid Hamite's political leaders, of the land of Ham, who see themselves, as leaders of their own people, who sit down and allow these European invaders to come into their forefather lands, to set up a city, where none of their own people are not allowed to walk and bread.

This would never happen if it was in Europe, if some Hamite's person was to say they are taking over a land area in Europe where no European people are not allowed, it would cause a war to brake out, and many of these Hamite's people would lose their lives, for wanting to do such a thing in their own forefathers land of Europe. Due to the fact that the land of Europe belong to the Gentile people of Japheth only, who were put there by Yahweh, after the flood of Noah, and also after the confusion of the language of the people of Nimrod, who were building the tower of Babel to reach up to heaven. So, the land of Europe belong to the people of Europe only, and the land of Ham belong to the people of Ham people only, and not to any other people of Europe, as they so see things to be under their control. But many of these foolish Hamite's politicians who see themselves as leaders of their own people, allow these European people to come in, and take over control of their lands to have things under their control. But many of these foolish Hamite's political leaders, do not have any problem with that, but only to fight and kill many of their own people, to put them in political office, for their own pocket, so as to become rich men, from the oppression of their own people. But when it come down to the people of Europe, who came in and take away their lands, they do not have the any problem with these people coming in and take over their lands, and the spirit to fight against these people. But only to fight, and kill each other, and let other people to used them as puppets, to keep their own people down, so they can drive around in a big Mercedes Benz, or a Rolls Royce, while the majority of their own people, are staving, and begging for bread. I am sorry to say that many of our Hamite's people are suffering from a very sad state of stupidity, and colonial slavery mentality of brain washing, that do affect their day to day thinking.

Chapter 7 - The Capturing of The Island of Indonesia

According to Volume 14 of the Encyclopaedia Britannica, in the 15th century, Vasco da Gama who was a Portuguese man, sail from the Cape of Good Hope that is now known as Southwest Africa, into the East Indian waters to make the Portuguese masters of Asia, and all of the Eastern seas of their conquests. According to volume 6 of the Encyclopaedia Britannica, Indonesia was first established as a European colony by the Portuguese in 1510. During the pursuit for world conquest and domination of people and their lands, they were later followed by the Spanish, Dutch, French, and later came the British to Indonesia to take part of the colonial conquest, like a set of conquering predators. According to volume 17 of the Encyclopaedia Britannica the Indonesian islands were formally call as the Netherlands, or the Dutch East Indies. The geographical land area eventually take on the name of Indonesia, that was given to the land area, by a German geographer in 1884. Volume 6 of the Encyclopaedia explained that the various European conquerors who went to the Islands of Indonesia was able to control the land by turning the local rulers against each other. This they did by using religious means to cast division, and wars among the various Hamites natives, then they would come in as peacemakers to established peace between the local tribes fighting among themselves, over religious wars. Eventually they would take over control as colonial rulers, without even had to fire a shot, or to use their swords to conquer.

This technique is what is called divide and conquer, in which many of the Gentile people of the land that become known as Europe, are very skillful people at, like that of Satan the Devil. The Encyclopaedia further went on to explained that the Dutch East India Company came with the pretense of wanting to trade with these various natives, when in reality; they were only buying the time to seize control over the Indonesian island of Java, Sumatra, and Moluccas. The Encyclopaedia explained that the Dutch East Indian Company setup their headquarters on one of the Indonesian island by the name as Batavia, which is known today as Jakarta, to oversee their captured colonies of Indonesia.

Volume 6 of the Encyclopaedia explained that at the end of the 17th century, the British lost their colonial stronghold of their Indonesian Island of Bantan to the Dutch. The Encyclopaedia explained that the Portuguese lost their colonial control of their Indonesian island of Timor to the Dutch, and the Dutch established economic, and political control over all the islands of Indonesia, and they became the over Lord, and master of all of the Indonesia Islands. When the Dutch became the over Lord of all the various island of Indonesia, they enslave many of the natives Hamite's people of the area, who were the true natives of the land, before the coming of the people of Europe, and that of many Chinese people who came later to be apart of the settlement of the of the island of Indonesian Island. Due to the the enslavement of the various natives, cause an uprising throughout the island of Java, in which many Chinese settlers took part in the uprising against the Dutch. However, because the Dutch had a strong nave force, they were able to put down all resistance against them, and by the time of 1749 they, the Dutch reign supreme over all the islands of Indonesia, and enslaving many of the population as they see so fit to do. This information was also taken from Volume 17 of the Encyclopaedia.

The same thing is true for the island of the Philippine, that take its name from the Spanish conquest, and became known as the Philippine Islands. Before the conquest of the island of the Philippine, many of the native people were Hamite's looking people, who were the true natives of the land, before the Spanish came along, and take over control of their islands. Also, when the British settlers of what became known as the United States of America, who came along and defeat the Spanish, and take over ruler ship of the islands, then they corrupt the minds of the many locals people, with sexual immorality, drugs, liquor, and with all sort of crime, and wickedness, and later these islands were taken over by the United States, after the war with the Spanish of 1898 to 1901.

The picture above is showing of some Hamite's people of the Philippine Islands, who were known as the Aeta Negros, fighting against the Spanish's solders who came to take over their islands. In which the Spanish and other European people were able to take over the island, so the name Philippine Islands was taken from the name of Philip II of Spain, and the islands became known as the Philippines Islands of Asia. This information was taken from the history of the Philippine book by David Barrows.

These pictures above, is showing of some of the original native of the islands that became known as the Philippines Islands.

Books that were written for the benefit of the Gentiles people of Japheth, who became known as the people of Europe. I must point out that I am very thankful, and great full to Yahweh very much, that I am now able to write from the various books that were written for the benefit of the Gentile people of Europe only. Books that fell from off their tables into my hands, that I am now able to write about many of our Hamite's people great history, and civilization, they have no knowledge of. So, as to bring much knowledge to the minds of many of Hamite's people minds worldwide of who they are, and where they and their ancestors is coming, that I have written about in this book. One must also realize that although reading, writing, and arithmetic was first started by the people of Ham's, yeah all the various books during the early colonial days of slavery were only written for the benefit of the Gentile people of Europe in mind only, because they were writing to each other, and they did not have us in mind and thoughts whatsoever. They also had many of the people of the world under their colonial captivity of slavery of conquest, and for them only to see things from their point of view only. So, many of us their conquered people were only thought of what they wanted us to know, and to see things from their concept only, and no more than that. So, the various books that fell from off their tables into my hands, have equip me with the various information to write this book of mine, the Untold Forgotten Great Civilization of the people of Ham. One must also realize that during the early colonial days of slavery, of the people of Ham, many of these books I have written from, were only written for the benefit of the Gentile people of Europe only, because they were only writing to each other, and they did did not have us in mind.

So, many of my ancestors who have gone by, were not permitted to go to school to learn how to read and write in any of the Gentiles people language of Europe, whom they were enslave by. So, many of us their offspring who are around today, were only educated to speak in the European dialect as our language, that were haded down to us to go by. Also, this was for us to see ourself as their educated people, from what we had learn from them, to see things their way. This was also for us to communicate with them, and for as to be able to do their work, and exist in the conquered colonial world of today.

It was against the laws of the people of Europe, for any of their slaves, and we their off springs, to learn to read and write in any Gentile people language of Europe, who we were enslave and rule by. Many of my ancestors were not even permitted to speak to their own children in their own native mother tongue, which mean language. They only wanted our ancestors, and we their offspring who are around today, to be able to understand when we were given certain command to do this or that, so right away we would understand what was required of us to do, to please them, and to carry out our duties, and that was all. The main reason why they did not allow the slaves to speak in their mother tongue, it is because they the slave masters wanted to make sure they would understand what the slaves was speaking about, that they were not trying to plot against them to cast an uprising of a slave rebellion, or to escape. I must also point out that from what I have read from the various history books of the Gentile people writing of Europe, if a slave master wanted to teach any of his slave, how to read and write in any of the European language, of their slave masters, who they were rule and control by, It would have cost this European person to lose their life. Or to be put in prison, for going against the system, for not to teach any slave how to read and write, in any of the language of Europe. So, many Hamite's people of today who see themselves as educated people, do not even realize that learning to read and write in any of the Gentile people languages of Europe, came about many years later after slavery was abolish. It was also design for us to learn what they wanted us to know, and to see things from their point of view only, and that is the reality of the matter. So, many of us Hamite's people of today, who see themselves as educated people, from the little chance that were given to some of us, for us to learn what the people of Europe want us to know and understand from what they teach in their schooling system, for their many student to understand, it was many years after slavery was abolished.

This was for us to see ourselves as educated people, from their brainwashing of their false history, of lies. Even in the early part of when slavery was abolished, and that did depend and what countries of Europe these slaves

So, when Alexander and his Greek people came and take over the land of Mizraim, from the power of the Persians, then they name this land of their conquest, from the power of Darius III as Aigyptos. This name Aigyptos, that became known as Egypt, in the Anglo-Saxon dialect, that did came from the writing of the Romans. Also, from the Greeks, where the Romans, the Angles and the Saxon people got their education from, that came down to the time of the Roman rulership of the Latin language. According to (Genesis Chapter 10 and verse 6), there it mentions that the land that is now known as Egypt was named after Ham's second son, whose name was known as Mizraim. (Genesis Chapter 10, and verse 13), there it mentioned the names of the various the sons of Mizraim, which were known as Ludim, Anamim, Lehabim, Pathrusim, Naphtumhim, and Casluhim. According to the Scripture Map of 1890, and compared the Scripture Map, with that of the world map of today, there it shows the land of Ludim, who was the first son of Mizraim. This land area of Ludim is also where the country of Carthage was located, before the kingdom of Carthage was destroyed by the Roman army, when reading from various volume of the Encyclopaedia Britannica. Reading from a map of volume 20 of the Encyclopaedia, showing the land of what is now known as Algeria, Morocco, and Oasis. This land area that is now known as Algeria, and Morocco is remarkably close to the land area of Carthage. So, this land area of Ludim later became known as the land of Carthage, Algeria and Morocco of what is known today as North Africa. This land area of Carthage was before the country of Carthage was destroyed by the Roman army. According to this map of volume 20 of the Encyclopaedia, the land area that is now known as Morocco, Algeria and what is now called as the Oasis, was known during Roman time as the land of Numidia, that was very close to the land area of Cartage. This land area that is now known as Algeria, Morocco and the Oases, was the land (Genesis 10, and verse 13) explained as the land of Ludim, who was the first sons of Mizraim, that is also showing on the Scripture Map of 1890, showing the land of Ludim.

I recently visited the country of Morocco, in August of 2023, and when I landed in the country of Morocco, I was surprise to see the land of Ludim as a little French city of Europe, that is rule by many French people, along with other European people who are there, and who see themselves as native of what in now known as Morocco. The funny thing about this story, when walking down the street of Morocco, it was very hard for me to see any of the original dark skin Hamite's people of the area.

This is because many of these dark skin Hamite's people of Morocco have totally washout themselves into many looking half-bread European people of what is now known as the country of Morocco. I do believe that the name Morocco and Algeria came from the conquest of the French Germanic people. Just like how the name Arabia, and Arabian people came from the Greeks, Romans, to the French people as the Arabian people. Speaking of these Ishmaelite people who is mixup with the blood of the Greek, Roman, Turks, French, and with that of the other Gentile European barbarian people, who came from out of the Greek and Roman conquest. The funny thing about this story, many of these half-bread people of Morocco see themselves as European people, because they have no knowledge of who they are, and where they and their ancestors is coming from. Verse (14 of Genesis Chapter 10), went on to explained that out of the family of Casluhim came the family who were known as the Philistim, that become known as the Philistine people of Mizraim. This family of Mizraim was living in the so-calls Middle East, that is still known today as the Gaza Strip, which was the land area of the Palestinian people, with the various cities of the Philistine people that is now under the control of Israel, and other Gentile European people of the so-call Middle East. These places are also under the power of the control of the so-call Arab people of Ishmael, known today as the Muslim people of Saudi Arabia. This was with their various conquered colonies of people, who became known as the Muslim and Arab people of the so-call Middle East of their conquest. I must also point out that many of these native tribes of the area, were also destroyed by Yahweh, when he miraculously fought for the children of Israel against the Philistine army, and other native Hamite's kingdoms of the area at the time. Due to the fact that Yahweh was not pleased with many of the kingdoms of the people of Ham, that gone by, of the area, because many of these ancient kingdoms of the people of Ham were idol worshipers of many graven images, as there gods. Also, with that of witchcraft, that were known as sorcery in the Scripture, that many Hamite's of that time did practice as a way of life.

This practice of witchcraft is still practice today, by many Hamite's people in different part of the world. So, the native Hamite's people of what became known as the Palestinian people, and many of the people of the so-called Middle East, were the true natives, of the land, long before the ancient children of Israel came along.

This including the people of Ishmael, who were known in Jacob's time as the Ishmaelite people of Ishmael, but who are known today as the Saudi Arabian people, of the so-call Middle East. Many of the people of the so-called Middle East, and what became known as North Africa, are a mixture with that of the blood of the Persians, Greeks, Romans, Turks. Also, with that of the various barbarian's kingdoms of the people of Europe, who came from out of the brake up of the Roman Empire, and became strong, and powerful kingdoms of people of the area. These people have also left many of their descendants behind, as a part of their melting pot people, of the area, one sees in these places of today, of the so-call Middle East. In the case of David and Goliath, Goliath was from the family of the Philistine people as the Scripture clearly explained. Sad to say that many of the native people of what is now known as the land of Palestine, and the Middle Eastern people, are a total washout people, with more so that of the Gentile man blood running through the veins of these people. This is because they the Gentile people were chiefly the conquerors of the land of Ham, and the land of Canaan, that is now known as a part of what they call as the Middle East, and the Middle Eastern people. The ancient children of Israel, and the Ishmaelite people were also conquerors of the land of Canaan, and the land of Ham, yet, many of the children of Israel mothers, were Hamite's women, who gave birth to this family of people, of what became known as the children of Israel. Also that of the Ishmaelite people, who are known today as the Saudi Arabian Muslim people, of Mohammed. So, the conquest of the children of Israel, and the Ishmaelite people over their Hamite's neighbors would not have been such a washout, because many of those people of the ancient world, were dark skin looking people, like that of the rest of their Hamite's people, whom they also came out of. Also who many of these people were living around in that time.

This is the reason why many of the people of the so-called Middle East, and what became known as North Africa, are so red, in pink skin in complexion, and some of these people are in brown skin in complexion, because of the mixture of the Gentile European man blood running through these brown skin people veins. I must also point out that the Mohammedans have also conquered most of the land of Canaan, and north of the land of Ham, all the way to what became known as Nigeria of today. This was with the Quran and the sword, so many of the tribes of the area, became known as the Muslim people, because of the conquest of the Mohammedans Muslim people of Ishmael.

Many of the Philistine people, and other Canaanite people who might be around in todays time, it is because many of their ancestors did not get destroyed, when Yahweh was destroying many of the native people of the land of Canaan for the children of Israel, and for other Abrahamic seeds. Many of the Canaanites and other Hamite's tribes of the area, who did not get destroyed by Yahweh, for various Abrahamic seeds, did become a part of the Mohammedan Muslim people of today. Or the Arab family of today, because they were also conquered by the Mohammedans, and many of whom see themselves as the Muslim family, because they have no knowledge of who they are, and where they are coming from. As I did also explain in this book, that the name Arab people came from Greek, Latin, and the French, who were also some of the ruling power over the so-call Middle East, and what become known as North Africa, of their conquest.

This is a book I have also written, that is called THE FOLLOWERS OF MOHAMMED. These followers of Mohammed became known as the Mohammedans, and the Muslim people of today. With their religious belief of Islam, that they have indoctrinate many of their captive people to the worship of their god Allah. I have incorporated this book, to help to enlighten many people of today, who do not have any knowledge, of how Islam came about, by way of Mohammed and his followers. These followers of Mohammed became known as the Mohammedans, and the Muslim people of what became known as the Saudi Arabian people. According to the Webster's New World Dictionary, the dictionary explained that word Moslem is an Arabian word, which means a true believer in the faith that was established by Mohammed. As I did explain earlier in this book that the word Arab, and the word Arabian people came from Greek, Latin, to the French people, as the Arab people, that gave birth to the word Arabian. Who were some of the colonial rulers, and conquerors of what became known as North Africa, and the so-call Middle East. I would also like to point out that although the Mohammedans Muslim people of Mohammed, have conquered many people, with the sword and the Quran, for them to become Muslim followers of Mohammed. Also have given them this religious belief of Islam to whole on to, there is no way their religious doctrines could have come from Yahweh, who is the creator, and Father, and givers of all things. My reason for making this of kind of statement, it is because Abraham said to Yahweh pertaining to Ishmael his first son, that is recorded in (Genesis Chapter 17, and verse 18), that he wish if Ishmael, could live, or walk perfect before Yahweh.

At verse (19 of Genesis Chapter 17), there Yahweh went on to say to Abraham, that Sarah his wife shall bear him a son indeed, and Abraham must call his name Isaac. Yahweh went on to say to Abraham, I will establish my covenant with him, which mean His Laws, and Commandments." What Yahweh was saying to Abraham is that as far as His Laws, precepts, and His Commandments were concerned, that became known as the Scroll, the Scripture, and later of what become known as the Bible. This was by the Greeks translators of Europe, which mean a book, He was going to bring it about by mean of Isaac, and his seed, from where Jacob came out of.

This promise of Yahweh was also pass-on to Jacob seeds, who became known as the children of Israel, which simple mean children of Jacob. Because Jacob name was change to Israel by an angel of Yahweh, so Jacob descendants became known as the children of Israel, after Jacob new name of Isreal. So, there is no way Yahweh go back on His Word, and let the Ishmaelite's people of Ishmael to bring about a Holy book they call as the Koran, that they say was written by their god Allah. According to (Genesis Chapter 25, verses 26 and 27), Isaac had two sons, his first born was known as Esau, and his second was known as Jacob. Yahweh chose Jacob, and named him Israel, and Jacob's offspring became known as the children of Israel. Or better put the children of Jacob, who became the people of Yahweh. Yahweh also gave the children of Jacob His Laws, and His Commandments, and chose from them His prophets, and Apostles, who became the mouthpiece of Yahweh, to them, the children of Jacob. So, that these Laws and Commandments they did received, were to govern their lives that they did received from the prophets, and the Apostles of the servants of Yashua, to keep thought out all their lives. Those who did believed on the teaching of Yashua, that was given to them as the Word of Yahweh, that did become known as the New Covenant Law. Notice that Yahweh did not choose any of Ishmael seeds, or any of the seeds of Esau to become any prophets, or Apostles of His. He did not give them His Commandments, His name, and His Laws for any of their seeds to keep throughout all their lives, as He did with Israel who He called as His people. Although He did give the people of Esau, and the people of Ishmael special treatment, compare to the other Hamite's people who they also came out of.

Also, who they were living around in the so-call Middle East, and what became known as North Africa, by way of the Roman conquest. According to (Roman Chapter 9, and verse 13) there the Apostle Paul was quoting from what Yahweh had said to the Prophets, and to the Apostles. By saying that as it is written, meaning in the Scripture, "Jacob have I love, but Esau have I hated". So, Yahweh did not choose any of Esau seeds, or any of the seeds of Ishmael to be any of His Prophets, or Apostles of His. Some people might say Yahweh is prejudice, and show favoritism, but one must realize that Yahweh is the boss of life to all people, because He make all people, and all things, and He also do what pleases Him, and that is the reality of life. Whether we like it or not, because no one can question what Yahweh do this, or why He do this or that.

If a person was to be so presumptuous, to question the Word, and the authority of Yahweh, it would mean sure death for that person, who would do so, who is the highest over all the world of His creation. Who do not need anyone, but everyone have to answer to Him for their action, and their deeds of what they say and what they do. Yahweh also mentions in the Scripture book of Exodus by saying, what can the clay said to the potter? We are His clay, and He is the potter, because a potter in ancient Mizraim makes bricks and pottery out of clay. So, this is the reason why Yahweh used that example to show that He is the maker of us all, and there is nothing we can ask of His action. Because it would be disrespectful to Yahweh, and it would mean sure death for that person who would be so presumptuous to question the authority of the Highest. Who is the ruler of the universe, and who do not need anyone, but we cannot live with out Him, and that is the reality of life. Furthermore, at (Exodus Chapter 33, and verse 19), there Yahweh said to Moses, that I will be gracious to whom I will be gracious, and I will show mercy to whom I will show mercy. So, it is up to Yahweh who He will choose from who He will not chose, and no man can dear to ask Him why He do this, or why do you do that, if that were possible, they would not be around in life. I must point out that men cannot even question the authority of other men, of why they do this, or that. This goes for men who became kings, and politicians in our today's time, that was set up by the Gentile people of Europe wheresoever they went and conquered in the name of Christianity. And set up their system of ruler ship over other people for them to see things their way. Many of whom did became their subjects and captives, much less to question the authority of Yahweh, who do not need anyone, but everyone must answer to Him, whether they like it or not. Even some ordinary men who are not in any authority, many people cannot even question them of why they do this or that, it would bring about hostility, muchness Yahweh who do not need anyone.

King Nebuchadnezzar of Babylon learns the hard way, when he came to the reality of the power of Yahweh, when he was disciplined and chastise by Yahweh for his arrogant, and proud behavior. Yahweh made him to eat grass like animals, then he came to his senses and made the statement at (Daniel Chapter 4, and verse 34 to verse 36), by saying that all the inhabitants of the earth are as nothing before Yahweh. Nebuchadnezzar went on to say, Yahweh doth according to His own will, in the army of heaven, and among the inhabitants of the earth.

This is what Yahweh said to Abraham concerning Ishmael his son, that is mentioned in verse (20 of Genesis Chapter 17), Yahweh went on to say to Abraham" as far as Ishmael is concern, I have heard what you have said". I will bless him and make him fruitful, and I will multiply him exceedingly. Twelve princes shall he beget, and I will make of him a great nation of people, but as far as my Covenant is concern, I will establish it with Isaac whom Sarah shall bear unto you at this set time next year). So, based upon the statement Yahweh made with Abraham, there is no way could the Saudi Arabian people of Ishmael, who became known as the Mohammedans, and the Muslim people, could establish a true worship to Yahweh. That became known as Islam, to the worship of their god Allah, as away of life for their many captives people to follow as their religious belief. Also, a book they called as the Koran, that they say is the commandment of Allah, that many people of today associate this name of Allah, to be that of Yahweh, who they say is on e God of the universe. That is of the followers of Mohammed, who became known as the Muslim people, and who they say, has His precepts and commandments of Allah, that many people were thought that this god Allah his Yahweh. So, this religious philosophy, and laws of Mohammed, to his flowers, which it is a mare commandment of men, that came down from Mohammed, to his followers, who became known as the Mohammedans, and the Moslem people. Yahweh made Himself very clear in (Genesis Chapter 17, and verses 21), that His Covenant, which mean His Laws, and precepts shall be established with Isaac, where Jacob came from, that eventually became known as the Scroll, and then the Scripture, which mean writing.

Later the Scripture became known as the Bible, by way of the Greek translators of the of Gentile land of Europe. What Yahweh had said in the Scripture, it is stronger than welding, because welding can break or cut, but what Yahweh had said, it cannot be broken, or cut. Nothing cannot be taking away from what He had said, unless of course, He Himself change His own mind. Which He seldom do, and, He do not change His mind like most people do. Moreover, Yahweh is not the author of confusion, but He is of the order of truth and righteousness, and true worship must be to Him only. He does not change His Word or His mind like most people do, and no one can question His authority of why He do this, or why He do that. According to the Webster's Third International Dictionary, there it mentioned that the word Muslim, or Moslem came from the French people, that is spelled as mousseline.

In the Latin language that came from the Romans, that became known as the Italian language of today, this word Muslim or Moslem is spelled as Muslin. In what became known as the Arab language of today, this word Muslim or Moslem is spelled as Mawsiliy or Mosul, and this word Muslim also came from Alsama, which according to the dictionary, it is a French word, that means to resign oneself to Allah. I would like to let this fact be known that in the time of Mohammed, these people who became known as the Arab people, and many Hamite's people of the land area, were idol worshippers of their many gods. Who were not worshippers of Yahweh, because they had no knowledge of Him, and of His Laws, and His Commandments, for them to keep throughout all their lives. Like that of the people of Isreal, who He gave His Laws and Commandment to, for them to keep throughout all their generation. According to the A to Z index of the Encyclopaedia, there it explained that this god Allah is a deity that became a god for the Muslim people, of Mohammed. This word god, was pass on to the Greeks, Romans, Asia, and many Hamite's people as their gods. So, this Muslim god Allah, that many people associate with that of Yahweh, as the one God of the universe. It is of idolatry worship to that of Satan the devil, and his fallen angels, who are known in the Scripture as the daemons. Which they have converted many of their captive people to become believers of their religious worship of their god Allah. This title of the word god was taken from the word Elohim, which this title was taken from the name of one of the Canaanites gods who were known as Beal.

Who many of the children of Israel did worship at one time as their god, when they came from out of the land of Mizraim. So, when they the children of Israel went to living in the land of Canaan, many of them became worshipers of strange gods, that came from the Hamite's people, who they were living around in the so-call Middle East, and what become known as North Africa. This was from where many of the ancient children of Israel mothers came out of. Many people of that time did not know anything about the worship of Yahweh, and His Laws, because He only had revealed Himself to Noah, Melchisedec, Abraham, Isaac, Jacob, and the descendants of Jacob, who became known as the children of Israel. The rest of the people of that time had their own various gods, who many of them use to worship, and serve, and called up on, by whatever names they gave to these gods, of graven image.

To give one a good example of the idolatry worship that did exist there in what became known as North Africa, and also what became known, as the so-call Middle East of the land of Canaan, in the time of Jacob. According to (Genesis Chapter 31, and verse 19), there it shows that Rachel Jacob second wife had stolen her father image, he had worship as his god, in what became known as the so-call Middle East of the land that become known as Iraq. This land of Haran that became known as Iraq, is where Abraham and his father Terah had stop off, after they left from Babylon. Where he was born, and raise, until when Yahweh told him to leave from Babylon, and to go to where the Canaanites people was mostly, to take over their lands. So, according to verse 30 of (Genesis Chapter 31), there it explained that Jacob's uncle Laban, accuse him of stolen his god. Because there were many gods of the Canaanites, the people of Haran that become known as Iraq, the Babylonians, Assyrians, and the people of Mizraim that became known as the Egyptians people. This is also true with the people who became known as Asia, the people, Greece, and Rome, they all had their own gods, who they use to worship and serve. This was also, among the rest of Gentile family of who came from out of the brake up of the Roman Empire, they all had their own many gods, and goddess, whom they use to worship, and who were not worshipers of

Yahweh. Because many people of these days, had no knowledge of Yahweh, of His Laws and precepts for them to live by. So, from this Chapter, one can clearly see that in the time of Jacob, before the Mohammedans came into existent, there were many different gods, who were worship in the so-call Middle, East, and what become known as North Africa, as well as Europe, and Asia.

So, it depends on what gods these Mohammedans Muslim people are speaking about, whether it is Yahweh the only true creator of all things, or the various idolatry gods that many people of that time did worship. Even in our modern time of today, many people still worship their many gods. So, this religious philosophy of the Mohammedans Muslim people of Saudi Arabia, that they have conquered, and converted many of their captives to become religious worshipers of Islam, of their god Allah. With the sword, and the Koran, it is only the commandment of men, and it is totally a false worship. It is also not from Yahweh, the ruler and the creator of the universe, to whom alone all worship belong, true the name of Yashua His Son. Who became the sacrificial Lam for the sin of the world, that Yahweh did set up by Yashua, and his disciples.
 So, many of these common gods that were worshiped in that time, is now infused with the spelling of the capital word for God, that was taken from the title of the word Elohim. That did replace calling on the name of Yahweh, to whom alone all parse and, worship must be given to, true Yashua, and not by Mohammed, or anyone else for that matter. I do hope that these Ishmaelite's people of Mohammed is not making a mistake between the common gods that was infused with that of the spelling of the capital word for God, that stand for Yahweh only. The Mohammedans have infused the worship of their god Allah, with that of the worship of Yahweh, that they called as the one God of the universe. Many of these religious believers, and followers gave themselves rules, laws, and commandment of men that they called as divine doctoring of whatever gods they had worshipped, and serve. They also did ordain various priests to the services, and worship of these gods or deities. Like in the case of the Roman Catholic Church, and other religious organization that came down from paganism, and idolatry worship, that is blended with the religious world of today. That also became known as Christianity, to many people, who were taken captives by the Gentile people of Europe to be come rich people from their many captives. This is also, true by the Mohammedans Muslim people of Mohammed, to their god Allah, who many people were conquered, and indoctrinated, and brainwash to become followers of their conquerors religious doctrines. These laws and philosophies, that were forced upon them by their conquerors, they have no knowledge of what was true or false. Besides, they had no choice or saying in the matter, because it meant their life or their death. So, many of their captives people became Muslim followers of the Mohammedans, and his Muslim followers, to save their lives, and to be able to exist in the religious world of the Mohammedan Muslim people. This was a way of life, to please their conquerors, as it is in today world.

These Muslim captives had to embrace these doctrines as divine laws that they were thought to believe, without any question. Because they did not have any saying in the matter of what were thought to them, because it meant their, life or death. These doctrines, and belief were pass on down the line, from generation to generation, and It became a way of life for many of these people, who became known as the Mohammedans, and the Muslim people, as their faith, and religion to the worship of their god Allah, of Mohammed.

I would like to also point out that the word religion is a European word for worship, and it does not mean that this religious person is a worshiper of Yahweh. One who is keeping to His Laws, and Commandments, and also who is following the teaching of the New Covent Law, Yahweh did set up by way of Yashua His Son. So, this religious person could be a worshiper of the devil, a man, a cow, or anything for that matter, that they whole onto as their religious belief. I must also point out that there is only one faith, according to (Ephesians Chapter 4, starting from verse 4 to verse 5 and 6). There the Scripture mention that there is only one body, and one Spirit, meaning the Spirit of Yahweh, and the body of believers of Yashua. Those believing sheep of the people of Yashua, who are following his teaching, he gave to his Apostles, and the keeping of his commandment, will be able to enter into Yahweh Kingdom that is to come. They will become the citizens of Yashua ruler ship, of Yahweh Kingdom, and that of Yashua. The chapter went on to say, as ye, which mean you, are called in one hope of your calling. One Lord, referring to Yashua, who did become the sacrificial lamb of Yahweh, for the sins of Isreal, and that of the world of other people. One Lord, one faith, and one baptism, that is of the following and the keeping of the commandment of Yashua, he gave to his Apostles to teach other believers, who would later believe on him true their teaching, and writhing. That all these believers, who follow his teaching, and who is obedient to his commandment will become the children, and the family of Yahweh, true Yashua His Son. So, the Scripture went on to say, there is one God, who is the Father of us all, and who is above all, and through you all, and in you all, which is speaking of Yahweh who is the Father of us all.

This is first for the children of Israel, and for the rest of the people of the world, those who believed on Yashua, will become the spiritual Israel of Yahweh, along with the natural Isreal, who is the people of Yahweh. According to (Acts Chapter 4, and verse 12), there the Scripture explains that neither is there salvation in any other person, meaning Yashua, who became the sacrifice lamb for sin. For there is no other name given under heaven among men where we must be saved from the wrath of Yahweh that is to come. So, this name that the Scripture is speaking of, is Yashua, who is our king, High priest, and the mediator of the New Covenant Law, that is of Yahweh that Yashua did set up true his Apostles.

Yashua is also the greater Moses, who came down from heaven, who was sent to the tribe of the Yehudahites, and the Benjaminhites, who were left there in the land that became known as Israel. Who the Gentile European Germanic people name as Jews, and the Jewish people. This name Jews, and Jewish people was taken from the Latin word Judah of the Romans, from where the name Judah, was taken from. This Muslim faith, and their religious belief, and philosophy, is that of Mohammed, and his followers, who became known as the Mohammedans, and the Muslim people to the religious belief of their god Allah. I must point out that this religious belief of theirs, is a false faith, and a false hope, that will not get anyone anywhere, but destruction from Yahweh. One should also realize that the Word of Yahweh is what did become known as the Scripture of truth. Yahweh alone is the ruler of the universe that everyone must give account to, who has everyone lives in His hands. He determines the time and the seasons, and the future to come, and that is a fact of life, whether one believes it or not. The dictionary went on to explained that the word Islam mean to be in submission to the will of Allah. If the Mohammedans or the Muslim people is speaking about Yahweh they called as the God Allah, their submission that they mention, would mean to pay attention to His Holy Word the Scripture. Also, to take in knowledge of Him from of what is written, there. For it is the Word of Yahweh to everyone who believe, because Yahweh is the author of the writing of the Scripture, that become known as the Bible, by the Greeks translators. More over, Yahweh is not dealing with unbelievers, but He is only dealing with believers who keep His Laws, and His Commandments.
The prophecies of the Scripture that are written there, it is of truth, and the keeping of the Laws of Yahweh, is for our own benefit, and good in this life, to please Him, otherwise it will men our death and destruction. There are guidelines there for every believer, to build their life and faith around, to save them, from the destruction of the wrath of Yahweh that is to come on this world, of unbelievers. This is because of all the evilness that is taking place in our world of today, so the Scripture is for our own good, and benefit. Especially the New Covenant Law that was establish by Yashua before his death, that is known as the New Testament Law.

Sad to say that many people who were conquered, and converted to the religious belief of Islam, many of their captives, who call themselves as the Islamic, people. Many of them, do not believe in the Holy writing of the Scripture, as the Word of Yahweh, the Father of all things. But they more so believe in the writing of Koran, as the word of their god Allah. The point I am trying to bring out here is this, in the early time of the Scripture, there were only ways to worship, and that was either a person was a worshipper of Yahweh, or a worshipper of some idols, that many people of that time did call as their gods. So, the worshiping of many idols of the ancient world, that many people did called as their gods, which was only the worshipping of Satan the devil, and his falling angels, who are known in the Scripture as the Demons. Many people of that time were idol worshippers; except for the ancient child of Israel, who had the knowledge of Yahweh. Many of the children of Isreal were not true worshipper of Yahweh neither, because many of them chose to worship idol as their gods. Rather than Yahweh, whom they had knowledge of, as the creator of all things, and of the universe. According to the

Webster's New World Dictionary, for centuries the Turks was the principal champions of the spreading of Islam, so what the dictionary is telling us, is that the people of Ashkenaz who became known as the Turkish people, were the spreaders of Islam. But these people of Ashkenazi were at one time had control over the so-call Middle East, and what became known as North Africa, were idol worshippers of their many gods that came down from the people of Greece. Reading from volume 28 of the Encyclopaedia, what I gathered from the reading of these pages, is that the people of Turkey accepted Islam in the time of 985 AD. When Islam was already started by Mohammed, and his followers, many centuries before that time of the Turks. So, Islam became a part of their religious belief they did accepted from the followers of Mohammed, who were known as the Mohammedans, and the Muslim people of Mohammed. Many of these Turkish war lords came from the Byzantine Empire, of what later became known as the Ottoman conquest.

Which was really what was left of the old Roman Empire of Eastern Europe, that did become known as Asia Minor. This old Byzantine Empire later became known as Constantinople, and Easton bull of the Turkey area of Europe. Volume 9 of the Encyclopaedia Britannica went on to explained that the Ottoman Empire was created by some Turkish tribe men from the Anatolia area of Europe.

This came about during the decline of the Byzantine Empire of 1300, and it continued until the establishment of the republic of Turkey, in 1922 AD. So, in reality Islam was started with Mohammed, and his followers, who became known as the Mohammedans, and the Muslin people of Mohammed. This was way before the people of Turkey came to the knowledge of Islam. Who later accepted Islam by way of the conquest of the Mohammedans Muslim people, with the sword and the Quran, as the faith of Mohammed, and the prophet of his god Allah. According to Volume 22 of the Encyclopaedia, there it explained that Islam world and its religion, belong to a Semitic family, and it was made popular by Mohammed in the 7th century AD. According to Volume 21 of the Encyclopaedia, there it explained that, the Semitic people volume 22 refers to, came from Southern Mesopotamia, that became known as Iraq. According to the Encyclopaedia, these people were also known as the Sumerians, but first I must say that the name Mesopotamia came from the Greeks, of their time of ruler ship over the land of Canaan, that became known as the Middle East, and Isreal. This word Mesopotamia, meant to the Greeks, a land that is between two rivers, which is speaking of the Euphrates River, and the Tigris River, of the so call Middle East. So, this land area is where the various kingdoms of Nimrod was located, of what became known as the so-call Middle East. Which were the land area (Genesis Chapter 10, and verse 10), spoke of, as the land of Shinar. This land area of Shinar later became known, as the Persian Gulf, of the so-call Middle East, where Nimrod had his various kingdoms there. I am not quite sure if the Encyclopaedia gave the right spelling for the word Sumerian, that should have spell as the Samaritan, which was a part of ancient Israel, that came about after the death of Solomon.

Because Solomon did not please Yahweh well, but instead went and worship the various idolatry gods of his Hamite's wives. Also of his sweethearts, whom they the children of Israel was living around in the so-call Middle East, and what become known as North Africa. Whom they the children of Israel also came out of, from the many granddaughters of the people of Ham. I must also mention that this statement the Encyclopaedia made about the Semitic people, who they calm was from Southern Mesopotamia, of what they now called as Iraq, it is a total false statement, that is not of truth. My reason for saying this, what is now known as Iraq, was one of the kingdoms of Nimrod, that were known as Haran, in the time of Abraham and his father Tera.

Abraham father came from ancient Persia, now known as Iran. So, when Abraham and his father Tera stop off in the land of Haran, that became known as Iraq, by the conquest of the Mohammedan Muslim people. This was when Abraham left from his country of Babylon, where Abraham was born and raise, until when Yahweh told him to leave from Babylon, and to go where the Canaanite people were mostly living, to take over their lands Yahweh gave to him. So, what became known as the city of the Samaritans, was a part of the ancient kingdom of Israel, that were given to the ten tribes of the children of Jacob, that did became known as the kingdom of Israel. The Kingdom of Jerusalem was given to Rehoboam, who was a son of King Solomon, for him to rule over the tribe of Yehuda, and the tribe of Benjamin, because of the sin of King Solomon, who did not please Yahweh well. Because he went and worship the various gods of his many wives, and concubines from the Hamite's people of Canaan. Also, that of other Hamite's women from the land of Ham itself that became known as North Africa. So, the kingdom of Israel was split into two different kingdoms, with Jeroboam ruling over the kingdom of Israel in Samaria, and Rehoboam ruling over the kingdom of Jerusalem. As it is so recorded in the Scripture book of (I Kings Chapter 11, starting from verse 1 to verse 43). Before the children of Israel, this land area were the land of the Canaanite people, and other Hamite's people of Ham, who were living there, and who had their kingdoms there. So, there were no such a people who were known as the Semitic people, as the Encyclopaedia would have many people of today to believe. It is a false makeup name, and a false statement. I am not quite sure if Mr. Mohammed was a true descendant of the people of the land of Ashkenaz, now known as the land of Turkey. Who the Encyclopaedia say gave birth to this religious belief of Islam, or he was a true descendant of Ishmael, I cannot say for sure. But according to volume 22 of the Encyclopaedia Abu al-Qasim Muhammad, or Abd al- Muttalib ibn Hashim, who were born in Mecca around 570 AD. Or in the time of 610 AD, who became the main religious leader of Islam, after the death of his father who was known as Abd Allah.

So, after the death of Muhammed father, he was put in the care of his grandfather, who was known as Abd al-Muttalib. But because the atmospheric condition of Mecca was not healthy for him, he was given as an infant to a nurse from a nomadic tribe of the area, to take care of him. He spent some of his time living in the desert, and he also lost his mother at age of six year old, whose name was known Aminah, and his grandfather at the age of eight.

After the death of his mother and grandfather, Mohammed came under the care of his uncle, whose name was Abu Talib, who was the head of tribal clan of Mecca. He also did accompany his uncle on a business trip to the land of Zidon now known as Syria. This was in the time of 595 AD, and while Mohammed was on this business trip to what became known as the land of Syria with his uncle, he was put in charge of the belonging of a rich lady by the name of Khadijah of a tribal clan by the name of Asad. This lady was impressed by the present of young Mohammed, that she offered to marry him. Young Mohammed got married to this lady who at the time was about the age of 40, she bore Mohammed two sons, and four daughters. But while Mohammed was married to Khadijah, he did not have any more wives until her death in 619 AD. I want to point out that I was watching You Tube, and this person of You Tube mention that it was the Roman Catholic Church who gave birth to Islam, because Mohammed wife Khadijah were a Roman Catholic believer, before she got married to Mohammed. Furthermore this story seam to be true, because the Roman Catholic Church came from out the Roman, who also had ruler ship over the so-call Middle East, and what became known as North Africa, long before Mohammed came on the seen of life. So, if Mohammed was around in the time of the Romans, and try to set up this religious belief of his, he would have been put to death by the Romand, for going against their system. According to Volume 22 of the Encyclopaedia page 1, this marriage of Mohammed to Khadijah was a big turning point in the life of Mohammed, because according to the custom of the Ishmaelite people of what became known as the Saudi Arabian people, minors did not inherit dead left properties, weather it was of father or grandfather. But by his marriage to Khadijah, who was a rich lady, he was able to obtain enough capital to engage in business activities.

The poverty and the disappointment of Mohammed young early life, help him to meditate upon the tension, and the poverty of many poor Meccans people, who were under the pressure of the wealthy Meccans society, of what became known as Arabia. Volume 22 of the Encyclopaedia went on to explained that while Mohammed was growing up as a young man in the city of Mecca, he was thinking about the prosperous merchants of Mecca who had all the wealth of the land to themselves. While most of the hard-nary people were living in poor condition. While he was thinking about these things, he claimed he had a vision of a majestic being, he later identified as the angel Gabriel, telling him he is chosen to be a messenger of Allah.

From Mohammed claimed of his vision of the angel Gabriel, he also claims he had different messages of revelation, from time to time, until the time of his death. He also claims he had verbal massages directly that came from Allah, whom they say is the one God of the universe. The Encyclopaedia explained that some of these messages were kept in the memory of Mohammed, and his followers, and sometimes these massages were written down. According to volume 22 of the Encyclopaedia, in the time of 650 AD, these messages Mohammed did received were collected, and written down in what became known as the Quran, or the Koran. After these messages of Mohammed, the Koran became the sacred Scripture book of Islam, and continues to be the Holy book of Islam to this day. The Encyclopaedia explained that the believers of Mohammed, from the time of his messages, believe the Quran was a divine revelation came from the god Allah, that was written in his own words. According to this same volume 22 of the Encyclopaedia, after the claim of Mohammed of his various visions, he gathered some of his friends who did accepted his claim to be a Prophet, of his god Allah, and they went and joined him in prayer in the worship to his god Allah. The Encyclopaedia mentions that many men of Mecca used to worship many gods, but a few of them believed that men was in needed a supernatural power. Many merchants in the time of Mohammed, believed that most things could be accomplished by wealth, and by human planning. So, after some opposition against Mohammed in Mecca, he and some of his followers went to live in Medina. While Mohammed and some of his followers were living in Medina, many Yehudahites of the tribe of Yehudh, who become known as the Jews of today.

These Yehudahites citizens of Medina did opposed Mohammed claimed to be a Prophet of the god Allah, or Yahweh. For at least five years, Mohammed had no direct power over the social group of Medina. But in the closing years of his life, the achievement of his military success, was of great conquest over the other social group and people of Medina. Also over the other bordering countries that were near to Medina. These military conquests of Mohammed gave him absolute power of control over the people of Medina, and other souring areas of Medina. Mohammed claimed the revelation he received at Medina, frequently contain legal rules for his community of Muslim believers, that had political question, on rare occasion to satisfy their political desire, of what was right or wrong.

For the first 18 months in Medina Mohammed spent settling, down, and he was given a piece of land where he built a house that had apartments that was grouped around a central courtyard for each of his wives. The Muslim community of Medina often joined Mohammed in prayer in his home, which after his death; became a Mosque of Medina for his Muslim worshipper to pray in. There was also a group of men who left from Mecca, and went to Medina to see Mohammed, who did appeared to be fellow Muslim believers. These Muslim believers were given the approval from Mohammed to set out on a normal Arab fashion of razzias. The word razzias is another word for a raid, or sudden attack on other Mecca's caravans who were on their way to what become known as Syria. According to the Encyclopaedia, Mohammed himself led three of these razzias, or raid in 623AD, in which these raid fail. Probably because of traitors that may have betrayed the Muslim movement to their enemy of Mecca, who did opposed Mohammed to be the prophet of his god Allah. At last in January of 624, a small band of men were sent eastward with a sealed order, telling them to proceed to a place that was known as Nakhlah, that was near to the city of Mecca, to carry out their raid, or attack on any of the people of Mecca passing by. This raid or attack was a successful attack made on some caravan coming from the country of Sheba known today as the country of Yemen. Volume 22 of the Encyclopaedia explained that, by this raids of these Muslims on the caravan coming from Yemen, they had violated pagan ideas of sanctity. Thereby making the Meccans to be aware of the seriousness of the threat coming from Mohammed. This word sanctity, which according to the Webster Colligate Dictionary, this word is a Latin word that stand for holiness of life, a person should show in their character of life toward another person, in their daily activities of their lives. According to volume 22of the Encyclopaedia, Mohammed changed his general policy of respect toward the Yehudahites of Medina, by braking off all relationship with them.

The earlier Muslim believers of Mohammed days, used to face the city of Jerusalem in their worship to Allah. But according to the Muslim believers, Mohammed did received a revelation helping him to understand, they should position their faces toward the city of Mecca, in their daily worship and prayer to Allah, instead of Jerusalem. Due to this change of the Muslims of Medina turning their face toward Mecca in their worship, many Meccans was ready to support Mohammad in his religious endeavor.

The Encyclopaedia explained that in March of 624 AD Mohammad was able to lead about 315 of his men on a razzaia, or attack, on some wealthy Meccans caravan who were returning from Syria to Mecca. These caravans coming from Syria was led by Abu Sufyan, who was the head of a Meccan clan, with also some other Meccans leading a force of about 800 men, who wanted to teach Mohammad a lesson. On March 15, 624 AD, near a place called Badr, the two forces met in battle, that neither of them could withdraw without disgrace. During this battle at least 45 Meccans were killed, including one of the leaders, by the name of Abu Jahal, and other leading men of Mecca. Mohammad and his men took 70 Meccans as prisoner, while only 14 Muslim were killed. This victory of Mohammad appeared to his followers as a divine vindication of his prophet hood, to show he had the support of the god Allah behind him as his messenger. Mohammed and his Muslim community were exalted in the spirit of victory, and in the spirit of the victory, Mohammed and some of his followers went and assassinate some people of Medina, because they were not supporters of his prophethood, as the prophet of his god Allah. Mohammed also made minor disturbances for an excuse to expel some Yehudahites people who operated the local market in Medina. Because they were not supporters of his claim to be a prophet of his god Allah. In 624 AD, Mohammad led a larger Muslim force on a razzias against some hostile nomadic tribes with some success. Mohammad realized that the Meccans were bound to try to avenge their defeat, so Abu Sufyan put together a Meccan army of about 3,000 men, in March 21, of 625 AD. They entered the area of Medina, and the Muslim group of Medina encouraged Mohammed to go out and fight against these Meccans.

According to the Encyclopaedia, Mohammad led an army of about 1,000 men, and when he reached the hill of Uhud, which were on the other side of the Meccan army camp. Which was on March 23, of 625 AD, the forces of the Meccans was driven back with considerable losses. As the Muslims chased after the forces of these Meccans, the Meccan managed to launch a side attack, on some Muslim who left from their position were thrown into confusion. Some of these Muslims who were trying to make it back to safety, many of them were cut down by the Meccan, but Mohammad was able to save the bulk of his force from the cavalry of the Meccans.

This war between the Muslim, and Meccans did not result in a clear victory, or losses for either side, because the Meccan killed the same number of Muslims as they had loss of their own men. Both sides prepared for a decisive encounter. The Encyclopaedia explained that in two cases a small party of Muslims was tracked down, and was ambushed, and many of them lost their life in the battle. Mohammad and his Muslim followers went and expelled another set of Yehudahites group from Medina, because they did not support his claim to be a prophet of his god Allah. In April of 627 AD, Abu Sufyan led a force of 10,000 men against the Muslim in Medina, which was the strong hold of Mohammad and his followers. But on this occasion, Mohammad ordered the crops of Medina to be harvested, and a trench to be dug to defend the main part of their frontier from the Meccan army. For about two weeks the army of the Meccans besieged the Muslims of Medina, but while they try to cross trench to reach the Muslim of Medina, but the Meccan, failed do so. So, at this time grass for the horses of the Meccan forces were getting scarce, and after a night of wind and rain, the great forces of the Meccans started to melt away. The Meccan failed to dislodge Mohammad and his men, whose position was now highly strengthened. For more than two years there had been no opposition to Mohammad in Medina, chiefly from Abd Allahibn and others. But Mohammad eventually had a showdown with Abd Allahibn Ubayy who had joined in spreading slander on one of his wives, whose name was Aishah. But after the confrontation, it was revealed that Abd Allah had little support in Medina.

So, he became reconciled with Mohammad after the siege of Medina, he was again accepted in the Muslim family of Medina. Mohammad went and attacked a Yehudahites group who were known as the Qurayzah, who he thought were in opposition to his claim to be a prophet of Allah. When these Yehudahites men surrendered to

Mohammad, the men were all savagely executed, and their women, and their children were sold into slavery. Mohammad wanted to win over his countrymen of Mecca to become Muslim, but he did not want to destroy them, but to bring economical pressure on them. Mohammad did not realize that in converting the Arabs of Mecca to become Muslims, he was equipping his countrymen with the idea of raiding and conquering other people to become Muslim as he did.

The Encyclopaedia explained that, in the eyes of the followers of Mohammed who became known as the Mohammedans, and the Muslim people of today. It was not a good idea for Muslim to be carrying out raids against other Muslims. All though Mohammed did install into his followers the idea of carrying out raids, and conquering other people to become Muslims. Yet he thought it was not a good idea for Muslim to be fighting and conquering another Muslim, because it would cause division and not unity among Muslim. According to volume 22 of the Encyclopaedia, in a dream Mohammad saw himself performing the annual pilgrimage to Mecca, which in March of 628 AD, he set out to do just that. Driving animals that were to be offered as sacrifice, but he was disappointed because no more than 1,600 of his men would accompany him to Mecca. The Meccan were determining to prevent the Muslim followers of Mohammad from entering their city of Mecca, but Mohammad and his men were stopped at a place that was known as Huday Byah. This place was close to the city of Mecca, until Mohammed was able to work out a treaty with the citizen of Mecca. A treaty was established with the understanding that hostility was to be stop, and also, the Muslim would be allowed to make their Pilgrimage way to Mecca, without any problems. About two months later Mohammad led some of his forces against some Yehudahites who were operating a farm of Khabar, that was not too far from Medina. After the invasion by Mohammad and his forces, they told the Yehudahites they could remain in their lands, under one condition, and that is they must send half their harvest to the Muslim of Medina. The Encyclopaedia explained that, throughout 628-629 AD the power of Mohammad become even stronger, because of his various military successes.

Due to the successful conquest Mohammed had made, led many people to become Muslim followers of Mohammed, and his religious organization of Islam. The religious attraction to Islam was now becoming more and more popular, and prosperous. The conversion to Islam of that time were more so for material motive, and for fare of persecution from Mohammed, and his Mohammedans followers who become known as the Muslim people. The Encyclopaedia explained that many of the idol worshippers of Mecca of their many gods was now on the decline, because of the exposure of Islam. The Encyclopaedia explained that several leading men of Mecca went to Medina, and become Muslim follower of Mohammed.

A new leader who had takes over from Abu Sufyan, who was one of Mohammad opposing leaders of Mecca, but he did not accomplish very much as far as followers was concern. Due to the treaty Mohammad made with Abu Sufyan, before he was replaced with the new leader of Mecca, it did remove some of the pressure of raids against the caravans of the Meccans by Mohammed and his followers. Shortly after the treaty with Abu Sufyan, Mohammad went and married to the daughter of Abu Sufyan, whose Muslim husband died in Ethiopia. After the marriage it led to a stronger bond between Mohammed and Abu Sufyan, who began to negotiate a peaceful surrender of Mecca to Mohammad and his followers. It was probably when Mohammad went to Mecca on a pilgrimage in 629 AD that he became reconciled with his uncle, who was known as Al Abbas. Mohammed take his uncle sister-in-law to be one of his wives, and her name was Maymunah. The Encyclopaedia explained that, there was an attack made by the allies of the Meccan, against the allies of Mohammad in November of 629 AD. Which caused Mohammad to break off his treaty with the Meccan of Mecca. After Mohammad break off his treaty with the Meccans, he made a secret preparation of putting together and army of 10,000 men to march on the city of Mecca, in January of 630 AD. But Abu Sufyan, and one of Mohammad's fathers in laws, together with other leaders of Mecca went out to meet with Mohammad, and submitted themselves to him. Mohammed promised these leaders of Mecca that he would grant them a general amnesty. But some people of Mecca were excluded from this amnesty. When Mohammed enters the city of Mecca, there was virtually no resistance against him. Although two of his Muslims followers were killed, and a few of his enemies of Mecca was also killed, but he was able to have things under his controlled.

The Encyclopaedia explained that, Mohammed left Mecca as a persecuted Prophet, and later he return in triumph, and gain the interest of most of the people of Mecca, although he did not insist on them becoming Muslims, but many of them did so. Mohammed became the strongest military man in Arabia, and many tribes of what is now known as the Arabian people, send representative to Medina, seeking to become Muslims. According to volume 22 of the Encyclopaedia, Mohammed benefit from the defeat of the Persian Empire, and from the Byzantine Christians Empire of 627-628 AD, of the old Roman Empire of the Turkey area.

Whereas in Sheba that become known as Yemen, and in other places of the so call Persian Gulf area, minorities did rule on the Persian support against the country of Byzantium, but many of them turn their attention to Mohammed for support. The country of Byzantium that was mention is in what became known as the country of Turkey, that were known as Asia Minor, during Greco Roman time. These people did came under the rule ship of the Roman Empire, after the defeat of the various generals of Alexander the Great, and their descendants to the new power of Rome. The Encyclopaedia explained that, the greatest of all the raids Mohammed did carried out, was the march to the Syrian border at the end of 630AD. When he take 30.000 of his men on a month's journey to the Syrian border, and he was able to bring them under his controlled. This invasion of the land of Zidon that became known as Syria, ends up in a treaty with the people of Syria, and it became the models for all treaty agreement for people who were conquered by their conquerors. Due to the vast army Mohammed had under his control at the time, it gave him success of power, to conquer the land of Zidon, now known as Syria, and other countries of the area. Some of the people who were near Syria, who were Christians, and who were under the influence of the Byzantines people, who had ruler ship over them, became Muslim followers of Mohammed. Due to Mohammed's conquest of Syria, the earlier friendship that did existed between Mohammed, and the Christian people of Ethiopia, were changed to hostility. The Encyclopaedia point out that before the death of Mohammed, there was armed opposition against him in various part of the country of Arabia, but the Islamic state of Arabia were strong enough to deal with these uprising. After the death of Mohammed, he left most of Arabia united, and were moving for the expansion into the country of Syria, and what became known as Iraq, for these people to became Muslim followers of Mohammed.

According to volume 22 of the Encyclopaedia, Mohammed who was in poor health for some time did, not made any arrangement for his successor, but because of his death in Medina in June of 632 AD, provoked a major crisis among his followers. Mohammed who was the chief significant establisher of the religious state of Islam, in his lifetime, he was able to create a federation of Arab tribes. Within less than 20 years after his death, they were able to defeat the Byzantine and what was left of the Persian Empire. The Byzantine, and what was left of the Persian empire did occupied a vast territory, from what became known as Libya, to Persia, that did developed into an Arab Islamic Empire of Arabia, by the Mohammedans Muslim people of Mohammed.

The Encyclopaedia explained that Mohammed established the religion of Islam as the very foundation of Arab unity, and that this religion and social character of Islam would expressed itself as a religious community. According to their, philosophy, this religion was commission by Allah to bring about its own value system to the world through Jihad. According to the Encyclopaedia, the word Jihad that was mentioned, meant a holy war, or a struggle. The success of the early generation of the Muslims, with in a 100 years after the death of Mohammed, in 632 AD, gave them the ability to conquer a large part of the globe. From Spain to central Asia, India, and North Africa to Nigeria, under a new Arab Muslim Empire that became known as Islam. According to volume 22 of the Encyclopaedia, this period of Islamic conquest, and empire building, did mark the first phase of the expansion of the Islamic religion to the various countries I have mentioned above. This Muslim religious community did discriminated against the followers of other religious group. They also, won rapid converts, because of their military might, and the Yehudahites, and the Christians communities were assigned to a special part of their captured communities. They were referred to, as those people who believed in the

Scripture, they called as the people of the book. These religious Christians were given religious freedom, but they were required to pay a special percent of capital tax, that were called as the Jizyah. But for those other group of people who were considered as pagans, or idol worshippers, they were required to accept Islam or die. Many of these Christians communities of their conquered lands, eventually became Muslims followers to avoid paying the tax.

I must point out that, I did not cover all the history about Mohammed, and his earlier, and later followers, who became known as the Mohammedans, and also what became known as the Muslim people of Islam. I would like to say that, whether Mohammed had the various visions he claimed he had, one cannot say for sure. But one thing I do know, and do believed, that according to the writhing of the Holy Scripture, there is no way there where it mentions of Mohammed to be a Prophet of Yahweh. Furthermore, all the various Prophets Yahweh did used, except for Enoch, Noah, Job, Abraham, Isaac, and Jacob, all the other Prophets Yahweh did used, were taken from among the ancient children of Jacob, who become known as the children of Israel.

Also, all the Apostles Yahweh had chosen by way of Yashua, to write the New Covenant part of the Scripture, that the Greeks, and the Latin people called as the New Testament, were taken from among the children of Israel. So, there is no way any of the prophets of Yahweh could have come from out of the seed of Ishmael. According to the statement Yahweh made with Abraham, about which of his sons He was going to let His Laws, and His commandment, that became known as the Scripture to come true. One can see the fulfillment of the promise Yahweh did made with Abraham concerning Isaac, and his seed, who become known as Jacob and Israel, from where all the prophet of the writers of the Scripture came from. These Ishmaelite people of the land of Raamah, that eventually became known as the land of the Saudi Arabia people. Are a mixed-up people with that of the blood of the Persians, Greek, Roman, Turks, and with that of the rest of the Gentile families of Europe who came from out of the brake up of the Roman Empire. Who also had conquered the so-call Middle East, and what became known as North Africa. So, by the mixture of these various conquerors blood, running true these Saudi Arabian people of Ishmael, gave birth to a new nation of people, one sees today in the various parts of what became known as the Middle East, and what became known as North Africa. Although Yahweh did not choose Esau and his seeds to be any Prophets, and Apostles of His, yet He did gave the seed of Esau who became known as the Edomites people special treatment over their Hamite's people they also came out of. Whom they were all living around in the land of Canaan, and what become known as North Africa. At the time of the conquest of people and their lands, and the spreading of Islam by the Mohammedans, many people of that time who were conquered had two choices, and that is to accept the Quran as the word of Allah. Also Mohammed as the prophet of Allah, and his religious philosophy as a way of life for them to follow.

If their conquered captives did not accept their philosophy about the Quran, and Mohammed as the Prophet of Allah, it would mean their death. So, many people had no choice but to become followers of Mohammed who became known as the Mohammedans, and the Muslim people of today. I must also point out that, the Mohammedans was a part of the destruction of many of the great civilization of the people of Ham. Yet they came from out of the people of Ham, who were their neighbors, they were living around, in what became known as the so-call Middle East and what became known as North Africa.

Because Hagar, the mother of Ishmael came from the land of Mizraim that became known as Egypt. Also, Abraham who is the father of Ishmael, he also came from out of the family of Cush, by his mother side of people off Babylon, and Cush was the first son of Ham. So, Abraham was a Cushite man by his mother side of people, of Babylon, where he was born, and raise of the people of Nimrod. When Yashua was here on earth, preaching and teaching among the Yehudahites who were left there in the land of Israel, who became known as the Jewish race of people of today. He did not lead an army of soldiers with swords against them, who did not believe on him that he was the Mashiah. The Son of Yahweh who was sent to them, for them to accept his teaching as the living truth. But rather at (John Chapter 10, and verse 27, and verse 28), there Yashua simply said to them, who did not believe on him that he was the one sent by Yahweh. He simple said to them that "his

90

sheep knows his voice, and he know them, and they follow him, and he will give them eternal life. Which simple mean life everlasting, and they shall never perish, neither shall any man pluck them out of his hands". It was Yahweh who had sent Yashua to the Yehudahites, and the Benjamites who was left there in Israel, to save them from their sins and death, and to give them everlasting life. By virtue, his blood, death, and the resurrection from the dead, that did establish the New Covenant part of the Scripture, that all believers, and unbelievers of today are under this New Covenant Law. Yashua also said to them at (John Chapter, 6 and verse 44) "no man cometh unto him, except the Father which had sent him draws them onto him, and he will raise them up in the last days. Meaning at time of the resurrection of the dead back to life". The reason why I gave these Scripture as an example, is to show the different of qualities between that of Yashua, and his Apostles. In comparison to that of Mohammed and his followers, who became known as the Mohammedans and the Muslims people of Mohammed.

Who went about slathering people for them to become believers, and followers of Mohammed, and his religious philosophies of Islam of his god Allah. Also, with their religious philosophies of their laws, and commandment of men, that were given to their captives of converts for them to believe in. Otherwise, if they did not accept their philosophies and laws they would die. The Israelites Prophets, who were the forerunner before the coming of Yashua, did not bring an army of men with swords and the old Covenant part of the Scripture to the ancient children of Israel, who were around in those days, for them to believe, what they were saying was the truth.

Nor did Yashua seek to become a colonizer, or a conqueror of many people and their lands, as did Mohammed, and his Followers did, who became known as the Mohammedans and the Muslim people. As well as the Gentile people who became known as the European people, with their Cross of Roman Catholicism, that became known as Christianity, for their captives to accept as Christianity as their religious belief. Who went about conquering, and enslaving many people in the name of Christianity to become rich people, and to have control over their captives lands. So, from this statement, one can clearly see from what I have written, who Yahweh did send, and who is true and who is false. This little history of truth I have written about Mr. Mohammed, and many of his earlier followers. Who became known as the Mohammedans, and the Islamic people, might be offensive to many of these kinds of people who see themselves as the Muslim believers of Mohammed, and his followers. But the truth must be told, weathers these believers like it or not. One can kill a man for telling the truth, but no man can kill the truth. The truth will always prevail, although it might become offensive to some people, who do not like to hear the truth. Who also do not know any better, yet the truth must be told. The reason why many of these Muslim believers of today might become offended, it is because they do not have any real knowledge and understanding of how this religious establishment of Islam came about. One should not be offended by the truth, because as Yashua said in (John Chapter 8, and verse 32), "you shall know the truth and the truth shall set you free". This truth that Yashua mention is free from falsehood, and from false doctrines of men that keep many people in ignorance and darkness. Many Hamite's people of the world of today, need to know the truth, the real true history of things.

Because we as a people of Ham, has been deceived by so many people, and many of us Hamite's people of today, are still in totally darkness of the real truth. Furthermore, people should not become worshippers, and followers of men, but they should become worshipper of Yahweh, and followers of Yashua, of his teaching he gave to his Apostles his servants to teach other believers. This was to save them who believe from the wrath and destruction of Yahweh that is to come on all the Un Yahweh like people, that were translated as Un Godliness, and upon all the Un Yashua like people. (I Corinthians Chapter 15, and verse 21), there it is stated that, for since by man cometh death, meaning Adam, by man cometh also the resurrection of the dead, meaning Yashua. Who came to earth as a man in the form of the first man Adam, who has cause death, and sin upon all his offspring's.

(I Corinthians Chapter 15, and verse 22) went on to say that, for as in Adam all die, even so in Yashua shall all be made alive, that is if they are believers, and follow of his teaching he gave to the Apostles, his servants to teach other believers. Also, by they living their lives to please Yahweh, and Yashua, but for the unbeliever's everlasting punishment, and destruction. So, it is not by Mohammed or by any other person for that matter. But it is all about Yahweh, and His Holy word the Scripture of truth, and His Son Yashua, who is our king and High Priest to Yahweh, and our master. People should not become followers of men, that will only lead them to destruction. Furthermore, if one should examine throughout the history of mankind, people have always wanted to become followers of other men, as their leaders, that many of the times, led to the destruction for many of their followers, and also of the leaders. This is true for Adolph Hitler of Germany, and many of his followers. Also, for Alexander the Great and many of his followers, and for many other men who love to be follower of other men as their leaders to destruction. Yashua make it quite clear in (Matthew Chapter 23, and verse 9) by saying, call no man your father upon the earth, for one is your Father who is in heaven, speaking of Yahweh. Also at verse 10, call no man your master or leader, for one is your leader and master, and that is speaking of Yashua himself. Yahweh made it clear through the various prophets of the Old Covenant part of the Scripture, that He was going to send His chief spokesman, and that spokesman was Yashua, and not that of Mohammed. It is Yashua whom Yahweh anointed as the Mashiah, which mean savior of the world of mankind, and the future King of all Kings, and Lord of all Lords, and High Priest to Yahweh.

(John Chapter 3, and verse 16) went on to say, for Yahweh so love the world of mankind that He gave, or send His only begotten Son, that whosoever believe on him will not perish in the destruction to come, but will received everlasting life. (Micah Chapter 5, and verse 2) there this prophecy was written about Yashua long before he came to earth. The prophecy went on to say, "but you Bethlehem Ephrata, though you be little among the thousands of Judah, yet out of you shall he come forth to me, who will be ruler in Israel, whose goings forth have been from of old, from everlasting".

(Psalms Chapter 2, starting from verse 6), there it read like this, "yet have I set my King upon my holy hill of Zion, meaning Jerusalem. I Yahweh will declare the decree, the Lord Yahweh hath said unto me, you art my Son; this day have I begotten you.

Ask of me, and I shall give you the heathen for your inheritance, and the uttermost parts of the earth for your possession. You shall break them with a rod of iron; you shalt dash them in pieces like a potter's vessel, which is speaking of Yashua as the Son of Yahweh. I would also like to say that a potter is a person who in ancient Mizraim, makes things out of clay. There the Scripture went on to say, be wise now therefore, O you kings: be instructed, ye judges of the earth, serve the Lord Yahweh with fear, and rejoice with trembling. Kiss the Son, lest he be angry, and you perish from the way, when his wrath is kindled but a little. But blessed, are happy are all they that put they trust in him". (Isaiah Chapter 61) and verse 1 went on to say, the Spirit of the Lord Yahweh is up on me, because the Lord Yahweh hath anointed me to preach good tidings unto the meek, which mean humble ones. Yashua also mention that He, Yahweh hath sent him to bind up the brokenhearted, to proclaim liberty to the captives, and to opening of the prison to them who are bound, which is speaking about Yashua. Yashua is also known in the book of Revelation Chapter (19, and verse 13), as the Word of Yahweh. This is not speaking of Mohammed, or anyone else for that matter, but of Yashua, who was Yahweh mouthpiece who came in the form of a man to the ancient Yehudahites who were left there in the land of Israel. This was as how Moses was the mouthpiece of Yahweh to the Israelites people, who were there in the land of Mizraim, now known as Egypt. (Deuteronomy Chapter 18, verse 15), there Moses spoke to the ancient children of Israel, by saying to them, that Yahweh was going to raise up unto them a prophet from the midst of them. One of their own brothers like unto him Moses, unto him the people should listen to.

Many Muslim believers I have spoken to here in the United States, believe that this Scripture I have mention above was speaking about Mr. Mohammed as the one who Yahweh was going to send, or raise up. But I am sorry to disappoint these Muslim believers, who believe this prophecy was speaking about Mohammed, but this prophecy of the Scripture was speaking about Yashua who Yahweh was going to send to the people of Isreal.

Chapter 11- The Hamite's People From The Island of Jamaica Who Became Known As The Rastafarians.

This is a book I have also written, that is called The Rastafarian philosophy of the worship of Hail Selassie. I have incorporated the story of these people worship to Hail Selassie this book, The Untold Forgotten Great Civilization of the people of Ham. I wrote about the Rastafarian philosophies, and their religious doctoring of belief, because I was born and raised in Jamaica, living in the Kingston area when the Rastafarians movement was taking shape back there in the early fifties. During this time of the early fifties, many of these people were brutalize, and beaten up by the police force of Jamaica, because of the way they grow their hair very long, and because of the smoking of marijuana as a part of their religious worship to Hails Selassie. These people worship Hail Selassie as their god, who they say is the conquering lion of the tribe of Judah, and a part of their religious worship to him, is the smoking of marijuana, and growing their hair very long. I could remember some time during the fifties, in the Kingston area, at a marketplace known as Carination market. A Blue Seam police officer hit a Rastafarians man in his head with his night stick, we people in Jamaica called as batten, and kill the man. The reasons why the Blue seam police officer hit and kill the Rastafarian man, was because the police officer told the Rastafarian man to move and keep on moving. This Rastafarian man told the police officer he must not touch him, because he is the Lord anointed, and he has not ascended to his father as yet.

So, the police officer grabs this Rastafarian man and said to him, are you anointed? And he hit this Rastafarian man in his head with his night stick weapon and killed the man. This Rastafarian man may have read the Scripture, and did not fully understand what Yashua had said to Mary, when he was risen from the dead when he made this statement to her, back there in Israel. Or he may have heard the statement made by someone else, and did not have a good understanding of this statement he had made to the police officer, that Yashua did said to Mary. This statement the Rastafarian man made to the police officer, can be found at (John Chapter 20, and verse 17), where Yashua make this statement to Mary after he was risen from the dead on the third day, which was on a Sunday as many people know it as today.

Due to the death of this Rastafarian man, it cast a big riot to break out in the Carination market, when a Red Seam police officer, who is a higher ranking officer, to that of the Blue Seam police officer, came to take statement from the venders of the market, who saw what took place. So when this Read Seam police officer came to take statement from the venders, who saw what took place between the Blue Seam officer, and that of the Rastafarian man. But the various venders were angry at this Read Seam police officer, because of the killing of the Rastafarian man, by the Blue Seam police officer, who they could not get to beat up, for the killing of this Rastafarian man. I must mention that I was eyewitness to the riot when the Red Seem officer came to take the statement from the various venders who were there, and who saw what took place, between the Rastafarian man, and the Blue Seam police officer. I must point out that I was not present when the Rastafarian man was killed, but I was there when the Red Seem officer came to take statement. I would like to say that when it comes down to many of the police officers of Jamaica, and in other Hamite's countries, and other islands of the world, where our ancestors were taken as slave, and brought us forth, these Hamite's police officers of the European police force system, are suffering from a bad state of slavery mentality, and that of stupidity. Of the way many of them treat their fellow brothers, and sisters, who also came from out of the slavery experience, as they did. But many of them for get where they, and their ancestors is coming from, because they are now apart of the European police force system, and have a good pay check coming in, every week, or a month. This is also because of their Gentile European police badge that was given to them as a sign of authority over their brothers, and sisters of their dwelling.

Many of these stupid police officers of Jamaica, and also in the land of Ham, known as Africa, and in many islands where our ancestors were taken as slaves, need to come to the reality that the police force system of Jamaica, and in the land of Ham, and elsewhere. Was established for the protection of the European settlers, or the colonist as they were called in those days. It was not set up for the protection of the slaves, or the various natives who were conquered, and many of them were enslaved to death, or they were just slater off their islands, and their lands was taken away from them by the people of Europe, to get rich.

The police force system of the people of Europe, was also set up as a protection from other European settlers, who many of the time wanted to rob, and kill other European people for what they had, that they wanted for themselves. So, many of these foolish Hamite's police officers who go about taking advantage, and brutalizing their own people. Due to their European police badge that was given to them as a sign of authority, over their fellow Hamite's citizens, need to stop and think about where their police badge of a sign of authority came from. I was told by other venders who were there at the market place about the killing of this Rastafarian man, and what took place. This philosophy, and the belief of the Rastafarian people, is totally a false doctrine, of their religious worship to Ras Tafari Makonnen, who become known as Hails Selassie. Because Ras Tafari Makonnen which was the name of the man who became known as Hails Selassie, was not from the tribe of Yehuda that became known as the tribe of Judah. This name Judah came from the Romans, and other various European translation of the Scripture, that became known as the Bible. These Yehudahites, and Benjamites became known as Jews and the Jewish people by the Angles, and Saxon Germanic people, who named these people as Jews, and Jewish people. That was taken from the Latin name Judah, and Yehuda was the fourth son of Jacob. Rastafari Makonnen was from the land of Seba that became known as Ethiopia by the Greeks conquest from the Persian. Who was the over Lord of the land of what became known of North Africa, East Africa, and the so-call Middle East, to what became known as Asia. So, Rastafari Makonnen was a Cushites descendant from the first son of Cush, who were known as Seba, (according to Genesis Chapter 10, and verse 7).

Rastafari Makonnen was also not a god, but he was just a mare sinful man like the rest of us males, who were created in image and likeness of Yahweh. The conquering Lion of the tribe of Judah that the Rastafarian believer's claim to be that of Hail Selassie, is no other than Yashua, who became a man by the will of Yahweh, to please Yahweh. Also, to sacrifice his life for the sin of Israel, and of the world of other people at large, who were born through the family line of David, and David himself was from the tribe of Yehuda, that was translated as Judah by the Romans. (2 Samuel Chapter 7, and verse 16), there Yahweh promise David that He was going to establish his throne forever. So, Yashua came to earth as a man, true the family line of David to fulfill the various prophecies of the Scripture that were spoken of him, by Yahweh true the various prophets of Israel.

Yashua, also came as a man to fulfill the promises Yahweh made to David, to inherit his throne as king, who will rule as king over all the earth in the place of David, as Yahweh did promise David, that is throne will stand forever. It is also recorded in (Micah Chapter 4, reading from verse 1, to verse 2), there the Scripture went on to say, but in the last days it shall come to pass, that mountain of the house of the Lord Yahweh shall be established upon the hill, and all people shall flow to it. He will teach us of His ways, and we will walk in His parts: for the Law of Yahweh shall go forth out of Zion, which is speaking of Jerusalem as Zion. And the word of the Yahweh from Jerusalem, where Yashua will be reigning as king over all the earth. I must point out that this last days that is mentioned in Micah, is speaking about our time we are presently living in, as the last days, before the wrath of Yahweh strike, that will bring about changes to our earth. With all of its evil, and violence as a way of life, as it is so present in this world of today. Furthermore, this kingship of Yashua is a part of the fulfillment of (Psalms Chapter 2, starting from verse 2), there the verse went on to say, the kings of the earth have set themselves up together, and the rulers take counsel together, against the Lord Yahweh, and against His anointed. Which the verse was speaking of Yashua, as Yahweh anointed. Verse 4 went on to say, he that sitteth in the heavens shall laugh, the Lord Yahweh shall have them in duration, then shall He speak unto them in His wrath, and vex them in His sore displeasure. Yet have I set my king upon my Holy hill of Zion. I Yahweh will declare the decree; the Lord Yahweh hath said unto me, you art my Son; this day have I begotten you. Which He was speaking of Yashua. Ask of me, and I shall give you the heathen for your inheritance, and the uttermost parts of the earth for your possession. Thou that mean you, shalt break them with a rod of iron; you shalt dash them in pieces like a potter 's vessel.

Be wise now therefore, O ye kings: be instructed, ye judges of the earth, serve the Lord Yahweh with fear, and rejoice with trembling, kiss the Son, lest he be angry, and you perish from the way, when his wrath is kindled but a little. But blessed, or happy are all they that put their trust in him. This verse of the Scripture is not speaking about Rastafari Makonnen, who became known as Hail Selassie, but the verse is speaking about Yashua, who is the Son of Yahweh, and our raining king, and master over all the earth. One can see that this prophecy of the Scripture is speaking of earthly Jerusalem, where Yashua will be ruling over David throne, as King of all Kings over all the earth.

The reason why Yashua is called as the Lion of the tribe of Yehuda, that became known as the tribe of Judah, that is mentioned in (Revelation Chapter 5, and verse 5), it is because he is the one who at his second coming, who shall conquer all the kingdoms of this world. He himself shall rule as King of all kings, and Lord of all Lords over all the people of the earth, except when it comes down to Yahweh Himself, who is over all things. It was Jacob who spoke about Judah as a lion, and this statement can be found in (Genesis Chapter 49 and verse 9). I must point out that the word Genesis, mean beginning from what I have came to understand. At verse (10, of Genesis Chapter 49), Jacob went on to say the Scepter, which is the rod of a king that represent his authority, and ruler ship in those days, shall not depart from Judah, nor a law giver from between his feet, until Shiloh come. Unto him shall the gathering of the people will be. This Shiloh that Jacob spoke of, that was to come to the people of Israel, is no other than Yashua who became known as Jesus and Christ in the Greek, and Latin language of the Romans. This gathering of the people that is mentioned, is not only they of the children of Israel, but it will be all the people of planet earth, who are believer in Yashua. Who is following his teaching he gave to his Apostles, to teach other believers, that they may become a part of his sheep, and a part of the people of Yahweh, true Yashua His Son. The Scripture clearly mentions that without the sacrificial blood of Yashua, that was shed for many, there can not be any forgiveness of sin by Yahweh. I must also point out that no one can enter into Yahweh new incoming Kingdom that will be reigning over all the earth, unless they are a believer, and followers of Yashua teaching, and his commandment he gave to his Apostles to teacher other believers.

These believers who is closely following the teaching of Yashua, to please Yahweh, and Yashua, will not be destroyed from this earthly paradise that Yahweh have in mind to bring about. The gathering of the people of the world who believe, and be obedient to his teaching he gave to his Apostles, will be his subjects. Those who do not believe on him, and who are not obedient to his teaching will be destroyed from out of this Kingdom of Yahweh, and Yashua. This is what Yashua said in harmony in what is written above. This statement can be found at (Matthew Chapter 25, reading from verse 31 to verse 34), there Yashua went on to say, when the Son of man shall come into his glory, and all the holy angels with him, then shall he sit upon the throne of his glory: and before him, shall be gathered all the nations of the earth.

He shall separate them one from another, as when a shepherd divided his sheep from the goats, he shall set the sheep on his right hand, but the goats on his left hand. Then shall the king say unto them on his right hand, come you blessed of my Father, in heart the kingdom prepared for you from the foundation of the world. I must point out here that there will be no plea barging, and no payoff like what it is taking place in the Gentile European court system of today. Where a person can pay off the judge, and get cretin respect, because he or she has money, and have cretin authority ship. Everyone will have to answer to the king for his or her own deeds, and belief during his or her life time here on earth, when that time come. One can also read (Matthew Chapter 13, starting from verse 40 to verse 42) to see what Yashua said about the end of this world, when he shall sits as king in his kingdom, judging the people of the earth. At (Revelation Chapter 6, and verse 2), there the Scripture went on to explained that, and I saw and behold a white horse, and he that sat on him, a bow and a crown was given unto him, he went forth conquering and to conquer. This person that sat upon this white horse is the one that the Scripture called as the Lam, or the Lam of Yahweh, which is speaking about Yashua, as this Lam of Yahweh. Who at his second coming will conquer all the kingdoms of this world, and who will reign as king. At (Revelation Chapter 19, and verse 13), there it speaks of Yashua as the word of Yahweh, whose vesture is dipped in blood, and this blood will be the destruction of the worldly UN-Yahweh like people, who are not

95

worshipers of Yahweh. Those who do not follow the teaching and commandment of Yashua he gave to his servant the Apostles.

These Rastafarian worshippers of Hail Selassie have deceived many people of the island of Jamaica, and elsewhere to believe in their vain foolish philosophy, of the worship of Selassie, that have spread like wild fire worldwide. But as the saying goes, one fool makes many more fools, and this is a true saying, in the case of these Rastafarians worshipers of Hail Selassie as their god. Hail Selassie who was one of the former kings of the land of Seba that became known as the land of Ethiopia, by way of the Greek conquests, was not a god, but he was just a mare man, who was created in the image, and likeness of Yahweh. This Rastafarian philosophy, and their doctrines was started in the Jamaica, in the early Forties and Fifties, when certain Hamite's men who was trying to identify with their roots in the land of Ham now called as Africa. These Rastafarians believers also base their ideas, and belief on the repatriation movement that was started by Marcus Garvey, in 1914 AD, who came from the island of Jamaica.

Marcus Garvey was not a member of the Rastafarian group of the worshippers of Hail Selassie. From what I have read from a book that is call Marcus Garvey and his vision of what become known as Africa. This book were written by John Henry Clark, and was published by Vintage Books in New York City. According to this biography of Mr. Garvey, in 1907, was involved in the Printer's Union strike of Jamaica, and after the unsuccessful strike ended in defeat for the printers. He went to work for the Government of Jamaica printing Office, and not long after that he edited his first publication that was called The Watchman. In 1909 Mr. Garvey made a trip to Costa Rica, where he observed the exploitation of many poor Hamite's people of Costa Rica, who he called as the Negros. Marcus Garvey even started a movement to help these Hamite's people in their poor condition of Costa Rica, by appealing to the British Government to do their best to improve the condition for these poor Hamite's workers of Costa Rica. While he was in Costa Rica, he even made several attempts to start a newspaper to expose the condition of many of these poor Hamite's workers of Costa Rica. But many of those Hamite's workers had no funds to help him in his endeavor, so the paper went nowhere. Mr. Garvey also went to Panama, Nicaragua, Honduras, Colombia, and Venezuela, and while he was in these places, he was doing his best to see if he could bring about some changes, and education to many of these poor exploited Hamite's people of the area.

I must point out that I did not cover the complete history about Mr. Garvey, and his doing, trying to bring about some changes, and education to many Hamite's people he meets, who he call as the Negroes. According to the name he was thought to see himself, and other people who look like him, by the people of Europe, as the Negroes, Black people, and the African people in the various schooling system of the people of Europe. So, Marcus Garvey was encouraging his Hamite's people he came across, to encourage them to look back to their forefather's land, as a movement, where they can be a freer people, shaping their own destiny, of life. So, one can see from what is written about Mr. Garvey, that he was a productive, and a responsible Hamite's person, who had the zeal to want to unite as many Hamite's people as possible, he came across with. Wheresoever they may happen to be, and to encourage them to look back to the land of their ancestors, for their well bean, and their betterment, that he know of as the land of Africa. Where they would have their own governmental system looking out for the needs of their own people.

So, Mr. Garvey was not involved in any Rastafarian foolishness, like that of many Hamite's people of Jamaica, who believed in this Rastafarian way of life. Matter of fact I doubt it very much, if there were any such a group of people in Jamaica in the early days of Marcus Garvey, who was known as the Rastafarian people. According to a book called Marcus Garvey, and his Vision of Africa, that was written by John Henry Clarke, Mr. Garvey came to the United States in 1916, when he was unable to get the support, he needed from the Hamite's people of Jamaica. Because of their slavery, and colonial mentality many Hamite's people of Jamaica are suffering from. Moreover, many Hamite's people of Jamaica have no unity and no togetherness among themselves, so this is one of the reasons why Mr. Garvey came to United States, with the expectation, hoping to meet up with

Booker T. Washington. But when Marcus Garvey reaches the United State, Booker T. Washington had died. According to the biography of Marcus Garvey, he came to the United States in the Harlem area of New York City, where he started his movement, and had the backing of about two million supporters. He also had different business in the Harlem area of New York City, where he was encouraging many Hamite's people of the New York area, to become more self-supported people, by them having their own little businesses, and also, for them to look back toward their forefather land he knew as, of Africa, for their well bean.

Marcus Garvey was born 1887, in St Ann's Bay of Jamaica, and he died in London in June of 1940, after his deportation from the United States, in 1927 for mail fraud. The biography of Marcus Garvey went on to explained that after he had served two years out of his five years 'prison sentence. Pertaining to the stocks for the Black Star Liner ship, he had bought for the repatriation of many Hamite's people of the United States back to the land of Ham, the land of their forefathers, for their own well bean. But unfortunately Mr. Garvey was sabotage by the United States Government, and other Hamite's people of the United States, who did not shear his views of the repatriation of the Hamite people of the United States back to their forefathers land, he new as as Africa. Marcus Garvey wanted to repatriate as many Hamite's people as possible, he could get in touch with, from all part of the so-call New World of the Gentile people of Europe, where our ancestors were taken as slaves. It was in his desire to take them back to the land of their forefathers, providing they were willing to go with him. Sad to say that Mr. Garvey did not succeed in his plans for the repatriation of many Hamite's people back to their homeland from where they were taken from before.

Due to the fact that there were certain Black leaders in the United States, who were working against Mr. Garvey plans, for the repatriation of many Hamite's people from the United States, to the land of their ancestors. Leaders such as A. Philip Randolph, and WEB Dubois, who were against Mr. Gravy plan of his repatriation movement, of the Hamite's people of the United States back to the land of Ham. These men were head of the organization that is called the N.A.A.C.P., that stand for the National Association for the Advancement of the Colored people of the United States. Or as they were also known as, the Negros, and the Black people of the United States. These Negros leaders did not share the views of Marcus Garvey, in his separation of the Hamite's people of the United States, from their Gentile European counterparts. Because their belief was for the Hamite's people of the United States to be integrated with that of their Gentile counterpart, to be a part of their melting pot people. Also, they did not share the view of Mr. Garvey, who wanted to return as many Hamite's people of the United States, back to their homeland of their forefathers he had in his mindset.

Which I think it would have been much better for many Hamite's people of the United States, if he had succeeded in his movements. These men worked against Mr. Garvey, as a secret agent with the Government of the United States, to bring about the downfall of Mr. Garvey, so he could not succeed with his plan of the repatriation of the Hamite's people from the United State, to their forefathers 'land. After I have been living in the United States for many years, and view different States, and see how many Hamite's people are struggling to live, and survive from day to day. In this system of high cost of living, and all sort of discrimination, and exploitation in many ways shape and form. In my opinion, many Hamite's people who are living on the streets here in the United States, picking up soda cans, bear cans, and scrap metal to sell to the recycle scrap yard so as to create some kind of finance, to support themselves.

Many of these Hamite's people who have no jobs, and many of whom do not have any skills, so as to be employed by the European job market system of the United States, to make a living. So, this picking up of soda cans, bear cans, and scrap metal, is their only source of making a living, in a system where one must have money to pay rent, buy food that they need to eat and survive every day, otherwise, they would literally die.

They cannot grow their own food, because the lands are mostly own and control by the Gentile European people of the United States, they have stolen from the various natives. Who were here before they came along, and enslave, and slater off many of these people and take away their lands to gain wealth. Furthermore, as I have mention before, that the system of the United States was set up, and design for the Gentile European people benefit of the United States, to grow the food, and to send it to their Gentile run supermarkets. So, many of their citizens who have the money, can go to these places, and buy what they wanted to eat and live. So, if one do not have any money to buy what they want to eat, they cannot eat. There are no fruit trees, and food trees that are grown here in the United States for many struggling Hamite's people to go and pick from to eat, like that of Jamaica. Also, in other Caribbean Islands, and in many parts of the land of Ham, where many of these fruit trees, and food trees are grown. Furthermore, if any of these food trees, and fruit trees were grow here in the United States, it would be mostly owned, and control by the Gentile European people, and their Governmental system of the United States. Because they own all the lands they have stolen from the natives, who were here before they came along, and kill off many of these people, and take over their lands. I must also point out that if there were many of these fruit trees, and food trees grown here in the United States, that a Hamite's person could go and pick from, like that of Jamaica. These trees would be mostly own by many European people of the United State, and if any Hamite's person were to go and pick their fruits, or their food trees, they would be shot on the spot, or go to prison for the rest of their life for trespassing.

So, many of these poor Hamite's people of the United States are literally bite in the dust, and waiting for the police to come and lock them up, for whatever crime they might commit against the system. Due to their poverties-ness, and struggling, and the ignorance of many Hamite's people of the United States are suffering from, this is the reason why many of them wine up in the prison system of the European people of these United States. More over the prison system were built for their many captives slave people, who did became their citizens of their establishment. So, the prison system of the United States was not built for the many European settlers, who came to this part of the world from Europe to share the British people conquest over the natives of their lands. This was also, to enjoyed the fruit of their stolen lands from the power of the Spanish who were the over Lord of their stolen lands, they had kill off, and enslave many of the natives to death, and take away their lands.

The prison system of the European people of the United States, were design and built to make money, as a form of a business from their many captives people who became their citizens to get rich. Where the police force make money from many Hamite's people going in, and out of their prison system. The European court system make money from many Hamite's people going, and out of their prison system. Also, the lawyers of the European court system make money from many of their Hamite's people go in, and out of their prison system, and their jail system. The prison warden also get paid, and the bond people make money from many Hamite's people going in, and out of the European person system. Including the probations officers, they all make money from many Hamite's people going, and out of their prison system, that were design and built for them to fall into. So, in my opinion, if Mr. Garvey had succeeded in his repatriation movement for many Hamite's people to leave from the United States, back to their forefather land. I think it would have been much better, for many poor Hamite's people of the United States, come pair to what I have see with many poor Hamite people of the United, who are literally biting the dust, and struggling to survive. Also standing on the soup kitchen line, waiting to get a little handout, and sleeping under some bridge, or living on the Street. The Rastafarian people doctoring was started after the death of Marcus Garvey in 1940, that was based upon Mr. Garvey philosophy of the repatriation of the Hamite's people back to the land of Ham, that became known as Africa. According to volume 5 of the Encyclopaedia Britannica, the word Ras mean a prince, so Ras Tafari Makonnen, which was the name of Haile Selassie, before he was given the title of Negus, which mean a king of the land of Seba that became known as the land of Ethiopia. According to the New World Dictionary of the American language, the title of the word hail, mean to salute, or to greet someone, or to welcome someone, or to name a person by way of tribute, as to a leader.

Such was the case of the man who were known as Ras Tafari Makonnen, better known as Haile Selassie. According to volume 5 of the Encyclopaedia, Ras Tafari Makonnen was born July 23, 1892. He was the grandson of Sahle Selassie who was a ruler of the kingdom of Shewa, or Shoa in the land of Seba that became known as Ethiopia. Sahle Selassie who was raining over the kingdom of Shewa, from 1813 to 1847, according to volume 5 of the Encyclopaedia. And Sahle Selassie was also the grandfather of Emperor Menelik the second, whose reign was from 1889 to 1913.

Volume 5 of the Encyclopaedia explained that Ras Tafari Makonnen, was a son of Ras Makonnen, who was the chief adviser to Emperor Menelik the second. According to this same volume 5 of the Encyclopaedia, Menelik daughter who were known as Zauditu, was made Empress in 1917, while Ras, which mean Prince, was made a ruler, and heir to the throne of Ethiopia. So, in 1928, Ras Tafari Makonnen received the title of Negus, when Menelik daughter Zauditu died. Two years later Ras Tafari Makonnen was crowned Emperor of Ethiopia, in November of 1930. Volume 5 of the Encyclopaedia explained that Ras Tafari Makonnen took on the name of Hail Selassie in 1930. The Encyclopaedia explained that there was no explanation of how Ras Tafari Makonnen take on the name as Hail Selassie, but the Encyclopaedia went on to say that it might have been a part of the Trinity. I must explain that the word Trinity is a Latin word, that came down into the various Gentile European language of Europe, by way of the Roman conquest of Europe, and that of the Roman Catholic Church. Also, by what become known as the Christianity, that came from paganism, and idolatry worship of their many gods. I must also printout that Ras Tafari Makonnen was not a god, and he was no part of any trinity, as how many Rastafarian believers might think. Also, the expression that the Encyclopaedia gave about him, but rather he was just a mare sinful man like the rest of us human been who Yahweh had created. Yahweh is not a part of any trinity, but He is by Himself, and there is no other Yahweh, but only one Yahweh as the Scripture clearly explained.

So, all our hope, and worship belong to Him only, because He is our creator, life giver, and our Father. This knowledge about Yahweh, it is if one can understand the reading of the Scripture for themselves, there they will see that there is only one Yahweh, that were translated as Lord, and God. This word God was taken from the word Elohim, that mean my God, that is speaking of Yahweh only. At (Isaiah Chapter 45, and verse 6), there Yahweh makes it quite clear by saying to the ancient children of Israel, that they may know, from the rising of the sun from of the west, that there is no one else beside Him. There Yahweh went on to say, I am the LORD that was translated from the word Adonai, that replace calling on the name of Yahweh. Yahweh also went on to say that, I formed light and I created darkness, I make peace, and I created evil, I the LORD Yahweh have done all these things. Furthermore (Exodus Chapter 20, and verse 3), there Yahweh spoke to the ancient children of Israel, by way of the prophet Moses, by saying to them, that He is the LORD, meaning Yahweh, and they must not have any other Gods before Him, or beside Him.

This statement Yahweh made to the children's of Isreal, also goes for us too, because we are also a part of His creation. I am quite sure that there is no written record, where Ras Tafari Makonnen told the Rastafarian believers, or anyone else for that matter, that he was a god, or any part of the so-call trinity. The Rastafarian believers have taken different things from the Holly writing of the Scripture, and applied these things to Hail Selassie. Such as the word Jah, which the word Jah is short for the word Jehovah. This word Jehovah, is a Gentile European false name that were given to Yahweh, that replace calling on the name of Yahweh. This false name of Jehovah has cast allot of confusion to many people of today, who might read a copy of the various translation of the Scripture, that became known as the Bible, by way of the Greeks translators of Europe. So, may people who came under the Gentile European captivity, of colonialism, and slavery, may not understand where these name, or titles came from, that is mention in what become known as the Bible. Also, many people of today, may not have any knowledge of where the word Lord came from, that is referring to Yahweh as the Lord. Also the word Elohim, that mean my God, that were added to replace calling on the name of Yahweh. I must also point out that Yashua is also Lord, which is only a title, and the angles are also Lord, and man is also lord.

But man is of a lower standard of the word Lord, when it comes down to Yahweh, Yashua, and that of the angles. Because as Yashua mention in the writing of the Scripture, that who is of the heaven, is above all the people who are of the earth. The Rastafarian believers have also taken this Gentile European name, and applied it to Hail Selassie as Jehovah God, Jah Ras Tafari, Hail Selassie I. The question I would like to ask these foolish Rastafarian worshippers of Hail Selassie, how can they worship a man as a god. When Ras Tafari Makonnen is also one of the creations of Yahweh, just like themselves? Although Hail Selassie is dead, and buried in his grave, he must answer to Yahweh, and Yashua, in the day of the resurrection of the dead back to life, to answer for all the things he did while he was alive here on earth. This statement about the resurrection of the dead that Yashua mention, can be found at (John chapter 5, verse 28, and verse 29), where Yashua spoke of these things to the Yehudahites at Jerusalem. By saying to them, marvel not at this: for the hour is coming, in which all who are in the graves, shall hear the voice of the Son of Yahweh. They shall come back to life, to give an account for all the things they did, while they were alive here on earth. They that have done good deeds, unto the resurrection of life, but they that have done evil deeds, unto the resurrection of damnation".

According to the Webster's Colligate Dictionary, the word damnation means everlasting punishment. The Rastafarian believers have also taken the word dreadlock from the Scripture, and applied this word to themselves, as dreadlock. According to the Webster Collegiate Dictionary, the word dread means to fear, so, this is the same word dread that is also translated in the Scripture as dread. But the word dread in the Scripture mean to fear Yahweh extremely. This word locks that the Rastafarian believers as apply to themselves, was taken from the book of (Judges Chapter 13, and Verse 4, to verse 14), explain that where the angel of Yahweh was sent to the mother of Samson. and his father whose name was known as Manoah. The angel told his mother, and father that no razor must not go on the head of Samson, because he was a Nazrite unto Yahweh before he was born, which mean he was a chosen vessel to Yahweh before he was born. There the Scripture explained that, Samson was a Nazarite unto Yahweh from his mother's womb, until the day of his death.

So, no razor as ever cut the hair of Samson head, that is referred in the Scripture as his locks, until he told Delilah his wife, who were a Philistine woman from the tribe of Mizraim, where his strength lies, that it was in his hair. So Delilah cut off the hair of Samson, and he became weak, and he was conquered by the Philistine army. According to the book of Judges, Samson told Delilah that if she were to cut off his seven locks of his hair from his head, his strength would be like any other man's strength. This is where the Rastafarian believers got the term locks from, and practice not to cut their hair, because of what they may had read from the Scripture, and did not have the full understanding of what they were reading about. Many Rastafarian believers have used this word dreadlock, without understanding the true meaning of the word, and where it came from. They the Rastafarian believers have also taken the title of the word King of Kings, and Lord of Lords that was given to Yashua by his father Yahweh, that is mentioned in (Revelation Chapter 19, and verse 16).

They have applied this title to Hail Selassie, as King of all Kings, and Lord of all Lords, which it is a false title they have given to him, and they are only deceiving themselves. According to the Rastafarian believers, and the Encyclopaedia Britannica, Hail Selassie was a direct descendant from Emperor Menelik the First.

First of all I could not come a across any kind of recorded information about this person who was known as Menelik the I, who the Encyclopaedia, and the Rastafarian believers claim was a son of King Salomon, and the Queen who come from the land of Sheba. So, this statement, and belief of these worshipers of Hail Selassie, it is a vain, and false belief. Volume 8 of the Encyclopaedia explained that Menelik II who was a king of a district in Ethiopia by the name of Shewa or Shoa, was a direct descendant of Menelik I. According to the Encyclopaedia and the Rastafarian believers of the worship of Hail Selassie, Menelik the I was a legendary son of King Solomon, and the Queen who came from the land of Sheba, known today as Yemen. I would like to point out, that I did check the L to Z Index of the Encyclopaedia Britannica, to see if I could come up with some information about Menelik I, but unfortunately I could not find any information about this person, who they say was a son of King Solomon, and the Queen who come from the land of Sheba. From what I have read, and gathered from the Encyclopaedia; they believe the land of Sheba to be that of what is now known as Ethiopia, which it is a totally false statement. So, this statement that is made by the Encyclopaedia, and also by the

Rastafarian believers, is also false statement, and lie that have no truth in it, although the Encyclopaedia mentioned about this person. As I have mentioned before that the land of Sheba is today known as Yemen, where the Queen of Sheba came from, and she was not from the land of Seba that become known as Ethiopia. Although these people were all Cushite's offspring, who were not living too far away from each other, as what is shown on the Scripture Map of 1890, showing the land of Sheba. Yet she did come from the land of Sheba, and not from the land of Ethiopia. Furthermore, there is no Scriptural record to prove this statement, that is made by the Encyclopaedia, and these Rastafarians believers, that King Solomon, and the Queen who came from the land of Sheba had a son by the name of Menelik I. So, again this statement is not of truth, but it is a false statement, and a false history of lies.

There is also no Scriptural record to show that King Solomon, and the Queen who came from the land of Sheba had a romantic affair, and by venture of this romantic affair, they had a son, whose name was known as this or that. If this statement were of truth, the Scripture would have mentioned it, just like how the Scripture mentioned at (First Kings, Chapter 7, and verse 8) that King Solomon first wife was the daughter of the Pharaoh. Who was ruling as king over the land of Egypt, during the time of King Solomon reining as king over the kingdom of Israel.

Also, just as how the Scripture mentioned at (II Samuel Chapter 11, and verse 2, to verse 6), reading from (Chapter 12, and verse 1 to verse 14), where the Scripture mentioned that King David took the wife of Uriah, who was from the tribe of the Hethites people. He had sex with her, and she conceived, and bare a son for King David. Due to this wicked David did to Uriah, in taking away his wife, and had him kill in a battle of war. Yahweh was not pleased with David, and because of this deed of his, the child died according to what Nathan the prophet told David of his deeds. However, after the child died, she conceive again, and bare a son by the name of Solomon to David, and Yahweh spare Solomon life, because He found favor in him, and Yahweh let him become king after the death of his father David. Yahweh is the author of the writing of the Scripture, who did not have the writers of the Scripture to hide this story from the world of other people, who would later read the Scripture for themselves, to see all these things that was done by King David. Yahweh left it there to be known, to the rest of the other people of the world, who would eventually read the Scripture to come to the knowledge, to know of these things David did. Yahweh is not the author of hypocrisy, but He is of truth, and there is no deceit in Him, this is the reason why He had these things to be written in the Scripture, so that everyone would know of it, for themselves. Also, this is the reason why He did sent Nathan the prophet, to David to tell him of his secrete deeds. Moreover, no one can question the authority of Yahweh, of His decision, and His action of why He allow this or that to take place, He please Himself of what He do, and that is finial. According to I Kings Chapter 11 starting from verse 1, after Pharaoh daughter who was the first wife of Solomon, he had many other wives, and concubines, and Princesses from among the various granddaughters of the people of Ham. Who he and the rest of the children of Israel was living around, and who they all so, came out of. These Canaanites people were also the natives of the land, long before the ancient children of Israel came about.

Also, other nation of people who came later, and became citizens of the land. This is clearly recorded in the Scripture for anyone to see, and for the benefit of those people who would read the Scripture of truth, to gain knowledge from what is written there. Furthermore, the Scripture at (I Kings Chapter 10, and verse 1), show that when the Queen who came from the land of Sheba, heard of the fame of Solomon, concerning the name of Yahweh his God, she came to prove him with hard questions. According to (Chapter 10, of I Kings), she arrived at Jerusalem with a great train of camels, bearing spices, with much gold, and precious stones from her land of Sheba.

Also, when she came to Solomon, she talked with him of all that was in her heart, and Solomon answered all her questions. The Scripture went on to explained that when the Queen who came from the land of Sheba, saw all the Wisdom of Solomon, and the house he built for himself. The meat of his table, and the setting of his table, and also, of his servants, and the manner he went up to the house of the temple of Yahweh, there in Jerusalem, there were no more spirit left in her. The Scripture went on to say that, she said to King Solomon, it was a true report she heard of him in her own country of Sheba of his acts, and of his wisdom, but she did not believe all what was told to her, until she saw all these things for herself. So, there is nothing in (First Kings Chapter 10), to lead anyone to believe that there were a sexual romantic affair that took place between the Queen of Sheba, and King Solomon. So by virtue of this romantic affair, they had a son whose name this or that. So if it were so, about King Salomon and the Queen who came from the land of Sheba, the Scripture would have mentioned it, just like how the Scripture mentioned many other things that the children of Isreal did that did not please Yahweh. So, this statement that comes from the Rastafarian believers, and the Encyclopaedia Britannica, about King Salomon, and the Queen of Sheba, who they said had a son for Salomon, it is totally a false statement and a lie. Yahweh make it quite clear to the ancient children of Israel, through the prophet Moses, at (Deuteronomy Chapter 6, and verse 4), that hear o Israel, the LORD Yahweh is one Yahweh, and you most loved the LORD Yahweh with all your heart, and with all your soul, meaning with your whole self. This commandment Moses gave to the children of Israel, goes for us Hamite's people too, because there is only one Yahweh over all the people of planet earth, of His creation, who we all must give an answer to, for ourselves, of all the things we have don in this life, weather it is good or bad.

Yashua spoke to the Yehudahites who were left there in the land of Israel, when he came to them as a man, by quoting to them from the book of Deuteronomy, by saying the same words to them that Moses had mentioned to the ancient children of Israel, when Yahweh take them from out of the land of Mizraim, that became known as Egypt. There Yashua mentioned to the Yehudahites at (Matthew Chapter 22, and verse 37, to verse 38), that they must love the Lord their God with all their soul, and with all their mind, this is the first and great Commandment that apply to all people.

It is sad to see how the Rastafarian believers of the island of Jamaica, and in other islands of the Caribbean have influenced the mind of many Hamite's people, to become believers in their Rastafarian foolishness, of the worship of Hail Selassie. This foolishness of the Rastafarian believers, have also spread itself into what became known as the United States. Also in many other places to become believers, and worshippers of Hail Selassie, with their foolishness, and madness, of this Rastafarian philosophy. This is also, with their dreadlock philosophy, that is of pure nonsense, that makes many of them to look very direful, because of their long hair of their head. According to (I Corinthians Chapter 11, and verse14 and 15), there it mentioned that a man must not have long hair like women on their heads. (I Corinthians Chapter 14, and verse 15), went on to explained that long hair upon a man head, is a disgrace to his body, but long hair upon a woman head is a beauty to her body, because her hair was given to her by Yahweh as a covering for her head, and for her beauty. We the people of Ham has been deceived and misled by the Gentile European people, and by the Mohammedans Muslim people to believe in their lies and falsehood, and we sure do not need our own people to add to the deception. We the people of Ham need truth, and not falsehood, we also need the love, and the mercy of Yahweh, who have our lives in His Hands, and we certainly do not need the wrath of Yahweh upon us as a people. For the worshiping of idolatry, and that of a man, because we as a people have been suffering long enough, for the many doings of our ancestors that gone by, and for our own sinful self. So, to worship, or to have any other God beside Yahweh mean destruction, and we certainly do not need His wrath up on us as a people, for what is translated in the Scripture as UN Godliness, which mean UN Yahweh like people. (Psalms Chapter 1, and verse 6) mentioned that the way of the UN Yahweh like people, that was translated as UN Godly, shall perish.

So, we the people of Ham do not need false worship, but we need true worship to Yahweh, and to study His Holy Word, to apply it to our daily lives, to gain knowledge, and understanding of Him. Because He is our creator, and life giver, and not to have knowledge of His Words the Scripture, and His Laws, and His requirement for us, mean destruction from Him. The deception of the Rastafarians people in the Island of Jamaica have cause quite allot of young people, and older ones to believe in their Rastafarians foolishness as a way of life, especially seeing that we as people of Ham need much knowledge, and understanding of the way we as a people must live our lives to please Yahweh, that it may go well with us as a people.

Many of us Hamite's people are are in totally darkness of this knowledge, and understanding of Yahweh, for us to live our lives by. So, to turn away from the worshipping of Yahweh, and to turn to the worship of a man, or anyone else besides Yahweh, as the Yahweh of our life, it is crazy, and weird. Furthermore, the life stile of many Rastafarians people, with their marijuana smoking, as a part of their everyday religious worship, and life to Hail Selassie, have caused many people in the island of Jamaica to lose their minds, due to their marijuana smoking, and their carefree living of stupidity. I do hope the Rastafarians believers, with many other Hamite's people of today, may turn to Yahweh in true worship, also, with that of many people of the world at large, may turn to Him in true worship before it is too late to do so. I also want to explain that I was watching a documentary of this historian by the name of Mr. Casely Hayford, explaining about the Ark of the Covenant he was told is in the land of Seba, known as Ethiopia. First I would like to say that this story about the Ark of the Covenant Yahweh gave to the children of Israel, at Mount Sinai, of His Laws, precepts, and Commandments, that they claim is in the land of Seba, known as Ethiopia, it is a false statement, that have no truth in this story. My reason for making this kind of statement, it is this, Yahweh gave Moses a strict commandment that is mention at (Numbers Chapter 3, and verse 6 to verse 13). There Yahweh said to Moses that He have taken the tribe of Live, who was one of the sons of Jacob, that became known as the tribe of the Levite's. This was to have the service of the tabernacle of the children's Israel, that eventually became known as the temple. They the tribe of the Levites were to do all the service of the tabernacle of the congregation service, from where Moses and Aaron came from.

So, if the Sebans people of Cush, who become known as the Ethiopian people of today, if they were to touch or carry the Ark of the Covenant of Yahweh, or anything pertaining to do with the service of the temple or of the congregation of the children of Israel. They would surely lose their lives by the power of Yahweh for doing so, for this service was only given to the Levites tribe of the children of Israel only. To give one a good example of how strict the word of Yahweh is, and His Commandments, there at (I Samuel Chapter 5, starting from verse 1), Yahweh allow the Philistine army of the people of Mizraim to capture the Ark of the Covenant from the children of Israel, because of the sins of Eli two sons, who were the priest at the time of young Samuel. These sons of Eli were known as Hophni and Phinehas, according to (Chapter 2, of 1 Samuel, starting from verse 22 to verse 24).

There the verse explained that these two sons of Eli lay, or have sex with the women at the assemble door of the tabernacle of the congregation of the children of Israel. So, because of the sins of these two sons of Eli the priest, Yahweh allow the Philistines army to capture the Ark of the Covenant of Yahweh, from the people of Isreal, so that these two sons of Eli would be killed by Philistines army. The killing of the two sons of Eli was to destroy the house of Eli name for the sins of his sons forever. Meaning that these sons of Eli would not be able to produce any offspring, to carry on the name of Eli, because of their sin they have committed. The way Yahweh saw it; Eli put his two sons before Him, in not taking acting against them for their deeds. So, the Ark of Yahweh was captured by the Philistine army, and the two sons of Eli were also killed by the army of the Philistine people. The Ark of Yahweh was also taken by the Philistine army, and they brought the Ark of the Covenant of Yahweh to Ebenezer, and Ashdod, of the house of their god, whose name were known as Dagon. (Chapter 5 of verse 1 of I Samuel), went on to explained that the hands of Yahweh were upon Dagon, and upon the Philistine people at large, because of the Ark of the Covenant of Yahweh that was in the midst's of the Philistine people, He had only given to the children of Israel. (Verse 7 of Chapter 5), went on to explained that when the Philistine men of Ashdod saw that the hands of Yahweh were upon Dagon, and upon the Philistine people at large, they mentioned that the Ark of Yahweh shall not abide among them. In the eyes of the Philistines people, they must send away the Ark of Yahweh from among them, before they all be consume by the power of Yahweh. (Verse 9 of Chapter 5), of 1 Samuel explained that after the Philistine people carry the

Ark about, for the hands of Yahweh was upon their cities, and upon the people, booth great and small with a great destruction, so they sent away the Ark to city of Ekron.

There the people of the city of Ekron cried out, by saying, they have brought the Ark of Yahweh to slay them. So, the people sent and call for all the Lords of the Philistines, for them to send away the Ark from them. According to verse (7 to verse 13 of Chapter 6 of 1 Samuel), the Ark of Yahweh was put upon a cart that was pull by two cows, that no yoke of burden did not put upon the necks of these two cows, to do any kind of work. After the Ark was place upon the cart that these two cows were pulling, the Ark was taking back to the people of Israel, at Bethshemite. (Verse 15 of Chapter 6 of 1 Samuel) explained that it was the men of the Levites who take down the Ark from the cart that was pull by these two cows.

According to verse (19, and 20 of 1 Samuel Chapter 6), there it explained that Yahweh smote the Israelites people of Bethshemite, because they went and look into the Ark, and it was only for the Levites to do so, and not for any of the hardy people of Israel to do so. Verse (21 of Chapter 6 of 1 Samuel) went on to say that, the people of Bethshemite sent messengers to the inhabitants of Kirjathjearim that they must come and take away the Ark from them, because it was return from the Philistines people. To further show the seriousness of the Commandment, and the Words of Yahweh that is mentioned at (2 Samuel Chapter 6), starting from verse I, there one would see that when David became king, he and the rest of the children of Israel went to the house of Abinadab, to take the Ark to Jerusalem. While David and the rest of the people was going along, the Ark shuck, as if it was going to fall from the cart to the ground, that was pull by these cows. According to verse (6 of 2 Samuel Chapter 6), Uzzah put forth his hands to stabilize the Ark from falling, as he had thought. By so doing, he was struck down by the power of Yahweh, for it was only the Levite's was to handle or touch the Ark, or anything to do with the tabernacle of the congregation of the people of Israel. Verse (10 of 2 Samuel, Chapter 6) went on explained that because of the death of Uzzah, David was afraid to take the Ark with him to the city of David, speaking of Jerusalem. According to verse (11 of 2 Samuel Chapter 6), because David was afraid to take the Ark with him to Jerusalem, he left the Ark at the house of Obededom. According to verse (12 of 2 Samuel Chapter 6), it was told to David how Yahweh blessed Obededom for the keeping of the Ark at his house.

Verse (10 of 2 Samuel Chapter 6) explained that David went to the house of Obededom, and have the Ark to remove from the house of Obededom to Jerusalem. My reason for going so deep into the history of the story of the Ark of the Covenant of Yahweh, it is to show that it is not possible for the Ark of the Covenant of Yahweh to be in the land of Seba, now known as Ethiopia. Another reason for me making this statement, as I have explained from the book of Numbers to the book of Samuel, that the carrying of the Ark was only for the Levites tribe of the people of Israel to do so only. So, if the Sebans people of Cush was to carry, or to touch the Ark of the Covenant of Yahweh, He had only given to the children's of Isreal, they would surely lose their lives. Just like the Philistines people who came from out of family of Mizrain, who lost their lives, for carrying, or touch the Ark of the Covenant, that is recorded at (Genesis Chapter 10, and verse 14). Who did touch or carry the, Ark and many of them was slain by the power of Yahweh for doing so.

So, this story about Menelik I, who the Rastafarian, and the Encyclopaedia claim was a legendary son of King Salmon, and the Queen who came from the land of Sheba, who they say was responsible for bringing the Ark of the Covenant to Ethiopia, it is a false fairy tale story, without any truth in it. So, this orthodox church of Ethiopia where they claim the Ark of the Covenant is kept, it is a branch of the Roman Catholic Church's, that take on the title as the Greek Orthodox Church, that sprang from paganism, and idolatry worship. Just like that of the many churches of today that came from out of the Roman Catholic Church, and also from out of Protestantism of Europe.

The Names Jesus and Christ where did it come from? According to the Webster Colligate Dictionary of the Fifth Edition, there it explained that the name Jesus is spelled in the French language that originally came from the Latin language of the Romans as Jezus. In the Angles and Saxon writing that also came from the Latin language of the Romans, the name Christ is spelled as Krist. So, in the Latin language of the Romans, the word Christ is spelled as Christus, and in the Greek language Christ is spelled as Christos, and it is also spelled as Iesous in the Greek language. In the Hebrew language, the name of Christ is spell as Yashua, and it is not Jesus and Christ as how many people who became captive, and slaves of the Gentile European Christianity for them to get rich, from slave labour, and the capture of people and their lands. Many of whom were taught to believe in the various churches doctrines, that came down from Europe, of what they did establish worldwide as Christianity, because of their conquest, of many people, and their lands. So, many people who came under the colonial slavery captivity teaching of the Gentile people of what become known as Christianity of Roman Catholicism. They have accept these teachings as truth, because they knew no better, and beside they had no saying in the matter, because it meant their lives, or death. According to a publication that I did received from the House of Yahweh in Texas, that is called the Amazing discoveries. On page 5 of this publication, there the page explained that in the original Hebrew writing of the Scripture, the meaning of the name Yashua, meant Yahweh is salvation. So, it is not Jesus and Christ, as how many people were thought to believed, and to accept as truth, according to the teaching of the Roman Catholic Church, that became known as Christianity. The reason why Yashua make the statement in the Scripture that he is the way the truth and the life, that became known as Roman Christianity. It is because it is stated at (John Chapter 3, and verse 16), that Yahweh so love the world of mankind, that He gave, or send His only begotten Son, that whosoever believe on him will not perish from the destruction to come, but will received everlasting life. As far as this everlasting life is concern, that is mentioned, it depends on if these believers live their lives, in the keeping of the commandment, and the teaching that Yahweh gave to Yashua. In which Yashua in turn gave this teaching to his Apostles, to teach other believers, that became known as the New Covenant Law, for all believers to fallow throughout their lives.

So, this faith of the believing in the teaching of Yashua, in a believer day to day life, was to please Yahweh, and Yashua, who is our king, Lord, and master. This is what the Gentile Catholic Church believers put a label on, that they name as Christianity, of Roman Catholicism. That is mix up with paganism of their laws, and commandment to govern their many church believers lives, who became known as Christians people. This is also true for their many captives, who became their slaves, and many of whom were converted to Roman Christianity of the Roman Catholic Church, as a way of life. According to the Webster Colligate Dictionary, there it mentioned that the name Christian was taken from the Latin word Christianus. So, when this name came down into the Angles and Saxon Germanic delict, it become known as Christendom. So, as I did explained many times in this book that being a Christian, or calling oneself a Christian, and, going to some church organization that was set up by the Gentile people of Europe, for believers to go to these places of worship. It does not mean that he or she who goes to some churches, and calling themselves a Christian, is living their lives by the teaching of Yashua, to please Yahweh, and Yashua. Because many of these churches, or religious organization was set up to make money, and to be a place to go to meet other people, so as to be a part of that religious organization. So, it is just like going to some club of gathering to meet other people. Since I have been living here in the United States for over forty years, and visited different churches, I have come to the knowledge that many of these pastors of the various churches have various girlfriends, plus their wives in the church. Also, I have come to the knowledge that many of these church pastors here in the United States, are homosexuals, practicing sodomy in the church, many of whom see themselves as good Christian people, followers of Christ.

Which this practice of sodomy is totally against the Law of Yahweh of the teaching of the Scripture of truth, for a believer to practice in their lives. Especially a pastor who supposed to be a teacher, and an example of the truth of the Scripture. These doings of these pastors is totally against the teaching of the Scripture, and the New

Covent Law, for a believer to live their lives by. That was set up by Yashua true his Apostles for believers not to do. Furthermore, this girlfriend and boyfriend relationship that were set up by the people of Europe, that is very prevalent in the various churches, and also in the European system of their colonial world true slavery.

So, this boyfriend, and girlfriend relationship is called fornication in the Scripture that is against the teaching of the Scripture, because from the days of the creation of the world by Yahweh, He only had created husband and wife, by Adam, and Eve, who were the first couple. Yahweh had only established husband, and wife, and not boyfriend, and girlfriend relationship, as how it was established by the people of Europe, from the slavery days, to our present time. It is also mention in the Scripture, that Yahweh shall judge all fornicators and adulters. So, going to some churches, and calling oneself a Christian, and are not living by the Laws of the teaching of the Scripture, they are only wasting their time, and deceiving themselves by calling themselves as Christian, which mean followers of Christ. Some of these church goers who are not following the teaching, and Laws of the Scripture, really see themselves as good Christian people, because they go to some church, and listen to their pastor, and pay their tides, and offering to the church. The ways of the teaching of the Apostles, was given a title by the Gentile believers that came from the early believers of Rome. So, the right terminology for a believers should be based upon the word of faith in the worshiping of Yahweh, and also in their following of the teaching of Yashua that one must apply to their daily lives, and not in the name of Christianity, that mean nothing at all. If that person do not live their lives to please Yahweh, and Yashua in according to the teaching of the New Covenant Law, they are only wasting their time, by calling themselves a Christian, and going to some church. Because being a Christian do not mean that one is a true worship of Yahweh, but only a believer who is following the teaching, and the Commandment of Yahweh, and that of Yashua in their daily lives to please Yahweh, and our Lord Yashua.

So, what became known as Christianity, was taken from what was known in Israel as the Way, by the teaching of Yashua, to his disciples, that was called as those who follow the Way, speaking of Yashua as the Way to the Father. The Scripture clearly teach that Yashus is the way to please Yahweh, and that is the reality of being obedient followers of Yashua, and true worshipers of Yahweh. When many Gentile people of Europe became believers of the teaching of the Apostle Peter, who were sent to Cornelius by the spirit of Yahweh, according to (Acts Chapter 10, starting from verse 14, to verse 34). Also, later by the Apostle Paul, who were made a minster to the Gentile people of Europe by Yashua, when he was risen from the dead. Then the Way of the teaching of the Apostles was given the name as Christianity, by the Gentile believers of what became known as Europeans people, in the city of Antioch of Turkey.

According to (Act, Chapter 11, and verse 26), there it explained that the believers of the Apostles were first called as Christians in the city of Antioch in the city of Turkey, and Turkey was also called as Asia Minor during Greco Roman time. But the right name for the land of Turkey is known in (Genesis Chapter 10, and verse 3), as Ashkenaz, who were the first son of Gomer, and Gomer is known today as the land of Russia, according to (Genesis, Chapter 10, and verse 2). Also that of the Scripture Map of 1890, showing the land of Gomer, that is now known as Russia, of the ancient world of the sons and daughters of Japheth, who was the last son of Noah. According to Volume 1 of the Encyclopaedia, there it clearly explained that the city of Antioch was called Antioch Pisidian, that was a city of Phrygia, of the Anatolia area of Turkey. This label as the Way, was given by many Yehudahites, who did not believe on Yashua, that he was the Son of Yahweh. This was also, by the Scribes, Pharisee, and the high priest, who did not believe on Yashua, that he was the Son of Yahweh, who were sent to them, the Yehudahites, and Benjaminhites of the children of Israel, to save them from their sin and death. So, these followers of Yashua who were his disciples, and later become known as his Apostles, were also known as those who follow the Way, meaning Yashua. (Acts Chapter 4, and verse 12) there it clearly stated that there is no other name given among men, under heaven, where we as people can be saved from the coming destruction of Yahweh, that is due to come on this world, because of the sins of many people who do not live their lives to please Yahweh.

Yashua is the greater Moses of the New Covenant order, of the Scripture, to all believers who believed on him that he is the Son of Yahweh, and those who follow his teaching, he gave to his Apostles, his servants, to teach other believers. That all believers who are obedient to his teaching of the New Covenant Law, that Yahweh did set up by way of Yashua, and his Apostles, will be save from the wrath of Yahweh that is to come. (Hebrew Chapter 1, and verse 1), there the Scripture went on to say, Yahweh who at sundry time, which mean long ago time, and in diverse manner. Which means different ways, and different times, have spoken in time past unto the fathers by the prophets, meaning the prophets of ancient Israel. But in these last days, He have spoken unto us by His Son. This us that the Scripture spoke of, were the Yehudahites, and the Benjaminhites of the children Israel, who were left there in the land of Israel, when Yashua came to them as a man.

It was just like when Yahweh sent Moses as His mouthpiece, or His spokesman to the ancient children of Israel, who were there in the land of Mizraim that became known as Egypt. So, if the people did not listen to Moses, it would mean they have rejected Yahweh himself, and that would mean sure death for that person, because Moses was the mouthpiece who were sent to them, in the land that became known as Egypt. Much less Yashua, who is the Son of Yahweh, and who came down from above, that is over every one who are on the earth. What Yahweh did was to put Yashua spirit into the whom of Mary to be born as a man. This was to take the place of the first man Adam, who has brought sin and death upon all his offspring, because of his disobedience in not keeping to the commandment Yahweh gave to him, not to eat from the tree of good and evil. But instead chose to listen to his wife Eve, who was deceived by the serpent, who was really Satan the devil in disguised as a snake. So, all the people of planet earth of today, who are obedient to the New Covenant Law that was set up by Yashua, and his Apostles, will become a part of the family of Yahweh true Yashua, His Son. Who was the greater Adam, and the greater Moses to all believers, who believe on him, and follow his teaching he gave to the Apostles his servants. Yashua also came to earth to fulfill the various prophecies of the Scripture that was spoken of him, by the various prophets of Israel, who Yahweh did used to be His spokesman. Or His mouthpiece to the Yehudahites and the Benjaminhites, who were left there in the land that became known as Israel, before he came to earth to fulfill the wishes of Yahweh.

Yahweh had also sent Yashua to the Yehudahites, and the Benjaminhites who were left there in the land of Israel to be their savior, and that of the world of mankind at large, because without Yashua there cannot be any forgiveness of sin, as it is so clearly stated in (Acts, Chapter 4, and verse 12). One can see the fulfillment of this prophecy taken place before our very eyes of the gathering of the believers, who came from the Way, many of whom became known as Christian, by the Gentile people of Europe. That is if these Christian people truly follow the teaching of Yashua, in their day to day lives, to please Yahweh, and Yashua. It is also mentioned in the House of Yahweh publication, that is called the Amazing discoveries, that they are many errs they have found in the various modern translations, that became known as the Bible. That in many ways are different from the original Hebrew Scripture that were only given to the ancient children of Israel.

This same publication went on to explained that leading Bible scholars, admit that, what became known as the Bible, by way of the people of Greece, who had translated the Scripture from Hebrew, to Aramaic, of the Canaanite writing. To that of the Greek Septuagint Version, that came down into the Latin Vulgate Version, that did also came down into what is known today as the King James Version. With many other translations that came down from the Gentile people of Europe, these Bible scholars found out that they are over 20,000 errors they have found in the various modern translations of what is now known as the Bible. From what I have read from this same Yahweh House of publication, in many of today's versions, words and phrases were added or deleted. So because of this, it makes it nearly impossible to understand the true meaning of many important verses of the original Hebrew Scripture, that many of these translations came down from. It is also stated that the Scripture was first written in Hebrew, and then translated into Aramaic, which was that of the writing of the Canaanite Phoenician people. Then into Greek, and Latin, and finally into what become known as the English language, that came from the name of the Angles, and Saxon people of Germany. Which these writings originally came from the alphabetical writing of the Phoenician, the Hethites, and the people of Mizraim that become known as the Egyptians' people. This House of Yahweh publication went on to explained that when many of these translators, was translating the Scripture into what become known as the Bible. These translators' added footnotes, and later other copyists, or scribes, and translators would write these footnotes in to their manuscripts. Which was later included the text by others translators. So, many of the ancient Hebrew manuscripts were either left out, or were un-translated, or were completely remove.

This is the reason why the name of Yahweh do not appear in many of the translations of today, but it is only mentioned as Lord, God, and Jehovah God, that do appear in many of the translations, which are only titles, and it is not the name of our creator Yahweh. But it is only titles and false name that was given to Him by various Gentile's translators of Europe. Yashua is the only way to Yahweh, by approaching Yahweh true the name of His Son, to give praise, and thanks to His Holy name, for all the things He has given us, His creation here on earth.

 I would like to let many of my Hamite's people to know, who became followers of Mohammed or anyone else for that matter, that there is only one way, one can escape the coming destruction, by Yahweh, and that is to become obedient followers of Yashua, and his teaching, he gave to his Apostles, to teach other believers. Who become knowledgeable of the New Covenant Law that was set up by Yahweh, true Yashua, and his Apostles, and know one else. Yashua said at (Matthew Chapter 7, and verse 24) that whosoever hearth these saying of his, and do them, he will liken him unto a wise man who built his house upon a rock, and when the rain descended, and the flood come, and the wind blew, and beat upon that house, it fell not, because it was founded upon the rock. Yashua went on to say, that everyone who hearth these saying of his, and do them not, shall be liken unto a foolish man, who built his house upon the sand, when the rain came, and the flood came, and the wind blew, and beat upon that house, it fell, and great was the fall of that house. I would like to say that this rock that the wise man did built his house upon, was the Word of Yahweh, and the teaching of Yashua, that is the New Covenant Law, which is the Scripture of truth. Yashua went on to say at (John Chapter 17, and verse 2), while he was praying to his father, and his God, by saying as you have given him power over all flesh, that he should give life everlasting to many as Yahweh has given him. (John Chapter 17, and verse 3) there Yeshua went on to say, and this is life everlasting, that they might know you, the only true Yahweh, and Yeshua whom you have sent.

My reason for mentioning these Scriptures, is to show to many of my fellow Hamite's people, who were converted to Islam, many of whom have become followers of Mohammed, and his religious philosophy, that became known as Islam, by his followers. Who later became known as the Muslim people, with their religious philosophy, of Islam, as a way of life for these believers to live by. This also, goes to other religious people, who were converted to their conquerors religious belief, that there is only one hope in this life, and that is to make our peace with Yahweh, true the name of Yashua, His Son, and to follow his teaching only, as a way of life to live by, to please Yahweh, and our Lord Yashua.

Powerful Civilizations and Inventions of the people of Mizraim, who became known as the Egyptian people. This was before the word science, and technology came into existence by the Gentile people of what is now known as the Europeans people of Europe. I would like to point out that the people of Mizraim had powerful civilization in the early beginning of the history of the human family, before the Greeks, and the Romans, who they the Gentile people of Europe say, it was the Greeks, and the Romans who had started the civilization of the world. These Gentile people has been used the word science, and technology, to describe knowledge, advancement, craft, and skills, also in the making of things, like medicine, mathematics, and writings, and so on. Although these things were started by the people of Mizraim, and others of the people of Ham of the so-call Middle East, and what become known as North Aprica, long before the word science, and technology came into existence by the Gentile people of what is now known as European people of Europe. Though I do not believe in the word science, because the word science only came into existence during the time of 1150, to the 1800, by the Gentile people of what is now European people of Europe. In the time of 1800, the word science came about by way of Charles Darwin, who was a British scientist, and an evolutionist. So, from what I have read from the Encyclopaedia Britannica, these Celtic people who became known as the British people, with other Celtic people of Europe, they could not read and write for themselves, until they were conquered, enslave, and given literacy by the Greeks, the Roman, and by the Roman Catholic Church.

Before the conquest of the Greeks and the Romans over these Celtic barbarian people of Europe, they could not read and write for themselves, so as to come up with the word science and technology. But it was due to the enslavement of the Greeks and the Romans who at one time had ruler ship over their brothers of Europe. So, they the Greeks pass on what they had learn from the various kingdoms of the people of Ham, that gave literacy to the rest of the people of Europe, that gave birth to the word science and technology, that was taking from the word craft and skills, that was used in the various ancient kingdoms of the people of Ham that gone by. So, how can a people who were uneducated came up with the word science and technology, that originally came from Latin word scientia, which this Latin word stand for knowledge, and skills.

During the early civilizations of the various kingdoms of the people of Ham, that gone by, this word science was known to them as craft and skills that is mentioned in the writing of the Scripture many times, as craft. That originally came from the Phoenicians, and other kingdoms of the people of Ham, before the word science, and technology came about, by the people of Europe. Due to this word science by Charles Darwin, with many of his fellow scientist believers, it has cost many of their free slave people, who were indoctrinated by the European schooling system, to see themselves as the educated people of the European system. This was for them to believe in their vein foolish theory, of evolution that they say that the world was started with the big bang explosion, and then everything came into been. This was from their foolish mindset, that they have thought to other people, who came under their captivity of ruler ship. This philosophy of Charles Darwin, with his fellow scientist believers, who also believe in his theory of how everything came in to existence, in our world of today. It has misled many people from the true knowledge of the creation of Yahweh, of how all things came into existence in our world by Him. This word science was also passed down the line to many people, who the Gentile people has conquered, enslaved, and taught us their ways, of beliefs of their educational system, to suit themselves in the various school system of their's. This was done, so as to gear our minds to think in the way we were educated by our teachers, to suit the Gentile European people schooling system. According to Volume 26 of the Encyclopaedia it explained that Latin did not become the official language of imperial Rome, until the time of 6th century BC, when it became an official language of Rome. According to this same volume 26 of the Encyclopaedia, the language at that time many of the early Roman had spoken, during the period, was that of Greek.

So, these evolutionists, and their scientist also believe that men evolve from monkeys and apes, as how they having been teaching in their schooling system, and also in their dictionary. So, because of their brainwashing teaching, it have cause many people who were educated by them, not believe in the creation of Yahweh, of how all things came into existence by Him, according to the teaching of the Scripture, that became known as the Bible, by the people of Greece. The question I would like to ask these evolutionists, scientists, and these so-called wise men of today, if their theory is true, that men came from monkeys and apes, why it is today, monkeys, and apes are still in the form of monkeys and apes, as how Yahweh made them to be?

Also man, who were created in the image, and likeness of Yahweh, as how it is stated in the Scripture of truth, is still looking like men, and not in the form of monkeys and apes, as how they having been teaching the world of people who came under their captivity. There is an old saying that goes like this, you can fool some of the people some of the time, but you cannot fool all the people all the time, the truth of the Scripture will always prevail, because it is the power, and the Word of Yahweh, to everyone who believed. The truth of the Scripture must come to light, and they the Gentile people of Europe cannot stop it. Although they have been trying to do so for many centuries, in many ways and form of skimming, in trying to keep their conquered people in darkness, from knowing the truth of the Scripture for themselves. Yet many of us, their captive people of today, are far more enlighten about the true teaching of the creation of Yahweh, from the Scripture of truth, than in the time of our ancestors of yesterday, who they had taken as their slaves and captives, and to keep them in ignorance and darkness. Many of these evolutionists, of Doctor Charles Darwin, and other scientists, who do not believe in the creation of Yahweh, that everything starts with Him, and everything ends with Him. This is the reason why they the scientists, and other evolutionists of today came up with the theory of Mother Nature, who they say created this and that. According to the Webster's Collegiate Dictionary of the Fifth Edition, the word Mother Nature came from early Latin language, that was known as Deus to them, the Romans. According to the dictionary, the meaning of the word deity stud for a god, or a goddess of nature that came down to the various Celtic barbarian kingdoms of the Gentile people of Europe. As Mother Nature who were under Roman ruler ship, of their teaching, and belief. This teaching of theirs have also pass on down to the minds of their many captive people, who came under their ruler ship of their schooling system, they did establish true slavery and colonialism.

So again, we have been going along with whatever they have thought us to believe in, because that is what is taught in their schooling system, and many of us their captives know no better. So, we just simply go along with what we have learned from these people, that became a way of life for many people who came under their system of things. It is also meant getting a good paying job, according to the European people educational system, many of us were brought up under their system, to be able to exist in their modern world of today.

Also, for us to accept their educational teaching as facts, otherwise, it would be exceedingly difficult to exist in their modern world of today, so, as to be able to find employment, and to put food on our tables. These wise men, and their scientists, also came up with the theory of ten million, or ten billion years ago "this was" and "that was", when none of these men was around in those time, so as to give an account of what was. But they only came up with a state of deception, and falsehood to deceive many people who came under their captivity. Also, for many people to look up to them as the people who have all the knowledge, and wisdom of today. So, it is extremely easy for them to deceive us, their many captive, because many people go to their various schools, colleges, and universities of the Gentile people system, to be educated, and school by them, so, a to get their degrees, and to see things from their perspective. Also to be able to exist in their system, they were able to established by ways of colonialism, and slavery to get rich. So, form their educational system, many of us their captives people had received, we see things their way, because they are the ones who are in control of world affairs, who also see themselves as the master race of the human family. From my experience in trying to distribute the first edition of this book that came out in 2009, I found out that many of my educated Hamite's people would rather believe in the philosophy of the scientists, more than to believe in the writing of the Scripture of truth. Which is the Law of Yahweh, that were only given to the children of Israel, for them to follow, and live by, in their everyday lives to please Yahweh. That it may go well with them, if they were to stick to His Laws, and Commandments. So, many of these educated Hamite's people would rather to believe in science, and the scientist's stories, more than to believe in the writing of the Scripture, that was translated by these same Gentile people of Europe, that they say my book is based upon.

Many of these foolish educated Hamite's people, who do not believe in the writing of the Scripture, fail to realize that this is the very same book of the Scripture, that we all are going to be judge by the things that are written there in. Whether we are believers or not, and this is a fact of life, and it is not a scientifically theory. We all must give an account of our deeds, and belief to Yahweh, and to Yashua, because Yahweh has giving Yashua power over all the people of the earth, to be Judge, and this statement is according to (John Chapter 5, and verse 22).

Furthermore, Yahweh is not dealing with unbelievers, but He is only dealing with believers, who are wise in the Scripture, to save many who believe, from His wrath of destruction that is to come. As how Noah and his family were a strong believer in the things Yahweh had said to him, although there were no written Scripture at that time, to help him to understand the intended destruction that was due to come from Yahweh. But he did believed the Word of Yahweh, that was spoken to him, although he did not see those things, until the flood came and take away all those UN Yahweh like people, who did not, please Yahweh well. (Proverbs Chapter 1, and verse 7), there it mentioned that the fear of Yahweh is the beginning of knowledge, but foolish people despise this knowledge, of fear, wisdom, and instruction of Yahweh. Which is the Scripture of truth, that our lives are based upon, which is also, the book of knowledge, and enlightenment. Also (Ecclesiastes Chapter 12 and verse 1), there the Scripture went on to say this, remember now your creator in the days of your youth, while the evil days come not. Also verse (13, and 14 of the same Chapter), there it went on to say, let us hear the conclusion of the whole matter of life, fear Yahweh and keep His Commandment: for this is the whole duty of man. For Yahweh shall bring every work of man into judgment, with every secret thing, whether it is good, or whether it is good or bad. So, again the scientists, and their evolutionists, and the various wise men of today, will not be able to save themselves, or anyone else who lesion, and believe in them, from the wrath of Yahweh that is to come. I must also point out to many of my fellow educated Hamite's people, and others who do not believed in the writing of the Scripture, but whoso, believed more in what the scientists of their philosophy say, how this or that came about. I must also point out that Yahweh do not need any one of us, or the scientists for that matter.

But we need Him, and we cannot live without Him, because He is the source of life, whether we believe it or not. Yahweh can also make people out of stone, if He so wish to do, to become worshippers of Him, who would please Him well. Many of my educated Hamite's people of today, believed that science has far more facts, and can prove things much more than what the Scripture say, that they say my book is based upon, that was written by believers who wrote the Scripture. Many of my educated Hamite's people of today need to take a good lesson of example from the Hamite's people who were living in the city of Nineveh. When Jonah was sent to warn them of the intended destruction that was coming from Yahweh to them.

They did believed Jonah, and turn away from their wicked, and evil ways, and was saved from the wrath of Yahweh, because they did believe. All though Yahweh later destroyed the country of the Assyrian, with the city of Nineveh, and many Hamite's cities, and countries of the area of the so-call Middle East, as it is called today. Along with the kingdom of Babylon, that is the reason why these cities are no longer around with us today, because they were conquered, by various conquerors Yahweh did used to bring about the destruction of these countries, and cities. These people of the country of Assyria could have chosen not to believe in what Jonah was saying to them, but to believe more so, in their wise men of their days, and they all would have been destroyed before the finial destruction of the Assyrian came about. Like that of the Hamite's people of the cities of Sodom and Gomorra of the land of Canaan, who Yahweh destroyed for all their evil ways, and deeds, that did not please Him well, that left no trace of them, as a people. Many of these educated Hamite's people of today, also believed that science can prove the creation of man, from D and A, that according to them is far more accurate than what the Scripture teaches, that became known as the Bible, that give the history of how the human family came in to being. I would also like to point out to many of my fellow educated Hamite's people, who see things this way, who believed in the scientist, and their vain theory of how this or that came into being. All these

111

scientists, and the archeologists, are not Yahweh, who is the creator of all things, and by Him all things existed. Including all the scientists, and other wise men of today, who do not believe in the writing of the Scripture, and who do not believe in Yahweh. All their scientifical theory, with their modern inventions of today came from the Gentile family of Europe.

That was spread to other people around the world by their conquest, of the world, and its people, and their lands, that came under their control. So many of their captives who came under their influence of their schooling system, for them to see things their way, according to their belief, that many of us have copy from them. It is the Word of Yahweh that become known as the Scripture, that foretold of the future of what is going to be, and what was before us of ancient time, because He was around in those time, and He knows what the future hold, because He invented time and events, and the future begin with Him, and end with Him. This is a fact of life, weather one believes it or not, and it is not a scientifical theory. Furthermore, Yahweh holds the future in His hands, because there cannot be any future without Him, and this is the reality of life, weather one knows it, or believed it or not.

Many of my educated Hamite's people of today, are just like the ancient children of Israel who were rap up in the philosophy, and the doctrines of the Scribes, and the Pharisees, who were the religious wise leaders of their days. They would rather to embrace the doctrines, and the philosophies of the Scribes, and the Pharisees, more than to believe in the prophecies concerning the coming of Yashua, and his teaching. Which was the way of life to everyone who did believed on him, and his teaching. This is the reason why Yashua said to his disciples at (Mathew Chapter 15, and verse 14), that they must leave the Scribes and Pharisees alone, Because they were blind leaders of the blind, and if the bind leads the blind; they all shall fall into the ditch, or the it pit. The same is true for many people of today, because many people love to put their trust, hope, and belief in men, who seem to know how, this, or that came about. When these men were not even around in life, of those days, so as to know how this or that came about. Yashua was indeed the Word of Yahweh who were sent to them, that was promise lone ago, before he came earth to fulfill the various prophecies of the Scripture, that were written of him. But these Israelites were more so rap up in the doctrines, and the philosophy of the Scribes, and the Pharisees, more than in the teaching of Yashua, who was indeed the Word of Yahweh who were sent to them. One of the reasons for this problem, it is because many people love to trust, and to glorified in men, who seems to impress them with their words, of charm that penetrate their hearts, and minds to be rap up in their philosophy of doctrines'.

It was the same way with Eve, and the serpent, who was Satan the devil in disguise, who came in the form of a snake, and started to trill her with his charm of words. By telling her that if she was to eats from the tree of knowledge, of good and evil, she and Adam will become wise like Yahweh, knowing good from evil. This statement can be found at {Genesis Chapter 2, and verse 17}. Due to her foolish mistake, as well as Adam in listing to Eve his wife, who were deceived by the serpent, in not to obey the Words of Yahweh, we their offspring, who are around today are going to suffer the same faith. Because people seem to want to glorify in men who seems to impress them with their doctoring of philosophy, who they consider as scalars, and wise men, who think they knows how this or that came into being. I also, came to the realization from trying to circulate the first edition of this same book that came out in 2009, that many of my Hamite's people would rather go to the various bookstores to by books that was written about sex, violence, and killing, than to take interest in my book that is dealing with our history, and knowledge of who we are as a people.

Also of the great civilization we as a people are coming from, that many of us of today have no knowledge of many of the things I have written about in this book. The way many of them see things, these books of sex, and violence seems to cart their imagination, and attention. I can understand why many of them think the way they do, it is because they were born and raise, and brought up into a system that was built up on guns, violence, killing and sexual immorality. That was brought about by way of these Gentile people of Europe, who left from Europe, and established their ruler ship, that were pass on to many of us their free slave's captive's people minds of today. Who became their citizens, and it became a part of our cultural, and ways of life. The first thing that many young boys and girls who were brought up under the European colonial world, especially in what became known as the United States, is for them to have a toy gun for them to play with. Later when these boys, and girls grow up into man hood, and woman hood, they replace the toy gun for the real gun.

So, from a child many people who were brought up in these societies, their mind was set and train, and geared toward killing by the guns of violence. Or from whatever violence tools they see and learn from these Gentile European people television, and their movies of their establishment of killing, of violence, and sexual immorality. There is an old saying that a man is a victim of his environment, where he or she was born and raised in. This is a true reality that has taken it told on many of our Hamite's people minds, and other people who were brought up under the Gentile European colonial system of things that became known as the United States. This is of their violence, wickedness, and evil ways they have establish wheresoever they went and conquer in the name of Christianity, and religion, by using the Bible as their tools. This is the case of many Hamite's people who were born, and raise in the United States, and in many other parts of the Gentile European people colonial world of their system, where our ancestors were taken as slave, and leave us behind. We have copy and learn the ways of these Gentile people of Europe, and have been corrupted by these people beyond measure.

Who did present themselves to us, and the world of other people at large, who came under their captivities, to see them as an angel of light, but who were the devil, and his agent in disguise. From my perspectives, many Hamite's people love too much to glorify in men, who seem to impress them with their doctrines of philosophy, and wisdom. That seems to penetrate their minds, and heart to see these men as professor of knowledge, who has all the knowledge of the world, how everything came about.

But as the saying goes, one fool makes many more fools, and this is the case that effect many of have us Hamite's people minds of today. Also, others people, who came under the colonial captivity, of the people of Europe, to see these scientists, and their archaeologist as the wise men of today. To tell them what the future holes, and what was before we came into being. These are some of the very same things that Yashua warns his Apostles, and other believers of Israel, and many of us believers of today, to be aware of these philosophers of men, and their doctrines. Those of us who are believers in the writings of the Scripture, need to be careful of these philosophers who many people look up to for guidance, and direction as for as life, and the future is concern. This is why it is recorded in (Matthew Chapter 7, and verse 15), where Yashua said, beware of false prophets, or false teachers, many of whom in my opinion came in the form of the scientists, and other wise men of today, who many people look up to as men who has all the answers about life. Of how this or that came about, when they were only born yesterday, in comparison to the creation of the world, and the time when the Scripture were given to the children of Israel. In my opinion many these scientists, and their archaeologists, are deceivers as the Scripture had foretold about these false prophets, and false teachers, where it is mentioned in (Matthew Chapter 24, and verse 11) where Yashua went on to say, for many false prophets shall arise, and shall deceive many. It is also mentioned in (Matthew Chapter 24, and verse 24) that they shall arise false Christ, and false prophets who shall show great sign, and wonders, in so much that if it were possible, they would deceive the very elect, or the chosen ones. This word elect was translated as the Saints, as I have mention many times in this book, by the various churches. Yashua also point out at (Matthew Chapter 24, and verse 22), that except the days are cut short, there would be no flesh save alive, but for the elect's sake the days are cut short. What Yashua was saying in (Matthew Chapter 24) that if the days of life were not cut short, no one would be able to survive on alive on planet earth.

This is the reason why many people of today have the saying that time seems to be flying so fast, because as they look around, the months and the years is finished. This is because as Yashua said, if the days were not cut short, no flesh, or people would save alive on plaint earth. This is because of these scientists, and their philosophies, of how they see things, of their ways, to gain more power, and wealth, by wars of conquest.

These scientists with their modern technological capability, have the capability to destroy all life on the planet earth, with their nuclear bombs, and with other chemical weapons they have develop from their evil minds. They have brought about to cast total destruction of all life on planet earth, because of their evil mind set, of greed, and selfishness for wealth, and power, and to control other people, and their life, and lands. It would only take one mad man to start the nuclear war, and there would be no more people saves alive on planet earth, as Yashua had point out. But as he had said, the days are cut short, to prevent this catastrophe from taking place. Yahweh has everything in plan for His Kingdom Government, that will come and rule by Yashua, to bring in peace, and tranquility over all the earth. It is only a matter of time before all these things take place according to His will. Many Hamite's people also point out to me during my distribution of the first edition of this same book, that came out in 2009 the scientists can make airplanes, computers, and rockets going to the moon, and they can also prove D, and A of how people came about. So, many of them would rather to believe in science, and the scientists, more than what is written, and thought in the Scripture. What many of these foolish Hamite's people fail to realize, and understand, is that these are the very fulfillment of the prophecy of (Daniel Chapter 12, and verse 4), that knowledge was going to increase, with other prophecies of the Scripture, that are being fulfilled before our very eyes, that many people don't seem to really understand.

(Luke Chapter 21, and verse 24), there the Scripture mentioned about the time of the Gentile reign, and domination over the earth, and also over Jerusalem, until the time of the Gentile people powers come to their end. This end of the Gentile reign over the earth, will come to its end, by way of Yahweh Kingdom, at Yashua send return, to take over ruler ship of the earth, from these Gentile political powers. As it is so pointed out at (Revelation Chapter 6, and verse 2), about he that sat on the white horse, who went forth conquering, and to conquer, which this prophecy, is referring to Yashua at his second coming. It is also mentioned in (Daniel Chapter 12, and verse 4) that knowledge was going to increase, which have brought about all these modern scientifical technology of invention, of today, that many people are not even aware of. They give glory to these scientists for their invention, as if to say that they the scientists make themselves. They also, give glory to these men, as if to say they themselves give themselves knowledge, and wisdom, and various capabilities to bring about all these modern technologies of today, that they called as science.

As I have also explained, many times in this book, that many of these modern technologies of today, came from the ancient world of the various kingdoms of the people of Ham, Yahweh had destroyed, because He was not pleased of their doings. It is Yahweh who is the one who give knowledge, wisdom, and understanding, and who also has allow all these modern inventions of the Gentile people of Europe to come into existence. This was to fulfill the various prophecies of the Scripture, that knowledge was going to increase, which has brought about all these modern technology of today. I would also like to point out to many of my Hamite's people, and others who became captives of the Gentiles European people, of their teaching, and their philosophy of what they teach us to believe in, from their vain belief, and point of view. Of how they think this or that came about, when there were not even around in those time, so as to give an account of what was. I must also point out that men did not create themselves, but rather we were all created, and put here by Yahweh, and we all must give an account of our self before His judgment seat, and the judgment seat of Yashua. This is for all what we have done, and say in this life, weather it is good or bad. I am quite sure, the scientists, or many of these wise men of today, who do not believe in the writing of the Scripture, and Yahweh, will not be able to save us, or themselves from the wrath of Yahweh that is to come. The wise mens of Pharaoh days of ancient Mizraim, that became known as the Egyptians people, could not save themselves, of the land of Mizraim, from the wrath of Yahweh that were poured out on them by Yahweh. Because of the enslavement of the children of Israel, and for their own evil doing that did not please Him well. It will be the same way in our modern world of today, where many of the scientist, and their wise men, will not be able to save themselves, and many people who look up to them from the wrath of Yahweh that is to come. Many of whom believe in their philosophy, from the wrath of Yahweh that will come on all the world of the unbelievers, and of the UN Yahweh like people. Yashua also point out at (John Chapter 8, and verse 47) that he who is of Yahweh hearth the word of Yahweh, which is speaking of the Scripture of truth.

But he that is not of Yahweh hearth not the word of Yahweh, because he is not of Yahweh, but he is of the devil. (Psalm Chapter 146, and verse 3), there it mentioned that, put not your trust in Princes, nor in the sons of men, or from my point of view, in these scientists, and their archeologists, in whom there is no hope or help, because they are only men. The Chapter went on to say, his breath goes out forth from is body, and he returned to his earth or his dust where he came out of before.

In that very day, his thoughts perish, but happy is he who has the God of Jacob, whose name is Yahweh for their help, who has made heaven and earth, the sea, and all that are therein. I must also point out that the people of Mizraim, the Canaanite, the Assyrian, the Babylonian, and also the Philistine people of Ham, all had powerful civilizations long before the word science, came about, by these Gentile people of Europe. One should also realize, and understand that many of the modern advancement, and achievement that the Gentile people called as science, and technology, was started with Canaanites, the Cushites, and with the people of Mizraim. Also, with that of the other various kingdoms of the people of Ham, long before the word science and technology came into being by the Gentile people of Europe. So, this word science and technology was called as craft, and skills, by the people of Ham, long before the word science and technology came into been by the Gentile people of Europe. Such as mathematics, reading, writing, the making of medicine, the making of the wheel. Art, jewelry, sword, ships, furniture's, and the making of chariots, that ran on wheels, from the chariots, with horses, and buggies, that gave birth to the modern-day Motorcars of today, which was started by the Gentile people, of what became known as the land of Europe.

This technology of the making of motorcars, was later copied by the Asiatic countries, of what became known as Asia, who also started the making of Motorcars they did copy from the people of Europe, that became a part of their industries of today. One can safely say that it was the people of Ham who had started what became known as technology, and the technology of music, if I may use this word technology. Because the word technology is a modern word, a term that was used to describe art, inventions, crafts, music, and the word science. Today, whenever the Gentile people of Europe speak of inventions, or technology, they mainly speak of the people of Europe, the Greeks, and the Romans, who they claim to have started the invention of things, and the civilization of the world. I can safely say the Gentile people of who became known as the Europeans people, have been teaching us, and the world of other people who came under their captivity, a bunch of lies over the centuries, to see things their way. The Scripture bare record of the much development, and of the many great civilization of the people of Ham, even before the Greeks, and the Romans, whom they say started the civilization of the world. Let us continue to examine the many great inventions of the people of Mizraim, the people of Mizraim were also responsible for the invention of writing, along with the Phoenician Canaanites people of Zidon.

That is mentioned in the Scripture as Sidon, now known as the land of Syria by the Greeks, conquest, and also by the Romans. This writing ability of the Phoenician, the people of Mizraim, the Hethites, and that of Carthaginian people of Mizraim did spread to the Gentile people of Europe, that also did came from the Babylon people of Nimrod, who also gave literacy to the people of Greece, and in turn to the other people of the Gentile land that become known as Europe. The people of Mizraim were also responsible for the making of furniture, the building of the Pyramid, which had taken the skills of mathematics, and craft. The embalmment of the dead that lasted for thousands of years, that became known as the mummies of Egypt. These mummies they the Gentile people of Europe, often time show on their movies, and their television program, as the mummies of Mizraim, that is now known as Egypt. Also the making of money as a form of their exchange, long before many of the Gentile countries of Europe started the using of money, as their medium of exchange. The people of Mizraim were also responsible for producing the first Physician of Medicine, and what become known as doctors of today. His name was known as Imotep, who was the father of medicine, by the saying of these same Gentile people of Europe. If anyone questions my statement that the people of Mizraim had the capability of the making money, that was started long before the Gentile people of Europe thought of the idea of making of money for themselves, as a medium of exchange. If one dough my statement, of what I had said, i that the people of Mizraim were using money long before the people of Europe came to the knowledge of the making of money, they can turn to (Genesis Chapter 42, and verse 28).

There it is mentioned that Joseph, who became the governor over the land of Mizraim during the time of the famine, when his brothers left from Canaan to go to Mizraim to buy corn for food, they used money as a form of their exchange to buy their food. There the Scripture explained that the servants of Joseph put back the money of his brothers in their sacks. The people of Ham were producing medicine out of herbs, and plants long before the Gentile people of Europe knew of these things, in which, most of the knowledge of the making of medicine, was passed down the line to various tribes of the people of Ham, that they the Gentile people of Europe called as bush medicine, and which doctors, because they had no knowledge of these things. The family of Cush, who became known as the Cushites people, had been making chariots, and jewelry long before their Gentile counterparts started the making of these things, as a part of their industry of today.

Even before the Greeks, and the Romans, who they say started civilization of the world. According (Jeremiah Chapter 43, starting from verse 10, to verse 13), Yahweh used Nebuchadnezzar king of Babylon to destroy the kingdom of Mizraim, that did become known as Egypt. So, after the conquest of the kingdom of Mizraim, Mizraim became a colony of the country of Babylon. This was before Babylon were destroyed by the Persian, and later the kingdom of Babylon were taken over by Cyrus of Persia, and became a colony of Persia, according to the fulfillment of the dream King Nebuchadnezzar of Babylon had, that is recorded in (Daniel Chapter 2, and verse 39). About the silver part of the image of Nebuchadnezzar dream, that stud for incoming power of Persia. Who was to come up, and destroyed Babylon, and take over the power of Babylon, and all her colonial territories. So, after the conquest of Babylon, then the kingdom of Mizraim came under the power of the Persians to be their colony of control. So, later when the power of the Persians was destroyed by the brass power that stud for the power of Greece, that came up in the form of Alexander the Great, and his army of Macedonia of Europe. Then the kingdom of Mizraim became the colony of Greece, by way of the conquest of Alexander the Great, and his generals. So, it was Alexander who made one of his general by the name of Ptolemy, to be governor over the kingdom of Mizraim, that became known as Egypt, which the name Egypt it's a Greek name, that were given to the land of Mizraim by the people of Greece.

So, when Alexander died at age 32, then Ptolemy maid himself king over the land of Mixraim, and when Ptolemy died, his dynasty continue on, until the time of Cleopatra the 7th, who came from the lineage of Ptolemy. This dynasty of Ptolemy continue on until the time of the Romans, who were to come up, and conquer Greece, according to the image of King Nebuchadnezzar dream. This dream is of (Daniel Chapter 2, and verse 33), about the iron legs, that stud for the coming up of the power of the Romans, who was to come up and destroyed the power of Greece. So, the name of the land of Mizraim became known as Agyptus, by the Greeks rulers, and the name Egypt came into the Anglo Saxon dialect of the Germanic people of Europe, that came from the Greek name Agyptus. So, doing the Greek rulership over the land of Mizraim, Greek laws, and custom, and their culture was robber off on the people of Mizraim, as a Greek way of lives, for the people of Mizraim to live by.

According to volume 20 of the Encyclopaedia, the last Greek dynasty that rule Mizraim, was that of Cleopatra the 7th, Who were known as Cleopatra Queen of the Nile. Who came from the linage of Ptolemy, and who was involve with Julius Cesar, and Mark Antony, before Rome take over Mizraim as their colony. After the Greek power fell to the new power of Rome, who was describe in the dream of Nebuchadnezzar at (Daniel Chapter 2, and verse 41), as the iron leg. Which was the fourth kingdom power who was to come up out of the dream of Nebuchadnezzar. Also that of the vision that Daniel the prophet had, that is mention in Daniel Chapter 7, and verse 7, about the fourth beast, that stud for the power of Rome. So, the kingdom of Mizraim came under the power of Rome, after Octavian Augustus defeated Cleopatra, and Mark Anthony in 30 BC, in the Greek Turkey area of Europe, and the kingdom of Mizraim became a price kingdom of the Romans. According to volume 18 of the Encyclopaedia Britannica, despite the struggles, and quarrels over the land of Mizraim, by the colonial rulers, the land of Mizraim was quite wealthy, and was trading with the West, meaning Western Europe. The

Encyclopaedia also explained that the city of Rome was very much depended on the country of Mizraim for their wealth, and food supplies. Also the kingdom of Mizraim was treated as a special colony of Rome, and it was also a prize colony that were governs by Octavian himself. Octavian did not allow any of the ruling senates to have any dealing with this prize colony of his.

The kingdom of Mizraim later fell to the power of the Turks, of what was left of the old Roman Empire of Eastern Europe, who also became a part of the Mohammedans family of the Muslim people of Mohammed, of 639-868 AD. Eventually the land of Mizraim did became the colony of the Mohammedans people of Ishmael, who became known as the Saudi Arabian people. So, the custom, and laws of the land of Mizraim became known as the Muslim laws, and custom, that is still govern the land of Mizraim today. The land of Mizraim was also conquered later by the British people, and the Angles, and Saxon dialect became a part of their vocabulary of speaking, that be came known as the English, or the Angles dialect that is spoken in many parts of what became known as the land of Egypt.

Chapter 14 - Prophecies of the Scripture That Shape the Event of Things, And Time

Another reason why many of the various kingdoms of the people of Ham did not remain until today, it is because of the prophecy about the Kingdom of Yahweh that is coming, to take away ruler ship of the earth from these political ruling systems. This political ruling system came about by means of these Gentile European colonial, slavery system, of their power of conquest. This political system was set up by the Gentile people of Europe, wheresoever they went and conquered, and set up their political system, in the name of Christianity, mainly to their own interest, and gain to get rich. This Kingdom of Yahweh that is coming, is mentioned in (Daniel Chapter 12, and verse 4), where Daniel was told to shut up the word, and seal up the book, even to the time of the end that we are now living in. This Gentile European political ruling system will be taken away by Yashua at his second coming, with his angels to take over control of earth affairs from these political systems that was setup by the Gentile people of Europe throughout their colonial conquest of the world. There are many more prophecies that were spoken against the kingdom of the people of Ham, that have been fulfilled already, and it still have its effect on us Hamite's people lives of today. One of this prophecies I am speaking about is found in (Isaiah Chapter 20, starting from verse 2 to verse 5). There Yahweh went on to say to the prophet Isaiah, "like as my servant Isaiah had walked naked, and barefoot for three years, for a sign, and wonder upon Egypt, and upon Ethiopia", so shall the king of Assyria lead away the Egyptians prisoners, and the Ethiopians captives. Young and old, naked, and barefoot, even with their buttocks uncovered, to the shame of Egypt."

Verse 5 of the same Chapter of Isaiah went on to say, "and they shall be afraid, and ashamed of Ethiopia their expectation, and of Egypt their glory." (Ezekiel Chapter 29, and verse 12 to verse 15), went on to say, speaking of Egypt, "and I will bring again the captivity of the Egyptian, and I will cause them to return into the land of Pathros, into the land of their habitation, and there they shall be a base Kingdom. Neither shall it exalt itself any more above the nations, for I will diminish them, that they shall no more rules over the nations."

I did search the Scripture Map of 1890, showing the land of Mizraim that is now known as Egypt, to find the area of the land of Mizraim where the Scripture called the land of Pathros. But unfortunately, I could not find the location of the land of Pathros, because many of the old names of the land of Mizraim has been changed. Also some of the land area of the land of Mizraim has been taken over by the Suez Canal that was built. The word base according to the Webster Colligate Dictionary, means to be made low, or to be put to the very bottom of things. So, the kingdom of Mizraim was made into a low kingdom, in comparison to the state of power the kingdom of Mizraim used to have. This was in the early days before the Scripture, or the Scroll that became known as the Bible, were given to the ancient children of Israel, also, before all these Gentile powers of today come about. These prophecies of the Scripture have taken its toll on the people of Mizraim, and the people of Ham at large. Today, the people of Mizraim do not even speak their own language anymore, they speak the language of Arabic, and English, as their main source of communication. This is because they were all conquered by various colonial conquerors, and last of all, by the Mohammedans, and the British people, of the Angles, and Saxon Germanic dialect. Their original form of communication, and writing, which were known as Hieroglyphic, many of them cannot even write it, because of colonial conquest, and slavery, by many different conquerors to full field the prophecy that was mention. Also, today the people of Mizraim have become a totally washout people, with more so that of the Gentile European man blood running true their veins. The reason for this is, because they the people of Mizraim were conquered by so many different European families of people, who have left their many offspring's behind, as the new natives of the land, one sees in what is now known as the land of Egypt. As for the Assyrian people who were mentioned in (Isaiah Chapter 20), who were to take away the people of Mizraim as their captives, these people of Assyria, were from the Cushite's family Cush, of the kingdom of Nimrod.

So, the taking away of the people of Mizraim as their captives would not have cast such a washout as a people of today. Because the Assyrian people themselves were dark skin people, like that of the rest of their Hamite's people, who they were living around, not too far away from the land of Mizraim. Whom the Assyrian people also came out of, that became known as North Africa, and what is now called as a part of the so-call Middle East, and Middle Eastern people.

This is in comparison to that of their Gentile captors, who are mostly of pink skin, and red skin complexion, and who have left their marks on the people of Mizraim, and on the Hamite's people of the so-called Middle East, and what became known as North Africa, and East Africa. (Daniel Chapter 11, and verse 42, and 43), there the Scripture spoke of he," this he" that the Scripture spoke of, represent a man, or an army of a nation of people, who were coming to take over the land of Ham, and its people. This he or nation of people who were coming to take over the land of Ham, they were going to corrupt the people, who they were coming to conquer. This was going to be, by flatteries, strategies, lies, diplomacy, psychology, violence, and force. Verse 42, and 43 of the same Chapter went on to explained that, "he shall stretch forth his hands also upon the countries, and the land of Egypt shall not escape". But he shall have power over the treasures of gold, and of silver, and over all the precious things of Egypt. Also, the Libyans, and the Ethiopians shall be at his step." I do believe that this prophecy of Daniel Chapter 11, was speaking about the various Gentile European powers, who were to come up, and take over control of the land of Ham, and its people, with corruption, lies, violence and force. They the Gentile people of Europe have done just that, since the time of their colonial conquest of the land of Ham, and the world at large that, came under their colonial conquest of ruler ship, of power. Since the taken over of the land of Ham by the Gentile people of what become known as the Europeans people, they have turn many of these people into sodomites, lesbians, war mongers with the glory of the guns to kill more people faster. This is also, for various political gain, and to control, by using the various warring factors, and leaders to their own advantage. This cast this unity, suffering, and confusion among many of the people who are living there, in the land of Ham. They have used many of these so-call political leaders of the land of Ham as their poppets, for their own interests and gain. Many of these poppets leaders of the land of Ham, as allow many of these colonial rulers to come in, and used them as a tool, to get their resources of their land.

Also to keep their own people down in poverty, and many of these political figureheads of the land of Ham, see themselves as leaders, and rulers of their own people. But many of whom are only there in office for their own pockets, while they take payoff and bribes, so, they can drive around in a big Mercedes Benz, and have a big fat bank account in some European banks, while many of their own people are suffering, staving, and begging for bread.

Many of these studied an foolish Hamite's who stock up their money in some European bank, don't realize that if they should died, all their money go right over to benefit the European communities who own many of these banks. Many of these so-call educated Hamite's political leaders of the land of Ham, who claim they are educated. Because they went to Cambridge, Yale, or some school of the United States, and Canada to study these European people laws of greed's, selfishness, as if to say that education was started in Europe, among the Gentile people of Japheth. When, what became known as education of reading, writing, and arithmetic, was started in the land of Ham, among the people of Ham. This education system of the people of Ham, was later spread to the Gentile land that became known as Europe. In which the people of Europe give the world of people, who came under their captivities, the impression to believe that reading, writing, and arithmetic, that became known as education, and science, was started in Europe, which is far from the truth. I was watching a documentary on You Tube, explaining that when the British take over Nigeria as their colony, they would set up puppet's rulers. These puppet's rulers was to rule in the interest of the British people, also, that these politicians would rule in the interest of their own pockets, as well. So, from these puppets politician, that were established by the British, gave birth to the corrupted political system of Nigeria of today. That many of these men only go into office, for their own interest of their own pockets, and they do not have the love for their own suffering brothers, and sisters at hearth. The French did the same thing that gave birth to a Hamite politician man by the name of Blaise Compare of Burkina Faso, and many of his kind of people. Who rule in the interest of France, and in his own pockets, while many of their own people of Burkina Faso are poor, and suffering to survive, from day to day. I must point out that, I went to the country of Burkina Faso, in 2016, and I spent one month there, and I saw the suffering of many poor Hamite's people, struggling to make ends meet, as a way of life, and many of whom live in shocks.

 I also want to mention that the Saudi Arabian people of Ishmael, who have establish the religious belief of Islam, from the so-call Middle East, to Nigeria, with the sword, and the Koran. This was for their own interest, and gain, by using foolish stupid fanatic people, like the Buckaram Muslim people of Nigeria, to slater off many of their own people, so as to establish a Muslim Government, of Nigeria, in the interest of the Saudi Arabian people of Ishmael.

This was for them to become followers of Mohammed, and to the worship of their god Allah, and to have things under their control, as a Muslim way of life. The funny thing about the story of these Buckram people, they don't seem to have any problem with the Gentile European people, coming, and taking over the land of Ham, to be their possession. But they do not have any problem killing, and oppress many of their own brother's, and sister's to establish a Muslim system in the interest of the Saudi Arabian people of Ishmael. The land of Ham belong to the people of Ham only, just like how the land of Europe belong to the people of Japheth only, who became known as the people of Europe. These Gentile European people of Japheth, have corrupt many Hamite's people mines of the land of Ham, to be comes tobacco smokers, drug addict, alcoholic, winos, thefts, murders, prostitution, and pornography users. Also, with that of child prostitute, and that of child pornography, and gambling, as a way of life. Many of these things I have mention, above, was un heard of, among many of our ancestors that gone by, before the coming of the people of Europe. I was watching a documentary on the internet by a Gentile man of Europe, who was the reporter about the sexual corruptions of the country of Kenya. He was explaining of how many Gentile European men, left from Europe, and the United States, and went to Kenya as tourists. Many of these European men, used little babies, and little children as their child prostitutes, on various beaches of Kenya. The reporter went on to explained that many of these little children's become child prostitutes, because many of their parents are poor. So, because these Gentile tourist's men have the means of the money power, they exploited these little children to become prostitutes, to give them sexual pleasure, with that of sodomy that is now known as homosexuals.

According to this reporter, none of these men who were engage in this child prostitution ring, was ever brought to justice, because the way the government of these countries see things, they do not want to spoil their money-making tourist's business. So, the trend continues, because of the love of money, and their tourist's industries business. Many of the countries of the land of Ham, and in the Caribbean depend on the tourist's business, to bring in wealth into their system, of corruption of prostitution to pollute, many of the people minds of these places. I have even seen this same documentary mentioned on the television, about many Gentile European tourist men, who left from Europe, Australia, the United States to go to the Philippine islands, and Cambodia, where they can have as many child prostitutes.

This was from the age of 6, 7, to 15-year-old, to give them sexual pleasure, because many of these children's parents are extremely poor, so many of these child prostitutes see these Gentile European men as a mean to escape from out of their poverty, because they have the money power. Also, many of these child prostitutes, and teenager of Cambodia, and the Philippine Island, hopping that many of these Gentile men who they have sex with, will eventually married to them, and to take them from out of their poverties. So, as to bring them to the United States, and Europe, where they will have a better life of wealth, where in my opinion they are living in a fantasy world of dream. So, from what I have written, one can see the fulfillment of the various prophecies I have mention, taking place before our very eyes. By the Gentile family, who are known as Europeans people, corrupting many of their captives people minds with all sort immorality, of UN Goldenness. Many of the wild animal life of the land of Ham have also becoming extinct, because of these Gentile people of Europe, who are there, many of whom, have been killing off many of the animals for sport, and game as they call it.

This is also to gain wealth, because they are a people who are the lovers of money, the lovers of the shedding of blood, and the lovers of the pleasure to killing. (Jeremiah Chapter 6, verse 22, and verse 23), there the Scripture speaks about a people "from the North Country", who is a very cruel, and wicked set of people, who have no mercy." Europe is also known in the Scripture as the people of the North, who are a very wicked, and cruel set of people, who have no mercy. Many of these prophecies, were spoken against the land of Ham, and his people, have caused many of our great civilization, skills, talents, and wealth to go to benefit many of our conquerors. They have used us, and our talent, and skills to their own gain, glory, and advantages. This also have caused many of our Hamite's people to want to washout themselves into the Gentile European looking people.

According to (Genesis Chapter 10, and verse 7), the first son of Cush was known as Seba, and the land of Seba is known today as Somalia and Ethiopia. I would like to mention that from the reading of (Genesis Chapter 10, and verse 7), there the Scripture did not mention anything about the land of Somalia. But only about the land of Seba that became known as the land of Ethiopia, which the name Ethiopia it is a Greek and Latin name. So, the name Somalia was a given name to a part of the captured land of Seba, by way of the Mohammedans, who became known as the Muslim people. According to Dictionary of the Bible, written by John L McKenzie, there he explained that the name Ethiopia came from the Greeks. This Greek name continued during the time of the Romans until present time. Dictionary of the Bible explained that the Greeks before the Romans spelled the name of Ethiopia as Aethiopia, so I do believe that the name Somalia came from the conquest of the Mohammedans Muslim people, who had conquered a part of the land of Seba, and name it Somalia. They have also converted many of these people to their religious belief of Islam, by way of the sword, and the Quran to the worship of their god Allah. According to (Genesis Chapter 10, and verse 7), there the Scripture explained that the second son of Cush was known as Havilah, but the Scripture Map of 1890, did not show the land of Havilah on the Scripture Map.

But according to (Genesis Chapter 2, reading from verse 11), there it mentioned that a river came from out of the Garden of Eden, and this river was parted, and became four different heads of rivers. The first river head that came from out of the Garden of Eden, did compassed, or surrounded the whole land of Havilah. This river head that the Scripture spoke of, was known as Psion that is mentioned in (Genesis Chapter 2). This land that is mentioned in (Genesis Chapter 2, and verse 11), was named after Cush's second son, whose name was known as Havilah. I do believe that the land of Havilah is now known as the land of Nubia. My reason for making this kind of statement, it is because the Scriptural Map of 1890, along with the reading of (Genesis Chapter 10, and verse 7), shows that all the family of the people of Ham in that time used to live very closely together in the land of Ham, and Canaan.

Also, the Scripture Map shows that the sons of Cush used to live very closely tother, in the land area of their father, whose land area was known as the land of Cush. The land of Cush is known today Sudan, where Cush were living. This is according to the Scripture Map, of 1890, showing the land of Cush on the map, of the ancient world that gone by. (Genesis Chapter 2, and verse 11), went on to explained that the second river head that came from out of the Garden of Eden, did compassed the whole land of Seba that is known today as Ethiopia. So, when I look at the Scripture Map, and compare it with the world map of today, the land of Seba is now known as Ethiopia, that is very close to the land of Sudan, which was the land of Cush, the father of Seba, and Havilah. So, from what is written in (Genesis Chapter 2, and verse 11), one can clearly see that the Garden of Eden were somewhere in what became known as East Africa. I must say that although they Gentile people of Europe, have try to keep this knowledge away from the minds of the people of Ham, yet Yahweh in His own time as brought out this knowledge to light. To benefit many of the people of Ham, and also that of other people of the world at large, so as to come to this knowledge of truth. Because the Garden of Eden was nowhere in what became known as the Gentile lands of Europe, as how these Gentile people of Europe would have many people of today to believe. My reason for making this kind of statement, it is because in the various translations of the Scripture, that became known as the Bible, that was translated by these Gentile people of what became known as the European people. They have always showed the various characters of the Bible, looking like the Gentile people of Europe. This they do, to fool many people of today, who do not have any knowledge of where the Garden of Eden was, for them to believe that the Garden of Eden was somewhere in Europe.

Because when one read the Scripture, and seeing these Bible characters in the Scripture looking like the Gentile people of Europe, right away a person who do not have much knowledge about the true history of where the Garden of Eden was. Would think to themselves that all people on planet earth came from the Gentile people of Europe. Who they may have believe was the original people, Yahweh had created in the beginning of time, and put there in the garden of Eden. They would not have the knowledge, or the understanding of the reading of the Scripture, that the Garden of Eden where all the human family is coming from, was somewhere in what became known as East Africa.

This was before Yahweh did destroyed all those people during the time of Noah, and his family, who Yahweh spared their lives, to repopulate the earth, that did bring about all the people of today, who are living on planet earth. They the people of Europe, do these things to deceive many people who do not have the true knowledge and understanding of where the Garden of Eden were located. So, many people of today who do not have much knowledge of the ancient world, would think to themselves that the Garden Eden, were in Europe. Because when a person read the Scripture, and see all these Bible character looking like the people of Europe, right away they would think to themselves that Adam, and Eve were some European looking people. Also that the Garden of Eden was somewhere in Europe, when it was in the land of Ham, and not in Europe. So, in that time there were no Kenya, Uganda, the Congo's, or that of the many various modern colonial names, that was given to the various countries of the land of Ham, that are shown on the modern world maps of today. As how they are so named, to deceive many people who do not know any different about the true history of the land of Ham, and his people. I must also point out that the ancient people of Nubia, or the land of Havilah were very skillful in making things out of gold, long before the Gentile people of Europe started the making of these things out of gold, as a part of their modern industry of technology of today. These Nubians people were also conquered by the Mohammedans when they did conquered the land of Havilah, and named the land as Nubia. According to (Genesis Chapter 2, and verses 12, and verse 13), there the Chapter explained that the land of Havilah was a land of gold that had all sorts of precious stones. But sad to say that most of the gold, and precious stones are all gone since the conquest of the Gentile people of Europe, and also that of the Mohammedans Muslim people, of what became known as the Saudi Arabian people, of the so-call Middle East.

According to (Genesis Chapter 10, and verse 7), the land that was known as the land of Sheba, was named after one of Cush's grandsons, whose name were known as Sheba. Sheba was the first son of the fourth son of Cush, whose name was known as Raamah. From the land of Sheba came a lady who was known as the Queen of Sheba, because she was the Queen, and a citizen of the land of Sheba. The land of Sheba is known today as the land of Yemen, because the land of Sheba was also conquered by the Mohammedans Muslim people, who had conquered the land, and name the land as Yemen.

This was after the breakup of the Persian, Greek, Roman Empire, and that of the Turks conquest, who also had ruler ship over the so-called Middle East, and what became known as North Africa. These people of the land of Sheba were also converted to Islam by the Quran and the sword, by the Mohammedans Muslim people, of Saudi Arabia, to the worship of their god Allah. The land of Sheba is located at the very foot part of the land area of what became known as the land of Saudi Arabia. Which this land area of the country of Sheba, is very close to the land area of Seba, known today as Ethiopia. The land of Ophir is also mentioned in the (Scripture book of Isaiah Chapter 13, and verse 12), as the land of gold. This information is also showing on the Scripture Map of 1890, as the land of Ophir, that is at the very bottom of the land of Sheba. Near to the land area of what is now known as Ethiopia, which was a land of gold. As I had mention before that all these people of the land of Sheba, was related to Cush. I must also point out that according to the reading of the Scripture, the land of Sheba was a very rich, and powerful kingdom before the land of Sheba was conquered by the various conquerors mentioned above. To prove my point that what I am saying about the riches of the ancient kingdom of Sheba is true. At (First King Chapter 10, starting from verse 1 to verse 2), there the Scripture explained that the queen who came from the land of Sheba, brought some of the riches from her land, when she went to visit King Solomon at Jerusalem. Again, most of the riches of the land of Sheba are all gone since the conquest of the Gentile people of Europe, also that of the Mohammedans Muslim people of the land area that became known as Saudi Arabia. (Genesis Chapter 10 and verse 7), went on to explained that the second grandson of Cush, were known as Dedan. According to the Scripture Map of 1890, showing the land of Dedan, that is very close to the borderline of the land area of his father Raamah, that did became known as the land of Saudi Arabia.

These people of the land of Dedan were also conquered, and converted to Islam by the Quran, and the sword, and became known as the land of the United Arab Emirates. This country of the land of Dedan is also known today as the land of Dubai, and the Arab, and Muslim people. This land of Dedan is not too far away from the land of Shinar, which was the land area of Nimrod, who was the last son of Cush. This land area of Shinar is known today as the Persian Gulf, when comparing the Scriptural Map of 1890, with that of the world map of today.

The land of Raamah was not too far away from where the Ishmaelite people were living, which was really in the land of Raamah, that became known as the land of the Saudi Arabian people of Ishmael. This was because a little part of the land area of Raamah, was given to Ishmael by his mother Hagar to settle on, because at the time of Ishmael and Hagar, these people were one family of the people of Ham, living very closely together. This land area of the people of Ishmael, was name after the ninth son of Ishmael, whose name were known as Tema. This information about Team, can be found at (Genesis, Chapter 10, and verse 8). The Scripture explained that the sixth, and last son of Cush was known as Nimrod. This land area of Nimrod, is known in Genesis Chapter 10, and verse10, as the land of Shinar, where Nimrod had four different kingdoms in the land area of Shinar. This land area of Shinar, is in the land area of Canaan, that became known as the so-call Middle East, and the Persian Gulf. This name Persian Gulf were given to the land of Shiner, as the Persian Gulf, by the Gentile people of Europe. This was to cause confusion, and to deceive other people, who may not have this Scripture knowledge, about the land of Shinar, as I do. I am not quite sure if the renaming of the land of Shinar was done by the Persians, who did conquered the so-called Middle East, and what became known as North Africa, Babylon, all the way to the Greek Turkey area of Europe, as a part of the Persian Empire. This happens when they the Persian became powerful, and take over power of Babylon's, as the prophecy of (Daniel Chapter 2, and Daniel Chapter 7) did foretell of the conquest of the Persian, of the kingdom of Babylon. So, the renaming of the land of Shinar could have also done by Alexander the Great, and his generals, who did take away power from the Persians, when he conquered the so-called Middle East, and what become known as North Africa from the Persians, all the way to Persia, and what became known as the land area of India.

Looking at the Scriptural Map of 1890, showing the land of Shinar, that was close to the waterway that became known as the Persian Gulf, where Nimrod had various kingdoms there, that was in the land area of what is now known, as a part of the so-call Middle East. Furthermore, (Genesis Chapter 11, starting from verse 1 to verse 2), clearly explained that all the families of the three sons of Noah were living very closely together in the land area of Shinar. Which was the land area of the various kingdoms of Nimrod, and speaking the same language, before they the Gentile people were scattered into the Gentile land of what became known as the land area of Europe.

So, all the Gentile people knowledge, craft, and skills, that they now named as science, and technology, came from the people of Ham, who they were living among for centuries, before they were scattered by the power of Yahweh into what is now known as the land of Europe. The Scripture Map also shows the land of Elam, and the land of Persia, where Shem had settled after the flood of Noah, that was not too far away from the land area that was known as the land of Shinar. The Scripture Map also shows the land of Raamah, and Dedan that was very close to this strip of waterway that is presently known as the Persian Gulf. According to (Genesis Chapter 10), the beginning of the kingdom of Nimrod was started in the land of Shinar with the city of Babel, which was in the land of Shinar, where the people were building a tower to reach up to heaven, which is known in the Scripture as the Tower of Babel. According to (Genesis Chapter 11, verse 4, to verse 8), Yahweh came down and confused the language of the people, who were building the Tower of Babel to reach up to heaven, causing them to stop from building the Tower of Babel, because they could not understand each other's speech. This same (Chapter 11 of the book of Genesis) went on to explained that all the people of that time, who were building the Tower of Babel, used to speak the same language, and were living closely together. Verse (8 of Genesis Chapter 11) explained that after Yahweh scattered the people throughout the earth, to stop them from building the Tower of Babel. So, from then came about the different languages many people speak today, that came from the original stock of the people who were building the tower of Babel to reach up to heaven. According to the Scripture Map of 1890, the city of Babylon was in the land of Shinar, so the name Babylon came from the city of Babel, where Nimrod, and his companions were building the Tower to reach up to heaven.

Looking at the world map of today, and comparing it with the Scripture Map of 1890, the land of Babylon was not too far from the land of Haran, now known as the land of Iraq. This land of Babylon became known today as Kuwait, because this land area was also conquered later by the Mohammedans after the Persian, Greeks, Romans, and the Turks. From these sons and grandsons of Cush gave birth to what was known as the Cushites Empire. This was from the land of Canaan, to the land of Ham that did became known as North Africa, to what become known as East Africa.

Then came along the rest of the Gentile family who came from out of the brake up of the Roman Empire, and spread themselves over what became known as Africa, and the so-call Middle East, as their colonies of their conquests. According to (Genesis Chapter 10, and verse 10), the other cities of Nimrod were also located in the land of Shinar, which was the city of Erech, Accad and Calneh that was in the land of Canaan, closer to Persia, and what became known as the land of Saudi Arabia. Which was indeed, the land area of Raamah, the fourth son of Cush as the Scripture Map of 1890 clearly show on the map. According to the Scripture book of (Micah Chapter 5, and verse 6), there it mentions that the kingdom of Assyria, which was also one of the other kingdoms of Nimrod, was also located in the land area of Shinar. According to a big King James Version of the Bible, I have in my position, that was printed in 1946, in section that is called Dictionary of the Bible, there it mentioned that the city of Nineveh which was the capital of city of the kingdom of Assyria, was located near the Tigris River area, of the so-call Middle East. According to the Encyclopaedia Britannia this city of Nineveh was destroyed in 612 BC by the Medes, the Persians, and the Babylonians, who were under Persian rule ship at the time. The final, destruction of the people of the city of Nineveh, was by a people who were known as the Scythians. According to volume 10 of the Encyclopaedia, there it explained that the Scythians people, originated from what is known today as Iran. Which was the land of Persia, who later migrated to Central Asia, and southern Russia, during the time of the 8th, and 7th century BC. When looking at the Scripture Map of 1890, there it show that this city of Nineveh was very close to the rear of the land of Haran, that is now known as Iraq. I must also mention that when Yahweh told Abraham to leave from the city of Ur of Chaldea, which was a city of Babylon, where he was born and raised. Abraham just left from the part of the land of Canaan, to go to the other side of the land area of where the Canaanite people were mostly living.

This was to take over the land of the Canaanite people, Yahweh did gave to him, and his descendants after him. So, Abraham just left from one part of the land area of Canaan, to go to the other side of the land of Canaan, where the various kingdoms of the Canaanites people were located. According to (Genesis Chapter 11, and verse 31), when Abraham left from the city of Ur of Chaldea of Babylon, with his father Terah, and also with his nephew Lot, and Sarah his wife, who was also his sister by his father side.

They stopped off in the land of Haran, now known as Iraq, and Terah died in the land of Iraq at the age of 205 years old. I must also mention that Terah had a son, whose name were known as Haran, but according to (Genesis Chapter 11, and verse 28), Haran died in the city of Ur of Chaldea of Babylon. So, the name Haran was the original name of the country of Iraq, before the country of Haran became known as Iraq. So, the name Haran, of the country of Iraq, did not come from the name of Terah son, whose name was known as Haran. So, Abraham and his family did stopped off in the land of Haran, and took up residency there, before he went over to other side, where the Canaanite people were living. According to (Acts Chapter 7, and verse 4) there it mentioned that while Abraham was living in what became known as Mesopotamia, which is now known as the area of Iraq. He ands his family members were living in the city of Charran. When looking at the world map of today, there is no more mentioning, or the showing of the kingdom of Assyria, which was to the rear of the land of Iraq. The reason why the land area of Assyria is no longer showing on the modern world maps of today, it is because the land area of Assyria was taken over by what became known as Iraq, and it became a part of the land area of Iraq. The reason why there is no more showing of the land area of Assyria on the world map of today, it is because as I have mention before that many of the old names of the various countries mention in Scriptural time have change by various conquerors. I would also like to point out that, the land of Haran that became known as Iraq, were also conquered by the Mohammedans Muslim people, before the conquest of Haran by the Mohammedans, and the land was called Mesopotamia by the Greeks. Who had conquered the land area of Haran from the power of the Persians, who had all the so-called Middle East, and what become known as North Africa, as a part of their empire.

This was way before the coming up of the Mohammedans Muslim people of Mohammed. According to volume 8 of the Encyclopaedia, and volume 21 of the Encyclopaedia, there it explained that the name Mesopotamia meant to the Greeks, a land that is between two rivers, which was speaking of the Tigris, and the Euphrates Rivers area. Volume 21 of the Encyclopaedia went on to explained that the name Iraq, is associated with the name of A-Jumhriy-Ah or Iraqyah, which was the name of a person who came from what is known today as Saudi Arabia.

I would also like to say that this land of what is now known as Iraq, was the same land area where Abraham sent his eldest servant to take from there a wife from among his family members, who were living there for his son Isaac, who was living among the Canaanites, and the Philistine people of the area of the Garza strip. This was the same land of what is now known as Iraq, where Rebekah sent her youngest son Jacob to stay with her brother there, until the wrath of his brother Esau was cooled off. This statement about Jacob and Esau was taken from (Genesis Chapter 27, and verse 42 through to verse 45).

According to Genesis Chapter 10, Canaan was the last son of Ham, from where the Canaanites families came from. This family of the Canaanite people were living in what is now known as a part of the so-call Middle East, of what is now known as Syria, Israel, Jordan, and Lebanon. The Phoenicians people came from Zidon, and Zidon himself was the first son of Canaan. But according to the Practical Polyglot Family Bible of 1875, in the section that is called the Household Dictionary of the Bible, there it explained that the name Sidon it is a Greek, and Latin name, that were given to the first son of Canaan, who was known as Zidon. From what I have read from the Encyclopaedia, in the Hebrew language, the name of Canaan's first son was also known as Tidn, but the spelling of his name in the Canaanite language is spelled as Zidon. It is more appropriate in the language of the Canaanite people who was also known as the Phoenician people, who came from the family of Zidon. So, the second son of Canaan were known as Heth, who gave birth to the Hethites tribe of people, who came from Heth, and Heth was the second sons of Canaan. Many of the Canaanites people who might be around in today, times are now known as the Middle Eastern people, Palestinian people, and the Arab people. Which these names are totally a false makeup name of the offspring of Canaan, who might have survived until today. My reason for expressing myself this way, it is because many of the Canaanites tribes, and their kingdoms were destroyed by Yahweh, on the behalf of the children of Israel, and for other Abrahamic seeds. So, many of the Canaanites tribes were also destroyed for Lots two sons, who were known as the Moabites, and the Benammi. From the tribe of Benammi gave birth to a people who were known as the children of Ammon, according to (Genesis Chapter 19, and verse 37, to verse 38). These tribe of people of Lot also had their kingdom in the land of Canaan.

Many of the Canaanites people, if any of them are still around in todays time, are now known as the Arab, and the Muslim people of Mohammed, and his followers. Because the land of Canaan was also conquered by the Mohammedans, after the Persians, Greeks, Romans, Turks, along with the other various European people who come from out of the brake up of the Roman Empire. So, if any of these Canaanites people might be around in today's times, they have become a part of the so-call Middle Eastern people.

Also, many of these Canaanites people, if any of them are still around in today time, have become a washout people of the melting pot of the various conquerors blood of the land of Canaan I have mention above. According to volume 25 of the Encyclopaedia Britannica, there it explained that the region of what the Roman did name as Palestine, was the eastern part of the Mediterranean. which did consist of what is now known as Israel, Jordan, and what is now known as Egypt, not for getting the land area of Carthage also. According to this same volume 25 of the Encyclopaedia Britannica page 402, there it explained that the Romans also did called what became known as Syria as Palaestina, from the second century AD, in which Syria was a Roman province also. So, from what is written, one can clearly see that the name Palestinian people, it is a false make up name, that were given by the Romans at the time of their conquest, and ruler ship over the land of Ham and Canaan. From what I came to understand by reading of different volume of the Encyclopaedia Britannica, the name Syria came from the conquest of Alexander the Great, and his generals, who came from the country of Macedonia, of the Gentile land of what became known as Europe. So, when these Greek people conquered the so-called Middle East from the Persian rulership, then this land of what became known as Syria meant to them, as little Greece. Because there was such a large population of Greek settlers who had settled there in the land of Zidon. According to the Household Dictionary of the Bible, the Phoenician people were the owners of the city of Tyre, and the Tyrian people were known as the Zidonians.

This dictionary also explained that the word Phoenicians was another name for the Canaanite people. According to the Webster Third New International Dictionary, there the dictionary explained that the name Sidonian, which did came from the name of Sidon, which is speaking of the descendants of Zidon. The Latin name for Zidon is spelled as Sidonii, but in the Greek language, the name Sidon is spelled as Sidonios, and in the French, and Hebrew language it is spell as Sidon. These people of Zidon were also known as the Zidonians who became known as the Phoenicians people, who were living there in the land of what is now known as Syria. According to the Webster's Colligate Dictionary, there it explained that the name Syria came from Latin, French, and Greek, and in the Greek language the name Syria is also spell as Syriakos.

According to (I Kings Chapter 16, and verse 31(, Jezebel, who was the wife of King Ahab, who was a king of Israel during the time of Jezebel, she was from the family line of Zidon, who was known as the Zidonians tribe of Zidon. According to this same Chapter that was mentioned, Jezebel was the daughter of Ethbal, who was a king of the Zidonians tribe of people. The last son of Canaan were known as Heth, from where the Hethites tribe of people came from, and they were also living in the land of Zidon, which is known today as the land of Syria. Household Dictionary of the Bible went on to explained that the Phoenician people were conquered by the Persians, the Greeks, meaning Alexander the Great, and later by the Romans, and other Gentile people of Europe, who came from out of the breakup of the Roman Empire. According to volume 9 of the Encyclopaedia, there it mentions that the ancient region of the Phoenician people, apart from their various colonies they had, was Jubal, but the new name of the city of Jubal was known as Byblos, which was also called as Jebeil. Which was an ancient seaport of Beirut Lebanon. This city of Byblos is where the Greek gave the name Bible, because the Papyrus plant that the Scripture was written on, were sent from the Phoenician city of Byblos to the Aegean Sea area of Greece. So, from what I have gathered from reading the Encyclopaedia Britannica, the Papyrus plant that the Scripture was written, on originally came from the land of Mizraim, that became known as Egypt. So, the name Bible simply meant to the Greeks a book. This city of Zidon was also known as Sayda, and the Phoenician people had called their city of Tyre as Tsor, but the Greeks named the city as Tyre or Tyros, which eventually became known as the city of Tyre. According to the Encyclopaedia, the Phoenician people had called another of their cities as Beirut, but the name Beirut was later changed by the Greeks to the name of Berot. But the Phoenician city of Beirut eventually did received back its Canaanite name as Beirut Lebanon. Volume 2 of the Encyclopaedia, explained that the city of Byblos or Beirut Lebanon, was one of the chief seaports for shipping cedar, and other valuable things to the land of Egypt.

The city of Beirut Lebanon, did became a great trading center, and the people of Egypt did called this city as Kubna. This city of Beirut Lebanon was also called Gubla in the Akkadian language of the Assyrian people of Nimrod. Volume 9 of the Encyclopaedia Britannica, explained that they are not sure of what the Phoenician people may have called themselves in their own language, but they think the Phoenician people may have called themselves Kanaani, or Kinahng.

The Encyclopaedia also explained that the word Canaanite in the Hebrew language, had a secondary meaning, which stands for the word merchants. It is also stated that the Phoenician city of Beirut Lebanon was a commercial, and religious center that was connected to the land of Egypt, from the 4th Dynasty. According to this same volume 9 of the Encyclopaedia, this time was from about 2,613 to about 2,494 BC; where there was an extensive trading that were taking place during the 16th Century BC. In which the people of Egypt eventually lost their strong hold over their Phoenician territory. According to the Encyclopaedia, in 9th Century BC, the independency of the Phoenician people was again threatened by the advancement of the Assyrian army. The Assyrians took over control of the territory of the Phoenicians people, until 538 BC, when the territory of the Phoenician people came under the ruler ship of the Persian. Who had take over power from the power of the Assyrian, and the land of the Phoenician people became their territory. The land of the Phoenicians people was also incorporated, and taken over, and become known as Syria by the Greeks, who defeated the Persians, meaning Alexander the Great, ands his army. The Encyclopaedia explained that the Phoenician people were a well-known set of colonizers, but by the time of the second Millennium BC, they had extended their influence along the area of what was known as Jeffa. According to the Encyclopaedia, the name Jaffa was changed to Yafo, which is a city of present-day Israel, known as the city of Tel Aviv. I must point out that what the writers of the Encyclopaedia failed to realize, and understand, is that the Canaanite people were the true natives of the land of what is now known as Israel. Although their land was given them by Yahweh, also the Moabites, and the Benammi people of Lot, who became known as the Ammonites tribe of people. Also, this blessing of Abraham were pass to the Ishmaelite people of Ishmael, who became known as the Saudi Arabian people, because of the promise Yahweh had made with Abraham, concern his first son Ishmael.

Also, this land of Canaan did consist of the various kingdoms of the different sons, and grandchildren of the people of Ham, who were living there in the land of Canaan, because the people of Ham during that time, was a large family of people, who were living very closely together. From the land area of what became known as East Africa, to what became known as North Africa, to the land of Canaan.

So I cannot understand how the writers of the Encyclopaedia can say that the Phoenician people were a set of colonizers of the city of Jaffa, which is now known as the city of Tel aviv, which indeed was their land area, of the ancient world that gone by. The Scripture Map of 1890, that is showing on the book cover of the Untold Forgotten Great Civilization of the people of Ham, also show the land area of the people of Ham, of his descendants borderline, of that ancient world. So, from what I have read from volume 9 of the Encyclopaedia, the Phoenicians people also had their kingdoms in a part of the land of what become known as the land of Turkey, that were known as the Anatolia. According to a map that is showing in volume 20 of the Encyclopaedia, showing the land area of Anatolia, which was in what become known as the land of Turkey of Europe. Where the Phoenicians, and the Hethites people of Heth, also had their various kingdoms there. Volume 9 of the Encyclopaedia also explained that there were several settlements of the Phoenician people, who were living in Spain. The people of Carthage of what became known as North Africa, also had rule ship over the land area of what did become known as Spain, until they were driven out by the Roman, when they became a power full set of people to deal with. Volume 9 of the Encyclopaedia explained that the Phoenician people before they were destroyed, were exporters of cedar, pinewood, and fine linen that did came from their city of Tire. Also, the Papyrus plant they did turned into paper, that the Scripture was written on, that did came from their city of Byblos, of Lebanon. The Phoenician people were also exporters of cloths, that were dyed with the famous Tyrian purple, that were made from snails.

They were also exporters of embroidery cloths that were made in their land of Zidon, now known as Syria. The Phoenician people were also exporters of wine, metal works, glass, salt and dried fish. They were also shipbuilders, and masters of sculpture of ivory, and wood. They were also was goldsmiths, and glass blowers that were also started by the Phoenician people. The Encyclopaedia also explained that the Phoenician alphabetical writing system, that did consisted of only 22 letters, was used in their city of Byblos, as early as 15th Century BC, that was later copied by the people of Greece, who became known as the Greek people, of the Gentile land of what is now known as Europe.

The Phoenician writing system later became the ancestors of the modern Gentile European alphabetical writing system, that gave birth to the writing of the English language. The Phoenician writing system also gave birth to the writing system of the various Germanic tribes of people. Also the Spanish writing system, and even the Latin writing system, that gave birth to what was called as the Romance language of Europe. Which did come from the Romans, the Greeks, and also from the Phoenician, Hethites and the writing system, of the people of Mizraim, now known as the Egyptian people. According to volume 29 of the Encyclopaedia, there it explain that the word alphabet came from the first two letters of the Greek word alphabet, which is spill as, alpha, and beta, that was first referred in its Latin form, as alphabetum. The word alphabetum came from Tertullian, who was a theologian Christian, who were born in the land of Carthage, in about 155-160 AD, according to volume 11 of the Encyclopaedia, who died around 220 AD in Carthage. Volume 11 of the Encyclopaedia went on to explained that Carthage at the time of Tertullian was second to Rome as far as culture, and education was concern, to that of the West, meaning Western Europe. Volume 29 of the Encyclopaedia explained that, as far as the theories of the alphabet origin is concern, evidence of the alphabetical source came exclusively from the land bordering the eastern Mediterranean shores. Which is speaking of the Canaanites land of the Phoenician people, of what is now known as Syria. This time was from about 1700, to 1500 BC, of the land of Canaan that is now known as Israel, and the so-call Middle Eastern people. Volume 29 of the Encyclopaedia explained that ie Greeks, and the Romans did considered five different nations of people, who were the inventor of the alphabetical writing system. Which were the Phoenicians, the Egyptians, the Hethites, and the Assyrians, and the Cretans people, and the Hebrew people.

I would also like to point out that, the people of Create could have been a Hamite's people who came from out of the family line of the people of Mizraim, now known as the Egyptian people. My reason for making this kind of statement, it is because when I was living in London during the early sixties, there were quite allot of people who came from the island of Cyprus, to live in London, as immigrants. Many of these people had woolly curly hair, just like that of many Hamite's people who is now known as the so-call African people, and the so-cal Black people, who have tight curly hair.

The island of Cyprus is not too far away from the island of Crete, when looking at the world Atlas, showing the island of Cyprus and the island of Crete, that is in the Mediterranean area, near to the country of Turkey. So, the people of Crete could have been an Hamite's people of the ancient world, who did also pass on their knowledge of writing and reading to the people of Greece, as did the Phoenicians, the Hethites, and the people of Mizraim, who also did so. Volume 29 of the Encyclopaedia further explained that the Phoenicians alphabetical writing system that was also called as Ahiram inscription, was found in their city of Byblos in what is now known as Lebanon, which was dated from about the 11th century BC. Volume 29 went on to explained that there is no doubt that the Greek did copy, and recopy the Phoenicians alphabetical writing system, that gave birth to all the writings that came down to the Gentile land, of what became known as Europe. The Phoenician writing system was also found in Cyprus, Malta, and Sicily, before the island of Sicily became a Roman province. Also, in Sardinia, Spain, and the city of Marseille that is a part of what is now known as France, as well of what become known as North Africa. According to this volume 29 of the Encyclopaedia, the Phoenician Aramaic writing scripts also found their way into Southeastern Asia, in the Persian scripts, that is known as the Iranian writing, which was known as the Pahlavi writings, that were used for the writing the pre-Islamic Persian literature. According to this same volume 29 of the Encyclopaedia, the Phoenician writing scripts did also find their way into Central Asia, in the second half of the first millennium AD. This writing were known as Kok Turki script, that were used from the 6th to the 8th century AD, by various Turkish tribe's men, who were living in the southern part of Central Siberia of Europe. Also, in northwestern Mongolia, and in northeastern Turkistan, in which this alphabet writing was the prototype of the early Hungarian alphabetical writing system.

This same volume 29 of the Encyclopaedia went on to explained that, the Phoenician people writing, did influence Tibetan, and that of the adopted writing of the Mongolian empire. So, the Phoenician Aramaic alphabet writing system, was also the prototype of the Brahmi script, of the land of Bharat that became known as the land of India, which did become the parent of nearly all the Indian writing.

According to this volume 29, of the Encyclopaedia, there it explained that the rise of Islam in the 7th century AD, and their conquest of a wide area of the earth gave them the opportunity to spread their holy book of the Quran to the so-call Middle East, North, and Central Africa. As well as to South East Asia, and in the southeastern part of Europe. As I had mention before that according to the Webster Colligate Dictionary, the word Arab came from Latin, Greek, and the French people as Arab people. So, the letter Ar, stand for the word Arab, which these people became known as the Arab people. Which was chiefly speaking of the area of what became known as the Saudi Arabian people of Ishmael. So many people of today who see themselves as the Arab people, were only conquered people, who were indoctrinated into the Islamic philosophy of Mohammed, and his followers, who became known as the Mohammedans, and the Muslim people. This writing alphabetical system of the people who became known as the Mohammedans 'and the Muslim people, also came from the people of Mizraim who became known as the Egyptian people. My reason for stating this fact, it is because Ishmael mother Hagar came from what is now known as Egypt. I am quite sure that the learning and the education of Ishmael, came from his mother Hagar, also from the people of Mizraim who he was living around while he was growing up as a young boy to manhood. This was in the land area of Raamah, now known as the land of Saudi Arabia, and Raamah was the fourth son of Cush. This alphabetical writing system of the so-call

Arab people, also came from the Phoenician script, and the various Hamite's kingdoms of the land of Canaan, now known as Israel, who had a great impact on these Saudi Arabia people of Ishmael, culture, and ways of life.

According to this same volume 29 of the Encyclopaedia, the Arabic alphabet writing system probably originated sometime in the 4th century AD, but the earliest extant of the Arabic writing came from the Greek, Syriac to the Arabic of AD 512. This volume 29 went on to explained that the two form of Arabic writing that did developed, in the Muslim period, were the Kufic that came from the town of Kufah, in what is now known as Mesopotamia that also became known as Iraq, by the conquest of the Mohammedans Muslim people. The Encyclopaedia also explained that the Phoenician people used to worship many gods, that were made of gold, and other items. One of the Canaanite gods that many of the children of Israel used to worship as their god, were known as Baal Peor, which is mentioned many times in the Scripture.

I must also mention that many of the people of that time, and even in our current time, were not worshippers of Yahweh who gave them all that knowledge, wisdom, and skills. Simply because many people of that time did not know anything about the worship of Yahweh, apart, from the children of Israel. Whom He gave His name, His Laws, and His commandments to keep true out all their generations. I must also point out that the conquest of Spain by the Moors that came from the Mohammedans, Who became known as the Muslim people. Was way after the decline of the powers of the Phoenician, and the Hethites, and the Carthaginian powers, ruling over a part of the Gentile land that is now known as Europe. So, the powers of the Mores also came about after the breakup of the Roman Empire of Western, and Eastern Europe. Also, after the various powers of what become known as North Africa, and what they name as the Middle East came to its end, by way of various conquerors who Yahweh did used to destroy the various kingdoms of the people of Ham, who He was not pleased with.

According to (Genesis Chapter 10, and verse 15), there it explained that the last son of Canaan was known as Heth, from where the Hethites tribe of people came from. According to volume 5 of the Encyclopaedia, there it explained about the people who they spelled, and called as the Hittites tribe, who they say were a member of an ancient Indo-European race of people. Which this statement of their is a totally a false statement and a lie. My reason for saying it is a false statement, and a lie, it is because there were no such a people who were known as the Indo Hittites race of people during Scriptural time. like how the Encyclopaedia, and other writings of the Gentile people of Europe would have many people of today to believe, and think of their false history of lies. So, when the Encyclopaedia described the Hethites as the Indo European race of people, what they are actually saying, is that these people, who they spelled as Hittites, were an Indian descendant people. Who came from the land of Bharat, now known as India, into the land area that is now known as Europe. The truth of the matter is that these people they called, and spell as Hittites, came from the land of Zidon now known as Syria, which was a tribe that came from Heth. Heth himself was the father of the Hethites tribe of people, that the Gentile people spell as Hittites, who was the last son of Canaan. These Hethites people had no originality with the land of Europe, or with the land that became known as India.

These Indian people of the East, who are now known as the Asiatic people of today, came from Shem, who was the first son of Noah, who had settled into that part of the world when Yahweh confuse the language, and scattered the people true out earth. This was to stop them from building the Tower of Babel. So, the Hethites people of Canaan, who they spell as Hittites, have no connection with the people of what the Gentile people called as the Indo-European people. As how they would have many people of today to believe in their lies of false history. Many of whom came under their colonial captivity of false teaching, and lies. In our our modern times of today, the Gentile people have given these people of Shem a new name, and a new identity of the land area they call as the Asiatic people of Asia. Which there were no such a people who were known as the Asiatic people of ancient world, before the Scripture were given to the children of Israel by Yahweh.

So, the term and name as the Asiatic people, it is a false identity, and a false name that was given to these people of Shem, by the people of Europe. According to this same volume 5 of the Encyclopaedia, the Indo Hittites race of people, were living in an area of Europe that were known as the Anatolia area of Europe at the beginning of the second Millennium BC. So, this word second Millennium BC, that was mentioned, stands for two thousand years. As I have mentioned before that the area of the world that was known as Anatolia, was in what is known today as the land of Turkey. The spelling of the word Hittites is totally a wrong spilling in the way the Encyclopaedia spelled the word Hittites. My reason for saying this is, all the people on planet earth of today came from the three sons of Noah, and their wives, who were known as Shem, Ham and Japheth, and this was after the flood of Noah. So, there were no Indo Hittites race of people who came from the three sons of Noah during that time. According to (Genesis Chapter 10, and verse 32), all the families of the earth of today, came from Noah three sons, after the flood of Noah, and the earth was divided between them, and their offspring's. According to the Scripture Map of 1890, and the Encyclopaedia map of volume 20, showing where the Hethites and the Phoenician people was living, which was the land of Zidon and his brother Heth, and their many descendants that is now known as the land of Syria, to the Jordan area, to Lebanon of the so-call Middle East. According to the Webster's Third International Dictionary, there the dictionary explained that the name hindu or hindoo was taken from the word India, that originally came from the Latin language, of the Romans, and that of the Greeks. This name India was passed down the line to the various Germanic Celtic barbarian people, who became known as the French, and the Anglo Saxon people. Who also came from out of the brake up of the Roman Empire, and who were educated by the Roman, and the Roman Catholic Church, who had ruler ship over these people.

Before the conquest of the Greeks of what became known as India, these people of the land of Bharat were known as the Hindu people by the Persians, who also were their next-door neighbors, all of whom were the descendants of Shem, the first son of Noah. According to the Webster Colligate Dictionary, there it also explained that the word Indo came from the Greek that also came down into the French language, as Indos. In the Latin language of the Roman, the name Indo, and Indos became known as Indus, and India, that stud for the people of Bharat, who became known as the East India people.

According to volume 6 of the Encyclopaedia, there it also verified that the land of what is now known as India, were known as the land of Bharat, before the land was conquered by the Various Gentile European powers of the land that became known as Europe. Last of all these Gentile conquerors, who came and conquered the land of Bharat, to be a part of their domain, were the Portuguese. Then came the British, and conquered the land area from the Portuguese, that did become a British colony. When the Greeks conquered the land of Bharat, then they named these people as Indo people. When the Romans came and conquer Greece, and take over their territories, then they named these people of Bharat as the land of India. So, one can clearly see from the tracing out from the Scripture, and the Scripture Map of 1890, and even the map of the Encyclopaedia Britannica, that there were no such a people who were known as the Indo-European Hittites. Whom the Encyclopaedia, and other writings of the Gentile European people, describe these Hethites people as Indo-European. Who they say these people settled down in what became known as the land of Europe, as they would have the world of people of today to believed in their lies of false history. Although the Encyclopaedia, and the dictionaries of the various writings of the Gentile people spoke about these people, as the Indo European Hittites, which there is no truth in their story.

They have totally deceived many people who came under their captivity of schooling, with false information, and false history of lies, of their teaching. (Genesis Chapter 10, and verse 2 to verse 5), clearly explained that these Gentile people of what is now known as Europeans, were known in Scriptural time as the Gentile people of Japheth. So, there is no connection between the people of India, and the Gentile people of what is now known as European people, who they would have us to believe as being the Indo-European Hittites people. According to the Encyclopaedia, by the time of 1340 BC, these Hittites became one of the dominant powers of the so-called Middle East, that was also called at one time as the Near East people. To give one another good example of how hypocritical, devilish, wicked, and deceptive these Gentile people of Japheth has been to the world of people, who came under their captivity, with brainwashing, and false teaching, of lies. I say this because they the Gentile people of today, are the ones who have all the written records of the ancient world, of what was, and of the various records of the modern history of today.

Yet, according to the Polygot Family Bible of 1782, that was written by these same Gentile people of what became known as the United States of America. There it is written by J.R. Jones, in the office of the Library of Congress, in Washington, DC, in section that is called the Household Dictionary of the Bible. There it clearly mentions that the Hethites the Encyclopaedia spelled as Hittites, and the Indo-European people, were a descendant of the last son of Canaan, who was known as Heth, and Heth was the father of this tribe of people. The Polygot Family Bible went on to explained that Abraham brought from this descendant of Heth, a field, and a cave that were known as Machpelah, that did belong to a person by the name of Ephron. Who was a son of Zohar, and Zohar himself was a member of the Hethites family. (Genesis Chapter 2, and verse 9), explained that Abraham bought this cave from Machpelah to be a burial place, to bury his wife Sarah, and also, other family members, who would later follow in death. Verse (19 of Genesis Chapter 23) states that Abraham buried his wife Sarah in the cave of the field of Machpelah, in the city of Mamre that was also known as the city of Hebron in the land of Canaan, that is now known as Israel. According to (2nd Samuel Chapter 11, and verse 3), there it shows that Uriah who was a member of the Hethites tribe, who was also a soldier in the army of David, and who was the husband of David's sweetheart whose name was known as Bathsheba. Bathsheba became the mother of King Solomon of the children of Israel, and she and her first husband Uriah came from the family line of the Hethites tribe of Canaan. According to (2nd Samuel Chapter 11, starting from verse 4 to verse 27), there the Scripture mentions that King David had sex with the wife of Uriah, because she was a very beautiful woman to look at. So, she became pregnant by David, and David tried all sorts of tricks to have Uriah to sleep with his wife Bathsheba, by so doing, he could pass off this pregnancy of his to Uriah, as his child. However, because Uriah did not fall for any of David's tricks, David decided to have Uriah to be killed in a battle of war. According to the Chapter, David gave Uriah a note to give to the general of his army.

This note was for the general to put Uriah at the front line of the battle, and to have the rest of the army pull back from Uriah, so that he would be killed in the battle of war, and after the death of Uriah, David take the wife of Uriah to be one of his wives. According to volume 5 of the Encyclopaedia, the Hittites tribe probably came from the area of the Black Sea, which is the Greek Turkey area of Europe, which is totally a false statement, and a lie.

The Encyclopaedia further explained that the Hittites first occupied Central Anatolia, and made it their capital. The early king of the old Hithites kingdom was known as Hattusilis the first, who reigned from about 1650 to 1620 BC, and who extended the Hithites control over much of the area of Anatolia, and what become known as Syria. Volume 5 of the Encyclopaedia explained that the writing of the Hethites system was called Hieroglyphics; and this writing of the Hethites begins at the upper right-hand corner of their alphabetical writing system. The Encyclopaedia explained that there appears to be no direct connection between the Hethites Hieroglyph writing, and the Hieroglyph writing of the people of Mizraim who became known as Egyptian people. I must point out that I did not cover all the various writing, and history about the Hethites tribe from volume 5 of the Encyclopaedia. Also, about the Greeks, and the people of Ashkenaz, known today as Turkey, who also did received their education from the Phoenician, the Hethites, and the people of Mizraim of their writing abilities, that was passed on to the Romans, and that of the rest of the Gentile land that became known as Europe. The Roman civilization is a continuation of the civilization of the people of Ham that did extended itself to what become known as Europe, by way of the Greeks, and later to the Romans. The reason why I mentioned the Hethites who also gave their civilization to the people of the Greece, and the Turkey area of what is now known as Europe, it is because the Hethites tribe that the Encyclopedia spelled as Hittites were livening in the Anatolia area of what is now Turkey, near to a people who were known as the Phrygian. Volume 9 of the Encyclopaedia explained that, the Phrygian people perhaps came from a people who were known as the Thracians. However, I did check out the L to Z Index of the Encyclopaedia, to see if I could find some information about the Thracian people. But unfortunately I could not find any trace of history about these people background.

According to volume 9 of the Encyclopaedia, the Phrygian people did settle down into what was known as northwestern Anatolia, in the late second two thousand BC, after the Hittites moved their capital to another part of the Anatolia area that was known as Gordium. Volume 5 of the Encyclopaedia, explained that what were known as Gordium, was an ancient Anatolian city, that was located along the bank of the Sangarius River of what is now Turkey. This city of the Hethites people became a flourishing capital for the people of Phrygia from the 9th to the 8th century BC, that were a religious center of the city of Midas.

According to volume 8 of the Encyclopaedia, there it explained that the city of Midas flourish from about 700 BC, with a question sign, in what is now known as Turkey, that was ruled by a Phrygian king who was known as Gyges. According to the Encyclopaedia, King Gyges was mention in Greek literature, by Herodotus who dedicated his throne at Delphi to one of the Greek gods of Greece. According to volume 5 of the Encyclopaedia, there it mentioned that King Gyges ruled the area of Lydia, of western Anatolia from 680 to 648 BC. Volume 9 of the Encyclopaedia explained that between the 12th, and 9th century BC, the Phrygian people formed a scattered settlement that did became known as the Mushki people. According to a record from the Encyclopaedia, about the history that were taken from the Assyrians people, the Phrygian people did dominate the entire area of the Anatolia peninsula. According to volume 1 of the Encyclopaedia, the Phrygian people civilization was heavily borrowed from the Hethites people of Heth. The Phrygian god Attis, along with the Great Mother Cyble, who were known as the mother of the gods to the Greek people, and also to the Latin people of Troy, of the Greek Turkey area of Europe. Who became a part of the religious gods of Rome, that came from the Phrygian people. From these two sons of Canaan that was mentioned, came the family of the Canaanite people, such as the Jebusite, Amorite, Sinites, Girgasite Arvadite, the Hivite, the Arkite, and the Zidonians. There were also the Canaanite kingdom of Admah, Zeboim, Lasha, and the kingdom of Sodom, and Gomorrah, that was near the Dead Sea, and the valley of Salt, in what is now known as Israel.

According to a map of the Encyclopaedia, showing this place that was not too far from the land area of Jordan. This information is also, according to the Scripture Map of 1890, showing the land of Sodom and Gomorrah that was near the Dead Sea area of the land of Canaan. There were also the Canaanite kingdom of OG, and also the kingdom of the country of Bashan, whom the children of Israel, with Moses kill, and take over their lands. This was when they the children of Jacob, came from out of the land of Mizraim, now known as Egypt.

This statement is according to (Numbers Chapter 21, verse 34, and verse 35), where it is mentions about the kingdom of Sihon, who were a king of the Amorite tribe, who were living in the land of Canaan that was known as the city of Heshbon. According to the Scripture Map, this place was near the River Jordan, that was also known as the River Arnon. According to (Deuteronomy Chapter 2, and verse 24), there it mentions that Moses, with the rest of the children of Israel who were with him, with the power of Yahweh, killed the king of Sihon, and take over his land, and his kingdom. This was the same citation for the kingdom of the Amorite tribe, who were living in the city of Heshbon, who the children of Israel kill with the power of Yahweh, and take over their cities, and it became a part of Israel. The reason why I mention with the power of Yahweh that was behind the ancient children of Israel, as the Scripture clearly mentioned. It is because many of the Amorites, and other Hamite's tribe of the land of Canaan, were known as men of giants, and giant tribe of people. So, there is no way the children of Israel by themselves could have defeated these tribes of people in battle, by themselves, if the power of Yahweh was not with them. Even the children of Israel testified of themselves, when Moses sent out spies from the Jordan area of Jericho, for them to go and check out the land of the Canaanite people. The report they brought back to Moses that is recorded in (Numbers Chapter 13, and verse 33), is that they saw the sons Anak, who were of the giant tribe of the Canaanite people. They the children of Israel went on to explained to Moses, that they saw the tribe of the Anakim, and they the children of Israel were like grasshoppers in the eye, and sight of these people, because they were a very tall set of people, before they were all destroyed by Yahweh, for the children of Israel. There were also the kingdom of the Emims who were known as a giant tribe, that is mentioned in Deuteronomy (Chapter 2, and verse 10).

There the Scripture mentioned that Moses told the children of Israel when they were in the Jordan area, they must not interfere with the Moabite people of Lot, who were living in the land of the Emims. Because Yahweh destroyed this tribe of the Emims, and gave their land to the Moabite people who named this tribe as the Emims. The reason why Yahweh destroyed this tribe of the Emims, and gave their lands to the Moabite people, was because Lot was the father of the Moabite people, and Lot was the nephew of Abraham. Even Lot wife were from the city of Sodom, that were in the Jordan area of the land of Canaan, where Lot and his wife were living.

According to (Genesis Chapter 12, and Chapter 13, to verse 10), when Lot and Abraham left from Ur of Chaldees of Babylon, to go where the Canaanites people were mostly living, to take over their land, Yahweh gave to him Abraham. Lot went with him, and take up residency in the city of Sodom. So, Lot two daughters were from a Canaanites woman of Jordon, when he became a citizen of Sodom. According to Deuteronomy (Chapter 2, and verse 10), before this tribe of the Emims was destroyed, they were known as a giant tribe. They were also tall as the giant tribe who were known as the Anakims, who were considered as a giant tribe of people of Canaan. According to Deuteronomy (Chapter 1, verse 28, and Chapter 2, verse 11), there it mention of the people of the Anakims, who were a giant tribe, like that of the Emims people of Canaan. (Deuteronomy Chapter 9), starting from verse 1, there the Scripture explain that Moses told the children of Israel, when they were going into the land of the Canaanites, that they were going to pass over Jordan, to go, and possess nations who were mightier than themselves, whose had great cities, that were great, and fenced up to heaven. These people were a great tribe, and were tall as the Anakims giant people of Canaan. Who they the children of Israel knew of, and who it has been said, "who can stand before the children of Anak, which is speaking of the Anakims tribe of Canaan, because these people of the Emims were giants tribe, like the Anakims. The Anakims was also a giant tribe from the land of Canaan, who were destroyed by Yahweh for various Abrahamic seed, that became a part of the so-call Middle Eastern people as it is called today. (Genesis Chapter 10, and verse 19), there the verse explained that the borderline of the land of the Canaanite people, was from the land of Zidon known today as Syria, which is near to the country of Turkey of Europe. The Chapter also mentions that the Canaanite land was also from the area of Gerar to Gaza, which was the land of the Philistine people.

Also, near the land border of Mizraim, and near to the borderline of the land area of the people of Shem, who were known as Elam, and Elam became known as Persia, that is now known as Iran of Asia. Sad to say that many of these names of the land area I have mentioned above are no longer around with us today, because many of these people were destroyed by Yahweh; and their lands were given to Israel.

Many of the names of the land of Canaan, and the land of Ham have been changed by various conquerors to suit themselves. This is the reason why many of these conquered lands of today, do not have the Scriptural names that is mentioned in the Scripture, as how they use to have during Scriptural time. This is because of colonial conquest by the children of Israel, Persians, Greek, Romans, Turks, the and by the Ishmaelite people of Ishmael. Also that of the rest of the Gentile European people who came from out of the brake up of the Roman Empire. I must also mention about the kingdom of Jericho where Rahab the harlot was living, which were a Canaanite kingdom of the Jordan area, according to (Joshua Chapter 2, and verse 1, also (Joshua Chapter 6, and verse 17). Sad to say that many of these tribes of Hamite's people were wiped out, along with the Philistine people, who originally came from out of the family of Mizraim, who had their kingdoms in the Grazer strip of the land of Canaan. This was because of the children of Israel, and for other Abrahamic seeds of the land, because Yahweh was not pleased with many of these people of Ham. Many other Hamite's tribes were also wiped out on behalf of the descendants of Lot, and Esau's children, all who had Hamite's mothers, who gave birth to the various descendants of these people I have mentioned above. These people of Abraham, and Lot became a nation of people in the land of Ham, and Canaan, who had their descendants there with the local Hamite's native women, of the area.

Many of the Canaanite lands are known today as the land of Israel, and they have taken their toll on the Canaanites, who did not get wiped out, during the time of the children of Israel taking over the land of Canaan. Many of the Canaanites people who did survived from the Israelite taken over of their lands, later became known as the Muslim, and Arab people of today, because many of them was later conquered by the Mohammedans, and became a part of the Muslim family of Mohammed. According to (Genesis Chapter 21, and verse 21), Hagar the mother of Ishmael take a wife from her own people of Mizraim for her son Ishmael, to be his wife. So, this would make the people of Saudi Arabia, a full-blooded Hamite's people, although they themselves are a part of Abraham who came from the city of Ur, of the Chaldees of the city of Babylon.

Even Abraham's, and his mother side of people, were from the people of Ham, because Terah, the father of Abraham came from the family of Shem of the East, of Persia, who had different children with various native Hamite's women of the city of Ur, of the country of Babylon. One could check out the genealogy of Terah, that is recorded in (Genesis Chapter 11, and verse 24), there they will see that Terah came from the family of Shem of what was known as Elam, and Elam became known as Persia. Eventually the name of Persia was change and became known as Iran, by the conquest of Alexander the Great, and his army, who came from the country of Macedonia of Europe. I would like to say that many of the Saudi Arabian people of today have become a washout set of people, with more so that of the Gentile European man blood running through their veins. This is because they too were conquered by the Gentile family of Europe at one time, and became a part of their melting pot of people. The promise Yahweh made with Abraham concerning his son Ishmael, that He was going to make the people of Ishmael into a great nation of people for Abraham's sake. They have all came true for the people of Ishmael, because Ishmael was Abraham first son, and this was because Abraham believed, and obeyed the voice of Yahweh, and pleased him well. So, this blessing that was granted to Abraham's they have used it, to conquer and manipulate many of their fellow Hamite's neighbors, with many other people whom they had conquered with the sword, and the Quran to be come followers of Mohammed.

They have also converted many of their captives to their religious belief of Islam. I must also mention that the kingdom of Jerusalem, that is still known today as the city of Jerusalem, was a Canaanite kingdom, before the children of Israel take away this city as their own, and it became known as the city of David. I would also like to point out that these ancient kingdoms of the people of Ham were there, in what is now known as the Middle East. These people of Ham, were not Gentile European looking people, as how they the Gentile people of Europe, would have many people of today to believe. That these ancient people of Ham, and their kingdoms, that gone by, were not European looking people, as how they have been teaching the world of people who came under their captivity, to believe that these people were of the stock of the Gentile people of Europe. "Due to the fact that many of their conquered people do not have any knowledge of who these people were.

So, they indoctrinate their many captive people, to believe that these people, were from the Gentile set of people of Europe, or they from the Asiatic people of Shem, who came from the East known today as Asia. The reason why many of the people of the world of today, can be easily deceived, and brainwash by these Gentile people, it is because many people have no knowledge of these historical facts, I have written about in this book. It is, also, because many people of today were educated by the Gentile people of Europe, for them to see things their way, according to their philosophy that they have been teaching to many people, to believe as fact. Many of whom came under their captivity of their schooling system of lies. Many people of today do not know any better, than from what they were taught by their Gentile European teachers, and their professors of their many lies. This is from their skimming, and deceptions they have taught to many of us their captives people to believe in their lies, at their various colleges, and universities of their higher learning, for their many captives to see things their way. These people I have mentioned above were from the seed of the people of Ham, who were around long before the Greeks, and the Romans. Who they the Gentile people of Europe, have taught their many captives, and slaves people to believe that it were the Greeks, and the Romans who had started civilization of the World. Sad to say that because of the various promises Yahweh made with Abraham, Isaac and Jacob, concerning the land of Canaan that became known as Israel, they have all come true upon the Canaanite people, and others of the kingdoms of the people of Ham at large. The Canaanites, and other Hamite's tribes of the land of Canaan, who might be around today, they have totally lost their homelands, and their identities.

Their many descendants who might be around today, have become a total washout set of people, looking more so like the Gentile people of Europe, and do not even know who they are. Also where they are coming from as a people, just like many other Hamite's people of today, who are scattered around the world through slavery and colonialism. Many of whom were given many false names, and identities, for them to go by, and for them to see themselves as such. Likewise, many of the Canaanite, and other Hamite's tribes of the land of Canaan, were given new names, such as the Palestinians, and the Middle Eastern people, and the Arab people to deceive any of these people who might still be around today.

There were also the kingdom of Lot's two sons, who had their kingdoms in the land of Canaan, known today as the Middle East. These two sons of Lot came about when Lot left from the land of Sodom to go and live in the mountain area of Zoar, according to (Genesis Chapter 19, and verse 31 to verse 38). There the Chapter explained that these two sons of Lot, came about when the first daughters of Lot, gave their father wine to drink, so that he would become drunk, and they could have sexual intercourse with him. Their reason for doing so, was because they thought to themselves that there would not be any more men left to come in to them, to bare children, because of the destruction of Sodom and Gomorra. So, the first daughter of Lot became pregnant, and gave birth to a son whose name was known as Moab. This is where the tribe of the Moabite people came from. According to (Deuteronomy Chapter 2, starting from verse 9 to verse 13), there Moses told the children of Israel when they came from out of the land of Mizraim, that they must not attack the family of the Moabites people. Also, they must not contend with them in battle, because Yahweh gave them the land of Ar as their dwelling place. According to this same Chapter of Deuteronomy, Moses told the children of Israel when they came near the coast of where the Ammonites tribe were living, that they must not attack them, because Yahweh gave this land to the Ammonites people of Lot, as their dewing place. The name of the second daughter's son of Lot was known as Benammi, from where the Ammonites tribe came from. So, before Yahweh gave this land to the Ammonites tribe, there were a giant tribe of the land of Canaan, that the Ammonites people of Lot name as the Zamzummims tribe of Canaan. According to this same Chapter of Deuteronomy, these people of the Zamzummims, tribe, were a great people, and many of them were tall as the giant tribe of the Anakims people of Canaan. But Yahweh destroyed these people, and gave their land to the Ammonites tribe of Lot.

Moses also went on to say to the children of Israel when they were in the area of Mount Seir, that there were another tribe of Canaanite people who were the natives of Mount Seir. But according to (Deuteronomy Chapter

2, and verse 12), there the Chapter mentioned that these tribes were also destroyed by Yahweh. Their land was given to the people of Esau, who were known as the Edomites people of Esau, in Scriptural time. The reason why Yahweh destroyed this tribe of the Hoirms, and gave their lands to the offspring of Esau, was because Esau was the brother of Jacob, who became known as Israel.

These descendants of Esau had their kingdoms in the land of Canaan, by various Hamite's mothers, who gave birth to this people, who became known as the Edomites tribe of Esau. According to Genesis (Chapter 36, and verse 2 to verse 3), there the Scripture explained that Esau's first wife were known as Elon, who was the daughter of a Hethites tribe from the land of Canaan. According to this same Chapter, Esau's second wife name was known as Aholibamah, who also was a Canaanite woman, from the tribe of the Hivites people of Canaan. The Scripture went on to explained that Esau's third wife was from the family of Ishmael. So, from these three Hamite's women, came about what was known as the Edomites tribe of Esau. I must also point out that although the Edomites tribe of people had Hamite's mothers, who gave birth to this nation of people, who became known as the Edomites people. Yet the seed of the women is not counted after the woman's seed, but it is only counted after the man's seed. This is the reason why they are only known as the Edomites people of Esau. The reason for this is, according to (Genesis Chapter 2, and verse 23), there Adam said, pertaining to Eve his wife, this is now bone of my bone, and flesh of my flesh she, shall be called Woman, because she was taken from out of man. So, the seed of the man is counted, but not that of the woman seeds, became she came from out of the man, and she was created in the image of the man, to be his wife, and companion. Also, at (I Corinthians Chapter 11, and verse 9), there the Scripture mentions that the woman was created for the man, and the man was made in the image, and the glory of Yahweh. So, this is the reason why the seed of the woman is not counted after the woman seeds, because the woman was made in the image of the man, and came from man to be his wife. This is the reason these people are only known as the Edomites tribe of Esau, the Israelite family of Jacob, and the family of Shem, because Terah the father of Abraham came from the people of Shem, of Persia.

This has been the way of life from when Yahweh created Adam and Eve, and their offspring's that came down from them to us today, that the children take their names from their fathers, and not from their mothers. So, in the time of Adam, the children were known as the people of Adam, and not from the name of their mother Eve. These are some of the things that did affect many of the kingdoms of the people of Ham even to this day, many of our great civilizations and kingdoms have been destroyed, or were conquered by different conquerors. Many of our remaining family of the people of Ham, who might be are around with us today, have become a washout people, into the Gentile European looking people of Europe, of their melting pot people of many shades of colors. Many of whom are known as the Latinos, and the Hispanic set of people, or whatever new names the Gentile people of Europe feel to give to their many melting pots people, of their former slave's colonies of their New World, where these people were born and rase. Or from wheresoever, they went and conquer, and set up their ruler ship, over many of their conquered people lives of their system. So, many of these mixed bread people, who came from out of the slave women, and that of the slave master blood, think to themselves that they are better than many of their Hamite's people, who they also come out of. This is because they have more opportunities, and are not the oppress people of today, like that of the many darker shades of the true blooded Hamite's people, who they also came out of. The destruction of one of the cities of Nimrod, that were known as Babylon, was prophesied in the book of (Jeremiah, Chapter 50, to Chapter 51), long before Yahweh use Cyrus, and Darius the Persian, and the Medes to bring about the destruction of Babylon.

The destruction of the city of Nineveh was also prophesied in the book of (Nahum Chapter 3, and verse 7) before it finally came about on the city of Nineveh. One can also read (Chapter 2, of the book of Nahum) pertaining of the destruction that was prophecy about the kingdom of Nineveh. Many people of today might ask the questions: what have become of the various powerful Kingdoms of the people of Ham I have mentioned about in this book. How come they are not a part of the many modern powerful kingdoms of the Earth of today? As I have mentioned before, that there are many prophecies of the Scripture that were spoken against many of the various kingdoms of the people of Ham that has been fulfilled already, and it has taken its toll upon us as a people.

Prophecies that were fulfilled upon the kingdoms of the people of Ham. The very first prophecy that I am speaking of, came from Noah himself, that still has it effect on many of us Hamite's people of today. The prophecy I am speaking of, is found in (Genesis Chapter 9, and verse 27). There it is stated that Noah, the father of Shem, Ham and Japheth, planted a vineyard, and he became drunk, when he drank from the grapes of his vineyard. So, because Noah was drunk in his tent, when he drank from the wine of the grapes of his vineyard, he became naked in his tent. According to the Chapter of the book of Genesis, Ham saw his father's nakedness, but did nothing to cover his father nakedness. But instead, went outside of the tent, and told his two other brothers, who knew nothing about the situation. Verse 23 explained that, Shem and Japheth took a garment, or a sheet and laid it upon both of their shoulders, and walked backwards, and covered their father's nakedness. And they saw not their father's nakedness. Verse 24 of the same Chapter went on to explained that Noah awoke from his drunkenness of his wine, and knew what his younger son had done to him. It seems to me that Yahweh must have revealed the action of Ham to Noah, because Noah was a prophet of Yahweh, and Yahweh was with him. According to the reading of (Genesis Chapter 9, and verse 27), there was no other person around in the place where Ham and Noah were, so as to explain to Noah the action of Ham take in not covering his father nakedness, but who went outside, and told his two other brothers. This was because Shem, and Japheth was outside of the tent, and new nothing of the situation, so this revelation to Noah must have come from Yahweh Himself. The Scripture went on to explained that because of the action of Ham, who did not take the action to cover his father nakedness, Noah cursed Canaan who was the last son of Ham, but he did not bless or curse Ham.

At verse (26 of this same Chapter), Noah went on to say, "Blessed be the LORD God of Shem, and Canaan shall be his servant." At verse (27, Noah went on to say that Yahweh "shall enlarge Japheth". So, Noah blessed Shem, and Japheth for their good deed they had done to him. So, the blessing that Noah spoke of, came upon Shem, that were pass on to his seeds, known today as the Asiatic people of the East. Also, the blessing of Japheth was passed on to his seeds who were known in Scriptural time, as the Gentile people, of what became known as the people of Europe.

If one should examine the prophecy of the Scripture, I have spoken of, and take notice of the prophecy that was mentioned by Noah, there they will see and understand that the people of Shem of what became known as the people of Asia, also the Gentile people of Japheth who became known as the European people of Europe, are a very prosperous and successful people of today. Although they the people of Europe have, skimmed, and rob their way true life, to become rich, and successful people. Yet the word of Noah stands sure. That is if one can see the effect it has on the Asiatic people, and that of the Gentile people of today. By the way of the success of the Asiatic people, and that of the Gentile people, who became known as the European people of Europe. Although many of the countries of Asia at one time were under bondage of slavery, and colonialism by the Gentile people who became known as the European people. So, many of the Gentile European people skills, of their modern technology, they themselves did received from the people of Ham, was pass on down to many of the countries of Asia, to enable many of them to become the industrial giant, many of them are today's. Also, they the Gentile people have rob, steal, and colonies, and enslave many nations of people to make themselves to become rich and powerful people, that did add to their blessing and advancement of today. They have also robbed many of the wealth's from the people of Ham, that did became their position, and colonies to make themselves become rich people. This is in comparison to many of the early kingdoms of the people of Ham, who at one time, in the very early beginning of the history of the human family, were a very rich, and powerful people. But now all this power, and richness have disappeared from many of the people of Ham, because of the fulfillment of the various prophecies of the Scripture that were spoken, and fulfill upon upon the various kingdoms of the people of Ham, I have mention.

It has taken it tool on us as a people, and many of our rich kingdoms, are all gone, and whatever little kingdoms that are left around with us in today's times, are struggling to become financially stable. Many of whom depend deeply on the Gentile people, and that of the Asiatic people for assistance, and their technology, that were known to the people of Ham as craft and skills. That is now enjoyed by the Gentile people, and by the Asiatic people of Shem as their technology of skills. This is the reality of life with many Hamite's people who are around in today's time, whether we like it or not. Many Hamite's people of today do not have any knowledge of many of these things I have written about in this book.

I want to point out that I was listening to a radio station pertaining to the story of Ham, that was told by a Gentile European man, according to this European man philosophy he was saying on the radio station, is that Ham had sex with Noah when he saw his father nakedness. Which the Scripture did not explained nothing like this story this European man was saying on this radio station. So one have to be very careful in listening some of these false information that come from many of these people minds set that is not of truth, but just mare speculation that come from their own belief.

The Sebans people who became known as the Ethiopians 'people, who are the many descendants of the first son of Cush, who were known as Seba, according to (Genesis Chapter 10, and verse 7). These descendants of Seba became known as the Ethiopians peo ple of today, which this name Ethiopia, it is a Geek and name, Latin name, that were given to the land of Saba. There were also the prophecy of (Isaiah Chapter 45, and verse 14), there Yahweh went on to say to the prophet Isaiah, that the labor of Egypt, and the merchandise of Seba, better known as the land of Ethiopia as the Sebans. Which is speaking of the descendants of the people of Seba, men of stature, which mean very tall people in height, they shall come after you in chains. They shall make supplication onto you, saying surely God is in you, which is speaking of the children of Israel. So, although Yahweh was not pleased with many of the kingdoms of the people of Ham, and He did destroyed many of the people of Ham kingdoms, and their civilization. Yet Yahweh has reserved good intention for the Seban's, and many of the people of Ham at large, who will turn to Him in true worship, true the name of His Son Yashua. So, these Hamite's people who are worshippers of Him, and who are call by His name, will be a part of the family of Yahweh true the name of His Son Yashua, so long as they stick to His Laws and commandment of the New Covenant part of the Scripture. Yahweh as also spoke about the Assyrian, and the people of Mizraim, by saying at (Isaiah Chapter 19, starting from verse 23 to verse 25), that blessed be Egypt my people, and the Assyrians the work of my hands, and Israel my inheritance).

So, what Yahweh is saying at (Isaiah at Chapter 19), that although He have punished, and destroyed many of the people of Mizraim, and also that of the Assyrians, and many of the people of Ham at large for Israel, and for their own UN Yahweh like qualities. That did not please Him, that was translated as UN Godliness in many of the Bible. Yet every Assyrian and the people of Mizraim, and the people of Ham at large, who will turn to Him in true worship, and who are also call by His name, will have a part in the righteous Kingdom of Yahweh that is to come. It is also recorded in (Psalms Chapter 68, and verse 31), there prophecy went on to say that Princes shall come out of Egypt, and what became known as Ethiopia, shall soon stretch out their hands to Yahweh.

I must also mention that many of the people of Seba, who became known as the Ethiopians people, as been stretching out their hands to Yahweh in worship with that of the ancient children of Israel long ago, so this prophecy had been fulfilled already. Many of the people of Seba are still stretching out their hands in worship to Yahweh, true the name of His Son, many of whom call themselves as Christians, which the name Christians, were taken from the Roman Catholic Church. Which simple mean followers of Yashua, that were translated as Jesus and Christ, that was taken from what was known as the Way in Israel. So, although many of them may not be knowledgeable about Scripture, and the true name of Yahweh, yet every Sebans who turn to Yahweh in truth worship, will be accepted by Him. A good example of how far back the worship of the people of Seba go to Yahweh, at (Jeremiah Chapter 38, and verse 7, to verse 12), there it explained that it was an Ethiopian man by the name of Ebedmelech, who was a servant of King Zedekiah of Israel, who went and pull Jeremiah out of the pit, so he would not die. When Jeremiah was put there by his own tribe of the Yehudahites, who were disobedient to the Laws, and the Commandments of Yahweh. Also (Acts Chapter 8, and verse 27 to verse 38), there it's mentions about the Ethiopian eunuch, who had great authority, and who were under the ruler ship of Queen Candace of the land of Seba, that became known as Ethiopia. He was one of the first outsiders of Israel to learn of the resurrection of Yashua from the dead. This was by Philip the Apostle, as he was reading the Isaiah Scroll, when he left from the worshiping of Yahweh in Jerusalem, and he was on his way back to Ethiopia. I am quite sure he did takes back the knowledge of the resurrection of Yashua, and the good news of the incoming Kingdom of Yahweh, to many of his countrymen of the people of Seba.

Many of whom became known as Christians in today's time, according to the colonialism of the Gentile people of Europe. This is the reasons why many of them are still worshipers of Yahweh in today's time. Yahweh has not cast off the people of Ham, who seek after him in true worship, true the name, and the teaching of His Son. Of the New Covent Law, Yashua gave to his Apostles, his servants to teach other believers. Also, (Amos

Chapter 9, starting from verse 12), there Yahweh went on to say, that they may possess the remnant of Edom, which He was speaking of the children of Israel, who He was going to allow to return back to the land of Israel, as a new nation of people.

The Scripture went on to say that they shall also possess these heathens, who were not worshippers of Yahweh, but now who are now called by His name. These heathens which the Scripture spoke of, were the many Hamite's nations of people, who were Israel neighbors, and who were not worshippers of Yahweh like that of the children of Israel of the ancient ancient world that gone by. But many of whom have now turn to Yahweh in true worship, true Yashua His Son. This heathens that the Scripture spoke about, were also, the many people of Shem, who are now known as the Asiatic people, of what the Gentile people of Europe name as the Asiatic people of the East. These heathen people, also included the many Gentile people of Europe, who are now known as the European people. Many of whom were not worshipers of Yahweh, but many of whom had their own gods, but now many of them have turn to Yahweh in true worship, true the name of Yashua His Son, who were a part of the heathens people that the Scripture spoke of. According to the Webster Collegiate Dictionary of the Fifth Edition, the word heathen is an Anglo-Saxon word, that was taken from the word (heathen). The dictionary explain that this word is connected to the word heath, which mean, one who lives in a country who do not acknowledge the God of the Bible, or a person who is a pagan, or an idol worshiper. So, from this statement that is mention in (Amos Chapter 9, and verse 12), one can see that Yahweh has open the door to many Hamite's people of today, who want to turn to Him in true worship, so as to be identified with His Holy name, and to be apart of His people, and His Kingdom, that is to come, true Yashua His Son.

It is also stated in (Romans Chapter 10, and verse 13) by the Apostle Paul, that whosoever shall called upon the name of the Lord, shall be saved. This name of the Lord that the Scripture spoke of, is not that of the name of the Lord Yashua, who also have the title of the word Lord, which this word Lord is only a title. But what Romans Chapter 10, and verse 13, is speaking of, is the name of the Lord Yahweh, who is the creator, and life giver, to whom all worship, and praise belong, true the name of Yashua, His Son. So, Yahweh is taking out of the people of the nations of the world, a people for His name, who are called by His name, and who are true worshipers of His name. While Yashua was here on earth with his Apostles, he mentions at (John Chapter 17, and verse 6), in payer to his Father, and his God, by saying that he has manifested Yahweh name, which mean to make known of Yahweh name to his Apostles, Yahweh gave to him from out of the world.

That they too, and many of us of today likewise will be knowledgeable of the name of Yahweh, and to be true worshippers of His name. The Gentile family of Europe has taught the world of people at large who came under their captivity, that they have civilized us Hamite's people, and other people who they had conquered, to become a part of their citizens, and colonies of today. What they forgot to say and teach us, is that there is a modern civilization, and there is an ancient civilization, and the modern civilization of the Gentile people of today, came from out of the ancient civilization of the people of Ham that gone by. The reason why the modern civilization of the Gentile people of Europe came into existence of today, it is because of the fulfillment of the prophecy of (Daniel Chapter 12, and verse 4). This prophecy of Daniel went on to explained that "many shall run to and fro," meaning that people will be going to this place or that country, seeking a better way out of their circumstances of life, and that knowledge was going to increase. Many people of today do not even know, and understand that many of the modern technological advancement that many of the Gentile people have brought about, in today's time, that hey called as science and technology, it is only within the last two hundred and fifty, or three hundred years ago. This is because of the fulfillment of this prophecy of (Daniel Chapter 12, and verse 4), where the Scripture mentions that knowledge was going to increase. This increase has brought about all this modern technological advancement that they the Gentile people of Europe, called as science and technology.

This knowledge of the Gentile people was also pass on to many of the Asiatic countries, due to the fact that they the Gentile people were looking for cheap labor to do their work. Why do I make this statement? If one should check and see if they can find this available information, they will see and understand that many of the modern technological advancement that they the Gentile family of Europe have made, and called as science, and technology, it is only within this period I have mentioned above. Before this period there was no television, radio, computers, airplanes, motor cars, cellphone, or rockets going to the moon. The modern-day medicines that many of the Gentile people have made, in today time's, were not available before the period I have mention. Although I have come to the knowledge, and the understanding, that the gas mask, and the traffic light signal were invented by a Hamite's man of the United States, by the name of Garrett Morgan. Unfortunately, when I checked out the dictionary, and the A-to-Z index of the Encyclopaedia Britannica, to see if I could find any information about this person, I could not find any available information about him whatsoever.

Many of the modern-day war machines that they the Gentile people of Europe have brought about, were not available before this period I have mentioned above. This prophecy of (Daniel Chapter 12, and verse 4) is not only speaking about the modern-day technological advancement of the Gentile people, of who is now known as Europeans people of Europe, of what they call as science and technology. It is also speaking about the knowledge of Yahweh, and His Son Yashua; and His Holy word the Scripture, and His Kingdom that is to come. However, many of the people of today still do not have a full knowledge, and understanding of Yahweh, and of His Holy word the Scripture for themselves. This is because many people of today are deceived by the various doctrines that came down from the Roman Catholic Church, and that of Protestantism, who were former Roman Catholic Church believers. Many of whom had broke off from the Roman Catholic Church, and form their own religious organization. This is also true for the Mohammedan Muslim people of Islam, who have also, conquered many people to become followers of Mohammed, and his religious belief of Islam to the worship of his god Allah. Yashua had foretold in the Scripture, at (Matthew Chapter 24, and verse 11) that many false prophets shall arise, and shall deceive many people, and this is true. Yet, many people of today have far more knowledge about Yahweh than in the Old, and New Covenant time of the Scripture.

Due to the fact that in those days, Yahweh were only dealing with the children of Israel, who only had the knowledge, and the understanding of His Laws and Commandments that no other people were that fortunate to know of. For they were the only set of people He gave His Laws, His Commandment to, and to know other people. All the other rest of the other nations of people of that time, had their own gods, and goddesses who they used to worship, and served.

I would also like to mention that many of the modern technological advancement that they the Gentile family has brought about in today's time, came from out of the mindset of their many captives, and enslaved people, who became their citizens, and properties, they have gain much knowledge, and skills from. Their ideas they have used to develop into their modern technology, that many people see today that they have learnt from their many captives. Although many of the time they may not acknowledge it to be so, and display themselves as if to say they did have all these knowledges before.

One can see from what I have written, that the modern day technological advancement of the Gentile people of today is tying in with the fulfillment of (Daniel Chapter 12, and verse 4). (Daniel Chapter 8 and verse 25) went on to say that "through his policy," meaning the Gentile family of Europe, they "shall cause craft to prosper in their hands. Also he that mean they, shall magnify themselves, and in their hearts, and by peace, they shall destroy many. So, this craft of skills that were given to the Gentile people of Europe, is what they name as science, and technology, as if to say that this craft, and skills were started by the people of Europe. This is also true, because it has been done just like that, from the early colonial days of slavery to our present time, by the Gentile people of Europe, using psychology, diplomacy and strategy to keep down and destroy many of their captives people, in different ways and means. This is if one has the eyes, and the historical knowledge, and the mine set, to know, and to see, and to understand these events that is done by these Gentile people of Europe. By using psychology, diplomacy, and strategy to keep many of their captive people down. Also, to destroy many of them, who became their captives, and slaves, and citizens of today, in many ways shape and form. The he and they that the Scripture is speaking about, is the Gentile people of Europe, with their modern day, technological advancement, and their modern-day army of war machines, who shall also stand up against the Prince of Princes, but they shall be broken without hands, as it is so point out in the Scripture." The Prince of Princes that the Scripture has mentioned is no other than Yashua, who became known as Jesus and Christ by the Greek and the Romans at his second coming, who is the Son of the supreme King of the universe, from whom all things flow. There is only one set of people, who is ruling over the world of today, that is match up to this prophecy of the Scripture, and that is the Gentile family of Europe, who have control over the world, along with the Asiatic people of today. They have done many of these things that are mentioned in the prophecy of (Daniel, Chapter 8) to many nations of people who came under their captivity of colonialism and slavery. They the Gentile people also has all the modern-day technological war machines, and the capability of the making these things, that is mentioned in the prophecy of (Daniel Chapter 8). The second set of people who are in control of world affairs of today, are the Asiatic people. But many of the Asiatic countries were one-time former slave, and colonies of the Gentile people of Europe, during their colonial era, of conquering many nations of people, who came under their captivity of colonialism.

Many of the Asiatic countries of today are the more tolerated people they the Gentile people of Europe have allow to be in second position to them. They have also pass on many of their technological skills, and know how to many of these people of Asia. Which did help them to develop into second place of world power behind the Gentile people of Europe. The people of Europe has allowed many of their modern technological knowhow to pass on to many of the Asiatic countries, simple because they were looking for cheap labor to do their works. Also, they the people of Asia are not the targeted people of today that they want to keep down, like many of us Hamite's people, who they have been praying up on for centuries. After many of the Ascitic countries did received their independent from the people of Europe. This is one of the reasons why many of the Asiatic people of today, can go into any of the Gentile European people neighborhood, and open their own little businesses there, without any problem from these Gentile people, who are living in these neighborhoods. It was not possible during the early colonial days of the Gentile people mapping up the countries of the world among themselves to be their empire, of colonies. Because in those days they the Asiatic people were their targeted people who they use to pray upon, whether they are Indian, or the Chinese people, there is no problem for them in today's time. This is in comparison to many of us Hamite's people who are now their targeted people of today. We the Hamite's people can mostly open our own businesses mainly in many of our own people neighborhoods, because many of the time if we were to go into the various European people neighborhoods to have our business there, many of us would be arras by the Gentile police men, and also, by the other Gentile European people who are living in these neighborhoods. In the early colonial days, before many Hamite's people were brought over to take the place of the various native's, as the new slaves.

It was the various Asiatic people of their New World, who they had called as Indians, who they were praying upon, and who were their first slave of their New World. Also their targeted people who they use to hunt for, and prey upon, spat upon, and were considered less than human beings. They even used many of the native's people as sport, by hunting them down, and collecting their heads to be rewarded as a trophy for the successful hunters. Not many people know that it was the various Asiatic people of what became known as their New World of the Americas, and the so-call West Indies, were the first slave for many of the Gentile people of Europe, of their conquered New World, as they did call it.

This was way before many of our Hamite's people were brought over to take their place as the new slaves to serve these Gentile people of Europe, as their new slaves, of their captured lands. Also, during the early colonial days of the Gentile people of Europe, many of the Asiatic countries of Asia, came under their conquered ruler ship as their pray, of their slaves, and colonies of their conquests. Although they the Gentile people of Europe had tried their very best to hide this knowledge of history about the enslavement of the various natives, from the other rest of people who came under their captivity. This is also true for many of the Asiatic countries that they had rule ship over, many of these people have no knowledge that many of them were former slave and colonies of the people of Europe. Yet Yahweh as allow this knowledge I have written about, to shine true these pages of this book, The Untold Forgotten Great Civilization of the people of Ham. Unfortunately, they then Gentile people of Europe, only teach us, and the world of other people who came under their ruler ship, that we the Hamite's people who named as the Negros, Black people, and the African people were their first and only slave, they were praying upon, and who were brought over to serve them, in their conquered New World. So, they do not bother to teach anything about the natives who they had enslaved to death, and take away their lands, and to see themselves as the new natives of their conquered New World. Also, they the people of Europe, did not bother to teach in their school, colleges, and universities, that the reason why many Indian, and Chinese people are scattered about in their New World of the Americas, and what became known as the West Indies, it is because many of these people were taken to these places as slaves, and cheap labor to do their works, and to serve them. But they kept this kind of knowledge of history, as a secrete under the carpet.

But they only teach the world of people who came under their captivity, that we the Hamite's people, who they name as African, Negros, and the Black people, were their only slaves they had brought over to serve them. So, the world of other people, do not have any knowledge of these history I have written about in this book, that it was many of the Indian, and the Chinese people who were brought over from Asia to the so-call New World, of the people of Europe, as their slave, and cheap labors to serve them. So, many of the natives who are around in today's time, do not know anything about these histories, I have written about, because many of them were not thought of these things, and they do not have any knowledge or idea of these of these history's I have written about.

It is also mentioned in (Daniel Chapter 7, and verse 25), that these same Gentile people of Europe, will seek to change things, and times, and laws, and they have done just that, starting from the Greeks, to the Romans, to the present-day Gentile family, who came from out of the breakup of the Roman Empire. They have even changed the world map, and the land description from how it is shown on the Scripture Map of 1890, of the land Ham and his people. Also in the book titled, A Political History of Tropical Africa, showing a map, of the land area of what they had called as Tropical Africa, during the Portuguese, and other European conquest of the the land, of what they called as Africa, that were of a bigger size, than what is showing on the modern world of today. This map I have mention, of what is called as Tropical Africa, did began from the borderline of what is now known as Turkey, and a part of the Mediterranean area, all the way to what is now known as South Africa. This map of Tropical Africa is not in harmony in what is shown on the modern world map of today, of the so-called Africa, that is much smaller in size than what is shown on the map I have mention. Also pertaining to the Gentile European advancement of today, at (Romans Chapter 10, and verse 19), there Yahweh said He was going to provoke Israel "to jealousy, by them who were no people," and by a foolish nation I will anger you," said Yahweh". So, what this prophecy of the Scripture is speaking about, is that they the children of Israel, were suppose to be the ruling power over the world after the fall of the various Hamite's kingdom. But because they did not kept the Laws and Commandment of Yahweh that were given to them. So, the powers the Gentile European people have today, came about to provoke Israel to jealousy. According to Deuteronomy (Chapter 28, starting from verse 1 to verse 13), there the Scripture mention that the people of Israel were supposed to be the head of all people. Ruling over everything, and everyone after the downfall of the various kingdoms of the people of Ham, that were brought about by means of the children of Israel, and other Abrahamic seeds.

Also, by the Gentile people of who became known as the land of Europe. Yahweh had promised the ancient children of Israel, that they would be the head of all people if they had kept His Commandments, and stick to His Laws and precepts. But they did not do so, otherwise, they would have been in control of the world affair of today, rather than they the Gentile people of Europe, who are now in control of the world affair of today. (Deuteronomy Chapter 15, and verse 6) there it mentions that the people of Israel would lend to many nations of people, but they would not borrow from no other nations.

They would rein, or rule over other nations, but no other nations would rule, or rein over them, if they did kept the Laws, and the Commandments, and the statues of Yahweh. But they did not do so, otherwise many of them would not have suffer the calamity and the destruction many of them had experience in Europe, by the Gentile people. So, the Gentile people of those days were not a powerful nation of people during the early civilization, and kingdoms of the people of Ham, in that early period of the human history, that is known as ancient civilization. My reason for making this statement, Yahweh did reveal to King Nebuchadnezzar of Babylon, a dream he did not understand. Of the various powers that was to rise up, and have dominion over the earth, after the fall of Mizraim, the Philistines, Assyrians, and the various Canaanites kingdoms, including Nebuchadnezzar kingdom power of Babylon, that was ruling at the time of Nebuchadnezzar dream. Until Daniel the prophet helped him to understand what his dream was all about. This dream Nebuchadnezzar had, is also tying in with the vision Daniel the prophet had, that is mentioned in (Daniel Chapter 7, starting from verse 1 to verse 9). Which was speaking about the same thing of Nebuchadnezzar's dream. But the vision that Daniel the prophet had was described in a different way from the image Nebuchadnezzar saw in his dream. Nebuchadnezzar dream was about this great image he saw that did represent the various world powers that were to come up, and become strong after the fall of Babylon to Persia. Daniel went on to explained to Nebuchadnezzar's at verse (37 of Daniel Chapter 2), by saying that, his kingdom of Babylon was this head of the gold that he saw in his dream. This head of gold was the first of these kingdoms that was to rise up after the fall of Mizraim to Babylon. Daniel went on to explained to Nebuchadnezzar at (Daniel Chapter 2, starting at verse 39) by saying that after the fall of his kingdom of Babylon, there was going to arise another kingdom that would be inferior to his kingdom of Babylon.

This kingdom that was to come up after the fall of Babylon, which was the silver part of the image that Nebuchadnezzar saw in his dream, that stood for the power of Persia, and the Medes, by way of Cyrus the Great. Verse (32 of Daniel Chapter 2) went on to explained that after the fall of Babylon to the silver part of the image of Nebuchadnezzar's dream, that stood for the power of Cyrus the Great of Persia, and his dual kingdom power of the Medes.

So, after the fall of Mizraim to Babylon, then came the Persians who came and take over Mizraim, and Babylonian, and all the colonies of Babylon, including the power of the Assyrians, all the way to the Eastern part of the Gentile land of Europe, to the Greek Turkey area of Europe to be their colonies. After the power of the Persian, and the Medes, then came up the brass part of the image of Nebuchadnezzar's dream, that is mentioned in (Daniel Chapter 2, and verse 33), that stood for the power of Greece. Who came up in the form of Alexander the Great, with his army, and generals of Macedonia. So, this brass part of Nebuchadnezzar dream came up, and become strong in the form of Alexander the Great, and his army, who take away power from Darius the third of Persia. Then the power of Greece take over all the colonial territories of Persia, including the kingdom of Mizraim, all the way to the land of Bharat that became known as India. Then the kingdom of Bharat, Mizraim, and the so-call Middle East became the Macedonian empire of Alexander the Great. Verse (33 of Daniel Chapter 2) went on to explained about the leg of iron, and the clay part of the image of Nebuchadnezzar's dream that stood for the power of Rome, who was to come up, and take over power from the brass power of Greece. The first set of people to have control over the north part of the land of Ham, that did become known as North Africa, were the Assyrians, and the Babylonians, and this was before the power of the Persians, Greece, and the power of the Romans. Who was to become strong, and take over control of Mizraim after the fall of Greece to Rome. Before Alexander's father died, who was known as Philip II of Macedonia, he had conquered all of Greece, who were always fighting among themselves for the control of Greece, and the Turkey Russian area of the Gentile land of Europe.

The power of those days, were between the Phoenician, the Hethites, the people of Mizraim, and that of Carthage, and the people of Greece, fighting among themselves for the control of the Mediterranean, and various colonies of the Gentile land of Europe. After the assassination of Alexander's father by the people of Greece, then the control of Greece came under the authority ship of Alexander and his generals, controlling all Greece to the so-called Middle East, and all the way to Persia and the land of Bharat that became known as India. After the death of Alexander the Great at age thirty, his various generals take over power of his conquered empire, who were always fighting among themselves for the control of the various territories of Alexander the Great of his empire.

So, after the fall of the various kingdoms of Alexander's generals, and their descendants, then came up the growing power of Rome, as this leg of iron, that is mentioned in (Daniel Chapter 2, and Daniel Chapter 7), who became strong, and conquered the brass power of Greece. Then the Romans were able to take over all of Greece, and her colonial territories, and enslaved many Greek people after the destruction of Carthage by the Roman. Matter of fact, when reading from volume 20 of the Encyclopaedia Britannica, there it explained that when the Romans became strong, and take over Greece, many Greek slaves were taken from Greece to the Eastern part of the Mediterranean area, as slave to the Romans. Then they the Romans made the island Delos, that is in the area of Greece, to be a slave market, for buying and selling Greek slaves, that was established there in 166 BC. Where many Greek slaves were sold from this marketplace by the thousands per day. Some of these Greek slaves were sold to various Latin communities, and to other native people of Italy who were given Roman citizenships. According to volume 11 of the Encyclopaedia Britannica, Spartacus who they the Gentile people of what became known as the United States, who they often show in their Hollywood movies, was a Greek slave, who was a Gladiator of the Roman army, before he and his slave army were destroyed by the Romans. So, the last dynastic of one of Alexander Generals who came under the ruler ship of Rome, was the Ptolemaic dynastic of Mizraim, that was ruled by Cleopatra VII. Who came from the linage of Ptolemy I, that was taken over by Octavian Augustus Caesar after the defeat of Mark Anthony and Cleopatra in the area of Greece.

So, the clay part of Nebuchadnezzar's dream, that was to come up from out of the iron leg of Rome, stood for the various Celtic Barbarians tribes of Europe, who was to come up from out of the brake up of the Roman Empire, and conquered many people, and countries of the world to be become their colonies of their empire. This was after the conquest of the Turks, which was what was left of the old Roman Empire of what was known as Asia Minor, and the so-called Middle East, and North Africa. Then came along the Mohammedans Muslim people, with the Quran, and the sword, and conquered all the so-called Middle East, all the way to what become known as Nigeria. Also, a part of Asia, Spain, and they were also trying to conquer France, but they were defeated, according to what I have read from various volume of the Encyclopaedia.

After the conquest of the Turks, and the Mohammedans, then came the Portuguese, and the rest of the Gentile powers, who came from out of the breakup of the Roman Empire of Western and Eastern Europe, and conquered the land of Ham with its people. The last beast of "Daniel Chapter 7, verse 7" was that of the power of Rome, and its beastly political system that is still ruling the world today. This political system that I have mention, came from out of Greece, and Rome that was pass on down the line to these various horns or the clay part of the prophecies of (Daniel Chapter 2. Also, Daniel Chapter 7) that is pertaining to the various Celtic barbarian Gentile European powers of today. Who also came from out of the brake up of the Roman Empire of the Gentile land of Europe, and became strong colonial power. These beastly power of ruler ship, was first started with the people of Mizraim, that became known as the Egyptians, the Canaanites, such as the Phoenicians, Hethites, also the Assyrians, and the Babylon people of Nimrod, all of whom were Hamite's people of their various kingdoms.

In this prophecy of (Daniel Chapter 2, starting from verse 34 to verse 35), there it mentions about the Kingdom of Yahweh, which is to come, that was describe symbolically speaking, as a stone that was cut out without hands. This stone of the Kingdom of Yahweh that is mention in Daniel Chapter 2, which did smite the image Nebuchadnezzar saw in his dream, that will take away ruler ship of the earth, from these clay part of the hones of these Gentiles powers who is ruling over the world of today. This stone that was mention, represents the Kingdom of Yahweh that did broke in pieces the golden crown of the power of Babylon. The silver power of Persia, the brass power of Greece, and the iron leg that stud for the power of Rome. It will also break in pieces the clay part that represent the various political powers of the Gentile people of today. Who came from out of the breakup of the Roman Empire, and set up their political system of ruler ship during their colonial conquest of the world, of slavery, and exploitation that came down to our present time of today. According to "verse 35 of Daniel Chapter 2", this stone that represent the Kingdom of Yahweh, will become a great mountain, and will filled the whole earth, and this is the same Kingdom of Yahweh that Yashua thought is disciples to pray for, that is mention at "Matthew Chapter 6, and verse 10".

(Revelation Chapter 11, and verse 15), there it mentions that the kingdoms of this world, did become the Kingdom of Yahweh, and His Christ, meaning Yashua, who became known as Christ, and Jesus in the Greek and Latin language of the Romans. So, it shall be Yahweh, and Yashua who will reign forever, over the earth, and that is to come, according to the Scripture of truth. Also (Matthew Chapter 25, and verse 31), there it mentions that when the Son of man, which is speaking of Yashua; shall come in his glory, and all the Holy angels with him, then he shall sit upon his throne of his glory: and before him shall be gathered all the nations of the earth. He shall separate them one from another, as when a shepherd divided his sheep from the goats. So again, this is speaking about the Kingdom of Yahweh that will take over ruler ship of this world, as Yahweh righteous government, ruling over the kingdom of mankind by Yashua, and his elects, which is speaking of the Apostles class of people as the elects. Daniel Chapter 2, and verse 44, went on to explained that in the days of these government of kingdoms, who came from out of Greece, and Rome, who is ruling over the world of today, "shall the God of heaven set up a Kingdom, which shall never be destroyed." But this Kingdom of Yahweh that is coming, shall not be left to other people as when a king died and leave his throne, and his kingdom to his son or to other family members, but this Kingdom of Yahweh shall break in pieces all these earthly kingdoms, and it political governments. This Kingdom of Yahweh shall consume them all, and this Kingdom of Yahweh shall rule forever. So, everything in this life is according to the prophecies of the Scripture, that is being fulfill every day, before our very eyes, this is if one have the knowledge, and the spiritual mindset, and the spiritual eyes to see all these signs of the time that we are now living in today, that is taking place, before our very eyes. (Revelation Chapter 21, starting from verse 1), there Yahweh mentioned that there will be a new heaven and a new earth where righteousness will dwell.

So, the Scripture went on to say, that He that sat on the throne, which is speaking of Yahweh, said I will make all things new. Yahweh went on to swear by Himself, by saying that I am Alpha, and the Omega, which the word Alpha and Omega it is a Greek word that was translated from the book of (Isaiah Chapter 44, and verse 6), that mean first and last. So, what Yahweh is saying that, He is the first, and He is the last in everything, which mean everything start with Him, and end with Him.

So, one can clearly see from what I have written, how Yahweh planned things out to be, of the coming up of these Gentile powers of Europe, and the destruction of them by Yashua at his second coming.

Chapter 22 - The Blessing Of The Gentile People, Who Have Turns The World Upside Down With Confusion And Corruption.

The blessing of the Gentile people of Japheth, who became known as the European people of today, who also have turn the world upside down with their corruption of immorality, and wickedness of all sort, that they have spread around the world by way of their conquest of people and their lands to get rich. Also, of their violent nature, that cause confusion to the minds of many different nation of people, who came under their captivity of ruler ship. Many of whom have copy the ways, and lifestyle of violence, wickedness, and corruption of these Gentile people of Europe to make money. The destruction of their corruption they left behind on the minds of their many Hamite's captives, with that of other people, who did came under their captivities of conquest of and ruler ship. It has cause many of their captive people to be infected with their lifestyle of corruption, and wickedness, also that of their sexual immorality of all sorts, that they have spread around the world by ways of their conquests of people and their lands, and that of their tourism business. Especially in what became known as the United States of America. It is very sad, and pitiful, to see how these Gentile people of Europe have spread their corruption everywhere, they went out to conquer in the name of Christianity. As a form of their deception, that they left on the minds of their many captives, to infected them with their lifestyle of corrupted, and all sorts of immorality. This is also, in many other parts of the world where our ancestors were taken as slave, and brought us fourth, and leave us behind, and we have adopted these people ways and life stile.

It is a very sad and pitiful, to see what many of our Hamite's people's who born and raise in the various slave colonies, where our ancestors were taken as slave, and leave us behind, to see what many of their offsprings have turn out to become. Copier of the Gentile European people life stile of corruption, and immorality. Also, many of whom has become drug dealers, drug addicts, wine nos, thief's, murders, prostitute, along with male prostitute. These sort of things I have mention above, many of our ancestors who were brought over to these sores, knew nothing about these things, of these European corruption. Also, that of their homosexual and lesbianism life stile that they have adopted from these Gentile European people, who had profess themselves to be an angel of light, to their many captives, but who were the devil in disguise. These Gentile people also went to different people, from different part of the world, of their conquest, with the cross of Christianity, to save sole for Christ, as they had put it.

Which was only a sham to rob, steel, and enslaved, and to conquered many people, and their lands with corruption and violence, and to gain wealth. It is a known fact that wheresoever the Gentile people of Europe went, and establish their colonial system, over other people, and their lands, they have always make sure they spread their philosophy of homosexuality, lesbianism, and their prostitution ideology to many of these native people minds, as a way of life. Many of whom became their subjects, as a way of life to spread their corruptions to the mines of their many captive's, of these places. The Gentile people of Europe have even pass laws making homosexual's, and lesbianism legal, in which this lifestyle of their, is abomination in the eyes of Yahweh for a man to lie with another man, or for a woman to have any kind of sexual activity with another woman. But the Gentile people of Europe has been pushing these kinds of mentality on many of their captive people minds, who came under their ruler ship, as a way of life. Also, by their tourism business, to spread these things as a way of life, to many places of their tourism, of their corruption. (Leviticus Chapter 18, and verse 22, and Leviticus Chapter 20, and verse 13), there Yahweh make it quite clear, that if a man lies with another man, as he does with woman kind, booth of these men who have committed this abomination: they booth shall surely be put to death, and their blood shall be upon their own heads. Many of these things I have mention, were brought about by the Gentile people by way of their conquest of the world, of people and their lands they have introduce to their many captives, for them to see as a normal way of life, according to their lifestyles of corruption, and immorality.

The blessing of Japheth that Noah spoke about, is recorded in (Genesis Chapter 9, and verse 27), where Noah mentioned, that Yahweh "shall enlarge Japheth." This enlargement of the blessing of Japheth came upon his seeds, who became known as the Gentile people, of Europe. To enlarge someone means to make them wider, larger, bigger, or greater. So, this enlargement of Japheth came upon his seeds that gave them the opportunity to conquer, and to corrupt the world of people who did came under their captivity, with all sorts of immorality. From their conquest of the world gave, them the privilege, and the opportunity to deceive, mislead, and corrupt their many captives people minds with all sorts of corruption, and evil. I have even read where some Gentile men of Europe have deceived various women from various poorer parts of Europe, by offering them job opportunities in the United, States, Canada, and other prosperous countries of Europe.

When many of these women reach out for these jobs' opportunities, they were taken as captive, and force to become sex slave of prostitution, to bring in money for their captors. One can imagine how many other non-Gentile European women, they have taken, and forced them into prostitution of sex slavery, for theirs captors, to bring in more welt. Because that is a part of the Gentile European people culture of Europe, and ways of life, to deceived, and capture people with their craftiness, and wickedness, so as to turn them into slaves to bring in profits. They the Gentile people have also brought about gambling, piracy, alcoholism, drug pushers, and drug addicts, all in the name of making money, for them to get richer, from the life, and misery of their many captives, and victims who become hook and these drugs of theirs. They have also brought about tobacco smokers, that became known as cigarettes, that they did copy from the Arawak's people, to make big profit, and to get rich from the selling of these things in Europe. Also, in their New World among themselves, and among their various conquered people, who became their captives, and citizens to become rich. Due to their invention of cigarettes, and tobacco smoking business, it has cause allot of destruction for many people who became hooked on the habit of the smoking of tobacco, as a way of life. By so doing, it as cost cancer, and other diseases, all because of their greed for wealth, and money for them to become rich, and powerful people. The funny thing about this story, all the people who were corrupted by these Gentile people of Europe, of their various doings, and life stile we have copped from them. We all are going to be punished by Yahweh, and Yashua for all these evils we have copy, and learn from these people, that did become a part of many people lifestyle, and cultures of today.

These Gentile people of Europe have brought about abortion clinics to suit their promiscuous sexual society, of unwanted pregnancy, they have established wheresoever they went, and conquered in the name of Christianity. Their many captive's people minds were influenced by what they have learned from these Gentile European people, through their television programs, and their Hollywood movies. Also, in the various Gentile European people world of today, the motto is for a woman, or a man to have as much sex as possible with different women, when she become pregnant, and they do not want to have the child, or children, have an abrasion and that would take of all the problem. Before the Gentile people left from their Gentile land of what became known as Europe, to go out and conquer many people and their lands with corruption, violence, liquor, drugs, and also, all sorts of sexual immorality.

These things were a part of their daily lifestyle in Europe, that did rub-off on many of their captive people minds, who came under the Gentile European people captivities. They Gentile people also teach many of our women to dress up like them, according to their fashion, of sexy look, they had invented from their vain mindset, that they advertise on their television to look sexy, as they put it. So, as to put on hot pants, mini-skirts, and tight up clothes that many of our women wear in today's societies, as a part of their fashion of sexy look, especially in what became known as the United States. This is to draw attention to themselves like a prostitute woman, seeking to attract the attention of men. Even in many of the churches I have went to in the United States, I have seen many women wearing tight up pants, or trousers, and some of these women even wear miniskirts to these churches as if they are going to a club, or to some dancehall. Not realizing they are going to a place of worship, to Yahweh, and it is acceptable by many of these pastors of these churches I went to in the United States, who see themselves as men of God. Many of these pastors who see themselves as men of Yahweh, should teach many of these ladies who come to their churches that this is not the way for a woman of Yahweh to dress to come to a place of worship to Yahweh, as they see themselves leading the flocks. It is also mentioned in the Scripture that a woman must not wear man clothes, and a man must not put on woman clothes.

But in this modern colonial world of the people of Europe, they have thought many of their captive's women, especially in what become known as the United States, to put on tight up pants for them to look sexy, so as to draw attention to themselves for men to see them as this sexy woman with beautiful figure. So, it is no more like how it uses to be in the old days before the Gentile European colonial, system of their immorality of their sexual look, of their modern colonial world, so as to draw attention of their sexy look to the minds of their many captives people, as a way of life. In my opinion I think many of these women who go to these churches wearing these garments, was to a track the attention of those pastors, and other men of these churches of their sexual looks. Some of these women who dress themselves up in this kind of fashion, and go to the various church, just do not know any better, because of the society they were born and raised, that influence their mind to think that it is alright for them to dress in this kind of way. So, it has become a way of life for many of them, because as the saying goes, monkey see, and monkey do, so people fallow other people, and that is a very sad part of life.

So, this is what as happen to many of these sisters who wear these kinds of dressing to go to the various churches, and think to themselves that it is ok, because they just do not know any better. Due to the fact that, many of these women are not taught by their pastors that this kind of dressing is not right for a lady of Yahweh, and a follower of Yashua, to dress in this kind of manner to come to a place of worship. Also because of the corrupted society they were born, and raised in, that as a great influence, and impact on the minds of many of these young women of today to dress up in this kind of way. Furthermore, it is the pastor's duty to educate these women who go to these churches dressing in this kind of manor, to point out to them that this is not the way to dress to come to worship Yahweh. Because this is a place of worship, and it is not a club, or a dancehall, of the worldly fashion, that is of Satan the devil, because a person cannot be a worshiper of Satan the devil, and at the same time be a worshiper of Yahweh. These Gentile European people has introduce to the minds of their many captives people who came under their system of rulership, boyfriend and girlfriends relationship, which the Scripture strongly condemned this kind of action as a fornication. It is also mention in (Ephesians Chapter 5, and verse 3) that fornication and all sort of uncleanness, or covetousness, let it not be name among you, who as become believers. So, the Scripture went on to say that Yahweh shall judge all fornicators and all adulterers. So, in this Gentile European conquered world of today, it is no more an husband, and wife relationship, as how Yahweh had established things to be, from the very beginning, when He created Adam, and Eve as a normal way of life. But now it is a boyfriend and girlfriend corrupted way of life that were introduce to the minds of their many captives people, for them to follow and see as a normal way of life.

It is also mentioned at (I John Chapter 2, and verse 15, to verse 17), love not world, or the worldly things that is of Satan the devil, for if any man loves the world, or the things of this world, the love of the Father Yahweh is not in him. Verse 16 of the same Chapter went on to say, for all that is the world is the worldly fashion of things, that is of Satan the devil, also the love of pleasure that is not of Yahweh, but it is of the world that is rule by Satan the devil. Also, the lust of the flesh, and the lust of the eyes, and the pride of life, which is not of the Father Yahweh, but it is of Satan the devil of this world that is under his control. So, this pride of life that the Scripture is speaking of, is the glamour of life, and worldly wealth that bring prestige, and glory to those people who has all this wealth and glamour to themselves.

Verse 17 went on to say, and the world with is doing is passing away, and the lust thereof: but he that do the will of Yahweh abide forever. Many Hamite's people who were born, and raised in the United States, and in many other parts of their colonial world. Has fallen victim to the Gentiles people lifestyle of alcoholism, smoking, drugs, violence, and all sorts of immorality of corruption they have copied, and learn from these Gentile people of Europe, who had a great influence, and in pack over their lives, and minds. They have even turned many of their free salves people of their society into users of profanities. Many of these things I have mentioned above were unheard of among many of my ancestors who were brought over to these lands, to take the place of the various natives, as the new slaves. This was to learn things of their faith, of their crookedness, corruption, and immorality of all sots, that they did present to their many captives people as a good Christian people. Unfortunately, many of their Hamite's free slaves 'people of the United States, and in many other European ruled societies of the world, of their colonies, where our ancestors were taken as slave, and leave us behind. We have fallen victims to their deeds, and we have copied, and learned many of the European people ways, and customs of their lifestyles of robbing, stealing, and killing to get rich, so as to live easy lives in their system. These Gentile people of Europe are all so about the love of money, violence, the shedding of blood to get rich, that did produce the cowboy's era of the 1800. Also, that of the pirates, and the gangsters that became known as the mobsters of today. They are also lovers of wars to gain more wealth, and to bring in new colonies, and the pollution of the earth with their chemical scientifically knowledge of destroying the earth, and the water supplies.

I was watching on YouTube where they were showing an island of the Pacific that is called the Marshal Island, where these Gentile European people of the United States, and their scientist has carryout various Nuclear bomb tests, that as coast the island to become poison with radiation. Because of their Nuclear bomb test of the radiation, that is present on the island. This Nuclear radiation has poisoned the water, plants, food, and the various Hamite's people who are living on the island, to brake out with cancer, and all form of sickness, from the radiation poison, they were expose to. According to this documentary of You Tube, this island is no longer safe to live on, and many of the various natives had to evacuate from off the island, because of the radiation poison that is present on the island.

When I was attending plumbing school in Newark New Jersey, I came to the knowledge that the water supplies that come true the water pipes in one house, it is recycle sewage water that many people of the United States drink from the water tap. This is without many people of the United States realizing that they are drinking recycle sewage water with all kind of chemicals they put in the sewage water to clean up this sewage water. This is one of the reason why many people of the United States are suffering from all kind of sickness, and diseases from drinking this recycle water, because a man is not Yahweh who can perform miracles, so as to clean up this sewage water. The Gentile European people of their thirst for wealth, power and greed, has left many people from many of their ex-slave colonies struggling for survival, because of their exploitation, and their high cost of living, that many people who are living in these society, can hardly cope with life. To survive from day to day, living in their established societies of the world, where many of us find ourself living, and called home. Whether it is to buy food, pay gas bill, electric bill, oil bill, house repair, permits, sign permits, closing, parking tickets, rent, and taxes and court fees, it is all for these people to get rich from their many captives who became their citizens, living under their system. This also included, paying hospital, and doctors expensive bills for these doctors, and the hospital to make money, to be come rich people, from their many patients who attend these facilities. It is all for them to gain wealth, and it is a struggle just to exist in their established conquered colonial world of today, of their making of money from their many conquered x slave people to get rich.

I would like to point out that if a person were to go to the court system of the United States for parking tickets, or for any form of tickets, if they do not have the money to pay for the tickets to the court, they will go to jail or prison, because system of the Gentile people of Europe was built, and design to make money from their many captives people, who became their citizens, living under their system. So, the only way a person can get freedom, and justice in their court system of the United States, or in any of the European colonial system. They must have money to pay to their court system, that they had set up throughout the world to get justice, or freedom, other wise there is no freedom, or justice to be given. So, if a person do not have money to pay to their court system, jail or prison will not miss this person, because the European people motto, is to bring in wealth into their systems, from their many captives people, in any way shape, and form possible.

So, this is the reality of the ways of life throughout the European colonial world of today, where many of us their captives find ourself living in. This is because they are in control of everything, and their greed for wealth make life becomes unbearable to survive on a daily base. Living in their systems, because of their increasing of pricing to gain more wealth, and to bring in more profits into their system, that they cannot take with them to graveyard, when Yahweh say it is time for them to leave this earth. When I sit down, and examine life, and realize that Yahweh has have giving us food in abundance, vegetable, and fruits that cannot be numbered, without any price to be paid. Yet because of these Gentile European people, and their greed of their colonial establishment, true slavery, and colonialism, it has left many people suffering for daily necessities. Here in what become known as the United States, which is one of the riches colonial slavery establishments of the Gentile British people. This is with other European people, who came from Europe to establish what is now known as the United States, that were built on crockery, violence, wickedness, and explication of many of their captives people to be come rich people. Many of their x slave free people, who became their citizens, are suffering, living on the street, sleeping under some bridge, or on the sidewalk, and eating out of the garbage cans. Due to their high cost of living, and their crookedness to bring in more wealth from their many captives. Many people are ignorant to these facts, that their system was designed for the wealthy, and what they classified as the high class, and middle-class, to live from off the poor.

Also, what they call as the working-class, and the lower class people, because they are poor, and was exploited, and rob by them the predictors, who see themselves as the high class people, of their colonial world system. (I Timothy Chapter 6, and verse 7), there it makes it very clear, that everyone came into this word naked without any form of wealth, and it is certain we cannot take anything out of this world, when Yahweh said it is time for us to leave this earth. There were no high class, or low-class people when we all came into this world as a baby, naked without a cent, by the power of Yahweh. So, this high class and low-class people came about by these Gentile European people, robbing, stealing, and enslaving, and oppressing many other people. So, that they can live off their many captives people, as a parasite, for them to become wealthy, and rich people.

Many of their conquered people who they consider as the peasants, the and low-class people of their societies, it is because they have taken everything from their many captives, and their many captives depend on them to survive. To be able to find job opportunities, to put food on their tables, to sustain themselves, in their expensive world of today. I would like to give an example of the struggling, I have come to realize of many poor Hamite's people of the United States have to go true, living in this European colonial establishment. I had a general contractor license from New Jersey, and when I left New Jersey in 2010, to go to the South, to check it out, to see what life was like there. I came to the reality that I could not use my general contractor license in the State of Georgia where I resided, and for me to get a general contractor license of Columbus Georgia where I was living, it would be impossible to obtain. From the view point of the city inspector, who was a Gentile European man, I would have to have a certificate showing of the various colleges I went to. Also, of the various degrees I took while I was attending colleges for me to be able to get a general contractor license, to work, and to have my own company. Plus, I would have to have references from various employers I had work for after I left from college, otherwise, it would be impossible for me to obtain a general contractors license to work in my own construction business. The point I am trying to make here is this, many poor Hamite's people of the United States, have just begun to explore in the education system of the Gentile European people of the United States.

In comparison to the time of the twenties, thirties, and the sixties, when many poor Hamite's people of the United States, and elsewhere could hardly afford to find the money to send their children to the general public schools. Let alone to be able to fine money to send their children to colleges, and universities, to learn this or that subject, and that trades to get a good paying job in this Gentile European people system of their conquest. So, these opportunities of their colleges, and universities, were more so design for the benefit of their own European people, who became citizens of these United States. Because many of their own people could find the money to pay to send their sons, and daughters to these colleges of their higher learning, to be able for them to learn this, or that skills, that is needed in the Gentile people European world of today. So, as to be able to find good paying employment, and to be able to get a general contractor license, to have their own little business, to better their standard of living. In which many of the general contractors of the these United States is that of the European people background.

So, the way I see it, with many of these read tapes, and laws of Georgia, and throughout the United States, it was design to keep certain of their Hamite's citizens down, from been able to have various skills, and to have their license, to be able to work for themselves, in whatever trades they may had learned from their father's to be able to better their standard of living. So, many Hamite's men who could not get the opportunity to go forward in life, because of these red tapes, and money they do not have to pay their way trough the European system of pressure, and red tapes. Many of them turn to alcohol, or drugs to drown their sorrows of disappointment, and set back in their daily lives, living in many parts of these United States. The funny thing about this story, many of the educational system of the people Europe, came from the Romans, and the Greeks. That intern came from many of the ancient kingdoms and civilization of the people of Ham that gone by, that they the Greeks, and the Romans had learned and was able to pass on to the rest of the Gentile people of Europe. Which was without any form of pressure from us, while they were learning from us. There were no barrios, or red tapes to stop them from learning, and to go forward in knowledge and skills in life. Yet as soon as they become the dominant rulers of their modern worldly systems of colonialism, that they had set up, it is all about allot of red tapes, and pressure to keep many of us their captives 'people down, from going forward in life. Another reason why many of the ancient kingdoms of the people of Ham did not remain until our present time, it is because of the fulfillment of the prophecy, about the time of the Gentile reign, that is mentioned in (Luke Chapter 21, and verse 24). There it is also mentioned that "Jerusalem shall be trodden down by the Gentiles family of Europe, until the times of the Gentiles people power be fulfill," are come to their end. So, the Gentile people domination over the earth started from the Medes, to the Greeks, to the Etruscans, the Romans, and to the rest of the Gentile family who came from out of the breakup of the Roman Empire.

These Medes people that were mentioned, came from the family of Media, and the Media people came from the family of Madai, who were one of the sons of Japheth, according to (Genesis Chapter 10, and verse 2). The Scripture Map of 1890, also show the land area of Madai, Media, and the Medes people, who were living right in the land area of Elam of Persia, close to what is known today as the Caspian Sea of Europe, and near to the land of Gomer, know today as Russia.

The land of the Medes people is known today as the land of Iran, because of the conquest of Alexander the Great, and his generals, who came from Macedonia, of the Gentile land of what is now known as Europe. According to volume 3 of the Encyclopaedia Britannica, Alexander the Great defeated Darius III of Persia, and conquered the Persian Empire in 331 BC. Darius was also killed by a fellow by the name of Bessus, according to what I have read from the Encyclopaedia Britannica. Later came the conquest of the Romans, the Turks, and last of all the Mohammedans, who came and conquered what is now known as Iran, India, and a part of China. They the Mohammedans Muslim people, of Mohammed, also conquered apart of Europe, and North Africa, all the way to what become known as Nigeria, with the Quran, and the sword. I am not quite sure where the name Iran originated from, but looking at the Scripture Map of 1890, and comparing it with the world map of today, the land of the Medes people was also close to the land area of Magog. Magog himself was a second son of Japheth, who was the father of the Gentile people, of what became known as the land of Europe. This is by comparing the Scripture Map of 1890, with that of the world map of today, showing the land of Magog that is known today as Tabriz that is in the area of Iran. Also, near to the land area that were known as Madai, and Meshech, which is apart of the various family of Japheth. The first son of Japheth was known as Gomer, and the land of Gomer is known today as Russia, as mentioned. The other sons of Japheth were known as Javan, Tubal, Meshech, and Tiras. In harmony with that of what the Scripture Map of 1890 showing, is that the land of Javan is right in the area of what became known as Greece. So, the people of Greece came from the seed of Javan, who are known today as the Greek people.

According to (Genesis Chapter 10, and verse 4), one of the sons of Javan were known as Elishah. The Scripture Map also shows the land of Elishah that is right in the area that became known as Greece, near to the landmark of his father Javan, that was not too far away from the land of Ashkenaz that became known as the land of Turkey. This land of Ashkenaz who was the first son of Gomer, and the other sons of Gomer was known as Riphath, and Togarmah, but the Scripture Map did not show the land area of Riphath, and Togarmah on the Scripture Map. The Scriptural Map also shows the land of Tarshish, who also was one of the sons Javan, and the land of Tarshish is known today as the land of Spain, and Portugal. But the Scriptural Map did not show the land of Portugal on the map, because during the time of these sons, and grandchildren of Japheth, there were no Portuguese people.

Their were all so the descendants of Tarshish, according to what Genesis Chapter 10, and verse 4, explain about the various sons of Javan. The other sons of Javan were known as Kittim, and Dodanim, but the Scripture Map of 1890, did not show the land area of Kittim, and Dodanim on the map, during the time of these sons, and grandchildren of the people of Japheth. So, there were no Portuguese people, but they were all the people of Tarshish, who were one of the sons of Javan. The Scriptural Map of 1890 also show the land area of Tiras, that is right near to the land area of Elishah, and Ashkenaz, known today as Turkey. In harmony with that of what the Scriptural Map is show, the land of Tubal was close to the land area of Turkey that is known today as Trabzon, and this land area of Trabzon is also close to the land area of Armenia, when compare the Scriptural Map with that of the world map of today. According to what the the Scripture Map is showing, of the family of the people of Japheth, and compare the Scripture Map with that of the world map of today, the land of Meshech is right in area of the Black Sea, and the Caspian Sea, that is a part of the land area of Russia of today. Also with various names, such as Armenia, Tbilisi, Azerbaidzhan, and Georgian. (Genesis Chapter 10, and verse 5), went on to say that by these sons, and grandchildren of Japheth, were the Isles of the Gentile people divided in their lands, everyone after their tongue, which mean language, or dialects, in their families, that became known as the land of Europe. So, this name Europe came from Greek mythology, according to the Webster Colligate Dictionary.

So, no matter what the dictionary, or the Encyclopaedia's of today might say in their various writings of the dictionaries, and the Encyclopaedias that the meaning of the word Gentile, mean the people of the nation, or none Jews. Which their information is a totally a false information of the word Gentile people, in comparison to what Genesis Chapter 10, and verse 2, to verse 5, gave of the meaning of the Gentile people. Who are the various descendants of the people of Japheth that became known as the people of Europe. So, in my opinion, the people of Europe give the definition of the word Gentile people, that they have written in their dictionaries, and in their Encyclopaedias, as the people of the nations, or none Jews. This was to suit themselves, of their brainwashing of lies, they have thought to their many captives people, who came under their colonial captivity for them to see things their way.

According to Webster Colligate Dictionary of the Fifth Edition, there it explained that the word Europe came from the word Europa, that came from Greeks' mythology, that meant to them, the god Zeus, who came down in the form of a white bull, and carried off the Phoenician princess, swimming with her to the island of Crete. Where she became his wife, and gave birth to Minos, Rhadamanthus, and Sarpedon.

As I have mention before that the Phoenician people were Canaanites, who came from what is now known as the land of Syria, of the so-call Middle East of today, so the Phoenician princess came from what is now known as Syria, byway of the Greek people conquest of their land. To give one a good example of the wicked nature of these Gentile people of Japheth, who became known as the people of Europe. I was watching a documentary on Direct TV, about a set of people of Gomer, who became known as the Russian people of Europe. These Russian people went to conquer the land that became known as Alaska from the native Eskimos people, who were a Chinese looking people of what became known as Asia. These people were the original natives, who were living there in what is now known as Alaska, that these Russian people went, and killed off many of these natives people from off their lands. Some of these people take up refuge, on a mountain top, and somehow, the Russians became aware that some of these Eskimos people were on the mountain top, hiding from them. These Russian people take their big cannon guns, and blast many of these tribal people to bits, who were there on the mountain top, hiding from them. After these Russians people killed off many of the native people, they take over control of the land, and later sold out the land to the Gentile European British people, of what became known as the United States, that did become a part of their states of control. According to a statement I have taken from a book called Basic English Review while I was attending Columbus Technical for a while, there it mentions in this book, that United States bought Alaska from the Russian in 1867, for 7.200.000.00 for this captured land from the Russians.

To give one another further examples of the wicked nature of these Gentile people of Japheth, according to volume 8 of the Encyclopaedia, the British and the French fought two wars with the Chinese people of Asia, these wars that were fought became known as the Opium wars of 1839-1842. The Encyclopaedia explained that the reason for the wars, was because the British, and the French were pushing opium drugs on the Chinese people, that they had called as trade business.

So, in other words they were big drug pushers, and drug dealers, pushing their drugs of poison on these Chinese people of what is now known as Asia. Volume 8 of the Encyclopaedia explained that in 1839, the Chinese Government of China tried to stop the opium trade from coming into their country, because the opium business was destroying the life, and mines of their many natives people, who were using the opium drugs. The action the Chinese government take to protect the interest of their people from the Opium drugs, of the British, and the French, caused the British to declared war on the Chinese people, for trying to stop their form of drug business from coming into their country. Volume 6 of the Encyclopaedia, explained that during the opium war, the British were able to capture the Chinese island of Hong Kong, from the Chinese people, and it became apart the British colony of control. I also came to the knowledge that when many of the Dutch, French, and the British came to what is now known as North America, speaking of what is now known as (Canada, and United States) to take away some of the land area from the Spanish, who had the so-call New World all to themselves for over 100 years. So, when many of these early European settlers, or colonists as they were called, came over they brought over blankets that were infected with the smallpox disease. They gave these disease blankets to many of the natives, so that many of these natives who take these infected blankets from these European invaders of their lands, would die off quickly. Many of whom had survived from the brutality of the Spanish, and the Portuguese, who did not get killed off, or who were enslaved to death by the Spanish, and the Portuguese, were given these smallpox blankets. The reason why these wicked Gentile European people did these things, was because they were hoping that when many of these people take these infected blankets, many of whom had survived from the slaughtering, and the enslavement of the Spanish, and the Portuguese, would become infected with the smallpox disease and die off. So, they could easily take away their lands, and see themselves as the new natives of these captured lands.

The same is true for the land that became known as Australia, and New Zealand, by Captain James Cook, and many of his British settlers, or colonists, as they were called. Who take over the land of Timor that became known as Australia from the Aborigines people, who were the true native of the land, before these Gentile British people came alone and take away their lands, and see themselves as the new natives of what became known as Australias.

This is also true for the lands of the Maoris, of what became known as New Zealand of today, these Gentile British people appointed themselves as the new natives of this part of the world, of the Pacific, from the natives Maoris. When the British went to take over what is now known as Australia, they enslave, and hang many of the men, and even cut off many of the men penis, so they would slowly bleed to death. Those who did not get kill off by the swords, and the guns, were enslave to death. Also, many of the women was raped, and spars were push up their virginal, so that they would slowly bleed to death. They have also corrupted the minds of the rest of these people who did not get slaughtered off, with sexual immorality, such as homosexuals, lesbianism, pornography, liquor, smoking, violence, drugs, and the glory of the guns to kill more people faster. While I was watching Direct TV, they were explaining, and showing of a documentary of how many of these European men of Australia would go into the various villages where many of these Aborigines women were living. They would have sexual intercourse with many of these women, and when many of these women became pregnant, and gave birth to many half breeds babies. As soon as these children grew up to be a certain age, the government of Australia made it a law, that the European police officers could go into these villages, and forcefully take away these half breed children from their mothers. They would take many of these children to other Gentile European neighborhoods, where they would be kept in camps that were run by Roman Catholic nuns, as the overseers of these camps. The reason why the Government of Australia takes away these children forcefully from their mothers, it is because the Gentile people of Australia have been trying, with all sorts of means to eradicate, and to exterminate many of these dark skin people from the soil of Australia. This they do in different ways and means, from life itself, but unfortunately, to their surprise, many of these people are still around today, although they had tried their very best to eradicate many of these people from the soil of Australia.

The idea by them taking away these half breed children from their mothers, and placing them into European neighborhoods. They were hoping that when these children grew up into adulthood, they would melt out back into full-blooded European people of Australia. So, many of the darker skin natives people would no longer be around, because they had killed off many of the men, so that the population would no longer keep on reproducing itself, as how Yahweh had made things to be.

This was also an attempt to turn the half breeds children's against their darker skin brothers and sisters, who had survived from the brutality, and the wickedness from many of these British settlers, who went to their land as strangers, and take away their land by force. The documentary explained that some of these children even ran away from these camps, and walk hundreds of miles back to their mothers 'villages, and many of them were caught, and forcefully returned back to these camps under police guard. This is one of the reasons why many of the times when they show the people of Australia on their television, they mostly show the Gentile European people of Australia as the natives, and the Aborigines people are rarely mentioned, because in eyes of these British settlers they do not exist. The same is true for the Maoris of what is now known as New Zcaland, many of these people have become extinct, and if any of these people are still around in todays time, they have become a part of the British people melting pot, of half-breed looking people of New Zealand. The European people of Australia, and New Zealand would like to give many people of the world of today, the impression, who are not knowledgeable about the history of Australia, and New Zealand. To think that the Gentile European people who are there today, were the original natives of the lands. This is because wheresoever the people of Europe went out to conquered, they have always see themselves as the new natives of these lands. This is the reason why they gave themselves different names from these places, they have conquered, such as the Canadians, Americans, South Africans, South American people, and the New Zealand people. The same is true for the land area that became known as South West Africa, by the Dutch, with other European settlers, who take way the land from the Portuguese, who had name the land area as Cape of Good Hope, before the coming of the Dutch, French, British, with other European settlers. While these European people have control over the land of what became known as South West Africa, they have tried their very best to eradicate, and to exterminate many of these Hamite's people from off their lands, that were given to them by Yahwe

The same is true for apart of land area that did became known as German South West Africa, of Namibia. These Germans people left from Germany to go and conquered different land area in the land of Ham as a part of the European people plan to capture the land of Ham, and his people to become their colony of position. So, these Gentile European people, are a set of predators, who have been praying upon the the rest of the human family for centuries.

These Germanic people wanted more lands to settle their German people on, so Namibia which was a part of the German colony of South West Africa, these people went and massacre, and enslave many Hamite's tribe of the area, who were known as the Aria people. This is also, with another tribe of the area, who they try to extinct and whip clean from the land, so that they could take over the land and whatever else these people had, and to see themselves as the new natives of what became known as Namibia. To show the barbarism of these European Germans people, who went to the land of Namibia, after they had slater off many of these natives people from their land, then they cut off many of these people heads, and send it to Germany, to put in museum, and on post card. This was to show that in their mind set, they are a superior people, to us Hamite's people, who they called as the Africans people, and the Black people. While these Gentile European people have control over what became known as South West Africa, they would make sure there is a big European community. The men would go around to the local villages where many of the Hamite's women were living. They would bread up many of these women, this was to create many half breads looking people, whom they named as the colorers people of the area. The Chinese, and the East Indians people from India became the second-class citizens to that of the Gentile people of Europe, who are there. While many of the half breed, or the collared people, as they are called, become their third-class citizens, and the true blooded Hamite's people were made to be the foot cloth that everyone would walk upon, and wipe their feet on. Alexander the Great, and his generals did the same thing when he and his soldiers had sexual orgies with many native women of North Africa, the so-called Middle East, and Asia. He also married off 10,000 of his solders to the local women of the area, producing many brown skin people, one see today in the so-call Middle East, Asia, North Africa, and what became known as East Africa.

So, from the Portuguese, the Dutch, French to the British, they have all try their best to melt out many of the people of Ham, into their melting pot of different shade of people. They have also did these things, in India, Indonesia, Hawaii, and also many of the natives of their New World that became known as the Americas, and the West Indies. Or wheresoever these European people went out to conquer, to become their colony, they always make sure that they created many shade of people, of the area. I would also like to give another example of the wicked and evil nature of these Gentile European people of Japheth.

On April 6th, which was a Sunday morning, I was watching a documentary on the television about the genocide that took place in the German Belgium colony, of what became known as Rwanda. According to this Gentile European man, who was the reporter, telling the story of how this genocide develop. This reporter went on to explained that during the time of the conquest, and the ruler ship over the country that become known as Rwanda, these German people put these tribes against each other, by telling one tribe, they are a superior people to that of the other tribe. Also that they the other tribe they consider to be the inferior tribe, were a part of the monkey family, and they were less intelligent to that of the superior tribe. This reporter went on to explained that this monkey family, they consider to be less intelligent to that of the superior tribe, they put to work as force labor of slavery. While they of the superior tribe, would have many privilege, of opportunities, in comparison to that of the tribe they consider to be less intelligent, and a part of the monkey family. So, by this devious, and evil mentality of these Gentile European Germanic people, brought about the genocide that took place in what became known as Rwanda, that cause 800.000 people to lose their lives, who were slathered off by their neighboring tribe. All because the instigation that were put in these people mind, by these Gentile European Germanic people, to cause division and war among these tribal people, of the land of Ham. This little story just goes to show that, wheresoever these Gentile people of what became known as the Europeans people, went out to conquer. They have always able to put people against each other, to suit their own wicked, and greedy deeds, that is call divide and conquer and rule. They have been doing these things from the colonial slavery days, of their conquest of the world, of people and their lands.

They have also been able to put different political rulers against each other, to their own gain, as puppets to suit their own interests. They have done so it in India, and South Africa, and in what become known as the Caribbean, of the West Indies. They also did these things in the island of Jamaica, by putting the Indian, and the Chinese people who were brought to the island as slave and cheap labor, against many Hamite's people, who were also taken to the island as slave. So, the Indian, and the Chinese people in the Caribbean, and in the Guiana's, were giving more opportunity to become more successful people, in comparison to that of their Hamite's counter parts of these places.

This is one of the reasons why many of the Chinese, and the Indian people of these places, are more financially better off than many Hamite's people who were also take to these place. They have also done many of this division in other places of their conquest that became their conquered colonies of people, by putting people against each other to achieve their objectives of wickedness. Unfortunately, it would only takes one fool to start the fire of their seed of hearted, they had planted in minds, and heart of their many captives people. Sad to say that many of our foolish Hamite's people fall in this category of following their skimming of Satanic devises of divide and conquer. To give one another good example of the lies and the cunningness of these Gentile people of Europe, I was watching a documentary on You Tube, by this European lady who is living in Jamaica, she was reading from a book that she said it were written by a Chinese man of Jamaica, who he claim that it was him who had started the making of beef patty in Jamaica, which is far from the truth. My reason for saying this is, I could remember when I was growing in the Kingston area of Jamaica during the fifties, many people use to make patty in their back yard, to give to their friends and family, and to sell to other people as well. So, this statement by this European lady, and this Chinese man, is notting but lies, that is far from the truth. Also I went to the country of Ghana in August of 2023, and from my observation many people of Ghana make a patty that they called as a meat pie. So, many people were taken from Ghana, and in different part of what became known as West Africa, and I am quite sure they did take along with them to the island that became known as Jamaica, their culture of the making of what became known as beaf patty. That is spread around the world by many Hamite's people who became known as the Jamaican people. This included many Jamaican dishes that were spread around the world where ever many Jamaican people went and pass on their ancestors culture food to the world of other people.

The people of Europe have always try to take over whatever the Hamite's people have started, and call it their own. Also, to give one another example of the wicked nature of these Gentile people, of what became known as the United States, many people worked very hard to get a mortgage, to buy their own homes, of the American dream they may never get the chance to pay off within their lifetime. This is because of how the Gentile European people of the United States setup the interest rates, that many of the times it is much too high. Many of mortgage companies rip off many home buyers by giving them inflated rates, and adjustable mortgages.

This they do, so in the long run many of these home owners would fail to pay their mortgage, and they would take back the property in foreclosure, and to sell the property again to make more money. This is how the system of United States was established by these Gentile European people, who came to this part of the world of their conquest to make money. So the system were designed that the middle class as they called it, and wealthy people to live from off what they call as the working class, of the poor people. Even many of the real estate lawyers, and real estate's agencies, and the mortgage companies work together to rip off many people. Especially those people who are not knowledgeable about the mortgage system, and the real estate laws of the Gentile people, of the United States, they did established. So, it is laws that were made by thieves for thieves. I can truly testify to these experiences since I have been living in what became known as the United States, because I have been a victim of these skimming of this system. If a person were able to live long enough to pay off their mortgage on their home, they would pay for it fifty times over from what they had initially paid during the closing. This is because of the interest rate, and the system that were built up on crookery, and wickedness to get rich. While a person is paying their mortgage for the first 10 years, they are mostly paying the interest on their mortgage loan, and very little goes toward paying the principle of the loan. Many people in the United States work extremely hard to own their own homes, but they may never live long enough to pay off their mortgages.

The day that many of these homeowners become sick, old, or unemployed, and can no longer afford to pay their mortgage, the mortgage companies, if they are still paying their mortgages, will take away their house, and put them on the street to live. The same is true for a person who has finished paying off their mortgage, and if they become sick, old, or unemployed, and can no longer afford to pay the taxes to the city, or States where their house is located. Which these taxes constantly keep on increases year after year, to the city where their houses are located. The city or, States would take away their homes for taxies, and their properties will be auctioned off to the highest bidder. They put many of these homeowners on the street to live, and they will become known as the homeless people, or streets people, living, and eating out of garbage cans, because they can no longer afford to pay the taxes on their homes.

The funny thing about this story, when these Gentile European people came to what is known today as the United States, they came here with their two long hands, with their swords, and their guns to take away the land from the natives. They did not pay them any money for the land, but just simply take away their lands, and to see themselves as the new natives. Yet as soon as these people set up their system of laws, and regulations, many of their captives, and their free slaves 'people who were born and raised in their system, become their tax, and rent paying people to make wealth from off their many captives to become rich people. The same is true for other free slave's people who left from many parts of their ex-slave colonies, and become legal residents, and citizens of the United States; right away they become their tax, and rent paying people, to bring in more revenue into their system. I also want to point out that a home owner of the United States cannot work on their own property, and less they pay to get a permit from the city or State where their home is located. If they should work on their home without these permit from the city, they will get a summons to go to court to answer for their repair on their home without a permit. They will also have to pay a heavy fine to the court, for working on their home, without first obtaining a permit do so. The same is true for people who cannot afford to pay their water bill, on their property to the city where their properties is located, the city will make the water bill become taxes, and they will eventually lose their homes in tax sales for the water bill.

My question to these Gentile European people of the United States, how much money did they, pay to Yahweh for the rain He sent from heaven? How much money did they pay to Him for the rivers, and the streams, and for the land they had fought, and killed off so many tribes of people for? The same is true for a house owner who needs to have some repairs done on their property, if they do not have the money to do the repairs, an inspector from the city where they are living, can give the house owner a summons to go to court. When, they go to court, the judge may fine the house owner a certain amount of money for the violation for none repairs, and if they cannot afford to pay the fine, and do the necessary repair, the fine the judge put on the homeowner will increase in interest rate to a large sum. Eventually if they cannot pay the fine, and do the repairs, they will lose their home in tax sales.

Also, an inspector from the city can give a homeowner a summons for having trash on the sidewalk, or a broken sidewalk that needs to be repaired by the homeowner. When the home owner go to court, and get fined by the judge for the violation of the none repair, if they cannot afford to pay the fine, and do the repairs, the fine will increase in interest, and eventually they will lose their home for the fine that was imposed upon them by the judge. I can truly testify to many of these experiences, because I had properties in Newark New Jersey, and I had to go true these various experiences with the city of Newark. Plus, many times I had to go to the municipal court, to answer for violation of the sidewalk, and other repairs. I also herd, and learn of other cases of other people, and their properties in the court system of Newark. Although many Hamite's people might left from various parts of the Gentile ex-slave colonies, of their world, and to come to lived, and work in the United States, to better their standing of living. There is a price to be paid to the Gentile governmental system, and that is taxes, exploitation, and rip-off in various forms. Many Hamite's, people who left from various parts of the Gentile European people ex-slave colonies of their world, and come to live, and work in United States, the land of opportunity. They need to realize that it is not all peaches and ice cream living in these United States, as how many other Hamite's people might think. There is allot of pressure, rip off, that a person have to go true on a daily base, living in the United States, the land of opportunities. The disrespectfulness that many Hamite's people of the United States show toward their fellow Hamite's people, who come to the United States from various parts of the European people colonial world to make a living.

In comparison to that of the Gentile people, who has far more love and respect toward their fellow Gentile people, who come to the United States, from various parts of their conquered world. Whether to live, or just to visit, it is totally a big difference, to that of many Hamite people, who were born, and raise in these United States. In comparison whenever other Gentile European people come to the United States from Europe, or from any other part of their colonial world where their ancestors went out to conquer. The Gentile people of the United States would make quite, sure that their fellow Gentile European brothers, and sisters are well come with open harms. As to say well come, by brother's, and sister's to our forefathers capture lands, that were left for us.

They would even make quite sure the neighborhood their fellow Gentile people will be going to live in, is that of a Gentile people European people neighborhoods, whether they are Gentile European Jews, or any other Gentile European people for that matter. They would go out of their way, to make quite sure their fellow Gentile

European brothers and sisters will live comfortably. They would even go out of their way to give them any assistance they could give to them. Whether it is business opportunities, or any help they could give to them, wether it is to find a good paying job, or anything for that matter, they will go out of their way to make sure their fellow Gentile European brothers, and sisters is extremely comfortable. But when it comes down to the Hamite's people who were born, and raised in these United States, it is a total different ball game. Rather many of them coming over to greet many of their fellow Hamite's brother's, and sister's, who were dropped off at different slave ports of the world, by the Gentile people of Europe, as they did. So as say to say, "welcome my brother's, and sister's, to a reunion of a part of the family of Ham that were broken off. Hoping we could get together, and try to build up our forefathers land, for us, and for our children to come, so that many of us who would want to return there could do so, also, for the future generation that is to come. But instead, many of them say to their brother's and sister's who come to the United Sates, that they must go back you foreigners. What many of these foolish Hamite's people who were born, and raised in these United States, fail to see, and realize, is that they themselves are also foreigners, like many have us their brother's and sister's who came to live, and work in the United States, to better their condition of life. Due to the fact that we as a family of the people of Ham, were not originated from this part of their captured New World of their conquest. From many of the natives people who were living in this part of the world before they came along and take away their lands.

But we as a people of Ham was dropped off at different slave ports, of their conquered world, in which many of us embrace these lands, as our native lands. This is because we were born and raised in these lands, and many of us do not have any knowledge of who we are, and where we are coming from. I cannot understand how many of these Hamite's people of the United States can see themselves as natives of this land, because they were born and raised in these United States. What about the true natives who were born, and raised in what become known as the United States, before many Hamite's people were brought over to take the place of the various the native, as the new slaves? Many of these foolish Hamite's people of the United States fail to see and realize that the Gentile community, along with the Asiatic people makes sure that they control all the business industries, and they live and get rich from off the support of many of these Hamite's people of the United States. Many Hamite's people of the United States work for these people, and when they get their pay, they go right back and spend all their money with the Gentile, and the Asiatic communities, who has all the stores, and businesses places in their neighborhoods. When Monday morning comes back around, they must push out again to start the cycle all over again. So, it is just like a conveyer belt, that come from them, and goes right back to them again. The sad thing about this story, none of the Hamite's people money stays in their communities, among their own people, so as to creates jobs opportunities for their own people betterment, to better their standard of living, and to create job opportunities for their own people to become more wealthier people. But rather they always looking to the Gentile people of the United States and Europe, to put bread on their tables, and all their monies go over to benefit, the Gentile European people, and that of the Asiatic people communities. So, as to enrich their surroundings, and to make them more wealthier people. This is because many Hamite's people of the United States are not mentality conscious people about themselves. Speaking from an economical, and self-awareness point of view, but rather they always going to these Gentile European people, and that of the Astatic people to give them job opportunities, to put bread on their tables, rather than them keeping their money in their own communities, so as to better their own people standard of living. So, as to open their own little businesses, to help many of their own people to find jobs opportunities among their own kind, like many of the East Indian, Chinese, and the Gentile people of Europe do.

If many Hamite's people of the Unite States did have the unity, and the love among themselves, like that of many of the Chinese, and Indian people, of Asia, as well as the Gentile people of Europe, many of whom have money would help their less unfortunate brothers and sisters to open their own little businesses, so as to help to employ some of their own people to better their standard of living. This would also help to train other Hamite's people to become skillful people, in this trade, or that trades that other Hamite's people do not have. So, as to help to pass on their skills, and knowledge to other Hamite's people, who are less fortunate than themselves. This would help many of their less unfortunate brothers, and sisters to have their own little businesses, to become more self-supported people. Rather than they always looking to these Gentile European people to give them job opportunity to better their standard of living. These Gentile European people of what become known as the United States, are so wicked, and evil, that when they killed off a native tribe who were known as the Mohegan's. Who used to live in the areas of what is now known as Canada to Boston, then they glorified this massacre of these people, by making a movie that was called Last of the Mohegan's, because many of these people were no longer around in life. When many of our ancestors who were granted a certain kind of freedom, they could not afford to buy their own homes, and lands, so as to have somewhere to live. So many of them become their free slave's or peasants people of those days looking for whatever little huts they could find, so as to have somewhere to live, and they had to pay rent to their former slave masters who became their lords, and bosses. So, it were just like a repeat of those days of the Romans, who were the slave masters, ruling over their brothers, and sisters of the Gentile land of Europe. Many of whom were free slave's, and peasants, who had to work on their landlords', or their x slave masters' plantations, so they could have something to eat, and somewhere to live.

In my opinion, the Gentile people of Europe are a predator's kind of people, who has been preying upon the rest of the human family, and upon the animals they killed off for sport. It is a historical fact, that wheresoever the Gentile people of Europe went, and conquer, and set up their system of ruler ship, they always caused many of the animals to become extinct. This is because of their love of wickedness, and their love for shedding of blood, and killing that seem to excite them with a trill. Then they turn around, and show many times on their television, they are trying to save the animals who had survived from their brutality, of slaughtering from extinction, from their own selves, and doing.

I would like to point out that before Yahweh revealed Himself to Abraham, who were a Cushite's man, from the country of Babylon, by his mother side of people, of the kingdom of Nimrod. Where he was born and raised, until when Yahweh revile Himself to him, that He is the creator of all living. All the families of Abraham were idol worshippers of their many gods, before they came to the knowledge of Yahweh, the creator, and sustainer of all living. This including many of the people of Shem of the East, who is known today as the Asiatic people. Many of these Shemites people of what is now known as Asia, are still idol worshipers of their many gods, who are not worshipers of Yahweh, because they have no knowledge of Him. Who has created all people for His glory worship, and praise, that belong to Him only, true the name of His Son Yashua. So Abraham father Terah, came from Elam, that became known as Persia, that is now known as Iran, who were living among the people of Ham in the so-call Middle East of Babylon, now called as Kuwait of the so-call Middle East. This was by the conquest of the Mohammedans Muslim people of what became known as the Saudi Arabia people. So while Terah were living in Babylon, he had different children with various Hamite's women, who gave birth to Abraham, Sarai, Nahor and Haran, and Sarai was the half-sister of Abraham, who came from another Hamite's mother of the land of Babylon, and Sarai also did became the wife of Abraham. Just in case someone might ask the question of what do I mean, by saying that Sarai who became known as Sarah, was the half-sister of Abraham, and she became his wife? If one was to question this true story of what I have written, they can turn to (Genesis Chapter 20, and read from verse 2 to verse 8).

There one will get the full understanding that Sarai who became known as Sarah, was the half-sister of Abraham. One can also read (Genesis Chapter 20, and verse 12), there they will see that Abraham make it to be known to Abimelech, who were a king of the Philistine people, that Sarah was the daughter of his father, but not the daughter of his mother, and she became his wife. I must point out that Yahweh did not disapprove of this relationship between Abraham and his sister Sarai, to bring about the seed of Isaac and Jacob.

Also, to bring about the people Yahweh did take to be His own people, because of the faith of Abraham, in believing Him, that He Yahweh is the creator of all things, and of all living. So, because of Abraham obedience, in pleasing Yahweh, and believing the Word of Yahweh, he became a friend of Yahweh. I must point out that no one can dear to question the authority and the decision Yahweh makes, of why He do this or that, or why He allow this or that to to take place. He do all things to please himself, and what He say is finial, and that is the reality of life, whether we believed it, or like it, or not. Later when Yahweh take the children of Israel from out of the land of Mizraim, and gave them His a Covenant at Mount Sinai, that became known as the Scroll, and later as the Scripture, of the Old Covenant Law. Which mean writing of His precepts that eventually became known as the Bible, by the people of Greece. He told them at (Leviticus Chapter 20, and verse 17) that if a man takes his sister, his father daughter, or his mother daughter, and see her nakedness, in other word, having sexual relationship with her. It is a wicked thing; in the sight of Yahweh, and they booth shall be cut off in the sight of their people, which mean to be put to death by Yahweh. So, Yahweh do not any longer approve of a man having any kind of sexual relationship with his sister, or any of his near kin of his relative, as he did with Abraham. One must realize that Yahweh is the boss of life, and He do whatever pleases Him, and no man can ask Him why He allow this, or why He allow, that to take place. If that were possible, they simple would not be around in life, because they would be a dead men, for been so presumptuous, to question the authority of the most High, who is the ruler of the universe, and of all people.

I would like to point out that men cannot even question the authority of other men, weather they be kings, or governors, or any kind of political rulers, or any ordinary men for that matter, of why they do this, or that. Much less Yahweh who is over all things, and who is all might, and all power. Who also have everyone life in His hand, and who everyone have to answer to. Furthermore, everyone must be careful of what he or she say, or think about the action of Yahweh, so they do not bring sin, and death on their own self, for speaking against Yahweh. Or cursing Yahweh which is called blasphemed, in speaking against the Holy Spirit, which is speaking of Yahweh of Himself, who is the Holy Spirit. Yashua said in (John Chapter 4, and verse 24) that Yahweh is a Spirit, and they that worship Him, must worship Him in sprit, and in truth.

So, if a person were to curses the Holy Spirit, which is speaking of Yahweh, he, or she would be cursing Yahweh Himself, and according to the Scripture, there is no forgiveness for that. So, that person who cure the Holy Sprit, which is Yahweh, is a walking dead man, that is doom forever. So, from Abraham, Yahweh chose Isaac, and from Isaac Yahweh chose Jacob, whom He later named as Israel, according to (Genesis Chapter 32, and verse 28). The children of Jacob later became known as the children of Israel, after Jacob's name was changed to Israel by an angel of Yahweh. So, although these children of Israel's mothers were from the daughters of Ham, who gave birth to this nation of people, who became known as the children Israel, because, Jacob name was change to Israel. However, they are only known as the children of Israel, because the seed of the woman is not contented after the women seed, but it is only counted after the man seed. This is the reason why they are only known as the children of Israel, because Jacob name was change to Isreal. Jacob also had twelve sons, and one daughter while he was living with his uncle in the land of Haran, that became known today as Iraq. This name Iraq came about by the conquest of the Mohammedans Muslim people, of what is now known as the Saudi Arabia people of Ishmael. So, Jacob had six sons and one daughter by his first wife whose name was known as Leah, and Leah were the eldest daughter of his uncle, who were his mother's brother. Jacob second wife name was known as Rachel, who was the sister of Leah. But Rachel was barren for a while; and she eventually bore two sons for Jacob. During the time when Rachel were not able to have children, she gave her handmaid whose name was known as Bilhah to Jacob, so she could bear children by Jacob on her behalf. Bilhah were a native from the land of Haran that is now known as the land of Iraq, where Abraham, and his father Terah had stopped off when they left from Ur of Chaldees of Babylon.

According to (Genesis Chapter 30, and verse 9), Leah also gave her handmaid to Jacob, so she also could bear children by Jacob on her behalf, because she also had stopped off bearing children for a while. This handmaid of Leah bore two sons for Jacob, and she also was a native from the land of Haran known today as the land of Iraq. Before the time of Jacob there was no set of people, on planet earth who were known as the children of Israel, which simply mean sons and, daughters of Jacob. Rebekah who was the mother of Jacob, and Esau, was the daughter of Bethuel, according to (Genesis Chapter 24, and verse 47). Bethuel was the son of Nahor who were Abraham second brother, according to (Genesis Chapter 11, and verse 26). Bethuel's mother's name was Milcah, according to (Genesis Chapter 11 and verse 29), and she became the wife of Nahor, who was Abraham second brother. Milcah was the daughter of Abraham third brother, whose name was known as Haran, who died in his nativity of Ur of the Chaldees of Babylon, and she became the wife of her uncle Nahor of the seed of Terah. These children of Jacob, became a nation of people in the land of Mizraim, now known as the land of Egypt, who left from there to go and take over the land of the Canaanites, according to the book of Exodus. According to (Genesis Chapter 41, and verse 50), Joseph's wife was the daughter of an Egyptian high priest, who were one of the Egyptian gods, who were known as On, and the name of Joseph's wife was known as Asenath. She gave birth to two sons for Joseph, who was known as Manasseh, and Ephraim, who became a part of the twelve tribes of the children of Israel. According to (Genesis Chapter 38, and verse 2 to verse 5), Yehuda wife, or his lady, was a Canaanite woman, and her name was known as Shuah, and she had three sons for Yehuda, according to (Genesis Chapter 38, and verse 24 to verse 27). There the verse went on to explained that Yehuda had two other sons by his daughter-in-law, whose name was Tamar, and she also were a Canaanite woman. So, from these two Canaanite women, who had five sons for Yehuda, who became known as the tribe of Judah in the Latin language of the Romans. Also, Jews, and Jewish people in the Anglo Saxon dialect, that became know as the English language, and also, in the French Germanic people dialect, who became known as the France people.

This Germanic tribe, were known before as the Francis people, who became known as the French people. In the Hebrew language of the children of Israel, this tribe of Yehuda were only known as the Yehudahites of the children of Yehuda, who were the fourth son for Jacob, and Leah. This word Jews, it is a broken form of Latin, that were taken from the Latin word Judah, because these Germanic people got their literacy of education, of reading, and writing from the Romans, and the Roman Catholic Church. Before the time of the Romans, and the Roman Catholic Church, these Francis people who became known as the French people, could not read, and write for themselves, until they were conquered, and ruled by the Romans.

It was the same way with many people of what became known as the Caribbean, or what became known as the West Indies, by Columbus. Also, in what became known as the Americas, that were rule by the Spanish, Portuguese, Dutch, French, and later by the British. So, many of our Hamite's people, who were taken as captive to their so-call New World, of the people of Europe as slaves, we speak a broken form of our conquerors language, that we had learn to communicate with them, to do their works. This were during the slavery days, that came down to our present time of today, so this slavery communication that many Hamite's people had learn, it became our languages, many of us Hamite's people speak today, as our form of communication. So, it was the same way with many of the people of the Gentile land of what is now known as Europe, they had learned their slave master's language that was rap up with their own dialect that became their own official language of today. There were eleven other tribes tribe of the people of Jacob, and the tribe of Yehuda was only one tribe. So, the term Jews, as a set people, that applies to the people of Jacob in today's time, it is totally a false identity, of the children of ancient Israel, because there were eleven other tribes who did make up this family of Jacob. I must also mention that King Solomon had many wives, concubines, and princesses from among the Canaanites, and other Hamite's tribes of women, who the children of Israel were living among in the land of Canaan. According to (2 Samuel Chapter 11, and verse 3), King Solomon's mother whose name were known as Bathsheba, she, and her first husband Uriah, were from the Hethites family of the Canaanite people, who the children of Israel were living among in the land of Canaan, and who many of them came out of.

According to (Exodus Chapter 1, and verse 5), all the family of Jacob who did left from the land of Canaan, to go and live in the land of Mizraim, now known as Egypt, in the land of Goshen, were seventy souls including Jacob himself. This was because Joseph himself was already living in the land of Mizraim with his family. Looking at the Scripture Map of 1890, showing the land of Goshen, but unfortunately, when comparing the Scripture Map with that of the world map of today, the world map of today do not show the land of Goshen. Due to the fact that the land area of Goshen might have became a part of the Suez Canal that was built in 1889. Moreover, these Gentile people of Europe, have changed the world map from how it is shown on the Scripture Map of 1890.

They do these things to cast confusion among many people of today, who do not have any knowledge about the ancient world of that time, that as brought about the present civilization of today. Because they the Gentile people of Europe, love to change things around, to deceive many people of today, many of whom have very little knowledge, of the ancient world that gone by. So, as it is so prophecy in the Scripture, that they the Gentile people, of what is now known as the people of Europe, shall seek to change things, and time, and they have done just that, starting from the Greeks, to the Romans, to the present day Gentile family of what became known as European.

When compare a map that is in the King James Version of what became known as the Bible of 1890, that I have in my position, there it shows the land of Goshen that, was in the land of Mizraim, now known as Egypt. Where the children of Israel were living, before they were taken out of the land of Mizraim. This land of Goshen was close to the land area that is known today as Saudi Arabia, which this land area was the land of Raamah, who was the fourth son of Cush. This was also with other Hamite's people, who were living in the land that became known as the land of Saudi Arabia, and Israel. When I examined this map in the King James Version of the Bible, and compared it with the world map of today, the land of Mizraim were a much a bigger size land area, in that time, than what is shown on the modern world map of today. This land of Goshen was also closer to the Jordan area of the land of Canaan, and some of the land area of Mizraim was taken over by what is now known as Sudan, and Libya. These Israelite people of the land of Goshen, in the time of the ancient children of Israel, were not red, or pink skin looking people, as how one might sees, many of these people of today, who are known as the Jewish people, in pink, or in red skin complexion. Many of whom are looking more like the Gentile people of Europe, in red, or pink skin complexion, and many of whom see themselves as the White race of people of today. My reason for making this kind of statement, about the children of Israel, in the time of Joseph, it is because the Israelite people in Joseph time, were not red skin, or pink skin looking people, has how many of them are looking today, who are known as the Jewish race of people.

This is because when Joseph was the governor over the land of Mizraim, his brothers came to him from Canaan, to buy corn for food because of the famine that were there in the land of Canaan. However, his brothers could not even recognize him, different from the other Mizraimhites people who were there with him, in the land of Mizraim. This was because at that time of Joseph, these Israelite people were all dark skin looking people, until when Joseph made himself known to them, that he was Joseph their brother.

According to (Genesis Chapter 50, and verse 13) Jacob died in the land of Mizraim that became known as Egypt, and he was buried in the cave of Machpelah, in the land of Canaan, by his sons who take their father body to be buried there. The point I am trying to make here is this: the ancient children of Israel in the time of Joseph were dark skin looking people, like many of the Indian people of Shem, of what became known as India, and also that of the dark skin people of Ham, known today as the Africa people, Negros, and the so-call Black people. These names came about by the Gentile people of what is now known as European people, who name these people as the Black people, African people, and the Negroes. I am not trying to say that the ancient children of Israel were Hamite's people, because they were not from the seed of Ham. Although many of the sons of Jacob had Hamite's mothers, Hamite's wives, and sweethearts who gave birth to this nation of people who became known as the children of Israel. As I have mention before that the children's take their name from their father's, and not from their mother's. So, although the children of Israel mothers were Hamite's women, who gave birth to this nation of people, yet the seed of the women is not counted after the women seed, but it is only counted from the man seeds. This is the reason why they are only known as the children of Jacob, the children of Isaac, the children of Abraham, and the children of Shem, because Terah the father of Abraham came from Persia of the people of Shem, that became known as Iran, of Asia. Reading from (Genesis Chapter 10, and verse 22), where the Scripture spoke of Elam, who were the first son of Shem, so the land area of Elam later became known as Persia, and the land of Persia later became known as Iran, after the conquest of Alexander the Great. One might ask the question, how comes the children of Israel of today, who are known as the Jewish people, are looking so much like the Gentile people of Europe, in pink skin, and in red skin in complexion.

The reason for this is, it is because they the Yehudahites, and the Benjamites of the children of Israel, who became known as the Jews, and the Jewish people, have been living for a long time among the Gentile people of Europe. For many centuries, and interbreeding their seeds with that of the Gentile people of Europe. So, this is the reason why they the Yehudahites, and the Benjamites people of today, who are known as the Jewish race of people, are looking so much like the Gentile people of Europe, in pink skin, and red skin complexions, and some of them are in light brown skin complexions. This is because they have been melting out themselves into the melting pot of the Gentile people of Europe for many centuries.

Also, before many of the Yehudahites, and the Benjamites women were taken into Europe as captives by the people of Greece, and later by the Romans, many of them used to interbreed their seed with that of the Greeks, and the Romans. Who did have ruled ship over the land of Israel, and that of the so-called Middle East, and what become known as North Africa. One could take a good example of the many Hamite's people who were taken captive by the various Celtic barbarian kingdoms of Europe, who came from out of the brake up of the Roman Empire, and became strong, powerful nation of people. Who also had their influences over many of their captives people throughout the world of their conquest. This was from the Portuguese to the Columbus era, many Hamite's people who have been living among the Gentile people under their colonial control of ruler ship. They have been mixed up their seeds with that of the Gentile people of Europe, this has brought about many of the half-breed looking people of today. One might see with that of the Gentile European man blood running true their veins. Such as the Puerto Ricans, the Santo Dominance, and many other Hamite's people from the various Spanish, and Portuguese slave colonies, where many of our Hamite's people were taken as slave, and brought about many of these halfbreed looking people of today. Many of whom were given the name, as the Latino and the Hispanic people. This is also, in what became known as the United States, South, and Central America, and in the West Indies of the Caribbean, where many of our Hamite's people were taken as slave, and inter breed their seed, with that of many of their slave masters.

So many of these halfbreed people, who were given the name as the Latino, and the Hispanic people, because many of them look just like that of many of the Gentile people of Europe. Because of their melting pot of different shade of people, with that of the European man blood running true these people veins. Not forgetting the many Hamite's people who were also taken as captives from what became known as North Africa, to the land of Italy, by the Romans as slaves, when they the Romans were able to defeat the Carthaginian army, in what became known as North Africa. So, many of these enslaved Hamite's women children, were later melted out into what became known as the Italian family of people of today. Also, many of these half breed people of today mainly came from the slavery experience their ancestors went through, with their Gentile European slave masters having sexual relationship with their many Hamite's slave women.

Who gave birth to these many shades of different colors of people, this happened when many Hamite's women were raped, or were forced to have sexual intercourse with their slave masters, and his associates. From the many Hamite's women the slave masters had as their concubines, helped to bring about the many half breed looking people of today, over the period of five or six hundred years after the Columbus era. In comparison to the many Yehudahites, and Benjamites people, who has been living for a longer period of time, among the Gentile people of Europe. They have become a part of their melting pot people, who became known as the Jews and the Jewish people of today. Yahweh had said in (Jeremiah Chapter 16, verses 14, and 15), "that behold, the days come said Yahweh, that it shall no more be said that as the Lord liveth that brought up the children of Israel out of the land of Egypt". But rather, as the Lord liveth who had brought up the children of Israel from the land of the North, and from all the lands He had driven them. This was for their disobedience, in not keeping to His Commandment, and His Laws He had made with their forefathers, when He had takes them by the hands to bring them from out of the land of Mizraim." As I had mentioned many times before, that the land of the north is the Gentile land that became known as the land of Europe. Where Yahweh allowed the Greeks, and the Romans to take away many of the tribes of the Yehudahites, and the Benjaminhites as their captives and slaves into the Gentile land that became known as Europe, for not pleasing Him. So, because Yahweh was not pleased with many of their doings, this is the reason why they were driven into the land of the North, of the Gentile people, to fulfill the prophecy of Jeremiah, that was mentioned. According to volume 26 of the Encyclopaedia, the persecution of many Jews, went true in different part of the Gentile land of Europe, this were during the time of 800-1200 AD, that gave birth to the word ghetto, that many of these people were forced to live in.

This was because of pure jealousy, and covetousness from many of these Gentile people of Europe, who were offended by the progress, and wealth these people were making. Volume 26 mentioned that during the time of 800 to 1200 AD, many Jews had multiplied, and settle in the Lombardy province of northern Italy. This were of the river valley area of the Rhone, and the Rhine area, of the Danube area of the Gentile land of Europe.

Volume 7, of the Encyclopaedia mentioned that these Lombardy people, were a Germanic tribe, who had conquered, and ruled this kingdom of northern Italy from 568, to 744 AD. These Lombardi's people were a Germanic tribe, who had form a settlement with another Germanic tribe, who were known as the Suebi people of northern Italy. This was from the I century AD, and their homeland originally were in the north part of Western Germany. During that time, they fought various battle against the Romans, and against other tribes, and eventually they move their settlement to the northern Danube area, of what is now known as Austria, during the 5th century AD. These Jews as they are called enter Britain after the Norman, or Vikings conquest of 1066 AD, and they settled in various parts of Britain, and became wealthy people there. Many of these Yehudahites, and the Benjamites, were used by various governments of Europe, who were badly in need to raise cash. They use many of these people to raze their necessary funds they needed, and eventually turn on them when the time was right for them to do so. While these Yehudahites, and the Benjamites, who became known as the Jews, were living in the Gentile land of Europe many of them were massacred during the time when the crusaders were preaching, especially in the Rhineland area of Germany. These crusaders were Roman Catholic Christians, as they saw themselves. Many of these Jews were accused by these Gentile Christian of Europe, of sacrilege, and child murders. Many of them were also persecuted because of these various beliefs, and suspicion many of them had against these people. According to the Webster Colligate Dictionary of the Fifth Edition, there it explained that the word sacrilege came from Latin, and Old French that meant one who steals sacred things.

So, many of these Yehudahites, and the Benjamites in the Gentile land of Europe were also suffered from a suspicious accusation made against them by a Christian group, who were known as the Cathari. According to volume 2 of the Encyclopaedia, this grope of the Cathari flourished in Europe from the 12th, to the 13th century AD, and many of these Cathari were Catholic Christians, who were control by various bishops. Volume 26 mentioned that the fourth Lateran Council gave these Jews a special badge, many of them had to where, and they were barred from various employment by the government. Due to the penalization of these people, they were forced to live in ghetto areas of many large towns of Europe, but although they were penalize, it still did not stop their progress.

So, because of their success, it leads to more precaution against them. According to volume 7 of the Encyclopaedia, the Lateran Council that was mentioned, were any of the five ecumenical councils of the Roman Catholic Church, that were held in the Lateran Place in Rome. The first of these councils was held in 1123 AD. Volume 26 went on to explained that despite the penalization that was put on these people, they continue to flourish, and because of that, many Christian's merchants of Britain became very jealous, and hostile to these Jews as they were so call. In 1290-1306 AD, many of these Jews were expel from Britain to France, and because many of them were force out of Britain, it causes their numbers to increase largely in the Germanic land, that brought about allot of suffering, and death for many of these Jews that the Encyclopaedia called martyrdom. This persecutions against these people, was because of pure jealousy, and covertness by many of these Germanic Christians of Europe they had against these people. In Spain, the toleration of these people gave way to widespread persecution, conversion, and prison meant that meant hardship, and death for many of these people who became known as the Jews. So, these were some of the conditions many of the Yehudahites, and Benjamites people had to go true while they were living in there in the Gentile land that became known as Europe. I must also point out that many Hamite's people who had left from the West Indies durian the fifties, and sixties went true similar experiences. But not as bad as what many of these Yehudahites, and Benjamites went true, who became known as the Jews, and the Jewish people. During my time of growing up in London, if a Hamite's person were to buy a nice car, or to have a nice house, they better make sure many of their British coworkers do not know they have this nice house, or nice car.

Otherwise, the news might reach the hearing of their boss, and they would lose their jobs, because the bosses would think that this Hamite's worker is getting rich. During the sixties, many Hamite's men who had nice cars were many times arras, and beaten up by the police of London, for driving these nice cars. I was told by an employer who I was working for at an Auto Body shop in London, that in his opinion, the only car a Black man should be driving, is one where the fenders is hanging off and looking very ragged. Because they did not want to see many of us left from the stage of biting the dust, and begging them for bread.

I was also working at another Auto body shop in London, and I went and purchase on finance a used Ford Zodiac car from a used car dealer, which this Ford Zodiac car was one of Britain luxury car at the time, and it was nearly new. I happen to take this car to where I was working, and one of my bosses said to me, what a piece of cheek, dear me invading the rich man word, because I had this nice car. Then he turns and ask me, if I could loan him my car for the weekend, so that he can go and impress his in laws with this nice car of mine, and I must keep his old car for the weekend, until he brings back my car on the Monday when we meet back for work. I told him yes, he could borrow my car for the weekend, to go and impress his in laws, while I will keep his car until the Monday when we meet back at work, and he would give me back my car, and I also would return back his car to him on that said Monday, and this actually took place. So, this little story of my experience I went true while I was living, and working in London, I have express in these pages of this book, just goes to show one the kind of grudge full mentality, and envious feeling, may of the Gentile British people had against us as a people. When they see us as trying to better our standing of living, from the way they had intend for us to being. Also, during the fifties leading up to the sixties, an Hamite man might be walking down the street mining his own business, and suddenly they would be attacked, and beaten up by a British group who were known as the Teddy Boys, with chains, knife, and other objects. So, this situation carryon until sometime in the sixties, when some Jamaican men, had a confrontation with this grope, that became known as the Noting Hill Gate riot of London. Due to this confrontation with these Jamaican men with these Teddy Boys, they left off from attacking many Hamite's people, because they said these Jamaica men were no game to play with. Then they turn on the Indian who were coming into London, and call it packie bashing, because many of these people would not fight back.

Speaking of the tribe of Yehuda, and the Benjamites, who became known as the Jews, and the Jewish people, the Scripture went on to say "I will bring them again into their land I gave to their fathers,". Meaning the land of Canaan that become known as the land of Israel. Also, at (Isaiah, Chapter 49, and verse 22), there the Scripture went on to say "thus saith the Lord Yahweh, behold I will lift mine standard to the people. This was speaking of the Gentile people of what is now known as European people, and they shall bring your sons in their arms, and your daughters shall be carried upon the shoulders."

The meaning of this statement that were mentioned in the Scripture, is that the people of what became known as the land of Europe, were given the responsibility to bring back the children of Israel from the land of Europe. Or from wheresoever they were driven by Yahweh for their disobedient, in not keeping to His Laws, and Commandments. It was these Gentile British settlers of what became known as the United States of America, and also other British people, who had fulfilled this prophecy of Isaiah, in the reestablishment of the kingdom, and state of Israel in 1948. Also, it was these same Gentile people who take away the land area of Israel from the Mohammedans Muslim people, or the Arab people, of Saudi Arabia, who had control over the so-called Middle East. It was also these same Gentile people who used their ships, and their airplanes to bring back many of the Israelite families from Europe, America, or wheresoever; they were driven by Yahweh for not sticking to His Law's, and Commandments. In which He used these Gentile people to take them back to the land of Israel. So, there is a big difference between the children of Israel who were living in the time of Joseph, and the Israelites who were living in the time of the Greeks, and the Romans. Also, the melting out of the children of Israel continued after the downfall of the Roman Empire, to the various barbarians 'Celtic tribes of Germanic people, who many of these people were living among in Europe for many centuries. To give one a good example of how truthful the prophecy of the Scripture is, Yahweh had said to the prophet Isaiah, that He was going to lift His hands to the Gentiles people, and they shall bring back His sons, and His daughters in their arms, back to the land He gave to their forefathers. I must mention that had it not been for Yahweh, who were watching over the Yehudahites, and the Benjamites of the children of Israel, who became known as Jews, and the Jewish people, to fulfill the prophecy of Isaiah, by these Gentile people of Europe. They would have been a totally lost set of people, as far as their culture, and their identity is concerned.

Matter of fact, many of the cultures, and ways of life of the present-day Jewish people as they are called today, are based on the cultures, and ways of life they had adopted from the Gentile people of Europe whom they have been living among for many centuries. These adopted cultures has passed on down the line, from generation to generation, to the present-day generation of the Israelite people, who speaks Yiddish as their official language, rather than Hebrew, which were the official language of the ancient of Israel.

According to volume 5 of the Encyclopaedia, there it explained that the Hebrew language is a Semitic language, of north central, and northwestern group of people, who is closely related to the Phoenician, and the Moabite people. Which are often, place by scholars to be that of a Canaanite background. I must point out that there were no such a people who were known as the Semitic people as how the Encyclopaedia would have us to believed. As I have mentioned before that the children of Jacob who became known as the children of Israel, came from the various granddaughters of the people of Ham, that Jacob, and Abraham came out of, that in turn came from Terah of the East, of the people of Shem. According to this same volume 5 of the Encyclopaedia, the Hebrew language was spoken in ancient time in the land of Canaan that the Romans did named as the land of Palestine. So, according to them, the Hebrew language was carryon by Aramaic language that begun somewhere in the 3rd century BC. Many of the children of Israel of today, who are known as the Jewish people, are learning to speak the Hebrew language of ancient Israel, rather than the Yiddish language, many of them think is Hebrew. Many of the Yehudahites, and the Benjamites of today who speak the Yiddish language as their official language, do not even know that this dialect of the Yiddish language came from a Germanic tribe, and not from ancient Israel. According to the Webster's Collegiate Dictionary of the Fifth Edition, there it explained that the Yiddish dialect came from High German, that was developed under Hebrew, and Slavic influence, that was spoken by Russian Jews, in Central Europe, and in the United States of what became known as America. I would also like to say that the Yehudahites of the children of Israel have a new identity, who are now known as the Jewish people of today, which it is a totally false identity. Because there were no such a people, who were known as the Jewish people, during the time of Jacob, and Joseph.

So, this statement I have made, might be very offensive to many Yehudahites, and Benjamites of the children of Israel of today, who see themselves as the Jewish set of people, because many of them do not have the real knowledge of their true history of the ancient children of Jacob, who became known as the children of Israel. So, the right terminology of expression for the offspring of Jacob, should be known as the Israelite people of Jacob, which simply means the children of Jacob, or from whatever tribe of the sons of Jacob they came out of originally.

So, where did the name Jews came from? According to the Webster's Collegiate Dictionary of the Fifth Edition, there the dictionary explained that the word Jew that was also spelled as Joo, but in the time OF, which stand for Old French, this word Jew was spelled as giu or jueu. The Encyclopaedia also explained that these Francis, or Frank's people who became known as the French people of today, who were a part of the Celtic barbarian tribe of Germanic people, could not read and write for themselves. So where did the word giu or jueu came from? It came from the Angles, and Saxon dialect of West Germany, at the time that were known as ME, which stands for Middle English, and also, from OF, which stands for Old French, that in turn came from the Latin language of the Romans, that were known to them, the Romans as Judah, and Judaea's. In the Greek language, this word Judah was spelled as Ioudaios, and in the Hebrew language the word Judah is spelled as Yehuda, that belongs to the tribe of Yehuda only. According to the Webster's Collegiate Dictionary, the term Jew simply means anyone belonging to the tribe of Judah, or the Hebrew race whose religion is Judaism. I must point out that this statement from the dictionary about the Jewish religion, is not in harmony with the true teaching of the Scripture of truth,   which were written only by the children of Israel, who Yahweh did used to write the

Scripture. My reason for making this kind of statement, it is because Yehuda, who was a part of the family of the sons of Jacob did not choose Yahweh, but rather it was Yahweh who had chosen Yehuda, and his descendants to be the family line of people where His name should be put among to be worship. Also, the kingdom of Yehuda was in the city of Jerusalem, where Yahweh did put David as king to rule over the tribe of the Yehudahites, and others of the children of Israel at large. It was Yahweh who also did chose Yehuda as the tribe from where Yashua, His Holy Son was to be born as a man, to be the savior of the children of Israel, and for the world of mankind at large.

Moreover, the worshiping of Yahweh is not about religion, or religious philosophies of men, also that about church religious doctrines, that govern many people's lives of today. But it is all about worshiping Yahweh according to what is written in the Scripture, and to follow the teaching of His Son Yashua, he gave to his Apostles. This was to teach other believers that became known as the New Covenant Law of the Scripture to save many who believe, and follow its teaching from destruction of Yahweh that is to come.

So, these religious church doctrines of are mair commandments of men, that came from out of Roman Catholicism, of the Roman Catholic Church, also from that of Protestantism, who were former Roman Catholic Church believers, of the Gentile land of Europe. Roman Catholicism came from idolatry worship, and paganism of the Gentile people, from where Christianity came out of, that were spread to wheresoever the Gentile people went, and conquered in the name of Christianity. By using the Bible as their tool, to their own advantage, to gain wealth, and to control the minds of their many captive's, in the name of Christianity. Also, of their spreading of their wickedness, and deception around the world that have brought allot of the corruptions to the minds of their many captives people, as a way of life. As, I have mention before, that word religion is a Gentile European word for worship, and it does not mean that a religious person, are a church goer, is a true worshipper of Yahweh, who is following the teaching of the Scripture, in their day-to-day life to please Yahweh. So, to have a religion, or to be a religious person, means nothing at all, but to be a true worshipper of Yahweh means everything in this life, and in the life to come, as far as our life, and future is concerned. These writings of the Apostles of Yashua were supposed to be known as the New Covenant Law of the Scripture, that were later called as the New Testament by the Greeks. The word New Testament it is a Greeks, and Latin word, that replace the word New Covenant, Yahweh did promise in (Jeremiah Chapter 31, and verse 31). Where He said He was going to make with the kingdom of Israel, and the kingdom of Yehuda, as the New Covenant Law. So, this New Covenant Law was translated by the Greeks, as the New Testament Laws for other believers to follow. Moreover, in the time of Joseph, and Yehuda these people who are known today as the Jewish race of people, were only known as the children of Israel, and the various tribes they came from. So, why are these people only known as the Jewish race of people of today?

The reason why they Greeks came up with this name of Ioudaios, it is because at the time of Alexander the Great, when he came, and conquered the so-called Middle East, in about 334-332 BC, with his army, and generals from Macedonia, only the tribe of Yehuda was left there in the land that became known as Israel. So, when other Greek settlers came in later, this tribe of Yehuda became known as Ioudaios, to the Greek people of Greece, who had settled in the so-called Middle East, and what become known as North Africa.

So, there is no such a thing as the Jewish religion, first, the children of Israel did not choose themselves to be the people of Yahweh. They did not gave themselves laws, and commandments to follow, they did received from Yahweh through the prophet Moses, and other prophets of the children of Israel, Yahweh did used to speak to them. If it were left up to them alone, they would have been just like the rest of the other Hamite's people, who they were living around, and who they originally come out of. Many of whom were idol worshippers of graven images, and which craft workers that Yahweh was not please of.

Chapter 25 - The Carrying Away of the Kingdom of Israel by the Assyrian Army.

The carrying away of the Kingdom of Israel by the Assyrian army that were in the part of the land of Canaan, that did become known as Samaria. (First Kings Chapter 11, and verse 11), there Yahweh told King Solomon in a dream that He was going to take away, or split the kingdom from out of his hands, because he did not keep the Laws, and the Commandments of Yahweh, but instead went and worshipped the various idolatry gods of his Hamite's wives, and sweethearts. Although Yahweh appear to King Solomon twice in a dream, telling him he must not go after these strange gods of the people of the lands, who were living around him, but he did not listen. The various times Yahweh spoke to King Solomon in a dream, can be found at (First Kings Chapter 3, starting from verse 6, to verse 7, and Chapter 11, verse 1 to verse 13). There Yahweh told King Solomon that He was not going to take away all the kingdom from out of his hands in his life time, but He was going to give one part of the kingdom to his son, for David, His servant's sake. Also, for the sake of Jerusalem's, because He had chosen that city of David to put His name there. (I Kings Chapter 11, and verse 12), there Yahweh went on to say to Solomon, He was not going to take away the kingdom from him, for David his servant's sake, but He was going to take it out of his son's hands, in his time of reigning as king. According to (First Kings Chapter 11, and verse 31), there it mention, Yahweh gave Jeroboam the son of Nebat ten tribes of the children of Israel, for him to rule over as king, in the city of Samaria, and this was after the death of Solomon. (First Kings Chapter 12, and verse 1), went on to say the tribe of Yehuda, and the tribe of Benjamin were left with Rehoboam for him to rule over, as king, in the place of his father Solomon, in the city of Jerusalem. So, two separate kingdoms came about after the death of Solomon, that became known as the kingdom of Yehuda, and the kingdom of Israel.

After the various evil doings of Jeroboam, and the other kings that came after him, Yahweh allowed the Assyrian army to carry away the people of the kingdom of Israel as captives, into the land of Assyria. Only leaving the tribe of Yehuda, and the tribe of Benjamin in the city of Jerusalem, for David His servant's sake. (Second Kings Chapter 17, and verse 6), there the Chapter went on to explain that, in the ninth year of king Hoshea, ruling as king of Samaria, the Assyrian army came, and carried away the Israelite people of the kingdom of Samaria into the land of Assyria.

According to (Second Kings Chapter 17, and verse 18), Yahweh allowed the Yehudahites people of the kingdom of Jerusalem, to continue living in the land He gave to their forefathers for David's his servant's sake, until He was ready to remove them from out of His sight. One can read about the carrying away of the children of Israel from their kingdom of Samaria, at (2 King Chapter 17, and verse 6), by the Assyrian army. So, when Alexander the Great, and his army came, and conquered the so-called Middle East, and North Africa, only the tribe of Yehuda and the tribe of Benjamin were left there in the land of Canaan. So, the Greeks named this tribe of Yehuda as Ioudaios. Later, when the Romans became strong, and conquered Greece, and take over all their colonial territories, then they named this tribe of Yehuda, as Judaeus, that did became known as the tribe of Judah. After the fall of the Roman Empire of Western Europe, by the Visigoth Celtic barbarian Germanic people, then these Yehudahites, and Benjamites who were dispersed among the various Germanic people for their disobedient, in not pleasing Yahweh. So, the word Judaeus came into the Francis people dialect, who became known as the French people, from where the name Jews, and Jewish people also came from. This name Jews, and Jewish people, also came down into Middle English dialect, that came from the Angles, and Saxon people of Germany, that became known as Jews, and Jewish people as well, which originally came from the Latin word Judah. I also want to explain that the enslavement of the children of Israel in the land of Mizraim, that became known as the land of Egypt, was the fulfillment of the prophecy of (Genesis Chapter 15, and verse 13). There Yahweh spoke to Abraham in a vision by saying, "know for surely that (your seed), meaning the children of Jacob, who became known as the children of Israel, shall be a stranger in a land that is not theirs. They shall serve them, and they shall afflict them for four hundred years, and after that they shall come out with great substance. At (Exodus Chapter 9, and verse 16), there Yahweh spoke to Moses the prophet pertaining to Pharaoh, who was ruling as king during the time of the children of Israel's Exodus out of the land of Mizraim.

By saying, "for this reason I have raised you up, [meaning Pharaoh], to show in you my power, that my name may be declared throughout all the earth." I must also mention that according to (Genesis Chapter 25, starting from verse 1, to verse 2), Abraham's second wife was known as Keturah, and she became Abraham's wife after the death of Abraham first wife Sarah. So, Keturah were from the family of the people of Ham, from the so-called Middle East, and she had six sons for him. The names of his six sons Keturah bore for him, was known as Zimran, Jokshan, Medan, Midian, Ishbak, and Shuah. I must point out that when it comes down to the worship of Yahweh, there is no such thing as a religious man, or a religious woman, it's either a person is a worshiper of Yahweh, who is following the teaching of the Scripture. Also the New Covent Laws Yahweh gave to Yashua His Son, and Yashua intern gave this Law to his Apostles to teach other believers, for them to keep throughout their lives. This was to please Yahweh, and Yashus, as a part of the New Covenant Law, that did replace the Old Covenant Law Yahweh did set up by way of Moses. So, there is no in-between with the worshipper of Yahweh, it either a person is a Yahweh worshiper, or a devil worshipper, who is worshipping the devil, and his angels who are known in the Scriptures as the demons. That came down in the farm of the various religions, and religious church doctrine of their organization. The Scripture that became known as the Bible, by the Gentile European people of Greece, who became known as the Greek people, that they the Romans Catholic Church put a label on, that became known as Christianity. So, the teaching of the Apostle Paul, who were made a minster to the Gentile people of Europe by Yashua, became known as Christianity, of their scheming to get rich, from their conquered people, and their lands. So, the Apostle Paul was made a minster to the people of Europe, by Yashus to bring them from out of darkness, and to bring them into the light, and the knowledge of the Scripture. Also, for them to become worshipers of Yahweh, and His Laws, that they did not know anything of before, because they were idol worshipers of their many gods. Notice that it is mentioned in (Isaiah Chapter 60, and verse 2) that there will be gross darkness to the rest of the people of the world, of the knowledge of the Scripture, and the worship of Yahweh.

But this light of the knowledge of the Scripture, and the worship of Yahweh was only to the Yehudahites, and the Benjamites who became known as the Jewish people of today. There in (Isaiah Chapter 60), it is also mentioned, that the Lord, which is speaking of Yahweh, shall arise upon you, and His glory shall be seen upon you, which is speaking of the Yehudahites, and the Benjamites, who became known as Jews, and Jewish people. Verse (3 of Isaiah Chapter 60) went on to say, and the Gentile people of who became known as the European people, shall come to your light.

The meaning of this statement, is that the Gentile people, were given the opportunity to come to the light of the knowledge, and the writing of the Scripture, that were only given to the children of Isreal. So, when the Gentile people of Europe came to the knowledge of the writing of the Scripture, then they put a label on it, that became known as Christianity of Roman Catholicism, of the Catholic Church. This is of the Scripture, and the worshiping of Yahweh, that they did not know anything of before. To show the truthfulness of this prophecy of (Isaiah Chapter 60), who was the people who went around spreading Christianity to the world of people, true conquest, slavery, and colonialism to get rich? This by them using the Bible as their tools, to conquer, that they put a label on, that became known as Christianity, to their many conquered people, who came under their conquered ruler ship. Is it not these Gentile people, who are known today as the people of Europe? It is also mentioned in (Isaiah Chapter 61, and verse 6), speaking of the Yehudahites and the Benjamites who became known as Jaws. But you shall be named the priest of the Lord Yahweh, and you shall eat the riches of the Gentile, and in their glory shall you boast yourself. So, again, to show the truthfulness of the prophecy of the Scripture, whenever there is a Jewish holiday throughout the Gentile people conquered world, many of these business places are close in the honoring of these Jewish holidays. (Jeremiah Chapter 5, and verse 7), there Yahweh spoke of Israel by saying, how shall I pardon Israel for this, because they have forsaken me, and swear by them that were no gods? When I have fed them to the full, then they committed adultery, and assembled themselves by troops in the houses of the harlot's. They were like fed horses in the morning, and everyone lust after their neighbor wife's, shall not my soul be avenged on such a nation as this?

Verse (18 of Jeremiah Chapter 5) went on to say, and it shall come to pass, when they shall say wherefore doth the Lord our God do all these things to us? Then shalt you answer them by saying, like as you have forsaken me, and served strange gods in your land. So, because of this very prophecy, they the Yehudahites, and the Benjamites were disperse of in Europe, and in other lands for not pleasing Yahweh. (Jeremiah Chapter 6, and verse 19), there the Chapter went on to say, hear o earth, behold I will bring evil upon this people, speaking of Israel. Even the fruit of their thoughts, because they have not listened to my words, nor to my Laws, but rejected it. Therefore, thus saith the Lord Yahweh, behold I will lay stumbling block before this people.

The father and the son together shall fall upon them, and their neighbor, and their friend shall perish. (Verse 22 of Jeremiah Chapter 6), Yahweh went on to say, behold a people cometh from the north country, a great nation shall arise from the side of the earth, they shall hold on bow and spear, and they are a very cruel and wicked people, who has no mercy. This is speaking of the Gentile people of Europe, who are known in the Scripture as the people of the north country, who became known as the people of Europe, who are a very cruel, and wicked people. So, Yahweh was going to bring these people against the daughter of Zion, speaking of the Yehudahites, and the Benjamites, who become known as Jews, and Jewish people of today. Because of them not keeping to the Laws, and Commandment of Yahweh. (Jeremiah Chapter 1, and verse 15), there Yahweh went on to say, for low I will call the family of the kingdom of the north, and they shall come, and set everyone his throne at the entering of the gate of Jerusalem. (Jeremiah Chapter 5, and verse 18), there Yahweh said, in those days I will not make a full end of the Yehudahites, and the Benjamites, so this is the reason why they the Yehudahites, and the Benjamites, were gathered back in the land that became known as Israel. From different nation of people that they were disperse among, for their disobedient in not keeping to the Laws, and Commandments of Yahweh.

The Gentile people of Europe who have infused their pagan holidays of the Christmas, story of the birth, and coming of Yashua, to be born as a man on December 25th, that is known as the Christians holidays of Christmas. Or better put, as the followers of Yashua day, because this is what Christianity should mean, followers of Yashua in the Hebrew language of the children of Israel, that was known as the Way. Speaking of Yashua who is the Way to the Father Yahweh. I must point out that Christmas is all about the making of money for their merchants, at their places of business, many of whom are mostly from the Gentile European people background. Also from many of the Asiatic people, who also have their business place in many of Gentile European people conquered lands, that became their colonies. They make a lot of money from their many captured x slave people, who became their citizens, who they had psyched, and indoctrinated into the Christmas spirit, of their tradition, of buying gifts, and the giving of gifts. So, quite naturally, the Christmas season is always a happy, and a joyful time of the year, for many of these merchants, and store owners at their place of business. Due to the fact that during this time of the year is when they make their big profits, and get richer, and count their millions, they had made from many people who were indoctrinated into the Christmas spirit. One should not be surprised to come to know about this knowledge of the Gentile family of Europe, using psychology, diplomacy, strategy and deceptions, on the minds of their many captive people, who became their citizens to make money from.

If one have any knowledge of the Gentile people of Europe, and their history, they will come to the realizatdion that the mindset, motto, philosophy, psychology, strategy, and the skimming of these people, is to make money, and get rich, in any way they can do so. For this said reason of their greed, selfishness, and wickedness, slavery and colonialism were established, for them to get rich, from the blood, sweat, and tears, and the life of their many victims. Who they live off like a parasite, to become wealthy and rich people. Also, to scrape the riches from their various colonies of the world, to send to Europe, to enrich the land of Europe with their various conquered commodities, that they had stolen from these colonies of theirs.

How did the Christmas festival of celebration came about? According to volume 16 of the Encyclopaedia Britannica, and volume 3, of the Encyclopaedia, there it explained that the Christmas story has three different sides to it. One of these stories about Christmas came from the time of the Romans, and from the Indian god Mitra. Last to add to the Christmas celebration were Saint Nicholas, who became known as Father Christmas. Volume 16 of the Encyclopaedia explained, that the exact circumstances of the beginning of the Christmas day, story is uncertain. The Encyclopaedia explained, that from Rome the feast day of the Christmas celebration was spread to the other churches of the West. Meaning the Roman Catholic Churches of Western, and Eastern Europe, of the Roman Empire, and also of the Greek Turkey area of Europe, that was called Asia Minor. Also, to the so-called Middle East, and what became known as North Africa. Last to adapt to the Christmas celebration, were the church of Jerusalem, that were under the ruler ship of Juvenal the Bishop of Rome, this was from 458, to 424 AD. The Encyclopaedia explained that in the Armenian churches of the Roman Empire, Christmas was never accepted, but the birth of Yashua was celebrated on January 6th, after the Christmas celebration was established in the eastern part of the empire. Volume 3 of the Encyclopaedia explained, that the Christmas celebration of Jesus birth, which according to them was supposed to be on December 25th. Which did connect to the Roman pagan agricultural sun god, of the midwinter season, of the Roman Catholic Church celebration, as the birthday of Yashua, according to their belief. Volume 18 of the Encyclopaedia, explained that for a period during the Roman religious 'system, coins, and other monuments continue to associate themselves with the Christian doctoring, with that of the worship of the sun god. In which Constantine were a dedicated worshiper of this sun god, before he became a part of Roman Catholicism, of the Catholic Church.

Constantine pass on to the various popes who came after him, the title as the chief priests, that came from the word Pontifex Maximus, of the Roman religious 'system. Under the subheading of the survival of the Roman religion, of the ecclesiastical Christian calendars, of the various priests, and bishops that were originally known as the Episcopal, of the Roman Catholic Church. They retained numerous remnants of the pre-Christian festival, that became known as Christmas. More outstanding of these festivals was Saturnalia, with its blended element, from where the Christmas story came from.

Also, from the birthday of the Iranian Indian god Mithra, that volume 8 of the Encyclopaedia mentions, it was connected to December 25, in which this December 25 was also the birthday of the Iranian, Indian god Mithra. According to volume 10 of the Encyclopaedia, there it explain that this Roman festival of Saturnalia, is associated with that of the Roman god Saturn. The Encyclopaedia explained that Saturnalia, or Saturn was the most popular, and the most merriest time of the year of the Roman festivals. It as it influences on the celebration of what became known as Christmas, and New Year in the Western world of the Gentile people of Europe. This celebration of theirs was spread to their various colonies of theirs, and it became a part of their conquered slave's people culture, and ways of life, of their celebration of the Christmas season story. According to volume 10 of the Encyclopaedia, Saturn is a Latin word for the word Saturnus, in the religion of the Romans, which was a god of sowing seeds. This god was compared with the Greek agricultural god, who were known as Cronus, so Saturn were a great festival that became known as Saturnalia. It was celebrated on December 17th, but it was later extended to seven more days, which came out to be December 24th. The Encyclopaedia explained that the festival of Saturnalia was the merriest festival of the year, in which all works were stopped, and business places were closed. Slaves were given temporary freedom to say, and do whatever they wanted to do, and certain moral restrictions were eased, and presents were freely exchanged. The Encyclopaedia explained that the weekday of what is now known as Saturday, it is a Latin word for Saturni, who was a Sun god. The second side of the Christmas season story of celebration was based upon the birthday of the Iranian Indian god Mitra.

According to volume 8 of the Encyclopaedia, Mitra that is also spelled as Mithras, but in the Sanskrit language of the people of India, his name was spelled as Mitra. Mitra were also a mythology god of light, that were also known as the sun of righteousness to the people of India, and Iran. The Encyclopaedia explained that the worship of the god Mitra, was spread from India to what became known as the Middle East, Spain, Germany, and Britain. The worship of the god Mithra dated back to the 14th century BC, where his worship was taken throughout the Greek Hellenistic world, of Alexander the Great, and his Generals of his Macedonia kingdoms, and colonies. During the time of the 3rd century AD, the worship of the god Mitra was carried, and supported by Roman soldiers of the Roman army.

It were the chief rival to the newly developing world of what became known as Christianity. Volume 16 of the Encyclopaedia, explained that the Christian choreographers of the 3rd century AD, believed to themselves that the creation of the world take place at the spring of what they had called as equinox. Which this word equinox was believed to be March 25th, according to their belief. According to the Webster Colligate Dictionary, the word equinox is a Latin, and a French word, that means night. According to their philosophy of belief, this is the time of the year when the sun crosses the equator, and day become night, and everywhere is of the same equal length, that accrued sometime in March 21st, or September 23rd of each year. According to the Webster Collegiate Dictionary, the word chronograph is an instrument that was used for measuring, and recording of time, and events. By so doing these Christian choreographers came up with their conception, that the death of Christ, must have occurred on the same day of his birth. Which was to them, nine months later at the winter solstice season, which came out to be December 25th, according to their belief. According to volume 11 of the Encyclopaedia, the solstice season that was mentioned, is based upon the movement of the sun, when it is further away north or south from the equator. Volume 10 of the Encyclopaedia, explained that the Roman religious calendar system was based upon the worship of a few of their main major gods, and goddess of their deities. So, the goddess Juno, and the goddess Minerva were chief among these gods, and Jupiter was a sky, and weather, god according to the belief of the Romans. Which they did established elaborate priesthood class to take care of the worship of these gods. At the head of this priesthood class was the college of the three pontiffs, who became known as the Pope of his office. There were also, 15 other priests who were to take care of the worship of these lesser gods.

The early Roman religious calendar was based upon 10 lunar months of the year that was established upon the movement of the moon. But later the 10 lunar months' system was replaced by the Romans copying the Etruscans religious calendar that was base upon the 12 months 'solar system, of the year, that came from the movement of the sun. The Encyclopaedia explained that during the Roman New Year, which was January I, houses were decorated with greenery, and lights, and gifts were given to children, and to the poor.

Volume 10 of the Encyclopaedia explained that the observance of the celebration of Christmas was later extended to the various Celtic barbarian Germanic tribes, and also to other Celtic tribes of Western, and Eastern Europe. The conquest of this Germanic tribe who were known as the Teutonic, with others Germanic people, helped to spread the Christmas spirit, that they themselves did received from the Roman Catholic Church. The Roman conquest of other Celtic tribes of Europe helped to make the Christmas festival more popular throughout Europe. This Roman festival were also passed on to other people, whom the Celtic barbarians people of Europe, did conquered, and enslaved, and many other different nations of people, to be a part of the Christmas festival of celebration. This Christmas spirit of celebration became a part of their conquered people culture, of the celebration of the Christmas story, as a way of life of each year. Of buying, and giving of gifts, and the sending of gifts to friends, and other family members. Volume 10 of the Encyclopaedia explained that food, and fellowship, the Yule log, greenery tree, gifts and greeting were all a part of the festival of the winter season they had called as the Christmas season. According to the Webster Collegiate Dictionary, the Yule log tree that was mentioned, was a large log that was cut off from a tree, that kept burning on the earth, from Christmas Eve to Christmas day. This celebration was a part of the Angles, and Saxon Germanic people tradition of West Germany, of the celebration of the Christmas festival season. Since the time of what became known as the middle Ages in Europe, the evergreen tree has been used as a symbol of the survival of the Christmas tree. From what I have gathered from reading the dictionary, and various volume of the Encyclopaedia Britannica, in the time of Old English, Christmas was spelled as Cristes maesse, in the dialect of the Angles and Saxon people of Germany, but later it was spelled as Christ's mass.

Volume 3 of the Encyclopaedia explained that according to the Roman almanac, or calendar, the Christian festival of the Christmas celebration was started in Rome in about AD 336. In the Eastern part of the Roman Empire, they had a festival of celebration that occurred on January 6th, that they held as a memorial of the appearance of God, in both the birth, and baptism of Yashua, who became known as Jesus, and Christ. In Jerusalem, this doctrine was not accepted, and they only celebrated the birth of Yashua, but no particular date was given.

During the 4th century AD, the celebration of Yashua birth on December 25 was gradually accepted in many of the eastern churches, but in Jerusalem the opposition to the Christmas celebration lasted much longer, but eventually it were accepted. In the various Armenian churches, Christmas were never accepted, and Yashua birth was celebrated on January 6th AD. The third part of the Christmas festival of celebration, was that of Saint Nicholas of Barior, or Saint Nicholas of Myra, who became known as Santa Claus, and Father Christmas. According to volume 8 of the Encyclopaedia, there is no historical record about the life of Saint Nicholas, except that he probably became a Bishop of the city of Myra, of the 4th century AD. The Encyclopaedia also explained that the city of Myra was in the country of Lycia, of what is now known as the country of Turkey. As tradition has it, Saint Nicholas was born in the country of Lycia, in the seaport of Patara. According to the Encyclopaedia, when Saint Nicholas was a young man, he traveled to the land of what the Roman did name as the land of Palestine, and went he went back to the country of Lycia, he became a Bishop of the city of Myra. Later he was put into prison by Emperor Diocletian who was a persecutor of the Roman Catholic Christians. He was finally released under the reign of Emperor Constantine the Great, and later attended the first Christian council of churches that was held in Nicaea in Cyprus, in 325 AD. I must point out that the council of churches that were mentioned above, was that of the Roman Catholic Churches that was known as the church, or churches of those days. Volume 8 of the Encyclopaedia, did not explained how Saint Nicholas died, but according to the Encyclopaedia, in the 6 century AD, a shrine was made for Saint Nicholas in the city of Myra.

From there in 1087 AD, Italian solders brought the remains of Saint Nicholas to be buried in the city of Bari, of what is now known as Italy. The word shrine according to the Webster's Collegiate Dictionary, means a box, the tomb that contains the remains of a person who was approved to be a Saint by the Roman Catholic Church. That one might see around many Roman Catholic Churches, and homes of their believers, as well as their businesses places. Volume 8 of the Encyclopaedia explained that the removal of the remains of Saint Nicholas to the city of Bari, on May 9th, greatly increased his popularity. So, the city of Bari became one of the most crowded pilgrimage center of the time, in the honor of worship and praise to Saint Nicholas. The Encyclopaedia explained that the transformation of Saint Nicholas into Father Christmas, or Father January, occurred first in Germany.

Later it was spread into other countries of Europe, where the Reformation churches, or the Protestant churches were in the majority. One of my reasons for writing about the Saint Nicholas story, it is to show to the people of Ham, and other people of the world, whom the Gentile people of Europe had captured, and indoctrinated, and enslave our minds to be become worshippers of Saint Nicholas. Also, of their many other pagan gods, of their holidays that many of us their captive's people celebrate with sincerity. Also, with other false doctrines of things that they the Gentile people of Europe had believed in, that they had taught to many of us their captives people, who came under their colonial system of ruler ship. Or what we, and many other people who came under their captivity, had copy from them, and we became believers of their religious doctrines, and culture that was pass down from them to us. To give one a good example of what I am speaking about, when I was growing up as a little boy in the Kingston area of Jamaica, there were a song that was taught in my school, and I suppose other children may have sung this song at their school. Or at their homes about Saint Nicholas, who became known as Father Christmas, and Santa Clause. The song I am referring to goes like this, "Jolly Old Saint Nicholas lean your ears this way, and don't you tell a single soul what I am going to say. Christmas Eve is coming soon now you dear old man. Whisper what you will bring for me, tell me if you can. Down the chimney broad and black with your stocking you will creep. Johnny wants a pair of skates; Susie wants a dolly. Nelly wants a storybook; she thinks doll is folly. As for me dear Santa Claus my brain is not very bright. Choose for me dear Santa Clause, what you think is right."

Different relatives used to say to me, I must put up my stocking on the wall, so that Santa Claus can come and put my present into my stocking, which was a total nonsense, but at the time I did believe that Santa Claus was true. Volume 8 of the Encyclopaedia explained that many people in Europe named their sons after the name of Saint Nicholas. Their reason for naming their sons after Saint Nicholas is a part of reverent, respect, glory, and worship to him. I must point out that there is no Scriptural date stating that Yashua was born as a man on December 25th. The Scripture book at (Colossians Chapter 1, and verse 15), clearly explained that Yashua is the first born of every creature Yahweh has created.

Furthermore, Yashua himself point out after his resurrection, when he went back to heaven, to site on the right-hand side of Yahweh, that is mentioned at (Revelation Chapter 3, and verse 14), that he is the beginning of the creation of Yahweh, or the first creation of Yahweh. The point that I am trying to bring out here is this, Yashua did not only had an earthly beginning, but in harmony with the writing of the Holy Scripture, there it stated that Yashua was always in the beginning of the creation of the world with Yahweh his creator. This was before Yahweh put the spirit of Yashua into the womb of Mary to be born as a man here on earth. To please his Father Yahweh, and to do His will, by sacrificing of his life for the sins of the Children of Israel, and for the world of mankind at large. Also, that Yashua would become the second Adam in whom all the people of the earth shall gain everlasting life true him. Those people, who believed on him, and obey his teaching he gave to his Apostles to teach other believers, will become the people of Yahweh, and Yashua, in the new order of things to come. Furthermore, the Scripture book of (Hebrew Chapter 1, and verse 10), clearly mentions that Yashua was a master builder with Yahweh, because he helped to lay the foundation of the world with Him. Not that Yahweh needed any help to do anything, or to make anything, but Yahweh chose to do so, because he is the boss, and what He says goes. So, when Yashua came to earth to be born as a little baby boy, and to grow up and to become a man, and then died, he only came to please his Father, and to fulfill the will of Yahweh and His wishes. This was to offer his life as the perfect sacrifice for the sins of the children of Israel, who would believe on him, that he was the promise Mashiah who was to come to them. Who was the promise savior of the world of mankind, to save many who believe, and obey his teaching, from the wrath of Yahweh that is to come.

It is also written in (John Chapter 3, and verse 16), that Yahweh so love the world of the people, that He gave, or send His only begotten Son, that whosoever believe on him, would not perish from the wrath to come, but will receive everlasting life. Because as it is so written in the Scripture, that without the sacrifice blood of Yashua, there can be no forgiveness of sin by Yahweh. (I Timothy Chapter 2, and verse 4), clearly explained that there is one mediator between Yahweh, and men, and that is Yashua, better known to many as Jesus Christ. According to the Webster Collegiate Dictionary, the word mediator means one who mediates, or acts as a go between parties.

So, in the case of Yashua, he acts as a go between men, and Yahweh, to save those who believed on him, and those who follow his teaching from the wrath, and destructions of Yahweh that is to come. Yashua also came to earth, to be born in the family line of David, to inherit, and sit on David throne, as Yahweh did promise David, at (2 Samuel Chapter 7, verse 13, and verse 16), that He Yahweh will establish David throne forever. So, Yashua also came to earth, to in heart David throne, on that will be at his second coming, to be the king over all the earth. In a small King James Version of what became known as the Bible, that was published by Thomas Nelson Inc, that I have in my position. In this little Bible there are a few pages that give the reader an inside history of how the Scripture, that became known as the Bible by the people of Greece. Also how the Scripture came into the English language, from the Latin Vulgate version of the writing of the Scripture that came down to the Romans, who did had control over Europe. Also, there were many different events that were taking place during the time of BC, to the time of early AD. On page 32 of this little Bible, in a section that is called the Bible chart, there is a number five with a question sign. The reason for this question sign, of this little Bible, there it mention 5 BC with a question sign, with the subheading of the savior comes. The translators start by saying that Jesus Christ was born when the Christian calendar was set up, and it was intended that the year of his birth should have been AD 1. According to the Webster Colligate Dictionary, the word AD is a Latin word that stands for Anno Domini, which mean in the year of our Lord Yashua. This paragraph went on to explained that there were a mistake made in the date that was assigned to King Herod, which came shortly after Yashua was born. According to volume 5 of the Encyclopaedia, Herod that was mentioned, were also known as Herod the Great. His Latin name were known as Herodes Magnus, who were born in 73 BC, and died March, or April of 4 BC in Jericho.

Which this place of Jericho was of the Jordan area, of the land of Canaan that became known as Israel. So, from what I have gathered from the reading of volume 5 of the Encyclopaedia, is that in the time of the New Covent Era, Herod was known as a tyrant, in whose kingdom Yashua was born as a baby boy in Nazareth. Who were the one who was seeking to take the life of Yashua, because he felt threaten of his kingship by another king.

This same volume went on to explained that Herod was born in what became known as southern Palestine, and his father were known as Antipater, who was an Edomites, or an Arab from the area of the Dead Sea. I must point out that I am not quite sure this statement the Encyclopaedia give about Herod father as an Edomites is of the right information. My reason for saying this, it is because the Edomites tribe that the Encyclopaedia mentions, came from Esau, who was the brother of Jacob. The mothers of these Edomites people came from two Canaanites women, and from a daughter of Ishmael of the people of Ham. Furthermore, the name Antipater is associated with the people of Greece, who became known as the Greek people. My reason for saying this, it is because a man by the name of Antipater, who were a general of the army of Philip the II, of his Macedonian empire, who help to secure the Macedonian throne for Philip son, when Philip was assonated. So, Philip's son became known as Alexander the Great, and this man was Greek. So, technically speaking, King Herod that was mentioned was not from the tribe of Yehuda, but he was of a Greek descendants, who were ruling as a king of Judea. According to what I have read, Herod had given his support to the invading army of Pompey, in what became known as Palestine, in the time of 106-48 BC. Herod was also a supporter of Julius Caesar, who did appoint him ruler of Judaea in 47 BC, and who also gave him Roman citizenship. So, in 40 BC there was a civil war that was taking place in Herod territory, and he had to flee to Rome, and it was the Senate of Rome who made him king of Judaea, and who gave him a strong army to secure his kingship. According to the volume, in the year of 37 BC, at the age of 36, Herod became the an challengeable ruler of Judaea, a position he kept for 32 years.

According to this same little King James Version of the Bible, this date of King Herod was used to calculate the date, and time of Yashua birth, which led to this mistake in setting up the Christian calendar by the Romans. During Roman time, Herod was one of the richest, and the most powerful of the various protected colony kingdom of Rome. The Encyclopaedia explained that after the death of Herod, in what became known as the land of Palestine, his kingdom was divided among his three sons. One of his sons were known as Philip, who was given ruler ship over a part of the province of Israel, and he rules from 37 to 4 BC. According to this same volume of the Encyclopaedia, there were another son of Herod, whose name was known as Herod Antipas, who was given ruler ship over Galilee.

Also over an era that was called Peraea, and he rules from AD 39, and this was the same Herod who had John the Baptist beheaded. There were another son of Herod who were known as Archelaus, and who were given ruler ship over Judaea, and Samaria, and an area that were known as Idumaea. But he was removed from his position by the Romans, for his oppressive rule ship in AD 6, and he was replaced by a Roman governor. According to this same volume 14 of the Encyclopaedia, there were two other Herod, who had ruler ship during the New Covenant era. One were known as Agrippa I, and another was known as Herod the king, who ruled from AD 37, to AD 44. He was the one who had James the brother of John killed, and who also had Peter arrested, according to what I had have read from the Encyclopaedia. The other Herod was known as Agrippa II, who was a king of a place that was known as Trichinosis, from AD 50 to 100 AD. According to this same paragraph of this Bible document, to correct this error about the birth of Yashua, it must be given as 4 BC, or maybe it can be assumed that he was born on December 5th BC, with a question sign. I must point out that these Gentile European translators were only speculating, who had no sure knowledge of what they were writing about, as far as the date when Yashua was born as a man here on earth. Furthermore, as I have mentioned before, that there are many Scriptures to prove that Yashua had a heavenly beginning, before he was sent to earth by Yahweh, to be made known in the flesh to Israel. To grow up as a man, and then sacrificed his life for the sin of Isreal, and for the rest of the people of the world. Yashua did not told his Apostles to celebrate his birth, as a form of an holiday, or an feast day. But rather he told them they should celebrate his death, as a memorial to him until he returns. At (1 Corinthians Chapter 11, verse 24, and verse 25), there the Apostle Paul was explaining that he was sent by Yashua to be a minister to the Gentile people, of what become known as the land of Europe.

This was to bring them from out of darkness, and from the worshipping of idols, and demons, and to bring them to the light, and the knowledge of the writing of the Holy Scripture. Also for them to become worshippers of Yahweh. The Apostle Paul was quoting from (Matthew Chapter 26, and verse 26 to verse 28), when he was explaining to the Yehudahites who were living there in Europe, also, to many Gentiles people, who became believers, that on the night while Yashua was celebrating the Passover, before he was nailed to the tree by the Romans.

He took bread, and blessed it, and gave thanks to his Father, and his God, and he also said to his disciples, "take eat, this is my body." He also take the cup, and gave thanks to his Father, and gave the cup to his disciples, and said to them, "drink you all of it. For this is my blood of the establishment of the New Covenant" that became known as the New Testament, by the Gentile people of Greece. That was shed for many for the forgiveness of sin. At (1 Corinthians Chapter 11), there Paul was explaining to the various people who he was speaking to, by saying to them, that Yashua said to his disciples that they must keep on doing this celebration of his death, until he returns to judge the world of mankind for their deeds. This is the same celebration of Yashua death that the Roman Catholic Church celebrates, and call as communion. To many people who do not know what the word communion means, nor understand the importance of this feast that was mostly for the Apostles class. Who were known as the elects, or the chosen ones, that is now translated as the Saints. According to the Scripture, one must be very careful, how he or she eats, and drinks at Yashua table, because this eating, and drinking at the Yashua table, were mostly for his disciples, who were known as the chosen ones, of the elects, and the little flock. It is also mentioned at (1 Corinthian Chapter 11, and verse 29) that whosoever eat, or drink at the Lord Yashua table unworthy, eat and drink damnation to themselves, not discerning the body of Yashua. Furthermore, this UN Yahweh Pagan Gentile European holiday that became known as Christmas, has nothing to do with the birth of Yashua coming to earth, to be born as a man. Just think about it, this holiday of celebration, of getting drunk, committing fornication, and adultery, going to rum bars, clubs, house parties, as many people has the saying, having a good time. Where there are sodomites, lesbians, prostitutes, winos, murderers, and all sorts of wicked, and UN Yahweh like people.

Also, UN Yashua like people, who claimed they are celebrating the birthday of Yashua. This psychology, and strategy of the making of money, that the Christmas spirit season is all about, has nothing to do with Yashua, and his Father Yahweh, who is the God of Yashua, and of all people. Yashua said in (John Chapter 17, and verse 14), when he was here on earth praying to his Father, that he, and his disciples were no part of that worldly UN Yahweh like system, that did exist there in the time of the Romans, ruling over what is now called as the Middle East, and North Africa.

I am quite sure that Yashua has no part in this present-day political UN Yahweh like system, that in my opinion is far more corrupted, and more UN Yahweh like, and more wicked than when he was here on earth. The question I would like to ask is this: how can all these worldly people, I have mentioned above claim they are celebrating the birthday of Yashua, who is righteous and Holy? If the Scripture did even give an actual date of when Yashua came to earth to be born as a baby, and to grow up as a man, how could the world of people all over celebrate this date or day? When he was only speaking to those chosen few of his disciples, who were from the tribe of Yehuda, and from the tribe of Benjamin, of the children of Israel, who were left there in the land that he was sent to? Who are known in the Scripture as the elects or the chosen ones. Also, Yashua clearly said at (Matthew Chapter 15, and verse 24), that he was only sent to the lost sheep of the house of Israel. At (John, Chapter 4, and verse 22) there Yashua clearly said that salvation is of the Jews, or for the tribe of Yehuda, from where the name Jews was taken from, that came from the Latin word Judah. Moreover, when Yashua was here on the earth, he did not have any dealing with the whole world of UN Yahweh like people, but only those chosen few believers of the tribe of Yehuda, and the tribe of Benjamin, who were left there in the land of Israel, who did believe on him, that he was the Son of Yahweh, who were sent to them.

The Gentile People Pagan Holidays of Easter, that came from Roman Catholicism, of the Roman Catholic Church. According to the Webster Collegiate Dictionary, their it explained that the meaning of the word Roman Catholicism, simply means the way of the Roman Catholic Church, and their philosophy. Of their belief, of teaching, they have taught to many people, who came under their captivity to see things their way. Many of Roman Catholicism of their belief, and teaching were not based upon true teaching came from the Scripture, but it was based upon their religious Theologians philosophy, doctoring, and commandments of men. That came from out of the Roman Catholic Church, of their worship to their many gods. As I had mention before that the word Theo gave birth to the word Theologians, that came from the name of Theo, who was a god of Greece, that came down into the Roman religious 'system of their many gods. A good example of some of their pagan worship, that were infused into what became known as Christianity, is Good Friday, which is based upon Easter. According to the Webster's Collegiate Dictionary, there it explained that Friday as we know it as today, came from the Anglo-Saxon goddess who was known as Frigedaeg. In the French dialect she was known as the goddess Frig. The dictionary also explained that Easter as it is known as today, came from the Anglo-Saxon goddess, who were also known as Eastre, and n Old French she was known as Teut, who was a goddess of spring. Volume 26 of the Encyclopaedia, explained that many of the ancient gods of these people survived either as demons, or by having their function transferred into Christian Saints.

Fertility right were given to the various gods, who were attached to the various Christian festivals of holidays in the honoring of these gods, and goddess feasts days. Such as eggs, and rabbits for the Easter celebration. According to volume 4 of the Encyclopaedia there it explained that Easter is the principal festival of the Christian Church year of Roman Catholicism. This is of the celebration of the resurrection of Yashua, who became known as Jesus, and Christ. The Encyclopaedia went on to explain that the origin of this Christian Easter celebration goes back to the beginning of Christianity, which is totally false.

My reason for making this kind of statement, it is because, as I have mention in various pages of this book, that what became known as Christianity, came from the Way in Israel of the teaching of Yashua to his Apostles. So, there were no Easter among the Apostles of Yashua, who were the early, and true believers, and followers of him, who were known as those who follow the Way. Speaking of Yashua who was known as the Way in Israel, by the high priest, Pharisees, Sadducees, and Scribes. Who did not believe on him that he was the Son of Yahweh, the one who was sent to them the Yehudahites, and the Benjamites people of Isreal. Who became known as the congregation of believers, that were translated as the church, by the Gentile people of Europe. I must also point out that when reading from the Scripture, there is no where there where the Apostles of Yashua, described themselves as the church, or a Christians, but rather they describe themselves as the followers, and servant of Yashua, and true worshipers of Yahweh, that was called as the faith in Yahweh. To whom alone all worship belong. But the word church came from the Roman Catholic believers, and from the Greeks word Kyriakon, which were a place for the gathering of various business activities. So, the Apostles of Yashua were not paganism, of idolatry worship, or that of any form of falsehood of the Roman Catholic Church, but they were true believers, and followers of Yashua, and true worshipers of Yahweh without any form of hypocrisy. They the Apostles of Yashua, were not like that of many Gentile European believers, who became known as Christians, and Christian countries of Europe. Many of whom profess to be followers of Christ, as many of them saw themselves, but many of whom were hypocrisy, evil, and wicked people, followers of Satan the devil. Apart from Judas who was known as the son of perdition that the prophecy of the Scripture did fulfill on, as it was so prophesied of him, showing of his hypocrisy, and deceitfulness.

The Encyclopaedia went on to explained that Western Christians, which is speaking of Western Europe, celebrate Easter on the first Sunday after the full moon of Paschal, that occur on equinox. Which this word equinox, is March 21, of each year, according to the Encyclopaedia. According to volume 9 of the

Encyclopaedia, there it explained that Paschal that was mentioned, is also spelled as Pascal, which is a Latin name for various Roman Catholic Popes.

According to volume 4 of the Encyclopaedia, the Easter celebration can fall between March 22, and April 25 of each year. These dates were established after much disputed between the various ecclesiastical priests, and bishops of the Christian Church of Rome, that came down to the 8th century AD. Which is speaking of the Pope and his office. I would like to mention that the word bishop according to the Webster Colligate Dictionary, came from the Anglo-Saxon dialect, that were taken from the Latin word Episcopal. Which mean according to them, an overseer, or head of the Catholic Diocese Church, which is the office of the Pope, or the priest. The Eastern Orthodox Churches of the Eastern part of the Gentile land of Europe, is an extension of Roman Catholicism of the Catholic Church, that was given the name as Orthodox. This Roman Catholicism of the Orthodox Church, have a different calculation for the time of Easter, that can fall on one or four weeks after the Western celebration of Easter. These Gentile church fathers, as the Encyclopaedia classified many of them of Roman Catholicism to be, who came up with their own philosophy of the Easter story. These church Canon laws, of what become known as Christianity, it was design to govern their church believers lives, of their laws, of the does, and do not. Many of their church laws, and philosophies was later passed on down to many people, who became their captives, and slaves of the Gentile people of Western, and Europe. This was a church way of life to their various pastors, and priests, for their believers to follow, as a Christian was of life, of their religious system, that became known as Christianity. According to volume 16 of the Encyclopaedia, there it explained that in the time of 190 AD. Bishop Victor of Rome threatened to excommunicate Christians of Asia Minor, who were following the memorial custom of the observance of Easter on the day of the Jewish Passover. Rather than at Rome on the Sunday after the first full moon, after the spring of equinox.

 I have already explained in the Christmas story about the meaning of the word equinox, this is the reason why I did not bother to mention the definition about equinox in this section of the Easter story. I have gained much knowledge from the reading of a booklet that is titled who is Baal? This booklet came from the House of Yahweh Worship in Texas. Reading from volume 1 of the Encyclopaedia, about the goddess Astarte who was a Canaanite goddess, the impression I have gotten from reading these documents, it seems to me that the name Easter, was taken from the name of the Phoenician goddess, whose name was known as Astarte.

Who was worship in the land of Zidon, or Sidon, which the word Sidon it is a Greek, and Latin name for Canaan first son of Canaan, who was known as Zidon. This land area of Zidon, is what became known today as the land of Syria, by Alexander the Great, and his Greek settlers. So, this goddess Astarte was worship by the Phoenician, Hethites, and in the land of Mizraim as well. This goddess Astarte was also worship by the Etruscan people of what became known as the land of Italy. These Etruscan people were allies to the Phoenician people of Canaan, and also to the people of Carthage. This was way before the Latin people of Rome came along, and take over ruler ship of the land area of what become known as Italy. This was from the various natives who were living there, before they the Romans came, and conquer the land that did become a Roman province. These Etruscans people was living in the land area that became known as Italy, with many other tribes, who were living there, way before the coming of the Romans. Who came, and captured the land area from the various natives who were living there, before they came along. They the Etruscan people used to worship the Phoenician goddess in one of their cities by the name of Pyrgi. This Etruscan goddess was known as Astarte. The reason why this goddess name may have came down into the Angles, and Saxon people dialect of Germany, as Easter, it is because the Germanic people education came from Latin, and Greek, which originally came from the Phoenician people writing alphabetical system. Also, from the Hethites Canaanites people, and from the people of Mizraim alphabetical writing system, that did become the educational system of Europe. Which they the Greeks had copy from the Phoenician alphabetical writing system, and it became their alphabetical writing system to the rest of the Gentile land that became known as Europe. So, when the Romans take over Italy from the Etruscans, and other tribes who were living in the land area.

Then this Phoenician goddess came down into the Roman religious system, that were pass on to these Germanic people, as a part of their religious system, to the goddess Astarte. This also included with that of many Greek gods that came down in the Romans religious system, that gave birth to the religious system of Rome, from where the Roman Catholic Church came out of. This religious system of the Etruscans, and the Greeks was later spread to Western, and Eastern Europe, by the Roman Empire that did became their provinces.

This Latin language of the Romans was later passed on to the various Germanic Celtic barbarian's tribes of Western, and Eastern Europe, who were educated by the Roman, and the Roman Catholic Church. It seems to me that they have changed the spelling of the word Astarte into an E. Which became known as Easter, in the Angles, or the English language, as it is known as today. One should not be surprised of the changing around of the spelling of words, and names that came down into the English, or the Angles language of today. Like in the case of the word English, that originally came from the name of the Angles, Saxon people of Germany, which they have changed around from Angles to English, that should have spelled as Angles with A, for the name Angles. Also, the spelling of the name Hittites, that should have spelled as Hethites. These descendants of Heth, became known as the Hethites people, who they the Gentile people of Europe spell as Hittites, and who they say was an Indo-European people, which is nothing but lies, and false history. According to the Gentile people, and their writings of history, many of the civilization of Europe came from them, the Hethites, and the Phoenician people of Canaan. Also from the people of Mizraim, now known as the Egyptian people. Also, the spelling of the word Aprica, which is now spelled as Africa, in the English language, that originally came from the Romans name Aprica, that was apply to the northern part of the land of Ham. This was due to the Roman conquest over the Carthaginian people of Ham, of what became known as North Africa. According to the Webster Colligate Dictionary of the Fifth Edition, the word Astarte came from Latin, French, and from Greek, who were a goddess of the Phoenician people. This goddess was worshipped as a fertility, and a sexual goddess of love. This goddess Astarte was also a goddess of war, and she may have been the same goddess that were known as Anath. Who were a goddess of the Aramaic people, that was also spelled as Atargatis, so the Aramaic language came from the Canaanite people.

This goddess was also worship in the land of Mizraim as the goddess Astarte, and she was also, known as the goddess Ugarit among the Hethites people of Canaan. Easter, and Easter Sunday, and Good Friday were all infused into what become a part of the various Christian holidays, that many of the Gentile free slave's people, were taught to embrace as the Holy weekdays of Christianity, of Roman Catholicism.

These holidays of the years of the Gentile European people were design for them to make big money from these holidays, that they have introduce to their many captive, and free slave people mines of today. I must point out that Easter is based upon the Passover celebration of the children of Israel, who came from out of the land of Mizraim, known today as Egypt. The blood of the lamb was put on the doorpost of the children of Israel, so that the angel of death who killed all the first born of the people of Mizraim, would see the blood, and Passover the doors of the children of Israel. This celebration of the children of Israel is what became known as the Passover. This Passover celebration Yahweh gave to the children of Israel, for them to keep throughout all their generations, as a memorial, to remind them they were taken from out of the land of Mizraim as slaves. Many people who have been captured, and conquered by the Gentile family of what become known as the Europeans people, were indoctrinated to accept and to believe in many of their pagan festival holidays. Such as Christmas, Easter, Good Friday, New Year, and what is now known as the Thanksgiving Day of the United States. According to volume 11 of the Encyclopaedia, there it explained that what became known as the Thanksgiving Day, was established in the autumn of 1621 AD. When Plymouth governor whose name was known as William Bradford, invited some of the native over, who they call as Indians. This was for them to join them in what they had called as the Pilgrims three-day festival of recreation, and feasting of their bountiful harvest season of that year. So, again, the Gentile people have established Thanksgiving Day for their many captives, and free slaves' people of the United States, who became their citizens, to celebrate this holiday of their conquest over the natives, of their lands.

Also, this Thanksgiving holiday was design to make money from their many conquered people of what became known as the United States, all in name of making of money from off their many captives people, who celebrate this Thanksgiving Day as a commercial form of celebration, of buying gifts, and giving gifts. I must also point out that people must give thanks to Yahweh every day of their lives, for all the things He has given to us, His creation here on earth, without any form of price to be paid. Apart from giving Him true worship, and parse to His Holly and wonderful name, as the Yahweh of our life. Without the commercial aspect of the making of money, for their many merchants, and store owners at their place of business to get rich.

Volume 16 of the Encyclopaedia, explained that during the early days of the expansion of the church, the (Roman Catholic Church), they had to accommodate itself to the modes of thought, language, and behavior of their many new converts. Many of these converts brought with them their former pagan ways, and beliefs into what became known as the church, and Christianity. The strategy of the church was to accommodate itself to the thought, language, and behavior of these many converts, so when many of these people became converts, many of them brought in their former paganism ways into the church. This was much the same way in the Roman world, where Christianity spread abroad true the conversion of many people. Much more so in the Germanic lands where a complete tribe accepted the faith. Reading from Volume 16 of the Encyclopaedia, there it explained that when Charlemagne of the Frankish kingdom became emperor of the Roman system, that was spread from Italy to France, and various part of Europe, he had power over the Roman Catholic Church, and he appointed bishops, and popes of what was to be accepted in the church. According to volume 26 of the Encyclopaedia, there it explained that when Otto I of Germany conquered northern Italy, in 962 AD, he and his grandson, who were known Otto III regarded the territory of the papal system of Rome as a part of their province of domain. They appointed, and remove popes as they so choose to do. This was to please themselves of what became a part of the ecclesiastical council of the Church of Rome, as a political body, of their influences. Christianity is of Roman Catholicism, of it do and don'ts, that were not base upon Scriptural teaching, that came from Yahweh, and Yashua to his Apostles. But rather, this religious system of theirs, came from their own doctoring, of what they see as right or wrong, from their pagan religious views, and laws that came down into the church, that were known by the Greek as Kyriakon. Volume 16 of the Encyclopaedia mentioned that as Christianity expanded from the Mediterranean area to various converts.

Many of whom did not leave their religious pagan belief behind, but many of them brought into the church their various pagan gods, such as the Roman god of war, who was known as Mars. According to their belief, this god was transferred into Michael the archangel, who led the heavenly host into battle against the dragon, who is Satan the devil. In many of the early churches of Europe, a good example of their pagan belief, was that the archangels materialized themselves as Santiago, Saint George, and Saint Michael.

Durian the Middle Age, many of the Germanic tribes from the Baltic to the Slavic area of Europe, many of their former gods was transferred into Saints, such as Saint George who rescued a lady after slaying the dragon. Many of their belief they had brought into what become known as Christianity, of their mythology, and legends of their belief. Many of the ancient gods of these people survived, either as demons, or by having their functions transferred into Christian Saints. Volume 16 of the Encyclopaedia mentioned that many of these Christians of Rome of the 3rd century AD, build shrines, or in other words a worship place for Peter, and Paul, who they did approve to be a part of the early Christians Saints of Roman Catholicism. According to volume 16 of the Encyclopaedia, the worship of Mary, as a part of the body of Saints, and as the mother of God, as they did put it, were introduce during the 3rd century AD, that became a part of the worship of the Catholic Church believers. Volume 16 of the Encyclopaedia also mention that Constantine built the basilicas, this was for the worship of Peter, and Paul, who were a part of these Saints of the Roman Catholic Church. According to the Webster Colligate Dictionary, the word basilicas meant, a public hall of assembly, an early Christian church of Saint Paul Basilica of Rome. Where people would gather to worship these Saints of the Catholic Church. Many of these early Christians of Rome were so involve in their idolatry belief, and that of which craft to these Saints, that bones of many of these men, who were consider as Saints, by the time of 400 AD, particular Saints were invoked from the grave for needs, for health, and for fertility. So, the action of many of these early Christians of Rome, were mix-up with which craft they had called as Christianity.

Many of these Saints were also known as martyrs, which the word martyrs meant according to the Webster Colligate Dictionary, one who voluntarily suffer death, refusing to renounce their religion. So, many of these martyrs or Saint was worship as gods, which is of idolatry worship to a men, for all worship belongs to Yahweh only. When this Germanic barbarian leader who were known as Alaric's Goths invaded and sacked Rome in 410 AD. Many Christians of Rome asked the question, why did Peter, and Paul failed to protect their city of Rome, durian the invasion of the Goths? So, in other words, Peter and Paul were worship by many of these early Christian of Rome as gods. After the event, many of these people believed the old gods of Rome, who were givers of success, and miracles, were offended by their neglect of their worshipers, not worshiping them as the way they used to do in early former days.

Volume 16 of the Encyclopaedia mentioned that to please these early Christian of Rome, the church found it necessary to provide similar assurances of success of miraculous, and patron from these Saints. According to their belief, by the time of the 6th century AD, wonder working shrines, and cloths that touched what they had called holly relics. Pictures of icon of Saints were invested with numerous spiritual powers, into the church to satisfy the spiritual needs of these Christians. Due to the belief of idolatry worship of the early Christians tradition of Rome, even highly educated figures, such as Augustine, and Pope Gregory, who also were known as Pope Gregory the Great. He was very sympathetic to this popular movement of idolatry, and witchcraft, because it was a means of winning various barbarian's tribal men, and their families over to Christianity. A bishop by the name of Ulfilas whom volume 16 of the Encyclopaedia describes as a member of the Goth tribe of Germanic people, who converted the Goths tribe into the Arianism faith, of the Catholic Church, in 340-350 AD. According to volume 1 of the Encyclopaedia, the word Arianism came from Arian who held some leading position in the early Catholic Church of Rome, who also was an emperor of Asia Minor of the Turkey area. The Encyclopaedia explained that the Arianism philosophy was that Christ is not of the same divine nature as that of Yahweh the Father. But he is a created being of Yahweh, so the Son could not be of the same equal position like that of the Father, which is right. Due to his teaching that did not go so well with the belief of the Catholic Church, he was condemned by the Catholic Church Council of Nicaea of AD 325, and was put out of the church. His teaching of belief later became known as the Arianism.

Because the Catholic Church believers believed that Yashua, who became known as Jesus and Christ, is on the same equal standing with that of Yahweh, who is the creator of Yashua, and Father of all things. So, this is the reason why they the Roman Catholic Church came up with the trinity, who they say is a part of this triune Gods, which is totally false, and it is not in harmony with the teaching of the Scripture of truth. I must also, point out that the Holy Ghost that they the Roman Catholic Church translate, and teach to their various church members, as a part of this trinity. Is the Holy Spirit of Yahweh they teach to their members as another God of this trinity, which is a total false teaching of lies.

According to volume 16 of the Encyclopaedia, there it explained that the Goths of their Arian teaching of faith, was pass on to other Germanic tribes, such as the Vandals, the Franks, and other Germanic family of people. It is just like how it is mention in many of the churches of today as the trinity, that they say is Yashua, who is a part of this trinity, of the God Head body. So, many of the churches, it is a business place for making money from their many members, who do not have much knowledge, and understanding of the teaching of the Scripture for themselves, to know any different from the falsehood that they were thought to them to believed in.

The Gentile paganism celebration of what they called as the Valentine Day, that is based on sexual love, and romance. From what I have gathered from reading volume 12 of the Encyclopaedia, the Valentine day story has various sides to it. The first side of this story about Valentine, is a man, who was born in Rome by the name of Valentinus, which is a Latin name, at unknown date, that the Encyclopaedia did not give much details about this person, who they say was a Pope for forty days during the time of August to September of 827 AD. He was an archdeacon, which meant according to the Webster Collegiate Dictionary, a chief deacon, who was next in rank below that of the bishop, who was the Pope of St, Paschal of Rome. According to the Encyclopaedia, this man was a beloved person for his goodness, and piety to the poor, and because of that, he was elected as Pope in August of that year, but his rain were short live, because he died very shortly after. The second side to the Valentine Day story, is what became known as St. Valentine's Day, that was set aside as an observance of this day of February 14, of each year, for buying gifts, and giving gifts to sexual lovers, that has nothing to do with the true love that come from Yahweh to all mankind. Of His creation, that we as His creatures should show toward each other as true love. The Encyclopaedia explained that this Saint Valentine's Day celebration custom, has no connection to do with that of St. Valentines, or his life story. This Valentine's Day of celebration was first established from the 14th to the 16th century AD, leading up to the 1800. This was for buying gift, and sending greeting cards to lovers. By the time of the 1800, this romantic celebration became a big business for making money, for buying gifts, and sending greeting cards to lovers of the Gentile European system of sexual love.

They had introduce to many of us their conquered free slave people mines of today, who become their citizens to make money from this celebration of sexual love, and romance. The third part of this Saint Valentine's Day story came from the 3rd century, of Rome, which was a feast day of February 14, that was connected to two religious 'legions, who the Roman Catholic Church classified as Saint, and who was given the title as martyrs. According to the Webster's Colligate Dictionary, there it explains that the word martyrs is Angles, Saxon, and Late Latin word. So, these religious figureheads of their's, one who was a priest, and the other was a physician who had suffered death during the persecution of the Roman Catholic Christians, by emperor Claudius II.

These men was buried in Via Flaminia of what is now known as Italy. The Encyclopaedia went on to explained that Pope St. Julius I built a basilica over the grave of these men, who were considered as Saints.

Chapter 29 - The Greeks and Etruscans Religious System That Came to Rome

The Greeks and Etruscans Religious system that became that of the Roman religious 'system. In the region of the Greek communities of southern Italy, there were many Greek gods who were introduce into the religious system of the Roman. Along with the various other gods the Romans had gotten from the Etruscan people, that they did adopted as their gods, of their religious system. A good example of the Romans engrafting Greek gods into their worship, is when the Romans brought in the Greek god Apollo into their religious system, in the late 5th century BC, according to volume 18 of the Encyclopaedia. In the southern part of Italy, the goddess Ceres who was a deity of nature, and she was also identified with the Greek goddess Demeter, who was a goddess of grain of sowing of seeds, during the threaten time of famine, according to their belief. According to the Encyclopaedia Britannica, many of the temples of Rome were built in Etruscan stile, also, with many Greek ornaments that stud on the Aventine Hill of Rome. According to volume 3 of the Encyclopaedia, Cumae which was an ancient Greek city that was 12 miles from of the city of Naples, was one of the oldest Greek mainland colonies, in southern Italy. Volume 18 of the Encyclopaedia explained that this Greek city of Cumae plays a great part in the introduction of the worship of the god Apollo, to the tribe of the Sibylline people, who were a part of the various natives of the land that became known as Italy. In the 1800, the land area of what was given the name of Italy, by the conquest of Napoleon Bonaparte of what is now known as France. Also, when the Romans take over what is now known as Italy, from the Etruscans, and from other tribes who were living there, before they, the Romans came, and take over the land area. Many of the Sibylline people, and their gods also became a part of the Romans religious system, that came down in the religious system of the Catholic Church of today.

When Augustus became emperor of the Roman conquered land, of what is now known as Italy, he glorified the god Apollo as a portion of himself, and of his army. This glorifying of the god Apollo by Augustus was intended to highlight the worship of this god of peace, and civilization to the glory of Rome, accord to their belief. Reading from volume 18 of the Encyclopaedia, there it explained that the goddess Fors, or Fortuna, whose temple was on the Tiber hill area of Rome, this goddess was a goddess of farming that eventually became the goddess of luck.

This goddess was identified with the Greek Hellenistic goddess, whose name was known as Tyche, who was a goddess of fortune, and luck to the people of Greece. The Encyclopaedia explained that Fortuna temple was on the Tiber hill area of Rome; and it was one of the few temples where slaves were given the permission to enter. According to the Encyclopaedia, two of the Etruscan gods by the name of Vulcan, and Saturn, which was a god of fire that was identified with the Greek blacksmiths god, whose name was Hephaestus. This god was an agricultural god, with that of the Greek god Cronus, who they say was the father of Zeus. Volume 18 of the Encyclopaedia explained that it was an Etruscan king who began to build the most elaborate Roman temples that was devoted on the Capitoline hill of Rome to the Triad gods, from where the word trinity was taken from. These tried gods were known as Jupiter, Juno, and Minerva, who were a part of the various gods of the Etruscan people of what became known as Italy. The goddess Asclepius, or Aesculapius was introduced into the religious worship of the Romans in 293 BC, to fight off a deadly disease that was affecting the Romans in that time. According to Volume 5 of the Encyclopaedia, the Great Mother Cyble was also brought into the religious worship of the Romans, in 204 BC, at a time that was extremely critical in the Roman history. This was when the land area that became known as Italy was invaded by Hannibal the Great, and his army during the second Punic war with that of the Romans, and the Carthaginian. Volume 5 of the Encyclopaedia explained that this Great Mother Cyble was also known as the Great Mother of the gods, and she was a Greco Roman goddess that had various names. From about the time of the 5th century BC onward, her full official Roman name was known as Mater Deum, or Magna Idaea, which meant to the Romans the Great Idaean Mother of the gods. The story that was told about this Great Mother Cyble is that she was worshiped in the country of Phrygia during Greco Roman times. There is a map in volume 20 of the Encyclopaedia, showing the country of Phrygia, that was in the Turkey area of Anatolia, that was called as Asia Minor.

During the Hannibal invasion of Italy in 204 BC, the Romans followed a sibylline prophecy, that was told to them that the enemy could be expelled, and defeated if the Idaean mother was brought into the city of Rome, together with her sacred symbol, which according to their belief was a small stone that was fallen from heaven. According to volume 20 of the Encyclopaedia, the sibylline people was a tribe from the land area of Italy, who were there before the Latin people of the Romans came along.

According to volume 5 of the Encyclopaedia, this Mother Cyble was also, identified with the various gods, and goddess of Rome, such as Maia, Ops, Rhea, and Tellus. During the time of the invaded army of Hannibal the Great, the Romans held a large worship to Mother Cyble, because they were in distress, that their army were not able to stop the invading Amy of Hannibal. The Romans were in such a deep distress of how the war was going against them, and because of the distress they were in; they resorted to various measures that were designed to gain divine favors from the gods. This was to help them with the war against Hannibal, and his army of elephant and men. These gods were represented by the various statues that were paired out in the manner, and custom like that of the Greeks. The pairing out of the various gods, were Jupiter with Juno, Mars with Venus, together with the other various minor gods, and goddesses that were worship at this gathering. During the later years of the Republic of Rome, epically under the rain of various emperors, the people of Rome had a strong desire for the worship of other gods. This was more than the various gods of the Etruscans, the Greeks, and the various gods of Romulus. Due to this thirst that the people of Rome had for new gods, they turn their attention to seek gods from other countries to satisfy their desire. This need of the people of Rome was first met with the worship of the goddess Isis. This goddess Isis were worshipped in the land of Mizraim known as Egypt. The worship of the goddess Isis was Hellenized, and were adopted by the Greeks, and the Romans, and Later her worship was spread to the West, meaning Western Europe. Volume 20 of the Encyclopaedia explained that the image of the goddess Isis was one of the various idolatry goddesses that were worship in the land that become known as Egypt. According to volume 20 of the Encyclopaedia the goddess Isis was one of the most widespread images that was worshipped throughout the Greek Hellenistic world, that later had its influence on what became known as Christianity. This image of the goddess Isis was later adopted by the Roman Catholic Church, that became known as the Christian church, where all the various churches of today sprang out of.

Volume 20 explained that the figure of the Virgin Mary statues that one might see in many of the Roman Catholic Churches, it is actually that of the image of the goddess Isis, they the Romans had taken to themselves to worship as one of their goddesses of Rome. This goddess Isis, appear as the virgin Mary, the earthy mother of Yashua, according to their belief.

This image of the goddess Isis is what they the Roman Catholic Church associate as the Virgin Mary, the mother of god, that is mentioned in the Catholic Church's to their worshipers, for them to believe in. Which this teaching of the Roman Catholic Church, it is a false teaching, of idolatry worship, because all worship belongs to Yahweh only, true the name of Yashua His Son. In that time of the Romans searching for other gods, to add to their worship, mystery religion came on the scene, that did seem to offer a personal salvation that did flourished everywhere, so did magic. According to volume 6 of the Encyclopaedia, the name of the goddess Isis originally came from the Greeks, but in the language of the people that became known as the Egyptians, her name was spelled as Aset or Eset. Volume 6 of the Encyclopaedia explained that the name Isis, which is a Greek name, was taken from the Hieroglyph writing of the ancient people of the land of Mizraim. The word Isis, or Aset, or Eset, meant in the Hieroglyph language of the people of Mizraim a throne, because according to the volume, throne was feminine in gender with that of the people of Mizraim. Its personification was that of a woman, the mother of a king, the royal throne was in effect, was the creator of a king. The Encyclopaedia explained that little is known about the history of the early beginning of the worship of the goddess Isis, that did began in the land of Mizraim. Volume 6 of the Encyclopaedia explained that even in what was known as the Pyramid tests, that is dated back to the time of 2,375 to 220 BC, the goddess Isis was really mentioned. Except as the mourner of her murdered husband, who was known as the god Osiris. The worship of the goddess Isis probably began in the area that was called as Lower Egypt, and it was spread throughout the rest of the country. The goddess Isis had received widespread worship as the mother of fertility, and had important temples throughout the land of Egypt, and later her worship was spread to the land of Havilah now known today as Nubia.

After the Romans take on many foreign gods to worship, as their gods, lastly to come into the Roman religious worship, was that of the god Mithra. Volume 8 of the Encyclopaedia, explained that Mithraism, which meant the worship of the god Mithra, who were an Indian, and a Iranian god of sun, justice, contract, and war in ancient Persia. During the Roman Empire of the 2nd and 3rd century AD, this deity was honored, as a symbol of loyalty to many of the emperors of Rome. In the religion of the people who became known as the Iranian people, this god Mithra was the most important of their gods, because he was a god of contract, and agreement between people, also was a god of oath.

Most important of all the worshiped that came into the religious system of Rome, was the worship of men, that was extremely popular in the army of the Romans. The worshipping of the sun as a solar god was quite common among many of the emperors of Rome, including the emperor Constantine, whom the Encyclopaedia says started what become known as Christianity in the Roman world. The Apostle Paul were sent by Yashua according to (Romans Chapter 15, and verse 16), to be a minster, and teacher of the Gentile people of what became known as Europe. This was to bring them from out of darkness, of idolatry worship, of devil to the true worship of Yahweh, the creator of all things. When the Latin people of Aeneas take overpower from the Etruscans that became known as the Romans, they brought in many Greek gods, and Etruscan's gods in their religious system that become known as Roman Catholicism, that did became known as the Roman Catholic Church. According to volume 26 of the Encyclopaedia, Christianity became the legal state religion of the Roman Empire when Constantine pass an edict of laws, in 313 AD, to make this religion the official religion of Rome. According to this volume 26 of the Encyclopaedia, the word Catholicism, where the word Catholic was taken from, came from the Greek word Katholihos, which meant to the Romans, the primacy position of the bishop, or the episcopes of Rome, who was the Popes of Rome. According to volume 16 of the Encyclopaedia, until about 250 AD, most Western leaders of the Catholic Church spoke Greek, and not Latin. Volume 16 of the Encyclopaedia went on to say that, a good example of those early Greek speakers that became a part of the main Latin theologians, came from what became known as North Africa. One of the names of these theologians was known as Irenaeus, and Hippolytus. According to volume 9 of the Encyclopaedia, Peter who the Roman Catholic Church nominated as a Saint, was the first Pope of the Roman Catholic Church, in the time of about 64 AD.

I must point out that his statement from the Encyclopaedia is totally a false statement, that is not in harmony with the writing, and the teaching of the Scripture of truth, that was only given to the children of Israel to be a Law, for them to live their lives by. This was to please Yahweh, and to save them from His wrath of destruction. According to volume 26 of the Encyclopaedia, Roman Catholicism claim to have a continuity with that of the New Covenant Church, of what they did name as the New Testament church. Which is speaking of the believers of the Apostles, who became known as the early church, by the Gentile people of Europe.

This statement the Encyclopaedia made that the Catholic Church came from the days of the Apostles, is totally a false statement that have no truth in it. My reason for making this kind of statement, it is because the very first time that any of the Apostles had any dealing with any of the Gentile people of what became known as Europeans. Is when the Apostle Peter was sent by the Holy Spirit of Yahweh to Cornelius, who was a Roman centurion, who was station at Caesarea. This statement is found at (Acts Chapter 10, starting from verse 1 to verse 37). I must point out that what was known as Caesarea, is nowhere in the Gentile land that became known as Europe, but according to volume 2 of the Encyclopaedia, this place was an ancient part of the land of Canaan that is now called as Palestine by the Romans. This place is now a part of the land area of Israel. This place is in the southern course of what is now known as Haifa, and this place became a Roman capital, in AD 6, which was a province of the Yehudahites who became known as the tribe of Judah by the Romans. Jews, and Jewish people by the Angles, and Saxon Germanic people. This city was a Phoenician settlement that were known as Straton's before the conquest of the Greeks, and the Romans. This city was later rebuilt and enlarges by Herod the Great, who was a king of Judea, and who were of Greek descendant, and a client kingdom of the Romans. According to "Acts Chapter 11, and verse 2", after Peter meet with Cornelius in Caesarea, and told him about the good news of the Kingdom of Yahweh, and about the resurrection of Yashua from the dead. He returns to Jerusalem to meet up with the other Yehudahites believers, who were complaining against him, because he went to speak with a Gentile person from the land of Europe. Peter went on to explained to these Israelites believers, that he was sent by the Holy Spirit of Yahweh to Cornelius. So, there is nothing in (Chapter 11 of the book of Acts) to say that Peter went to Rome to speak with the Romans, and by so doing, he became a bishop, or a Pope of Rome.

Furthermore, it was not left up to the Apostle Peter, or any of the Apostles to choose another Apostle to replace this one, or that one. This replacement of any of the Apostles, was left up to Yahweh, and Yashua. Also, all the Apostles were from the seed of Jacob, who became known as the children of Israel. If one should fine such a statement in any of the modern translation of the Scripture, that became known as the Bible, that many of the Apostles were that of the Gentile people of Europe. It was put there by the Gentile people of Europe, because they the Gentile people of Europe were the translators of the Scripture into their various languages. Also to that of many of us their conquered ex-slave people, who speak their language, as our language.

This is because they the Gentile people were given the opportunity to come to the light, and the knowledge of the Scripture of the children of Israel, that were prophecy in (Isaiah Chapter 60, and verse 3). There the Scripture explained that the Gentile people were going to come to the light of the children of Israel, which is speaking of the Scripture of truth, because Yahweh used the children of Israel only to write the Scripture. Furthermore, it would be against the teaching of their master, who is Yashua, for any of his Apostles to set up themselves as a political figurehead of the Gentile European political ruling system. Volume 26 of the Encyclopaedia, made the statement that Peter was the first Pope, or bishop of Rome, and that all of the other Popes came down after him, and succeeded him as Pope. Which this statement of theirs, it is a totally false statement of lies, that have no truth in it. The Encyclopaedia also claims that Peter was put to death by Nero, and he was buried in Rome. Again I must point out that this statement the Encyclopaedia made about Peter, is totally a false statement that have no truth in it whatsoever. My reason for saying this is, there is nowhere in the writing of the New Covenant part of the Scripture to support this kind of philosophy, that the Roman Catholic Church, and that of what Encyclopaedia make about Peter. Who they say became the first Pope of the Roman Church after Yashua went back to heaven. There is also, nowhere in (Acts Chapter 2), which was the beginning of the ministry of Peter, and also of the others Apostles of Yashua, where they mention that Peter became a Pope during the time of what the Gentile people translated as Pentecost. Which this Pentecost story they had mention, was during the out poring of the Holy Spirit of Yahweh, that was poured out on the Apostles during the Passover celebration of the children of Israel. This is what they the Gentile people translated as Pentecost. I must also point out that Peter did not chose himself to become an Apostle of Yashua, but rather he was chosen by Yashua to be one of the chief Apostles of his, because Peter did believe that he Yashua was the Son of Yahweh.

Who was sent to them the Yehudahites, and the Benjaminhites of the children of Israel, who were left there in the land that become known as Israel. Furthermore, Yashua made it quite clear that is recorded at (John Chapter 17, and verse 16), that he and his Apostles were no part of that political system of the Romans, that did existed their during the time of the Romans, ruling over the so-call Middle East, and what become known as North Africa.

Also, the Apostle Paul makes it quite clear at (Galatians Chapter 1, and verse 8), that Peter was given the ministry ship to the circumcision, meaning to the Yehudahites, and Benjamites of the children of Israel, who were known as the people of the circumcision. The Apostle Paul made it quite clear, that he was given the minster ship to the uncircumcision, meaning to the Gentile people of what became known as the European people of Europe. This time was before Paul who were known as Saul, who became a believer of Yashua, that he Yashua is the Son of Yahweh, the one who were sent to them the Yehudahites, and Benjaminhites of the children of Israel, who were left there in the land. There is no mentioning of any Roman Catholic Church during the early Apostleship of Peter, that is mention in (Act chapter 2). The first people that Peter, and others of the Apostles were ministering to, was that of the Yehudahites, and the Benjaminhites of the children of Israel. Who were left there in the land of Isreal, when Peter started his ministry ship to them. Philip was later sent to the Ethiopian eunuch before the Apostle Paul was made a Minster to the Gentile people. This was to bring them from out of darkness, to the light, and knowledge of the New Covenant order, and the worship of Yahweh, and the knowledge about Yashua. I must also point out that this statement the Encyclopaedia, and the Roman Catholic Church make about Peter, is totally a false statement that has no truth in it, because there is nowhere in the Scripture where it makes mentioned, that Peter became a Pope, of what become known as the Roman Catholic Church. The Apostles Paul was explaining to the Galatians who were Israelites, and other European believers, that the Gospel was giving to him, to the uncircumcision, and Peter was given the Apostles ship to the circumcision. The Apostle Paul went on to explain that the same was mighty in him toward the Gentile people, meaning Yahweh. According to volume 9 of the Encyclopaedia, the word Pentecost came from the Greeks, which was the 50th day that was called Whit Sunday.

The Encyclopaedia explained that Whit Sunday was a big celebration for many people of Europe, who became known as Christians. According to volume 9 of the Encyclopaedia, this celebration of Whit Sunday was held on a Sunday that fell on the 50th day after Ester, which is also a part of the European paganism belief of Easter. This celebration of Pentecost was held as a memorial of the outpouring of the Holy Spirit of Yahweh, that was poured on the disciples of Yashua, which did occur on the Israelite Passover celebration, that they the Greek, Romans, and other Gentile people, who came from out of the Greeks, and Roman conquest, continue to call as Pentecost.

This celebration of the Yehudahites, and Benjaminhites of the children of Israel did take place after the death, and the resurrection, and the ascending of Yashua back to heaven, that is mentioned in "Act chapter 2". This Passover feast of the children of Israel that the Gentile people of Europe called as Pentecost, was a celebrated feast of thanksgiving for the first fruit of the wheat harvest, that they the Gentile people of Europe associated with the remembrance of the Passover of the children, of Israel from Mizraim {Egypt, Yahweh gave to them to celebrate as a memorial throughout all their generation. Volume 9 of the Encyclopaedia explained that the actual time when the Pentecost feast was first celebrated in the Christian churches of Europe, is not known. This Pentecost festival of celebration was held in the 3rd century, by a fellow whose name was Origen, who were a theologian, and who was the head of the Catechetical school in Alexandria Egypt. Also, by Tertullian who were a Christian priest, and a writer of Carthage. In the time of the early church, meaning the Roman Catholic Church, Christians often referred to the entire 50-day period following Easter, as Pentecost. Where baptism was carried out at the beginning of Easter, and at the ending of the Pentecost season. Eventually Pentecost became a more popular time for baptism in northern Europe, and also in Britain, where the Pentecost feast were commonly called as White Sunday. Rather than Whitsunday as it were commonly called by the Greeks. The reason why the Pentecost season were called as White Sunday in Britain, was because of the special white garment that were worn by the newly baptize believers of Britain. In the rein of Edward 6th, in 1549, the first prayer books were officially called Whitsunday, and the name continue in the Anglican Church, that became known as the Church of England.

"Revelation Chapter 13, verse 1 and 2" there it read like this, and I stood upon the sand of the sea, and saw a beast rise up out of the sea, having seven heads, and ten horns. Upon his horns ten crowns, and upon his head the name of blasphemy. This beast which was liken to a leopard, and his feet's were as the feet's of a bear, and his mouth as the mouth of a lion, that is mentioned in (Revelation Chapter 13, and verse 1 to verse 7), was speaking of Rome. Who were this last beast of Daniel Chapter 7, and verse 7), who were to have dominion over the earth after the fall of the power of Greece to Rome. This dragon who is described as Satan the Devil in "Revelation Chapter (12, and verse 9)", gave him his power, and his seat of great authority.

The seven heads, and ten crowns that is mentioned in Revelation Chapter 13, was the various Gentile European powers who were to come up from out of the breakup of the Roman Empire of Europe, who is ruling over the world of today. Such as the various Celtic Germanic barbarians' people, who became known as the French, Dutch, Angles, and Saxon people of Burton, that became known as the British people, and the English people. Also, the Austrian, Danish, Swedish, Iceland's, Polish, Russia, Spain, Portugal, Turkey, Italy, and Romania. All of whom come from out of the breakup of the Roman Empire of Europe. (Revelation Chapter 12, and verse 9), mentioned that Satan the Devil gave power and great authority to the beasts. Which was the political power structure of Babylon, Persia, Greece, and Rome. So, from the Roman political system that came from out of Greece, to Rome, spread throughout their colonial conquest of Europe. These barbarians 'kingdoms that came from out of the breakup of the Roman Empire, became strong colonial powers, that spread their political system of ruler ship of their governmental control throughout the world of people who did came under their colonial conquest of the world. (Revelation Chapter 14, and verse 9), there the Scripture went on to say that the 3rd angel followed them saying, with a loud voice, if any man worships the beast, and his image, and receive his mark in their forehead, or in their hands, the same shall drink of the wine of the wrath of Yahweh. (Revelation Chapter 13, and verse 16) mentioned that the beast, or the beastly system of the Romans Empire, that these Gentile powers of today sprang out of. Cause both small, and great, rich, and poor, free, and bond to receive the mark of the beast in their forehead. (Verse 17 of Chapter 13 of Revelation) mentioned that, no man could buy or sell, save he who has the mark, or the name of beast in his forehead, or the number of his name in their possession.

To give one a good example of how truthful, and accurate the prophecy of the Scripture is, (Revelation Chapter 13) is speaking of the Gentile political system of today, that came from out of the brake up of the Roman Empire. For in order for anyone of today, to do any kind of business, work, or to buy, and sell in this Gentile political system of today, they must have the mark of the beast in their possession. Otherwise, if they do not have the mark of the beast in their possession, they will go to prison, or having to pay a very heave fine for not having the mark of the beast in their possession.

The mark of the beast I am chiefly speaking of, is the various licenses, and permits, that one must have in their possession to be able to buy and sell, or to do any kind of work, and business in this Gentile run political system of things of today. This applies throughout their conquered political world, that they the Gentile people of Europe have established wheresoever they went, and conquered, and set up their political system in the name of Christianity. Especially in what become known as the United States of America. Because if one do not have these licenses, and permits, in their position, and try to do any kind of businesses, work, or to buy and sell, they would simply go to prison, or having to pay a heavy fine. For not having these licenses, and permits in their position, before they can do any kind of work, and business. Otherwise they would surely go to jail, or prison, for going against the system of the Gentile people, and their laws of greed they did set up to bring in more revenue into their system. Before the modern colonial period of the raining of these Gentile powers that came from out of the Roman Empire. I cannot remember ever reading from the Scripture, or the Encyclopaedia where it makes mentioned that in the time of BC, or early AD, one had to have a license, or permit to buy and sell, and to do any kind of work, or to do any kind of business. These laws very much applies in what become known as the United States of America. For in order for a person to do any kind of work, on their own property in this Gentile European system of what became known as the United States, they must have these license, and permits, from the city or states where they are living. Otherwise, if they do not have these licenses, and permit, to show to the city inspectors who come to their properties, to see if they are doing any kind of work without these licenses and permit. When they go to court, they will have to pay a heavy find, or go to prison, if they do not have the money to pay to the court system, for not having these licenses, and permits to work on their own properties.

But the prophecy of the Scripture must be full field, as Yashua mentioned in (Matthew Chapter 26, and verse 54). So, these Gentile people of what became known as the land of Europe, have corrupted the true teaching of the Scripture, and they have also deceived many nations of people whom they have captured, conquered, and enslave to see things their way. Many of whom did not have any knowledge of the Scripture for themselves, to know any different from what they were thought. One should not be surprised to learn about many of these things I have written about the Roman Catholic Church, because it is the fulfillment of the prophecy of "Revelation Chapter 17, starting from verse 1, to verse 10".

There the Scripture mentions about this symbiotically whore, who was described as mystery Babylon the Great, the mother of harlots, and of all the abomination who is sitting on many waters. According to (Revelation Chapter 17), the many waters this whore is sitting upon, is the many nations of people who this whore is sitting on, that came under the captivity of the Roman Catholic Church, and that of the Gentile family of Europe, who have control over many nation of people. Many of whom came under the Gentile European colonial system, and who had drunken of her bad wine of her false teaching, many people were expose to, and received. Due to the colonial slavery system, and the conquest of the world by the Gentile people of Europe, who came from out of the brake up of the Roman Empire, which is a continuation of the Roman system that have its influence, and power on the world of people of today. They have pass on their teaching they themselves did received from Rome, and from the Roman Catholic Church, that they had pass on to many of us their conquered people. Who later became their subjects, and slaves of Roman Catholicism of the Catholic Church system, that became known as Christianity. According to volume 10 of the Encyclopaedia, Roman Catholicism that became known as the Roman Catholic Church, traces its history back to the Apostles of the first century AD. That also came from out of the Eastern Orthodox Church of the Roman Empire of Asia Minor, which was the Greek Turkey area of Europe. Who were able to exist due to the relative tolerant attitude of the imperial authorities of that time, and a steady flow of converts that was attracted to the church, because of the charity of the church.

Volume 16 explained that due to the conversion of Constantine after the reign of Diocletian, he was able to bring in a new beginning in the Christian church of Rome, that did develop the empire into a Christian state. Which did provide the way for the Christian culture to spread from Byzantium, which is the Turkey area of Europe, to the medieval culture of Western Europe. During this reign of Constantine, it brought in a new era to the church, and laws was pass in 314 AD to make the Roman church the official religion of the Roman world. During the devolvement of Roman Catholicism of the 3rd century AD, that became known as Christianity. Various Popes of the Episcopal, which is a Latin word, for the word bishop, who gave themselves primacy authority ship, that in their eyes they liken themselves to be in the position of Peter, who they say was the head of the Apostles.

They also gave rules and regulation that was known as edits, or Canon laws to govern their member of what they had called as the universal church, that became known as the Roman Catholic Church. In other words, these men set up commandments of men, who were also known as the ecclesiastical body, which were priests, and bishops that became known as the clergy's of today. According to volume 26 of the Encyclopaedia, by the time of the 10th century AD, Roman Catholicism became known as Christendom by the conversion of many barbarians 'tribes of Western Europe. Volume 26 also mentioned that the Middle Ages saw the rise of universities of Catholic learning, that came from many Arabs scholars. As I did mention before, that according to the Webster Colligate Dictionary, the name Arab came from Greek, Latin, and also to the French people as Arabe. Who were some of the former colonial rulers of what became known as North Africa, and the so-cal Middle East. So, this name Arab were chiefly speaking of the Ishmaelite people, who became known as the Saudi Arabian people of Ishmael. Who also became known as the Mohammedans, and the Muslim people, who has spread themselves by way of conquest, and slavery, to establish the faith of Mohammed to many of their converts, who became known as the Muslim people of Mohammed, as the prophet of his god Allah.

According to the Webster Collegiate Dictionary, what became known as the church, was taken from a Greek word Kyriakon, which meant an assembly of citizens, or a gathering of a group of people, which did not have anything to do with any form of religious worship. According to Dictionary of the Bible, there it explained that the Anglo-Saxon words for church, such as in Britain, and in Scotland, were known as kirk. Also in various German dialects, the word church were known as kirche, and in the Dutch dialect, this word church were known as kerk, that was taken from the Greek word Kyriakon. From what I came to understand from the reading of the dictionary, and the Encyclopaedia Britannica, in the time of the Greeks, this word Kyriakon were used, and this group of people had no religious affiliation as such, but it was more so for various business activities, and for other usages. This word Kyriakon was not used for any worship, like how many people of today who go to various churches, claiming they are going to these places to worship, as a Christian people. So, the word Kyriakon was translated as the church, by the Gentile people of Europe, that is mentioned in (Acts Chapter 2, and verse 47). That meant the early believers of Yashua, who were mostly Yehudahites, and Benjaminhites believers, who were known as the congregation of believers. Who were under the ruler ship of the Greco-Roman society in Israel, that the Romans did name as Palestine.

Many of the early believers of Yashua, use to gather in various other believers 'houses, to worship that was call as the congregation of believers, that later became known as the church, by the Gentile Roman believers of Antioch of the Turkey area of Europe. This is also, by the present-day Gentile family of today, who came from out of the brake up of the Roman Empire, and form these church societies, in a way to make money, form their various members, as tide and offerings. The reason why many of the early Yehudahites, and Benjaminhites use to gather in various believers 'houses to worship, that was translated as the church in various Bibles. It was because of prosecution from the religious leaders of Isreal, who did not believe on Yashua, that he was the Son of Yahweh, who was sent to them.

So, many believes of Isreal did not go to the temple where Yahweh put His name there to be worship, because it was of fear of persecution from the religious leaders of Israel. So, there is nowhere in the writing of the Scripture where it make mentions that John, who later became known as John the Baptist, by the Roma Catholic Church, established a place that were called a church, for the Yehudahites believers to go there to worship Yahweh, who he did baptized in the River Jordan. In the book of (Malachi Chapter 3, and verse 1), which is the last book of the Old Covenant part of the Scripture. There it explained that the Yehudahites, and the Benjaminhites believers in Malachi time, leading up to the time of John, used to worship Yahweh in the Temple that was built by Solomon, where Yahweh did approve for His name to be put there to be worship in Jerusalem. The reason why the word church was used in the book of Acts, it is because during the time of the Romans ruling over the Greeks Turkey area of Europe, the word church was used by these believers. Also over the so-call Middle East and what become known as North Africa, because of Roman Catholicism of the Catholic Church. So, the word church was used by these believers of the area. One must realize that the Scripture was translated from Hebrew, to Aramaic, to Greek, and to Latin. The Scripture was later translated down into the various barbarian dialect of Western, and Eastern Europe, who themselves was under the religious doctrine of Roman Catholicism, of the Roman Catholic Church. Where many of us their captives' people of today speak their language, as our main form of communication, that did came down from Greek, to Latin of the Roman ruler ship. So, this is the reason why the word church came down into the Angles, and Saxon dialect, that become known as the English language, that is used as the word churches of today.

In the King James Version of the Bible, the word church became known as Circe, that was taken from the Greek word Kyriakon, that became known as the church, that came from the Roman Catholic Church. During the time when Yashua was here on earth, the word temple, and Synagogue was used, because according to the Webster Colligate Dictionary, the word Synagogue came from Greek, Latin, Middle English, Old French, and East Central. Which the word East Central was a part of the Roman Empire of the Greek Turkey area of Europe.

From what I have gathered from the dictionary, and the Encyclopaedia Britannica, the word Synagogue did not come from ancient Israel, that spoke Hebrew, but this word Synagogue came from the Gentile people, who had translated the Scripture into their various languages.

According to the Webster's Collegiate Dictionary of the Fifth Edition, there the dictionary explained that the word synagogue, came from Late Latin, Greek, and Old French. The dictionary explained by saying that, in the Jewish religion, this word synagogue meant a local assembly of Jews organized chiefly for public worship. I must point out that, the Apostles of Yashua, who wrote the New Covenants part of the Scripture, that is now called as the New Testament. There is nowhere in their writings where it makes mention that the various Apostles built, and form a church, that was called as the Baptist Church, or any other churches that came down from the Gentile people of Europe. The Scripture clearly explained that the Apostles use to worship Yahweh in the Temple that was built by Solomon, where Yahweh put His name there to be worship at Jerusalem. (Act Chapter 3) mentioned that the Apostles use to preach in the temple to other Yehudahites, and Benjaminhites who were left there in Jerusalem. Also, from house to house, as the Spirit of Yahweh gave them power to do so. Sunday, and Sunday worship that came from Christianity, how did it came about? According to the Webster Colligate Dictionary of the Fifth Edition, the word Sunday came from the Angles, and Saxon dialect that came from the word sunnandxg, that was adopted to replace the Israelite Sabbath. Sunday became a Holy day of worship for the Adventists, and other churches, how did it came about? According to the Webster Colligate Dictionary of the Fifth Edition, the word Sunday is an Angles and Saxon word that spells as sundi. This word became the first day of the week of the Christian Sabbath, as we know it as today, as Sunday. Volume 11 of the Encyclopaedia explained that Sunday, was the first day of the week in the Christian religion, that came from Protectionism, and from Roman Catholicism, which was called as the Lord's Day. Which was the weekly memorial of the resurrection of Yashua from the dead. The Encyclopaedia explained that the practice of Christians gathering for worship on Sunday, date back to the time of the Apostles of Yashua, but the actual date, and time is not known.

I must point out that when the Encyclopaedia make this statement, that Sunday worship date back to the time of the Apostles, this statement of theirs is totally a false statement, and a lie, that have no truth in it. My reason for making this kind of statement, it is because the Apostles of Yashua were from the family of the children of Israel, who used to worship and kept the Sabbath Day Holy. As they were commanded by Yahweh true the prophet Moses to do so.

When Yashua, and his Apostles were here on earth, they used to worship Yahweh in the temple on the Sabbath day, that Yahweh gave to Moses, to give to the children of Israel, as a day of worship to Yahweh. Also for them to keep throughout all their generation, so Sunday worship came from the Roman Catholic Church, that was pass down the line to the various Celtic barbarians Germanic people of Europe. Also, to others Celtic people who came from out of the brake up of Roman Empire, and who were conquered and control by the Romans. So, the Roman Catholic Church Christianized many of these barbarian people of Europe, to acknowledge this day as a day of worship. So, when these Gentile European people came from out of the breakup of the Roman Empire of Western, and Eastern Europe, and became strong nation of people. Then the people who they did conquered, became their subjects, and slaves, and they just simple passed on this Sunday day of worship to them, to embrace as a day of worship, according to their religious belief, of Christianity. The Encyclopaedia explained that before the end of the first century AD, the writers of the book of Revelation, which the Scripture clearly explained that it was the Apostle John, who wrote the book of Revelation. By saying that he was in the Spirit on the Lord Day, which he was referring to the Sabbath day, Yahweh gave to them, the children of Isreal to be a worship day to them. So, the dictionary went on to explained that Sunday as we know it as today became the first day of the week of the Christian Sabbath. This worship day of Sunday was set up by the Roman Christians, that was based upon the memorial of the resurrection of Yashua from the dead. So, the Apostle John was making references to the Sabbath Day of Yahweh, where he, and rest of the children of Israel did worshipped Yahweh on this day, he was referring to that is recorded in the book of Revelation.

To prove my point that this was the day John was making referring to as the Lord's Day, meaning Yahweh day. At (Exodus Chapter 16, starting from verse 23, to verse 26), also (Acts Chapter 13, and verse 44), there it shows that the children of Israel, and the Apostle use to gather to worship Yahweh on the Sabbath day, that they kept throughout all their generation. So, when John made the statement at (Revelation Chapter 1, and verse 10), that he was in the Spirit on the Lord's Day, when he received the Revelation from the angel that Yashua sent to him. He was referring about the Sabbath day of the Lord Yahweh, who gave the children of Israel this day, as a day of worship.

(Revelation Chapter 1 starting from verse 1), clearly explained by saying that the Revelation of Jesus Christ, which Yahweh gave unto him, to show unto his servant's things which must shortly come to pass. Yashua in turn gave this revelation to his angel, to give to John the Apostle, who bare record of the word of Yahweh, which is the Scripture of truth, and the testimony of Jesus Christ, that he wrote about. This revelation to John by the angel, is after Yashua was resign from the dead, and went back to heaven to sit on the right-hand side of Yahweh, until the time of his second coming. When he shall return to take over ruler ship of the earth, from these political governments, who have ruler ship over the earth that was set up by means of the various Gentile European colonial powers. This was during their time of their conquest of people and their lands, and the world to get rich, and to have power over the earth. According to volume 12 of the Encyclopaedia, there it explained that the ancient Babylonian named each day of the week after one of the heavenly bodies as their gods, that was known to them, who many of them had worship. Which was the sun, moon, and stars, and later the Romans adopted these customs from the Babylonian as a part of their worship. The Encyclopaedia explained that the Romans for some period did used the 8 days of the week, in their civil governmental system. But it was the emperor Constantine in 321 AD, who did established the seven days 'week, that was first started by the Babylonians. That was later copied into the Roman calendar weekdays, as we know it as today. The Roman days of the week were known as Moon's day, Mars 'day, Mercury's day, Jupiter's day, Venus day, and Saturn's day. Which many of these names came from the name of their various gods, that were known to them as deities. These days of the week that was assigned by the Romans, such as Sun, Moon, and Saturn, so Saturn became known as Saturday, of today, which was later adopted as a corresponding day of the week by the Angles, and Saxon tribe of Germanic people.

Where the name English, or the Angles language came from, volume 12 of the Encyclopaedia explained that the other days of the week, as we know them as today, depend on the part of the world that is ruled and controlled by the various Celtic barbarians' people of Western Europe. Many of whom who called themselves Christians, and Christian countries of Europe, came from the Anglo-Saxon gods, of their deities, and from the Teutonic people mythology of belief. According to volume 18 of the Encyclopaedia, the Teutonic people that were mention, were a part of the Celtic Germanic barbarian tribes, of what became known as the European's people. According to volume 12 of the Encyclopaedia, the name Tuesday came from Tyr, or Tiu, or Tiw, which was the name of an Angles, and Saxon god, who was also a god of the Norse Germanic people, who was a god of war. According to their mythology of belief, Tyr was one of the sons of Odin, or Woden, who was a chief deity for the Norse Germanic people, that came from what is now known as Scandinavia. According to volume 8 of the Encyclopaedia, the Norse people, were a Germanic tribe that came from what is now known as Iceland, Norway, Denmark, Sweden, and Finland, who were the Old Norse people, and who were also known as the Viking people, and the Scandinavian people. Volume 12 of the Encyclopaedia explained that Tyr was one of the sons of Odin, or Woden, from where the name Wednesday was taken from. Volume 12 of the Encyclopaedia explained that Thursday originated from Thor's-day, who was a god of thunder, and this god was a god of war, who was worship by these Germanic people. Friday as we know it as today, came from the goddess Frigg's-day, and Frigg was the wife of Odin, and she was a god of love and beauty in the Norse mythology of belief. According to volume 5 of the Encyclopaedia, the goddess Frigg, or Friia, or Frija, in the Norse mythology of belief, was the mother of Balder, and she was worshipped by various Germanic tribes. According to volume 5 of the Encyclopaedia, Frigg or Friia were a goddess who was a promoter of marriage, and fertility in the Icelandic Germanic people's culture. From what I have gathered from reading the Encyclopaedia, the weekdays of the weeks, as we know them as today, came from these Gentile people of what became known as the Europeans people. They have infused their paganism of belief into what became known as Christianity.

By so doing, they have deceived many people who they had captured, enslaved, and converted into their religious teaching of falsehood of belief. Many of their x free slave people of today, who became their citizens of their ways of life, and belief according to what their captives were taught to believing in. Reading from volume 11 of the Encyclopaedia, there it explained that the word Sunday, and Sunday worship could have also come from a god of the land of Mizraim, who were known as the sun god Re. This god Re may have later pass on to the Romans as Sunday that many people of the ancient world, were a sun worshipers of this sun god. Which the emperor Constantine was a part of this belief, before he became a part of Roman Catholicism, of the Catholic Church.

One of my reasons for saying this is, during the time of the Roman Republic, they were always seeking other gods to worship, apart from the other gods of the Etruscan, and that of the Greeks, that the Romans did adopted into their religious system. This Sunday day of worship was later passed on to the various Celtic Germanic barbarians 'people, who were Christianize by the Roman, and by the Roman Catholic Church to adopt to this Sunday day of worship in their Christianity religion. So, when many of these people were Christianized by the Roman Catholic Church, then Sunday became a Holy day of worship to them that was copped from the Israelite Sabbath. Sunday worship, also became a worship day for their many slaves, and conquered people worldwide, that they did accept as Christianity from their many slave masters, and conquerors. Many of whom did see themselves as good Christians people, and good Christian countries of Europe. According to the Encyclopaedia, this god Re was one of the chief high gods of the land area that became known as Egypt. So, when Pharaoh Ikhnaton became ruler over the land of Mizraim, he totally reformed the Egyptian religious system, and did established the worship of the god Re-Horakhte, under the name of the god Aton. So, the name Sunday could have come from the people of Mizraim, from the worship of one of their gods.

The prophecy of Nebuchadnezzar dream was right on time, when Aeneas, who left from the city of Troy, who went, and established a settlement that were known as Latium. This settlement was established in land area that became known as Italy, so from this settlement of Latium gave birth to Romulus, who became strong, and conquered, and established the city of Rome, that were taken from his name. Eventually these Latin people of Romulus take over the land area that is known today as Italy. This taking over was from the various natives who were living there, before the land was conquered by the Romans of Romulus. These natives people became subjects, and citizens of Roman laws, that was pass on to them to live by, as a Roman way of life. According to volume 1 of the Encyclopaedia, when Aeneas left from the city of Troy, he went to the country of Carthage, Sicily, and finally to the land area that is now known as Italy. This was with his comrades, to established a settlement there that became known as Latium. Volume 1 of the Encyclopaedia explained that Aeneas was heavily involved with the defense of the city of Troy, against the Greeks who were the invaders. The association of Aeneas with the land area that became known as Italy, and the island of Sicily go back to the 8th century BC, with the various Greek colonies that were there in the land of Italy, and Sicily. Volume 7 of the Encyclopaedia explained that the town of Lavinum were an ancient town that were in the city of Latium. Which were a religious center for the early Latin people that were about nineteen miles south of the city of Rome. Roman tradition maintains that this religious place of Lavinum was established by Aeneas, and his followers, who followed him from the city of Troy, to what became known as the Latium communities of Italy.

This religious center of Lavinum that Aeneas established, were named after his wife, whose name was known as Lavinia. This religious place of worship of Lavinum was established for the worship of the household gods, and for the goddess Vesta. The Penates gods was worship privately as a protector of the individual household families. This worship place was a public place for the worship for the Latin community. From this city of Latium gave birth to a people who become known as the Latin people, from where Romulus, who were a descendant of these Latin people came from.

According to the Encyclopaedia, some 500 years later, Romulus went and established what become known as the city of Rome, that came from his name of Romulus, who they say was the first Latin king. According to volume 1 of the Encyclopaedia, Julius Caesar, and Octavian Augustus Caesar say they came from the descendants of Aeneas, who was the establisher of the city of Latium. This city was established on the Tiber hill area of what is now known as Italy. Volume 10 of the Encyclopaedia, explained that the name Rome came from Romulus, and Remus, who were two twin brothers of the establishment of what became known as the city of Rome. According to the mystical belief of these Latin people of Aeneas, these two brothers were the sons of Rhea Silvia, who was the daughter of Numitor, who was a king of a place that were known as Alba Longa in Italy. According to Volume 1 of the Encyclopaedia Britannica, this area of Alba became known as northwestern Italy, that was not too far away from the Tanaro River area that became known as the city of Rome. According to volume 10 of the Encyclopaedia, Rhea in the Greek religion was a goddess during the Hellenistic periods, and her worship spread throughout Greece. From what I have read about Romulus, and his brother Remus, the story about these two brothers seems to have a lot of Greek, and Latin mythology of belief, that is wrap up in this story about these two brothers who were raised by a female wolf, who also were their foster mother. According to this story, Numitor who was the grandfather of Romulus, and his brother Remus, who was dethrone by his younger brother, who was known as Amulius. So, when Amulius became ruler of the kingship of Numitor his brother, then he forced Rhea to become a part of the Vestal Virgins that is likening to a Roman Catholic Nun, before she was able to give birth to Romulus, and Remus. So, when Rhea Silvia was forced to become a part of the Vestal Virgins of the organization of the Latin people, she was forced to take a vow of chastity. This vow was to prevent her from giving birth to a rival of the throne, that her grandfather brother had stolen from him.

According to volume 12 of the Encyclopaedia, in the Roman religion, these Vestal Virgins were any of the six priestesses who represent the daughters of the royal household of the worship to the goddess Vestal. These virgins were chosen from the age of six, and ten years old, by the Pontifex Maximus, who was the chief priest, or the high priest of the Roman religious 'system to their various gods. This office of the Pontifex Maximus position became known as the Pope of Rome, who was the overseer of these Vestal Virgins.

These Vestal Virgins had to serve for thirty years, and they had to remain virgins, and after the service of thirty years, they were free to get married if they so wish to do. But only a few did so, because it was considered as bad luck to do so. These Vestal Virgins had to take care of the temple fire, and prepared foods, and take care of the temple objects of the inner sanctuary, and to prepare for the public worship of Vesta. If these Vestal Virgins did not attend to their duties, they were punished by flogging. Violations of their chastity vow would mean for that virgin who did so, to be buried alive. Despite Rhea Silver was made a part of the Vestal Virgins organization to prevent her from bringing an air to the throne of Amulius, she became pregnant somehow by the war god, who were known as Mars, and bare him twins. These twins became known as Romulus, and Remus. When Amulius found out that Rhea was pregnant with child, he gave the order that when she give birth, her child should be put in a container, and the infant would die by drowning in the Tiber River. According to this story that was told, when she gave birth to Romulus and Remus, they were put into a container to sink to the bottom of the Tiber River. But instead of the container sinking to the bottom of the Tiber River, the container floated down stream, and stop in an area that eventually became known as Rome, that was near a secret fig tree. When the container that Romulus, and his brother were floating in, it stops at the fig tree where they were a female wolf, and a woodpecker bird that was secret to the god Mars, and these creatures were there to receive them. The Encyclopaedia explained that the wolf gave suck to Romulus, and his brother Remus, until they were later found by a man who were attending to his animals by the name of Faustulus. Romulus, and his brother Remus were raised by Faustulus, and his wife, who was known as Acca Larentia. These twins grow up and became a leader of a band of youths, who eventually went and kill Amulius, and restore back the throne to their grandfather who was the brother of Amulius.

According to the story, Romulus build a town near the site where he and his brother was found, and when Romulus built the wall of the town, Remus jump over the wall and was killed by his brother Romulus. Romulus grew in power and might, and increased in popularity with the people of his town, and eventually the town became known as the city of Rome. Romulus, and the town he established offered sanctuary to people who were fugitives, and people who were exile from their place of birth, and he gave them the opportunity to become citizens of Rome.

Romulus held a big festival and invited a neighboring tribe to the festival of the Italian land area, who were known as the Sabine's people. While the festival was taking place; Romulus went with his men, and captured the women of the Sabine's people to be their wives. The woman of the Sabine's got married to their Roman Captors, this was to prevent a full-scale war between the men of the Sabine's, and the Romans over the captured of their women. The Romans, and the men of the Sabine's people drew up a peace treaty between themselves, and Romulus accepted a Sabine man by the name of Tatius to be a co-ruler with him, however Tatius died an early death, and left Romulus as the sole ruler of the city of Rome. After a long ruler ship of Romulus over the city of Rome, the belief that is held by the local people, is that he mysteriously vanishes in a storm, and change into a god. So, the people of Rome worship Romulus as one of their gods, who were known as Quirinus, according to their belief. Volume 20 of the Encyclopaedia gave a totally different version of this story about Romulus, and his brother Remus who narrowly escaped death. According to volume 20 of the Encyclopaedia, these two brothers asked the gods for a sign, to distinguish between them, which one of them was to find, and build a city? Romulus was chosen by means of divination, and who in the process of time killed his brother over a strong quarrel. According to the Webster Colligate Dictionary of the Fifth Edition, the word divination is a Latin, and French word of the foretelling of future of hidden knowledge. The word divination is also, rap up with witchcraft, sorcery devilism, that is known today as fortunetellers.

Who are working true the spirit of the devil, and his demons, who were former angles who were cast out of heaven with Satan to the vicinity of the earth, who became known as the devil. (Revelation Chapter 12, starting from verse 7 to verse 12), explained that Satan who become known as the dragon, and also the Devil, was cast out of heaven to the vicinity of the earth with his angels, who are known in the Scripture as the demons. My reason for mentioning (Revelation Chapter 12) is to show that Satan held high position in heaven, before he was cast out of heaven with his angels who followed him in his devises. My reason for associating fortunetellers with with Satan and is demons, it is because only Yahweh alone and His angles who He gave powers to can work miracles. Also certain men who Yahweh give certain power to can perform miracles. Due to the fact that men by themselves cannot work miracles, but only true the Spirit of Yahweh, or the spirit of Satan and his fallen angles, who are known as the demons, can men perform certain miracles.

So, according this story of the Encyclopaedia, after Romulus killed his brother, he became the first of seven traditional kings who rule the city of Rome from 754 BC, to the established meant of the republic of Rome in 509 BC. This story was gradually accepted as fact by the people of Rome, from the 6th century BC onward. The Encyclopaedia explained that much of the story about the early history of Rome was taken from the account of this fellow by the name of Livy, whose writing was from about 59 or 64 BC to AD 17. This writing of Livy was hundreds of years later after the established meant of Rome by Romulus that he wrote about. Due to the marriage union with that of the Sabianean women, and the men of Rome, the Serbians, and the Romans became one people. After the death of Romulus who died a mysterious death in 717 BC, according to the Encyclopaedia, a Sabianean man by the name of Numa Pompilius reigned as king after the death of Romulus until 673 BC. According to the account, Numa Pompilius became a devoted ruler to the city of Rome that was established by force, and by his laws of arm that they called as morality. So, it was Pompilius who organized the early religious system of Rome, that came from the Etruscans people. Pompilius was succeeded by a warrior king by the name of Tullus Hostilius, who take over the ruler ship of the city of Rome after the death of Pompilius in 672 to 641 BC. According to volume 10 of the Encyclopaedia, the store about Romulus, and his brother Remus probably came about during the time of the 4th century BC, that is mix-up with Greek, and Roman mythology of belief. Under the subheading of Greco-Roman civilization, volume 20 of the Encyclopaedia explained that from the early beginning of the 8th century BC, the Romans who were a minor set of people, who had settled on a few hills overlooking the Tiber River area.

The Encyclopaedia explain that in arts and politics, the Romans were a good copper of the Greeks who believed their skills, and talents were given to them by the gods, that made it possible for them to conquer and established an empire. They extended their domination over the Mediterranean basin, and expanded their empire into the other part of the Gentile land that became known as Europe. According to volume 20 of the Encyclopaedia, from a settler of peasants, and solders, the Romans were able to develop into a civilization that was pattern after the Greeks, and the Etruscans. In arts, and politics, the Romans were a good copper of the Greeks, who believed their skills, and talents were given to them by the gods, that made it possible for them to conquer, and established an empire.

The development, and territorial expansion of the Italian land area, by the Romans was very much influence by their neighboring country of Greece. These ancient tribes who were living in the land area of what is now known as Italy, take on a Roman identity, and Roman citizenship. Because they were all rule and conquered by the Romans, and became subjects to Rome, and they were all anchored in the various names and traditions that came from Rome.

This is a book I have also written, that is called the Scripture that became known as the Bible in the Angle and Saxon dialect that became known as the English language, by the translators of the Protestant Reformers. From the Latin Vulgate Version of what became known as the Bible. These men were former Roman Catholic Church members of the city of Rome. According to the Biographical Sketches of the Translators, these Reformers of the Bible that was taken from the King James Authorized Version of the Bible of 1890, One of these early Reformers that was known as John Wycliffe, who was born in the year of 1324, in Riding of Yorkshire of Britain. Wycliffe was born more than a century before Martin Luther was born, who were one of these first early Reformer, and a theologian, who first complete the translation of the Scripture into the English, or the Angles Saxon dialect, that became known as the Bible. In 1340 at the age of sixteen Wycliffe was admitted as a student at the Queen College of Oxford, that was established there, and he was later transferred to Merton College University. Many of his collage associates was involve in the study of the Christian philosophers of the Middle Age theologian that was known as the scholastic, and civil laws. While attending the university, he did not only confine himself to the study that was layout by the university, but he also studded the writing of learned men before his time. Also, the writing of the Sacred Scripture that was almost neglected by the various priests who were also known as the ecclesiastical Bishops of the Roman Catholic Church. So, Bishop Langham who was overseeing the collage after the death of the owner of the collage, had a very strong dislike for the Reformers that Wycliffe were a part of. He also deprived Wycliffe of the office position that was given to him by the owner of the collage before his death.

Wycliffe appeals to the Pope at the court of Rome, to straighten out the problem he was experiencing at the collage, but after four years the Pope made his ruling on the behalf of the Archbishop to stand. Later Wycliffe were appointed by the Chancellor, and governor of the University as a Professor of the Divinity. According to the Webster Collegiate Dictionary of the Fifth Edition, the word Divinity mean the quality, or state of been divine, deity or godhead. So, this was the greatest honor of this title the university could have given to Wycliffe, who was an excellent student at the university.

Wycliffe was devoted to much of his time in the Monastery studding the Scripture, to get more knowledge, and understanding from it. One of his philosophies he develops, was that the Catholic Church that were known as the church, should give up its worldly possession, and stick more to the guideline of the teaching of the Scripture to its members. During this time of Wycliffe, the Pope of Rome demanded from Edward III, one thousand marks as tribute, or tax money, as the acknowledgement that the sovereign of Britain was under the authority ship of the successor of Saint Peter. Speaking of the Pope who they say was the successor of Peter, according to the Roman Catholic Church philosophies of their belief. Wycliffe was called upon to take part in this dispute that was taking place between the court of Rome, and the crown of Britain. Edward declined to make the payment, and he was given notice to appear before the Pontiff for trial. Edward appeal to Parliament who decided to resist the charges by force, if it was necessary to do so. Wycliffe at this time verbally defended the king against the demand of the Pope tax on Edward. In 1374 he was sent as an ambassador to appear before the Pope of Rome, concerning the king affair, but after staying aboard for over two years, and carefully studding the policy of the Pontiff. Wycliffe returns to Britain, thoroughly convinced of the gross corruption of the Roman Catholic Church, who had it's rule ship, and control over the people of Britain. Wycliffe remarks of the corruption concerning the Roman Catholic Church affair he saw, while he was there in Rome, gave much offense to the various Roman Catholic clergies, so much so that in 1377, he was told to appear before the religious convention. He was label an heresies, because he spoke about the corruption, and the deception of the Roman Catholic Church that he saw from his observation while he were there in Rome, but the convention broke up in confusion without taking any real action against him.

Later in the same year the Pope demanded he should be arrested and kept in jail, until further order from the Pope office, but the University Wycliffe was attending was enraged of the Pope demand, and debated whether they should receive the Pope's messenger, or just to dismiss him disgracefully. But Wycliffe decided to meet with his accuser's face to face in Lambert of London, and this was to be in January of 1378. But whether his action would be pleasing to the Roman Catholic clergies were left to be seen. The queen mother intervenes on Wycliffe behalf, and they dismissed him by only telling him he must refrain from preaching his doctoring against the church. Also, his teaching of his philosophies against the various Roman Catholic bishops, or priests that many people of his day were thought to listen to, and to follow only.

During this time, Wycliffe was busy translating the Scripture into British people dialect, from the Vulgate Latin version that the Scripture were found in at the time. Wycliffe writing was based upon sound Protestant views, that the Scripture alone should be the supreme authority of guideline, to one faith, and practice in the in their daily lives. His enemies took advantage of some disturbance that was taking place at this University, in which they unjustly charged this disturbance to his teaching of his belief. Due to this accusation by many of his enemies they accuse him of, he was banished from the university in 1382, and after the incident, he went to live at Lutterworth, where he died in 1384. Wycliffe translation of the Scripture into the British language from the Latin Vulgate Version, were the glory of his life, and the truing point of the Pope losing control over Britain. Wycliffe was one of the most important agents in producing the Protestant movement, that was also known as the Reformation movement, more than a century before Martin Luther was born. Wycliffe planted the seeds for the Reformation movements with great boldness, and perseverance. He also put together those principles, which were to shake the Romani's Church of Rome from Britain. These Protestants, or the Reformers, were former Roman Catholic believers, who broke off from the Roman Catholic Church, because they were protesting against it teaching, and ways of the Roman Catholic Church they did not go along with. According to the Encyclopaedia, it was the Roman Catholic Church believers who named these ex Catholic believers, as the Protestants, which mean to protest. Another British Reformer were known as William Tyndale, who was born in the year of 1490, or 1494 in Gloucestershire of Britain. He went to Oxford University where he increases in the knowledge of speaking in different languages. Also, in the knowledge of the writing of the Scripture where his mind was firmly set, because he believes the Scripture alone should be the doctoring of every believer lives in the church.

In 1520, Tyndale went to Gloucestershire his native countryside where the influence of the Roman Catholic Church, were strong over Britain, and where the abuses of the Church were more frequent, and the ignorance of its ministers was more in extreme. Tyndale bold speaking of the things he saw with the Roman Catholic Church, made him become very unpopular with the bishops, and ministers of the church. He was secretly charged with having heretical opinions against the Roman Catholic Church. He was given notice to appear before the bishops, who rebukes him severely. Tyndale left Gloucestershire, and went to London, hopping to get the chance of his heart desire to translating the New Covenant part of the Scripture into the British people dialect.

The way Tyndale saw it, Wycliffe's early translation of the New Covenant part of the Scripture before his time was outdated, and it needed to be updated. This was because the Scripture was a seal book to many of his people of Britain, and they only had the knowledge from what the Bishops thought them. Who were the priest, and who were only concern about their own interest, and strive to keep things that way. They perverted his teaching to their own gain, and twist the meaning of what he was saying to their own purposes. So, because of this, Tyndale could not find anywhere in London to worked on his translation of the New Covenant part of the Scripture, and he was not welcome in Britain to do so neither. So, in January of 1524, Tyndale left London with the support of some wealthy merchants of London, and he went to Hamburg of West Germany, where he found help, and were able to work on his translation of the New Covenant part of the Scripture there. In May of 1525, he went to Cologne of West Germany to print up his translation of his New Covenant part of the Scripture, he was working on. But unfortunately for Tyndale a German man by the name of Johannes Cochlaeus who was a strong Roman Catholic believer happens to be in Cologne at of the time. Johannes came to the knowledge that Tyndale was printing up his translation of the New Covenant part of the Scripture, and he was determined to have the printing stop. So, he went to the city authorities, and persuaded them to have the printing stop, while he contacts various Bishops in Britain, to warn them to prevent Tyndale printed translation of the New Covenant part of the Scripture from reaching the British shore. Tyndale who was barred from printing his translation, went to the city of Worms in West Germany to have the printing done there.

In the spring of 1526, various copies of his translation were able to smuggle into Britain, where there were stiff opposition made against these printed copies, by the Catholic Church officials, who were known as the ecclesiastical body of the church. Their intention were to prevent these printed documents of Tyndale from circulating in the country of Britain, but their attempts to suppress these copies were not all to gather successful. Various number of people booth in Britain, and in other part of Europe was able to read copies of his translation for themselves. Though many of these copies was burn in the fire by the officials of the Catholic Church. While Tyndale remain in the city of Worms where he was writing pamphlets against the religious abasement of the Roman Catholic Church, and also, that he was in favor of the Reformation church movement.

Many of his pamphlets were circulated in Britain, and the bishops of London held a meeting, pass a decree of law, to stop any imported printed reading materials of Tyndale from entering in the country of Britain. They also made laws of stipulation to prevent any form of his teaching to enter in the English language, or into the Latin language, that they describe as heresies, from reaching the people of Britain. Apart from what was taught by them of the Roman Catholic Church. But their decree was not able to prevent various study books of Tyndale from reaching the people of Britain. Quite a few people who read coppys of his books, and accepted his views were burn at the stake in Britain. Yet there was great demand for his translation of the New Covenant part of the Scripture. Many of Tyndale enemies in Britain desire to have him brought back to Britain, to have him under their control, but he started to work on his translation of the Old Covenant part of the Scripture in 1530. But Tyndale was not able to finished his translate, and to published the first five books of Moses, that is called as the Torah, in the Hebrew language. This writing of Moses was also called as the Pentateuch, but the word Pentateuch came from Late Latin, and Greek, according to the Webster Colligate Dictionary of the Fifth Edition. Which meant the first five books of the Old Covenant part of the Scripture, that were written by Moses the prophet. Tyndale was not able to finish his work of his translation of the Old Covenant part of the Scripture, because men were busy seeking to arrest him. In 1535, in the city of Antwerp he was busy revising his translation of the New Covenant part of the Scripture, and circulating of his editions, of his work. While men were sent out from Britain to seek, and to arrest him. He was captured, and were put in prison, in the Castle of Filford, where he was closely confined. When many British merchants heard of his arrest, letters were also sent out from Oliver Cromwell for his release, but to no avail. He remains in prison for more than a year, and after much reasoning, he were condemned to death.

Although he knew he was going to die, he was not timed, and faithless, and in October of 1536, he was led out to be put to death, and he was bound to the stake, and his last word was, "Lord opens the eyes of the king of Britain", which he was referring to King Henry the 8th, who was then the king, and who were a strong Roman Catholic believer. Tyndale was finally strangled, and his body was burn at the stake. In the time of William Tyndale, the king of Britain had a close alliance with the Pope, and all classes of the people continued in submitting themselves to his authority.

But the power of the Pope, and the Roman Catholic Church ruling over Britain was on borrow time, with all its oppression and abuse was running out, and the man who was to do more than all the others to overthrow its power in Britain, was already born. Speaking of Henry 8th, who broke off from the Roman Catholic Church, and formed the Anglican Church, that became known as the Church of England. Volume 26 of the Encyclopaedia explained that, during the time when the Reformation was taking root, there develop a political quarrel between Henry 8th, and the Pontifex, better known as the Pope who was ruling over the British throne at the time. This dispute came about, because Henry who was national stallion, wanted a son to be his heir, and successor of the British throne. At the time Britain was not a part of the Salic law system, like that of other Germanic tribe of Germany, who prevented women from becoming successors to the throne of Germany. According to the Webster Collegiate Dictionary, the word Salic law means a cod of laws that did existed there among various tribes of Germany. The Encyclopaedia also explained that in France there existed this kind of law, that did forbid females from becoming successor to the throne of France. During this time in Britain, the British people just came from out of fighting a war, so there were fare that the struggle of this war might continue, if there were not a male successor, to take over the British throne after the death of Henry 8th. Catherine who came from the city of Aragon of Spain, was the first wife of Henry 8th, Who bare him numerous children, but only Mary survived, who became known as Queen Mary I of Britain. Who were also known as bloody Mary, because of her persecution against the British Reformation believers, because Mary who were a strong Roman Catholic believer, wanted to keep things that way. After Catherine gave birth to Mary, she did not gave birth to any more children for Henry, so the chances of Henry having a son by her to be his heir, were almost impossible.

Henry thought to himself that the best thing for him to do was to find a legal ground to divorce his wife. Henry come up with a clause to put away his wife, by saying that Catherine was first married to his brother Arthur, and after the death of his brother, she became his wife. Volume 5 of the Encyclopaedia explained that there were a law existed there in Britain, that was taken from the book of Leviticus, that did forbid the marriage of a man with his deceased brother's widow, but the Encyclopaedia did not explain in what Chapter, and what verse of the book of Leviticus were this statement found.

So, this statement the Encyclopaedia made is a religious philosophy of the people of Britain, and it is not from the Scripture of truth, of the Laws of Yahweh for a man to live by. The Pope who was ruling in the time of Henry 8th made a law stature against the matter of divorcement against a man, and his wife, so the question now arrives, whether the Pope will give Henry the ok for him to divorce from Catherine his wife or not. Catherine made the statement that there were no ground for divorcement, Henry should found in her former marriage to his brother, as a clause to want to put her away. Due to the fact that her husband had died, and there were no flaws for divorcement as for as she was concern, for she was free to married to another man if she so chooses. The Encyclopaedia explained that Pope Clement 7th who was the pope at the time, would have granted Henry his divorcement from his wife Catherine, had it not been that Catherine was the aunt of Emperor Charles 5th of the Roman Empire of that time. Pope Clement was under the authority ship of Emperor Charles 5th, who did not want to see his aunt to be put aside for another wife of Henry's. As for the Pope, he did not want to offend, or to provoke the emperor to grant Henry his divorcement from his wife. But so long as Henry takes the affair in his own hands, that would leave him in clear out of the picture. Catherine did appeal to Pope Clement stating that her marriage to Henry were no way illegal, because of her previous marriage to Arthur came to its end, because of his death, and she were free to marry again. I must point out that according to the Scripture book of "Romans Chapter 7, verse 2, and 3" Catherine was totally with in her rights. Because the Scripture make it quit clear, that the woman who has a husband, is bound by the law to her husband, as long as he live. Which meant the Law of Yahweh of the Scripture, to a man, and his wife, but if her husband died, she is free from the law to her husband, as far as the marriage goes. So, then, if while her husband lives, and she is married to another man, she shall be called an adulterous. But if her husband is dead, she is free from the law of her husband, if she is married to another man, she shall not be called an adulterous.

So, for seven years the Pope avoids giving his ruling on the matter, because of the authority ship of the emperor he was under. Thomas Cranmer who was born July 2-1489, in Aslacton in Nottinghamshire of Britain, who was one of the early translators of the Bible in the English language, who attend Jesus Collage in Cambridge, where he was appointed as a theological lecturer in religious studies. He was called upon to give his opinion on the subject, about King Henry 8th who wanted to divorce from Catharine his wife.

The speech he gave about the subject was completely in favor, with that of Henry's opinion, so because of his speech he gave, the king gave him the position of Archbishop of Canterbury, because his opinion was in harmony with that of Henry 8th. So, as soon as Thomas Cranmer became Archbishop of Canterbury, and he granted Henry his divorce from his wife Catharine, and conforms the king marriage ceremony to Anne Boleyn. The action of the Archbishop excited the various enemy of the Pope in Britain, but it was in the intention of the Pope to have Cranmer and others of his flocks, to be excommunicated from the Roman Catholic Church. Thomas Cranmer immediately set up a defense for himself, in the church movement of the Reformation. He was also able to get an act to pass by Parliament to abolish forever the Pope supremacy over the British kingdom of Britain. Thomas Cranmer also declared Henry 8th as the sole head of the Anglican Church, that became known as the Church of England. Thomas Cranmer next move was to have the Scripture to be translated into the English language, and to dissolve the various Catholic Monasteries in Britain. According to the Webster's Colligate Dictionary, the word Monasteries, came from the Romans, to the Anglo-Saxon dialect of West Germany, that meant a house of religious retirement, or a house of seclusion from the world for a person who is under religious vows. This high position, to which Thomas Cranmer had succeeded to, naturally made him many enemies, who had sought to ruin his position. But he was protected by the king, who appointed him executioner of his will, and regent of his kingdom. The word regent according to Webster Collegiate Dictionary, meant a ruler, or a governor, so the Parliament of Britain pass an act of law given Henry all authority ship over the affair of Britain, that was previously belong to the Pope, and the Catholic Church of England. So, Henry became the head of the Church of England, with Thomas Cranmer as the spiritual head of the organization. According to volume 2 of the Encyclopaedia, Catherine of Aragon were born December 16-1485, in Alcala de Henares of Spain, and she died January 7-1536, in Kimbolton of Britain.

She was the youngest daughter of a Spanish ruler by the name of Ferdinand II, of Aragon, and Isabella of Castile Spain. Catherine who got married to Prince Arthur who were the oldest son for King Henry 7th of Britain, but Arthur died shortly after his marriage to Catherine, and shortly thereafter she became the wife of Henry 8th, who was the second son for Henry 7th.

Before the death of Henry 8th, he had married to six different wives, Catherine of Aragon was the first wife, and then Anne Boleyn, who was the mother of Queen Elizabeth I, and who were his second wife. According to volume 1 of the Encyclopaedia, Anne Boleyn were born in 1507, with a question sign, and she was a sister of one of Henry's earlier mistresses, and Henry decided to get married to her after, he had put away his wife Catherine. Henry, who was getting tired of Anne Boleyn, because she failed to produce him a male child, he wanted, so he come up with a skim in 1536, to have her executed for adultery with other members of his court. In May 2, of 1536, Henry put his wife Anne Boleyn in prison into the Tower of London, and charges her of having adulterous relationship with various men. According to the Encyclopaedia, Henry also charged her for committed incest with her own brother. She was tried by a court of Britain, and were found guilty, and was beheaded May 19-1536, in London. Anne Boleyn father was known as Sir Thomas Boleyn, who later became known as Earl of Wiltshire of Britain. Anne Boleyn spent a part of her childhood days in France, and she returns to Britain in 1522, and lived at Henry's court. The Encyclopaedia explained that although Henry had lost interest in Boleyn, and started to look around his court for another woman of his fancy, if she did given birth to a son, it might have made all the difference in the world, as far as Henry were concern. It would have perhaps save her marriage, and her life. Volume 1 of the Encyclopaedia explained that Anne Boleyn had a miscarriage in 1534, and in January of 1536, she gave birth to a son who were born dead. So, this was the mishap for Anne Boleyn, in her marriage to Henry, in not producing him a son to be his hear. The Encyclopaedia explained that although the court that was set up to Judge Anne, and found her guilty, she may have been the victim of a court group that were set up and supported by Thomas Cromwell in Henry favor.

According to Volume 1 of the Encyclopaedia, in May 30 of 1536, Henry got married to his third wife, who were known as Jane Seymour, so Henry's marriage to Jane Seymour finally gave him his heart desire, by giving birth to a son, by the name of Edward 6th, but Jane Seymour died in childbirth in 1537. So, for the next 3 years, Henry spent looking around for another wife to replace the loss of Jane Seymour, his fourth wife were known as Anne, who was the sister of William Duke of Cleves of Germany. Anne was born September 22-1515, and died July 16-1557, in London of Britain.

Henry got married to Anne because he believed his marriage to her would create a political family alliance with her brother who was known as William the Duke of Cleves, who were also a leader of the Protestants movement of Western Germany. Henry believed to himself that this alliance with Anne's brother were necessary, because he felt in 1539, it did appear to him that the two Roman Catholic powers of the time, which were France, and the Holy Roman Empire of Germany, were about to join forces to gather to attack the Protestants followers of

Britain. This belief of Henry moved his chief minister, who was known as Thomas Cromwell, to make the arrangement for the marriage between Henry and Anne, to establish the union between Britain, and her Lutheran enemies of the Roman Empire of Charles 5th of Germany and France Volume 1 of the Encyclopaedia explained that in January 1, of 1540, Anne arrived in Britain to meet with Henry, to be her future husband, and they got married five days later, but Henry was disappointed because she was less attractive than he had hope for. So, Henry became very resentful toward her, because of her unpolished vocabulary of the English language, he was not pleased of. The anticipated alliance Henry was expecting between France, and Germany of the Roman Catholic Empire did not materialize. So, this marriage alliance between Henry, and Anne became a political embarrassment, and was finally put to an end by the Anglican Church men, in July 9-1540. Anne accepted the divorcement with quietness without any form of protest, and she were rewarded with a large income, with the understanding she must remain living in Britain. Anne eventually went to live in Richmond of London, and occasionally visit the court of Henry, until her death. The fifth wife for Henry was known as Catherine Howard, and she was put to death on February 13-1542, in London, because of her accused promiscuous lifestyle, as a queen of Britain.

According to volume 2 of the Encyclopaedia, Catherine who was one of 10 children for Lord Edmund Howard, who died in 1539, and who was a poverty-stricken younger son of Thomas Howard II, who was also known as the Duke of Norfolk of Britain. Henry became attracted to Catherine who was just a young girl in 1540, when Henry was planning to put an end to his political marriage to Anne of Cleves of Germany, to whom Catherine was just a maid of honor. Henry put an end to his marriage to Anne on July 9th, and in July 28-1540, Henry and Catherine gotten married privately. So, on August 8- of 1540, Henry made it known to Catherine that she was now the Queen of Britain, and for the next 14th months Henry was full of love with Catherine.

According to the Encyclopaedia, while Catherine was married to Henry, she was accused of having an affair with Frances Dereham who was her secretary, and also she may have committed adultery with Thomas Culpepper, though it were left to be proven. When Henry learned about these accusations of his new wife, he found it extremely hard to believe the various things he heard about her, and Henry became terribly angry with wrath of these revelation. So, in February 11-of 1542, Parliament sentenced Catherine to death, declaring her sentence to be of treason, for an unchaste woman to be married to the king. Two days later she was beheaded in the Tower of London. The sixth and last wife for Henry was known as Catherine Parr, who was born 1512, and died September 7-1548, according to the Encyclopaedia volume 2 of the Encyclopaedia there it explained that she was married two different time, before she became the wife of Henry. Her first husband was known as Edward borough, who died in 1529, and Catherine Parr were also married to Henry for four years, and then he died in 1547. She went and gotten married to Thomas Lord Seymour, and gave birth to a daughter, and then died. The death of Henry 8th in 1547, gave Cranmer the position to crown Edward 6th as the new king of Britain. According to volume 4 of the Encyclopaedia, Edward was born October 12-1537, in London, and he died July 6-1553, of tuberculosis, and Edward 6th was the only legitimate son for Henry 8th. During the time of Cranmer crowing Edward as the new king of Britain, he was very zealous in promoting the Reformation movement in Britain. Before the death of Edward 6th, John Dudley who were duke of Northumberland, gave his son the title as Guildford Dudley, that would give him the position to marry to Lady Jane Grey, and Lady Jane Gray were related to Henry 8th.

So, Dudley persuaded Edward the 6th, to will over the crown to Lady Jane Grey, and her husband, and totally leaving Mary, and Elizabeth out of the picture. Thomas Cranmer who were the archbishop at the time, who did presided over the ceremony of the crowing of Lady Jane Grey to the British throne, and Lady Jane Gray reign for a period of 9 days only, before she was dethroned by the army of Mary. Mary had the support of the masses of the people, and in July 19 of 1553, the Lord Mayor of London made it to be officially known, that Mary Tudor was the rightful ruler of the British throne. So, Lady Jane Gray, and her husband were arrested, and charge for high treason, and were put to death.

Mary intention with her advisers was not to put Cranmer to death for his support of putting Lady Jane Gray, and her husband to the British throne, but their real intention was to have him put to death for his longstanding in promoting Protestantism in the British Kingdom. The queen and her advisers had to wait until they could get Parliament to reinstate the law that was set up by Henry 8, and Edward 6th to burn people at the stake, who they had consider as heretics of the Roman Catholic Church doctoring. During the time of Henry reign, he was not impartial to burn people at the stake. Some Protestants, and some Lutherans followers, and some Roman Catholic believers who did not go along with his rules and regulations as the royal supreme head of the Church of England, were burn at the stake. According to volume 5 of the Encyclopaedia before the death of Henry, he became suspicious of the power of his chief Minister of the house of Parliament, who were known as Thomas Cromwell, who Henry helps to put him to death, in July 1540. In the year of 1555, the law for burning heretics to the stake was reinstated, and after a long trial, in which Cranmer defend himself against the various charges that were brought against him. He was eventually degraded from his Episcopal office, and were put in prison by Mary's government. Mary, and her Roman Catholic advisers tried in different ways, and means to have Cranmer to denounce his belief in Protestantism. Even in having him watching Ridley, and Hugh Latimer, who were former bishops, who became believers of Protestantism, to be put to death at the stake. The government of Mary was hoping that by the various pressures they put on Cranmer, he would publicly denounce his belief in Protestantism, and by so doing they would destroy Protestantism in Britain. But Cranmer held on to his belief in Protestantism, and the decoration was sign for him to be burn at the stake for his belief.

While they were making the preparations to have him to be burn at the stake, he went on to say that, the hands that signed for him to be burned should first be punished. Many of his enemies, who were at this gathering, did not like the answer he gave to them, so they drag him, and tied him to the stake, and lit the fire around him burning, around him. While Cranmer was tied to the stake, and the fire burning around him, he stretched out his right hand in the flame until it was consumed, by saying this is the hand that wrote it, and therefore it shall first suffer punishment.

According to this Biographical Sketch of the Translators, and Reformers, before Cranmer died, he was repeating the words of the Apostle Stephen, by saying Lord Jesus received my spirit, so he died at age 67. Another member of the Reformation movement of the Protestant churches, was a British man by the name of Miles Coverdale, who were born in Yorkshire of Britain in 1486, and he eventually became an Augustine Monk. While Coverdale was an Augustine Monk, he translated the Scripture into the British people dialect, while he was in exile for his belief in the Protectionism principles. He was given the permission to return to Britain, and he was given a position of an Almoner to Catherine Parr, who was the last wife of Henry 8th. According to volume 1 of the Encyclopaedia, an Almoner that was mentioned, was an officer who was responsible for giving out things to the poor, which was usually connected with a religious house, or other institutions of those days. Cloverdale became famous, because under his dedication in 1535, the first whole translation of the Scripture was completed in Britain, that were printed in Zurich, of Switzerland, and it were dedicated to Henry the 8th. In Cloverdale letter of dedication to Henry 8th, Coverdale mentioned to his Majesty that the Pope gave him the title of Defender of the Faith, only because his Majesty gave his bishops the permission to burn God's Word. Which is the root of faith, and to persecute the lovers, and the ministers of it", while in the meantime, the king claiming to have an intimate conviction of it, because of the title that were given to him as defender of the faith by the Pope. Cloverdale also mention in his writing of dedication to the king, that the king believed his administration was a part of the fulfillment of the prophecy, that were spoken of, that by the king faith, shall the word be defended. Also, that God Word with its ministers of faith, shall have its free course throughout all Christendom, specially in his ruling, meaning in Britain, or what became known as England.

According to the Webster's Collegiate Dictionary of the Fifth Edition, the word Christendom, came from AS, which is short for Anglo Saxon, which mean the whole body of Christians, or the church, which originally is speaking of the Roman Catholic Church, in the part of the world where Christianity prevails. Under the reign of Edward 6th Coverdale was made a bishop, but he lost his position, and were put in prison when Mary came to the British throne, after the overthrow of Lady Jane Gray in 1553-58, who take over ruler ship after the death of Edward 6th.

So, when Mary came to the ruler ship of the British throne, she became known as bloody Mary, for her persecution against the Reformers. So, at the plea of the king of Denmark, Coverdale was set free, and were given the permission to leave the British Kingdom. He returns to Britain when Elizabeth I came to the British throne, who reigned from 1558 to 1603, after the death of her sister Mary I. After Coverdale return to Britain, he was greatly attached to the religious belief of what was known as the Puritans, and he refuses to accept any longer the office of the bishop of the Roman Catholic Church. According to the Webster's Colligate Dictionary of the Fifth Edition, the word Puritans mean a religious group of people who existed during the reign of Queen Elizabeth I, so these Puritans believers, were opposed to the traditional, and formal practice of the religious order that was setup by the Roman Catholic Church system. These Puritans supports wanted a simpler form of faith, and worship, than that of what were established by the law of the land. Cloverdale were given a small living quarter that were later taken away from him, because of his principles of his religious belief, and he died in poverty in the year of 1569. According to this Biographical Sketch of the Translators, and the Reformers, of what became known as the Bible, of 1890. Many Reformers, and preachers of the Good News of the Scripture, were burn at the stake in Britain, and in other part of Europe, because they were a part of the Reformation movement, who broke away from the Catholic Church, and its teaching. Many were also burn at the stake for wanting to bring the knowledge, and the purity of the Scripture into the dialect of the ordinary people of Europe, which were under the influence, and the teaching of the Roman Catholic Church, and its Bishops.

Another of these early translators of the Bible, that came in to the English language, were a man by the name of Hugh Latimer, who were born in the time of 1470, in Leicestershire of Britain. His father were a farmer, and when he was fourteen-year-old, he went went to Christ Collage in Cambridge, where he was an honorable student. While he was at Cambridge Collage, he was very zealous in the religious belief of Roman Catholicism, and he was in total opposition to the Lutheran philosophy of Protestantism, that later became known as the Reformation movement. But later he was able to meet up with a former priest by the name of Tomas Bilney, who had read books about Luther belief in Protestantism, and he became a secret follower of the Reformation religious movement.

From this discussion with this former priest, Latimer feeling started to change from Roman Catholicism, and he had to face up to the reality of the various errors of the Roman Catholic Church, he had been educated into, to see things their way. He also became aware of the superstitious observance of the Roman Catholic Church, and he was very egger to expose it to others, of the various faults he came to learn about the Catholic Church. But he came to the realization that the bishops of the Roman Catholic Church were determining to ruin him, and the bishops would have certainly succeeded, had it not been that King Henry was his friend. Later Latimer became a preacher to the people of his associates, that make him to become extremely popular with the people of Britain, and this made him more heated among the various priests of the Catholic Church. He were frequently arrested by the command of the bishops, and he was ordered to give up his views about his feeling of the Roman Catholic Church, that he was a part of before, but he did not give in to their demands. Later he resigned from his position of been a bishop, and he went to live in the countryside of Britain, intended to pass out the remainder of his life there. But he had an accident that force him to go to London to seek surgical assistance, and while he was in London he was seized, and was put in prison in the Tower of London during the reign of King Henry 8th. But when Edward 6th came to the British throne, after the death of his father, Latimer was given his freedom, and became an extremely popular preacher among the people of Britain, and he also, had the opportunity to give lengthy sermons before Edward 6th. According to the Biographical Sketches of the Translators, and the Reformers, he was treated with great cruelty in the Tower of London, for him to change his views he had against Roman Catholicism.

But he refused from doing so, and he was excommunicated from the Catholic Church, and was condemned to put to death, with another fellow by the name of Ridley. The time, and the place was set for his execution, which was set for October 16th, 1555, in the city of Oxford, near Baliol Collage. Where Ridley was dressed up in his bishop robe, and Latimer in his prison clothes, were taken from their prison cell, and were tied to the stake to be burned. When the fire was lit, and Latimer saw the flame, he shouted to Bishop Ridley, and said to him, be of good cheer Master Ridley, and be a man, we shall this day light the candle by the grace of God in England, and I trust that it shall never be put out, and they both died in the fire.

Another early translator of what became known as the Bible, was known as John Huss, who were also one of the early Reformers, who got his surname from his native village of Hussinetz, which was in south western corner of Bohemia. According to volume 2 of the Encyclopaedia, the country and kingdom of Bohemia is in what were known as Czechoslovakia, of the Gentile land of what became known as Europe. This tribe of people was originally Germans Bohemians that existed there in Central Europe, with their land border, in what is now known as Austria, and their west side is Bavaria, and their north side was the kingdom of Saxony, that were borderline with another Germanic tribe by the name of Lusatia. According to this Bible of 1890, of the early Reformers, the history they had received about John Huss that were gathered from his early life is very scanty. Which were taken from simple record of many poor people who knew him well. According to their source of information they had gathered about him, he was born July 6, of 1373, and at the age of 16, he went as a poor boy to the University of Prague, where he became a Master of Art in 1396. In the year of 1400, he was appointed as a preacher at the University chapel of Bethlehem, that were newly built by the wealthy Bohemians for the spreading of the Gospel in their language. For the most part he was burning with the desire to spread the word of Yahweh, which to him was a commanding position to do so. Which he had performed very well, that the Archbishop of Prague became his enemy. The Archbishop succeed in having him sent back to his native village, where he spent his time studding the writing of Wycliffe, that were brought over from Britain with Jerome, who were a young student of Prague. His desire were to spread the Good News of the Scripture among his people, that move him to translate certain books of the Old, and New Covenant part of the Scripture in his own language.

Upon the death of his enemy, who were the Archbishop of Prague, he returns to the city Prague where he began to zealously to attack the abuses of the church, which was the Roman Catholic Church. Many of his people of Prague were in his favor, during his famous speeches against the doing of the church, and because of that many people of his country became more, and more filled with his doctrines. This was, until it brought about great disturbances among the people of Prague. Eventually the Bishops, and Deacons became terribly angry with Huss, and he was compelled to return to his native village. This was because of his speeches he gave against the Catholic Church, and its bishops, and deacons, and due to his various speeches, against the Catholic Church, he was not allowed to live in peace.

There were a council meeting, that were held against him, that command him to appear to answer charges that were brought against him for his speeches against the Catholic Church, and its bishops in 1414. He was promised a safe conduct by the Emperor, to return to his native village, but this promised did not come true on his behalf. Huss were condemned to death, by the official of the Catholic Church, on the charges of heretic. According to the Webster Dictionary, the word heretic, which is a Latin, and Greek word, that meant, one who holds heresy, or one whose opinion is held in opposition against the common teaching of the religious church, that promote division. Or one who deliberately upholds a doctoring that is different from that of the church, meaning that of the Catholic Church, where all the various churches of today came out of, also that of Protectionism. Huss were given the chance to change from his religious belief, after been condemn by the council of the Roman Catholic Church, but he held on to his belief, and would not change his mind. He was finally sentenced to be burned at the stake, with heaps of straws piled up around him, and the fire was lit, and his last word was, Jesus Son of the living God have pity on me. After his death, his ashes were scraped up and gathered, and thrown into the Rhine River. John Rogers were also one of these early Translators of the Bible into the British people dialects, and a former Protestant believer, who broke off from the Catholic Church of Rome. According to the Translators and Reformers, that was taken from the Authorized King James Version of 1890 AD, John Rogers who were born in Lancashire of Britain, in the year of 1500, and he went to Cambridge where he received a scholarship. He were sent as a Chaplin to a factory at Antwerp, in Germany to render important assistance to William Tyndale, and Coverdale, in their work of translating the Scripture into the British people dialect, from the Latin language of the Romans.

In 1537, a famous Edition of this Bible was issued into folded sheets of paper, that were known as the Folio, which the word Folio came from the Latin word of folium, which meant a leaf, according to the Webster Dictionary, and this Bible was called the Matthew Bible. According to page 6 of this Bible, of the New Testament part of the translation of Roger's work. This translation of Roger was call as the Pentateuch, that were slightly different from the Pentateuch of the translation of Coverdale. In the reign of Edward 6th, Roger return to Britain and was given a position in Saint Paul's Cathedral durian the time when Mary became Queen of the British throne. His outspokenness of the faith of the Gospel could not fail to cause offense, and he was put in prison, and before he was put to death, he was taken to Bishop Bonner, to be degraded by him.

While he was in prison, he asked one petition from this bishop, that he might speak a few words to his wife, and children before he was burn at the stake, but his petition was denied, and his last words to this Bishop, and the rest of Mary's servants, your action show the kind of charity you have. He was finally burn to death at the stake, in February 14th, 1555, in a place in Britain that was known as Smithfield. Laurence Sander were another one of these early Reformers, and he were from Britain, who were living during the reign of Queen Mary I of Britain. Mary was a very devoted member of the Roman Catholic society, who did not want the Scripture to reach into the hands of the local people of Britain, except what was taught only by the Roman Catholic Church society, and its bishops, and Priests. According to this Bible, Mary tried her very best to crush the translation of the Scripture from been translated into the British people language, from the Latin language of the Roman. But although she tried her best to crush the translation work, still there were devoted Reformers who did not feared to risk their lives, trying to bring the reading of the Scripture into the British people dialect. Such was the case of this man who were known as Lawrence Saunders, who were educated at Eton, at the king's college in Cambridge of Britain. According to this Bible, he was described as a Reverent, and after Saunders graduated from the University, he was engaged in the trading business, but in Edward 6th time of the Reformation, he resigned from his mercantile pursuits, and obtained a license, and began to preach.

He was a man of much ability, and this made him extremely popular with the people, of Britain, and he were appointed by the authorities as a lecturer, in the Cathedral of Litchfield. One Sunday of October 15th, 1553, he was delivering a sermon from his Parish Church pulpit, that created much excitement, he was arrested on that same Sunday afternoon, by the order of the bishop of London. He was put into prison for one year, and three months, by which time, he wrote several letters to various Reformers leaders for their support. He was taken before the Queen council for examination, and other bishops of Winchester of Britain, in which he made the statement to them that he is a free minded person, who is free from the authority of the bishops of Rome, with all of it's abuses. He was threatened by the council, for his speech, in which he replied, be aware of shedding innocent blood, and if it is the will of God for him to die by their hands so be it.

The councils, and the various bishops, who were there, were unable to force him to change his views, and his belief, and to give in to their demands of the Catholic Church. He were excommunicated, from the church, and were sentence to be put to death. On February 8th of 1555, he were taken out to be executed in an old gown, from his prison cell. Even at the stake before the fire was lit, they could not change his mind to give up his thinking of his belief, against the teaching of the Roman Catholic Church. When the fire were lit, his last word was, welcome the cross of Christ, and welcome the everlasting fire, by this time, the fire was spread around him, and he fall asleep in death. According to volume 23 of the Encyclopaedia, Martin Luther were another of these Reformers of Protestantism, this youth, who were informed about the last days, and the dreadful fair of this day that the Scripture spoke about. Were fortunate to come up on a copy of the Holy writing of the Scripture, that he held as a very dear treasure to himself. He was able to attend a Latin school in Germany, that were known as Mansfield, and Later Martin Luther spent a year at a religious Protestant church group, in Magdeburg, that was run by a group of believers. Who were dedicated to the study of what became known as the Bible, and a student, of the Scripture. Hans Luther who were the father of Martin Luther, who wanted his son to become a lawyer, he also worked in various copper mines to be able to purchase the various textbooks for his son courses, for him to become a lawyer. But Martin Luther without consulting his parents, decided to join the religious monastery of Saint Augustinian. According to the information taken from volume 23 of the Encyclopaedia, Martin Luther went to pay his parents a visit, and on his way, returning back, from the visit of his parents, in 1505, of July 2, he gets cart up in a terrible thunderstorm near his village of Stotternheim. Martin Luther cried out in terror, because of the fair of the thunderstorm that he was cart up in.

In his fair of the thunderstorm, he called for the help of Saint Anne, and he made a vow, that if he was to makes it true the storm, he was going to become a monk, so after he were able to make it true the thunderstorm, he decided to become a monk, because he was concern of the terror, and the agony of sudden death. So, he sold many of his books he was studying from to become a lawyer, and in July 17, of 1505, he entered the monastery at Erfurt of East Germany. In April of 1507, he was appointed to the position of the priest office, where he held his first mass in the early part of May of that year.

Luther went to the University of Wittenberg to become a student of theology, in 1510, and Luther was also one of the monks, who were chosen to go to Rome to appeal to the office of the Pope, to strengthen out some religious problem he were experiencing that did affecting his monastery. While he were in Rome, he were surprised to see the worldly lifestyle, of many of the bishops, or the priests, who should have been living like many of the monks, who were living plain, and simple life, with self-discipline. Luther appeal to the office of the Pope was not granted, and he returns to Germany, and eventually he became a professor at Wittenberg University, of Biblical theology. Before the death, and ill health of Luther, he broke away from the Roman Catholic Church, of Rome and became leader of the Protestant Reformation movement in Germany, in 1522. Luther began to work on his translation of the Scripture, in his native language, and he went on to say that his intention were not only to translate the book of John Gospel, but his intention was to translate the whole new Covenant part of the Scripture, that became known as the New Testament. Luther translated the whole complete New Covenant part of the Scripture, with the help of another German fellow by the name of Melanchthon. The Encyclopaedia explained that Melanchthon help to establish the educational system of Germany, who also were one of these early Reformers and Theologian. According to this Bible, the first effort to print the Scripture in Germany went back as far as the year 1477, in which there was little opposition to the work. These printed copies of the Scripture at the time in Germany were not very clear, in giving a good understanding to many people of Germany. So to promote the circulation of the translation of the New Covenant part of the Scripture, these copies were made to be sold very cheaply as possible, to the people of Germany. Luther vigorously went on to work on his translation of the Old Covenant, part of the Scripture, and in November 2- of 1522, Luther went on to say that "in his translation of the Old Covenant, he only reaches as far as Leviticus".

He also realize how much writing letters, and also looking after other businesses, can interrupt his progress, so Luther decided to shut himself up, and used some other means of communication with his associates. After Luther finished the five books of Moses, he went on to work on the other part of the Old Covenant part of the Scripture, and set a price that were reasonable for the public to porches it. Luther translation of the Old, and New Covenant part of the Scripture into the dialect of his Germanic people, cast the Roman Catholic officials to be up in arms.

Due to his his translation of the Scripture into his native people dialect, that were always against the principle, and the belief of the Roman Catholic Church organization of Rome. But the work of Luther was received with great joy by his people of Germany, and his translation were able to reach other part of the Gentile land of Europe, who understood the Germanic dialect. According to this Bible of 1890, Luther translation stud at the top of other versions of what became known as the Bible, with its simplicity, force, and dignity that had no rival, like that of the King James Authorized Version. Which did appeal to the finest example of people, who came in contact with it. Due to Luther work in his translation of the Scripture, into the dialect of the Germanic people, he became a legend in the mind of many people of Germany, and his translation of the Scripture helps to unite the dialect of the Swabian, and the Frankish Germanic people, into one nation of speech, that helps to preserve the unity of the German nation of its language, literature, and thoughts. The Encyclopaedia explained that the Swabian people whose historic region, was from southwestern Germany, including what is now known as the southern part of Baden, the Wurttemberg land area of Bayern, and also the area of eastern Switzerland, and a region that was known as Alsace of Germany. According to the Encyclopaedia, the name Swabia came from the Suebi people, who were a Germanic people, with the tribe of the Almanni, who had occupied the upper Rhine, and upper Danube region in the time of the 3rd century AD. The Franks under the leadership of Clovis were able to control the Almannis, with a customary laws of theirs, until about AD 500. By the time of the 7th century AD, Irish missionaries began to introduce Christianity to many of these tribal gropes of Germany. I must also point out that according to a map that is in volume 20 of the Encyclopaedia, showing the land area of Germany, the land size of Germany, was a far larger size during Roman time ruling over Europe, than what is shown on the modern world map of today.

Volume 4 of the Encyclopaedia, explained about the Frankish people, who were a member of a Germanic tribe, who invaded the Western part of the Roman Empire in the 5th century AD, and control what is known to day as France, and also, the Western part of Germany. These Frankish people were able to establish the most powerful Christian kingdom, of early medieval time, of what is now known as Western Europe. The name France, were taken from their name of Francia. According to the Encyclopaedia, these Franks people were divided into four groups, who were known as the Salians, the Riparian, the Chatty, and the Hessians.

This group of the Germanic people, who were living in the Rhineland area of Germany, in the 3rd century AD, invaded the area of Gaul repeatedly during the next 200 years of the Roman control of Western Europe. Volume 11 of the Encyclopaedia explained that many of Luther's critics, made the statement that his writing, and his books were too sharp, and cutting in which Luther replied by saying that they were right, in what they were saying, because he did not meant for his words to be soft or gentle. Reading from this said Bible; it seems to me that although Luther was a Monk, he did not care very much for the Roman Catholic establishment. My reason for making this statement, it is because Luther makes the statement, that he cares not about being accused of violence, for it shall be his glory and honor. Luther went on to say that, many times in the night when he was unable to sleep, he would ponder in his bed painfully, and anxiously about the Roman Catholic organization, and its Papists. As, they were called in that period, that they may be won over, and repent before the time of that dreadful judgment come. According to the Webster Colligate Dictionary, the word Papist meant, the office and dignity of the Pope, or the period of the governmental system of the Roman Catholic Church, of which the Pope was the supreme head of the church, and still is today. Many German solders gave Luther the title as the Pope, and by so doing; they take away the title from Clement, who were the Pope at that time. Various theologians of Germany, who were free spirit minded people, look to Luther as their leader. Also, many of the oppressed peasants people of Germany, were appreciative of Luther sympathy, in their helpless struggle for their rights against the Feudal chiefs. According to this Bible of 1890 AD, there it went on to explained that Luther made the statement, that where the Lord God build a church, the Devil make sure he also builds a Chapel close behind this church of God.

These were the word of Luther throughout his twenty-five years of trouble, and stormy life, and conflict until in the 15th of February, 1546, when he falls asleep in death. Many of the church religious philosophy of that time, was that men could erase their sins one by one through confession, and absolution in sacrament, and penance. According to the Webster Colligate Dictionary, the word penance, which is a Latin word, meant repentance in confession to the priest. During Luther ministry, he points out that the whole man is sick, but the church held the view that men is not too sick to make up for their bad deeds, by some good deeds. Another church teaching during the early time of the Roman Catholic Church, and the Reformers, is that God give to all a measure of grace, that if a man will lay hold on this grace of Yahweh.

The church further explained by saying that, these extra credits God would give, would constitute a treasury of merits from the Saints, from which the Pope could make a transfer to those who account were in arrears. This church philosophy of the Roman Catholic Church were called an indulgence. According to their belief, the grateful recipient member of the church, would contribute to the church. Volume 26 went on to explained that this arrangement of contribution to the church, became an extremely popular way of raising money for the church, and due to this mean of psychology of raising money by the church, the church was able to build big Cathedrals, hospitals, and even bridges, that were financed by the church. During the time of the Roman Catholic Church ruling over Germany, they established a law that were known as commutation, which this law were a law of physical punishment, or a fine of penalty that was imposed by the church. In which they claim this law, were a law from God, that were known as purgatory. According to the Webster New World Dictionary of the American language, the word purgatory was used in the time of Middle Latin, Late Latin, Old French, and Middle English. Which was a place that was teach in the various Roman Catholic Churches, that those who died in the grace of God, are waiting to pay for their sins, and to suffer temporary punishment in purgatory. I must point out that this doctoring, and philosophy of the Roman Catholic Church, and other Christians churches, that came from out of Roman Catholicism, have no Scriptural base, or ground for this king of teaching, and their belief. Which is totally a false teaching, and it is only the doctoring of the Roman Catholic Church, and it is not that of the writing of the Scripture of truth. In Luther days, the belief was that immediately after the release from purgatory, and for forgiveness, this was not only for penalties, but also for sins was granted. Due to this teaching Luther did received, as a Roman Catholic member, he was desperately concern about his standing before God.

The wood cut cross of the image of Christ, as the judge that is upon the rainbow of the cross, cause Luther to think about the person who were condemn to hell, that cause him to fill with terror. Luther concluded that by him becoming a monk, it would be the best way for him to acquire those benefits, which would add to the balance of his good account before God. So, he became a monk, and confined himself to religious study. I must point out that the word hell, that was translated in what is now known as the Bible, in the time of OHG, that stand for Old High German, was taken from the word Helen.

This word Helen, was also spell as hella, or holla, which was an underworld goddess that was based on the word Helen, which meant to cover or hide. The dictionary went on to explained that the word hell came from the Latin, that were spelled as celare, which meant to hide. The dictionary also explained that in the Bible the word hell meant where the spirits of the dead is, that is identified with the word sheol, and the word hades. But in Christianity the word hell mean the place where the devils live, and where various sinners, and unbelievers are doomed to eternal punishment after death. According to the dictionary, the word hades, came from Greek mythology, that was taken from the word Pluto, which the word Pluto means the god of the lower world, or the grave of the home of the dead beneath the earth. Or the ruler of the underworld, the resting place of the dead. So, the word Sheol according to the dictionary, is a Hebrew word, that meant the underworld, the place of the dead, the grave. So, the definition of the word hell came from Roman Catholicism of their paganism of their belief, that they had brought into the true worship of Yahweh, that became known as Christianity, that were translated as hell. So, according to the dictionary the word hell simple mean the common grave of the dead, that came down in the Angles, and Saxon dialect as Helen, or hell. Many of this information about hell, were also taken from the Webster Colligate Dictionary. So, when Roman Catholicism was established, they came up with their own laws of precepts to their meany church members, for them to go by as a way of life.

During this early period of the church, the bishops who were the priests, and the deacons decided to come up with what they had called as Scriptural Canon, which were only laws and commandments of men, and it was not laws that came down from Yahweh to govern the believer's lives. But it was only church laws, of what they think things should be, to govern their religious believer's lives. According to the Webster Dictionary of the American language, the word Canon came from Middle English, Old French, Middle Latin, East Central, and Greek. In the Greek language the word Canon is spelled as Canon, that stood for a rod, a measuring line, a law, or a body of laws of a church. One of this church precepts of laws that were established, were that the priests should live a life of celibacy, which means to remain as a single man, without having a wife, which there were no Scriptural Law for their belief, but it was just mare religious philosophies, and the commandment of the

Due to this law of the church, that was established, it had cast many of the men who became priests, not to be married, that led to many of them living a life of concubine age, and sodomy in the church, known today as homosexuals 'in secrete. The church also take the lead in pushing a war, that were taking place in Europe, at the time. This war were on the behalf of the various Christian princes of Germany, seeking to turn them against their common enemy, who were their surrounding neighbors, who did not believed in their form of religion. According to volume 26, the Encyclopaedia, the great peace campaign ended in what became known as the Crusade, in turn the Crusaders attracted many of dregs of Europe. The word Crusade according to the Webster Dictionary, came about in the time that was known as Middle Latin, and these Crusaders was mark with the cross, which is the religious symbol of the Roman Catholic Church. Also other churches that came from out of Roman Catholicism, of the Catholic Church. Over the centuries, as time went on, the Papacy, which mean according to the Webster New World Dictionary the position, and the authority, and rank of the Bishop, which is the office of the Pope, with the assistance of the monastic community. Which mean monks, and nuns, who were able to Christianize the Germanic tribe of the Visigoths, and others. By the action of the bishop's monks, and nuns, they were able to cement the ties between a distinctly form of Roman Christianity, that did became a part of Western European culture. That they did pass on to many of us, their conquered slave people, of their various colonies of the world. Volume 20 explained that the highest order of the Roman Catholic Church, is the office of the Pope, who were also known as the bishop of Rome, or the Pontifex Maximus. According to the Webster Colligate Dictionary, the word Pontifex, came from the word pontiff, that meant a way maker, a bridge, who is a member of the council of priests, that came from the central body of the Pontifical Collage, which is the highest priestly organization of Rome.

The word Maximus was taken from the word maximum, which meant the greatest, or the highest degree to obtain in the Roman religious 'world. According to volume 26 of the Encyclopaedia, what became known as Protestantism, began in northern Europe, from the 14 to the 1500 AD, sand this was in reaction to the Medieval Roman Catholic doctrines, and practices of their religious customs.

Which also came from the Eastern Orthodox Church of the Roman Empire, which were one of the 3 major forces from where Christianity came from. The Eastern part of the Roman Empire that the Encyclopaedia spoke of, consist of Romania, Macedonia, the Greek Turkey area of Europe, and what became known as the Middle East, and North Africa. The Encyclopaedia explained that after the various religious wars that had taken place in Europe, and in their various colonies of their conquered world, of the 1800 AD, Protestantism gained a strong foot hole that eventually influenced to a greater extent of the social, economic, political, and cultural life of many of the people of their colonies. Protestantism got its name from an assembly of x Roman Catholic believers, who were gathered in Germany in 1529 AD, to protest many of the Roman Catholic ways, and belief, they did not want to go along with. A protest was read against the revoked tolerance that were granted to Martin Luther followers, who were x Roman Catholic believers, that became known as the Protestants, that were taken away by the Roman emperor, who were Charles 5th. This protest were field on the behalf of 14 free cities in Germany, and 6 Lutheran princes who were followers, and believers of Martin Luther. Who decided that this decision of the emperor had no binding on them, because they were free states, and did not had to abide by the rule and regulation of the emperor, and they were no longer under Roman Catholicism. This group of people who made this protest became known as the Protestant, because they were protesting against the religious ways of the Roman Catholic Church, they did not want to go along with. According to volume 26 of the Encyclopaedia, the name Protestant was not only adopted by these protesters, but also by their opposers, who were their fellow Roman Catholic brothers, and sisters. The name Protestants were gradually applied as a general description to those people who became followers of the Protestant movement, especially those people outside of Germany. These Protesters take their appeal to the general council of all Christendom, and to the congress of all German nations.

By so doing, these Lutheran followers who made this protest became known as the Protestants. Before the year 1700, the broad usage of the word Protestants were accepted, though the word was not yet applied to the

Unitarians Christian believers. The British Toleration Act of 1689, were put into force to prevent the British Protestant subjects, from entering the church of England, that were also known as the Anglican Church. This Act of law did only allow for the toleration of opinions of the Orthodox Protestants.

The Encyclopaedia explained that the leaders of Protestantism, or the Reformation movement, as it were also called in that time of Martin Luther, John Knox, Thomas Muntzer, and Huldrychzwingli. Many other German followers of the Reformation movement, had preferred the name and title of the evangelist. In France, the followers of the Reformation preferred the name of Huguenots. Volume 26 of the Encyclopaedia explained that the name Protestants, were not only attached to the disciples of Martin Luther, but also, to the disciples of Huldrychzwingli, of Switzerland, who were born in 1484, and died 1531. After the death of Huldrychzwingli the leadership was taken over by John Calvin who lived from 1509 to 1564 AD. The followers of the Swiss Reformation, and those followers of the Reformation movement in Holland, Britain, and Scotland, specially after the 17th century preferred the name of Reformed. In the 16th century the name Protestant were used rather than the name Reformation, or the Lutheran. In the 17th century in Britain, the word Protestant were used to make a separation between those of the Orthodox Protestants, who were regarded by the Anglicans Church as the Baptist, Quakers, and the Roman Catholic. This word Orthodox were used by the Anglicans Church for all those groups who did claim to be Christian, but at the same time opposed Roman Catholicism, except for those of the Eastern churches. According to this Bible, that was Copyright in 1890, by A.J. Holman, and Company, there was a period in Europe that was known as the burning of the Scripture, that became known as the Bible. I must point out that page 8 of this Bible did not used the word as the Scripture, that became known as the Bible, but just used the word the burning of the Bible. According to page 8 of this Bible, the first English translation of the New Testament that were printed from the Greek Septuagint translation of the Scripture, were done in Antwerp Germany. Volume 1 of the Encyclopaedia explained that Antwerp was a province in what became known as Belgium, in which 1500 copies of this Bible was printed in 1526 AD.

Bishop Tunstall, and Bishop Wolsey went about destroying these translation of the Bible. A British merchant who were in the city of Antwerp, offered money to these bishops to buy all those translations of these Bible they were burning up. One of this Bishops answer the merchant by saying, that Mr. Packington do your best to take them from me, and with all my mind I intend to burn them up at Saint Paul Cross.

This time was before the death of William Tyndale, because Mr. Packington had spoken to Tyndale, by saying to him, I know you are a poor man, and you have a lot of books in your position, and because of these books, you have put your friends in danger, and your own self. Mr. Packington went on to say to Tyndale I have found a wealthy merchant who have allot of money, and he is ready to by all these books that you have, and Tyndale reply, who is he, Is he the Bishop of London? Tyndale went on to say, I know he will burn all these copies of the Bible I have worked so hard to translate into the ordinary British people dialect. Tyndale went on to say to this merchant that I am glad about the selling of these books, because by means of this sale, it would help me to get out of my debts. I am quite sure that the whole world will cry out against him, for the burning of God's word. Tyndale also makes the statement that this sale will also give him the over plus money, and the opportunity to correct any mistakes of his copy of the New Testament, and to print new ones. Tyndale went on to say, I trust that the second of these copies will be much better than the first. So, the burning of the Bible took place at Saint Paul's Cross in great quantities in the year of 1526 AD, and in 1529 other copies of Tyndale translation of the New Covenant part of the Scripture were resurfaces in Briton in large numbers that Dr. Stokesly, who were the Bishop of London, cause all these New Covenant translations to be bought up. Along with other work Tyndale did, to be brought to Saint Paul's Churchyard to be burn there, and this took place in May of 1531 AD.

Also, In 1538 AD, a British man by the name of Cloverdale, and a printer by the name of Richard Grafton had 2,500 copies of these Bible to be printed in French, and in the British language. But many of these copies was seized by the bishops, and other officials of the Catholic Church, and was thrown into the fire. But only a few copies were able to be saved from the flame of the fire. According to this Bible that was mentioned, in 1534

AD, Tyndale prepared and print in Antwerp a second, and more enlarged perfect edition of his New Testament, in which a copy of this edition is still in the British Museum.

According to volume 26 of the Encyclopaedia Britannica, and volume 12, the Methodists Church movements was started by John Wesley, with his younger brother, who were known as the Charles Wesley. Wesley was born in 1703 AD, and he was a former member of the Anglican Church that became known as the Church of England, that was started by Henry 8th. John Wesley attends Christ Church of Oxford University in 1720, and while he was there, he became an ordained priest, and he were a leader of a group of students who regularly attend sacrament, better known as Holy Communion. Wesley group was called the Methodists, because of their religious devotion to methodical study. In which they regularly vested the Oxford filthy prisons system of Britain, to shear the Scripture with prisoners. Teaching them to read, and to help them to find jobs after they were realest from person. Charles, and John Wesley help the group to grow in numbers, and this group became known as the Methodist. This religious group was also known as the Holy club, because of their regular communion services, and fasting two days per week. The Methodists also extend their services to workhouses, and to poor people distributing food, clothes, medicine, and books. Also running a school for the less unfortunate ones of Britain. According to the Webster's New World Dictionary, of the American language, the word Methodist came from the word Method, and this word Method came from French, Latin, and Greek, that stud for going after, or to pursuit. After the death of Wesley's father in April of 1735, he set out to go to the colony of Georgia, to become pastor there among the settlers, who were also known as the colonists. This was to carry out missionary work among the natives of Georgia who, they had call as the Red Indians.

This name Red Indians were given by the Gentile settlers of what became known as the United States of America. Due to lack of support from the establisher of the colony of Georgia, whose name was known as James Edward Oglethorpe of what became known as the United States. His missionary work was unsuccessful among the settlers, and also among the natives. The two brothers return to Britain, and came to the reality of their lock of genuine Christian faith. While they was in Britain, they went to seek help from a church member, who were known as the Brethren, who was station in Britain for a while, before they move to the colony of United States, to join up with the Moravian settlement who were there.

According to volume 8 of the Encyclopaedia, the Moravian Church movement that was a Protestant denomination that originally came from Bohemia, or Moravia of the Gentile land of Europe. These Bohemians were a Germanic tribe of people, whose country was in central Europe, that was close to Austria, Bavaria, Saxony, Lusatia, and Moravia. Some months later while John Wesley went to London, where he visits a friend by the name of Whitfield, who himself was a member of the Anglican Church of priests, who went true a conversion to that of Protestantism. Wesley invites him to go with him to the city of Bristol, to help him with the preaching work to the various coal miners of Kingwood Castle, where the human condition was at its worse. Wesley and Whitfield went with to Bristol to preaches to the local people in the open air, among many of whom were the outcast of the society of Bristol. This was the beginning of the Methodists outreach among the people of Britain. Whitfield, and Wesley worked together for a while, but later they separated from each other, because they had different religious belief. This different religious belief between Whitfield and Wesley, is that Whitfield believed in the in the doctrine of predestination, while Wesley believe that the love of Yahweh is universal to all people. According to the Webster Colligate Dictionary of the Fifth Edition, the word predestination means, the decree or the setting of Yahweh, from the beginning of time, respecting all events of men, whether it is to everlasting happiness, or to everlasting misery. Wesley believed that the belief of Whitfield in predestination was an error from the translators, who had translates the Scripture into what became known as the Bible, in the English language. From what I have gathered from reading the Encyclopaedia Britannica, for a while the leadership of the believers came under Whitfield, and then went back to the leadership of Wesley.

Under Wesley leadership the Methodists movement gains ground among those who had felt neglected by the Church of England. Wesley did not go along with many of the doctrines of the Anglican Church of England, because he believed that his teaching were based upon Scriptural doctoring, that man may gain salvation true the power of the Holy Spirit of Yahweh. That was translated as the Holly Ghost, of the prefect love of Yahweh, that is in Yashua, better known to many as Jesus Christ. Many of Wesley's helpers was various priests from the Anglican Church, including his brother Charles, who together helps him write more than 6,000 hymns.

 This was to express his message of the Methodists faith, to the public, and in private life to his British people of Europe. The Methodists movement formed a believer's society within the Church of England, but Wesley never intended for his followers to leave the Church of England, but as time went on the relationship between the Church of England, and that of the Methodists drifted apart. In 1784, there were shortages of ordained ministers in the colony, that became known as the United States of America. This was after the American Revolution war of 1775-1783, in which it was the British settlers, and other Gentile European settlers of Europe, who was fighting against the ruler ship of the British crown. Because they wanted self-rule, and they did not want to pay taxes to the British government anymore. During this time, the bishop of London refused to appoint Methodists as ministers to America, but Wesley wasted no time, and went straight away and called for an emergency meeting on a Biblical ground, that he believed gave him the right to ordain presbyters for the American cause. According to the Webster Colligate Dictionary, the word presbyter where the word Presbyterian came from, came from Greek, Late Latin, and French, that meant a priest, an elder of the Christian Church, that was also known as the ecclesiastical government of the presbyters body of believers. Thomas Coke who was a friend of Wesley, and also friend of Methodism's, who was Wesley right hand man, and a former ordained priest of the Anglican Church. Who was appointed by Wesley, as the superintendent of the new mission of North America. So, in 1787, during one of Coke nine vests to America, he also appointed other bishops for the colony of America, and Coke also appointed two other presbyteries for the American affair. By a deed of declaration, he also, appointed 100 men to govern the society, of the Methodists affair of the America's before his death. Coke became the president of the English conference of the America's in 1797, and in 1808.

Before the death of Coke he asked the prime Minster of Britain, who was known as Lord Liverpool, to make him bishop of the Anglican Church of India, but Coke request was dined, and Coke raises his own money, and was on his way to India, to carry out his Methodist missionary work among the people of India. But on his way to India he died, and did not accomplished his desire. The finial brake away of the Methodists Church from the Church of England, came about in 1795, which was four years later after the death of Wesley.

After the death of Wesley, the British Methodism, with branches in Ireland, Scotland, and Wales developed from a society into a church, with its system of conference, that take place yearly to control all the affair of the church. The Methodists movement in Britain was divided into districts, and into circuits of congregational groups. Various ministers was appointed to oversee the circuits, and each circuit was run by a superintendent, but much of the authority of the church, remain in the hands of the local overseers. The duties of sacrament, such as baptism, and the Lord Supper, that is known in the Roman Catholic Church, as Holy Communion. Also, the matrimony services, was carried out by the appointed minister of Methodism, and the other local preachers conduct most of the other services. This small group of Methodists rapidly grows throughout the 1800, into a membership of about 450,000 believers. When the Methodist group branch out to the colony of United States, and Canada, they take on different religious name, such as the Wesleyan, the Methodist New Connexion, and the United Methodist Free Churches. The Methodist New Connexion broke off in 1795, and from the main Methodist branch, that originally came from Britain, to the colony of the United States. The Primitive Methodist Church broke off in 1811, from the mainstream Methodist congregation, and the Methodist Bible Christians broke off in 1815, and the United Methodist Free Churches broke off in 1857 and from the main body of the Methodist organization, of the United States, and elsewhere. The smaller Methodist group was closer in contact with that of the working-class people, while the Wesleyan established leadership in trade union, and in politics. In 1907, the Methodist New Connexion, and the Methodist Bible Christians, and the Methodist Free Churches joined union together and formed the United Methodist Church throughout the British colonies of the world. In 1932, the Wesleyan Church, the Primitive Methodist Church, and the United Methodist Church came together, and formed the Methodist Church.

The Methodist Church along with other churches that was started in Britain, spread to their so-call New World, and did experience a drop-in number of memberships in 1910. The Methodist continue however to influence at large the national, and local life of many people of the colony of Canada, and the United States. Also, in many parts of the Gentile people conquered New World, with their evangelism of Methodism to their conquered people minds. The Methodist, and the Church of England did come to some form of reunion in stages, and it were accepted in principle, by the Methodist Churches of North America, in 1965- 1969, and in 1971.

The Encyclopaedia explained that Methodism was chiefly brought to America by Irish immigrants, who was converted by John Wesley, and Wesley also sent preachers to strengthen the societies of the church, in United States, and Canada. One of these successful preachers was a man by the name of Francis Asbury, who was a blacksmith. Asbury covered a vast area in his preaching journeys, and he also helps to organized many of the settlers, to settle in communities, who did believed in his preaching massage of the Wesley teaching. During the time of the Revolution war, Wesley damages his image in the mind of many of the settlers of America, by taking side with the British Government. But Asbury was able to restore back the image of Wesley in the minds of the new American republic, who was able to defeat the British their brothers. The advancement of the Methodist movement was somewhat interrupted, because of the slavery issue, that bitterly divided the Methodist Episcopal Church of the South, from that of the North. The Methodist Episcopal Church of the South, brought about a split in 1844, into two different churches, and after the Civil War of 1861-1865, was ended, both churches begun to increase rapidly in membership and material wealth. When the old issue of slavery, was no longer a divided problem, booth churches begun to grow closer, but it was not until 1939 that booth churches came together, and formed the Methodist Church of United States. The Methodist Church in the South lost its Hamite's members, who they had call as the Negros, and the so-call Black people. But when the church had a reunion, they came up with a stipulation of jurisdiction, to embrace all their so-call Afro American membership, whenever the citations make itself available.

The church central jurisdiction was later abolished in 1968, and the Methodist Hamite's members was fully integrated into the society of the church. Also, into the higher department of the church body. But this standard did not apply to the entire Methodist congregation in all part of the United States. The Church of the United Brethren, in Christ united with that of the Methodist Church, and became a part of the Methodist Church organization in1968. These believers was originally German Speaking Protestants ministers, who was influence by the Methodist doctoring, and their church order, of the 1800. But they were not able to bring in their German Speaking society into the Methodist. Due to the fact that the Methodist rule, was that only the English language should be used in their church services.

According to volume 26 of the Encyclopaedia, the Unitarians, and the Universalists religious movement, trace their heritage back to the established doctrine, and views that came from the early Protestantism, who came about in the time of 1500. This religious group established their various churches in Europe, Hungary, Romania, Poland, and in Britain. Later they also had various congregation in European, and in their overseas territories, such as the United States, Canada, and what became known as the West Indies. The Unitarians, and the Universalists association that was established in the Americas, see themselves free from the traditions, and commitment of the various rules, and regulation they would have to go true in their native motherland of Europe. They see themselves advancing into a more scientific truth, rather than in the old fashion Christian tradition of Europe, many of their ancestors before them experience while they were there in Europe. The Unitarians, and the Universalists in other lands, see themselves in similar position, but they were more attached to the ways, and belief of the early Protestantism, where their beginning started from. The Unitarians, and the Universalists held verity of views of doctrines, concerning the standing of Jesus Christ, who they say was a man who was adopted by Yahweh, to make known of His incoming Kingdom, true the tribe of Yudah, that were left there in the land of Canaan, that became known as Israel.

According to Volume 9 of the Encyclopaedia Britannica, there it explained that the Pentecostal Assemble of the world, was incorporated, and was formed in the United States, in 1916. When reading from the Encyclopaedia, it seems to me that the early believers of the Pentecostal Church, use to be a worshipper of God Church only, but later the organization had a dispute among themselves, where some of the members wanted the organization to be, called the Jesus only church. This dispute causes the church to have a division among it selves, and later it became an interracial church society. Some of the Gentile European American settlers, who saw themselves as the White race of people, wanted the church to be divided into a separate place of worship for the White race only. Also a separate part of the building for the Blacks, or the Negroes as what they had name their Hamite's slaves, who was brought over to their New World called of the America's. This division became known as the Pentecostal Church incorporated in 1924. The Pentecostal Church incorporated was started in 1916, and eventually they merged with that of the Pentecostal assembles of the Jesus Christ Church in 1945. This religious group of people, also became known as the United Pentecostal Church incorporated. The Pentecostal assemble of the world incorporated, differ from the ways, and teaching, that were setup by the Pentecostal group of their believers. This is that they only baptize in the name of Jesus Christ only, rather than in the name of the Trinity. Meaning Father, Son, and Holy Ghost, that came down from the Roman Catholic Church. Volume 9 of the Encyclopaedia went on to explained that the organization of Pentecostal Church assemble, was similar in organization to that of the Methodist Church, who had their headquarters in Indianapolis, of what became known as the United States. This branch that came from the Protestant denomination organization, was form the Chicago area of 1919. This was by a group of ministers who earlier refused to take on a member branch of the General Council of the assemble Church of God, that were form in 1914. This new Pentecostal group went on to established, and demonstrate their independence, by bringing about their policies, and their ordination to their members of what they should do, and what they should not do. Also, the issue of divorcement, and the remarrying status of their members.

Although the Pentecostal church group was not continually active in the overseas missionary work, yet they had a very extensive ministry among the various natives, who Columbus, and other Gentile European settlers, who came to their New World after Columbus, continuing called these people as Indians. There was also another Pentecostal organization, that were called as the Pentecostal Fellowship of North America Incorporated, who started in the Chicago area, in 1948, by eight Pentecostal members for the inter Pentecostal denomination fellowship. By the late 1970, this organization was governed by 13-member board executive committee. Like most other Pentecostal Churches, the denomination permits candidates for water baptism, and they even permit the baptism for infants. The Pentecostal religious movement, that came from the body of the Pentecostal Church, that was formed in the United States in the 19th, and 20th centuries. They established their own belief, that all Christians should seek the religious experience, of what they had called as the baptism with the Holy Spirit, that were translated as the Holy Ghost. The Pentecostal religious movement associated themselves with the experience of the pouring out of the Holy Spirit of Yahweh, that was poor out on the Apostles of Yashua, in the upper room. This citation took place on the Passover celebration of the children of Israel, they the Gentile people of Europe translated, and called as the Pentecost. This was the pouring out of the Holy Spirit of Yahweh, that is mentioned in "Acts Chapter 2, and verse 1, to verse 4". Volume 9 of the Encyclopaedia Britannica explained that the Pentecostal religious group of people, associated their belief with the speaking of tongues, that the Encyclopaedia called as glossolalia. I must point out that this speaking of tongues that is mentioned in (I Corinthians Chapter 13, and verse 1), also in (I Corinthians Chapter 14, and verse 2), that these Pentecostal people, and other religious church groups, associate themselves as speaking in tongues. Many of these religious group of people speak, and do not understand what they are really saying. This speaking of tongues that is mentioned in (I Corinthians), is not speaking about making allot of noise, like many of these people do, and call themselves speaking in tongues. But many of whom do not understand what they are really saying. This speaking in tongues in the time of the Apostles, meant speaking in different languages, that were different from the Hebrew language of the children of Isreal, that many of the Apostles were given the permission by the Holy Spirit of Yahweh to speak in other language, that were different to that of Hebrew.

The reason why the Holy Spirit of Yahweh gave the Apostle Peter, and others of the Apostles this gift, was to benefit many of those Israelites who was gathered there in Jerusalem from different nations, where their ancestors was taken as captives, and brought them fourth. They were gathered there in Jerusalem to celebrate the Passover, Yahweh gave to the children of Israel to celebrate throughout all their generations. So, many of their descendants who were there in Jerusalem, to celebrate the Passover, did lost their Hebrew language of their mother tong, to that of the various countries they were born, and raised in. So, this gift was given to the Apostles to benefit many of those Israelites, who were gathered there in Jerusalem to celebrate the Passover, Yahweh did commands them true the prophet Moses to celebrate throughout all their generations. So, this is what the Pentecostal religious group of people, and other religious church group of today called as speaking in unknowing tongues, and do not understand what they are actually saying. Many Pentecostal believers, believe to themselves that when they get baptized, they would automatically receive the supernatural gift of the Holy Spirit of Yahweh, that was poured out on the Apostles of Yashua, in the upper room of the Passover celebration of the Children of Israel, that they the Gentile people name as Pentecost. Such as the power of prophecy, which is the gift of foretelling of future events that is to come. Also, the gifts of healing the sick, and interpreting different languages, and razing of the dead that was only given to the prophets, and the Apostles of the children of Israel, and to no other people. It is the same citation with many Hamite's people of today, we have lost our mother tongs, true slavery, and colonialism, and we have adapted to the tongs, or languages of our slave masters, many of us Hamite's people of today speak, as our language.

We, their descendants who are around today, have no knowledge of our ancestor's language, they had before slavery, and colonialism were impose on many of them, that did came down to us today. The big different with the children of Israel, and with us Hamite's people of today, is that they had the eyes of Yahweh who were watching over them. To perform His Words, and His promises He had made with them true the various prophets of Israel, He did use as His mouthpiece to speak to them. While we as a Hamite's people of today, we must live out the various prophecies of the Scripture, that was spoken against many of the various ancient kingdoms of the people of Ham, of the so-call Middle East that Yahweh did destroyed, and in what became known as North Africa.

Due to the fact that Yahweh was not pleased with many of those people of their doings of witchcraft, idolatry worship, and many other forms of wickedness that Yahweh was not please of. Furthermore, Yahweh had spoken in Deuteronomy, and in other books of the Scripture, that the children of Israel was a special people to Himself, because they are of the seeds of Abraham, who was call as the friend of Yahweh. Who did obey His voice, and the Words of Yahweh, and who did please Yahweh very well. So, the Pentecostal believers believed to themselves that they possess the kind of faith like that of the Apostles, also that they might can do some of things the Apostles did by the Holy Spirit of Yahweh. Which in reality they were only deceiving themselves, and other people who listen to them, and believed in their false story that is not of truth. Sad to say that this is the problem with many of the churches of today, their pastors teach allot of false doctoring, to their various church members that they hold on to as true gospels. Because many of these Pastors, and preachers of the European Christianity, misunderstand the Scripture, and by so doing, they have deceived their many members with their false doctoring they hold on to as truth, that came down from the Roman Catholic Church, of paganism, and of idolatry worship of the people of Europe.his is the end of the Pentecostal story.

According to volume 26 of the Encyclopaedia Britannica, and also volume 1 of the Encyclopaedia, there it explained that the Baptist are a Protestant Christians Church grope, who believe, and shear the same views of most Protestants Churches. These Baptist believers insist that only believers of the faith should be baptized, and it must be done by immersion where the whole body is dipped under water. Rather than by the sprinkling, or the pouring out of water, like that of the doing of the Roman Catholic Church, where they sprang out of. During the Reformation of the Lutherans, and the Anglicans church, many of the believers who came from out of the Roman Catholic Church, accepted the Catholic views of infant baptism, of the sprinkling of water. But later the Anabaptists believers considered infant baptism to be unacceptable, and public confection is a sin, and faith were sealed by an adult water baptism. The Anabaptist movement became known as The General Baptist, along with the Particular Baptist Church organization of the 1500. These religious group were a members of a Protestant group, of British speaking denomination, who originated from out of the Puritan Church Reformed movement of Britain. According to the Encyclopaedia, the Puritan Church try to purge themselves from the tradition and teaching of the Roman Catholic Church, that was left there in the Anglican Church that they were a part of, before they became known as the Puritan religious group. This is where this religious church group of what were known as the Anabaptists, who became known as the Baptist Church, who got their name from the religious church group who were also known before as the Puritans.

There were two Baptists Church groups that begun in Britain during the time that was known as the Puritan Reform movements. According to the Webster Colligate Dictionary, the word Puritan came from Late Latin, and this was during the time of the reign of Queen Elizabeth I. Where some people was in opposition to the traditional ways of worship, that was set up by the Roman Catholic Church, and also by the Church of England. Many of these people had a desire for a simpler way of worship, more than that of the traditional ways that was established for them to follow, with that of the Catholic Church, and that of the Anglican Church that many of them was a part of. This Particular Baptist movement was strongly influence by the doctoring of John Calvin, who was one of the early Protestants Reformers.

The General Baptist, and the Particular Baptist group, shear the same views that only believers should be baptized. The different between the believers of the General Baptist, and that of the Particular Baptist, is that the General Baptist believed that the sacrifice Christ's suffered for was for sin of all people. It was not only for the elect class of people, who the Particular Baptist Church believers believe in, and teach it to their many members, to see themselves as the elect class of people. So, one of this groups became known as the General Baptist, and the other became known as the Particular Baptist, referring to themselves as the elect class of people, who did became known as the Particular Baptist. The Separatists, and the None-Separatist Church held on to the same views, when it come down to the self-governing of the church, they believed that only believers should govern the church, like that of the New Covenant order of the early believers of the Apostles. Through the work of the original Baptist movement, that was started in London. The other General Baptist congregation was formed, and spread to other areas of the Gentile European people overseas colonies, of what became known as their New World of the Americas, and the West Indies. The General Baptist doctrines basically came from the Armenians believers who believed that the atonement death of Christ was for all men, and it was not only for the elect's class. As I had mention before that the word elect's means chosen ones, who became known as the Saints, in many of the churches of today that came down from the Roman Catholic Church, and from that of the Protestants. The Separatists was a part of the Church of England, who believed to themselves that they must separate themselves from the Anglican Church. This break away from the Church of England, must break all ties with them, because in their opinion, the Church of England is a false church, and the braking away from them must be a complete uncompromised action.

The None-Separatists was a part of the General Baptist, and they felt to themselves that although they were aware of the corruption, and falsehood of the Church of England, yet in their eyes it was necessary as a member of the Christian community, to maintain some form of bond of unity with them. This Separatists religious group had a strong influence on the British Baptist community that did spread itself to their overseas colonies. Yet it was the General Baptist who was a more organized church group, who spread themselves from Britain. The General Baptists trace their beginning to the Baptist Church that was first started in London around the time of 1611, by Thomas Helwys, and his followers who return to London from Amsterdam.

According to the Encyclopaedia due to the religious persecution of 1608, that the Separatists went true in Britain, they had the desire to separate themselves from the Church of England, who was known as the Anglian Church. While they were living in Amsterdam, they adopted themselves to the belief of the teaching of the original leader of the church, who was known as John Smyth. Smyth who by studying the New Covenant part of the Scripture, decided that only believers should be baptized. Smyth explained to his congregation of Baptists believers that when he made a search of the Scripture, he could not find anywhere there where it makes mention that infants was to be baptized. So, for that reason, he take it upon himself in 1609, to baptize himself along with 36 other believers. While Smyth, and his followers was living in Amsterdam, they came across some believers who was known as the Mennonite communities, who became known as the Anabaptist community of Amsterdam. Due to his exposure of this religious community in Holland, he began to question himself if he made the right decision in baptizing himself. So, after some observation of the Mennonite Christian community, of Amsterdam, he came to the conclusion that the Mennonite communities represent a true set of believers, and he recommend to become in union with them. Due to his action of interest with this community, cause some of his member to be in rage, such as Thomas Helwys, and others of his group, who in 1611, or 1612, return to Britain and established the first Baptist Church in London. As for the Mennonite community of Amsterdam they eventually went out of business, and there were no more trace of them as a religious group. The Particular Baptist organization movement came from out of the Separatist Church, that was first established in 1616, by Henry Jacob.

The Separatist got their name from when they separated from the Church of England, in 1638, with various members from the Separatists Church who left from the leadership of John Spilsbury, and went, and form the first Particular Baptist Church. Within twenty years after the time of the Particular Baptist Church of Britain, they did increase in membership. During this time, many Baptist preachers was able to win over many converts to their side, many of whom was gathered around a campfire of the Puritan leader, who was known as Oliver Cromwell's with his army. The large membership of the Particular Baptist, and the General Baptist started to give way to the Quakers organization, that was established there in Britain. From what I have gathered from reading volume 26 of the Encyclopaedia, before the rise of Quakerism, this group of people was known as the Seekers.

Who had gathered during what was known as the Puritan Revolution in the reign of Charles I of Britain. This group of revolutionists or Seekers, as they was called, was waiting upon the Lord Yahweh, or Yashua to act on their behalf of their desperation of spiritual help. That should have come from the Church of England, or from the organization of the Puritan body. The center of the Quakers movement was in Swarthmore Hill in north western part of Britain, and during the time of 1660, the Particular Baptist, and the General Baptist was subjected to severe disruption, by the Angles Church. They was forced to operate in secrecy, until the Act of toleration was pass in London in 1689, that this Toleration Act gave relief to many people of Britain, the freedom from the Church of England rules and regulation. This act of toleration gave these religious worshipers to worship wheresoever they so choose, that granted them a measure of relief. After these experiences, the General Baptist were drained of its energy, of its members by skepticism, that develops within the church. They eventually dwindled down, and lost most of their members, and the church eventually closes its door. Some of the General Baptist members went and formed a new congregation in 1770, that was known as the New Connection Baptist, many of whom were influenced by the Methodist Church that was led by John Wesley. The Particular Baptist increase more in members, but the increase of their members started to decline, because the Particular Baptist held on to the belief, that salvation was more so for the elect's class, and they did not exert themselves to gain new converts. During the time of 1750, the Particular Baptist was also influenced by the movement of the Methodist, and they did develop new interest in evangelism, also in missionary work, that brought into the organization new members.

Due to the leadership of William Carey, the British Baptist Missionary society was form in 1792, and Carey went to India as the first Baptist missionary to performed missionary work among the British conquered people of India. I must point out that one must be very couscous when the word missionary is mentioned. Because during the early colonial slavery days of the Gentile people of Europe, many of these colonial conquerors, use to send out what they had called as, missionaries to their various conquered people. This was to preach to them about Christianity, by using the Bible as their tool to keep their captives in subjection to their will, while they themselves did not live up to any Scriptural teaching, nor did they believed very much in the writing, and the teaching of the Scripture. So, as to apply it to themselves to prevent them from doing so much wickedness, in the name of Christianity, and the church.

But rather many of them were murderers, thefts, alcoholic, winos, promoters of prostitution, also that of lesbianism, sodomites, pirates', and evolutionists. Many of whom did not believed in the Scripture teaching of the creation of Yahweh, of how everything came into being, by Him. But rather they have taught many of their captives, who they have indoctrinated to believe in their vein theory of evolution, of how they think the world came into being, with their big bang theory. This is because they did not have any faith, in the believing of the Word of Yahweh, and in His power, and in His might, that became known as the Scrolls, the Scripture, and later what became known as the Bible, by the Greek translators. But many of these missionaries of the Gentile land of Europe, as many of them did see themselves, were secret agents, acting on the behalf of their various colonial governments. Many of whom did see themselves as Christian people, and Christian countries of Europe, to gain colonies, and wealth true captivity, and slavery to get rich. They were only wolf in sheep clothing, who did not represent any Yahweh like qualities, or that of Yashua like qualities. But rather many of whom were deceivers, seeking to hide, rob and steal in the name of Christianity, to get the wealth of the land, and to enslave people to get rich, and to become powerful people, from their blood sweat, and tears of their many victims. The problem I have with the word missionaries, that were started back there in the early colonial slavery days, of the Gentile people of Europe, spreading what they had called as Christian missionaries, of their hypocritical, deceitful, and cunningness of their intention to get rich. This was from the blood, sweats, and tars of their many victims, who they claim they came to to spread Christianity to these uncivilized people of their conquest, as how they did see it. My reason for making this kind of statement, it is because, many of the Gentile countries of Europe, who went out to conqueror people, and their lands to get the wealth from the land as their colonies.

The first thing many of them would do, was to send out missionaries, to Christianize the mind of their many captives, so as to make them easy to control, and rule in the name of Christianity. This was from the Portuguese, Spanish, Dutch, French, and the British. They all did these things in their various conquered lands that became their colonies of conquered slave people, throughout the world, that did became their empire. The Baptists group was very influential in their religious, and in their political life in Britain, during the 1800. But their influence started to fade away after World War I. Baptist Churches was also established in Australia in 1831, in New Zealand in 1854, by British Missionaries Society.

In Canada Baptist Church were established there, by some British settlers of Massachusetts who went and organized this church in Nova Scotia in 1763. In Ontario, the first Baptist Churches were established there by a Gentile European man, who crossed the border of the United States, after the American Revolution war, and formed the first Baptist Church there. The Baptist Union of Britain, Ireland, and the Particular Baptist Church came together, and formed an organization union in 1813- 1891. The New Connection General Baptist Church, later merged together with that of the Baptist Union, and became one organization of Baptist Church. The strict doctoring, and philosophy of John Calvin, that became known as the Calvinism, who was one of the early leaders of Protestantism, from where the Particular Baptist base many of their church philosophy from. This philosophy of their's were gradually modified, and gave more room of freedom, of thought between it congregational members. Roger Williams established the first Baptist Church in Providence of Annapolis, which is the capital of Maryland, in 1639. This was after he was expelled by the Puritans Baptist denomination of Massachusetts Bay. Although William had various Calvinist views, before he became a member of this Baptist Church. He eventually came to the conclusion that all the churches, including his newly established Baptist Church, lacked true Apostle ships foundation like that of the early church of the Apostles, of Israel, who were the true followers of Yashua. William left his Baptist congregation in 1652, without any strong leadership, and it became a part of the General Baptist Church organization of the United States. The General Baptist Church of United States never gain great strength as an organization, and the Providence Church was look upon by many as a part of the Particular Baptist Church movement. The few General Baptist Church that did survived, never entered the mainstream of the American Baptist life, and they did not have a great impact on many of the early settlers, or the natives.

There were scattered General Baptist church activities throughout the colony of United States, but only the large General Baptist Church, that were located in Rhode Island in 1670, where the church was united, as an organization, and meet regularly. They did became a part of the main stream Baptist Churches organization of today. According to the Encyclopaedia, although the State of Rhode Island was the main stronghold of the Baptist religious center, that were started there in colonial America, yet the center of the Baptist life was in the State of Philadelphia.

The first congregation of the Baptist Church organization was formed in 1707, and this was in Philadelphia, as the new Baptist Church organization throughout the colony of what became known as the United States. The Baptist Church of the United States was a byproduct of the leftwing movement among the colonial Puritans. Who emigrate from Britain to their Gentile European so-call New World, of their conquest from the Spanish their brothers, that became known as North America. Some early Baptist believers, held the views that they had been unbroken succession of Baptist Churches, from the days of John the baptizer, to the time of the Apostles of Yashua. Other Baptists believers trace their early beginning to the Anabaptist movement that was started in the 16th century, by some radical Protestant believers, who had some views of their own, and who wanted to see some changes. I must point out that this philosophy of the Baptist believers, about the succession of unbroken Baptist Churches from the days of John, to the time of the Apostles, is totally a false statement, that have no truth in it, but it is all lies. My reason for saying this, there is nowhere in the writing of the Scripture of truth, where it makes mention that John who became known as John the Baptist. Established a Baptist Church, for the Yehudahites, and the Benjaminhites believers, of the children of Israel, who were left there in the land, for them to go there to worship Yahweh. Many of whom were left there in the land, when he went out to preach to them, about the coming of Yashua, and the Kingdom of Yahweh that is to come. Volume 1 of the Encyclopaedia explained that the Anabaptist where the name Baptist sprang from, were a member of a radical left-wing movement, that came about in the time of the 16 century, during the time of the Protestant Reformation movement in Europe.

The Encyclopaedia explained that the first generation of the Anabaptist movement of converts, had to go true a second baptism, and it was a crime, punished able by death, if a person did not abide by the rules of the church. The Anabaptist later put away the baptism of infants, and considers it to be an abnormal practice for them to do so, because this was the way it was when many of them were formally members of the Roman Catholic Church, before many of them broke away from there. Many of whom had baptize in the church, meaning the Roman Catholic Church, were converts from Greco-Roman paganism. Who were adults, who brought in their paganism ways into what became known as the church, and Christianity.

During the time of this Swiss Reformer, whose name was Huldrych Zwingli, the Anabaptists held on to the belief that infants was not punishable for their sins, until there was an awareness of the knowledge of good and evil, that would eventually come within them later. Then they could exercise their own free will, and later when they become older they could repent, and accept baptism. I must point out that this statement that was made by this religious group, of the Anabaptists, it is not of truth, according to the writing of the Scripture. My reason for saying this is, when Yahweh was destroying Sodom, and Gomorrah, that is recorded in (Genesis Chapter 19, and verse 24), He destroyed all the people of Sodom, and Gomorrah, whether they were infants or adults. As far as Yahweh were concern, they were all sinners who were doomed to died, because the children inherit the sins from their parents, they came out of. It was the same way, when Yahweh was destroying the people in the flood of Noah days, He destroyed children, and adults alike, because as far as Yahweh saw it, they were all sinners, and evil people. It is going to be the same way with us people of today, we have inherited the sins of Adam, and Eve our fore parents, and because of that, in the eyes of Yahweh, we are all are sinners who are doomed to die for all our sins. We have in hearted, and the sins we have committed agents Him, in our day to day lives. It was the same way when Yahweh was destroying all the first born of the people of the land of Mizraim, that became known as Egypt, that is recorded at (Exodus Chapter 10, and verse 30), He destroyed all the first born of Mizraim, whether they were infants, or adults. As far as Yahweh saw it, they were all sinners in His eyes who had to died. The same is true for the people of the land of Canaan, and for the various Hamite's cities, and kingdoms who Yahweh did destroyed. He destroyed booth infants, and adult alike, because they did not please Him, like that of Abraham, and many of the children of Israel who did please Him well.

The Anabaptists believers, believe that the church should be a community of redeemers, and should be separated from states, or governmental affairs, which to them existed only for the punishment of wrongdoers, and sinners. The Encyclopaedia explained, that the Anabaptists believers, was strongly against, any believers professing themselves to be Christians, and taking up of the sword, or the guns of a regular army, or to be in any kind of warfare.

Volume I of the Encyclopaedia explained that the Anabaptists, also refused to swear in the case of a civil oath, and because of their standing, many thousands of them were put to death in Europe. The Anabaptists believers did not see themselves set out to change the Medieval Church of Europe, but they were determined instead to restore the institution, and the spirit of the primitive church, that sprang from the teaching of the Apostle Paul. Who was made a minister to the Gentile people, of what became known as Europe. They also were convinced that they were living at the end of the ages. According to the Webster New World Dictionary of the American language, there it explain, that they was a time in Europe, that were also called as the Latin Medieval time, when the Latin language was use thought out Europe. Which was a time of 600, to 1500 AD, of Roman Catholicism rulership. Which many of the Anabaptist leaders of that time, saw themselves as spiritualist, who was leading a group of peasant's believers in a revolt against the system in 1527, that cast many of their leaders to be executed. Another Baptist leader, by the name of Hans Hut, died in prison in Augsburg in 1527, who was a principal radical leader of the Reformer of southern Germany. Another Anabaptist leader by the name of Balthasar Hubmaier, was executed in Vienna in 1528. There was also another Anabaptist leader by the name of Jokob Hutter, who had a growing group of believers, who did take on his name, and called themselves the Hutterites group. The Encyclopaedia explained that this group of the Hutterites survived, and are now located primarily in the Western United States, and in what became known as Canada. According to the Encyclopaedia, there was another Anabaptist leader who saw himself, as an Apostle, of the Netherlands, better known today as Holland, and he was known as Melchior Hofmann, who developed a very large following.

This teaching of Hofmann, was that the world would soon come to its end, and that the new age would begin in Strasbourg, where he was put in prison in 1533, and died there in 1543. According to the Webster Dictionary, the city of Strasbourg was located in North Eastern France, and Hofmann followers came under the leadership of Jan Matthijs, who also was a Dutch man from the Netherlands, and who died in 1534. The Anabaptists movement, and their disciples of Jan Matthijs settled in Munster Westphalia in West Germany in 1534, where they gain control of the city, and established a community of theocratic government, and practice polygamy. The word polygamy according to the Webster Colligate Dictionary, means a man who has more than one wife.

This city of the Anabaptist were later captured in 1535, by an army that was raised up by a German prince, and the Anabaptists leader were tortured, and killed. The Protestants, and the Roman Catholic believers increase their persecution against the two groups of the Anabaptists believers. This was throughout Europe, and the name of the two groups of the Anabaptists, was known as the Belligerent minority and the Pacifist majority. The

Pacifist Anabaptist group was located in the Netherlands, and also in North Germany, and they existed there under the leadership of a former Baptist believers. Many of their members saw their leaders as a divinely men, who they believed to be prophets, or Apostles. Due to their belief, many Baptist converts stood their ground, and always preparing themselves to give a full account of their faith before the Magistrates, to whom they were brought before. Their revolutionary ways of teaching, led to their drifting from one city to another, and by doing so, they increased their missionary movement of converts. Their action of movement soon cause the civil magistrates to take stronger action against them, and their leaders, many of whom died in prison, or who were executed. The Anabaptists group of Europe survived and eventually was accepted as a minority religious group. The Particular Baptist of America established five churches in Pennsylvania, and Particular Baptist Church was also established in Newport Rhode Island. This established meant was from 1641 to 1648, and this church was established by John Clark, who were a physician, and he also was a minister who adapt himself to many of the Baptist views. Others Particular Baptist Churches was established in Maine, New England, and in Massachusetts. One of these churches that was established in Massachusetts, was established by a Welsh man, who was under the leadership of John Myles.

John Myles tried to establish a Particular Baptist Church near Plymouth, but he was arrested and fined for conducting public meeting without giving the permission to do so. By first obtaining a license, to do his preaching, and he also did establish a Particular Baptist Church in Boston in 1665. According to the Encyclopaedia, Particular Baptist Church was also established in South Carolina in 1683-1684, and also in 1707, Particular Baptist Church was established in New Jersey, Pennsylvania, and Delaware. These churches came under the union of the Philadelphia Baptist Association. As time went on, the Philadelphia Particular Baptist organization provided spiritual leadership for the North Carolina Baptist organization, that were established there in 1751.

According to the Encyclopaedia, it was the Philadelphia Baptist organization of 1707, who went on to established new Baptist Churches throughout the colony of the of the United States. The increase growth of the Baptist organization multiplies in the midst 1700, that they did called as the Great Awakening. But by the time of 1800, there was 48 Baptist associations that did developed into a main stream body of united churches, of the United States. According to the Encyclopaedia, one of the main interests of the Anabaptists was to establish the missionary overseas work. This missionary work was carried out by Adoniram Judson, and Luther Rice, who was sent on their mission to India, and while they were on their way to their mission, studding the Scripture; they came to the conclusion that only believers should be baptize. When they arrived in India, Judson went to Burma, and Rice's return to the United States to help to put to gather the General Convention Baptist denomination. That were formed in 1814, that did established missionary homes, and their education, of their publication of their religious books, and articles. In 1826, General Baptist Convention restricted itself to the foreign missionary activities, that eventually became known as the American Baptist Foreign Mission Society, and the American Baptist Publication. The unity that was accomplished through these organization, were disrupted, due to the issue of giving freedom to the slaves of United States. That many Baptists Churches of the South did not feel comfortable with, like that of the Baptist Church of the North, many of whom did not mind given freedom to many of their slaves. This disruption eventually causes a split in the organization in 1845, when the Southern Baptist of Augusta Georgia separated themselves, from the Northern Baptist, because of their different in belief toward their slavery business.

But later the two organizations became known as the American Baptist, that did led their own separate way of religious doctoring. In the later part of the 1800, the Southern Baptist Convention begun to develop their missionary work, and publication. The finial separation between the Baptist of the North, and the Baptist of the South came about in 1907, by the Northern Baptist Convention. According to the Encyclopaedia, by the time of 1950, the Baptist group was renamed, and became known as the American Baptist Convention. Also, after 1972, they became known as the American Baptist Churches of the United States, that brought together the Northern and the Southern convention Baptist Churches together. During the slavery days, many Hamite's people who became known, as the Black race of the United States, became a part of their slave master's religious belief of teaching.

That gave birth to many Hamite's pastors of their various churches of today, of their Christianity teaching. So, if their slave master was of the Baptist religious belief, then their slave religious belief would be that of their slave master religious belief, of their teaching, of their organization. Although their slaves was not welcome to worship with their slave masters, at these religious place of their worship. After the emancipation of the slave labor Act of 1863, to the end of the Civil War of 1865-1866, of the United States, then many Hamite's people formed their own little Baptist Churches, or whatever religious organization they were exposed to, because of their slave master religious conviction. So, if their slave master was a Pentecostal believer, they would also become a Pentecostal believers, or Roman Catholic worshippers, and so on. These churches that were formed, and established by the various free Hamite's slaves of the United States, did served to be a social, and a spiritual center for many Hamite's people of what became known as the United State of America. This is one of the reasons why in many of the so-call Black Churches of the United States, their belief, and concept was design, and established from what they had learned from their former slave master's religious views. These religious believes that many Hamite's people of the United States did accept, as divine Gospel, may not have been according to the true teaching of the Scripture. But it was what they were thought to believe in, and what they was expose to, that they did accept as divine gospel from their slave master religious belief.

According to volume 26 of the Encyclopaedia, there it explained that the Presbyterians was known as the Reformed Presbyterians Church, that was started in Switzerland, in the 16 centuries. According to the Encyclopaedia, the Presbyterians also shear a common origin, that came from off the body of the Protestant Reformed movement, that was started in Germany. The Reformed, and the Presbyterian Churches are one of the major representative groups of Protestantism. The word reformed, is a more appropriate term in identifying those Reformed Churches, that was regarded as the Calvinistic doctoring of teaching, than that of Martin Luther of Germany. According to the Webster New World Dictionary of the American language, John Calvin was born in France, in 1509, and he died in 1564, and he was a leader of the Protestant Re formed movement that was started there.

The name Presbyterian according to volume 26 of the Encyclopaedia, came about as a collage type of church government that was run, and control by a pastor, and a ordinary church member that was called as an elder. The Presbyterian rules throughout various congregations, that came together as a national assemble, was commonly called a session of meeting. But not all Reformed Churches was that of the Presbyterian, in the form of government. According to the Encyclopaedia, only those kinds of churches, that used the name Presbyterian, are a part of the Reformed tradition.

According to volume 1 of the Encyclopaedia, in the early Romans Catholic Church, there was a period of preparation for the celebration of Yashua birth, who became known as Jesus, and Christ in the Latin, and also In the Greeks. This custom was held on Christmas, which was a celebration for his second coming of Yashua. This celebration was started on the last Sunday in the month of November, that was close to the 30th day of the month, that was called as Saint Andrew's day. Which was the beginning of the church year, meaning the Roman Catholic Church year. Volume 1 of the Encyclopaedia explained, that the actual date when this season of celebrated was started, is not clearly known. According to the Encyclopaedia, a bishop by the name of Perpetuus of Tour, in 461-490, established a feast before the Christmas celebration was started, and it was held in November, and it was call as Saint Martin's Day. The Encyclopaedia explained that although this season of celebration is no longer kept with the strictness at lent as it were, yet the Roman Catholic Church did forbid marriages during this season of the Advent. In many countries that came under the influence of the ruler ship of the Roman Empire, this season was started by variety of observances, such as the lighting of the Advent candles. The Adventist Christian Church as it is known as today, was one of several of the Advents Churches that was developed from the teaching of William Miller. This was some time of 1782-1849, that did come from the Roman word Advent-us. According to volume 8 of the Encyclopaedia, William Miller teaching was developed on the base of the second coming of Yashua, of the judgment of the wicked, who will be destroyed, and the chosen ones will be resurrected to live on a restored earth of paradise. That was to be establish in the time of 1860, according to William Miller thinking.

The congregational policy of the Seventh Day Adventists Church, of 1860, was to hold church services on a Sunday, but when the Advent Union merged with that of the Advent Christian Church, their policy was change to a different day of church services.

The Adventists Churches according to the Encyclopaedia, was a part of the various church groups that came from the various Protestants Churches, that was established in the United States of America, science the time of the 19th century. According to volume 8 of the Encyclopaedia, Miller was born February 15, in Pittsfield Boston Massachusetts, and he was a religious leader of a movement that were called as the Millerism. The Encyclopaedia explained that Miller livelihood was a farmer, but he also was able to hold the position of deputy sheriff, and justice of the peace. In the war of 1812, he was able to serve as a captain of the 30th infantry of the United States army. After Miller came from the army, he had a change of heart, and was converted, and began to study the Scripture book of Daniel, and also the book of Revelation, and he became a Baptist preacher. Which this Baptist denomination was that of his father before him. Miller came up with the idea that Yashua would return again sometime in March, 21 of 1843, or in March of 1844. This view of Miller was encouraged by various minister of his. Such as a man by the name of Joshua Himes of Boston, and many of his followers that amount to about 10,000, according to the estimation the Encyclopaedia gave of the time. Miller was accused by many of fanaticism, because of his stressing of the coming of Jesus Christ, which were very distressful to many of his hears of his time. Yashua did not return on the various dates, that was set up by Miller. So, he and his associates came up with another dates, which was to be October 22, of 1844, which these date of his came, and pass like a wind, without the return of Yashua on the date that was set by Miller. These dates of Miller was called as the great disappointment dates, among the Adventists of his time, that these members call for a conference to be held between the various Adventists, of 1845, to try and sort out the problem of these dates. The various Adventists believers who was gathered at this meeting place, found it very difficult to come up with a confession of these dates. This was also for them to form a permanent organization of the church. Miller also preaches to many of his believers that in the time of 1843, the world would come to its end, and he based his belief from the reading of "Daniel Chapter 8, and verse 13, to verse 14", where he had various publication made up, that were called the Miller movement of the sign of the time.

Some of Miller associates even went so far as to set the date of October 22, of 1844, to be the second coming of Yashua return, which left many people minds of those days, in doubt of what the future holds for them as far as Yashua was concern. These Adventist was called as the Millerhites by the newspaper press, and these Millerhites did believed that Miller set the right dates, but people interpreted what he had said incorrectly. The Millerhites went on to examining the book of Revelation, about the book of life, that is mention there, and they came up with the conclusion that after all the various events was accomplish, then there would be Yashua appearance, and this would begin his one-thousand-year reign. These Millerhites did not set a new date for the second coming of Yashua, but they believed that his coming would be personal, visible, and a glorious one. The Millerhites believed to themselves, that by they observing the seventh day worship, which they did believed to be a Saturday, rather than a Sunday, it would help to bring about the second coming of Yashua. The Millerhites headquarter was established in Battle Creek Michigan, in 1855, which became the official denomination center for the service of the Seventh Day Adventist in 1863. Volume 1 explained that the Adventists influence was also found among the Pentecostal, and the Holiness Church group, who did believe to themselves, they have the gift of knowledge, and the understanding of interpreting of the outpouring of the Holy Spirit of Yahweh, that was pour out on the Apostles of Yashua.

The Encyclopaedia explained that Charles Taze Russell, who started the Jehovah Witness organization, in the 1800, came under the influence of the Adventists idea. The Encyclopaedia explained that there was two different bodies of the Advent Christian Church organization, that was formed in 1861. The much larger body of this organization became known as the Seventh-Day Adventist Church, that were formed in 1863, with different small bodies of the organizations that used to worship on Sunday before they switch over to the Saturday worship.

According to volume 6 of the Encyclopaedia, there it explained that Jehovah Witness organization was started in the United States, by a Gentile European man, by the name of Charles Taze Russell. In Pittsburgh Pennsylvania, in 1872, that eventually spread worldwide. The Encyclopaedia explained that the name Jehovah Witnesses was later adopted, by Russell successor, who was known as Joseph Franklin. Franklin thought by using the name Jehovah Witnesses, it would make the organization a witness, and a servant of Yahweh; who they believe His name His Jehovah. So, by bearing His name, that appear in most of the modern translation of the Scripture that became known as the Bible, as Jehovah God, this would make them the people of Jehovah. I must point out that Mr. Franklin meant well, in wanting to be associated with the name of Yahweh, and to be his servant, but the name Jehovah, is not the name Yahweh did reveal to Moses of the children of Israel, as His own personal name. The name of Yahweh goes far way back, before the name Jehovah came into being, by the various Gentile European translators of the Scripture, that became known as the Bible, in the different language of Europe. The name of Yahweh even went further back than the Greeks translation of the Septuagint Version of the Scripture, and much further than the Vulgate Latin Version, that came down from the Greek Version, that eventually came down to that of the King James Version of 1611. These Gentile European translators, came up with this false name of Jehovah, that came down the line, from various translations, that was spread around the world by these Gentile people of Europe, to their colonies of their empire, and their conquered subjects, to believe in this false name of Jehovah God.

According to volume 1 of the Encyclopaedia, it explained that the name of Yahweh was used by the Yehudahites, and the Benjamites during the time of Joseph Maccabean, who rise up against the Greek Macedonian ruler ship over the land of Israel. These Greeks wanted to introduce the worship of their god Zeus, in the temple of Yahweh that was there in Jerusalem, in the second century BC, where the Maccabean Yehudahites rouse up in revolt against it.

It was Antiochus the IV, who wanted this worship of the god Zeus to take place in the temple of Yahweh, who was ruling as king in the land of Zidon, that became known as the land of Syria, who was the first son of Canaan. Antiochus the IV, also built a statue of the god Zeus in the temple of Yahweh, and he was a descendant of one of Alexander the Great generals, whose name was known as Seleucid of Macedonia. Antiochus IV had ruler ship over a part of the land of Zidon, the Turkey area of Europe, and the so-called Middle East, and a part of Asia that came down to him from the Seleucid dynasty. This was after the death of Alexander the Great, and also after the death of Seleucid himself. Antiochus in his zeal wanted to propagate Greek culture in Israel, who had the statue of the god Zeus to be built in the temple at Jerusalem, where Yahweh put His name there to be worship, by the people of Jacob, who became known as the children of Isreal. So, because of his presumptuousness caused the upholders of the tradition of Yehudahisim, who were loyal to the worship of Yahweh and the keeping of the Old Covenant Law, to rebel against him. This group of Yehudahites who rose up against him, and his comrades was known as the Maccabean, that take its name from Joseph Maccabees, who led this revolt. After twenty-five years of struggle, the Maccabean won back the way of Yehudahisim in Israel, from the Seleucids descendants. In that time there were worshipers of many different gods, in the so-called Middle East, and what became known as North Africa. Many Yehudahites, and Benjamites used to worship many of these gods, such as the god Beal, Molech, Zeus, Marduk, and others Yehudahites of the children of Israel, who were loyal to the worship of Yahweh continue to use the name of Yahweh in their worship to Him, that Yahweh gave to Moses, as His own personal name.

So, from what I have read from volume 1 of the Encyclopaedia, in that time of the worship of these many different gods, of graven images, that was worship in the so- call Middle East, and what became known as North Africa, there was no mentioning 'of a god by the name of Jehovah. The Encyclopaedia explained that before the conquest of Alexander the Great, and his generals, of the area of what became known as the Middle East, North Africa, and Persia, in The time of 333- 332-331 BC, the name of Yahweh was always used and worshipped by the children of Israel. Who were loyal to the worship of Yahweh, and the keeping of His Commandment, and His Laws. (Exodus Chapter 20, and verse 7); there the Scripture clearly explained, that one must not take the name of the Lord your God in vain, which the word Lord, and God it is a only a title, and it is not the name of Yahweh.

These translators should have express it as taking the name of the Lord Yahweh in vain, or in UN worship way that was translated as the name of the Lord God in vain. Which this word Lord were translated from the word Adonai which mean my Lord. This word Lord and God was taken from the Canaanite god Beal, that came down into the Angles dialect, that became known as the English language, as my Lord, and my God. The word God was also taken from the word Elohim, that was pertaining to one of the Canaanite gods, who was known as Beal. This word Elohim and Adonai came down in the Hebrew language of the children of Isreal, because as I had mention many times that the children of Isreal mothers came from the Canaanite women, the women of Mizraim, and also from the Babylon women who the children of Isreal were living among, and also who they also came out of. So, this word Elohim came down into the Angles, and Saxon dialect, that became known as the English language, as my Lord, and my God, referring to Yahweh as my God. Many of the children of Isreal use to worship this god Beal, although they were warn by Yahweh, by the prophets He did used to speak to them, that they must not worship these gods of the land they were going to take over. So, many of the children of Isreal who were loyal to the worship, and the keeping of the Commandment of Yahweh, continue to used the name of Yahweh, in their daily worship to Him. So, what the Scripture is speaking about in (Exodus Chapter 20, and verse 7), that a person must not use the name of Yahweh in a careless kind of way, or using profanity in calling on His name, or in any falsehood, by telling lies, or in any kind of deceitful way. But rather a believer must give praise thanks and worship to the Holly name of Yahweh, in a worship, and in a respectful way. So, although Jehovah Witnesses called themselves a "Witness, and "servant, of Jehovah, that should have expressed as Yahweh.

Though they meant well, yet the only set of people Yahweh ever makes reference to as His witnesses, His servants, and His people, was that of the ancient children of Jacob, who became known as the children of Isreal. To prove my point that it is so, if one should read (Isaiah Chapter 43, and verse 10), there they will see that Yahweh spoke to the ancient children of Israel, through the prophet Isaiah, "by saying to them that you are my witnesses saith Yahweh, my servants whom I have chosen: that you may know, and believed me, and understand that I am He". "Before me there were no God formed, neither shall there be after me."

So, they the children of Isreal, were the only set of people, who were knowledgeable of Yahweh, in comparison to the many Hamite's people, who they were living around in the so-call Middle East, and what became known as North Africa. Also that of the people of Asia, and in what became known as Europe. There Yahweh went on to say to the children of Isreal, that He form light, and He create darkness, and He also make peace, and He create evil: I the Lord Yahweh do all these things. (Verse 11 of Isaiah Chapter 43) went on to say, that I am the Lord which means Yahweh, and beside me there is no savior. The reason why Yahweh said these things to the ancient children of Israel, it is because they were the only set of people He gave his Laws, His name, His Commandments, and His statues to, and to no other people. They were also the only set of people who were knowledgeable of Him, in comparison to the many Hamite's people who they were living around in the so-called Middle East, and what became known as North Africa. Many of whom had their own gods, and who were not worshipers of Him, like that of the ancient children of Israel, and who they also came out of as a nation of people. Joseph Franklin Rutherford was born in 1869, and who died in 1942, and who took over from Taze Russell, and who sorts firmly to establish Jehovah Witnesses, as Jehovah God true people. Rutherford equipped many of his members with a portable phonograph player, so that many of his members, and converts would replay his sermon of speaking on their front porches, or in their living rooms.

Under the leadership of Rutherford, the democratic policy that were started by Russell, was later replace by a theocratic system, that is directed from the society headquarters in Brooklyn, New York. According to the Webster Colligate Dictionary, the word theocratic is a Greek word, that was taken from the word theocracy.

Which this word theocracy was also taken from the name Theos, which the name Theos was a god of Greece. This is where the word theologian were taken from, that came down to the Roman Catholic Church bishops, and priests, of their theologians philosophers, which is thought to many people who came under Roman Catholicism of their Christianity. This word theocracy meant to the people of Greece, a governmental of the gods, that was run by priests, and by his ministers, as his representatives here on earth. This view of the Greeks as a theocratic system of governmental ruler ship, over the earth by their gods, is not in harmony with that of the teaching of the Scripture.

This Kingdom of Yahweh will be a heavenly Kingdom government, that will be ruled by Yahweh, and by Yashua, as our king over all the earth, and Lords of all Lord, whether it will be that of men, or that of angel. This is in exception to Yahweh Himself, who is the boss overall things, and from whom all things flow. Moreover, this theocratic political system of today is control by the Satan the devil, and his demons, this is the reason why Yahweh is sending back Yashua to destroy the political system of the devil, and his representatives, who are in control of the political system of the world, which is also tying with many of church religious organization, of their philosophies to their various church members. Rutherford polices of running the organization of Jehovah Witnesses continue under his successor, who were known as Nathan Homer Knorr, who was born 1905, and died in 1977. Knorr who was the one who was responsible for the establishment of the Watch Tower Bible School of Gilled, that is in the New York area. This school was established for training of missionaries, and leaders who would oversee the publishing of the society books, and articles. This adult school educational program, were designed to help various Witnesses to conduct their own talks, or their speeches when they go from door to door, to witnessing to other people. According to volume 6 of the Encyclopaedia, under the supervision of Nathan Knorr, a group of witnesses came out with their own translation, of the New World translation of Jehovah Witnesses Bible. Later Knorr was succeeded by Frederick W. Franz. The Encyclopaedia explained that the Jehovah Witness as a religious group of people, have very little association with other religious denominations, and they as a group keep themselves separate from the political governmental system of the world. I must point out that the action Jehovah Witnesses take, in keeping themselves separated from the worldly political system, is right in harmony with the teaching of the Scripture. My reason for making this statement, it is because it is recorded at (First John Chapter 2, and verse 5 to verse 17), there the Scripture said, "love not the world, neither the things that are in the world". For if any man love the world, the love of the Father is not in him.

For all that is in the world, is the lust of the flesh, and the lust of the eyes, and the pride of life, that is not of the Father. But it is of the world, that his control by Satan the Devil, and his fallen angels, who are known in the Scripture as the demons. Furthermore, the Scripture went on to say, that the world's passeth away, and the lust there of, but he that do the will of Yahweh abideth forever.

Also, at (John Chapter 17, and verse 14), there Yashua was praying to his Father, and his God, by saying that he, and his disciples Yahweh gave to him from out of the world, were no part of the world. Which Yashua was referring to the political system that exited there in his time, that was ruled by the Romans, who had controlled over what is now called as the Middle East, and what became known as North Africa. I must point out that the Scripture is not say that a man should not work for his or her own living. Or to have a house, or a car, or some form of money in their lives, as a common necessity of life, because one must have money to buy whatever, he or she need for their wellbeing, so as to eat, and live. Especially living in this Gentile European conquered colonial world of today, where a person must have money to buy food, pay rent, pay taxes, parking tickets, and whatever fine the Gentile European court system might put on their citizens, who live under their system. So, money in itself is a necessity of life, epically in this modern world of the people of Europe, with their love, and greed for making of money. Also their skimming to get rich from their many conquered people, who became their citizens, and subjects. So, if a person do not have any money in this modern world of this Gentile people of Europe, it would be very hard, and difficult for that person to survive, and live from day two day. So, as to be able to buy the things they need to live and exist, from day to day, and that is a reality, living in this European conquered world of today. But what the Scripture condemn is the greed, and the love of money, that will move people to do all kind of evil things, just to get money to get rich.

What the Scripture is also speaking about mainly, is the sexual immorality, the political system of selfishness, wickedness, and greed for wealth, to get rich, that we cannot take with us to the graveyard, when Yahweh is ready to remove us from this earth. Also with it's violence, that were brought about by means of the Gentile European colonial world of their exploitation, of their conquered people, to get rich, that many of their conquered people has copped from them, as a way of life. Because as the saying goes, monkey see, and monkey do, meaning that people will always want to fellow other people doing. This modern world of the people of Europe, is now even more corrupted, evil and wicked than how it was, in the early days when the Scripture was given to the children of Israel. This corrupted system of theirs came from out of Rome, and Greece that many of the Celtic barbarian people were expose to, who became known as the Gentile European people of today.

The ways and life style of the Gentile European people, in turn spread to many people who became their captives, of their colonies, that they have adapted from their slave master ways, of skimming, and robbing to get rich. The pride of life that is mention at (First John Chapter 2), is to do with when a person becomes wealthy, and have some material possession in this Gentile colonial world of today, where some people become more prosperous than others. They get puff up, and try their best to keep down other people, as their foot cloth, or as their low-class people, because they feel to themselves that they are the high-class people of the Gentile society, who have all the wealth, and the fine things of life. Because they have a good paying job, and have some form of money, living the good life of the Gentile European people system. Many of their poorer people of their system, are the ones they make their wealth from, and live luxuriously from, and they become puff up with pride, because of their wealth. Many of their poorer people of their society, are the children of their former slaves, and conquered people who, they consider as their third-class citizens, or their garbage people of their societies. Because they have all the wealth of life, that they had stolen from many people who became their captive, and citizenship of today. Where many of their x slave, and conquered people, have no form of wealth, and are the poor ones. Many of whom are struggling to live, and survive in this Gentile European high class world, of their societies.

This is because many of their former slaves' children of today, are the ones they have try their very best to keep down, ignorant, poor and destitute, in comparison to many of the Gentile people of Europe, and that of the Asiatic people, who are consider as the high-class people of the European societies. Because they have all the opportunities, and are not kept down like many of us Hamite's people, and others, who are the poorer ones of their societies, struggling to survive from day to day, in this Gentile European colonial world of today. The Gentile European people system is all about the love of making money to get rich, in any way that they can do so in their colonial slavery system that they did established to get rich. So, if a person is poor, and struggling, in this Gentile European colonial world of today, he or she is considered as the low class, ignorant, and stupidest people, because they are poor, and they are the oppress people, of the Gentile European colonial system.

This is where the pride of life that is mention at (John Chapter 2), that the Scripture is speaking about. The Scripture clearly mention that we all came into this world without anything; and everything was put here by Yahweh for us all, and at the time of death we shall take nothing with us out of this world. Furthermore, there are no high class, or low class dead people in the graveyard, but everyone will be judge by Yahweh, and Yashua for their deeds while they were alive at the time of the resurrection of the dead. Those who are alive, when Yeshua come back, who are not of his flock, will pay the price for their Un Yahweh, and un Yashua like qualities, of there lives, from their day to day doing. I personally do not think that in the eyes of these Gentile European people, they see things this way, because of their greed for wealth, and their power to control things. So, the way they think, they are going to take all their stolen wealth with them to the graveyard, when Yahweh said it is time for them to leave this earth. The way many of them think, they are going to live here on earth forever with all their stolen wealth, because many of the Gentile people of Europe do not believe in Yahweh. They do not believed that He has set a time to judge everyone, according to their deeds. According to volume 6 of the Encyclopaedia, Jehovah Witness believers regarded the worldly political system, as Satan system, so for this reason they refuse to salute any flags, of any nations, and they do not perform in any military services, and they do not part take in any public elections.

I also want to point out that the various flags of today, as an identity of a countries, or islands, where many of us their conquered people were born and raise in, to see ourselves as natives of these conquered colonies of theirs. Were brought about by mean of the Gentile European colonial establishment, of their conquered world. This was for their many captives, and conquered people to embrace these lands they were born and raise in, as their country of origin. Which these false, are a deception, that many of their captives people whole on to, because many people were taken from different part of the world, to make up this European colonial flag system of today. Also, Jehovah Witness view many of the other religious church denominations as a part of Satan organizations, and for this reason they avoid using the term as minister, or reverent in their organization affairs.

Jehovah Witness also view themselves as a people looking for the establishment of the Kingdom of Yahweh, that is to come, as Yahweh rightful government, ruling over the kingdom of mankind, that will come about by Yahweh war of Armageddon. This war of Yahweh of Armageddon that is to come, is mention in (Revelation Chapter 16, and verse 16). I must point out that this view of Jehovah Witness, looking for the establishment of Yahweh Kingdom, is right in harmony with the teaching of the Scripture, that a believers should be looking forward to come. This is the same Kingdom Yashua taught his disciples to pray for that is to come, that is mentioned in (Matthew Chapter 6, and verse 9 and 10). Jehovah Witness is right in their views, looking for the Kingdom of Yahweh to come, to take over control of world affairs from these Gentile European political governmental system of today. Volume 6 of the Encyclopaedia explained that Jehovah Witness base their hope on the Scripture, as Yahweh time table, for world affairs, and the hope of mankind, as far as the future of mankind is concerned. Russell predicted that the year of 1874, should have been the year of Yashua invisible return, but his prediction was false, and did not come true. He also predicted that the year of 1914, was to be the year of Yashua second coming, and the end of the Gentile rein. To many people who might have read the Scripture, and came across the word Gentile, and do not know what the word really meant. So, when they go to check out the meaning of the word Gentile from the dictionary or the Encyclopaedia, they will get from the dictionary, that this word Gentile, mean none Jews, or the people of the nations.

So, the dictionary definition of the word Gentile, is totally a false definition, in comparison to the definition given in (Genesis Chapter 10, and verse 2, to verse 5), which states that the Gentile people are the descendant of the last son of Noah, who were known as Japheth. I must also point out that Mr. Russell was speaking falsely, when he made the statement to his Witness believers, that Yashua, was going to return to earth in 1914. My reason for making this kind of statement, it is because Yashua make it very clear in (Mathew Chapter 24, and verse 36), that of that day, and hour of his second coming, "knoweth no man. Not even the angles who are in heaven, nor the Son himself, but the Father only." Verse 37 of the same Chapter went on to say, but as the day of Noah were, soshall also the coming of the Son of man will be.

Many people will be eating, and drinking, and having a good time, as the saying goes, until suddenly the master appeared to give out punishment, to the unbelievers, and also to the UN Yahweh like people, and that of un Yashua like people, who do not live their lives to please Yahweh, and our Lord Yashua. Pertaining to the end of the Gentile rein that Mr. Russell spoke about, what Mr. Russell failed to understand, that he himself was a part of this Gentile family of people, that the Scripture spoke about, who are the people that is domineering over the earth of today. The end of the Gentile rein will not come to it's end, until when Yashua returns with the armies of heaven to take over control from these Gentile political system, they had set up true colonialism. They also, will be the one, who will gathered to fight against him at his second coming, as the Scripture foretold at (Revelation Chapter 17, verse 14, and also Revelation Chapter 19, verse 12 through to verse 16). There Yashua is described as the Lamb, the King of all Kings, and Lord of all Lords, who will take away the ruler ship of the world, from this Gentile European political powers. Also, from the various Asiatic powers who came up, after the Gentile European, powers that is ruling over the earth of today. Volume 6 of the Encyclopaedia explained that Jehovah Witnesses during World War II, were faced with many persecutions in Germany, and in other countries of Europe. Also, in the land of Ham, that the Romans named as Aprica, whose nationalism conflicted with that of the Watch Tower idea of government. The Encyclopaedia explained that each members of Jehovah Witness meet in a place they call the Kingdom Hall, and baptizing by immersion of water is a must, after these believers have studied the Scripture, and come to some knowledge of truth from the Scripture. Also, the organization of Jehovah Witness insists on high moral code, and personal conduct of its members, and they also disapprove of divorcement, except on the ground of adultery or fornication. The organization of Jehovah Witness also opposes blood transfusion, they say is based upon Scriptural ground, where Yahweh told the children of Israel, that is recorded at (Leviticus Chapter 3, and verse 17), that they must not eat fat, or blood.

Many members of the local congregation of Jehovah Witnesses are known as Kingdom publishers, who are expected to spend five hours per weeks, meeting at various Kingdom Halls, or meeting at other members' homes, papering themselves for the door to door preaching work, they call as field service. In the Jehovah Witness organization there are witnesses, who are known as pioneer's publishers, and these pioneer's publishers hold a part time job.

Many also do their best to devote 100 hours of their time, per month to their religious work of field service, as they called it, the preaching work. The Encyclopaedia explained that special pioneer publishers are full time paid salary employees of the Jehovah Witness organization, who spend at least 150 hours per months to the work of preaching, distributing magazines of the Jehovah Witness organization, they called the Watch Tower, and the Awake magazine. Also, each Kingdom Hall of Jehovah Witness organization is assigned to a territory, and each Witness has a particular neighborhood to work in. Each Witness take great pain to keep track of records of each person they had spoken with. Also, the number of times they make returned visits, to speak to different ones, hoping the returned visits would eventually lead up to Bible study with different individuals. I would like to point out that although a person, or an organization, might call themselves religious people. It does not necessarily mean they are true worshipper of Yahweh, doing His will, and keeping to His commandment, like that of Yashua, and of his Apostles, who did all things to please Yahweh. This word religious, was taken from the word religion, that came from the Latin language of the Romans, of their worship to their many gods. This religious people could be a worshipper of a deity, which mean a gods, or goddesses of Roman paganism, from where what became known as Christianity came out of.

This word religious, and religion is a Gentile European word for worship, of their many gods. So, to be a religious person, could be a worshipper of a man, idol, a cow, the moon, and the stars. Even Satan the Devil himself, and his angles who are called as the demons in the Scripture. According to volume 6 of the Encyclopaedia, Jehovah Witness most powerful headquarters is the Watch Tower Bible, and Tract Society of Pennsylvania, and it was started by Russell in 1884. The other two corporations are the Watch Tower Bible, and Tract Society of New York, and the International Bible student association.

My personal experience of attending the Pentecostal Church in Brooklyn New York, but my worst experience is with that of the Jehovah Witness Kingdom Hall of the East Orange area of New Jersey, where I use to attend. In 1975, I and my ex-wife went to a Pentecostal Church in Brooklyn, and we had the intentions to become a member of this church, and we even got baptized while we were there. While attending their church services, their belief and teachings was that Jesus is God, whom they prayed to, including all the other various churches I have visited while living in the New York, Jersey area of the United States. While attending the Pentecostal Church in Brooklyn, I became very confused at their teaching, because when I read the Scripture, the understanding I got from it, is that Yahweh is alone by Himself that was translated as God and Lord. Who is the ruler, creator and God of this universe, and of all thing, and Yashua is the Son of Yahweh. So, Yahweh is not another God of this so call trinity that came down from the Roman Catholic Church teaching of Europe. At the time I did not have the knowledge and the understanding as I do have now of the personal name of Yahweh, and also the personal name of Yashua, as I do know now. I found out much later after leaving the Pentecostal Church, and that of the Jehovah Witness organization. Eventually, I became very troubled at the teaching of the Pentecostal people, and I went to pray to Yahweh, and said to Him that I did not want to offend Him by praying to Jesus, and I did not want to offend Jesus by praying to Him, Yahweh. After a while I stopped from attending the Pentecostal Church, and I decided that I was just going to keep on reading the Scripture, rather than going to any churches, because I personally get more understanding and satisfaction from just reading the Scripture rather than going to these churches.

While living in Brooklyn and not going to any church, I had a dream that Yashua came to me, and in this dream and I was hiding, because I said I was not ready as yet. I also had a second dream, where he came to me and said I must go with him to visit the churches. Sometime after my Pentecostal experience, I left from Brooklyn, and moved to the East Orange area of New Jersey. While living in New Jersey I went to check out quite a few churches to see if I would get more satisfaction in harmony with that of the reading of the Scripture, in comparison to the teaching of the Pentecostal Church where I was attending in Brooklyn.

After going around to quite a few churches, and saw that most of the pastors just take a few texts from the Scripture, and speak on it, and claim they are preaching, and teaching the Word of Yahweh to their members. Many of whom most of the time don't even have a clue of understanding, of the true knowledge of the Scripture, so as to teach others, believers how to live a Yahweh, and a Yashua life stile, to please Yahweh, and Yashua. But many of these members just go along with whatever the various pastors say to them, whether it is right or wrong from their own point of view, and the collection of money from their members, to become rich men from their members ignorance. In many of the churches I went to, the standing procedure is all about singing, and clapping of hands, and giving their money in the collection plate, as tides and offering. Or in the collection baskets, and it is not about helping the various believers to get an accurate knowledge of the Scripture for themselves, so as to help them to live a Yahweh, and a Yashua life stile, as it is so required in the teaching of the Scripture. So, again I decided I was just going to stay at home, and read the Scripture, and try my best to live a Yahweh like life style, that is translated in the Scripture as Godliness, in the best way I can possibly do so. Sometime after my decision to stay at home where I was living in the East Orange area of New Jersey, one early Sunday morning, while I was still in bed sleeping, I had a dream, and in this dream, I was talking to a dark skin man dressed in white clothing, speaking to me from the clouds. I said to this man in the dream that I wish if the end could come now, because there are too many false prophets, and I do not know which one of them is telling the truth. The man in the cloud said to me that at least Jehovah Witness say God is God, and Jesus is Jesus.

In this dream I saw a little book in a man's hand sitting in heaven, with other men all of whom were dressed in white clothing. So, in this little book I saw my name McKenzie, but it was crossed with two lines across it, as when a person crosses a check with two lines. Also, in this dream there was a round circle, and different ones were sent up to heaven, and this person who was sending these people up to heaven looked like a Gentile

European man. He said to different ones, "look, you have baptized in the name of the Father, and in the name of the Son, go up and receive your reward." But when he came to me, he told me that I cannot go up, because I am a Muslim. I said to this man in the dream, who was sending different ones up to heaven, that I was never a Muslim, and when I were living in London my interest was to study history, and the man in the dream said to me I was crazy.

When I finally woke up that Sunday morning, I said to myself, that if Yahweh so good enough to give me a dream like this, all the way from heaven, then I am going to go to the Jehovah Witness Kingdom Hall. I must point out that long before all these experiences of my dreams, I had spoken with a Witness lady on the Street, but I never had any real interests in what she was saying about Jehovah Witness Organization. Although my ex-wife became a Witness, long before I had these dreams, and started to attend the Jehovah Witness Kingdom Hall myself. On that same Sunday morning I went to the local Kingdom Hall, but I was very careful in listening to what they were saying. Also checking the Scripture to make sure what they were saying, was in harmony with the teaching of the Scripture, and not coming from their religious organization. As time went on I was there for a while, but I was not participating in the regular door-to-door field service work, because I was afraid of people slamming their doors in my face, and getting mad with me for ringing their door bells, or knocking on their doors. One morning I had a dream that a census was taken up in heaven, and my ex-wife got two marks, because she was regularly in the field service, and I was not, and because of that I only get one mark, and one mark was not good enough. After this dream I started to go to field service more often than before, and the fear of people getting mad with me for ringing their door bells, and knowing on their doors went away from me, and I had no more of that fear. I used to have a regular Bible study with one of the elders at the Kingdom Hall, because that was a part of their policy, and I would always make sure that whatever this elder was saying to me at this Bible study, was coming straight from the Scripture only. And not from their Jehovah Witness Organization, and their religious philosophies of their point of view, of their teaching. This elder wanted me to stop from using the King James Version of the Scripture, that I had, and for me only to use their Jehovah Witness New World Translation Version of what became known as the Bible only. That was brought about by some Jehovah Witnesses person for their believers to use. But I flatly rejected it and stuck to the King James Version.

My reason for choosing the King James Version over the New World Translation of Jehovah Witness Organization, is because I had a good understanding of what I was read from the King James Version. I am not saying I did have a very good knowledge of all the things I have read in the King James Version, but I had a very good understanding of most of the things I had read.

Reason number two for sticking to the King James Version, it is because when the King James Version came out in 1611, many of my ancestors were in slavery, and it was not permitted for them, and their off springs to be able to read and write in the Angles Saxon dialect that became known as the English language. So, reading the Scripture was out of the question for many of them. Because they were not given the chance to learn to read and write for themselves, in any of the Gentile people language of Europe, whom they were in slave and rule by. So, this New World translation of Jehovah Witness Bible was more so to benefit the chinning time that we are now living in, according to what they want us to know and to believing from their point of view only. Their intention was to keep us down and ignorant, only wanting us to know what they think we should know from their point of view. So, when the King James Version came out in 1611, they were only writing to their own people, who were under the teaching of the Roman Catholic Church. Also, that of the Anglican Church, that was set up by Henry the 8th. So, the New World translation came out under the leadership of Nathan Homer Knorr, who took over the organization of Jehovah Witness in 1905, to 1977, and this was after slavery was abolished by the British. So, many Hamite's people of today who came from out of the slavery experience of the Gentile European people system, have very little knowledge about the Scripture for themselves. Except from what they had learn and copy from their Gentile European slave masters who had called themselves Christians and Christian countries of Europe. When the Scripture was translated from the Latin language of the Romans, into the English languages they did not have us in mind, so this good knowledge of the Scripture was translated for them, and their off springs who are around with us today. If it was not for the mercy, and kindness of Yahweh, who has give knowledge wisdom and understanding. Also a copy of the King James Version that came out in 1700 to, 1890, that I have in my possession, showing of the land of Ham, his sons, and grand children that is now known as the so-call Middle East, and what is now known and North Africa.

I would have never come to the knowledge of who I am as a person, and of the great civilization I and my ancestors are coming from before slavery, and colonialism was imposed on us as a people of Ham. If I was a person who were born and rise in the Jehovah Witness organization, and using their New World Translation of the Scripture that became known as the Bible, I would have never come to this knowledge of the great civilization the people of Ham are coming from.

I would have just have to go along with what they say, and what their translation is showing, whether it was true or false, because I would not have known any different from what their translation is showing and teaching. As a matter of fact, when I was attending the Kingdom Hall of Jehovah Witness, in the back part of the cover of their Bible, there is a map showing of a picture of a Gentile European man standing in what is known as Egypt, and the so-call Middle East. Also, a picture of a dark skin man standing in what became known as Ethiopia, from where the so-call Black people is coming from, according to their thinking of deception. So, what this Jehovah Witness Bible map is telling me, of a European man standing in what is now known as Egypt, and the so-call Middle East, is that the Gentile people of Europe came from what is now known as Egypt, and the Middle East. Also that the so-call Black people originated in the land area that became known as the land of Ethiopia. So, if I did accept this kind of information and teaching from this elder, I was studying with, and what their translation of their Bible map is showing of the ancient world that gone by. It would have left me totally brainwashed, and mislead from the real truth of what was, of the ancient world that is recorded in the King James Version of 1890. As I had mention, that while I was studying with this elder, he never like the idea of me using the King Jame Version, but only to used their Jehovah Witness Version only. Because according to their philosophy, the King James Version is an inferior translation in comparison to that of their New World Translation. While I was studying with this elder on a regularly basis, and going to the Kingdom Hall, he wanted me to accept his story where Yahweh said in (Isaiah Chapter 43, and verse 10), that the children of Israel are His Witnesses, that He alone is God and beside Him there is no other.

He wanted me to accept his story that this part of the Scripture of Isaiah Chapter 43, and verse 10 was speaking about Jehovah Witnesses as Yahweh group of people, which is totally false, and I rejected it, and did not go along with his story. This action of mine in rejecting this elder story did not put me in good standing with the local Kingdom Hall of Jehovah Witnesses where I used to attend. Furthermore, when I used to go in field service, doing door to door work with other Witnesses, they would always say to the person who opened the door of their houses," we are today placing a copy of the Watch Tower, and Awake magazine, on a contribution of fifty cents." If the person at the door says they did not have any money, the Witnesses would say to the individual, they would leave them an old copy of the Watch Tower and Awake magazine.

They would just say to the home owners, they would return at another time, when he or she has the money, to pay for the magazine. They would just walk away and go to another house, without even mentioning anything about what the Scripture had to say about the Kingdom of Yahweh that is to coming, and the time we are now living in. This was the reason why we were there, knowing at their doors in the first place, to expose to them what the Scripture have to say about the time we are now living in. I must point out that many times in field services, I heard different Witnesses make this kind of statement to people at their doors, without even mentioning anything about what the Scripture had to say. It was very upsetting to me, and many times I would say to different ones, we are not out here to sell magazine, but we are out here to teach the word of Yahweh to other people. Another time, I and a Witness went to knock on a door, a lady came out, and the Witness said to the lady, "we are placing our latest copy of the Watch Tower and Awake magazine on a contribution of fifty cents, when the lady heard this statement, she just slams her door and went back into her house, without even hearing a word of what the Scripture had to say about the Kingdom of Yahweh that is to come. Which was the real reason why we were there knocking on her door in the first place. Later, I came to the knowledge and the understanding that many of the Witnesses did not like to do field service work with me, because of my views of their actions in speaking to different people at their doors, about the price of their magazine, rather than what the Scripture have to say. This was due to what I had mentioned to different ones about giving people the impression, that Jehovah Witnesses are only sellers of magazine, rather than been teachers of the word of Yahweh, and His Kingdom that is to come. I eventually got baptized, and became a Witness of the local Kingdom Hall, but from the various experiences I had in the field services with different ones, I started to lose interest in attending the meetings at the local Kingdom Hall, and going to field services.

Another reason for causing me to lose more interest in attending the meetings, at the local Kingdom Hall, it was because one Wednesday night I was at the meeting, and a Hamite elder who was conducting the meeting, said to the congregation, "no one should intrepid the Scripture for themselves, except only the Society of the Organization of Jehovah Witness." When I heard that statement, I could not believe what I was hearing from this elder, so from then on, I started to attend the meeting less regularly than that of before.

After this experience of mine, one Friday night I was working on my car until way down in the Saturday morning, when I went to lay down to sleep. I had a dream, and it was like I was standing before the sun, and In this dream, it looks to me like it was real judgment. Also in this dream my ex-wife and my first daughter was standing at one side of the Kingdom Hall, with another elder standing next to them. So, I awoke from my sleep, and I said to myself, maybe the reason why I got this dream, it is because I am not attending the Kingdom Hall as before. So, I got up that same Saturday morning, and put on my clothes, and said to myself, let me run to the Kingdom Hall and go to field service, to do door to door work like I use to do. When I went out to field service, they put me to work with a lady to go from house to house, and while I was working with this lady I happened to mention to her that I had a very bad dream this morning. She turns to me and said, "God do not deal with dreams in today's time, but He is only dealing with the organization of Jehovah Witnesses, and their magazine, and she said to me, she think I should better speak to one of the elders about this matter." I did not answer her a word, because I did not go along with what she was saying to me. We kept on working, going from house to house, and we went and knock on a door. A man came and opened the door of his house, I gave him one of the Watch Tower magazines for free, and I was just about getting ready to share the Scripture with him, when the lady who I was working with take back the magazine from this man. The man got so upset, and closed his door and went back into his house without even, hearing a word of what the Scripture have to say, that I was about to share with him. The reason why this lady take back the magazine from this man, was because I did not charge him the fifty cents for the magazine. When twelve o'clock came, she hypocritically said to me, it was very nice working with me, and we went our separate ways.

One Sunday morning while I was still in my apartment, I heard the doorbell rang, so I went to open the door, to see who it was. It was two elders from the Kingdom Hall, so I open the door and invited them in. We went upstairs to my apartment, and when they went into my apartment, they took out a green cover book that contains the rules and regulation of the Jehovah Witness Organization. I simply turn to them and said, I do not go by that book; but I only go by what the Scripture have to say. These elders said to me that the statement I made, called for deist fellowship from the Jehovah Witness Kingdom Hall.

I knew the reason why these two elders came to my home, was because of the lady who I was working with in the field service, who I had told her about the dream I had, which she did not go along with. I said to these elders, "the only reason why I came to Jehovah Witness Kingdom Hall in the first place, was because of a dream I had that said to me, at lease Jehovah Witness say God is God and Jesus his Jesus. In comparison to the rest of the other churches who worship Jesus as God. One of the elders turned to me and said, "God do not deal with dream anymore in today's time, and it was the devil who gave me this dream to go to the Kingdom Hall." I turn to them and said, many times at the Kingdom Hall I heard different ones say that this person, or that person introduced them to the Kingdom Hall, and eventually they became a Witness. So, in my case, what must I say if a person was to ask me, why I became a Witness, and go to the Kingdom Hall? Seeing that it was because of the dream that I had, why I did go to the Kingdom Hall in the first place. As far as these Elders were concerned, I could say anything else, except to say that my dream came from Yahweh. I told them that I was not willing to go along with that kind of story. So, they said that they have to deist fellowship me from the Kingdom Hall. I turn to them, and asked, "on what grounds are you going to deist fellowship me on?" They came up with a tailor made Scriptural from the book of Jeremiah (Chapter 23, and verse 21 to verse 25), that I was a false prophet. I turn to them and asked, "what false things have I told you?" Moreover, I said to them that this Scripture verse that they have quoted to me, was speaking about the ancient children of Israel, many of whom were false prophets. They turned to me and said that I can appeal their deist fellowship decision, with other elders at the local Kingdom Hall. I did so, and a date was set for a hearing, like a person going before a judge to be sentenced to prison. When I went to the Kingdom Hall to have this hearing, there were some elders who were sitting down to act as judges, and right away one of these elders started to take sides with the other elders, without hearing what I had to say.

I turned to them and asked, "are you going to hear my side of the story?" They said to me that I should explained my side of the story, which I did. When I started to explain to them of my experience with the other two elders, who came to my home, and the reason why I came to the Kingdom Hall, was because of the dream I had. They turned to me, and said that they agree with the other two elders to deist fellowship me from the Jehovah Witness, organization, because Jehovah Witness do not believe in dreams.

From their point a view, dream come from a person mind, and also from the devil, and they also said to me that I was an anti-Christ, because I did not believe in Christ brothers. According to their philosophy, these brothers of Christ are the ones who are running the organization of Jehovah Witness. Also, that these brothers of Christ are responsible for all the printing material, and they are called as the Anointed ones, or the elects, which mean chosen ones. I turned to these elders and said, "I know from the reading of the Scripture, that the elects, or the anointed ones were of the Apostles class of people of Yashua. But I do not have any knowledge of any anointed ones, or elects is in the Jehovah Witness Organization. So, I cannot say so because I do not know of this to be so." I turned to these elders at the Kingdom Hall and asked, "what Scripture did I break?" They said to me none, but they came up with another tailor-made Scripture from the book of Proverbs that said, "be not wise in your own eyes." After all the bad experience I went through, I got very upset, and said to them, "forget about you people," and I walked away from the Kingdom Hall, and never went back there anymore. Due to the deist fellowship decision from the Jehovah Witness organization, my ex-wife and my two daughters have no form of affiliation with me, because it is against their beliefs for a member to have any form of association with members who are deist fellowship, from the organization of Jehovah Witness. This just goes to show how religious organizations, and their philosophies, can tear families and even communities a part. After the ordeal I went through with the elders at the Kingdom Hall, I went to see the elder who I used to study with when I first went to the Kingdom Hall. I explained to him about the various experiences I had encounter with the Witnesses, and according to his statement, from the day I have been attending the Kingdom Hall, I never totally followed the philosophies, and the rules of the Jehovah Witness organization.

He also mentions to me that I keep on using the King James Version of the Bible, rather than using their New World translation of the Scripture, even though he had tried very hard to stop me from using it. While I was just staying at home, and not going to any church or the Kingdom Hall, I had a dream, telling me that a new congregation was formed, and I became an elder. So, after this dream I had, I came to the understanding of the name of Yahweh, and Yashua, and the knowledge of the various books I have written, that I did not know anything of before, even while I was going to the Kingdom Hall.

I must point out that one must not become followers of men, or religious organizations, and their elders, but one must become followers of Yashua, who is our Lord, Master, King and High priests to Yahweh, as it is so stated at (Mathew Chapter 23, and verse 9). One can also read (Hebrew Chapter 8, starting from verse 1); to get a very clear picture of the high priest position of Yashua that is mention there in the Chapter. There at (Mathew Chapter 23, and verse 9), Yashua said to the Yehudahites, and the "Benjaminhites of the children of Israel, who were left there in the land that became known as Israel. Call no man your father upon the earth, for one is your father who is in heaven," meaning Yahweh. Verse 10 of (Mathew Chapter 23) went on to say neither be you called masters, or leaders, because one is your master, and leader, even Yashua, who was translated as Christ, and Jesus in the Greek, and Latin language of the Romans, that came down in the Angles, and Saxon dialect as Jesus Christ". So, what this Chapter is saying, there are many priests of the Catholic Churches, who gave themselves titles, such as Holy Father, and having people confess their sins to them. By so doing, they are setting themselves up as Yahweh, who is the Holy Father, because He created all people for His worship, and parses, and He is the sustainer of us all, and we cannot live, and edgiest without Him. Also, as Yashua said, call no man your leader, or master, for one is your leader, and master, speaking of himself.

This is the end of my Jehovah Witness ordeal of experience.

The false name of Jehovah that replace calling on the name of Yahweh, according to volume 12 of the Encyclopaedia Britannica, it explained that the artificial name that was given to Yahweh as the name Jehovah. Was taking from the word Yehowah that became known as Jehovah, in many of the translation of what became known as the Bibles. According to this same volume 12 of the Encyclopaedia Britannica, Christian scholars after the Renaissance, and the Reformation period, used or translated the word Jehovah from the name of Yehowah, that came from the name of Yahweh. From what I have come to understand, there is no J in the Hebrew language, of the children of Israel, so this name Jehovah in what became known in the English language, it is a false name that replace calling on the name of Yahweh. I also came to the knowledge that the word Renaissance mean a new beginning of light of learning of knowledge that came to the people of Western, and Eastern Europe. This was after the breakup of the Roman Empire that was the sustainer of light, and knowledge, to many people of Western and Eastern Europe. The word Lord that is pertaining to Yahweh, is a title that was given to men as the lowest of all Lords. The angels are also Lords, that is of a higher position than that of all men, who is of the earth, and the angel are also spiritual Sons and solders of Yahweh heavenly army. Our Lord Yashua, who is next in power and authority to that of Yahweh, he is also Lord. But Yahweh is the supreme Lord that is over all, that was taken from the word Adonai, and the word Adonai was translated as my Lord in the various Bibles of today. The word god with a capital G is also a title pertaining to Yahweh, that was taken from the word Elohim, that came from the Canaanites people of the worship of one of their gods, who was known a Beal. This word Elohim was later passed on to the children of Israel, the Greeks, and the Romans as a description of worship to their various deities, that was translated as gods, in the various translations of what became known as the Bible.

The title of the word Almighty, which is speaking of Yahweh, that meant all might and all power, which is also a title that was given to Yahweh. According to the Webster's Colligate Dictionary of the Fifth Edition, there it explained that the word Almighty came from the Angles, and Saxon dialect, that was known to them as olmiti. The word Most High, which is also a title that was given to Yahweh, which meant, the highest person of the universe that his overall of His creation, that everyone must answer to.

According to Dictionary of the Bible written by John L. McKenzie, there it mentions that the word Alleluia, which is a Latin word that was taken from the Hebrew word haleluyah, which mean to praise Yahweh, and to give Him glory and praise to His Holy and wonderful name, as the Yahweh of our lives. My reason for bringing out this little light, of information, it is to benefit many believers, and worshipers of Yahweh, who go to the various churches on a Sunday morning, and sing the song Alleluia, and do not know what the word really means. According to the Webster's Third International Dictionary, the word deity came from ME, which stands for Middle English, that was spelled as deity. When this word deity came down into MF, which stands for Middle French, this word was spelled as deity. In the time of LL, which stands for Late Latin, this word was spelled as deity, and in the time of the Greeks this same word deity was spelled as theotes. But when reading from the Encyclopaedia Britannica, there it explained that the word Theo's was the name of a god of Greece, and when this word came down into Latin, it was spelled as dues, which means the gods of the Roman world. Also, in the Latin language of the Romans, this word deity was known as divus that meant divine gods to the Romans. Dominus in the Latin language was taken from the word Adonai, that became known in the English language as my Lord, and Elohim as my God. In which they did suppress the name of Yahweh from speaking His name aloud, and by so doing adopting these titles, and false names that were given to Him. This word deity was also applied to the Greek god Zeus who was known as a sky god to the people of Greece. When this same word deity came down into OE, which stands for Old English, then this word was known as Tiw who was an Angles and Saxon god of war. This word deity was also known in OHG, that stands for Old High German dialect as Zio. This word deity was also known by the Old Norse people, as Tyr, which was a god of war, who are known today as the Icelandic people, and the Scandinavian people, who also was a Germanic tribe, of what became known as Europe.

I would like to make this fact to be known that the name Jehovah that is mentioned in many of the modern translations of what became known as the Bible, is a Gentile European false name that was giving to Yahweh. It was taken from the four Hebrew consonants of the word YHWH, that stood for the name of Yahweh that was taken from the Tetragrammaton. According the Webster's Third International Dictionary, the name Jehovah came from the abbreviation of NL that stand for New Latin. This word Jehovah was substituted for the name of Yahweh, that was taken from the word Yehowah.

According to the Webster Collegiate Dictionary of Fifth Edition, the word Tetragrammaton came from New Latin, and from Greek, that was taken from the word Tetra-gram, which meant letters. The word Tetragrammaton is a Gentile European word from where the name Jehovah was taken from. According (Malachi Chapter 1, and verse 6), there Yahweh went on to say pertaining to the various priests of the children of Israel, o priests that despise My Holy name for not expressing it aloud. By so doing, it would have benefit many believers of today to come to the knowledge of the name of Yahweh, rather than the false name of Jehovah that appear in many of the modern translation of what became known as the Bible. Malachi Chapter 1), there Yahweh said that from the rising of the sun, even unto the going down of the same, His name shall be great among the Gentiles. Also in every place incense shall be offered unto His name, and a pure offering: for His name shall be great among the heathen, saith the Lord oYahweh of hosts. The heathen that the Scripture spoke about were the various Hamite's nations, and also the various Asiatic Samite's people, of the East. Who are not too far away from the land of Canaan that became known as Israel, and the Saudi Arabian people of Ishmael, many of whom are idol worshipers, of their many gods. Many of these idol worshipers did also included many of the Gentile people of what became known as Europeans, who had no knowledge of Him whatsoever, but who had their own gods that they use to worship and serve. To give one a good example of how truthful the prophecies of the Scripture is, had it not been for volume 12 of the Encyclopaedia Britannica, that was written by these same Gentile people of what became known as Europeans. I would not have come to knowledge of the name of Yahweh, to give glory and praise to His Holy, and wonderful name, as the Yahweh of my life.

It is also true that it was these same Gentile people of what became known as European, who have brought about the false name of Jehovah, that did replace calling on the name of Yahweh, that has cast allot of confusion, and deception of the name of Yahweh. In my opinion, everyone should be knowledgeable in calling upon the name, of Yahweh who is our life, and Father of all creation. It is also written in (Zephaniah Chapter 3, and verse 9), there Yahweh went on to say, for then will I turn to the people a pure language, that they may all call upon the name of the Lord, which mean Yahweh, to serve him with one consent, and one accord.

(Amos Chapter 9 and verse 12), there Yahweh went on to say, speaking of the Israelites people, who He was going to allow them to return to the land, He gave to their forefathers. By saying they may possess the remnant of Edom, and all the heathen that is call by His name. (Romans Chapter 10 and verse 13) went on to say, for whosoever shall call on the name of the Lord Yahweh shall be saved, and this name of the Lord that the Scripture is speaking of, is the Lord Yahweh. (John Chapter 17, and verse 6), there Yashua went on to say while he was here on earth, praying to his Father, and his God, by saying, I have manifested your name, to the men you have given me out of the world. Which Yashua was speaking of the Apostles who did believed on him that he was the Son of Yahweh, the one who was sent to them, the Yehudahites, and the Benjamites who was left there in the land when Yashua came to them as a man. So what Yashua was saying is, that he has made known the name of Yahweh to his disciples Yahweh gave to him from among the Yehudahites and the Benjaminhites who did believe on him that he was sent to them, to be their savior. Yashua also mention in (John Chapter 12, and verse 28), by saying, Father glorify thy name, which the word thy mean yours. So, in other words Yashua was saying to his Father, and his God, by saying glorify your name, or let your name be known. This example just goes to show how it is so important for one to give parse, glory, and worship to the name of Yahweh. Who

248

is the Yahweh of our lives, by calling on His name in our daily worship to Him, and also applying His Holy word to our daily lives. According to this same Third Webster International Dictionary, the name Jehovah came from the abbreviation of CAP, and J&G.

According to the dictionary, the abbreviation of N means north, and northern, and the abbreviation of CAP mean capital and capitalize. I could not find the meaning of the abbreviation for the word J&G in the abbreviation section of the Webster's International Dictionary. But according to this same dictionary that was mentioned, the name Jehovah with a J, stood for a god by the name of Jehovah, who is the supreme deity, that was recognized, and worshiped by the organization that became known as the Jehovah Witness. They the Yehudahites and the Benjaminhites people of the children of Israel substituted the word Elohim for the name of Yahweh, because they had considered His name to be too scared to express aloud by anyone. They the Yehudahites and the Benjaminhites also substituted the title of the word Adonai to replace calling on the name of Yahweh, because they were afraid to express his name aloud.

In time of around 300 BC, after the death of Alexander the Great, the Yehudahites ceased to further use the name of Yahweh. According to volume 12 of the Encyclopaedia, the word Lord is a title that was translated as Kurios in the Greek Septuagint version of the Old Covenant part of the Scripture, and it did replaced calling on the name of Yahweh. With the word Adonai, that was translated in the various Bible as my Lord. According to volume 12 of the Encyclopaedia, there it explained that the name Yahweh was the name He revealed to Moses as His own personal name. Which was passed on down the line to other Gentile people of Eastern, and Western Europe, who came from out of the breakup of the Roman Empire. According to what I have gathered from reading volume 12 of the Encyclopaedia, after the Exile of the children of Israel from the land of Canaan, in the time of the 6th Century BC, to the 3rd Century BC, many Yehudahites, and Benjaminhites ceased to use the name of Yahweh, that was expressed aloud by the ancient children of Israel, before their time of the 6th and 3rd Century BC. The worship of Yahweh spread throughout the Greek, and the Roman world by the Yehudahites, and the Benjaminhites who were dispersed among the Gentile people of Europe, for their disobedience of not keeping to the Commandments of Yahweh, He gave to their forefathers. They the Yehudahites and the Benjaminhites who were scattered among the Gentile people of what became known as European, decided to use the noun of the title of the word Elohim, that was substituted for the name of Yahweh. They the Yehudahites, and the Benjaminhites further refused to express the name of Yahweh aloud, because of fear. By so doing they came up with the title of Adonai that was translated as Kurios, that appear in many of the translations as my Lord and Elohim as my God. Volume 12 further explained that from the time of the 6th, to the 10th Century AD, a Yehudahites group by the name of the Masoretes, who was located in Germany further worked to reduce the original text of the Hebrew Scripture of not expressing the name of Yahweh aloud.

They managed to replace the consonants of the four-letter word of the Hebrew vowel of YHWH, with that of the vowel sign of the Hebrew word Adonai, and Elohim that gave birth to the artificial name that appears in most of the translations of the Bible as my Lord and Jehovah God. According to a booklet I did receive from the House of Yahweh worship in Texas, there they explained that according the Encyclopaedia Judaica volume 7, the word Elohim that became known as God, and the word Adonai that became known as my Lord are titles.

These titles did replaced calling on the name of Yahweh that was taken from a Canaanite god who was known as BaalPeor, and this word Lord that was applied to BaalPeor was only titles. This little booklet also explained that many of the Canaanites names, and words came down into the Hebrew language from the Canaanites writing of Aramaic. From what I have gathered from this little booklet, the Hebrew name Jerubaal that appeared in the book of (Judges Chapter 7, and verse 1), came from the name of Baal. Also, the name Esh-baal, and Merib-baal that is mention in (I Chronicles Chapter 8, verse 33 and 34), was also taken from the name of Baal by the ancient children of Israel. I must say that I am not surprised at this statement that was made by this little booklet, because as I have mention before that the ancient children of Israel mothers came from among the Canaanites people, and also from other Hamite's women of what became known as North Africa. Many of whom were their mothers, and their neighbors who they were living around in the so-call Middle East, and what became known as North Africa, who gave birth to this nation of people. From what is explained, one can clearly see how much many people of today who came from out of the Gentile European slavery colonial system, and were Christianized by them to see things their way. We their many captives were deceived from the true understanding of the teaching of the Scripture, Yahweh did only gave to the children of Israel to benefit other believers, who fear Him, and who wanted to be worshipers of Him. (Revelation Chapter 16 and verse 13), there the Scripture went on to say "and I saw three unclean spirits like frogs came from out of the mouth of the dragon, also out of the mouth of the beast. (Revelation Chapter 16 verse 13 and 14) went on to say the "unclean spirits like frogs" also came from out of the false prophets", for they are spirits of the devils, working miracles, which go forth unto the kings [and politicians] of the earth.

Also of the whole world to gather them to gather to the battle of the great day of God the Almighty" and that is to come. In my opinion the spirit of the devil came down in the form of these scientists, and their many false historians, theologians, their religious church leaders, and the astrology people, many people who look up to these people for direction for the future and life itself.

Due to the religious doctrines that was spread around the world, by these Gentile European people, and also by the Mohammedans Muslim people, it has cause division among many people in what is known today as the Middle East, and what became known as Africa. Fighting, and killing each other over these religious doctrines of their colonial conquerors, that has nothing to do with the true worshipers of Yahweh who are livening their lives by the teaching of the New Covenant Law, Yahweh did set up by way of Yashua, and his disciples. My reason for bringing out these Scriptures, is to prove to many people that Yahweh has his own Spirit within himself, the devil and his angels also have their own spirits within themselves. Man, and the animals have their own spirit within themselves, but the spirit of man cannot do the things that the spirit of Yahweh can do. Yashua, who is the Son of Yahweh, and who is in second position to that of the authority, and the power of Yahweh, he also has his own spirit within himself. To prove my point that this is so, if one should read {Luke Chapter 23, and verse 46}, there one will see that when Yashua cried out with a loud voice, and said Father into your hands I commend my spirit. Having said so, he gave up his spirit, that is called as the ghost in many translations of the Bible, and then died. Just in case someone might ask the question of what do I mean by saying Yashua, better known as Jesus Christ is second in position to that of Yahweh in power, and authority. To prove my point that it is so, if one should read {First Corinthians Chapter 11 and verse 3}, there it stated, I would have you know that the head of every man is Christ, and the head of the woman is the man, and the head of Christ is God, and this is speaking of power, authority, and ruler ship. I must also point out that the animals also have their own spirit that Yahweh put within themselves, and the spirit of the animals is a different spirit to that of all men. The reason why I mention men and did not mention women also, it is because the Scripture clearly mention that from the man came forth the women, so the woman was made for the man to be his wife, and the man is the head of the human family of Yahweh.

Many of the Gentile people captives, and free slaves people of today's who were indoctrinated into their form of belief, and worship of their many gods that was infused into what became known as the Christianity. With their trinity Gods; with many false teaching and worship to their various gods of Europe that were intertwine with that of Christianity, that came down to many of their captives of today to believe in, as a way of life.

Speaking of what they called as the Father, Son and the Holy Ghost, that they called as one God in three persons. Or the triune Gods, that is speaking of Yahweh, Yashua and the Holy Spirit of Yahweh that they called as the Holy Ghost, as another God of this so-call trinity. The Holy Spirit of Yahweh was translated in many of the Bibles as the Holy Ghost, which is the Holy Spirit of Yahweh, and it is not another God of this so-call trinity. According to Dictionary of the Bible, written by John L. McKenzie, it is stated in page 899, that the word trinity came about in the 4th and 5th centuries AD, by the theologians into the church, which is speaking of the Roman Catholic Church, that spread to the various churches as this trinity Gods. Dictionary of the Bible clearly explained that in the writing of the Scripture, this belief of the Trinity was not teach in ancient Isreal of the Yehudahites and Benjaminhites believers of the worship of Yahweh, who are now known as the Jews and

Jewish people of today. Reading from the Encyclopaedia Britannica, there it explained that in Roman time, they were three major gods of Rome who were known as Jupiter, Juno and Minerva, and who were known as the tried gods, from where the word trinity was taking from. This belief of the trinity came down from the Roman Catholic Church that were known as the tried gods that spread to many of the various churches, as the triune gods, that they name as Father, Son and Holy Ghost. Three spirits in one God that was spread around the world by means of the Gentile European conquest, to many people who became their slaves, and conquered people of what became known as Christianity. One must not be surprised to come to this knowledge of awareness, because many of the Gentile people of Europe words, and their educational system came from the Romans, and the Greeks, who they were rule, and educated and control by. So, many of the Roman, and Greek belief became that of their own belief, as a way of life for them to fallow as a religious people.

Many people of today go to the various churches, seeking to get a better knowledge, and understanding from the Scripture, for them to become true worship of Yahweh, in accordance with the teaching of Scriptures. But unfortunately, they only get religious church doctrines that came down from their pastors, and priest, who they look up to as men of Yahweh. But they do not get the true knowledge from many of these men who see themselves as men of Yahweh, and Yashua, teaching the truth of Yahweh and Yashua, but many of whom are deceivers. Many of the time they only get false religious church doctrines from these men who they consider to be teachers of the Word of Yahweh.

Which many of the time it is only church doctrines of men philosophy, that came down from the Catholic Church, and that of Protestantism, of the Gentile land of Europe. I could remember one Sunday morning I went to a local church in the Newark, New Jersey, hoping to become a member of this church, which was a Baptist Church. While I was in the Sunday morning Bible class, I happened to mention that the name of God is Yahweh, and it is not Jesus as what they were saying, that is also taught in many of the various churches I went to. The members laughed me to scorn, and the deacons who was in charge of the Sunday school said to me, we do not worship Yahweh here, but we worship Jesus who is God. I did not say anything to these church members, or this deacon, but the next Sunday morning I take along the dictionary, and the Encyclopaedia to show to this deacon what the name of God is. This deacon did not want to see what I have to show to him concerning the name of Yahweh, but instead, he told me that there are many other churches down the road apart from his church. So, in other words, if I did not like their teaching, there is other churches that I could go to.

So, I collected my documents, and walked away from that church, and went to seeking other churches that I could settle down into. But unfortunately, many of the other churches I went to; believe in the same Trinity doctoring as the three Gods in one person, that they said appeared as Jesus Christ in the flesh. So, for a person to find a church that is teaching the true doctoring that were given to the prophets of the children of Israel, and that of the Apostles, it would be like looking for gold and diamonds, that is very hard to come by. My reason writing this little story about my experience of the various, churches, is to show to many people that the only way a person can become a member of a local church, they would have to go along with what they say, whether it is true or false, otherwise they cannot be there. I was speaking to another pastor of another church in Newark New Jersey area I went to on a Sunday morning, he was trying to convince me that the words "Alpha and "Omega" that appeared in the book of Revelations is speaking about Jesus Christ, who he said is the Alpha and the Omega, the Great God of the universe. So, I try to show to this paster that the word Alpha, and Omega is a Greek word that is speaking of Yahweh, that was translated from the book of (Isaiah Chapter 44, and verse and verse 6), where Yahweh said He is the first, and He is the last, and beside Him there is no other God.

So, this word first and last was translated by the people of Greece in the book of Revelation as the Alpha and the Omega, which mean first and last. So, what Yahweh is saying in the book of Isaiah that was translated in the book of Revelations as Alpha and Omega, is that everything starts with Him, and everything ends with Him, and beside Him there is no other. My purpose for explaining the truth about Alpha and Omega, is that it might benefit many Hamite's people who go to the various churches, many of whom have been totally deceived by the wrong doctrines they did received from their various pastors, who see themselves as men of Yahweh. Teaching their church doctrines that came down from the Roman Catholic Church, and that of Protestantism, from where all the churches of today came out of. Some of these pastors also see themselves as Apostles, and prophets of Yahweh, and Yashua to their many church members by deceiving them.

Many of these posters really believe to themselves that they are teaching the truth to their many church members as the Word of Yahweh, but many of whom don't realize that they are deceiving many of their church members with false doctrine of men. This is the reason why Yashua make the statement in (Matthew Chapter 15, and verse 14), by saying to his Apostles, speaking of the high priest, the Pharisees, Sadducees, and the scribes, who were the writers. Also, the religious men of Israel of those days, that they must leave them alone, because they are blind leaders of the blind, and if the blind lead the blind, they all shall fall into the pit. The same is true in our today's time, many of these pastors, priests and deacons, are blind leaders of the blind, with their religious doctoring that will cast many of their members who look up to them for leadership, and direction in gaining Scriptural knowledge to fall into the pit of destruction.

Chapter 41 - The Righteousness of Yashua, Who Did All Things to Please His Father, and His God.

When Yashua was here on earth, he did not do things to please himself, but rather he did all things to please his Father, and his God Yahweh, who had sent him to the tribe of Yehuda and the tribe of Benjamin, who was left there in Jerusalem. This was to do the will of his Father Yahweh, to be that perfect sacrificial lamb for the children of Israel, and for the rest of world of mankind at large. Who will turn to Yahweh in true worship, and to live their lives by His Word the Scripture, and His Commandment to please Him, and to save these believers from the wrath of Yahweh that is to come. I must also point out that although a believer who believes in Yashua, that he is the Son of Yahweh, and call themselves a Christian, that came from the Latin word Christus. Also from the Greek word Christos, and from the word Christendom, that came from the Anglo-Saxon Germanic people, that meant" followers of Christ." It does not necessary mean that he or she who calls themselves a Christians, is living by the teaching of the New Covent Law, that Yahweh did set up by way of Yashua. Also true his Apostles, to teach other believers, who is doing things to please Yahweh, and Yashua, as his true sheep's of his followers. Yashua made it very clear at (Matthew Chapter 7, and verse 21), by saying not everyone who will say to him on that day to come, "Lord, Lord, will enter into the Kingdom of Yahweh, that will be ruling over the earth, but only those people who do the will of his Father Yahweh who is in heaven.

Yashua also mention at (Matthew Chapter 7, and verse 13), that a believer, and a follower of him, must walk in the straight and narrow gate that lead to everlasting life, because broad, and wide is the gate that lead to destruction, and sad to say that the majority of the people of planet earth, are walking on this broad road to destruction. Whereas straight and narrow is the gate that lead toward everlasting life, and only a few people, out of all the people of planet earth will fine it. The important issue for a believer should be based on the Faith in Yahweh, and living their lives in Yashua like qualities, to please Yahweh. Not on the name of Christianity that came from out of the Roman Catholic Church, of paganism, also of idolatry worship, that became known as Christianity, by the Gentile people of Europe.

Even the Ku Klux Clan, and the Crusaders of the Roman Catholic Church, who call themselves Christians, and who went about slaughtering people, and burning people houses, all in the name of Christianity to control people. This was to send fear in the minds and hearts of people who they wanted to destroy, and get rid of as the servant of the devil, doing his will. The Mohammedans, who became known as the Muslim people, are in the same basket with that of the Roman Catholic Crusaders, and the Ku Klux Clan, many of whom went about slaughtering people, and burning people houses. This was to control them, and to send fear in the heart, and mind of many people for them to become Muslim, and also, for them to become follow of Mohammed, and his religious philosophies of his god Allah, as a way of life for them to follow. When Yashua was here on earth, he did not set such example for his followers to follow, but he did good things while he was here on earth, as examples for his followers to follow, to please his Father Yahweh, and to please Yashua himself. Yashua also mention at (Matthew Chapter 24, and verse 13), by saying that a believer, and a follower of his, must endure living faithfully, applying the Scripture to their daily lives, and to keeping on doing good things true the trial, and tribulation of this life. To please him, and his Father Yahweh, and the same shall be save at the end of their lives, or when Yashua come back to Jude the living, and the dead for their deeds. Yashua will be the one who will say well done good and faithful servant; enter into my father Kingdom. So, it is not like what the various church pastors of their various churches teaches their church many members, who became baptize believers. By telling them that they are save, and are going to heaven, to be with Yahweh, and Yashua, and to pay their tide, and offerings to the church for the many pastors to get rich. Also calling them Saint, that meant chosen ones, that was taken from the word elect, that was mostly applied to the Apostles, and the prophets of the children of Israel.

I must also point out that only Yashua, and Yahweh have the power, and the authority to say to a believer that they are save, and are well come to enter Yahweh new order of things to come. It is not for the various pastors of their churches, to say to their members they are save, and are going to heaven, because they are a baptize member of the church, and give their tide, and offering very regularly to the church. Many of these church pastors of today are totally deceiving their many members, with false teaching, and false hope.

Many of whom do not know any better, because many of them are rap up in the church philosophies, and doctrines that came down from the Roman Catholic Church, and from Protestants, of the Reformers, that many of these churches of today, and their teaching came out of. Even if a believer died, and buried in their grave faithfully, living their lives in the teaching of Yashua, that is now known as the New Covenant Law. That Yashua gave to his Apostles to teach other believers, that person resurrection is sure, because Yashua said at (John Chapter 5, and verse 28) that all who are in the grave shall hear his voice, and come back to life to be judge according to their deeds. So, there will be a judgment for the dead, and for the living, according to the teaching of the Scripture of truth. (Romans Chapter 8, and verse 1) mentions that there is no condemnation to them who are in Yashua, who walk not after the flesh, but after the Spirit of Yahweh, and the teaching of the New Covenant Law. That was set up by Yashua before his death, and his resurrection that is now called as the New Testament by the people of Greece. To prove my point that there is a difference between Christianity, and Yahweh like qualities, that was translated as Godliness, that was taken from the word Elohim, that meant Yahweh, that became known as Godly in most of the Bible translation of today. If one should read (Psalms Chapter 1, starting from verse 1), there it read like this," blessed is the man that walketh not in the counsel of the UN Godly. Nor standeth in the way of sinners, nor sitteth in the seat of the scornful, but his delight is in the Laws of Yahweh, and in the Laws of Yahweh he meditates day, and night, which is speaking of the Scripture of truth.

The Scripture went on to say, he shall be like a tree planted by the rivers of waters that bringeth forth his own fruit in his own season, his leaf also shall not whither, and whatsoever he doth shall prosper. But the UN Godly (or the UN-Yahweh like) people are not so, but are like the chaff that the wind driveth away. Therefore, the UN Godly, or the UN Yahweh like people shall not stand in the judgment, nor sinners in the congregation of the righteous, for the Lord Yahweh knoweth the way of the righteous, but the way of the UN Godly, or the UN Yahweh like people shall perish. So, it is not about been a "Christian", and calling oneself a Christian, that come down from the Roman Catholic Church, and that of the Protestant, of the Gentile people of Europe. But it is all about seeking to please Yahweh, and Yashua, who is our King, high priest, and the mediator of the New Covenant Law.

To live our lives according to the teachings of the New Covenant Law, that Yashua gave to the Apostles his servants to teach other believers. Yashua was also sent to Earth to establish the New Covenant part of the Scripture that is known today as the New Testament. This New Covenant part of the Scripture, that Yashua was sent to establish, is the fulfillment of the prophecy of (Jeremiah Chapter 31, and verse 31). There the prophecy went on to read like this: "behold the days come said Yahweh", when I will make a New Covenant with the house of Israel, and the house of Yehuda, that was translated as Judah. Not according to the Covenant, I made with their fathers, in the days when I took them by the hand to bring them from out of the land of Egypt, which my covenant they break, although I was a husband unto them," said Yahweh". So, the Old Covenant, and the New Covenant part of the Scripture is for the children of Israel as a whole. We the people of today, who believe, and worship Yahweh according to the teaching of the Scripture, and who live their lives to please Him, will become a part of the spiritual family of natural Israel. The people of Yahweh, and will be save from His wrath to come. We, the believers of today, are eating, and drinking from the table of the children of Israel, because the Scripture was given to them only. Which is the law of life for everyone who believed, because Yahweh make it quite clear that he was going to make a New Covenant with the house of Israel, and the house of Yehuda, that was translated as Judah, and Jews of today. At (1 Corinthians Chapter 15, and verse 21 to verse 28), there the Scripture read like this", when all things shall be subdued unto him," meaning the reigning of Yashua, having power and dominion over everything. Then the Son himself shall also subject himself unto him who did put all things under his feet, that Yahweh will be Yahweh to all people, having supreme power over all things of his creation, and everyone looking to Yahweh to satisfy their needs. The churches of today, with its various false teaching and deceptions to their many members, who came from out of the slavery experience, that is mixed-up with politics.

That came from out of the beastly system, that these Gentile people of Europe came out of, that came from out of the breakup of the Roman Empire, from where all the politics, and many of the church doctoring of the milking of money came from. To their various church pastors, for them to get rich, from their many members who have very little knowledge, and understanding about the Scriptures for themselves to live by.

Many of these church philosophy, and teaching came down from the Gentile people, to their various slave colonies of the world, who came under their colonial captivity of ruler ship, of false teaching, and lies to get rich. So, many people from their ex-slave colonies, who became pastors of their false teaching, and deceptiveness they had learn from their slave masters, who had called themselves Christians. They continue to practice the various skims, of the milking for money from their many church members, who do not know any better of what the Scripture is all about. Many of these church pastors also get their church members to be involved in the political affairs of the world that the Apostles, and Yashua was no part of while they were here on earth during Roman time. None of the Apostles of Yashua who he left in charge of the preaching work, of the good news of Yahweh Kingdom, who he did sent to be a minister to the Yehudahites, of the children of Israel, and that of the Gentiles people of Europe, were not wrapped up in any of the political affairs of that time. So, all the believers of today should be following the same examples, and teachings the Apostles, left in the Scripture as a guideline for all believers of today to fellow. Because they were following the examples and teaching Yashua laid down for all believers to follow to please him, and his Father Yahweh. It is Yashua with all his angels who are coming to destroy all the political system, that was setup by Satan the devil, byway of these Gentile European people, who came from out of the breakup of the Roman Empire. The political system of today came from out of Rome, where all these Gentile European powers, who are ruling over the world came out of. They have established their political system, throughout their various slave colonies of the world that became their empire, that many people of today are following. (Revelation Chapter 12, and verse 9), described the Devil as the dragon, and Satan, who have deceived the whole world, and who was cast out of heaven to the vicinity of the earth with his angels, who are known as the demons in the Scripture.

Just in case someone may ask the question of what do I mean by saying that the political system of today is backed up by Satan the Devil? To prove my point that this is so, according to (Revelation Chapter 13, and verse 2), there it mentions that the dragon, which is Satan the Devil, gave the beasts its power and great authority. The last beast that is mention in (Daniel Chapter 7, and verse 7) was Rome. Also, Daniel Chapter 2, and verse 33, where the verse speak about the ion leg of Nebuchadnezzar dream, where the political system of today came out of, that was pass on to these European people of today, who came from out of the brake up of the Roman Empire.

So, wheresoever the colonial powers of these Gentile people of Europe, went and conquered people and their lands, in the name of Christianity, they have always set up their political system for their colonies, and captives people to follow. This is the reason why in various countries of the world of today, the political system was set up by whatever European powers who had ruler ship over their various colonies, and they left their many half springs behind to carry on with their political system of their power. With various flags as a form of identity, to many of their former x slave's people of their colonies of the Gentile people of Europe captured world. My reason for mention about the various flags of identity's of today, of the various formers slaves colonies of the Gentile people of Europe. It is because during the time of BC, and early AD, I cannot ever remember reading from the Scripture, or any history book of that time, about any flags of any countries. Although in early Scriptural time various countries did came under different ruler ship of their conquerors, who had dominion over their lands of kingdoms, yet there were no national flags of those days. So this political system of the Gentile people of Europe, also filters down to many of their x slave people who became their political rulers of their slave colonial system, that they were born and raised in, and many of whom became political figure head, ruling over their brothers, and sisters of these former slave colonies. Many of their former captive's slave people, just follow along, with many who became political leaders of the Gentile ruling system over their fellow captive people, n many of the former Gentile European slave's colonies, that later became known as the Third World countries and islands.

Many of their former x slaves people fought, and killed each other over these politicians to put them in offices, and as soon as many of these political leaders get elected into office, they forgot about many of the poorer, and foolish people, who forth and kill each other to put them in office. Also, of the various promises they had made to them during their election campaign, to become rich men living off their subjects. This is the reason why it is stated in (Psalms Chapter 146, verse 3, and 4), "put not your trust in princes, or in the sons of men, or in the politicians of today for that matter, in whom there is no help or hope. But rather people need to put their trust, and hope in Yahweh alone, who is the creator, and giver of all things. I would also like to point out that it is Yahweh who has allowed these political governments to continue to rule over the earth, until He is ready to destroyed them.

Just like how He destroyed the political system of Mizraim, Babylon, Persia, Greece and Rome, and eventually these political governments of today will suffer the same faith. Grant it, there must be some form of government to rule over the people, this is the reason why Yahweh allows these political governments to rule until He is ready, to destroy them, and to bring about His own righteous kingdom, to take over ruler ship over all the earth. The reason why I made the statement about the churches using psychology of skimming on their many members to get rich, from their ignorance of not having a proper knowledge, and understanding of the Scripture for themselves. I myself have visited many churches in the United States on various Sunday mornings, and from my experience, I have concluded that many people in the various churches, are suffering from lack of knowledge of the Scriptures for themselves. They do not get a true understanding of the Scriptures from their various pastors, whom they look up to as men of God. To teach them, and to give them the true understanding of the knowledge of the Scripture. But rather they just get church religious doctrine to prepare their minds to give their tithes, and offerings, and to become a member of the church. The first thing many of these pastors, and deacons would do to gear the minds of their church members to give their tithes and offering, is to quote (Malachi Chapter 3, and verse 8 to verse 10). Verse 8, there the Scripture ask the question: "will a man rob God?" This question was put to the ancient children of Israel, who Yahweh made a Covenant with only, and to no other people of the world.

This tide, and offering that (Malachi Chapter 3) spoke about, were for the Israelites Priests, who came from the tribe of Levites, that was to sustain them, and for the up keep of the Temple of Yahweh. This tide and offering that (Malachi in Chapter 3) spoke about, was not only about money, but it was also about the giving of their tiding of their farms, animals, harvest, and the first born of their male sons. To prove my point that it is so, at (Deuteronomy Chapter 12, verse 5 to verse 7), there Moses was pointing out to the children of Israel when they were about to go into the land of Canaan. To take over the land of Canaan, Yahweh gave to them, and their seeds after them, Moses went on to say to them, unto the place which Yahweh your God shall choose out of all your tribes to put His name there, even unto His habitation shall you seek, and there you shall come, and you shall bring your burnt offerings, and your sacrifices, and your tide.

Also, your have offering of your hands, and your vows offering, and your free well offering, and the first things of your heard, and of your flocks. In this place Yahweh chose to put His name there to be worship, there you shall eat before Yahweh, and you shall rejoice in all that you put your hands unto. You, and your household wherein Yahweh hath bless you. So, it is not like what the various churches of today do, who used psychology, diplomacy, and strategy on their various members mind, who do not know any better. To get rich from their ignorance, of not knowing the Scripture for themselves, that was only given to the children of Israel only. Furthermore, Yahweh make it quite clear to Israel, and to the world of people at large, who would later come to the knowledge of the reading of the Scripture, by saying at (Deuteronomy Chapter 7, verse 6, and 7), for you are a Holy people unto Yahweh, speaking of Israel. Who has chosen you to be a special people for Himself, above all the people who are upon the face of the earth. Verse 7 went on to say, Yahweh did not set his love on you, nor chose you because you were more in number than any other people, for you were the fewest of all people. Verse 8 went on to say, but it was because Yahweh love you, and He kept the oath which He sworn unto your fathers, meaning Abraham, Isaac and Jacob. This is the reason why Yahweh brought you out with a mighty hand, and redeemed you out of the house of bondmen, from the hands of Pharaoh king of what became known as Egypt, to be His particular people. (Jeremiah Chapter 31, and verse 31), there it mentions that Yahweh was going to make a New Covenant with the house of Israel, and with the house of Yehuda. Not according to the Old Covenant, He made with them, when He took them by the hands to lead them from out of the land of Mizraim {Egypt}, but this Covenant would be a different Covenant from the Old one.

This Old Covenant was finish away with in the New Covenant that was established by Yashua, before his death, that was called as the Last Supper, and it was also done away with in Yashua. According to (Romans Chapter 10, and verse 4), there it mentions that Yashua is the end of the Old Covenant Law for the forgiveness of sin, to everyone who believe in the writing of the Scripture, of the prophets, and of the Apostles of the children of Israel. Who were the true servants, and ministers of the Word of Yahweh, and Yashua. I must also point out that, the term New Testament it is a Greek, and Latin word for the replacement of the word New Covenant, that Yahweh promise at (Jeremiah Chapter 31, verse 31 to Isreal.

 The word elects was also known as the chosen ones, that became known as the Saints in the various translation of the Bible, and also, in the various churches, that they applied to various members as the Saints, that came down from the Roman Catholic Churches. This is what Yashua said to his Apostles, that is recorded at (Matthew Chapter 28, verse 19 and 20)," go you therefore, and teach all nations, baptizing them in the name of the Father, and the Son, and the Holy Spirit. Teaching them to observe all the things he had taught and command them his Apostles to do. Notice Yashua commanded his Apostles that they should teach the people who would later become fellow believers of their faith, to observe, and to do all the things he had taught, and commanded them his Apostles to do. That other believers would become followers of their faith, doing and teaching likewise. Yashua is the High Priest of the New Covenant order, that is not only earthly, but heavenly also, according to (Hebrew Chapter 5 verse 5 and 6). Also (Psalms Chapter 110, and verse 4), there Yahweh swear by Himself, by saying that He will not repent or change His mind, but He made Yashua a high priest for ever, after the order of Melchizedek, who was a king, and a High Priest to Yahweh during the time of Abraham. So, when the churches of today mentions to their congregation about them having to pay tides and offering, or for them to give 10 percent of their earnings, they are only using psychology, and diplomacy and the mind of their many members, to deceive, and to rob them of their money.

Many of whom don't have much knowledge, and the understanding of the Scripture for themselves, because many people of today, are coming from out of colonialism, and slavery of the Gentile people of Europe. Also, that of the Mohammedans Muslim people of what became known as Saudi Arabia of Ishmael, who have also conquered many people to become followers of Mohammed, to the worship of his god Allah. So, it is very easy to deceive and to rob, many of their converts, because many of them do not know any better. Many people of today who came from out of the slavery experience, their ancestors went true before they came about, were train, educated, and brainwash, according to the Gentile European people teaching, they were expose to, and to believe. The same is true, for the Mohammedans who are now known as the Muslim people, for their many captives, to see things their way, and to become believe of their doctoring's.

This is also because of the fulfillment of the prophecy of (Isaiah Chapter 60), where it mentions that the Gentile people was going to be exposed to the light, and the knowledge of the Scripture of the children of Israel. At (Isaiah Chapter 60), there it said that there would be gross, or total darkness of knowledge of the Scripture, and the true worship to Yahweh, to the rest of the people of the world. So, is the reason why they the Gentile European people were given the opportunity to translate the Scripture that was only give to the children of Jacob, whom became known as the children of Isreal. I have also discover reading Up from Slavery, that was written by Booker T. Washington, in his book of his experiences of his day of slavery. When reading Up from Slavery by Booker T. Washington, the impression I have gotten from a statement he made, it seemed to me that many of the x-slave pastors of his day, of their Hamite's congregation, use to live from off the ignorance, and support of their many members. Many of who had no knowledge of what the Scripture was all about, but they tried their very best to get over on many of their members to become rich men from their ignorance. Many Hamite's people, and many others who were enslaved and taken captives by the Gentile people of Europe, to their New World of what became known as the Americas, and the West Indies, to learn things of their faith, as they did put it, have very little knowledge of what the Scripture is all about.

This also included many people of East India, and many Chinese people who were taken to their New World as cheap labors, and slaves, to learn of the Gentile people faith, and to serve them as their servants. Also, that of the many Arawak's, Caribs, and with many other native people of the so-called New World, who were conquered, and enslaved to death for them to become rich people from many of their slave labors. The remainder of these people who did survive from the brutality of the Spanish, and other people of Europe, they were Christianized to suit their purposes of their religious philosophies. This was of their deceits, and skimming to get rich, so as to live easy lives from off their many captives. What many people of today know about Christianity, and the church, meaning the Roman Catholic Church, or that of Protestantism, that many of the churches of today came out of, came from Roman Catholicism, of their philosophies, that came down to other Gentile people of their colonies of Europe. Who were under Roman ruler ship, that eventually came down to us their x slave people of today. When many of these Gentile people who were former slaves, and colonies of Rome, who later became slave masters of their various slave colonies of the world.

They just simply passed on what they themselves had learned from the Roman Catholic Church, that became known as Protestantism, to many of us their x-slaves people, as a church way of life. Many of us, who are the children of their former slaves, who later became pastors, and Ministers of their Gentile slave masters teaching, of their church doctrines, of their skimming, and deceptiveness to get rich. They continue with the practice of what they had learned from their Christian slave masters about tithes, and offerings, and calling themselves Reverent. Not even the Apostles of Yashua, who were his true, and faithful servants, whom many times he called as his brethren, did called themselves Revenants. They did not call themselves Reverent, or give themselves the titles of the word as Reverent, but rather many of whom were obedient servants to their death, and who had suffered many things before their death. So, when some Pastor or some church officials, call themselves a Reverent, they are putting themselves in the place of Yahweh to be worshipped, by their church members. Many of whom do not know any better, and who do not have any knowledge of the Scripture for themselves. According to the Webster Colligate Dictionary of the Fifth Edition, there it explained that the title of the word Reverent was taken from the word reverence. This word reverence was taken from the Latin language of the Romans, that was pass on to the French, that meant honor, respect and worship. So, this title of the word Reverent, belong to Yahweh only, because all worship belong to Him only, true the name of His Son Yashua. I must point out to many of my Hamite's people, who do not really know what the word reverent mean, the word reverent means to worship Yahweh, to give Him honor, glory and praise to His Holy, and wonderful name as the Yahweh of our lives.

There is nowhere in the writing of the New Covenant part of the Scripture that was established by Yashua, where he said that a believer, and a follower of his must pay tithes and offering, or to give 10 percent of their earnings to the church. If anyone should find in any of the translation of the New Covenant part of the Scripture, that a believer must give 10 percent of their earning to the church, it was put there by the Gentile people of Europe. Because they were the translators of the Scripture, into their various languages many of us their captives people speak today as our language. Also in that of other people languages, who came under the captivity, and ruler ship of the Gentile people of Europe. This is what Yashua said in (Matthew Chapter 5, and verse 43) that a believer, and a follower of his should do to follow his teaching of the New Covenant Law, that was established by him.

He said, to his Apostles, and to other fellow believers, that they must give to them who would ask of them, if they have it to give. Also from him who would borrow from him, or his neighbors, turn not away. So, what

Yashua was saying to his followers, that is recorded in the Scripture, is that they should become loving kindhearted people, sympathetic to each other needs, because everything that a man has in his life, was given to him by Yahweh. For we were all born, and came into this world naked without anything, and we all are going to leave here naked without anything, as the Scripture clearly mentions. I understand that the building, and the expense of the churches has to be taken care of, by the congregation of believers who attend these church meetings. But not to be ripped off, and taken advantage of by their various pastors, and ministers of the various churches, many of whom see themselves as leading the flocks. Many of whom use psychology, and deception to put a guilt trip on their member's minds, so that they can become rich men, from people who go to these places to worship Yahweh, and who do not have a full knowledge of the Scripture for themselves. I also want to mention that in many of the churches of the United States I went to, many of the Pastors live from off the support of their members, who pay them a salary to preach the word of Yahweh to them, as they put it. I must point out that many of these activities by these pastors, are not in harmony with the teaching of the Scripture of truth.

But it is only Christian religious church doctrines, that did not come down from the teaching of the Apostles of Yashua, but it came from the church, the (Roman Catholic Church). This action by many of these pastors of today, is only greedy men, misusing the Word of Yahweh to get rich, also to get over on other believers, who do not have much knowledge of the Scripture for themselves, to know any different. According to (2nd Thessalonians Chapter 3, starting from verse 7 to verse 10), there the Apostle Paul went on to say that, "for you know yourself how you ought to follow us". Meaning the teaching of the Apostles, who were following the examples, and the teachings of Yashua that was passed on to them, his early believers of Israel, and later to the Gentile people of land of Europe, by the Apostle Paul. For we behaved not ourselves disorderly among you, neither did we eat any man's bread for nothing, but we work with our hands, laboring, and travail night, and day, that we might not be chargeable to any of you. "This we command you, that if any man would not work with his hands for his living, neither should he eat."

I do hope this little enlightenment from the Scripture might help many church members, who go to the various churches, and give their monies to the pastors, as a salary for them to get rich, from their hard-earned money they need for them to survive, on to live on day by day. Many of these pastors of today, who call themselves preaching, and teaching the Word of Yahweh, I do hope their many members might become a little more smarter, and wiser about their deeds. What the Apostle Paul was saying in the Scripture, is that a pastor of today must work for his living, as did the Apostle Paul, and others of the Apostles of Yashua. Who worked for their living, to sustain themselves, and they did not become a peddler, of Yahweh Words, as many pastors of today do, to get rich, from their many of their members, who do not know any better. They teach the Word of Yahweh in truth and did not use it as a merchandise to make money, as many Pastors of today do to get rich. They did not become a burden, and a skimmers, to any believer on whom they were put over, to live easy lives from their faith in Yashua, and the worship of Yahweh. The funny thing about this story, many of these church members do not get much knowledge, and understanding about the Scripture from many of these Pastors, who call themselves Reverent, preachers, and teachers of the Word of Yahweh.

The Apostle Paul was made an overseer by Yashua, over the early Gentile believers, that the churches of today should have been following their examples, and teachings, that were laid down by the Apostle Paul. This religious belief of Roman Catholicism, was spread around the world by way of the European conquest of the world, also by their deception to gain wealth, and power through the Cross of Christianity. I must also point out that the Cross, (some with the image many church members of today believed it looks to be like that of Yashua. That many Christians, and churches use as a symbol of Christianity), it is totally an idolatry worship of Yashua. Furthermore, the image on many of these Crosses, is not that of Yashua. Yashua did not say in the writing of the New Covenant part of the Scripture, that any one should worship him as a god, that belong to Yahweh only. Who is the creator, and ruler of the universe over all things, and all people. But rather when Yashua was here on earth, among his Apostles, he appointed all worship to his Father and his God, to whom alone all worship and praise must be given to, through the name of his Son, Yashua.

This is what Yashua said about when one pray, there in (Matthew Chapter 6, and verse 6), he said, but when you pray, enter into your closet, or your room, shout the door, and pray to your Father who see in secret, and your Father who sees in secret, shall reward you openly. Notice that Yashus did not said in this Chapter, or in any part of the New Covent part of the Scripture that anyone should worship him as Yahweh. That was translated as God in many of these Bibles of today, that many churches, and their members pray to Yashua as a God that belong to Yahweh only. The cross that is on many of these Christian churches of today came from out of the Roman Catholic Church, which is of idolatry and paganism of the Roman world. This religious Christian symbol of theirs, was spread to Western Europe, Eastern Europe, North Africa, and the so-called Middle East, or wheresoever the Gentile people went and conquered in the name of Christianity, and set up their colonial system, over their conquered people. As I have mentioned before that the Roman Catholic Church came out of paganism and idolatry worship, which was infused into what became known as Christianity, that was taken from what was known in Israel as the Way, that meant followers of Yashua.

The word Messiah was taken from the Hebrew word Messias, that meant the anointed one of Yahweh, according to the King James Version of the Bible, in section that is called Dictionary of the Bible, that was copyright in 1964 by Nelson-National Printing company of the United States. Also, according to volume 8 of the Encyclopaedia, there it mentions that the word Messiah was taken from the Hebrew word Messias, that meant the anointed one of Yahweh, or the one who was sent by Yahweh to the Yehudahites, and the Benjaminhites who were left there in the land of what became known as Israel during the time of the Romans. The word Messias gave birth to what became known as the Messiah, that came from the British Protestant believers of Europe, who had to flee from the persecution of Queen Mary, who was a strong Roman Catholic believer, according volume 5 of the Encyclopaedia. Many of these Protestants Reformers had to flee to Geneva Switzerland, to work on their translation of what was known as the Geneva Bible, that was also called as the Breeches Bible. These men were working under the direction of Mile Coverdale, John Knox, and John Calvin, according volume 5 of the Encyclopaedia Britannica. The name Breeches, according to these translator's belief, was adopted by the way it was describe in (Genesis Chapter 3, and verse 7) about Adam and Eve who made themselves breeches to cover their nakedness, instead of aprons when they realize they were naked. I must point out that according to my copy of the Authorized King James Version I have in my position, there in Genesis Chapter 3, and verse 7, it did not used the word Breeches, but just used the word, they sewed fig leaves together, and made themselves as aprons to cover their nakedness.

 The Encyclopaedia also explained that in 1576 the Geneva Bible was imported in to Britain, and it also had its influence on the translation of what became known as the King James Version of the Bible. According to a King James Version that was copyright by Thomas Nelson INC, in 1970, there it make the statement that if it were not for the courage of many believing Jews, and many Christians. Speaking of the Gentile believers of what became known as Europeans people, one would not have the Bible in today's languages, for what became known as the Bible was often under attack to be destroyed.

I would like to point out to many people who might read a copy of this book, that it was not because of the many Yehudahites, who became known as the Jewish people, and also, the many Christian believers of Europe, who they say was responsible for saving the Scripture. That became known as the Bible, from being destroyed by many evil people, Satan was using, but rather it was due to the power of Yahweh, who was watching over His Holly Word that became known as the Scroll, and later became known as the Scripture, that meant writings. Also much later that became known as the Bible, to the enlightenment of the Gentile people of Europe, so as to fulfill the prophecy of "Isaiah Chapter 60, starting from verse 1 to verse 3" that the Gentile people shall come to the light of the Scripture, of the children of Isreal. So, the reason why the Scripture prevail into many of the various languages of today, it was because of the power of Yahweh, who was watching over His Holly Words, so it would be a light, and knowledge to many other people of today, as well. This also included myself, who has come to the knowledge of the name of Yahweh, His will, and His Kingdom that is to come. That this knowledge of enlightenment might save many who believed in the writing of the Scripture, and also, many of whom follow its teaching, to save them from the destruction of the power of Yahweh that is to come. According to this King James Version of this Bible, there it explained of how the Bible was translated into the English language, and why it is called the King James Version. The Bible went on to explained that for some five hundred years ago certain powerful churchmen, meaning various Roman Catholic bishops, and kings, did not want the people of Britain to know anything about the reading of the Scripture for themselves. Except what was taught by the various bishops, or the priests of the Roman Catholic Churches, who had power over the British kingdom, and over many people of Europe.

They did not want the people of Britain thinking about Yahweh for themselves, and the people were only taught of the religious philosophies, and doctoring of the bishops who were the priests of their church's. At the time, the Scripture was in the language of the Romans, who was ruling over the people of Britain, and only a few people of Britain at the time, who were educated, and could read, write, and speak in the Latin language of the Romans. One should also realize, and understand that many British people of that time, were illiterate, and who could not read and write for themselves.

 It was not until about the time of the 12th to the 15th Century, when many of these people became literate through the teachings of the monks, and the nuns of the Roman Catholic Church that enable many of these people to read and write for themselves. The Bible went on to say that in those days it was easy to keep the people of Britain from having a full knowledge of the Scripture for themselves, because printing was not invented as yet, and the Scripture had to be copied by hands. So, putting the Scripture into the language of the common people of Britain of that time, was often dangerous for the person who would try to do so, in losing their lives, or to be burn at the stakes for going against the Roman Catholic Church ways of teaching. It was also forbidden under the rule ship of Queen Mary of Britain, for anyone to translate the Scripture into the British people dialect. According to this King James Version, of the Bible, the first great translation of the Scripture into the language of the people of Rome, and also of her subjects, and provinces came about some four hundred years after the birth of Yashua. This was by Jerome, who translates the Scripture into the Latin language, that was widely spoken in those days. He translates it from the language it was found in, which was Hebrew, Aramaic, and Greek. According to volume 1 of the Encyclopaedia, it explained that the language of Aramaic, was spoken in northern and in the central part of what became known as the Middle East. This was from the 6th, and 7th century BC, which was the language of the Canaanites people of Canaan. The Encyclopaedia explained that the language of Aramaic eventually took over from the Akkadian language of the Assyrian, and the Babylonian people of Nimrod, and it became the official language of the Persian Empire. Because all of these former kingdoms were later conquered by the Persians, and became the Persian empire of their colonies.

The Roman Catholic Church continues to use the Jerome Bible, that was called the Vulgate Bible, that was translated from the Greek Septuagint version of the Old Covenant part of the Scripture, and also from the Jerusalem Bible, long after Latin cease to be in common use in Britain. According to volume 10 of the Encyclopaedia, the name Septuagint, came from the Latin word that was known as Septuaginta. According to volume 14 of the Encyclopaedia Britannica, it explained that the Greeks used seventy-two men from the tribes of Yehuda, to translate the Scripture into what became known as the Greek Septuagint version of the Bible.

These Hebrew translators labor over 100 years at Alexandra Egypt, in the third century BC before the coming of Yashua, during the time of the Greek ruler ship over what became known as the Middle East, and what became known as North Africa. The Encyclopaedia also explained that the language of much of the early church believers was that of Greek speaking people. This version was made originally for the Israelites people who were living in the land of Mizraim, who spoke Greek, and who were under Greek ruler ship. They translated it from the Torah, or the Pentateuch, which the word Pentateuch it is a Greek word, which stud for the five books that Moses the prophet wrote. It is stated that it was in the Greek Septuagint version of the Scripture, that the early believers of Yashua, who were Yehudahites, and Benjaminhites of the children of Israel came to the realization of the various prophecies concerning Yashua. According to the Encyclopaedia, many Israelites people later stopped from using the Septuagint version, because they considered it as an improper use of the Holy writing of the Scripture, that was only given to the Hebrew people of Israel only. The Encyclopaedia explained, that by the time of the 3rd century, various students of knowledge tried to clear up the various copy errors they had found in the Septuagint version, which by that time it was varied widely from copy to copy. Other writers exerted themselves to check the Hebrew writing of the Scripture, to try to straighten out the various errors they had found in the Septuagint version. The Encyclopaedia went on to explained that it was in the Septuagint version, and not in the Hebrew text that was the main foundation for the translation of the Old Latin. Also the Coptic, Ethiopic, Armenian, Georgian, Slavonic, and a part of the Arabic translation of the Old Covenant part of the Scripture was found in.

According to a Standard Revised King James Version of the Scripture, that was printed in the United States in 1901, in section that is called Dictionary of the Bible, there it explained that the word Hebrew came from the descendants of Eber. But according to (Genesis, Chapter 10, and verse 21), there the Scripture explained that Eber was one of the sons of Shem, who was the first son of Noah. Volume 4 of the Encyclopaedia explained that Eber was an Egyptian papyrus complicated medical texts that was dated from about 1550 BC, which was one of the oldest known medical works of the time. Volume 24 of the Encyclopaedia explained that the term Hebrew has nothing to do with a race of people, or an ethnic grope of people.

According to this same volume of the Encyclopaedia, the name Hebrew came from the name Habiru, which was spelled in different ways as Hapiru, which was a class of people who made their living by hiring out themselves to others for various services. According to Dictionary of the Bible, there it went on to explained that Habiru where the name Hebrew came from, was a dialect, or language that was widely spoken in UR of the Chaldees of Babylon. UR of the Chaldees of Babylon, is where Abraham came from, to what was known as Mesopotamia, which is now known as Iraq, where he also resided after he left from Babylon. The Dictionary of the Bible went on to explained that the Habiru group of people was a social group, of lower status in their community, rather than an ethnic group. I did not cover the complete story from Dictionary of the Bible about the people of Habiru, but I just took a few abstract to give the reader of this book, some enlightenment from where the name Hebrew came from. According to the Encyclopaedia, it was in the Septuagint version of the Old Covenant part of the Scripture that many Greek churches used as their version of the Scripture, in their daily worship of the knowledge of Yahweh that they came to. It was also in the Septuagint version that Jerome began his translation of the Vulgate Version, of the Old, and the New Covenant part of the Scripture, that became known as the New Testament. So, the people of Britain again had no Bible they could understand in their own dialect. Finally, when James the 6th of Scotland, who became known as King James I of Britain, came to the British throne after the death of Queen Elizabeth I. He gave his authorization for the Bible to be translated into the dialect of the common people of Britain in 1611, without anyone having to be put to death. This is the reason why it is called the King James Version of the Bible, because of King James who gave his authorization for the Scripture, that became known as the Bible, to be translated into the British people dialect without creating problem for any anyone would try to do so, and lose their lives.

According to volume 6 of the Encyclopaedia, James 6th was born June 1566, in Edinburgh Castle of Scotland, and James became king of Scotland, when he was only one-year-old, on July 24, of 1567, by some rebel lords of Scotland, when his mother who was known as Queen Mary of Scotland, who were defeated by these rebel lords. She had to flee from her throne on May 16, 1568 to Britain, and never saw her son again. James was made king of Scotland, when these rebel lords defeated his mother, and set him as king of Scotland as the new ruler.

James 6th of Scotland became known as king James I of Britain, after the death of Elizabeth I, in 1603, and James died March 27, of 1625. The Encyclopaedia explained that king James I were responsible for the establishment of peace in Europe, also for their colonial expansion in what became known as the United States of America. According to volume 7 of the Encyclopaedia, Mary Stuart who was Queen of Scotland from 1542 to 1567, and she was also Queen consort of France from 1559 to 1560. Her unwise marital, and political actions provoked a rebellion among the Scottish nobles of Scotland, in which it forced her to flee to Britain where she was eventually beheaded by the order of Queen Elizabeth I, as a Roman Catholic threat to the British throne. Mary Stuart of Scotland was the only child for king James 5th of Scotland, and his French wife, who was known as Mary Guise. The death of her father six days, after she was born, left her as Queen of Scotland, and king Henry 8th was her great uncle. My reason for writing this little story of how the Bible came into the British people dialect, it is because, like many British people of those days, there are still many people who go to the various churches of today, who do not have a clue of what the Scripture is all about. For they only go by the various belief of what they were taught by their pastors, or by their priests of their various churches, and congregation.

Many of whom do not really have the true knowledge, and the understanding of the Scriptures for themselves. These men who gave themselves various titles, such as Reverent, Priest, and Pastors, who teach commandments, and laws of men as Scriptural doctrines, to their church members for them to follow, and go by. Also, my reason for explaining about why it is called as the King James Version of the Bible,it is because various Hamite's people I have spoken with, believed to themselves that it was King James who wrote this translation of the Bible. Or have it written to suit is own purpose, which is not so, according to their thinking, and it is far from the truth.

Chapter 43 - The Forgotten Great Skils, And Crafts of The People of Ham That Became Known As Science And Technology.

Many people who might happen to read a copy of this book I have written, may ask the question: where is all the skills, and crafts I have mentioned the people of Ham used to have, and how come they do not have all these skills of today? First, to many of these people who might ask this question; I would like to answer by saying that it was because of the many prophecies of the Scripture that was spoken against the various kingdoms of the people of Ham. That has been fulfilled already, and it has taken its tolls on our kingdoms and us as a people of today. It is also because of the slavery experience, and the colonial conquest of our lands, and its people, that has further caused a brain drain of our knowledge, skills, and crafts to go to benefit many of our conquerors, that became known as science, and technology by the people of Europe, and other people who came under their conquest. The Gentile European family, along with the Ishmaelite people who are known today as the Saudi Arabian Muslim people, have also taken it toll on the civilization of the people of Ham. Although they the Ishmaelite people are a Hamite's people of themselves, because Ismael mother Hagar came from the land of Mizraim, that became known as Egypt. Ishmael father Abraham was a Cushite man, by his mother side of people of Babylon of the kingdom of Nimrod. If one should consider the period of conquests, and the enslavement of the people of Ham, by the Persians, Greeks, Romans, the Turks, and the Mohammedans.

Also, by the rest of the Gentile European family, who came from out of the breakup of the Roman Empire, that as further caused many of our craft, and skills to go to enrich their civilizations, rather than to in rich our own civilization. Just think for one moment, that if the land of Ham, and its people did not have so many conquerors, and enslavers, they would have long time been making motor cars, and airplanes long before these things came about byway of the Gentile people of what is now known as the Europeans people of Europe. Just to give the reader of this book some inside knowledge of the rich, and great civilization the people of Ham are coming from, that many people of today have no knowledge of.

There in (Ezekiel Chapter 28, starting from verse 2), there Yahweh when on to say to the prophet Ezekiel; say unto the prince of the city of Tyrus, which is speaking of the kingdom of Tire. Which was a Canaanite kingdom that was in the area of Lebanon, of the so-call Middle East. There Yahweh went on to say to Ezekiel, that he must say to the ruler of the city of Tire, that because his heart is lifted up, and he has said he is a god, he sit in the seat of gods, in the midst of the seas, which is speaking of the Mediterranean Sea. Yet you are a man, and not a god, though you set your heart as the heart of god. Verse 3 went on to say behold, you art wiser than Daniel: there is no secret they can hide from you. With your wisdom, and with your understanding, you has gotten gold and silver into your treasures, by your great wisdom, and by your trafficking you as increased your riches, and your heart is lifted up because of your riches. Verse 7 went on to say, behold therefore I will bring strangers upon you, the terrible of the nation, and they shall draw their swords against the beauty of your wisdom, and they shall defile your brightness. Verse 8 went on to say, they shall bring you down to the pit, and the grave, and you shalt die the deaths of them who are slain in the midst of the seas. One can read the complete Chapter for themselves to get a good understanding of what is written there. My reason for bringing out this prophecy of the Scripture, is to show of the various prophecies, that was spoken against the various kingdoms of the people of Ham. That has brought our destruction, and have cause us, as a people to be a washout set of people, because of many of these conquerors, and enslaver. Although the people of Ham were the inventors of slavery, of the children of Israel, and others, today slavery have brought our destruction, our civilization, and have cause confusion to many of us Hamite's people of today. That have cause us as a people not to know who we are, and where we are coming from, because of colonialism and slavery.

My reason for making this statement, it is because it was the people of Ham who had started writing, arithmetic, medicine, and what was known as physician, that became known as doctors in the Gentile European world of today. Also, the making of chariots, and wagons that had run on wheels, from where motor cars came from, that has brought much wealth, and riches to the Gentile families of Europe. Also, to many of the Asiatic people of Shem, that they have copy from the Gentile people of Europe, who had started the making of motor cars.

This was from the combustion engines, that originally came from chariots, horse, and buggy, and wagon that was started by the people of Ham. My reason for saying these things, it is because during the early civilization of the people of Ham, they were far more advanced in knowledge, crafts and skills, in making things out of iron, than our Gentile European conquerors, and enslavers who came up later, and have got many of these knowledge, and skills from us, the people of Ham. People like the Greeks, who got most of their knowledge, and writing abilities, and skills from the people of Mizraim, the Phoenicians, the people of Carthage, the Hethites, and the Babylonian Cushites people of Nimrod. In the case of the Romans, they have gotten many of their knowledge, and skills from the Greeks, the Phoenician, the people of Carthage, and the Etruscan, who were living in the land area that became known as Italy. This is also, from the Hethites people, of Canaan, who were living in what was known as the Anatolia area of Turkey. From where Anneas left from the city of Troy, and went and established what became known as the settlement of Latium, that gave birth to the Latin people who became known as the Romans. From where Romulus came from that gave birth to the name of Rome, that take its name from himself. Many of the Romans' knowledge that they had gotten was later spread to the rest of the Gentile land of Europe, who were under slavery, and colonial conquests of the Romans, and that of the Greeks, of the lands area that became known as Europe. Just think of the gifts, skills, and crafts that many of the people of Ham had at one time, my reason for making this kind of statement, it is because many of the people of Ham at one time had the capability of communicating through the beat of the drum. That was known as the drum speak. The beat of the drum would tell other villagers who were coming to their villages, if a person was sick, or dying or dead, the beat of the drum would pass on the message to others villagers.

The Gentile people of what became known as Europeans, did not possess any of this kind of skills, and knowledge like that of the people of Ham of what became known as Ghana of West Africa of today. Apart from the native people, who the Gentile European settlers of what became known as the United States, name these people as the Red Indians, who had sent war signals through the beat of the drum, and smoke signal. There was no other set of people, on the face of planet earth who had such knowledge, and skills like that of the people of Ham, and the natives, who the Gentiles European people named as Red Indians.

Sad to say that because of the fulfillments of the various prophecies, that were spoken against the various kingdoms of the people of Ham, it has cause slavery, and colonialism, of the people of Ham to be lost, or were taken over by the Gentile European people, and others, to benefit their societies. According to (Joshua, Chapter 17, and verse 16), there it mentions that the Canaanite people who were living in the valley of the land of Canaan, now known as Israel, had chairs that were made from out of iron. This knowledge of making things from out of iron, was way before the people of Europe came to the knowledge of making things out of irons. (Deuteronomy Chapter 9, starting from verse 1), there it read like this, here O Israel: you are to pass over this Jordan River this day, to go in to possess nations greater, and mightier than yourself, who has cities great, and fenced up to heaven. A people great and tall, which was speaking of the Canaanites tribe of the Anakims, whom the children of Israel knew of. And whom it had been said, who can stand before the children of Anak, because these people of Anak, who was the father of the Anakim tribe, were a giant tribe of the land of Canaan. This was with other various other giant tribes of the people of Ham, who were living there in the land of Canaan, along with the Philistine people, who came from out of the family of Mizraim. Who were living in the land of Canaan, before the land was taken over by the children of Israel, and other Abrahamic seeds. Moses went on to say to the children of Israel, understand therefore this day, that it is the Lord Yahweh your God, who go over before you, as a consuming fire, He shall destroy them, and bring them down before your face, so shall you drive them out, and destroyed them quickly, as Yahweh had said. Also, (Roman Chapter 10, and verse 19), there Yahweh said He was going to provoke Israel to jealousy by them who was no people, and by a foolish nation will I anger you. This prophecy was speaking of the Gentile people of Europe, who were not a powerful nation of people during the ancient kingdoms of the people of Ham. That was destroyed for the children of Israel, and for other Abrahamic seeds, who were living there in the land of Canaan, during the time of these ancient kingdoms of the people of Ham.

The meaning of this statement in the book of the Romans, it is that Yahweh was going to move Israel to jealousy by the powers of the various countries of Europe's, who are ruling over the earth today. Due to the fact it was the children of Israel who should have been ruling over the earth, after the down fall of the various kingdoms of the people of Ham, that Yahweh did use the children of Israel, and other Abrahamic seed to destroyed many of these ancient kingdom of the people of Ham, that gone by.

(Deuteronomy Chapter 15, reading from verse 6), there Yahweh promise the children of Israel that He would bless them, and they would lend to many nations, but they would not borrow from no other nations. The Scripture went on to say that they shalt reign, or rule over many other nations, but no other nations shall reign, or rule over them, if they had kept the Laws and Commandments of Yahweh. But they did not do so, otherwise they the Yehudahites, and the Benjamites, who became known as the Jews, and Jewish people would not have suffer so many things in Europe. Where they were scattered by Yahweh for their dissident, in not keeping to His Laws, and Commandments. Moses went on to say to the children of Israel while they were in the wilderness, going to the land of Canaan, speak not in your hearth that Yahweh had driven out these nations, because of your own righteousness. But it was because of the wickedness of these nations of Canaan, this is the reason why Yahweh drive them out before your face. This time was way before the Gentile people of Europe started the making of motorcars, and other things out of iron, they have gotten many of these skills from the people of Ham of the ancient world, that gone by that they name as science, and technology, as if to say that they were the people who had started all of these things.

Chapter 44 - The Inventions of the Hamite's people Music and Dance

The inventions of the Hamite's people Music of singing and Dancing, that gave birth to what they the Gentile European people of the United States call as the Negro Spiritual music. This Negro Spiritual music gave birth to what became known as the Blues, Jazzes, Country, and Western, music. Also what became known as Pop music, Sole music, Reggae music, with many form of music of today, that came from the Hamite's people suffering of these United States. This was of their joy, and sadness, that was a part of their ancestor's culture, of singing, and dancing, that came down to them, of the various form of music I have mention above. The people of Ham were also the entertainers, of singing, and dancing, to give entertainment to many Gentile European settlers, of what became known as the United States. This was during the early colonial days of slavery, to give them entertainment. This entertainment of the Hamite's people to ward these Gentile European settlers, was carry on to our present time. I must point out that I do not blame the Hamite's, people, who were born, and raised in what became known as these United States of America, for their kind of slavery mentality, many of them has toward us their brothers, and sisters. Who come from different parts of the European people conquered world, to these United States to make a living, because we as a people worldwide were indoctrinated against ourselves, to become haters, and enemies of our own selves. Also, to love others more than to love our own self, as the way it is in our world of today. The Gentiles European people are a very smart, and cunning set of people, they would go around to the various parts of their domain where many of their captive's slave people were living, and they would try to learn as much as they could learn from their enslaved people.

When time was right, they would do their very best to take over the various things they had learn from their captives people, which were a part of their captive's people everyday culture, and ways of life, before they were taken away from their native land as slave's. Whatever knowledge, they the Gentile people had copy from their slave's people, of their musical culture, and dancing, they would take it over, and called it their own musical culture, and they would give the music different titles, and different name. Whatever knowledge, and know how they have, or cultural gift that many of them possess, they would do their very best to prevent their various captives, mainly the people of Ham from learning any of their knowledge of know how that they call their knowledge of knowhow, as cultural gift, and trade secret.

 But they would only let their own people to learn of their knowledge of knowhow, and cultural gifts. The people of Ham who were brought over to the so-called New World of the Gentile people of their conquest, of what became known as the Americas, and the West Indies. Their customary ways of life before many of their ancestors were taken out of their forefather's lands, as slave's, was to express their feelings true music, songs, and dancing. Whether it was their love lives, suffering, or just plain happiness, signing, music, and dancing was a part of their everyday culture, and background, and ways of life of the people of Ham. So, that if someone was not a part of their cultural background, and did not have the understanding about the Hamite's people ways of life and culture. They would right away say that these people are a happy go lucky people, because we as a people of Ham, are always singing, and dancing. Most of the times, they do not know the real meaning behind the songs many of the people of Ham singing. I could remember when I was growing up as a little boy in the Island of Jamaica; many times, I would hear different people sings, because they were sorrowful at hearth. So, many people in the island would sign to cheer up their spirits, whenever they were sad. Many would also sing when they were working in the cultivated field, and this singing would give many of the Hamite's fieldworkers a sense of peace of joy, to help them to accomplish their work. This was a normal natural way of life for many Hamite's people in the land of Ham, of what became known as Africa. This was also the same in what became known as Jamaica, and what became known as the United States of America, or wheresoever the Hamite's people were taken as slaves. I myself many times I would sing whenever I was sad at heart, and this singing would eventually cheer up my spirit of sadness. It was the same way with many of the people of Ham, who were brought over from the land of Ham, to the land area that became known as the United States, to work on their Gentile European slave master's plantations, and forms.

Many of them would sing because of their sadness of heart, they were going through, because of their slavery experiences these wicked, and evil Gentile people of Europe, had put them true. This singing would cheer up their spirits, to help them to endure, and to carry on doing their work, under the wicked, and brutality hands of their Gentile slave masters. This singing of sadness gave birth to what was known as the "Negro spiritual music", that was so named by their Gentile European settlers, and slave masters of what became known as the United States of America.

This Negro music also gave birth to the Swing, Sole music, Gospels music, and what the European people of the United States, and Britain call as Pop music. Due to the fact that it came from out of their grief, sorrows, and their experience of suffering they were going true. This musical gift, was back up by the gift of their ancestor's culture, of music, of singing, and dancing. This singing of sadness was sometimes mistaken by their slave masters, that these people are a happy go lucky people, even in pain, and sorrows. Let us take Elvis Presley for an example, Elvis Presley grew up among the so-called Black people of the Memphis Tennessee area, and this music had an influence on Elvis Presley mind, and many other young Gentile European men, and women of his day. Elvis Presley like the music, and decided to become a singer himself, and as soon as Elvis Presley came on the music scene, they crowned him King of Rock 'n 'Roll, or King of the Blue, because they change the name of the music to Rock 'n 'Roll, during the Elvis Presley area of 1956, that came from the Blues. Their reason for doing so, they wanted to deceive many people of the world, who do not have any knowledge of how this music came about. This was for them to think that it was Elvis Presley, or some other Gentile European person of what became known as the United States, brought out this music. Technically speaking, the European settlers of what became known as the United States, became very envious, and jealous of the Hamite's people music. They would try their very best, to steal the music from the Hamite's people, by changing the name of the music, and giving the music different names, and different titles. This was the same way they have stolen the Hamite's people music of the United States, and gave the music a new title, and a new name, that is known today as the Country, and Western music. They the European people of the United States, have always showed, and given many people of the world the impression who watches their television programs, that Country, and Western music is that of a Gentile European music, that was started by some Gentile European people of the United States, or in Europe.

I used to listen to a radio station called the CBS Radio Station, of the New York, and the New Jersey area, and many times leasing to the station, they mention that one of the strategies many of the European radio station used to do, in the early fifties of the Rhythm, and Blues area. Whenever a Hamite person of the United States released a record, especially if it was a good record, they would make a copy version of the same record, by some other Gentile European singer.

They would not play the original version of the record on their radio station, but they would always play the copy version of the record. This was to give the listeners of their radio stations, the impression that the copy version by the Gentile European singer was the original version of the record. They would suppress the Hamite's people who wrote, and sing their songs from making a living from their own music, they had brought out from their sorrow, suffering, and grief. This was the same way with Pat Boon, and many other European singers of the United States. Another time I was listening to the CBS Radio Station on a Saturday evening, and one of their radio personalities from the station made the statement that Rock 'n 'Roll was started by Elvis Presley, during the early fifties. On another occasion, I was listening to CBS Radio Station in the Newark, New Jersey area, and they were playing a Hamite person record by the name of Bobby Day, that was recorded in the fifties. This record was done over by a British group by the name of the Dave Clark Five. They would always play the Dave Clark Five copy version of the record, but they would never play the original version of the record that was made by Bobby Day. The reason why the radio station did this, was to give their younger listeners of today the impression that it was the Dave Clark Five group who made the original version of the Bobby Day song, that was called "Over and Over Again." This is because the younger generation of today, would not have any knowledge that this record was recorded in the fifties by Bobby Day, because they weren't around in those days, and many of those singers are now decease. There is also another Rhythm, and Blues group from the fifties by the name of the Clovers; two of their songs were done over by a European American singer by the name of Bobby Vee.

On different occasion I was listening to the station, and I heard they were playing two of the Clover songs, that were done over Bobby Vee. They would always play the Bobby Vee versions, but they would hardly ever play the original versions of the Clovers record. The reason why the radio station would not play the original version of the record, it was to deceive the general public who listen to their radio station, to let them to believed that the Bobby Vee version was the original version of the Clovers songs. The two versions of the Clovers songs that I am referring to is call "Devil or Angel," and the other song is called "Blue Velvet" that was made back in the fifties.

The reason why many of these European people could afford to do these things that I have mentioned, it was because they were the ones who own the recording studios, the radio stations, and many of the times they were the managers of the various Hamite's singers of the forties and fifties, who made all the money from these Hamite's singers 'talents. Many of these radio station, and the mangers of the various Hamite's people music, made all the moneys from the Hamite's people music, and many of the time they the Hamite's singers did not really make as much money from their own music, as they did, and are still doing so today. In the Caribbean, and in many parts of the South American countries where many Hamite's people were taken as slaves, they gave birth to what became known as the Brazilian music. The Meringue, Tango, Rumba, Cha-Cha-Cha, and the music the European people called as the Latin, and Hispanic Music. In the Island of Trinidad, the Hamite's people who were taken there gave birth to what became known as Calypso music, that in many ways sound just like many of the so-called Latin, and Hispanic music of the various former Spanish, and Portuguese slave's colonies, and that of Brazil. I must also point out that the Hamite's people of the Island of Trinidad, gave birth to the Steal Ban drum music, that were made from out of old oil drums containers. In the Island of Jamaica, Rhythm, and Blues music gave birth to what was known as Blue Beat music, during the fifties. Later the Blue beat music became known as the Ska music that gave birth to Reggae music, that also came from what many people in Jamaica call as the Poco Mainan Spiritual church people of Jamaica. When I was growing up in Jamaica during the fifties, the music that was mostly played on the radio stations in that time, was Rhythm and Blues, and Calypso music. The Rumba, and Tango music came from the Hamite's people of the Island of Cuba, who were taken there as slaves.

I also want to point out that this so-called Latin, and Hispanic music did not started with the Spanish people of Spain, or with the various Arawak's, and Caribs people who was the natives of what became known as South America, Florida, and what became known as the West Indies of the Caribbean by Columbus. This so-called Latin music did not start with the real Latin people, who were the Romans. This Latin music was started with many of the Hamite's people who were taken to the so-called New Word, of the Spanish, and the Portuguese people as their slaves, and colonies of their New World, to learn things of their faith of wickedness and corruption.

This New World of the Spanish, and the Portuguese, were conquered from the Arawak's, Incas, Caribs, Aztec, Mayans, and other tribal natives of the area, that become known as the New World of the Americas, and the West Indies for the Gentile European people. This so-called Latin, and Hispanic music, and Brazilian music, did not started with the Portuguese people, who colonized, and take way the land area from the Arawak's and others various tribes who were living there, that they named as the country of Brazil. This Brazilian music did not start with the native Arawak's of Brazil, who Columbus, and other European people named as Indians. This Brazilian Music was started with the Hamite's people who were taken there as slaves. The Redeem, and the Blues, and the other various music I have mention, was not a part of the Gentile European people culture, and ways of life, as it was with the Hamite's people of Ham. So, when there were a session of singing, and dancing that was taking place in many of the so-called Black neighborhoods in the Southern part of United States. Many young Gentile males and females would go to many of these places to sit down, listen, watch and learn from these same Hamite's people whom they brutalize, and used like a tool. Walk upon, and spat upon, and called as Niggers. This word Niggers was taken from the Latin word Niger, that meant to the Romans, as dark skin people, that did also came down into the Spanish, and Portuguese dialect as Negro's, that become known as Black people. This Latin word Niger eventually, became known to the various Germanic people as Niggers, that really mean Black people to them, that was taken from the Latin word Niger. They the Gentile people of what became known as the United States, would go, and watch, and learn the technique of singing, and dancing from these Hamite's people. Many times they would try their best to copy the various steps of the Hamite's people music of singing, and dancing.

Many of the times they would show their own people on their television as the best dancers, and singers on stage, such was the case of Freddy Stair, and Ginger Rogers. Let us for a moment examine the dancing history of Freddy Stair, and Ginger Rogers, they often showed many times on their television, and in their movies as the best dancers on the stages. They did not tell their viewers that Freddy Stair, and Ginger Rogers used to go, and sit-down, watch, and learn from various Hamite's dancers, like Mr. Bow Jangles, the Mills brothers, the Nicholas Brothers, and many other Hamite's dancers who they used to sit down watch, and learn from.

My reason for mentioning these things about Freddy Stair, and Ginger Rogers it is because dancing, and rhythm, and music do not come naturally with many of the Gentile people of Europe, as it does come naturally with many of the people of Ham. So, for Freddy Stair, and Ginger Rogers to have the relative kind of dancing skills they showed them having on their television, and in the movies, I am quite sure they were taking some kind of dancing lessons from some Hamite's person of the United States, or they were watching some Hamite's person very closely. The reason why many Hamite's people have this kind of musical capability, it is because the Hamite's people in the land of Ham, their natural ways of life before many of them were taken out as slaves. Whenever they were sad, or happy, they would sing and dance, whenever someone visited their villages or town, they would sing, and dance to show a sign of welcome to these visitors or friends. So, this is the reason why the Blues, and Jazz that, gave birth to Soul music, and the Swing, was so good, it was because the Hamite's people, who were brought over to the United States, have suffered, robbed, and brutalize tremendously. Under the hands of these wicked Gentile European oppressors, and their slave masters. There was no place for them to run, so if they was to run to the left, they were there, and if they was to run to the right, they were there to give them nothing but pressure, and problems, so as to make their lives become miserable, and unbearable. So, the suffering of many Hamite's people of the United States was very great, and many of the times they would sing because they were sorrowful at hearth for what they were going true, and their expression of their feeling was through music, songs, and dancing.

Which was a natural part of their culture, that was passed down the line to them, by their ancestors true their blood line. What make their feeling came out so good, in music, songs, and dancing, it was because they were segregated into their own part of town. So, their roots were more stronger, and more bonded together then, then how it is in this diplomatically integrated society of the United States of today. Their rhythm, and their feeling, and their suffering, and their inner soul is what they all had in common. They also had more unity then, because they did need each other to survive in a system that was against them. They also had a little bit more of their ancestors 'culture back their then, than what many Hamite's people of the United States show to each other. Many of these Hamite's musicians, and dancers, became the entertainers to many Gentile European people of the United States, and also in Europe.

In which some of them were fortunate to make a lot of money from their Yahweh given gift, talent, and culture of their ancestor's music, of signing, and dance. Listening to the CBS Radio Station of the New York New Jersey area, many of the times, the disk jockeys would give their listeners of their radio station the impression that the Beetles, the Rolling Stones, and other British group, who came on the music scene during the Sixties, were the great singers, and musicians that did appeared on the music scene. The reason why the radio station gave this kind of impression, to their radio listeners, it is because they the European people have always tried to make out that their people are the best in everything that they do. What their radio audience did not know, and realize, and understand, is that the Beetles, the Rolling Stone, with other British group, who came about during the sixties, was because Britain itself was a dead place musically speaking. Their normal ways of life in the early fifties, and sixties, apart from many of them going to the bingo club, on a Friday and Saturday night, or the Opera Theatre. Some of the men, and women would go to the local pub bar to drink their liquor, and beer, and sing folk songs. They would also play the piano, and the harmonica, and drink their liquor, and beer, and many of the time started to fight among themselves. It was just like in many of the cowboy movies, of the 1800, during the Wild West of the United States, where they show many of these cowboys used to go to the bar salon, to drink their liquor, and bear. In many of these salon bars of the Wild West, there were piano players, and some would play the harmonica. While these cowboys were drinking their liquors, and beers, and listening to folk songs, and the piano playing, later they would start to fight, and kill each other for various reasons, or maybe the liquor tell them to fight, and kill each other. It was the same way in many of these pub bars of London, they would drink their liquors, and beers, and listen to the folk songs, with the piano, and harmonica playing, and then they would start to fight among themselves, especially the Irish men.

There were no other musical outlet, until in the fifties, and sixties when the migration of many Hamite's people, who left from Jamaica, and other Caribbean Islands that were under British rule ship, to go and work, and live in Britain. The reason why many Hamite's people migrated to Britain in the early fifties, and sixties from the West Indies, as it was so called by Columbus, and from other British colonies. It was because during World War II, Germany had caused a lot of damage to the British Isles, and they the British government wanted cheap laborers, from many of their various x-slave colonies, to come and work in Britain, to build up the economy of Britain.

This was by working and paying taxes, to the system, so as to built up the economy of Britain. Many Hamite's men who left from Jamaica, who had sound systems they used to play in various Rhythm, and Blues dancehalls, on most Friday, and Saturday nights in the Kingston area of Jamaica. They take along with them their sound systems, and their Rhythm, and Blues records when many of them migrated to Britain, during the early fifties and sixties. These sound system men, while they were living in Britain, used to have a lot of house parties, dancehall, and night clubs where they use to play their Rhythm, and Blues music on a regular scale, every Friday and Saturday night, just like when they were living in Jamaica. Many of these former sound system men, by their actions, cause Britain to come alive, musically speaking, where many young British men, and women would sometimes go to these places to learn how to dance to the Rhythm, and Blues, and Reggae music. Also to enjoy themselves in many of these night clubs, and dance hall.

Eventually, many of these night clubs that were later owned, and operated by many British people, would play Rhythm, and Blues, Soul, and Jazz music, although many of these British clubs, did not want to let any Hamite's people in to their clubs. These sound system men, and their Rhythm, and Blues music, and the various clubs, whether they were owned by Hamite's people, or by British people, gave birth to what became known as the Beatles, Rolling Stones, and many other British groups of the sixties. Although they the British people, did adopt to the music of Rhythm and Blues, Soul music, and Jazz, yet there is no comparison to that of the sound of the Hamite's people music, to that of the British music, that was copy from Rhythm, and Blues music.

The same thing is true for Holland, and Denmark, when I was living there in the sixties, many of the clubs I went to, the music that they used to play, was that of Rhythm, and Blues, Soul and Jazz music, but many of the various club owners, would not let any Hamite's people into their clubs. I must also mention that many of these British fellows who had formed their musical groups in the early sixties, were former Teddy boy's gangsters, who used to fight against many Hamite's people, who were coming into Britain from many different parts of their colonial slave ports. I must mention that the way the Gentile Europe people are, if they did possess these kinds of musical, and dancing skills like that of many Hamites people.

We the people of Ham, would have to pay them taxes, get beat up, and go to prison, if we were to go to their clubs, to listen to their music, watch them dance, and learn from them. As they came, and learned from us, without any problem, and anyone getting beat up, or getting kill, or go to prison, to listen to their music.

I would like to let many of my Hamite's people to know that Gospel music that many Hamite's people of the United States associated as a form of their music, come from the word Gospel. Which the word Gospel was taken from (Matthew Chapter 24, and verse 14), where Yashua spoke to his disciples about the Gospel, or the preaching of the Kingdom of Yahweh will be done, before the world as we know it as today come to its end. This Kingdom of Yahweh will eventually take over ruler ship of this world, from these worldly political systems, that was established by Satan the Devil, through these Gentile people of Europe. This is by way of their conquest of people, and their lands, they did established, true slavery, and colonialism to get rich. So, wheresoever these Gentile European people went and conquered, and set up their political system of ruler ship, of corruption, immorality, and wickedness, they had left on many of their captive people minds, as way of life, as it is today. My reason for mentioning the word Gospel, it is because may Hamite's people of the United States used the word Gospel music, without understanding the real meaning of the word Gospel, apart from associating it with their music. This Negro Spiritual music, also became known as Gospel music, because they were singing from their inner sole, of what they came to know about Christianity, and the church, that was back up by their ancestors singing, and dancing from the land of Ham. This Gospel music is also a form of worship to Yahweh, because in the churches, they learn about signing hems, and spiritual songs, to the worship of Yahweh, whom many of them were thought to believe as Yashua, who became known as Jesus, and Christ is the great God of the universe, who came in the form of the flesh.

(Psalm Chapter 66, and verse 1), there it mentions, make a joyful noise of singing unto the Lord, which this Lord that Psalm is speaking of, is Yahweh who is the Lord. So, what Psalm is saying that we people of Yahweh must make a joyful noise of singing all you lands, to Yahweh, which is speaking of all the people of His creation, and the worshipers of His name. So, this is what true Gospel music means, to sing praise, and worship to Yahweh, and to glorify His Holly, and wonderful name, as the creator, and sustainer of our lives. Although one is not certain of the actual starting date of when the Negro Spiritual music was started in the United States, as it was called back there then, that gave birth to many others form of music of today.

According to the volume 6 of the Encyclopaedia, it mentions that there was a plantation brass band that were form, as early as 1835, in what became known as the United States. The Encyclopaedia also explained that there was a Ragtime music that was the forerunner of Jazz music. As far as I came to understand, the Hamite's people of the United States started Jazz music in the New Orleans area, when at the time there were no Hamite's people who had any recording companies of their own. The Encyclopaedia explained that the first American Jazz band were that of a European American Jazz band, that was called the Dixieland Jazz Band, and they started to record their music in 1917. According to this same volume 6 of the Encyclopaedia, New Orleans was a city that had a long history of interracial mixture, or better put the melting pot people of the Gentile European people, of what became known as the United States. The Gentile people will always use their integration philosophy, to come in to us their captives people, to wash us out into their melting pot of different shade of people. They would always sit down, eat, and drink with us, and learn all they can learn from us, and when the time is right they will take over whatever we as a people had started, and called it their own. If one should dig deep into the history of United States, they would come to the reality, that it was the Hamite's people of the United States from the days of slavery, to the sixties, and beyond, who were the entertainers to many of the Gentile people of the United States, and Europe, by singing, and dancing to give them entertainment. As I have mention before that Latin was the language the ancient Romans spoke, and I am quite sure they did not know anything about this so-called Latin music of today. I am also quite sure, that there is no written record of history, stating that the Romans had a music that was called Latin music, as many people of today were thought to believed.

As a matter of fact, the ancient Romans were a warlike people, who knew nothing else but to make war, to shed blood, to seek power, and to control many people, and their lives, and their lands like that of the rest of their Gentile brothers, and sisters of today. The Spanish are brothers and sisters to the ancient Romans, because they were all sons, and daughters of Japheth, who was the last son of Noah. Moreover, they were all ruled, enslaved, and controlled by the Roman people of Rome. This is the reason why many of the language of Europe are known as the Romance language, because their education came from the Romans, and also from the Greeks, whom many of them were rule and enslave by.

I must also point out that many people in our modern world of today, don't even know that many of the modern musical instruments, that one might see in the various musical stores, that is also shown on their television, were create in the land of Ham by many Hamite's people who were there. Although many of us Hamite's people of today do not have any knowledge of these things, yet our Gentile European enslavers, who have miss-educated us, did not teach us, that when they went to the land of Ham to conquer there, they saw all of these musical instruments that were made by the local Hamite's people. That is used in the modern world of the Gentile people of Europe of today. They have taken many of these musical instruments, and modernized them into the form that many people see them as today, as a part of their industries. Musical instruments like the drum, the trumpet, the guitar, the tambourine, the flute, the banjo, tambourine, and many other musical instruments that many musicians play today, were taken from the land of Ham, by the people of Europe. If one should read (Numbers Chapter 10, starting from verse 1), there they will see Yahweh instructed Moses to build 2 silver trumpets. These trumpets were to be made for the blowing of the gathering of the people of Israel, when they were going true wilderness, toward the land of Canaan, the land of promise. Notice that the people of Israel had their beginning in the land of Canaan, also in the land of Mizraim that they came out of, and they were also scattered among the Babylon people of Nimrod for not pleasing Yahweh. So, all the children of Isreal knowledge of craft, and skills of making this or that came from Yahweh, and also from the land of Mizraim that became known as Egypt, where they came out of as a nation of people, from the many granddaughters of the people of Ham.

Today the people of Ham have given birth to many different forms of music, that one might hear playing in different parts of the world, due to the fact that wheresoever the people of Ham were taken as slaves, they take along with them their musical skills of signing and dancing. I would also like to mention that if one was to check out the deep root of the Opera music, that is known today as the Italian music, one might be very surprised to find out that this music may have also came from many Hamite's people who were living, and taking there into the land area, that became known as the Italy. This is because during the time of Hannibal war, with the Romans, there were quite a few Hamite's people who were living there in the Italian land area, also after the invasion of Hannibal, and even before the Romans conquest of the land area that became known as Italy.

There were also many Carthaginian people, who were acquainted with the land area of Italy, way before the coming of the Romans, who came and take over the land area, from the various natives who were living there. According to volume 20 of the Encyclopaedia, there it explained that the Phoenician people, and the people who are known today as Egyptian people, their alphabetical writing system was found among the Etruscan tribe. Who were a part of the various natives of the land area, of what became known as Italy. This was way before the Latin people of Anneas came along, and settle, and conquered the land area, that became as a Roman territory. According to volume 20 of the Encyclopaedia, there it stated that king Caere who was a king of the Etruscan city of Etruria, and in the city of Pyrgi use to be a worshiper of the Phoenician goddess Astarte. This just goes to show the connection the people of Ham had with the land area of what became known as Italy, long before the coming of the Romans. This time was way before the Romans came, and conquered the land, that became known as the Roman province, of Italy, that were taken from the various natives, who were living there before they the Roman came, and conquer the land area. So, this just goes to show that the people of Ham were always in touch with the land area, that became known as Italy.

This time was way before the powers of the various kingdoms of the people of Ham of the so-call Middle East, and what became known as North Africa, came to their end, by way of the various colonial conquerors, that Yahweh did used to bring about the down fall of these many kingdoms of the people of Ham. Many Hamite's men were also in the Roman army, during the period when the Romans take over ruler ship of Sicily, from the Carthaginian, who had three quarters of the island of Sicily under their ruler ship. The Greeks also had the other quarter of the island of Sicily under their control. This was before the Roman take away the island of Sicily from the Carthaginian, and also from the Greeks. Reading from the Greco-Roman history of volume 20 of the Encyclopaedia, I did not recall where it mentioned that during Roman time, there was such a music that was known as Opera music.

So, this Opera music must have come much later, after the breakup of the Roman Empire. Volume 20 of the Encyclopaedia mentions, that the people of Carthage were also allies to the Romans before they were conquered, and destroyed by the Romans. This was way before the Romans became strong, and conquered the city of Carthage, and killing 150,000 of the Carthaginian people, and take away 50,000, of the rest of the Carthaginian, that were left alive as slaves to what became known as Italy, and they also, burn the city of Carthage to the ground. The name Italy came about by the conquest of Napoleon Bonaparte, during the 1800, according to the reading of the Encyclopaedia Britannica. So, it is quite possible that the Opera music could have also come from the Hamite's people of Ham, who were taken to Italy as slave. Just in case someone may ask the question, where have all those Hamite's people have gone, who used to live in the land area that became known as Italy, and Sicily? To answer this question, I must say that many of those Hamite's people, who used to live in Italy, Sicily, Corsica, Sardinia, Spain, and even in what became known as France, have totally melt out themselves into the melting pot of the Gentile people of Europe. They have become a part of the European family of their melting pot people, of today. According to volume 9 of the Encyclopaedia Britannica, the Carthaginian people built a city in the Island of Sicily, that was called Palermo, or Panoramas in the 8th century BC. This city of Palermo, or Panoramas became a Carthaginian settlement, until the Romans captured this city from the Carthaginian people in 254 BC. Which became a part of the Roman Empire of Sicily. The Carthaginian people were also the ruler of the Island of Sardinia, and the land of Tarshish, that became known as Spain. This way before the Romans take over Spain, as a part of their colony, and pushed out the Carthaginians. The people of Carthage also had a city in France that was known as the city of Marseille France.

This was before they were defeated by the ancient Romans, and were taken as their captives, and slaves. The Romans took over the various cities of the Carthaginian people of the Mediterranean area, also in Europe that they, the people of Carthage had under their control of ruler ship. I must also explain that I am not writing about music specifically, to encourage the people of Ham to keep on going to night clubs. Dancehall, house parties, and rum bars, like so many Hamite's people of today like to do, and call it "having a good time. Many of these so- call good times, we have copped from the Gentile people of Europe, that they have spread to their colonies worldwide, as a way of life, that their many captives have copped from them, and it became a way of life, for many Hamite's people. These so-call good times, abets, are of worldly pleasure, and destruction that is of Satan the devil.

The Scripture condemn, many of these Worley pleasure, that many of the people of Ham, of the ancient world were involve with, that have brought the civilization of the people of Ham to destruction. Because many of the people of Ham love too much pleasure of distraction, that is of devilism. (Proverbs Chapter 21, and verse 17) explained that a person, who love pleasure, and who live for pleasure, shall be a poor man. (It is also stated in (Proverbs Chapter 9, and verse 13) that a foolish woman is glamorous, she is simple, and knows nothing. Sad to say that many of our Hamite's sisters of the United States, the Caribbean, and also of the land of Ham, have fallen into this category of living for pleasure, and carefree lives. That will eventually lead to destruction by Yahweh. They have inherited some of these things, such as liquor, rum bars, and carefree living from their Gentile European captures. Because many of these things I have mentioned, was a part of their custom, and way of life in Europe, before many of them left from their Gentile land of Europe, to go out and conquer many people, and their lands. Many Hamite's people of today, especially in what became known as the United States, just live for dancing, partying, drugging, and drinking their lives away, without any Yahweh consciousness, of their lives, as if to say that is all they are living for. They don't realize that we as people must give an account to Yahweh, and Yashua, for everything we have said, and done in this life, whether it is good or bad. Although music, and dancing is a natural part of the life, and culture of many Hamite's people. But in my opinion, there is only one thing a person can find in many of these places I have mentioned above, and that is UN Yahweh like qualities, and devilism, immorality, and finally, destruction from Yahweh of Himself.

Sad to say that too many of our Hamite's people, especially here in what became known as the United States, the land of Ham, and in many of the South American countries, and the Caribbean love to spend their lives living carefree living. Without any consciousness of Yahweh, and His Laws, and His principles that is recorded in the Scripture, as Godly lives, for a person to live by. The Scripture is the book of life, and the guideline, of how one should live their life to please Yahweh, for now, and for the future to come. These were some of the very things why many of our early, and ancient civilization, and the kingdoms of the people of Ham did not remain until our present time, because many of the people of Ham of the ancient world, lived UN-Yahweh lifestyle, that did not please Him, that was translated as Un Godly lifestyle.

This is due to their actions that did not please Him, that have caused many of our people to be dispersed out of their lands, to be scattered around the world true slavery, and colonialism. The Scripture is there to support me, on many of the things I have mention, about many of the early people of Ham, who were living in the so-called Middle East, and what became known as North Africa, before the Scripture was given to the ancient children of Israel. My main reason for writing about the historical part of our music, and dancing of the people of Ham, it is to set the record straight, of our musical heritage, that so many people have tried to steal away from us, the people of Ham, and call it their own.

The Scripture explained that the ancient people of Mizraim, and many other Hamite's people of the land of Ham, and Canaan used magic as way of life. I would like to let many people to know that magic is associated with sorcery, which is witchcraft, and separatism. When the word separatism is used, it is not speaking about the Holy Spirit of Yahweh, but what the Scripture is speaking about is the spirit of the Devil, and his angels, who were cast out of heaven, to the vicinity of the earth that is known as the spirit of the demons. These angels were spirit creatures of Yahweh heavenly army of His solders. One can read (Revelation Chapter 12, and verse 7, through to verse 10) to get a good understanding about Satan, and his angles, who were cast out of heaven to the vicinity of the earth, and who became known as the demons. There it explained about the dragon, who is known as Satan the Devil, who was a high-ranking angel, and who were put out of heaven, with his angels, who did follow him, in his devises. These angels are known as the demons, who were put out of heaven to the vicinity of the earth, who did follow Satan in his doings. Magic is also associated with witchcraft, and sad to say that, wheresoever the people of Ham were taken as slaves, they continued to practice this ancient Egyptian art, as a way of life against each other. To prove my point that what I am saying about the ancient magicians of Egypt is true.

One can read (Exodus Chapter 7, and verse 11), there one will see that Yahweh told Moses that when he goes before Pharaoh, he should cast down his rod before Pharaoh, and is rod or his staff would become a snake. So, when Moses cast down his rod before Pharaoh, his rod turned into a snake. Pharaoh called for his wise men, which in today's time these men would be called as scientists, although a scientist of today could not do the things that the magician, or wise men of ancient Egypt did. According to (Exodus Chapter 7), when these wise men, or magicians of ancient Egypt cast down their rods, or staff before Pharaoh to the ground, their rods became serpents. However, the snake of Moses 'rod swallowed up the snakes of the magicians of Egypt, because it was the power of Yahweh who was behind the snake of Moses rod, while it was the power of the devil that was behind the magician's rods of ancient Mizraim, that became a snake.

I have read from a book, that is called, The Complete history of Tutankamun, of his treasures of the land of Mizraim, that became known as Egypt. This book is by Nicholas Reeves, that was publish by Thames & Hudson. This book explained that when Lord Carnarvon, and Howard Carter open the tomb in 1922, of King Tutankamun, who had died for about five thousand years. It causes the course of the king to come on all those people who was involve in disturbing the king tomb. Due to this disturbance of the tomb of Tutankamun, it has causes to take the life of some of these men family member, who had nothing to with disturbance of the king tomb. In all it took the life of about thirty of these people, one after another, that they had call as the curse of Tutanhamum. So, this documentary of history that I read, Just goes to show how much the people of Mizraim, who became known as the Egyptian people, was so much wrap up in sorcery, and which craft, that became known as magic. Idolatry worship, and wish craft has cause the down fall of many of the various kingdoms of the people of Ham, to be taken over by other people. Who came up after our civilization, and became powerful, and enslave many of us, that has cast our destruction, and our down fall, of today. So, wheresoever the people of Ham were taken as slaves, to the so-call New World of the Gentile people of Europe, they continued to use these same practices of witchcraft against each other. This is because of their slavery mentality, jealousy, envy, covetousness, and stupidity, that many of them have against their own people.

Not wanting to see their own people to become more successful in life, and have more wealth than themselves. Sometimes many of these foolish Hamite's people use witchcraft to get even with another Hamite's person that they dislike. The funny thing about this, many of these foolish Hamite's people, who practice witchcraft against each other for various reasons, don't seem to have any problem whenever they see other set of people, doing better than themselves. Getting richer from their business support, that many of them would not even give to their own people, who has businesses in their localities. But when they are in needs, and are looking for a helping hand out, the very first people they would look to run to for assistant, is their own people, because the people of Europe, and other people, would not give them the time of the day. Much less to give them a handout, because they take care of their own people, and look out for each other, which is only a natural thing to do.

The kind of mentality that many Hamite's people have toward each other, is when they see another Hamite's person trying to better his, or her life, right away it becomes a problem of jealousy. But they don't seem to have any problem when they see the Gentile people of Europe, and other set of people, they give all their business support to, doing better than themselves. The people of Europe do not have this kind of mentality to each other, like many Hamite's people do have toward each other. They will not leave their own people to come and give us their business support, because many of them are not as stupid, and foolish, like many of our Hamite's people, who would do these things. They the people of Europe know that charity, which means love, start at their home first, meaning that one must love oneself first, and look out for their own people benefit, and interest first, before they can extend their love, or charity to other people. This action of looking out for each other first comes naturally among the animals, and other set of people, but when it comes down to the Hamite's people, it is a different ball game of stupidity. They would rather look out for other people, more than to look out for their own people, because many of them, are suffering from slavery mentality, stupidity, and inferiority complex. (Matthew Chapter 12, and verse 25), there Yashua said that every kingdom divided against itself is brought to desolation, and destruction, and every city, or houses that is divided against itself shall not stand, but fall. The same thing is true for us Hamite's people of of today, because we as a people are so divided amongst ourselves, and don't have any charity for each other. So, we cannot stand, but fall all the time, and many other people use us, and our talent for their own benefit, and gain, as a tool for them to get rich from our talent, and things we possess. The people of Europe, and other set of people, make sure that their charity, which mean love, begin at their home first, look out for their own people, and maybe they might give us some consideration, that is if Yahweh should speak in their hearts for them to do so.

The Gentile people of Europe, and other set of people don't mind getting our business support, because they live from off us, and use us to their own advantage and benefit, and gain to get wealth. So, we are like a feeding tree for them to make money from us, whether it is in music, sports, dancing, or whatever Yahweh given talent many of us Hamite's people might possess. We are the feeding tree that the Gentile people, and other set of people feed upon, and to become wealthy. They would never give us the time of the day, if it was left up to them alone, they would make sure that all their business support, and their wealth stay among their own people. They might give us some consideration, again that is if Yahweh was to speak in their hearts for them to do so. I can remember when I was living in Amsterdam, and Denmark in the sixties, many times I would go to look for rooms, and I would see sign saying, EUROPEANS ONLY. It was the same way when I went looking for work in Amsterdam, and Denmark, when they see me coming toward their office, to inquire if there was any vacancy of employment. I would see many of them waving their hands as to say, "Don't come, we don't need you here." When I put the laughter's behind me, and finally reaches their office, and asked if there was any vacancy, I was told by them, "we are very sorry, you cannot work here." So, the Gentile people of Europe, and other set of people, look out first for each other in everything they do. The only time they would give us a chance, and that is if they could make money for them doing so for their own benefit and gain, otherwise it would never happen. If it was a Gentile European person who go to a Hamite's company, for employment, they would have never gone through the experience I went through in Amsterdam, and Denmark. That Hamite's employer would treat this Gentile European person with such kindness, and respect. They would right away give him the job without any problem, whether he was qualified or not, but when it comes down to the various Hamite's people of today, they would give their support to anyone else, but their own people. Because as I have said, that they are suffering from slavery mentality, and stupidity, but when their back is against the wall, and in needed of a helping hands, the very first people they would turn to seek run to for help, is their own kind of people, because the other set of people, would not give them the time of the day.

It was the same way with many of the taxi drivers in Amsterdam, Denmark, and London when I was living there, many of the taxi drivers would rather leave a Hamite's person, who has been standing for hours looking for a taxi. But as soon as a Gentile European person come along, he or she would right away get a taxi without any problem of waiting for a long time. It was the same way when these Gentile European people came, and conquered this so-called New World from the various natives who were living there. They would made sure that their conquered lands was for them, and for their fellow Gentile people of Europe only. Although one might see many of these people fighting, and killing each other, for colonial conquest, of people, and their lands.

Yet when the smokes of the guns disappear, they would come together, and form a union of European powers, sharing their stolen wealth among themselves. The only time they would let some of us, their conquered slave people into their conquered society, that is when they need cheap labors, to come in, and work for them, to pay taxes, along with other various court fines, to build their up their economical system. I must also point out that I am grateful to the Gentile people, to have opened their doors of their establish conquered societies, to allow many of us their former slave people to come in and work as cheap labors. From different parts of their x slaves colonies, although it was to their own advantage, and glory to gain wealth. By so doing, it has help many of us, their conquered people, to come in and worked, to better our standard of living, and to learn many things in the process. In which many of my ancestors before us, did not have these opportunities like many of us have today, compare to how it was, after slavery was abolish. Leading up to the fifties, and sixties, when many of us their x slave people were living in poverties, without any form of employment to better our standard of living. It has also helped many of us their former slave people, to acquire various skills, and wealth that many of us did not have before. So, because of these skills, many of us was able to find good paying jobs, in their established societies to better our standard of living. In process, we also must give thanks, and parse to Yahweh, for the open of these doors of opportunities, that many of us still do not have today. Because if it was left up to the Gentile people of Europe alone, we would be still in slavery, and might have become an extent set of people by now. The same is true when many Gentile people left from Europe, to go and conquerors many Hamite's people, and their lands, they would make quite sure that their conquered lands belong to them, and other Gentile people of Europe only.

Who come to their conquered lands as distinguish guests, to share the wealth of the land among themselves. The various Hamite's people who became their captives, and servants, did not even have the right to walk in their own Yahweh given land, without being harassed, and brutalized by their Gentile European Kuku Cult Clan police force system. That was set up, and design for the protection of their own people against their conquered slave people. It was the same way when I was growing up in my early boyhood days in the island of Jamaica, in the fifties, many Hamite's people of Jamaica could not go to the various beaches, and hotels. It was mostly for the Gentile people of Jamaica, and other Gentile European tourists who come to the island to enjoy themselves, and to spread their corruption to the minds of their many captive people, who were living there on the island. I would like to also point out, that witchcraft, or sorcery of the people of Ham, has taken on different names depending on wheresoever our ancestors were taken as slaves. In Jamaica witchcraft is known as Obya. In Haiti it is known as Voodoo, and in British Guyana it is known as Obya, and in many other places it is known as Black Magic. I also came to the understanding that in the southern parts of the United States, witchcraft and Black Magic is known as roots. I am not quite sure what it is called in many other countries where other Hamite's people were taken as slaves. I am not trying to single out the people of Ham to be the only witchcraft workers, because many other set of people practice it too. Including many Gentile people of Europe, who indulge in divination, or observation of time, that is known today as astrology. I would like to point out that astrology began in the land of Mizraim, and in Babylon among various Hamite's people of the area, that were spread to other places around the world where many Hamite's people were taken as slaves, and continue to practice witchcraft among themselves. The Scripture also mentions about people who indulge in consultation with familiar spirits, that is known today as palm readers, and others who call themselves psychic people. The meaning of the term psychic people, is a person who is working, or doing things through the power of the spirit of the devil; that is not of the Spirit of Yahweh. The people who work by familiar spirits, or have familiar spirits, that call themselves palm readers, or who call themselves fortunetellers, are doing these things through the spirit of the devil, and his demons. The term familiar spirit means, a person who worked, or do things true the spirits of the demons, that is not of Yahweh Sprit, because only true the Spirit of Yahweh can miracles be perform, because man by himself cannot perform any miracles.

Many Gentile European people in what became known as the United States of America, practice witchcraft in the form of Halloween, Dracula movies, and psychics, and palm readers, which is also a part of separatism of the demons. Frankly speaking, magic, witchcraft, astrology, and fortunetellers was all started with the people of Ham, in the land of Mizraim, Babylon, and also among many of the Canaanites people of Canaan. The practiced of witchcraft, and astrology, the Scripture called it as stargazing, and observation of time. It is also stated in (Deuteronomy Chapter 9, and verse 4), where Moses told the children of Israel when they came from out of the land of Mizraim to go and take over the land of the Canaanite people, that it was not because of their own righteousness why Yahweh gave them the lands of the Canaan. But it was because of the wickedness of those Hamite's nations, who was living there. I would like to say that although many Hamite's people have washed out themselves, and are now looking like many Gentile people of the land of Europe, many of them continue to use witchcraft, in different ways. (Deuteronomy Chapter 18, and verse 10, to verse 12, also (Revelation Chapter 21, and verse 8), there it is stated that such practice as witchcraft, and sorcery, is abomination to Yahweh. And anyone who is practicing, or indulges in such things, will not inherit the Kingdom of Yahweh that is to come. I would also like to say, that there are many Hamite's people of the United States, who have helped to advance some of these modern technological skills, and knowhow of United States, but what benefit did their kind of people received, from their advancement, nothing?

This story was taken from a book I have written, that is called the War like people of Japheth, who became known as the Romans. The power structure of the Mediterranean was between the Hamite's people of Carthage, who had three-quarter of the Island of Sicily under their control, and the Greek who had the other quarter of the Island of Sicily under their control. This, was before the Roman became strong, and take over the island of Sicily, from the Carthaginians, and also from the Greeks. Also, the power structure of that time was with the people of Carthage, the Greeks, and the Etruscans, who had control over the Mediterranean area, before the Roman became strong, and takes over control of the Mediterranean from Carthage, the Etruscans, and the Greeks. The people of Carthage also had the Island of Corsica, Sardinia, Spain, the Anatolia area of Turkey, Cyprus, and a part of France as their colonies. This was way before the Romans up and became powerful, and strong according to the dream of Nebuchadnezzar that is mention in (Daniel Chapter 2, and verse 33). About the iron leg, that stud for the power of Rome, who was to come up, and have dominion over the earth, after the fall of Greece to Rome. Reading from volume 20 of the Encyclopaedia, there it explained that Etruscan power structure in the Italian land area did not continue because of the invasion of the Celtics barbarians, who invaded, and settled in PO valley area, of Italy, and destroyed many of the Etruscan civilization.

The Etruscan control of the city of Campania was also destroyed, in the late 5th century BC, by an Italian tribe, who were known as the Samnite tribe of the land area of what is now known as Italy. According to volume 20 of the Encyclopaedia, in the 4th century BC, the Italian peninsula take on a different face with that of the Umbrian- Sabellian tribe of Italy, who did control a good part of Italy. The Greeks of the city of Syracuse of Sicily, also had various colonies in different part of Italy, that was a part of the power struggle of Italy. Also with that of the new power of Rome, that was also taking shape. In the 4th century BC, the new power structure that takes over the Italian peninsula from the Etruscan, and the Greeks, was that of the power of Romans.

In the 6 century BC, in the reign of an Etruscan kings, who was ruling over the city of Rome, the city of Rome gain a deep Etruscan blue print of economic from the Etruscan people, before the Romans came and conquered the land area. Such as technology, arts, religion, and politics, as a ways of life, that became a part of the Roman society, that also came under the control of the Latin people. All though the city of Rome was now under the control of the Latin people, yet the city of Rome could be called the city of the Etruscans people. Because of their economic development, art and technology that they left behind to the Romans. While the city of Rome was growing under the power of the Latin people, there were constant rivalry between the various cities of the Etruscan, and that of the Romans. The city of Rome came under the attack of two Etruscan cities, that were known as Vulci, and Clusium. But in the 5 century BC the Romans reach out to their Latin communities, and form a Latin league, which Rome was the head of this Latin league. The city of Rome, and this Etruscan city, by the name of Veii had a constant border clashes, that lasted for at least one hundred years, until the city of Veii was finally defeated by the Romans in 396 BC, and became a part of their rulership. After the Romans defeated the city of Veii, they push themselves toward another Etruscan city, by the name of Etruria, and for another hundred years there was constant war between this Etruscan city and the Romans, until they were all conquered by the Romans. While Rome was getting strong, some Etruscan cities were able to hold on to their self-rule for a while, with their own government, and their own religious activities, and culture. Until 90 BC, when the Romans extended citizenship to all the various conquered tribes of the Italian peninsula.

While the Romans was growing in strengths, and power over the southern part of Italy, they were also becoming a Mediterranean power, that they and the Carthaginian were on good friendly term. The Romans went and capture, a part of southern Italy, that were known as Tarentum, and left a part of their army to oversee things there. The authority of Tarentum realize that they was dealing with a serious colonial problem, with that of the Romans, so they decided to appeal for help from King Pyrrhus of Epirus, of Greece, to bring the Romans to a state of reasoning. King Pyrrhus decided that this plea for help, was a good opportunity for him to use the occasion to unite the Greek Hellenistic cities of southern Italy, as a strong bond against the new advancing power of Rome. King Pyrrhus sent out an army of men, and elephants, that were able to defeated a Roman army, on two different occasions. This defeat of the Romans, was between 280- 276 BC, but the king victories over the Romans was short live, because when the king and his army went back to Epirus the Romans were able to defeat the Greek cities of Tarentum, and bring them under the alliance with that of Roman rules, and laws in 271 BC. By the time of the 3rd century BC, the Romans became the masters of the Italian peninsula, and was growing to become the new power of the Mediterranean. To take over from the Etruscans, the Carthaginians, and the Greeks. According to volume 20 of the Encyclopaedia, in 306 BC, the Romans, and the Carthaginians renewed their peace treaty of alliance before the big outbreak of hostilities came between them and Romans. The last peace treaty they, the Roman, and the Carthaginians sign, before they had their first big showdown of war. Was based upon the understanding that Carthage must not inter fair with the Roman rule over Italy, likewise, the Romans must not interfere with the Carthaginian rule ship over their part of the island of Sicily, or their ruler ship over of the island of Sardinia, Corsica and Spain. But after the treaty was sign between Carthage, and Rome, who were former allies of each other, for over forty years after the agreement between the Romans and Carthage was signed, the Romans continue to interfere with the island of Sicily. Volume 20 of the Encyclopaedia explained that many of the people of Italy, who were conquered by the Romans, came under Rome rule ship. They were given a certain amount of flexibility of diplomacy that was pleasing to the Romans. The population of the Latin colonies was made up of a people who were known as the proletarians, who were given duties to clear the conquered colonies of the Romans, and to bring the captured land under cultivation for the Romans.

Due to the vast colonial conquest of the Romans, the economy of the city of Rome develops rapidly, and they sorted to establish a Roman currency, to suit their wide colonial, and commercial empire. The war with King Pyrrhus of the city of Epirus, gave rise to the first Roman silver coinage, before the first Punic war with that of the country of Carthage, and the Romans. The city of Rome became a commercial city, competing with the Greek Hellenistic world, and that of Carthage. According to volume 9 of the Encyclopaedia, there it explained that the word Punic is a Phoenician writing that was developed by the Phoenician people of Canaan, and became known as Punic, and Neo-punic alphabets that came from the Phoenician language. This Phoenician writing that was develop, was used by the Berber tribe community of what became known as North Africa, until about the time of 6th century AD. Volume 20 of the Encyclopaedia, explained that the two first Punic wars with the Romans, and the country of Carthage came about because the Roman desire was to safeguard their conquered land area of Italy, from Carthage and Greece. The Carthaginian had control of a large part of the Mediterranean area, they also had three quarter of the island of Sicily, under they control, from the country of Carthage. The country of Carthage was located in the northern part of the land of Ham, now known as North Africa, and this was before the Roman became strong. The first Punic war between the Roman, and Carthage came about in 264-241 BC, because of a dispute that was taking place in a part of the island of Sicily, that was known as Messina. The city of Messina was near to the foot part of Italy, that was under the control of the Greek city of Syracuse of Sicily. When looking at a map in volume 20 of the Encyclopaedia, showing the island of Sicily and Messina. So, what cause the outbreak of the first Punic war between the Romans and the country of Carthage, was because of a band of mercenaries 'solders who left from their city of Campania of Italy, and who were employed by the city of Syracuse. These solders deserted from the city of Syracuse, and went, and occupied Messina, that was near to the city of Syracuse. Heron II who was a Greek ruler of the city of Syracuse put a blockaded around the city of Messina in 264 BC, but when the band of mercenaries' solders realizes they were hard press by the army of Heron, they appeal to Rome, and Carthage for help. The Carthaginian army arrived first, and takes position of Messina, and open negotiation with Heron on the behalf of the mercenary's solders.

The Romans also sent in their army later, after the Carthaginian took charge of the situation. But the Roman general who arrives on the scene, did not check out the situation of what was taken place there in the city, and he did not introduce himself properly to the officers of the Carthaginian army. But instead detain the general of the Carthaginian army. Due to the action taken by this Roman general, put Rome and Carthage at war against each other. The Greeks of the city of Syracuse gave their support to the Carthaginian against the Roman army.

Due to the action the Roman general took, creates a joint combination force, of the Carthaginian, and the Greeks of Syracuse, who went and attack the Romans in the city of Messina, which the army of the Romans were able to drive back this combine force of the Carthaginian, and Greek solders.

In 263 BC the Romans put to gather a strong army, and invade the city of Syracuse, and force Heron to seek peace with Rome, and to form an alliance with them. So, In 262 BC the Roman alliance army with that of Heron went into the Carthaginian part of the island of Sicily, and captures a city that was known as Agrigentum. But this Roman alliance army was not able to push out the Carthaginian from their various cities of the western part of Sicily, that were still under their control. In 260 BC the Romans built their first large fleet of battle ships, to battle with the Carthaginian, or any other opposing enemies. In an area of the Tyrrhenian Sea, near the land area of Italy, at a place that was known as Mylae, that is on the northern part of the island of Sicily, that were control by the Greeks. A Roman general by the name of Gaius Duilius defeated a Carthaginian navy fleet there. This defeat of the Carthaginian navy fleet gave the Romans the opportunity to put a Roman army on the island of Corsica, that was under the control of Carthage in 259 BC. The Roman was also able to expel the Carthaginian from the island of Corsica, but they were not able at the time to push out the Carthaginian out of the island of Sicily. In 256 BC, a big Roman navy fleet was sent out, and they defeated a Carthaginian navy fleet off the course of an island, that was near to Sicily, that was known as Cape Ecnomus. This place was not too far away from the country of Carthage, that was on the western part of Sicily, that was under control of Carthage. The Hamite's people on the land of Ham near the country of Carthage could not stop the invading force of the Romans from invading their land area of Carthage. The people of Carthage became very disturb of the invading force of the Roman in their land area. After a battle confrontation with the Romans, the authority of Carthage decided to seek for peace with their enemy, the people of Rome.

The terms for peace that a Roman general by the name of Atilius Regulus put on the people of Carthage were very severe, and unjust, and it was not accepted by the people of Carthage. Under the advice of a Greek captain of mercenary's solders, by the name of Xanthippus, who also had war elephants. He helps the Carthaginian to put together a very strong army to fight against the invaded army of the Roman. In 255 BC, this Carthaginian army of men, and elephants, that was under the command of Xanthippus, went to challenges Atilius Regulus to battle, with his army of elephants, and men. But Atilius Regulus, and his Roman army take up their position near their base of Tunis, to battle with the Carthaginian army, that was under the command of Xanthippus. But the bulk of Xanthippus Carthaginian army was destroyed by Atilius Regulus.

The Romans sent out a second fleet that reaches their base in the land of Ham in Tunis, and this fleet of the Roman navy was able to destroy a full Carthaginian navy fleet off an area that was known as Cape Hermaeum, that became known as Cape Bon. After the various defeat of the Carthaginian navy, and their army, the Romans turn their attention to completely push out the Carthaginian out of the island of Sicily. So, that the island of Sicily would be totally under the control of Rome. In 254 BC, the Romans set out themselves to do just that. They captured a strong Carthaginian city by the name of Panormus, that was in the Carthaginian part of the island of Sicily, but the Carthaginian was not able to send in reinforcement into their part of Sicily. So, that the war between them, and the Romans in Sicily came to a standstill for a while. In the time of 251-250 BC, a Roman general by the name of Caecilus Metellus forth a pitch battle with the army of the Carthaginian in Sicily. Near the city of Panormus that put an heave losses on the Carthaginian army. With this loss of some of the Carthaginian army in Sicily, cast them to lose a few more of their cities in Sicily to the Romans. But the Carthaginian still had a few other cities and basis in Sicily that they held on to for a while. In 249 BC the Romans came back with a decisive navy force, to put an end to the Carthaginian in Sicily, but the Carthaginians were able to strike blow for blow with the Romans, causing the Romans to lose 93 of their ships. By the time of 242 BC, the Romans start back their operation by sea to completely get rid of the Carthaginian out of Sicily. So, from private moneys from citizens of Rome, the Romans were able to put together 200 fleets of new war ships. These new war ships was to battle with whatever forces the Carthaginian could put together against them. The Carthaginian were able to put together a relief force to battle with that of the Romans, off an island that was known as Aegates, but many of their ships were cart in a disadvantage position, that causes many of their ships to sink, or to be capture by the Roman navy fleet.

Hamilcar Barca was made a general of the Carthaginian army in Sicily in 247 BC, according to volume 20 of the Encyclopaedia, but the Carthaginian lost most of their territory of Sicily to the Romans, except for an area in Sicily that was known as Lilybaeum. According to the Encyclopaedia, this place became known as Marsala, and Drepanum, and Trapani, where Hamilcar Barca was able to carry out a guerrilla war fare against the Romans, and capture Mount Ercte, in 247/246-244 BC, and also Mount Eryx. From this strong position he was able to give the Romans a hard time, and he was able to carry out a navy operation against the Romans in Sicily, and southern Italy. After the defeat of the Carthaginian navy fleets in 241 BC, by a Roman general who was known as Gaius Lutatius Catulus, Hamilcar Barca decided to make peace with the Romans, and ends the war in Sicily. The victory of the Romans over the Carthaginian gave them the opportunity to master the sea, and the surrounding area of the Sicily, and what they name as North Aprica. After the Carthaginian defeat of 241 BC they decided to open negotiation with the Romans for peace, and to give up the island of Sicily, and the Lipari Islands to the Romans. According to a map of volume 20 of the Encyclopaedia, showing the islands of Lipari, that was also known as Eolie islands. These were a set of little islands that is near the southern part of Sicily, close to the foot part of Italy. For the peace treaty with that of the Romans, the Carthaginians also had to pay the Romans a tribute, or a war tax of 3,200 talents of gold. After the first Punic wars of 241 BC with the Romans, cost the Carthaginians to lose their navy supremacy to the Romans. Due to the loss of the Carthaginian navy supremacy, cost them to lose their dominance over the area of the western Mediterranean to the new power of Rome. There were some discontent between the Carthaginian, and their mercenary's solders on their island of Sardinia, and because of this situation that was taken place there on the island. In the eyes of the Romans, this issue between Carthage and their mercenary's solders, was a breach of the war treaty they had established between themselves, and Carthage. Due to this breach of treaty, that the people of Rome accuse Carthage of, they decided to send in a Roman army to occupy the island of Sardinia. The Carthaginian mercenaries 'solders were ready to surrender the island of Sardinia to the Roman army, but Carthage was very much in opposition of the surrendering of the Island of Sardinia to the Romans. Due to the Carthaginian opposition to the Roman on their island of Sardinia, the Roman declare a state of war with Carthage, and take over the island of Sardinia, and the island of Corsica as their provinces.

'The loss of the Carthaginian navy fleet, and much of their army to the Romans, left them with no choice, but just to accept the loss of their islands, and whatever war penalty of taxies they the Romans feel to put on them as a form of punishment for losing the war to them. Although the Carthaginians lost their navy fleets, and most of their army in defeat to the Romans, yet the people of Carthage were able to find a new hope in Hamilcar Barca, after he ended the war with the Romans, and leave the island of Sicily to them. The government of Carthage sent Hamilcar Barca who was the father of Hannibal to the land area, the Scripture described as the land of Tarshish, now known as the land of Spain, and Portugal to establish a base there. In the mine of the Carthaginian government, this new base in Spain would give them a new wealth, and a new army to take the war to the Romans in their conquered land of Italy, to make up for their loss of their army, and their navy to the Romans. Also, the loss of their island of Sicily, Sardinia, Corsica, and other islands of the Mediterranean to the Romans in the first Punic war. While Hamilcar Barca was in Spain, he was able to establish a city that was known as Acra Leuce. The modern name of this city is now known as Alicante where he was able to make an extensive conquest in 237-229-228 BC. According to volume 5 of the Encyclopaedia, Hannibal was born in 247 BC, in the land area the Romans name as North Aprica, that became known as North Africa of Carthage. According to volume 20 of the Encyclopaedia, the story about Hannibal came from these two writers, by the name of Polybius and Livy. Who had the Latin information about the early life, and death of Hannibal before he was taken to Spain by his father, and his invasion of Italy. According to the information that the Roman had gathered, about Hannibal, he was taken to Spain by his father at an early age. His father made him swear to him before his death, that he would take the war to the Romans, in their conquered land of what became known as Italy. Hamilcar Barca was killed in a battle of war, in 229 BC in Spain, and after his death his work was carryon by his son-in-law, who was known as Hasdrubal, and by his son Hannibal after the first Punic war. Before the death of Hamilcar Barca, Hasdrubal became the commander chief, of the Carthaginian army of Spain, but Hasdrubal was assassinated in 221 BC, by members of the Carthaginian army.

Hannibal was made general of the Carthaginian army of Spain in 221 BC, and his command was approved by the army. After Hannibal became field marshal of the Carthaginian army, he went and make sure the Carthaginian grip on Spain was very strong in the interest of Carthage. Hannibal also went and get married to a Spanish princess by the name of Imilce, and then he began to conquer many Spanish tribes. Hannibal fought against a Spanish settlement that were known as Olcades, and he was able to captured the capital of this place, that were name as Althaea. Hannibal also went and captured another Spanish tribe, who was known as the Vaccaei people, who were living in the north western part of Spain in the time of 221 BC. When Hannibal captured the Vaccaei people, and their surrounding area, he named the seaport area as Cartagena, or Carthage Nova, and made there the capital base for of his Carthaginian army. Hannibal also won various victories over another Spanish tribe who was known as the Carpetani, who was living in the Tagus River area of Spain. In 219 BC Hannibal went and attacks a Spanish city by the name of Saguntum that was located south of the Ebro River. In the first Punic war of 264-241 BC, between the Romans and Carthage, the peace treaty that was established and put on Carthage, was that the Ebro River area of Spain must be free from Carthage domination. Because the Romans, and many of the people of the Ebro River area was on good friendly term. The way the Romans saw it, Hannibal attack on the city of Saguntum, was an act of war against Rome itself. The Romans at once sent ambassador to Carthage as a form of protest, against Hannibal action in the city of Saguntum. But Although the Romans protested against Hannibal action of the war of the city of Saguntum, yet they did not send in any of their army to help the people of Saguntum to fight against Hannibal and his army. After the city of Saguntum fell to Hannibal, the Romans demanded from Carthage the sunder of Hannibal to them. But when the sunder of Hannibal did not take place, as they demanded from Carthage, the dissatisfaction of the Romans started the second Punic war, that was carried out by Hannibal himself, on the behalf of Carthage against the Romans, on their own soil of what became known as Italy. In 219-218 BC, Hannibal spent the winter at the Carthaginian base in Spain, peppering to take the war in the heart of the Roman conquered land of Italy. Hannibal march his army true the area, the Romans named as Gaul, taking his army toward Italy, and leaving his brother Hasdrubal in command of a large army at their base in Spain. This was to defend Spain, and what became known as North Africa from any Roman attack.

According to volume 5 of the Encyclopaedia, Hannibal crossed the Ebro River area in April, or May of 218 BC, and he marched his army into the Pyrenees of what is now known as France, before the Romans had any knowledge of his action. According to Polybius, who was a Roman writer, when Hannibal crosses the Pyrenees with his army that consists of 90.000 solders, that were marching on foot. 12.000 solders who were riding on horse back, and quite a few war elephants that were met up with a stiff resistance from a tribe of the Pyrenees area, of what is now France. This opposition was from some local tribe men of the Pyrenees area, plus the desertion of some of his Spanish solders greatly reduced the size of his army, but he was able to reach the Rhone River area without allot of opposition, from the local tribe of southern Gaul of Switzerland. A Roman General by the name Publius Cornelius Scipio, learn of the movement of Hannibal, and he rush his army in the Rhine River area where he got the information about Hannibal traveling. But when Scipio, and his army reaches the Rhine River area, he was told that Hannibal, and his army already crosses the river, he and his army was marching toward the northern part of the river bank moving toward the Alps mountainous area going toward Italy. So, Scipio realize that he had miss the crossing of Hannibal, and his army over the Rhine River area. So, he decided to return to the northern part of Italy to wait for Hannibal, entering the land of Italy.

According to volume 5 of the Encyclopaedia, Hannibal used boats to crosses the river for him, and his men. But he made platform raft that was made from a plant weed, that was known as coracles, that was grown in different parts of Europe, to float the elephants on. According to the Encyclopaedia, this plant weed was also known as the coracles, that was grown in Gaul by local tribes that was known as commandeered weed. From this weed, boats, and raft was made, as well as wood, at the time. The raft that Hannibal made, and used to float his elephants on, was known as Jetties, by the local people of Gaul. Hannibal also put his horses on large boats, or just made many of them to swim across the river. During the operation of Hannibal, and his army, and animals crossing the Rhine River, there on the other side of the bank, an hostile tribe of Gaul, who was in opposition to the crossing of Hannibal, and his army passing true their territory.

Hannibal sent out a small army under one of his general, by the name of Hanno, to cross far up stream of the river, and to attack these hostile Gaul men from behind them. After the crossing of Hannibal, and his army, they were received by another friendly Gallic tribal leaders, who was known as the Boii, who had a deep knowledge of the Alpine mountainous area. By Hannibal meeting up with these friendly tribes of the Alps, turnout to be a blessing for him, because they knew their way true the Alps. Hannibal and his army crosses the Durance River, which flowed into the Rhine, and an area that was known as the island, where it was fertile, and populated. On this island there were a civil war that was taken place between two brother tribes.

When Hannibal and his army arrived on the scene, of this civil war, one of the elder brothers asked him to help them to solve his war problem, against the other brother tribe. In return for his help they did supplying him, and his army with food. Hannibal was very appreciated for the offer of the food, and supplies for him, and his army. After he, and his army has been traveling for the pass seven hundred, and fifty miles, for four months after leaving their Carthaginian base in Spain. After Hannibal help to solve the war problem with this two-brother's tribe, they left from the island of these two brother tribes, going toward Italy. A dangerous situation came from a Celtic tribe who was known as the Allobroges who role down big stone from high hills, and attack the rear of Hannibal animal train, causing both men, and animals to lose their balance, and fall to their death. After the incident, Hannibal went and captures a Celtic Gaul town, and made them to supply him with food, men, and other necessities for his army. After Hannibal left from the Celtic Gaul town, going true the Alps toward Italy, snow was falling making the partway of his traveling very dangerous. What make it even more treacherous, on the ground there was frozen ice that were there from the previous snow fall, that causes animals, and men to slip, and fall into fresh pile of snow. There were also landslides that block the narrow pathway for the animals, and the army that they were traveling true, that held up the army for a few days until the part way was cleared. Hannibal and his army was traveling for the past five months, after leaving their Carthaginian base of Cartagena Nova in Spain, with only 20.000 of his foot soldiers, and 6.000 men who rode on horse back. Also, only a few of the thirty-eight war elephants he had, when he left from Spain.

Hannibal and his army at last end up in the PO valley area of the Roman conquered land of Italy, after they went true all the various difficulties of the climate of the Gentile land of Europe. Traveling true the Alps and experiencing the various Celtic Gaul's barbarian people, who had tried to sabotage his army with various ambush. Also of the difficulties in commanding a multiracial army of different nationality, and languages that was not fed properly. Marching on their way towards Italy, they finally entered the PO valley area of the Roman conquered land that became known as Italy, by way of the conquest of Napoleon Bonaparte of France, during the time of 1800. When Hannibal and his army enter the PO valley area, they met up with a hostile tribe who was known as the Taurini, in which Hannibal attack the town of this tribe of people, and defeated them in battle.

After Hannibal and his army defeated this tribe of the PO valley, and was marching his army into the northern part of Italy, he met up with the Roman army of Publius Cornelius Scipio, who rush his army into the PO Valley area to protect the newly conquered colonial territory, of northern Italy from the army of Hannibal. The first clash between the army of Hannibal, and the Roman army of Scipio take place in an area west of the Ticino River area, where Hannibal Carthaginian Numidian force was able to stand their ground, against this vast army of Roman soldiers in battle. In this battle between the army of Hannibal, and General Scipio, Scipio was badly wounded, and his army retreated to the city of Placentia of the northern part of Italy. After various plans of Scipio fail to have another battle engagement with the army of Hannibal. The Romans decided to put together a combine army of General Sempronius, and the army of Longus, and what was left of the army of Scipio, to fight against the army of Hannibal. The army of Hannibal met up with the combine army of these Roman generals, on the left bank of the Trebia River south of the city of Placentia. This combine army of these Roman generals was severely defeated, on December of 218 BC. The victory of Hannibal army brought over to his side both Gaul's, and Celtic Ligurian tribe of northern Italy, to fight against the Romans. Hannibal army was made up of Celtic Gaul's, as well as many other Hamite's tribes from the area that became known as North Africa. After Hannibal army defeated the combine force of the Roman army that was sent out against him, he was able to defend his army against another Roman army that was under the leadership of Gaius Flaminius, at a place that was called Arretium.

Due to Hannibal wits, and skills, he was able to force Gaius Flaminius, and his army into an open battle engagement with him, and as the army of Flaminius was passing between the areas of the northern shore of Lake Trasimene where Hannibal, and his army were hiding to make the attack on Flaminius army. Hannibal moved his army from out of their hiding place, and attack, and killed thousands of Flaminius solders, and the remainder of what was left of his army, he force them to run in the lake, and many of them drown in the lake. The Romans sent out a reinforcement of about four thousand men, riding on horseback, under the command of Gaius Centenius, but this reinforcement was also attack, and destroyed by Hannibal and his army before they could get to joined up with the rest of the other Roman soldiers. Although Hannibal, and his Carthaginian army of different nationality were very victorious over the Romans in battle, yet Hannibal did not march his army on the capital of Rome. He claims he was too weary to take the war to the center of Rome, from where all the decision making of the land area of Italy came from. As for Hannibal himself, he had vain elusion, hopping many of the native people of Italy, who were conquered, and came under the ruler ship of Rome would joined up with his army, to fight against their oppressors, the Romans. By so doing, he was hoping it would lead to a civil war against the Romans. While the going was going good for Hannibal and his army, he did not march his army on Rome, but instead spent the summer of 217 BC resting at a place in Italy that was known as Picenum. But later he went and attacks the city of Apulia, and the city of Campania. Quintus Fabius, and Maximus Cunctaor did not allow their armies to have any sort of battle engagement against the army of Hannibal. But suddenly in the summer of 216 BC, Hannibal moves his army toward the southern part of Italy, and seized a large army supply at a Roman base, at an area that was known as Canne. After the Roman defeat at Canne, many of the Roman allies of the land area of Italy started to break away from the side of the Romans, and gave their support to Hannibal, and his army. The Romans, and Hannibal war at the city of Canne of Capua should have brought about the finial end of the war in Hannibal favor, because he had the Romans totally in this a ray, and had them running for their lives. Although Hannibal had all the support of the native people of Italy on his side, and the war against the Romans was in his favor, yet, he still did not move his army to march against the city of Rome, to attack the Roman headquarters. But spent the winter of 216-215 BC in the city of Copua. After Hannibal have been messing around, and taking it easy, his army started to lose control of the war of Italy, and the Roman started to get stronger. The Romans put together an idea, that was brought up by General Fabius into action, this idea of Fabius, was for the Roman army to defend those cities of Italy, who was loyal to the city of Rome.

Also, for their solders should try to recover whatever territories they could recapture from Hannibal, and his army whenever the opportunity present itself for them to do so safely. Many of those cities that fell into the hands of Hannibal did not fight with him against the Roman army, but some of them kept him inform of the activities of the Romans. Hannibal realizes to himself he did not have the vast amount of men, in his army, like that of the Romans, to spread out his army to cover a wide area, so he used caution, and attack when it was necessary to do so. Volume 5 of the Encyclopaedia explained that the army of Hannibal was not supported by the Government of Carthage, because the Roman navy forms a blockage in the sea area of Italy, and except for the capture of the city of Tarentum in 215 BC, the army of Hannibal gain minor victories over the Roman army. Due to the lock of support, and reinforcement Hannibal did not get from Carthage, in 213 BC, the city of Casilinum, and the city of Arpi that was captured by Hannibal in 216-215 BC, was recaptured back by the Roman army. By the time of 211 BC, Hannibal had to force himself to march his army toward the city of Capua, to free some of his men, who was trap by Roman soldiers. Although Hannibal, and his army was three miles away from the strong defense city of Rome, he did not make any attempt to march his army on the city of Rome. The city of Capua fell back in the hands of the Romans, in the same year of 211 BC. In the same year of 211 BC, the Greek colony of Syracuse of the island of Sicily fell in the hands of the Romans, and became their colony of Sicily, which giving the Romans complete control over the island of Sicily. By the time of 209 BC, the city of Tarentum that is in the southern part of Italy, fell back into the hands of the Romans. According volume 5 of the Encyclopaedia in, the mind of Hannibal, he was waiting around southern Italy, hoping to join forces with his brother Hasdrubal who he had left in charge of the Carthaginian army of Spain, but his hope was in vain. Volume 5 of the Encyclopaedia, explained that while Hasdrubal was in charge of the Carthaginian army of Spain, he tried his best to have complete domination over the Spanish land area, that was in opposition to the Romans. He also fought for seven years against the Roman army of Publius Cornelius Scipio, and the army of his brother who was Gnaeus Scipio.

In the summer of 217 BC, on the Ebro River, in an area that was known as Tarraco, Hasdrubal fleet of ship was destroyed by a surprise attack from this two brother's Roman armies. In 215 BC, the army of Hasdrubal, and Scipio had a battle confrontation at a place in Spain that was known as Dertosa which was a city that was located on the bank of the Ebro River. The Carthaginian army of Hasdrubal suffers a heavy loss in this battle with the Scipios, and four years later, the Carthaginian army of Hasdrubal recuperates from their defect, and came back, and put heavy losses on the Roman army of the Scipios, killing him and his brother, and drove the rest of the Roman army from most of Spain south of the Ebro River.

The younger son of Publius Cornelius Scipio, who was age twenty-five at the time, when he was put into full command of the Roman army of Spain. He arrived in Spain in 210 BC, and made a sneaky attack on the Carthaginian base of Spain. In 208 BC, the army of young Scipio was able to defeat the Carthaginian army of Hasdrubal, at a place in Spain that was known as Bacula. Hasdrubal was able to escape with much of his army, and enter the northern part of Italy in 207 BC, with nearly the size of Hannibal army, when he enters Italy in 218 BC. Hasdrubal was hoping to join up with the army of his brother, who was waiting around southern Italy to meet up with him, for them to march on the city of Rome. The army of Hasdrubal was made up of Celtic Gaul's, and Ligurian tribe men, as well as Hamite's men from what became known as North Africa. According to volume 7 of the Encyclopaedia, the Ligurian people came from northeastern Spain, of what is now known as southern France, and from the northwestern part of Italy. These Ligurian people was a member of the Celtic people, that stretch from Ireland all the way to the Baltic Sea area of Europe. The Romans who were under severe pressure, both from the heavy loses of their solders in battle, and from a financial drain of money, but they were able to put together an army under the generalship of Gaius Nero. Nero came to understand that Hannibal would not move his army further than the city of Apulia, until he was able to make some contact with the army of Hasdrubal. Nero were able to slip away with a part of his army, and went to reinforce another Roman army that was under the leadership of Levies who was engaged in a battle with the army of Hasdrubal in the northern part of Italy. While this battle was taking place between these two Roman armies, and the army of Hasdrubal, Hannibal had no idea that his brother was already there in the Italian land area, fighting against these two Romans Generals.

This combine force of the Roman army were able to put the army of Hasdrubal in a difficult situation, and forces his army to fight them openly on the bank of the River Metaurus. Unfortunately, Hannibal was nowhere around to assist is brother in this battle with these two Roman generals. Nero came on the sideline of Hasdrubal army, and cut off his retreat, and Hasdrubal was killed in this battle, and the rest of his army was destroyed. Many of the Greek communities of southern Italy who were loyal to the Romans, along with other Latin communities, held some of Hannibal men as prisoner for the Romans.

So, Hannibal came to learn of his brother death, when Nero orders the head of Hasdrubal to be cutoff, and throw in Hannibal camp. So, Hannibal came to realize that his brother was already in Italy, and was killed in battle. For several years Hannibal was able to resist the wrath of the Romans, because of the support of his allies of southern Italy, and because the Romans were exhausted from the losses of much of their men, and from financial strain of the war. Hannibal some how, came to the knowledge, that young Scipio gave his army the opportunity to leave Italy, without any action taken against them by the Romans army. Hannibal also came to the knowledge, that Carthage chief allies, who was the country of Numidia, now known as Morocco, and

Algeria, left from the side of Carthage to become a new ally of the Romans, that was led by Prince Massena of what is now known as Morocco. So, in 203 BC the Carthaginian army of Hannibal took the option that was given to him by Scipio, and he left from Italy, to go and help his country of Carthage who was left alone to fight against the Roman army of Scipio by themselves. When Hannibal went back to Carthage, he was accused by his countrymen of mishandling the war in Italy, against the Romans, and the Carthaginian Government did not right away put him back as a general of their army, but instead gave him the position of a civil magistrate. While Hannibal was given the position as a civil magistrate, he was able to use his position to overthrow the ruling Government of Carthage, and brought about new changes in Carthage. After a while Hannibal became very unpopular with cretin other political faction of Carthage. The Romans and Philip the fifth of Macedonia, also had a war engagement in 214- 205 BC, and due to the war engagement with Phillip, the Roman was further forced to stretch out their severely drain army to the area of Greece. But the Romans, and Philip were able to come to some peace treaty, and finally, the Romans was able to keep a Roman fleet in Greece. This was to maintain a patrol in the Adrian Sea, so as to keep an eye on Philip activity.

The reason why the Romans maintain a fleet in the Adrian Sea, was to prevent the army of Hannibal, and Philip to join forces together to fight against Rome, when they were at their weakest point. In this time of the Roman history, the food situation of Italy was not as plentiful as before, so the Romans had to turn to their colonial islands of Sardinia, and Sicily to make up for their food supplies to satisfy their needs. The Carthaginian control of Spain gave the Romans a sense of feeling, that any Carthaginian control of Spain, was like they were controlling the Italian land area itself. So, in the eyes of the Romans, they must do their very best to get reed of the Carthaginian out of Spain for good, by so doing, the country of Spain would be under their control. Rome also realize that from the country of Spain came a large amount of money, and solders that did go to reinforce the army of Hannibal. So, it was in their best interest for them to challenge the Carthaginian control of Spain. The Romans army under the leadership of young Scipio, was able to drive out the Carthaginian out of Spain in 206 BC, and there after Spain became a Roman province of territory. In 205 BC young Scipio return to Italy in his triumphant victory, of pushing out the Carthaginian army out of Spain, and to fallow up with his victory to take the war to Carthage.

Young Scipio went to the Senates to gain their approval for him to take the war to Carthage. At first the Senates was very reluctant in giving their approval, because of the dread of the image Hannibal, and his army left upon the people of Rome mine. Hannibal who was now in Carthage, made the Romans even more afraid to give their approval to young Scipio, to take the war to Carthage, that it might cost him his life, at the hand of Hannibal, and his army. But young Scipio was able to convince the Senates to give him their approval, because he and the rest of his army were able to defeat, and push the Carthaginian army out of Spain. Finally, the Senates gave their approval to young Scipio for him to take the war to the Country of Carthage. So, you Scipio went to the island of Sicily, and built up a strong army there, and in 204 BC, and he left from Sicily, and sail to the land area of Carthage. In the land area of Carthage Scipio, and his army was met with a combine force of the Carthaginian army, as well as the army of King Syphax of the country of what became known as Morocco. But the army of Scipio was stop on the shore of Utica where in the spring of 204 BC he was able to set his army free from the position they were pin down. When Scipio were able to remove from their location of the shore of Utica, he went, and made a surprise attack on the army camp of King Syphax, and his Carthaginian allies. The Roman attack on the combine force of Carthage, and King Syphax army brought about a total defeat of King Syphax army, who was Carthage strong ally. King Syphax was strip of his throne, and he became a prisoner at Rome.

After King Syphax was made a prisoner by the Roman army of Scipio, Scipio put Prince Masinissa as the new ruler of Numidia. Prince Masinissa had fought against the Romans in the army of Hannibal in the Second Punic War of 218 BC, in Italy, who suddenly became a traitor to his own people of what became known today as Morocco, and Algeria, whose land area, was very close to the land area of Carthage. According to volume 7 of the Encyclopaedia, Prince Masinissa was born in 240 BC, and died in 148 BC. He was a son of a chief, from the Massyli tribal group of what was known as Numidia, during Roman time. Prince Masinissa was brought up in the land of Carthage, where his father was a close ally of Carthage.

After the Romans defeated the combine force of the Carthaginian, and King Syphax of Numidia, the people of Carthage was able to put together a new Carthaginian army in 203 BC, and this army was also destroyed by Scipio, and his new ally who was Masinissa in an area that was known as the Great Plains. After the various defeats of disaster that Carthage experience with the Romans, they decided to seek for peace with Rome. But the severity for peace that Scipio put on Carthage, they decided before they accept his term for peace they would recall Hannibal, who was now a magistrate in Carthage, and put him over what was left of their Carthaginian army to fight against Scipio. Also, against Prince Masinissa, who was now an ally of Rome, as their finial try, and to break off their negotiation with young Scope. Hannibal was put in charge of the Carthaginian army in 202 BC, and the army of Scipio with their ally of Prince Masinissa, meets up with Hannibal army of mercenary solders, from Italy, as well as from North Africa in a place that was known as Zama. The army size of Scipio foot solders, was a little smaller in size than that of the army of Hannibal men, and war elephants. But the army of Scipio was well trained, and his men that were riding on horses, was more in numbers than that of the army of Hannibal. Scipio foot solders was able to escape the attack that was made by Hannibal war elephants, and they was able to break true the first center line of Hannibal army reserve. While Prince Masinissa was fighting alongside with Hannibal, in the war with the Romans in Italy, he remembers the funny tricks Hannibal did, while he was fighting against the Roman at the city of Canne, in Italy.

Where Hannibal was able to destroy thousands of the Romans, and send them running for their lives. Masinissa decided to use some of these same tricks of Hannibal against his army, and by so doing, he was able to destroy the rear part of Hannibal army reserves. Hannibal lost 20,000 of his men in this battle with Scipio, and with Prince Masinissa himself. But Hannibal himself was able to escape from the army of Masinissa, who was pursing after him. As for Hannibal himself, he was able to escape from the hands of Prince Masinissa, and the army of Scipio, of the defeat of the battle of Zama. This defeat of Hannibal at Zama haunts him for the rest of his life, and his hope of taking up arms against the Romans lived on in his mind. After Hannibal was able to escape from Prince Masinissa, and the Romans, he was able to survive from been captured by the Romans.

But he was somewhat rejected by the local ruling authorities of Carthage, of the way he handle the war against the Romans in Italy. While Carthage seek for peace, and did accept the peace term Scipio put on them, Hannibal was expose to the Roman by some of his countrymen, that he was encouraging Antiochus 3rd of the land of Zidon, that became known as Syria, to take up arms against them. The Romans at the time did not yet conquered the land of Syria, to be under their control, it was still under the kingdom ruler ship of the descendant of Seleucids Nicator I, who was one of the Generals of Alexander the Great. Who took charge of a part of the so-call Middle East, where Antiochus 3rd came from his linage, who was the ruler of Syria at the time of Hannibal, and the Romans. So, Hannibal became aware of what was told to the Romans, so he fled to Ephesus, which was also a part the Seleucids kingdom, that Antiochus had ruler ship over, of what is now Turkey in 195 BC. When Hannibal arrived in the city of Ephesus, he was first welcome by Antiochus III, because he himself was getting ready to have a war with the Romans. But when Antiochus thought about the way in which Hannibal conducted the war with the Romans in Italy, Hannibal became an embarrassment in his site, and he lost favor with him. Although Antiochus was not very favorable with Hannibal; he made him captain of a fleet of ships he had, that was in various Phoenician cities, of what became known as the Middle East. Hannibal was not very experience about navy affairs, and the Romans were able to defeat the fleet of ships that was put under his command. In a place that were known as Pamphylia, that is now a part of Turkey, finally the Romans was able to defeat the army of Antiochus in 190 BC, and one of the condition the Romans gave to him for peace, was that he most turn over Hannibal to them. Again Hannibal somehow learns of the term the Romans gave to Antiochus for peace with them. So, when Hannibal became aware of the Romans demand, concern him, he was able to escape from the kingdom of Antiochus, and fled to the kingdom of King Prusias, of the country of Bithynia, that was also located in the Anatolia area of what is now Turkey, near to the Russia border line.

This knowledge of the geography land area that I have explained about, is by looking at the map of the Encyclopaedia, and comparing the map of the Encyclopaedia, with that of the world map of today. Hannibal took shelter with King Prusias, who at the time was fighting a war against one of Rome allies, who was known as King Eumenes II of the city of Pergamum, of the land area of what is now Turkey.Hannibal joined the, war and fought on the side of Prusias against Eumenes II, but the Romans also joined themselves to the war, and fought on the side of Eumenes II, as their allies against Prusias, and Prusias was defeated. One of the demeaned the Roman put on Prusias for peace, was for him to turn over Hannibal to them. Hannibal somehow became knowledge of the Roman demeaned from Prusias concerning him. Hannibal was tired of running, and hiding from the Romans, so he decided that it was time for him to end his life, and to set himself free from the fare of falling into the hands of the Romans. So, Hannibal poisoned himself in the country of Bithynia, and died in a village that was known as Libyssa, in the time of 183 BC. So, Hannibal died in the land of Turkey, before the destruction of his country Carthage by the hands of the Romans in 147 BC. The people of Carthage lost their army, and decided to seek for peace, and to accept the peace term Scipio put on them. The peace term Scipio put on Carthage, was for them not to have any dealing with the land of Spain, and they also must give up all their Mediterranean islands they had under their control. They were also compelled by Scipio, that they must turn over to Rome all their war ships they had left in their position, and they must pay a war penalty of 10,000 talents of gold within fifty years. Scipio further demanded from Carthage that they must give up their independence in all war affair, and their overseas affairs. Carthage was very serious about keeping the peace treaty the Roman put on them, but in 201 BC, Carthage and King Masinissa, of what became known as the country of Morocco, had a hostile territorial dispute. In the eyes of the Romans, this dispute between King Masinissa, and Carthage, Carthage break the peace treaty in taking up arms against the country of Numidia.

Moreover, many of the people of Rome who were in the commerce business, and some Senators became very jealous of the prosperity Carthage was making in their business of commerce. Due to this jealous feeling of the people of Rome, and some of their Senators, the order was given that the country of Carthage must be destroyed. The Roman sent out a Roman army to destroy the country of Carthage, and despite the people of

Carthage was ready to give up hostages, and surrender all their weapons to the Romans for peace. They was force by the Romans to take up arms to defend themselves. To add to the insult, and the pressure the Romans put on the people of Carthage because of pure jealousy to show their power over CartThey further order the Carthaginian Government they must pack up, and move to some other location in the land area of Ham, where they would be barred from donning any form of business. When these statements were made to the Carthaginian people, they made a desperate last effort to made new war equipment to fight against the Roman army of Publius Cornelius Scipio in 149 BC. The Romans attack the city of Carthage for two years, and completely slathering the people of Carthage as they go along, until in 147 BC, the new command was given to Scipio Aemilianus, who was the adopted grandson of Publius Cornelius Scipio. Who was the former conqueror of Carthage. Aemilianus made a blockage of a narrow wall around the city of Carthage, to cut off all their overseas supplies, and he attacks the main entrance of the city where there was no way out. The slathering did not stop until Aemilianus was able to capture from house to house, and from Street to Streets. Volume 20 of the Encyclopaedia explained that according to the estimation of this writer by the name of Strabo, the population of Carthage before the mascara, was about a 225,000 people. But after the end of the slathering, there were only 50,000 people who were left alive, and the 50.000 was sold into slavery, and the city of Carthage was burn to the ground by the Romans. The Encyclopaedia explained that some of the land area of Carthage was taken over by Prince Masinissa, and a part of the land area of Carthage, was given the name of Thenae that became known as Tunisia of today. The Roman province of Numidia, and what became known as Tunisia, with the rest of their conquest of the north of the land of Ham, was given the name as North Africa, that did take its name from the Latin word North Aprica.

After the Carthaginian defeat at Zama, in 202 BC, Rome became the strongest power of the Mediterranean world. Had it not been for fulfillment of the prophecy about the coming up of Rome, of Nebuchadnezzar dream, of (Daniel Chapter 2). Also, of the prophecy of Daniel vision of Chapter 7, and verse 7, about the coming up of Rome), that had to be fulfill. Hannibal would have destroyed Rome, and all the Gentile people of Europe would have been ruled, and control by the people of Carthage, instead of the Romans. Also, all the Gentile land of Europe would have been speaking the Carthaginian language of today, rather than the Latin language of the Roman, where all the writing of many of the countries of Europe came from.

This writings ability of Europe also came from the Greeks, that originally came from the writing of the Hethites, the Phoenician and the people of Mizraim, who became known as Egyptian people, that did spread to the rest of the people of Europe. Due to the Roman conquest over the Gentile land that became known as Europe, this is the reason why many of the writing of Europe, is found in Latin, and Greek. The Roman writing also came from the Greeks, of the Troy Turkey area of Europe, that also came from the Hethites, and Phoenician people of Ham. The Romans took over power from the people of Carthage that they were able to conquer, and destroyed, because of the said prophecy of (Daniel Chapter 2, and Daniel Chapter 7, and verse 7). Hannibal also had many Celtic Gallic people, in his army fighting against the Romans in Italy. Neither Hannibal, or the Romans had any knowledge of the prophecy I have mention above, that did shapes the outcome of the war between Hannibal, and the Romans. Neither the various Gentile European people of today, who came from out of the brake up of the Roman Empire of Europe, had any knowledge of the prophecy I have mention above. Which did had an impact on the war between the Romans, and the Carthaginians. Yashua mention in the Scripture, at (John Chapter 10, and verse 35), that the prophecies of the Scripture, that were spoken by Yahweh, true the prophets, and that of Yashua, and that of his Apostles, cannot be broken, but shall surely come to pass. So, due to the prophecies I have spoken of, this is the reason why Hannibal made, so much mistake in Italy, and did not march his army to make a full end of the Romans, otherwise the prophecy about the Romans would not have been fulfilled. After the Romans conquered, and destroyed Carthage they move their effort toward conquering Greece, of the various kingdoms of the generals of Alexander the Great.

Also, of their descendants who was around in that time of the Romans, when they became strong, and take over power from Greece. Philip 5th had his first war with the Romans, but for the Romans to give their full attention toward the defeat, and the destroying of the country of Carthage, they made peace with Philip in 205 BC. This was with the intention with the intention to deal with him at a later time, when it was more convenient for them to do so. Philip knew the Romans had it in their intention to come back at him at a later time, when it was more convenient for them to make an end of his kingdom, but he did not have the power to destroyed Rome to prevent them from doing so. The kingdom of Macedonia where Philip was ruling as king, had a second war in 200 BC, with the Romans, because of some rumors that came to the Roman knowledge, about King Attalus I of Pergamum, who was an ally to Philip in his first war against Rome. This roomer came from a person of the island of Rhodes, who told the story that Philip made a secret plan with Antiochus $3^{rd,}$ to capture the wealth of Egypt, from Ptolemy $5^{th,}$ who was a boy king from the family lineages of Ptolemy I. Ptolemy I, who was one of the generals of Alexander the Great, who he made governor over the land of what became known as Egypt. Also, governor over the country of Libya, and what became known as Arabia, but after the death of Alexander the Great in 323 BC, Ptolemy 1, made himself king of Mizraim, and Ptolemy 5th came from his linage. Rome declared war on Philip, to force him to pull his armies from the position he had his army surrounding Greece. The Romans, and the Macedonian forth a few wars, in which there were peace treaties that were drawn up between Rome, and Macedonia. In the winter of 172-171 BC, a Roman army crosses over into Greece, and for three years they did not make great progress in conquering Greece. But in June of 168 BC, a Roman general by the name of Lucius Aemilius Paullus, defeated Perseus in a place that was called Pydna, and because of this victory the Roman army, brought an end of the Antigonid monarchy of Macedonia, that was set up by Antigonus I. Perseus was the oldest son of Philip 5th of Macedonia, and Philip 4th was the son of Demetrius II. Demetrius II was the son of Antigonus II, and Antigonus I was one of the general of Alexander the Great, who was also a general to Alexander father, who was Philip II. After the death of Alexander, Antigonus fought with other various generals of Alexander, over his conquered territories of Macedonia, along with other areas of Europe that became a part of his kingdom of territories.

Perseus was the last king of Macedonia, of 179-168 BC, who wanted to dominate Greece, by his Macedonian kingdom, but he was defeated, and spent the rest of his life in captivity in Rome. Due to the Roman conquest of Greece, the country of Macedonia was divided into four separate tributes of taxpaying independent republics countries. With different capitals, such as Amphipolis, Tessalonica, Pella, Heraclea, and the city of Lyncestis, and also, 150.000 of the men of Macedonia were sold into slavery. When compare the world map of today, with that of the map of volume 20 of the Encyclopaedia, showing the country of Macedonia, Macedonia is known today as the counter of Yugoslavia, Rumania, Hungary, and Czechoslovakia.

During the Roman conquest of Greece, the country of Athens was rewarded by the Romans, for their loyalties to them, but the country of Eprius was savagely destroyed, by the Romans, and those who did not get killed by sword, and spars were sold into slavery. Many countries of Greece was quite disturbed, and was uneasy after the defeat of Perseus of Macedonia, because all Greece came under the ruler ship of Macedonia, by the conquest of Philip II, who was the father of Alexander the Great. Later after the death of Alexander the Great, all Greece, and the Turkey of Europe area, came under the ruler ship of the various generals of Alexander the Great. Also, that of their descendants, that became known as dynasty. So, Rome were able to conquer all Greece, and the Turkey area of Europe. So, when the Roman conquered Greece, various countries of Greece became allies to Rome. Those countries of Greece who were not allies to Rome, their people were sold into slavery, and their position was taken over by Rome. The country of Corinth was also conquered, and robs of its wealth, and was destroyed by the Romans in 146 BC. Also, many of the inhabitants who did not get killed off, were sold into slavery. The king of Pergamum of the Turkey area who was known as Attalus 3rd, who was a client kingdom of Rome, when he died, he left his kingdom to Rome, because he had no heir to inherit his throne. All the various territories that were conquered by the Romans, became their province, which were governed by different generals, who was elected as consul, and who also were given the title as governors. Volume 20 of the Encyclopaedia explained that, the Roman Empire was established, and developed as the Roman government take full controlled of overseeing their administration of their conquered territories, and provinces.

In 238- 197 BC the land of Tarshish, that is known today, as Spain and Portugal, became a Roman province that was known as Nearer Spain, and Farther Spain. This was the start of the western part of the Roman Empire of the Gentile land that became known as Europe. In 146 BC, after 50 years Macedonia, Illyria, Achaea, Pergamum that was also known as Asia Minor, also what became known as North Africa, became a part of the Roman Empire. According to volume 1 of the Encyclopaedia, the name for the country of Achaea, is now known as Akhaia, that was in the area of Greece. Which were known as Peloponnese, where the kingdom of Sparta was located. In the 4th century BC, many of the countries of the Peloponnese area of Greece, did form an alliance that was known as the Achaean League. The reason why the Achaean League was formed during the time of the Greeks before they were conquered by the Romans, it is because, they the people of Greece was always fighting among themselves, to conquer each other territories. Because of their greed for wealth, and power, until they were all conquered by Philip the II, before he was assassinated. After the assassination of Philip II of Macedon, Alexander took up where his father left off, and all Greece came under his ruler ship. After Alexander died at age 32, his various generals and their descendants took over the power of Greece and all of the conquered territories of Alexander the Great. These former territories of Alexander and his generals, and their descendants did eventually fell to the Romans, and became their conquered colonial provinces, of their Empire. Each province was given a written rules, and regulations of laws, by each generals, or consul, who was the conqueror of that territory, that was back up by 10 Senators, who were acting in harmony within the regulation board of Senate. Each conquered colony had to go by the various laws that was established by the Romans, as well as paying taxes to the state of Rome. This term of rules that was lay down by the Senators, was called as the constitution, and it was up to the powers of the Senators to name each province, that would keep their independence, and that would mean if they were a client kingdom of Rome, ruling in the interest of Rome before they were conquered. Those countries who were loyal to Rome in their conquest of each territory, and were allies to Rome, would receive this kind of special treatment. These were cities that did assist Rome before the time of their conquest, or were already bound to Rome by treaties. The rules that the Romans lay down for Sicily, and the island of Sardinia, is that they had the responsibly to be an agricultural producing island for the Romans.

So, in other words, these people were given the job, without pay to be the producing islands for the food of the tables of the Romans. At the center of the Romans administration of their colonies, were the yearly appointed consuls, who were given the title as governors of each province, as well as financial secretaries that were responsible for the revenue coming from each province to the State of Rome. This is the end of the story of the Romans, and the war with Hannibal, and Carthage.

According to volume 18 of the Encyclopaedia, the name Gaul came from the Romans when they were able to conquered a tribe of the Celtic people, who were the native of what is now known as France, and Switzerland, who were a member of a Germanic tribe of the barbarian people. According to volume 5 of the Encyclopaedia, the Gaul people inhabited what is now France, Belgium, western Germany, and northern Italy. From the 5th century BC, these Gauls, or Celtic people migrated south from the Rhine River Valley of Germany, to the Mediterranean coast, and from the 4th century various Celtic tribe cross northern Italy to Milan, and to the Adriatic coast of Greece, and made their settlement there. According to volume 3 of the Encyclopaedia, the Celtic dialect dived into Goidelic, which came from the Irish, and the Scottish, and Manx that came from the Scottish. Gaelic, and Brythonic that came from Welsh, and the Cornish dialect that came from the Breton people, who became known as Britain. Later these British people became known as the English people and England, after the conquest of the Angles and Saxon people of West Germany. The country of Britain became known as Great Britain during the slavery colonial period, of the Gentile people of Europe conquering the world to be their colonies, and provinces. Britain became known as Great Britain, because she was able to conquer three quarter of the world geographical land area from the other Gentile European colonial powers to be her colonial territories of the various natives, who were living there in these lands.

According to the Webster's Third International Dictionary, their it explained that the name Gallic came from the word gale, that is speaking of the people of Ireland, Scotland, the Idles of Man who were a member of the Gaelic Celtic barbarian speaking people of Western Europe. The Briton people, who became known as and Britain, and the British people with France, Germany, Spain to the Baltic Sea area of the Gentile land that became known as Europe, where many of these Celtic barbarian people who had settled there, and form their own communities. These barbarian people could not read, and write for themselves, but they had a verbal communication among themselves as ay of life. According to this same volume 3 of the Encyclopaedia Britannica, this group of the Celtic people traces their dialect to a Celtic people, who were there before Christianity came to Western Europe. These Celtic people used to have what was called Druids, and this Druid was a priest to their various gods who they used to worship, and serve during those time. Also, many of these priests were call as the seers, or the word Vates, which mean the same thing according the Encyclopaedia. The Encyclopaedia explained that these Druids, or priests had no writing alphabetical skills of their own, but they more so relied completely on memory to pass on their teaching to others of their communities.

According to volume 3 of the Encyclopaedia, the Irish land of Ireland never became fully a part of the Roman Empire, and bY so doing they were able to preserve their Celtic culture. Far better than many others of their Celtic brothers, and sisters of Scotland, Wales, Cornwall, Britain, France, and other places of Europe that did succumb to Roman culture. These Celtic people who came under Roman captivity, did adopt to a Roman way of life, because of the Roman conquest of slavery, and colonialism that was pass on down to them from generation to generation. The Encyclopaedia explained that the Irish people of Ireland did not embrace fully what became known as Roman Christianity of the Roman Catholic Church, and eventually their Druid, or priest of their various gods disappeared, when they became a part of Christianity that spread over Western Europe. The Encyclopaedia also explained that the Roman Christianity brought to the people of Ireland the skill of writing, which if it was left up to them, the Celtic people of Ireland, they could not have developed this art, and skills of writing, reading and arithmetic for themselves for many generations that was to come. The Encyclopaedia explained that when many of these Irish men became learned men, and scholars, many of them became missionaries, but in the 9th century AD, during the invasion of the Vikings, many of the old monastic system crumbled.

Many of these learned men of Ireland had to fled from Ireland, taking with them, their valuable manuscripts, and eventually the Vikings were driven back, and stop. So, when Julius Caesar conquered these people whom he named as Gauls, that did consist of three different regions of settlement of these Gallic tribes who became known as the Gaul people of Europe. Which did consist of present day France, and Switzerland, also, the Aquitani tribe, who were living in southwestern part of France, the Belgae tribe who were living in the northern part of France. From what I have gathered from reading volume 22 of the Encyclopaedia, the Gaelic dialect started with the Irish, and in Scotland, and this dialect was a verbal form of communication, because many of these people were illiterate, and who had no form of reading, and writing abilities for themselves. Volume 18 of the Encyclopaedia, explained that the Gaelic, or Gaul Celtic people had many different tribes, such as the Helvetii, who were living in what is now present-day Switzerland, the Sequani, and the Lingones who were living far west of Gaul, of what is now France, and Switzerland. There were also the Arverni tribe who were living in what is now France, that was also known as the Auvergne, and the Aedui who were living along the Loire Valley of western Gaul. The Gaul, and other various Germanic tribes, as well as the people of Tarshish, who are now known as the people of Spain, and Portugal are also member of these Celtic barbarian people. According to the Webster Collegiate Dictionary of the Fifth Edition, these Gaelic, Celtic people, were a racial member, who had settled in Central, and Western Europe. According to volume 18 of the Encyclopaedia, in the Greek language, these Celtic people were known as Keltoi people. In the Latin language of the Romans, they were known as the Gaul's, which did apply to any of the various Celtic speaking tribe of the Gentile people, of what became known as Europeans. These Celtic people who had settled in central, and the western part of the Gentile land of Europe, were described as tall people, with many of them who had blond hair.

According to volume 18 of the Encyclopaedia, there it explained that, these Celtic people were an unknown people north of mountainous region of the Alps, and nothing were known of them, until in the middle of the first thousand BC, when they became aware of, by the civilize world of the Mediterranean people. According volume 18 of the Encyclopaedia, these Celtic barbarian people became aware of, when Hannibal left from Spain where he was living, when he cross true France, and Switzerland to the Alps going toward Italy. The Encyclopaedia also explained that during the time when these Celtic became the dominant people of the barbarian world of the Gentile land of Europe they extended themselves from Ireland, Britain, to the Balkan Sea, even as far as the Anatolia area of what is now known as Turkey. By the time of the fourth century BC, many Greek writers rate these people together with a tribe of Europe, who were known as the Scythians, with the Persian, to be among the most numerous barbarian people of the known world of that time.

According to the Encyclopaedia, although these Celtic people did not form a unified ethnic group, nor had great empire of those days, yet they were divided into many different tribes, with different dialects that became an important factor in the development of what is known as the European society, of their world of today. Volume 10 of the Encyclopaedia, explained that Scythians were a nomadic people, who originally came from Persia, and who migrated from central Asia to southern Russia during the 8th, and 7th century BC. The word Anglo Saxon, simply stands for these two Germanic tribes, who were known as the Angles, and Saxon people, along with a tribe who were known as the Tunis, and the Jutes of West Germany, who invaded Britain, and conquered, and ruled there. From them came the Angles language, that became known as the English language, of their dialect, and their name became known as England, and the English people, that should have known as the land of the Angles, and Saxon people of West Germany, because of their conquest of the land of the Breton people, who became known as the British people. I am not quite sure how they came up with the litter E, for the name England, and E for the name English language, that should have spell as the Angles Saxon dialect, rather than the name English language. But I am not surprise, because these Gentile people of what became known as the Europeans people, are a very skillful set of people, in chaining things around, and who can conceal things to suit their own porpoises. The English language, as we know it as today, is a borrowed language, that came from Latin, and Greek, that originally came from the Phoenicians, Hethites, the people of Mizraim, and the Assyrian, and the Babylon's Cushite's people of Nimrod.

The English languages as it is known as today, keep on adopting itself to new words every day, that came down into the English, or Angles vocabulary, from many of their captured slave people, to express themselves into what became known as the English language. I am quite sure the English language, that is spoken in today's times, has varied widely from the way it was spoken during the time of Alfred the Great, who were a king of the Saxon tribe of Germanic people of that time. Who were living in the land that became known as England, and Britain, and who could not read or write for himself. Volume 1 of the Encyclopaedia, explained that the Angles gave their name to what became known as England, as well as the word Englisc that later became known as English, by Saxon writers to establish their dialect of speaking.

This Germanic tribe of the Angles, were first mention by this Roman general, whose name was Publis Cornelius Tacitus, who came across these people in the 1st century AD, who were a worshipper of their god, who were known as Nerthus. According to volume 8 of the Encyclopaedia, this goddess was worship by various Germanic tribes of the Baltic Sea area. Their belief, and worship to her, was that she would come to her worshippers, riding in a chariot that was pull by cows. According to volume 1 of the Encyclopaedia, the Angles were a member of a Germanic tribe, who together with Jutes, and the Saxons invaded Britain in the 5th century AD. This was after the breakup of the Roman Empire, ruling over Western, and Eastern Europe. This brake of the Roman Empire ruling over Western Europe, was cost by a Germanic tribe, who were known as the Visigoths in 410 AD. The Roman Empire of Western Europe, also came to its end by the Vandals, and the Huns, that brought about the end of the Roman Empire of Western Europe, to the various barbarians Celtic people, of the Gentile land of Europe. Who became strong after the breakup of the Roman Empire, and conquered many nations of people, who became their slaves, and empire of subjects to get rich. During the conquest of Britain by the Angles, and Saxon Germanic people, they were settled in large numbers, in the kingdoms of Mercia, North Umbria, and in East Middle Anglia, that take it name from the Angles conquests. According to volume 1 of the Encyclopaedia, from the invasion of the Anglo Saxons people, the name of Britain became known as England, from the 5th century AD. In the time of the invasion by the Norseman, or the Northman, who became known as the Vikings, people, of their conquest of Britain in AD 1066.

Volume 12 of the Encyclopaedia, explained that the Viking tribe was a member of a Germanic tribe of the Scandinavian sea warrior people, who raided, and conquered a wide area of Europe after the breakup of the Roman Empire ruling over Western Europe. According to the Encyclopaedia, these people were chiefly from what is known today as the area of Denmark, Norway, Sweden, Iceland, and Finland, who raided, and conquer a wide area of Europe, after the conquest of the Romans, and the Angles, and Saxon people, who did invaded Britain, and conquered there. According to volume 2, of the Encyclopaedia, the British people were known as the Britons who inhabited Britain before the Anglo-Saxon conquest of the 6th century AD. Who come from a people who were known as the Cymric Celtic people, who they say arrived in the island of Britain at un known date of time.

The Encyclopaedia went on to speculate that they think these people may arrive in Britain around the time of the 7th, or the 6th century BC, which they do not know for sure. I did check out the name Cymric in the A to K Index of the Encyclopaedia, to see if I could come up with some information about these people. But unfortunately, I could not come up with any information about these people, who were known as the Cymric Celtic people. The Vikings raid started in 865 AD, when an army that was led by the sons of Ranger, who were known as Lord Book, who conquered the ancient kingdom of the Angles, that was located in East Anglia, North Umbria, and destroyed the Angles city of Mercia. Volume 1 explained that this writer, by the name of Venerable Bede, who distinguish the Saxon of Britain, who he called antique Saxons, which mean Old Saxon. Volume 1 of the Encyclopaedia, explained that Alfred the Great who existed from 849, to 899 AD, became king of the Saxon in a place in Britain that was called Wessex, during the time of 871, to 899 AD. During the time of his reign, he prevented Britten from falling into the hands of the Danish people, who was a part of the Vikings Germanic tribe of people. He also encourages learning of literacy for his people, of what became known as England, and the English people, because many of his people of Britain could not read, and write for themselves.

He also sees to it that the history of the Anglo-Saxon people was put into chronological order, that began during the time of his reign, which was about AD 890. The Encyclopaedia, also explained that from the early boyhood days of Alfred his mother encourages his interest in poetry, and he was also very eager to learn Latin, which stimulated his interest to visits Rome, which he did in 853-855 AD. He was also a great admirer of the great Frankish king, who was known as Charlemagne, who at the beginning of his reign revived learning of reading, and writing in Europe, after the fall of the Roman Empire that had brought light of knowledge to the people of Western, and Eastern Europe. The Encyclopaedia explained that while Alfred was growing up as a young man, he did not have any form of education of reading, and writing, but he sought after it much later in his life. Volume 20 of the Encyclopaedia, explained that feudalism came about after the fall of the Roman Empire of Western Europe, to fill the gap of learning. Such as the church, meaning the Roman Catholic Church. According to the Webster Colligate Dictionary, of the Fifth Edition, the meaning of the word feudalism, was a political system, that did existed there in Europe, after the fall of the Roman Empire, that became known as the Middle Ages.

This system was based upon the relationship of a lord, and his vassal, which the word vassal means a slave master, and his slaves, or his servants that, was known as vassal. This feudal system of the church, meaning the Roman Catholic Church, kept the light of religion, and learning alive, and what was left of the old Roman Empire system of civilization to Ireland, and Britain. Also, Central Europe, and what became known as Scandinavia. This feudalism system also provided professional government, where many of these barbarian's kings, along with Charlemagne who was one of the greatest ruler, of the old Roman system. The Angles and the Saxon, also got their education mainly from the Romans, and the Roman Catholic Church, who conquered, and enslaved and converted many of these people to, Roman Catholicism of the Latin language of the Roman, that became known as Christianity.

Chapter 51 - The Literately of The Gentile People of Western Europe by Charlemagne.

According to volume 8 of the Encyclopaedia, the word Middle Age came about after the fall of the Roman Empire ruling over Western, and Eastern Europe, that brought knowledge of light to many of these people of the area. After the fall of the Roman Empire of Western Europe, it created a thousand years of darkness of knowledge, and it was the Catholic Church that was the main institutions that kept the light of religion, and learning alive, of what was left of the old Roman civilization, to Western Europe. Due to the help of the Roman Catholic Church teaching, it did help to create stable government, that was hard to come by in those days of the various war lords, seeking to conquer each other territory to establish their own system of ruler ship. From the enlightenment of the Roman Catholic Church eventually gave way to a new beginning of learning, that was started by Charlemagne of the Frankish kingdom, who ruled from 768 to 814 AD, according to the Encyclopaedia. According to volume 20 of the Encyclopaedia, one of the greatest of these barbarian kings of that time, was known as Charlemagne of the Frankish Germanic kingdom. He provided military leadership, and established a governmental system like that of the old Roman Empire, that did control Europe. According to volume 3 of the Encyclopaedia, Charlemagne was also known as Charles the I, and he also was known as Charles the Great, and in the French language, he was known as Charles LE Grand, who was born April 2- 742 AD. He died January 28-814, who was a king of the Germanic tribe of the Franks. He also was a king of a Celtic people who were known as the Lombards people. This was from 774-814 AD, and he was able to unite these two tribe by conquering Western Europe, and rule as emperor from 800 to 814.

The Encyclopaedia explained that, besides expanding his political power, over Western Europe, he also brought about a cultural revival in his empire, that was called the Carolingian renaissance. Charlemagne also became a Christian king of the Franks Germanic people. He also conquer the Saxon, and other Germanic tribe, and Christianize them, and establish a part of his kingdom in the Roman conquered land of what became known as Italy, and this was after the death of his brother in 771 AD. Volume 20 of the Encyclopaedia explained, that from the military power structure of Charlemagne, it developed into various military aristocracy, where various members gave themselves nobles titles, in the fashion of that of the Romans.

Such as the title as the word comes; which stand for the word count; dux which stand for the word duke, which these names were a mare decoration of titles. He also became an emperor of what was left of the old Roman Empire system of Western Europe. This new beginning of learning of Charle Charlemagne continued making improvement from the time of the 12th to the 15th century AD. This is where many monks got their education from, by way of the Catholic Church, that eventually gave light of learning to many hard-nary people of Europe, that they had called as the Renaissance of Charles Charlemagne. According to the Webster Colligate Dictionary, the word Renaissance means a new beginning of learning to many people of Western Europe. I would like to point out that the word knights, was a military person that came from the Angles, and Saxon people dialect, that was copy from what was known as the Roman legionary. According to what I have gathered from reading various volume of the Encyclopaedia Britannica, explaining about the Roman Legionary, that became known as knights. These knights was a staff member to a king, or a queen, which was started with Augustus Gaius Octaves Caesar, as the Legionary during his reign, that was later copied by the Anglo-Saxon people, as the knights. Volume 20 of the Encyclopaedia explained that, many of these military aristocracies who had taken power as kings, or queens, did lack the machinery might, like that of the taxation of imperial Rome. Many of whom could not afford to pay to have a regular standing army, like that of the old Roman Empire system. The Encyclopaedia also explained that these body of men in that time, where heavily armored gears that was called cavalrymen. It was also called as Chevalier, in the French language, and knights in the Anglo-Saxon dialect, that became known as the English language.

From what I have read, and come to understand from reading various volume of the Encyclopaedia, these knights was an independent force, that was not a dependable instrument, like that of the old Roman legionary. I also came to the understand, from reading the Encyclopaedia, that these knights was a force that could be bought, if the price was right, as a mercenary solder, who sell their services for the right price. It was just like that of the many fast gunslingers of the Wild West of what became known as the United States, where many wealthy European settlers, used to pay these fast gunslingers for their services. This was to get even with other Gentile people who were standing in their way. Or to protect what they had from been stolen by other European settlers, of what became known as the United States. According to volume 18 of the Encyclopaedia Britannica, there it explained about the early learning of the educational system of the Renaissance, of Charlemagne, for his people of Western Europe, that gave them the ability, of reading and the writing skills. Many of who were totally illiterate, until Charlemagne took it upon himself to give literacy to the people of his empire. This was by the monks, nuns, and bishops who were known as the Episcopal of the Roman Catholic Church. According to the Webster Colligate Dictionary, of the Fifth Edition, the word bishop is an Anglo-Saxon word that was taken from the Latin word Episcopal. This educational system of Charlemagne, started from his empire of Italy, all the way to what became known as France. Later this educational system extended itself to Britain, by King Alfred the Great, who himself could not read, and write during the early time of the Renaissance of Charlemagne. According to the Encyclopaedia Britannica, it was due to the skills of reading, writing, and arithmetic that came from the Islamic translation, into the Latin language, that was pass on to Medieval Europe, that cause many of the barbarian people of Europe to come alive educational speaking. I must point out that the word Islamic came from the word Islam, that came from Mohammed and his early followers who were known as the Mohammedans, who became known as the Muslim people of today. As I have mention before that these people who became known as the Saudi Arabian people, were known as the Ishmaelite people during the time of Jacob, because these Saudi Arabian people, are a descendants of Ishmael. Who was the son of Hagar who came from the land of Mizraim, now known as Egypt, also, from Abraham who came from the country of Babylon, who was a Cushite's man from the Cushite's kingdom of the people of Nimrod, from his mother side of people, of the family of Cush. The point that I am trying to make here is this, these Ishmaelite's people, who are known today as the Saudi Arabian people, and the Islamic people, their educational system did not start with them, but it came from Hagar and her people of Mizraim, and the various kingdoms of the people of Ham that gone by.

This education system was pass on down to her son Ishmael, that was pass on to his seeds, who later became known as the Saudi Arabian people of today. The Phoenician Canaanite people of Canaan, way before the coming of Mohammed, and his Muslim followers came into existence, they had pass on their skills of reading, writing, and arithmetic to the people of Greece, Sicily, Spain and France. This educational system of the Phoenician, the people of Mizraim, the Hethites, became the educational system of what is now known today, as the Europeans educational system of Europe.

So, this reading, writing and arithmetic, that became a part of the educational system of the people of what is now known as the Saudi Arabian people of Ishmael, came from his mother Hagar, and from the rest of the people of Mizraim that they call as science, and technology of today. So, the point I am driving at is this, the educational system of the Gentile people of what became known as Europeans, came from the people of Ham, that very few people of today have any knowledge of. So, this statement volume 18 of the Encyclopaedia made about the educational system that came from the Islamic people, to the people of Europe, it is total a false statement, and a total nonce. Due to the fact that the Ishmaelite people education came from the people of Ham where Ishmael, and his descendants came out of.

This is a story I have taken from a few pages of a book, that is called The Talking Drum of the Willie Lynch famous speech, of the making, and the braking of a slave, that I have gotten from a gentleman while I was living in the New Jersey. I have incorporated some of this Willie story into this book, The Untold Forgotten Great Civilization of the people of Ham. This is to give the Hamite's readers of this book, of the Gentile European people mind set, toward us Hamite's people, who they had taken as their captives, and slave, and called as Negroes, Blacks, and the African people. There were a Gentile European slave master by the name of Willie Lynch, who had slaves in what became known as the West Indies by Columbus. That is now called as the Caribbean by these same Gentile European people, who have deceived the world of people who came under their captivity with lies, and false history of teaching. In his book that is called the Willie Lynch speech, of the making, and the braking of a slave, unfortunately I do not have the complete book in my position, but I only have a few pages, I have taken from his statement of the making, and braking of a slave. The book went on to explained that Willie Lynch came to the British colony of Virginia, by the invitation of some of his European slave masters of Virginia. This was to encourage them, how to make, and break a slave. It seems to me that, they were having some problem in the colony of Virginia with their slave population.

So, he gave his famous speech on the bank of the James River, in 1712, that was called as the making, and braking of a slave. This was of his methods of controlling his slave population in the West Indies. Willie Lynch went on to say to his fellow Gentile European slave masters, that there are various principles of steps that is needed to be taken, to make and break a slave. He went on to say that one of these breaking processes was that of the African women, and the controlling of the marriage unit, and their mind, and their language. Lynch went on to explained that while the Romans used cords, and wood as crosses for the purpose of supporting human bodies along their highways in vast numbers. They the slave masters of Virginia were using trees, and rope to hang their slaves on, because in his traveling, he notices slaves were hanging from various trees.

Lynch went on to explained to is fellow slave masters, that they were losing good profits, by hanging their slaves who were involve in the slave uprising, and runaway slaves that were caught. Willie Lynch went on to say that he was going to teach them his ways of controlling the slaves, without losing good profits of slave labor and lives. Some of his methods he was going teaching them, were to drive fear, and distrust among the various slaves. This was to instill in them to learn to love, and put their trust only in their slave masters, and in his kind of people, rather than them putting their trust in their own fellow slave's people, looking out for each other, and having hope in their own people. Willie Lynch was using the psychology of divide, and conquers, in what became known as the slavery mentality of today, that still very much affect many of our Hamite's people minds of today, in their day to day lives, dealing with each other on a regular scale. This mistrust, and fear that was to be driven into them, have caused many Hamite's people of today, especially in became known as the United State, not to have any real love, trust, and unity among their own people. The way many of them see it, it is only to rob, and steal, and sell drugs to their own people, so as to mess up, and destroyed their own people minds, with these drugs, that were brought about by means of the Gentiles European settlers, of the United State. This was to destroy the minds of many of their Hamite's people of these United States, who they want to keep down, and get read of, out of their system. I must point out that many of these Hamite's drug dealers who sell drugs to their own people, and rob many of them in the process, they can only do these things in their own people neighborhoods, but they cannot going to the Gentile European people neighborhoods, and sell their drugs.

If they were to do so, they would be killed, or to put in prison for the rest of their lives, but when many of these Hamite's drug dealers find themselves in trouble, and their back is against the wall, the very first set of people they would seek to run to for help, is their own kind of people. Whom they have been selling their drugs of poison to, and robbing them in the process. Many of them would rather put their trust, and hope, and love in many of the Gentile European people, who having been abusing, and brutalizing us for many centuries. The way it is in today's societies, among many Hamite's people of the United Stated, and elsewhere, the slave masters do not need to be around to push the fire of disunity among the various Hamite's people of today. The seed was already been planted in their hearts, and minds to have mistrust, and disunity among themselves, so it comes naturally. Lynch went on to tell his fellow slave masters, that if they were to follow his methods of dealing with their Black slaves, it would last for 300, or even a thousand years of them having distrust among themselves. The Hamite's people would always be looking toward their slave masters, to put their trust, and hope in them, to better their standard of living, and to put bread on their tables. Lynch went on to encourage his fellow slave masters by saying that distrust is stronger than trust, and they must put the old Black slaves against the young Black slaves. The dark skin slaves against the brown skin slaves, and those of the female with long hair against those that have short hair. This distrust of confusion would last for a thousands year, but it was necessary for them to learn to trust, love, respect, and depend only on their Gentile slave masters, and his kind of people, for their hope, and betterment of their lives. According to his philosophy he was teaching his fellow Gentile people, if they should apply these principles of his, it would not be necessary for them to keep on instilling this belief in them all the time. For they themselves will carry on teaching it to the next generation, and the cycle will continue repeating itself generation after generation to come. In the mind of Lynch, he compares the Hamite's people who he name as Negros, that they were to be broken in, like how a wild horse is broken, and tied for the productive good use of the economy of their system. He went on to say that the Negro women should be put to produce a crossbred of different shades of people, that would be good for the labor workforce, and they were to be taught to respond to a new language of psychology, and physical containment. Lynch pointed out to his fellow Gentile European slave masters, that a wild horse, and a wild Negros is very dangerous even when captured. For they will have the tendency to want to seek their freedom. In so doing, they might turn around, and might want to kill the slave master, and his family while they are sleeping.

Therefore, they must make sure the slaves sleep, while they are awake, and they should sleep, when the slaves are awake with someone watching their every movement. They should also pay extra attention to the female Negros, that this indoctrination she will received would later pass on to her young offspring's, so as to bring up a profitable workforce, suitable for the slave master's needs. They should keep the body, but they should enslave the mind of their male slaves. In other words, they should break their mind, and their spirit to resist against their slave master will. The next stage was to drive fear into the other Negro males, by stripping off one of their Negro male's clothes, in front of the other Negroes males, females, young and old. They should also tie a Negro's male hands, and feet to four horses, and set him on fire, so that the horses would pull him a part in front of their very eyes. The next stage was to take a bull whip, and beat the remaining Negro males to the point of death, in front of the females, and infants. They should not kill them, for they will be useful for future breeding. But they must be beaten to put the fear of God, and the slave master in their hearts, and minds. I must point out that I did not cover the full Willie Lynch story, but I just take a few abstracts from his famous speech, he gave to encourage his fellow Gentile slave masters of what became known as the United States, to deal with their slave population. Also, of the slavery embedment, of the slavery mentality that would carry on to the future generations that was to come.

The Hamite's leaders who classified themselves to be educated people, according to the Gentile European people educational system, that many of them were expose to, to see themselves as educated people. Many of whom have no knowledge of who they are, and where they are coming from as a people, but they were educated to see things from a European prospective. Due to the fact that many of these so-call educated brain wash Hamite 's leaders went to school in Britain, United States, Canada, and other parts of the Gentile land of Europe, to study their laws. Of custom of their greed, of exploitation of people, who they have ruled over. So, when many of these Hamite's people graduated from these universities, and colleges of these European people system, they go right back to the land of Ham, the Caribbean, and other places of the Gentile people New World, of their ruler ship, to oppress their own people with these Gentile European laws of greed. This is of their customs of greed, selfishness, taxes, and oppression they had learned from many of these oppressive, and wicked people of their schooling system. What many of these foolish educated Hamite's people who become politician, and leaders of their own people, need to realize, that reading, writing, and arithmetic that became known as education of the European people system. Did not started in Europe with the people of Europe, but it was started in the land of Ham, among the people of Ham, that did spread to Europe. Many of the times because of these oppressive European laws many of these Hamite's leaders had learn, and adapted from these people, lead to hardship, conflict and civil war in the land of Ham, among their own people who are there.

This citation also applies to many parts of the Gentile European people New World, where many of our Hamite's people find themselves living and call home, because of the slavery experience our ancestors went true, and leave us behind as the new citizens of their system. The Hamite's people of the United States need to become more self-conscious, of who they are as a people. They need to draw more closely, mentally, and physically speaking to the land of their forefathers, the land of Ham, where their true roots came from. Although many of our leaders, and rulers in the land of Ham are suffering from miss education, slavery, and colonial mentality, and stupidity, that have causes a lot of disunity, wars, and suffering among many of the people who are there.

This is because of their greed, selfishness, ignorance, and stupidity of their colonial learning they had receive from their colonial slave masters, of their form of education to oppress their own people with these European schooling they did received. Also, many of these political leaders of the land of Ham, who see themselves as educated people, allow many of their colonial master of the land of Ham to used them as puppets, by taking pay off, and bribes of their resources of their lands, and to keep many of their own people down in poverty. While they drive around in a big Merced's Benz, and have a fat bank account in some Gentile European people banks. Many of these foolish, and stupid Hamite's political leaders of the land of Ham, who have their money pile up in some European banks, do not even realize that if they should died, all their moneys go right over to benefit the people of Europe, who owned the banks, rather their own people. This also go for the foolish, and stupid Hamite's people like Booker A-ram Muslim people of Nigeria, and other Muslim fanatic of the land of Ham, who allow the Saudi Arabian people of Ishmael, to used them, to kill off many of their own people, so as to set up a Muslim State, and a Muslim Government in Nigeria, in the interest of the people of Saudi Arabia. This Muslim philosophy and ideology, was spread from the so-call Middle East, to Nigeria, and also in many other places by way of the Quran, and the sward. By the Mohammedan Muslim people of what became known as the Saudi Arabia people, for their captives people, to accept their religious belief of Mohammed, and the worship of his god Allah. Yet I would like to encourage many Hamite's people of the United States, that they must not only think of the United States as their homeland, but they must also think of the land of Ham, the land of their ancestors, as their homeland too.

My reason for making this kind of statement is this, if there should be a famine for food and water in the United States, the Hamite's people of the United States are the ones who will suffer the most. They would not be able to go into any of their Gentile European people neighborhoods, with their intention, they are going there to look for food and water, from these people, who do not have any love for them. Many of whom have control over all the things of the United States. Many of the Gentile European people of their neighborhoods, would literally take their guns and shoot down many of these Hamite's people like birds. For being so presumptuous to come into their neighborhoods looking for food, and water they want for themselves.

Also, in their eyes they would think that these Hamite's people who they name as Black people have the audacity to come into their neighborhoods where they are not welcome, and are not wanted in the first place. But if many of these Hamite's people of the United States were living in the land of Ham among their own people, and there should be a famine, I am quite sure they could go into any of their own Hamite's people neighborhoods, to look for food, and water without any problem, and anyone getting kill. In comparison to what it would be like, if this kind of situation was to take place here in the United States. Also, in other European rule societies where many of us find our self-living, in and call home. I am quite sure if this situation was to take place in the land of Ham, living among their own people, they would share whatever little food, and water they have with them without any problems, and anyone getting killed. In comparison to what it would be like, if there should be such a dilemma as what I had mention above, if it was to take place here in the United States. Also, many Hamite's people of the United States need to realize that the only way they can have something to eat, and drink, and that is if they have the money to go down to the various run Gentile European supermarkets, to buy what they need to eat and drink, otherwise, they would literally starve to death. The way the system of the United States was setup, it was not set up to benefit many of their free slave Hamite's people of today, because the system was not set up for them to grow their own food they need to eat and survive.

The way the system of the United States was setup, it was set up for their many Gentile European farmers to grow the food, and send it to their various Gentile European run supermarkets. So, that they, and their free slave people of today can go and buy their food from these places, if they have the money to do so. Otherwise they would not able to eat. Many of the time the prices of these food kinds are so expensive, that the average poor Hamite's person can hardly afford to buy the necessary food they need to eat and survive. Because of the greed of these Gentile European people, to gain wealth, and to bring in more profits. So, if a poor Hamite's person do not have the money to buy what they need to eat, they would literally starve to death. Or if they should take anything from these supermarkets that they would like to eat to save their life, they would go to prison, or be shot to death by the store owners, or by the police officer for taking the supermarket things they are selling.

If many of these poor Hamite's people of the United States was living in the land of Ham, among their own people, they would be free to grow their own food they need to eat, and live without any problem. In comparison to that of the United States, where the food is mostly grown by the Gentile European farmers, to sell to the general public. I am quite sure they would able to survive, with the help of Yahweh sending rain from above, without any problem, and anyone going to jail, for planting their own food without having any permits, or license from the city where they are living to do so, as how it is here in the United States. Also, if many Hamite's people of the United States were living in the land of Ham among their own people, I am quite sure many of them would be a far more freer people, without all the pressure, and the red tapes I have seen many Hamite's people of the United States have to go true living in these United States. They would be far more freer people to live wheresoever they would want to live, without the various exploitation of pressure, I have seen many Hamite's people of the United States have to go through on a daily base. Just to survive, and live the best way they can do so, in a system that is against them. As the saying goes, there is no place like home, where one can sit down under his, or her own fig tree, or their own vineyard, among their own people. Where one can feel a little more relax, and don't have to worry about the pressure living in this Gentile European run society of what became known as the United States. Where it mostly caters to their own kind of people benefit, of their exploitation to bring in more wealth into their system. I am not implying that the Gentile people of what became known as the European people were not conquered, and enslaved by others, because they have been. But the only difference between their captivity, and our captivities is that they were mostly conquered, and enslaved by their own people.

Such as the Greeks, the Romans, Angles Saxon, the Vikings, and other various war like tribes of Europe, seeking to control, and to gain more wealth, and to dominate over their own brothers, and sisters of what became known as Europe. But the enslavement many Gentile people of the land area that became known as Europe, went through by their own people was not for a long period of time. In comparison to we the people of Ham, who have been conquered, and enslaved by so many different foreign conquerors of people. One can safely say that the conquest of the Grecians, and the Romans over their own brothers, and sisters, on the continent of the land area that became known as Europe, did add to their advancement, and bettermenThe reason why I can safely say these things, it is because many of the Gentile European people's culture, writing, and languages came from the Greeks, to the Latin people of Rome, whom many of these people were ruled, and governed and enslave by. Let us take for argument sake the country of Burton, that became known as Britain, and England, because of the Angles, and Saxon conquest, where the name England, and English was taken from. This dialect that became known as the English language, is widely spoken throughout word of today. In turn, the Burtons, Irish, Scotts, French, Germans, Spanish, and the Portuguese, all got their education of literacy, from the Roman, and the Roman Catholic Church, and also from the Greeks, who they were rule, and control by at one time. Even many of the Gentile people of today, many of their modern technology, if I may use this word came from the people of Mizraim, the Canaanites, and other Cushite's Hamite's people at large. So, one may ask the question, of how the Greeks, and the Romans got their knowledge from the people of Ham? In my opinion, the Gentile people of Europe are a snake-like people, they will come in friendly to eat, drink, sing and dance with their captives, and when the time is right, they will turn around and conquer and enslave the same people whom they used to sit down, eat and drink, sing, and dance with, and learn from. Columbus who were from the Gentile family of Europe, did the same snake-like action to the Arawak's people, whom he named as Indians, of the area of the world he named as the West Indies. According to History of the West Indian People Book II, the Arawak's people came out to meet with Columbus, and his men with water for them to drink, and with friendliness, and compassion, when they came as strangers to their world.

They even told him where he could find gold, and after all their kindness, and friendliness, when gold was found, many of these same people were taken as prisoners, and slave. Many of them were enslave to death, by Columbus, and later by the Spanish who Columbus, and Vespucci was working for. Many of them were also enslaved to death, and their lands were taken away from them by the Spanish, the Portuguese, with other European pirates, who came and forth the Spanish, and take away some of their lands to be their colonies. Many of whom also enslave many of these natives to death. It is very sad to say that because of the Gentile family, who left from their land of Europe, to go out and conquer many people, and their lands in the name of Christianity, using the Bible as a form of their deception of tools, to get rich.

Many of the time these places of their conquest, and colonies have always become full of all sorts of Immorality, corruption, violence and wickedness, that was rubbed off on many of their captive's people, who were born, and raised in their established colonies of the world as a way of life. Many of whom have copied the Gentile European people ways of life, that was left behind, from the pirates to the cow boys' era, and the gangsters of the Rowing Twenties. This is also to our present time, with all sort of corruption that was pass on to many of their x slave people mind, as a way of life, for them to gain wealth. When I was growing up in Jamaica in the fifties, many people of the island had more love and unity among themselves in those days, because it was less European people, in comparison to a larger Hamite's population, that did continue on from the days of slavery. Furthermore, many of us of those days had more unity among ourselves, that our ancestors left behind, that was pass on to many of us who were there, that many of us had patterned ourselves after. But today, many of the people of the island of Jamaica have copied, and patterned themselves after the violence they see in the various Gentile European movies. Also their television program, videos, and their cowboy movies, of the Wild West, of the United States. Also, the gangsters, and the mobster's movies, of the American societies that seem to influence the minds of many people toward violence, stealing, robbing, and killing each other to get rich, especially the younger generation of today, compared to my days of the fifties. The island of Jamaica has become full of violence, and killing, because many of the younger generation who are there, have copied the violence they see in the movies, and on the television that influence their mind to become this kind of people they are today.

This violence also came about, because of the political system of Jamaica, that was set up by the Gentile British people of Europe, to rule over the island, where many people fight, and kill each other, over these politicians to put them in office. Because this is how the system was set up after slavery was abolish by the Gentile British people. The violence of Jamaica also came about because of many Hamite's people who left from Jamaica, and went to live in Britain, Canada, and the United States, and many of whom returned to Jamaica with their violence they had copied, and learn from these Gentile people of Europe, who they have been living among for a long period of time. Even the police force system of Jamaica, many of them are suffering from ignorance, slavery, and colonial mentality of stupidity.

My reason for saying this is, I was told by many of my family members who are still living there in the island, of the brutality of many of the police officers against many of their own Hamite's people who are there. Many of these police officers, take the law into their own hands, by becoming judges, juries, and executioners, by beating, and killing many of their own brothers, who they call as boys. With an insulting behavior that they have no respect toward their own struggling people, who came from out of the Gentile slavery system of the Caribbean like themselves. Many of these Hamite's police officers of Jamaica, have exalted themselves above their fellow Hamite's people, who came from out of the slavery experience like themselves. Because of their Gentile European police officer badges, that was given to them as a sign of authority ship, over their own people, to keep them in check. Also, because many of these police officers are financially better off, than many of their poorer Hamite's brothers, and sisters who are not employed by the government has they do. Having a paycheck coming every month or weeks, to enable them to live the good life of the Gentile European people system that they had set up true slavery and colonialism. Many of these police officers of Jamaica, don't really know that the police force system was set up for the protection of settlers, or the colonist as they were call in those days. It was not set up for the protection of the many Hamite's people, who were brought over to the island as slaves, nor was the police force of Jamaica was set up for the protection of the many Arawaks people, who were enslave to death. Also, many of whom were slaughter off the island, by the Spanish, and later by the British, and their lands was taken away. So next time that many of these police officers go brutalizing many of their own people, because of their European police badges, that were given to them as a sign of authority. They need to stop and think about many of these things I have written about, that many of them do not have any knowledge of, because they were not thought of these things, and many of them are suffering from slavery mentality, and colonial stupidity.

Many Hamite's people of Jamaica have copied, and patterned themselves of becoming drugs dealers to make fast money. These drugs they are selling to their own people of Jamaica, will in the long run only destroy the minds of many of their brothers and sisters who get hock on these drugs, because of their ignorance, stupidity, and carefree living, of Devil-ism. Many of these drug dealers have no Yahweh consciousness of how to live their lives to please Him, because many of us Hamite's people love too much pleasure, and carefree living, that will end many of us into destruction, like many of our ancestors gone by. It is also mention in (I Timothy Chapter 5, and verse 6) that she who lived for pleasure is dead while she lived, and sad to say that too many of our Hamite's people, both men, and women love too much pleasure, and also carefree living, that will lead many of us into destruction. This is one of the reason why many of the early civilization of the people of Ham did not remain until today, because Yahweh was not pleased with the doings of many of these Hamite's kingdoms of the so-call Middle East, and what became known as North Africa. It is also mention in (Leviticus Chapter 18, and verse 3), were Yahweh said to Moses to tell the children of Israel, they must not learn to do after the doings after the land of Egypt where they came out of. Nor after the doing of the Canaanites, in whose land they were going to take over, as the new citizens of the land. Because many of the doings of the early people of Ham were evil in the site of Yahweh. Many Hamite's people of Jamaica, who sell drugs to many of their own people, to make fast money, don't seem to realize that it is the mobsters, and gangster of the Gentile people of Europe, who are mainly the distributers of many of these drugs, to different parts of the world to gain wealth. By using local people, who do not have any care for their own people, who are buying, and selling, and using their drugs, but only to make money from these foolish people, who do not know any better. Who do not realize that they are destroying their own people lives and minds with these poisons, from these Gentile people of Europe. Likewise, many of these drug dealers of Jamaica who are selling their drugs to their own people to kill many of them off, with these drugs, to become rich men from their miseries of their carefree living of their stupidity that many of them have fallen into.

They do not have any sympathy for many of their own foolish people who have fallen victim to their drugs. For this reason, many Hamite's people who had left from the island, and went to live overseas, would love to want to return to help to build up the economy of the island, if the circumstance was different. But because of the violence, and the crime, and the drugs, many are afraid to return to the island, because they don't want to get caught up in such madness, and foolishness of the violence, and the ignorance of many foolish people of the island. I was watching Direct TV on the History channel, and they was explaining that back in the 1800, many of the Gentile European dock companies, who did used Hamite's workers on their dock site, they would give them cocaine drugs to make them work faster. Their reason for doing so was, to make them work faster to make big profits from their laborers.

After many of these Hamite's dock workers get hooked on the cocaine habit, it spread to their neighborhoods, and many of these drug users began to attack Gentile people, this was because of their drug habits, and their condition of poverties. The news reports explained that the police had to get special bullets made that was designed to penetrate, and kill these drug users who became violent against Gentile European people of the United States. This little story just goes to show how much many of these Gentile European people of what became known as the United States, sit down, and plan how they may go about destroying many of us, their free slave Hamite's people from the United States, who they want to get read of from their society. I was told by some of the older ones of Jamaica about the destruction that took place on a part of the Island of Jamaica, that is known as Port Royal. From what I have read from the book, A short History of the West Indies, this place used to be a place of pirates, prostitution, alcoholism, and violence during the slavery colonial period of the Gentile people of Europe of their lifestyle in Jamaica. Until three quarter of the island was destroyed by an earthquake, in 1692, and fell to the bottom of the sea; because of all the UN Yahweh like qualities, and wickedness that was taking place there during the time. To add further to the Gentile corruption, I could remember when I was growing up in Jamaica in the fifties, in the Kingston area, tourism, sailors, and prostitution was a big part of the economy on the island at the time. When the sailors come to Jamaica, mostly from the United States, the first place they would look for is the rum bars, and the local whorehouses, that came down from the colonial slavery days. Many women who were poor, sold themselves into prostitution as a way out of their poverty nests.

I would like to point out to many Hamite's people of the West Indies, and in the land of Ham, who depend on tourism as a way to make money, such as the airlines resorts, restaurants, and so on, that was setup by these Gentile European people to make money. Also, to further their knowledge, and experience of other people culture, and to pass on their corruption to the minds of many other people of the area. Who have adopted themselves to the Gentile European people ways of life, of their tourism business. Although tourism is good in one form, in bringing foreign currency into many of the islands of the Caribbean, and also in the land of Ham itself, that many people rely on to make a living, and many businesses places to make money.

Yet many Hamite's people of the various islands of the West Indies, and in the land of Ham itself, ned to realize to themselves, that tourism is another way to help to corrupt many of our people minds. With prostitution, homosexuals, lesbianism, drugs, the glory of the guns to kill more people faster. But many of our people, do not realize these things, but they are only looking from the money point of view. Many Hamite's people may not agree with me that tourism helps to spread corruption, and the ill nature that comes with it, because of the glory of the wealth that come from tourism. I do know that tourism is another way for the Gentile people of Europe to find leisure, also to spread their corruption to the minds of other people, because they have been doing so wheresoever they went and conquer, and set up their system, and many of their captives were influence by the corruptions of the people of Europe. They have also pass on their form of lifestyle, such as prostitution, homosexuals, lesbianism, pornography, gambling, smoking, rum bars, and the distribution of guns. Along with many drugs that have spread to the Caribbean, and in the land of Ham itself, by these same Gentile European people of their tourism business. Colonialism, and the tourism trade of the Gentile people, and their lifestyle of corruption of sexual immorality, in the Caribbean, and in the land of Ham itself, have caused the spread of HIV, and other sexual diseases to spread like wildfire among many people who are living there. This is the reason why it is written in (I Timothy Chapter 6, and verse 10) that the love of money is the root of all evil, and because of this love of money many people have pierced themselves through with many sorrows, that we as a people could do without. What the people of Ham need in the Caribbean, and in the land of Ham itself, is not tourism, but economic development, and industries, so many of the people would be able to find employment among many of their own people. To uplift their standard of living, rather than to depend on tourism as a way of life to make a living.

Many of the Asiatic countries of the people of Shem, were at one time under colonialism, and slavery of the Gentile people of Europe, but now many of them have develop themselves into a modern industrialize nation, employing many of their own people, rather than to depend on tourism, as a way of life to make a living. The land of Ham have many raw materials that the Gentile people, and other people want for themselves, which we should try to develop for our own benefit, rather than to depend on tourism to make a living. If we were a people who did have love, and unity among ourselves, like the Chinese, the Indian people of Shem, of what is now known as India, as well as the Gentile European people of Japheth, we could be doing much better with our resources, rather than to depend on tourism of the Gentile people for our economical well-being. Many Hamite's people who were taken from the land of Ham as slaves, were decent people, many of whom were married with husbands, wives, and children living off the land as how Yahweh made things to be, without any of these immoralities I have mentioned above. Although I have come to the knowledge, from the Scripture Map of 1890, that the city of Sodom, and Gomorra was in the land of Canaan, of the Jordan area, and what is now known as Israel. In the location of the Dead Sea that was destroyed by Yahweh for their UN Yahweh lifestyle. I have also learned from reading the Encyclopaedia that the lifestyle of many people of Europe at one time, were so loose, that many men who had wives had to let them wear what was called chastity belts, to prevent other men from having sexual intercourse with their wives while they were away. Many of these things I have mentioned above were former lifestyles, and culture of the Gentile people of Europe, before they left from their Gentile land of Europe to go out and conquered other people and their lands, so as spread their corruption to many people minds who became their captives. Many of their captives, and free slaves people of today, have become contaminated with their ways and lifestyle, of violence, crookedness, and sexual immorality that were rubbed off on many of their captives, and free slave people minds, who became a part of their citizens of their system. Many of the times, watching the news on the television, here in the United States, they often show many Hamite's men as the criminals, drug pushers, and thieves of their societies. But what they did not explained to their television viewers, is that they themselves are the problem that has caused many of these Hamite's men of the United States to become thieves, robbers, and drug pushers, that they show as the scum or dregs of this society.

They have used many Hamite's people of the United States to their own advantage, and when the time was right they let them lose without any form of skills and directions for them to fine employment, to better their standard of living, so many of them have fallen victim to the prison system that was design for them to fall into. From what I have come to realize, one of the reason why many of these Hamite's men of the United States become drug pushers, it is because many of the times, it is very hard for them to find employment, because many of them do not have any skills to be employed by their Gentile employers. Who has all of the various industries, and business for them to find employment from. The Gentile people will always employ their own people first, and give them whatever training, and opportunities they need to become skillful men in the job market field. In comparison to many Hamite's men who will not be able to get these training, as their Gentile counterpart will get. They will be the last to be haired, and the first to be fired, and that is the reality for many Hamite's people living in these United States. This is one of the reasons why many Hamite's people of the United States, must seek to establish their own little business, but more so, in the the land of Ham, among their own people, who are living there. That many of them will be able to find employment among their own people, to better their own standard of living. Many times, watching the television documentary, on the History channel, they explained that it was the mobsters, and the gangsters of the Gentile people, who were responsible for the drug trafficking business. They also point out that it was the mobsters, who were responsible for the prostitution rings, gun running, casino gambling, liquor distribution, and multiple murders throughout the United States. The various pirates of the Gentile people, who they have glorified for their evil deeds of violence and wickedness, who were given titles such as Sir Henry Morgan, Black braid, Sir Francis Drake, Sir Walter Raleigh, and the Buccaneers of the West Indies. Who were also a part of the Henry Morgan gangsters of pirates, who were living in various parts of the West Indies, and what became known as South, and Central America.

Many of these pirates used to rob, steal and kill many of their own Gentile Spanish people, to get wealth, and to steal colonies from the Spanish their brothers, who had the New World all to themselves for over one years, before the coming of the other Gentile pirates of Europe. Who came and fought the Spanish, to take away some of their territories of the New World, to become colonies of their native countries of Europe, where they came from. Many of their captives, and free slaves people of today have copied the Gentiles European people lifestyles ostruggling all their lives, and have nothing.

Yet, whenever they show these mobsters, and gangsters on their television, they always glorified these men as business men, and bosses of their crime world. That many of the time influenced the minds of many other people to want to follow their lifestyle of gangster-ism, and wickedness to get rich. Living under the European colonial system, with their laws of exploitation, with all sorts of oppressiveness, that they have put on many of us their captive people, such as taxes of various descriptions. Tickets for this or that, licenses for this, and license for that, these things was designed to bring in much revenue from their conquered people who became their citizens to make money off. Also, the many red tapes of laws that were design to keep certain kind of their captives people down from making too much progress in life, when they try to open the door to their own little business, to survive in their system of oppressiveness. I as a Hamite person, have personal experience of many of these red tapes, when going to their city hall, to seek about my license to open my own little business. It's all about a whole lot of red tapes that a person must go true, just to trying to open the door to their own little business. In my opinion many of these red tapes of their laws was designed to keep certain kind of their captive people down, such as many of us Hamite's people, who they do not want to see making too much progress, and eventually will become economically independent people. Able to employ ourself, and stop from biting the dust, and picking up soda cans, and bear cans, and begging them for bread, and always looking to them for employment like how many of us are doing in today time, living under their system. In other for a Hamite's person to break true the various red tapes of their laws of the Gentile European American system, they must have plenty of money that will speak for them.

Otherwise it is a struggle to survive in their system, of red tapes that was designed to keep us back, and this makes life become very difficult to live and survive in their system. Epically many of us Hamite's people, who are mainly the victims of their establishment. This also includes the various court fines, and parking tickets that were designed as a form of business of exploitation that they have put on many of us, their free slaves, captive people. Who became a part of their system of citizen's, to bring in extra revenue from their court system, as a form of business to make money. The high gas prices with the other form of bills that one as to pay, just to live, and survive in their system, because of their greed to gain more wealth. An Hamite person of the United States can to go to prison for

traffic, or parking tickets, especially if they do not have the money to pay to the court system for the parking tickets, and other various fines, of their many oppressive laws, they put on their many conquered people. Who became their free slave's citizens of today, so as to bring in more revenues. There was a time in the southern part of the United States, that a Hamite man could go to prison, or to be killed for a law that the Gentile European people of the United States did established, that was known as the Eye Rape Law. During that time, if a Hamite man was walking down the street, and a Gentile European woman was passing by, he better makes sure he is walking with his head looking down to the ground. Because if that Gentile European woman was prejudiced, and she screamed because she claimed the Hamite man was looking at her. When the police officer come to investigate the matter, that Hamite man could be arrested, and charged for Eye Rape. Beaten or be killed for looking at a Gentile woman, whom they classified as the most beautiful women in the world to look at, in comparison to other women. There are many ways of today that a Hamite man of the United Sates, can end up in the prison system without doing anything wrong, but just get arrested through trumped up charges by the police system, that was design for many of their x-slave Hamite's people to fall in to the prison system, to keep the population in check. Most of the people who are in the prison system of the United States are Hamite's people, because many of them have been the underprivileged people, who are suffering from poverties, ignorance, and slavery mentality, that many of them are suffering from. In comparison to that of their Gentile communities of the United States, who have for more opportunities, and are not the victim of the prison system, like in the case of many Hamite's people of the United States, who are the victim of these United States.

This make the crime rates lesser in the European communities of the United States in comparison to that of the various Hamite's communities of the United States, because they are the most oppress, and are the poorest of their system, that was built upon slavery, and exploitation to get rich. As I have mention that many of the Hamite's people of the United States have pattern themselves after the Gentile people life style of crime, violence, drugs, liqueur and ignorance. That has cast many of them to end up in the prison establishment that was built, and design for them to fall into. The prison system of the United States, was built for their captive's people, many of whom are now the free slave citizens of today.

The prison system was not built for the settlers, or the colonies, as they were call, who came from Europe, but it was built for many of their captive's people, who have copy their life style of crime, and robbery of the Gentile people of Europe. Not many people of today know that the police force system, as we know it as today, was not designed for the protection of the Hamite's people, who were brought over to the New World as slaves. Nor was it designed for the various natives, who were conquered, and many of them were enslaved to death, and there lands were taken away by the Gentile people of Europe to become wealthy people. The police force system came from out of the army system, and from the Sheriff Marshal system, that were designed for the protection of the various Gentile European settlers. Who came to this part of the world from their Gentile land of what became known as Europe. It was also designed to protect them from the uprising of their conquered people, who became their subjects, and slaves. The police force system was also established for the protection of other Gentile European people, who used to rob, steal, and kill many of their own people to get the wealth they had. This was because of their greed, selfishness, and their love for money, violence and power. Back in the days of the Wild West of the United States, in order for a European person who has wealth, chattels, and lands, to keep their wealth, and their life, they had to hire many fast guns slingers to stay around them. This was to protect them from their own people, who use to rob and kill many of them to take away what they had. When a Hamite person become a police officer, the first people they would try to show their Gentile given authority on, his is their own people, by brutalizing, and harass them, because they cannot brutalize any of the Gentile people with their European police badges of authority ship.

If Hamite police officer was to used his European police badge to brutalize, any European people of their neighborhood, all the European people in that neighborhood, including other European policer officers, would turn around, and beat this Hamite policer to death. For using his given police authority against their own European people. As I have mention before that many Hamite's people are suffering from slavery mentality, and inferiority complex, and stupidity, so this is one of the reason why many of our police officers do not have any respect, and love for many of their own suffering Hamite's people. But only to flex their muscles on their own people when they get the chance to do so.

In the American system of today, if a Hamite person who is innocent and is accused of some crime against the system, and they do not have any money to get himself, or herself a good lawyer, who as his, or her own interest at heart, may Yahweh have mercy upon that soul. Because they are going to go to prison, and stay there for a long time, because they do not have the money to pay their way true the system. The only way a person can get justice in the United States, and that is, if they have money to pay their way through the system, and get the right lawyer who will work in their favor. Otherwise, they will go to prison, and stay there for a long time, if they do not have any money to pay to get justice, and freedom. Because justice and freedom comes in the United States if one has money to pay, otherwise there is no justice to be given, and that person future is bleak. Sad to say that many Hamite's people of the United States, and in many parts of the Gentile world, where we happen to find ourselves. Must go and look for a European lawyer to defend our rights, and to go before these same European people, who became lawyers, and judges to get justice from them. These were the same people, who has been our oppressors, and destroyers for many centuries, and who do not have our interest at heart, but only want to see us down, as a people, so that they can exploit us to their own advantage. Most of the time, many of these Gentile lawyers do not have our interests at hearts, but only interested to take our money, and wrap up the case between themselves, and the judges. Who most of the time, are mainly from the European people background, and they all work and stick together as a group.

Even if a Hamite's person was to go and look for a Hamite lawyer, to represent his, or her interest in this European established system, many of the times, many of these Hamite's lawyers, are even worse than many of the Europeans lawyers, because many Hamite's lawyers are suffering from slavery, and colonial mentality. Stupidity and inferiority complex, and they do not have any love for their own struggling people at hearth, but just to take their money, and get richer. Number one, many of these Hamite's lawyers were educated from a European standpoint, and many of them do not have their Hamite's people interest at heart, but only to rip them off, and take their money, in comparison to other set of people, who look out for the interest of their own people betterment. The reason why I can write about these things, it is because I myself, have personal bitter experiences dealing with different European lawyers, and various Hamite's lawyers here in the United States, who has take my money, and did nothing for me.

One must also realize that we Hamite's people are living in a European system, that they have control over. So a Hamite's lawyer must sing their song, and go along with their program, otherwise they themselves may find themselves in jail, and the prison system. It is also very difficult for one to get back their monies they had pay to various lawyers here in the United States, even if they have taken advantage of their clients. The way the system of the United Sates was set up, if a person has been rips off by their lawyers, they would have to have money to pay to get another lawyer, to take their lawyer to court, to show to the judge what this lawyer had done wrong to him, or her. Also, this new lawyer has to have another lawyer as an expert layer, that is called affidavit of merit, to show to the judge what the lawyer in question had done wrong, and who was brought to court. This expert lawyer must get pay as well, and there is no guarantee that he or she who has suffers losses by their lawyer, will get back his, or her money. After paying the various court fees, and the various lawyers all their monies. Most of the time, many of these lawyers do not like to take another lawyer to court, because it is like going against the family of the organization of lawyer, and judges. Who most of the time, work to gather, and stick to gather as a group. So, it is like a Mafia system of the organization of lawyers. I was told by a European lawyer, who I had paid my money to represent me in a house I had bought in New Jersey area, that went into foreclosure. This lawyer told me that it is very hard for a person to get back money they had pay to a lawyer, even if he had done wrong to his client, because lawyers do not take other layers to court, it is like going against the families of lawyers, of the Mafia system.

The Gentile people of Europe are the ones who are responsible for the breakup of many Hamite's families 'lives of the United States, because of their perverted system, that promotes promiscuous lifestyle, that many Hamite's people of the United States were born and raised in. This corrupted system, of what became known as the United States, that many Hamite's people were born, and raised in, it has become a part of their day to day life of corruptions. That they have adopted themselves to from these people, who had great impact, and influence on their lives, and mind. Many of whom do not know no better, because as the saying goes, a man is a victim of his environment, where he or she was born, and raised in. This is the case of many Hamite's people, who were born and raise in these United States, who has fallen victim to their corrupted system they were born and rise in. The breakup of many Hamite's family of the United States, has caused many of these single mothers to raise up their children all by themselves. Many of whom later become juvenile delinquents, moving in and out of the prison system that was designed for them to fall into. I must point out that Yahweh did only originate husband, and wife, and He did not invented boyfriend, and girlfriend relationship as how it is so prevalent in this society of the United States. Or wheresoever the Gentile families of Europe, went and conquer, and set up their system of ruler ship of corruptions as a way of life for many people of their captive people to fallow. So, this boyfriend, and girlfriend relationship in the Scripture, is called fornication, and it is also mention in (Ephesians Chapter 5 and verse 3) about fornication, which is speaking of sexual relationship outside of married.

Because Yahweh did only create husband and wife relationship in the beginning of time. So, many of these children who were born from the participating of girlfriend, and boyfriend sexual relationship, end up without any proper fatherly direction for them to follow, so as to take them through life, in this perverted society, which is full of violence, crime, sexual immorality, and all sort of UN Yahweh like qualities of life. Many of these children from out of boyfriend, and girlfriend relationship live, and wasted their lives away, and end up in the prison system of the United States, because many of their fathers are somewhere else, with some other women making more babies, and living carelessly without any self-consciousness for themselves, and their off springs.

In the early days before our ancestors were brought over to the Gentile so-called New World as slaves, for them to learn things of their faith, as they did put it, their common ways of life were for a man to have children with his wife, or wives, and to bring them up in a respectable manner to take them through life. So, there is a big difference, between those Hamite's children, who were born and raised in the land of Ham, and in the Caribbean, in comparison to those Hamite's children who were born, and raised in what became known as the United States. Many of whom do not have any morals, no discipline, and no respect, for each other, and no love for themselves, or for their own kind of people. My reason for saying this is, it is because I have heard in many of their Rap songs, they called as" kill the Niggers", because many of them are suffering from slavery mentality, stupidity, and ignorance of not knowing who they are, and where they, and their ancestors is coming from. This is of the great civilization we as a people are coming from, before slavery and colonialism was impose on us as a people. Many of them developed this kind of mentality due to the system they were born and raised in, which influenced many of them to become this sort of people, I have mentioned above. Many of the Gentiles people of the United States don't want to see many of their free slave Hamite's people rise from biting the dust, and begging them for bread, and always looking to them for work, to better their standard of living, and to put bead on their tables. There is an old saying that goes like this, monkey see, and monkey do. So, because many Hamite's people were born, and raised in these United States, and have lives their lives for many centuries among these European people. They have totally copied their lifestyles, culture, and ways of life of these people, who had great impact, on their lives and minds.

This has helped to mold many of them into the kind of people many of them are today, without any self-consciousness for themselves. Furthermore, the Gentile people of the United States are in the majority, and the Hamite's people are in the minority, and the Gentiles people of Europe also rule their system they had established, for themselves, and for those people who they want to live in their conquered society. So, it is very easy for their culture, and way of lives to rub off on many of their conquered people. Many of whom do not know any better, and who always trying to copy the things they see the Gentile European people do, on their television, and in their Hollywood movies, also in their day to day lives.

It has helps to influence the minds of many Hamite's people, who always want to follow the ways, and lifestyles of many of these European people, who as a great impact on their minds, and lives. Many Hamite's people who were born and raised in the land of Ham among their own people, and many who were born and raised in the Caribbean, living among their own people. Is a far kinder, and helpful people to each other, than what I have seen with many Hamite's people of the United States, show toward their own people. All though many Hamite's people of the Caribbean and in the land of Ham itself, are suffering from the same slavery mentality, stupidity, and ignorance, of the colonial slavery mentality system, many them were born, and expose to, by our colonial slave masters. Yet many Hamite's people of the Caribbean, and of the land of Ham has more love for themselves as a set of people, in comparison to what many Hamite's people of the United States show to each other. Many of whom always trying to run away from themselves of who they are, and trying their very best to look like, and to be like that of the Gentile people of Europe of the United States. The kind of love many Hamite's people of the United States have toward each other, is only to rob, and steal from each other, and to sell their drugs to their own people. This is to destroy the minds, and lives of their own people, who they call the Niggers, with their drugs of stupidity. They take advantage of their brothers, and sisters who are the victims of the United States oppressive, and exploitation system. To give one a good example of how many Hamite's people of the United States do not have any real love and care for each other, unless of course there is some money to be paid out to get some help. I had an Auto body repair shop in the Newark area of New Jersey, and one day the rollup steal door trapped me inside the garage, and it was the only door to go in, and out of the garage.

I look through a peephole that was in the steal rollup door, and I saw a Hamite brother who was passing by, I called out, "brother please help me, I'm trapped inside, can you pull the chain to open the door for me?" His reply to me was, "do you have three dollars?" I was somewhat shock by his response to my plea for help, and I said to him, my "business is very bad at the moment, and I do not have any money to give to you." He said to me, I should stay inside of the garage, because I did not have the money to pay him, to pull the chain for me!" Sadness, and frustration came over me, because I didn't have any money to pay this brother, he refused to give me a helping hand. It was a good thing a neighbor who I knew was passing by, otherwise, I would have to stayed in the garage and died.

It is very sad to come to this reality, with many of our Hamite's people of the United States, because our ancestors before them, had love and unity among themselves, that did enabled them to bring about the present generation of the Unite States of today. If they did not have any love, and unity among themselves, many Hamite's people of the United States of today would not be around in today's time. Many Hamite's people of the United States, do not support each other in their own little businesses, so as to create job opportunities among their own people, to help them to better their own people standard of living. Why is it that the behavior of the Hamite's people of the United States is so different, in comparison to their brothers, and sisters who are living in the land of Ham, and in the Caribbean where many of our ancestors were taken as slaves? The answer this question, it is because many Hamite's people of the United States, have become alienated from their own kind of people, and many of them have become enemies of their own kind, and have copied most of the Gentile people lifestyle of selfishness, greed, and wickedness to get rich quickly. Many of them are suffering from the Willie Lynch teaching, that became known as the slavery mentality of today. This Willie Lynch teaching still affect many Hamite's people minds in their day to day life, that influence many of them to behave the way many of them do toward each other, on a day to day base.

Chapter 55 - The Invaders From of Europe

The invaders from the Gentile Land, of what became known as Europe. Many people of today don't have the knowledge, and the understanding that many of the Gentile people of who became known as Europeans people, had left from their Gentile land to go out and conquer other people, and their lands in the name of Christianity. Many of whom, were thieves, pirates, murderers, rapists, wicked and evil people, who have killed off many people, to get their gold, and diamonds of their lands to get rich and powerful. All in the name of the cross, and Christianity, using the Bible as their tools to conquer, and to keep their many captives in subjection to their will. So, in other words, they were imposters of what was known as the Way in Isreal, by the Yehudahites, and the Benjamites of the children of Israel. Who were the true, and early followers of Yashua, that became known as Christianity in the city of Antioch of Turkey. These early followers of Yashua were without any form of hypocrisy and deceitfulness, not like that of many Gentile people of Europe, who had professed themselves as Christians, to their many captives, but not in good deeds. Many of these early Gentile people of Europe, who had called themselves Christians, and Christian countries, who became known as the colonists, settlers, and pilgrims. Many of whom were alcoholics, winos, gold hungry people, who had the thirst for wealth, power, and to conquer people and their lands to get rich. Also, to spread their corruption to the minds of their many captive people who had survive from their brutality and wickedness, to see them as followers of Yashua. Who they name as Jesus and Christ, but who were wolf in sheep closing, who had no Yashua like qualities.

This is the reason why in places that became known as the United States, and in many other parts of the European so-called New World of the Americas, and the West Indies there are so much violence, crime, and wickedness, of exploitation that were left behind by the European conquerors as a way of life. Because this was the foundation left behind by the Gentile Europeans conquerors of Europe, who went to these places, and established their colonies of crookery, wickedness, and violence to gain rich. This is because of their greed, and their thirst for wealth, that these Gentile people left behind as an example among many of their off springs who are there, and also, among many of their ex-slave's people, who have copied their ways of robbing, and stealing to get rich.

Many of the natives, and their Hamite's freed slave's people have become their tax, and rent paying people to bring in more wealth into their system, this was to benefit their descendants who are around today. For them to get rich from the life, and struggles of their many oppressed, and conquered people. Before many Hamite's people were brought over to the New World of the people of Europe, to replace the natives as the new slaves. Their many captives were free from any form of taxation, and their rent paying system, that they had set up, and designed to bring in much revenue, from their conquered people. Who became their citizens of their established system, that they live off, and get wealthy like a parasite. Many Gentile people can leave from their Gentile land of Europe without, any form of wealth, and come to the United States, and became wealthy landlords overnight. This is from their rent paying system, that was setup for them to live from their many conquered people, who became their citizens, and their free slave people of today. The taxpaying system as we know it as today was established by many earlier conquerors before the Romans came on the scene, as a world conqueror, that was known as tribute. The word tribute is a Latin word, that was called by different names, and by different conquerors. This was before Rome was established by Romulus, and his companions, and it was a form of taxation that was paid in gold or other precious metals. That various conquerors had put on their subjects they had conquered. This tribute was a form of exploitation for those people who came under their ruler ship, of conquest, and had to pay their conquerors for piece to please them. So, when the Romans came on the scene, they made the taxpaying system more modern, and more fashionable. This system was adopted, by the various Gentile European powers, who came from out of the breakup of the Roman Empire of the Gentile land of Europe. So, this tribute of taxation was a form of exploitation to their conquered brothers, and sisters of Europe, who became their victims, and slaves of those days to bring in more wealth to the city of Rome. The landlord, and the tenant, and the rent paying system as we know it as today, came about when the Romans had control over the Gentile land of Europe.

Many of their Gentile brothers, and sisters who the Romans had under their control, became their slaves, and servants, that were known as serfs. This word serf is another word for a slave, who did came under the Roman system of captivity. These serfs, or slaves had to work in their agricultural fields, of plantations, and many of these serfs were drafted, and put in the Roman army to fight as Roman soldiers.

According to volume 16 of the Encyclopaedia, these drafted solders of the Roman army of their wars, was for them the Romans to gain wealth, power, and control over other people, and their lands, who they had conquered. According to volume 20 of the Encyclopaedia, under the subheading of Feudalism. This word feudalism, means according to the Webster Dictionary, was an economical, political, and a social system that did egxiested there in Medieval Europe, in which land was worked by serfs, or slaves. These serfs were bound to work on the land that was held by Vassals, in exchange for military, and other services that was given by their over lords, or masters. The word Vassals according to the Webster Colligate Dictionary came from Middle Latin, and Late Latin, that meant one who place himself, under the protection of another, as his lord, and who had vowed to serve him as his vassal. It is the same way in what became known as the United States of America, and in many other lands where the people of Europe went out and conquered, many of their captives people became their tax, and rent paying people. They also, train many of their captives to become solders, to go out and fight their wars of greed, power, and control, and to bring in more wealth, and colonies into their system. During the sixties the British brought out a magazine that was called the British Empire, and in this magazine they boasted of themselves how they had captured the savages, as they put it, from different countries, and train them to go out and fight their wars of greed, to gain power, and wealth, and to bring in more colonies.

George Washington did the same thing with various natives of what became known as the United States, when he was fighting against the British, his brothers, who he also came out of. He drafted many of the natives and put them into his army to fight against the British. Because he did not want to be any longer under British ruler ship, and having to pay them taxies, so the war became known as the war of independent. I would also like to point out that, many of these early settlers, who were fighting against the British Crown, of the Government of Britain, were of British ancestry, including George Washington himself. This war of George Washington was for the independent from Britain, because Britain at the time had fought in quite a few wars, and needed more revenue to stabilize the economy of Britain. Also, they the British needed more money for the military budget, so in 1764, the British Government imposes a tax on the settlers of the United States to bring in this needed revenue.

These British settlers did not like the idea of paying any extra tax to the British Government, including George Washington himself. Many of these British settlers of the United States had the desire to rule themselves, rather than having to answer to the British government, for this or that, and having to pay more taxes to the British crown. So, many of these wealthy settlers get to gather and decided to form a committee that became known as the Continental Congress of the United States, with George Washington who was the chief military man among his neighbors, friends and associates. This committee of the organization of the Continental Congress was formed to resist the Crown of the British Government. The funny thing about it, George Washington used many of these native people, who became known as Indian to fight in their war of interest against his fellow British countrymen. These were the same people who the early British settlers, and other Gentile European settlers, who came from different part of Europe, to what is now known as the United States, who used to enslave, and slather off many of these natives people, to get their lands. According to volume 29 of the Encyclopaedia Britannica Mecropedia, there it explained that George Washington was born in what became known as Westmorland County of Virginia, on February 22, or February 11, 17, 32. This same volume 29 of the Encyclopaedia explained that George Washington father who was known as Augustine Washington, went to school in Britain, and later Augustine Washington got married to Mary Ball who was a widow, and she became the mother of George Washington.

According to volume 9 of the Encyclopaedia, John Washington was the grandfather of Augustine Washington, who migrated from Britain in 1657, to the British colony of Virginia. My reason for bringing this little history about George Washington, and his family to light, it is to show that many of these early settlers, who were fighting against the British Crown for independence of what is now known as the United States of America. Were former British people, with other Gentile European people of Europe, who were a part of these early settlers. Many of whom used many of the native people to achieve their war objective, as how they have been using many of their free slave Hamite's people of the United States, to go out and fight in their wars of interest of greed. When many of these Hamite's solders return from fighting their wars of greed, they cannot even walk the street in peace, without been arras, and beaten up by their European police force system.

In Roman times, many of their Gentile brothers, and sisters who became their slaves, had to work under various Roman officers who became their Lords. Many of these slaves who became their properties, had to work on many of these Roman officer's properties of plantations. There were also Arch Bishops, who became very powerful landlords, many of whom had royal authorities that they had over other Gentile slaves, as servants, working for them as a part of the Roman Empire system of Europe. According to volume 18 of the Encyclopaedia, the Roman agricultural society that was in their various country sides throughout Europe, were cultivated by many serfs of Europe, on their big estates that were called Villas. Many of these slaves 'cultivators were bound by the Roman Governmental officials, to remain on the land of their cultivation, to maintain a tax paying system of their society. Even the papacy that were known during the Roman Republic time as the Pontiff Maximums, which is another word for the Pope, and his office of Rome. Many of these serfs eventually became known as free slaves, or peasants. The reason why these free slaves became known as peasants, is because they were given a certain amount of freedom, in comparison to other slaves who were still in bondage, and who were not given the title as free slaves, or peasants of that time. Many of these free slaves became known as peasants, because they owned nothing, and they were given the opportunity by their Lords, or slave masters to cultivate their own little farm. This opportunity that was given to many of these serfs to cultivate their own little farm, were done on their masters 'properties, so as to be able to sustain themselves, but they were equally expected by their Lords to look after, and cultivate their Lords villa, or farms.

Volume 18 of the Encyclopaedia further explained that it was during the invasion period of Rome, by the tribe of the Germanic Visigoths, in the time of 410, that brought an end to the Roman Empire of Western Europe. So, during the Germanic invasion period, there were three-fold of these free slaves, or peasant's class of people. While there were other slaves who were still in bondage, and were not given the title as free slaves. Among these free slave's class, was a Germanic people who were known as the Franks, who became known today as the French people. Also the Alamannis, Goths, Visigoths, Vandals, Saxon, and other Germanic tribes of Germany. Also, in Kent of Breton that became known as Britain, and England, there was also these free slaves ' classes who had limited amount of freedom, such as having their little huts, and a little piece of land to do their own little farming on. Many of these free slaves or peasant farmers of Europe, by the time of 1000 AD, their were equally expected to perform such work on their Lords properties, such as plowing, reaping and cutting. They were subjected to their Lords will, in much the same way as those other slaves who were not given the title as free slaves, or peasants. Volume 18 of the Encyclopaedia explain that in many parts of Europe, but more so, in the northern part of Germany, and also in the eastern part of Britain, many of these early free slaves, or peasants had formed an important part of the population of Western Europe. By the time of the 13th, to the 14th Century AD, many of these free slaves became free men in relationship to their societies, but they were subjection to their Lords will who were over them. By the time of the 14th Century, many of these free slaves had to pay a fixed rent, in the form of money, to their Lords, or their former slave masters so as to have somewhere to live. My reason for going so deep into the rent paying system, that were established by the Gentile Romans, over the rest of their Gentile brothers, and sisters of Europe. It is because we the people of Ham, and other set of people, who were taken captives by the people of Europe, who came from out of the breakup of the Roman Empire, and became strong, and powerful nation of people.

We the people of Ham, with many others of their free slave captive people, who became their citizens, subject, and their tax, and rent paying people, they had established throughout their colonies of the world. Many of us, their x slave people, had to pay them taxies, and rent, as a form of income for them to get rich, and for us to have somewhere to live. Because they own most of the lands of the world, they had stolen from many of the natives people, to be their lands of position. This rent and taxpaying system of today is a copy pattern of what were imposed on many of the Gentile people of Europe, by the Romans, and others of their captors, that came from their own people, who had many of them in bondage. These Gentile free slaves' people who came from out of the breakup of the Roman Empire, became powerful slave masters, and oppressors to different set of people, who they had conquered, and destroyed in many ways, and form for them to get rich.

So, many of us their free slave's people who became their subjects of their societies, of their tax, and rent paying people they had established to bring in much wealth from their freed slaves who were born and raise and became their citizens in their various slave colonies of the world. The tax and rent paying system is a form of exploitation to many of us, their captives, who became their free slaves people, and who had to find somewhere to live in their established societies of today. One should realize that before the rent, and taxpaying system that were brought about by the Gentile people of Europe, as a form of exploitation, and pressure to make money, all the people of the world were living free from off the land as a family unit. Without any form of taxation, and rent paying system, as the way Yahweh had made things to be, free and easy, without any price to be paid to live. Until the Gentile people came on the scene, and established their system of pressure that one must go through on a daily scale, living in their societies to exist. So, as to have somewhere to live, under their system of greed and selfishness. They have turn the world up sided down, and have cast allot of confusion, suffering, and sorrows in many form, that many of their free slave people of can hardly cope with life, to survived, and live in their tax, and rent paying system. One must realize that the Gentile people of Japheth are a greedy, and a wicked set of people, who have the thirst for gold, wealth, power, and control. So, because of their greed for wealth, power, and crookedness, it has cause a lot of people to live in misery. Due to the pressure they put on their many captives, and free slaves people in different ways, and means, in their societies of the world, to bring much wealth.

The Gentile people are like a parasite set of people, who like to suck the life, and blood from their many captured people, who later became their citizens, of their conquered establishment, who had to pay them various fees, just to live in their system. I would like to give the reader of this book another example of the pressure that one must go true living under the Gentile European system of their high cost living to bringing more wealth into their system from their conquered people. Sometime in March of 2012, I remove from the city of Columbus Georgia to go to the city of Atlanta Georgia, and to my surprise, I came to realization that for a person to be able to qualified to get an apartment, they would have to make three time, or four times the rent of the apartment. Otherwise they would never be qualified to get an apartment to rent in the city of Atlanta.

In reality the way it is in the city of Atlanta if a person cannot meet the rent standard that is set up by the landlords, of their properties, they would have to move out of the city of Atlanta, and seek to find somewhere else where it might be a litter cheaper to live, that will meet their financial needs if they can find it. So, if they cannot find anywhere else, to meet the rent they can afford, they would have to look to find another States, where the rental system might be a little cheaper to live. Or to live under some bridge, like I have seen so many people do in Columbus Georgia, and also in the city of Atlanta Georgia, and in many other parts of the United States, because they cannot afford the rent system. This living on the Street, or under some bridge, is anywhere in the world that is rule and control by the Gentile people of their colonial establishment, they did established to bring in much wealth in their colonial world of slavery. It was a good thing I had my home renovation box truck, I had rebuilt the engine from the block up, that I was able to live in it for a while, until I was able to get a senior city apartment, because at the time I was the age 66. So due to my age, I was qualified for the apartment I am presently living in, otherwise I would have to keep on living in my box truck until maybe, if I could find an affordable apartment, to fit my budget. Or to live under some bridge, like I have seen so many people do in the city of Atlanta Georgia.

When I mentioned that the Gentile family had destroyed the minds of their many conquered people in many ways, and means, one may not have the knowledge, and the understanding of the things I am speaking about,

317

because they were not taught about many of these things in their schooling, I have wrote about in this book. Many of the Gentile people have the knowledge of these things, but they kept most of these things as secrets among themselves, and they only teach other people, what they want them to know. They are the ones who have control over the schooling system, through the world, by mean of their colonial conquest. Those other countries of the world that is not directly rule, and control by them, many of the time is under their influence of teaching.

So, they make quite sure they teach their own people one set of knowledge of history, and many other people who came under their captivity a different set of teaching of history. This is according to whatever suits their purposes, and their intentions of what they think we should know.

This is to keep us their many captives people ignorant of their deeds. Also of the true history that gone by, that is far different from what they teach their students in their collages, and in their universities.

Chapter 56 - Food And Sickness From Eating These Gentiles Manufactures Fast Junk Food Every Day

Food and sickness from eating these Gentiles European manufactures fast, and greasy junk food every day, tat they had impose on many of their captives people, who were born and raised in what became known as the United States. Also, in many other lands where our ancestors were taken as slaves, and leave us behind, we have become subject to these Gentile European people junk, and greasy fast food. Also, their ways of lives that we have copy, and adopted from these people, that is not good. It is very sad to come to the knowledge of how these Gentile European people, of what became known as the United States, have strip many of their free Hamite's slave people who were born and raised in these United States of their ancestor's cultural food. They have copy and adopted themselves to the European American culture, and their fast and greasy food. They have imposed their food, and their culture to many of their captives people, who became their citizens as a way of life for them to adopt to their cultural fast, and greasy junk food, to bring in more wealth into their system. I would like to point out to many of my Hamite's people of the United States, that they should try to learn more about their ancestor's cultural food from other Hamite's people of Jamaica, and other islands of the Caribbean. Who mainly eat their ancestral kind of food that is grown from the ground, and from trees. Food that has to be cooked, or roasted on the fire, rather than what I have seen many Hamite's people of the United States mostly eat. That in my opinion will only make many of them become big and fat from eating these fast, and greasy junk food every day that was design to make money by their Gentile European captor's. Many Hamite's people of the United States, mainly eat the Gentile European fast and greasy food they were raise on.

 That in many ways are no good for them, but will only makes many of them to become very big and fat, and sick, for the doctors, and the hospital to make money from them eating their fast, and junk and greasy food every day. These foods I have seen many Hamite's people of the United States manly eat as their staple diet will, only make them in the long run suffer from many health's related problems, such as high blood pressure, heart and other health related problems, because of eating too much of this kind of fast, greasy, and salty food every day, that in many ways are no good for them. But it was design for the people that run these establishments to make a fast buck, while they will suffer the consequences in the long run.

The problem of eating too much of this Gentile European fast and greasy food every day, it consists of too much cheese, grease, butter, salt, sugar, processed manufactured food, fatty meat, and sodas. This Gentile European commercial fast food is only geared to make money from many from their former x slave's people, who do not know any better. But many of whom embrace this kind of food that will only destroy many of them in the long run. When I was growing up in Jamaica, many people would eat bread and cheese, or bun and cheese as a snack. Along with their daily cooked meals that comes straight from the ground, or from trees, as the way Yahweh made things to be, that has allots of nourishment for the eaters. From I left Jamaica and went to live in London of Britain, for twelve years, I have never seen people cook their food with cheese, as I have seen with so many Hamite's people of the United States do. Who cooked their food with cheeses. Whether it would be bacon and cheese, steak and cheese, ham and cheese, eggs and cheese, turkey and cheese, macaroni and cheese, and spaghetti and cheese, it is all fatty and grease food. Bacon is full of fat, cheese is full of fat, steak is also full of fat, and eating fried eggs everyday with its grease will only make a person become big, and fat that might lead to heart and other health related problems. Many times, here in the United States, I would go to the lunch trucks, that goes to various job sites, and buy a butter roll from the trucks. When I opened the roll, it is full of butter; that one could scrape out the butter and lay bricks with it. A person would become very big and fat, and sick from eating these butter rolls every day. During my time as a teenager, or a young man growing up in London of Briton, I have never seen any British people cook their food with cheese, apart from the regular cheese roll, or a cheese sandwich as a snack before eating their regular cooked meals. The staple diet for many Gentile people of the land that became known as Europe, it is mostly consists of meat, sausages, bread, ham, eggs, fish and plenty of cheese. Also white potatoes from where French fries and chips came from.

This name chips came from the British people, and the name French fries take its name from France. However, I came to the knowledge and the understanding from reading volume 9 of the Encyclopaedia, that white potatoes, where French fries and chips came from. Originally came from the Incas people of Peru, that were known to them as solanum tuberosum. This food was later copped by the Spanish over lords of the Incas people, who had introduced the white potato into Europe during the 1500s, because of a famine they had there in Europe, that left many people in Europe starving to death.

This adopted potato is also known as the Irish potato, White potatoes, King Edward potatoes and so on. Such things as rice, and other foods that many Gentile European people eat today as their staple diet, they did not know anything of this kind of food, but many of this kind of foods came from their captives, and conquered people. Which was a part of their cultural food, that the Gentile people of Europe have adopted to themselves to eat, as their kind of food. One should realize and understand that eating too much of this greasy food every day, especially living in cold climates, like many parts of the United States, Canada and Europe, where one do not get to sweat out of their body, like that of many people who are living in hot climates. The eating of these greasy food everyday will only make a person become big and fat from eating all these greasy and fatty food, that will stored up in one's bodies. Many of the sicknesses and diseases that come from eating this kind of food, it is because they the Gentile people of Europe do not leave things alone as the way Yahweh made things to be. But instead, because of their greed for wealth, they grow many of the vegetable with chemicals to make them grow much faster. So, that these food kind will be ready to ship to their local run Gentile European supermarket, to make big profits from the selling of these things. They also inject many of the animals and poultry with chemicals to make them grow much faster, so as to be ready to ship to the slather houses, to make big profits from the selling of these meats, that in the long run will causes a lot of sicknesses. The funny thing about it, when a person becomes sick in the United States, and go to the doctors, or the hospitals from eating this kind of food every day, right away it's all about making money for the doctors, and the hospitals. Not forgetting the pharmaceutical companies who make big money from the selling of their expensive drugs, they the doctors give to many people to lose the weight they put on from eating this kind of food, which most of the times do not work. Before Yahweh gave man meat to eat from cows, sheep's, goats and poultry, the first thing He gave man to eat were herbs of the field that is known today as vegetables, and this was before the flood of Noah.

This statement about the herbs of the field that Yahweh gave to man for his food, can be found in (Genesis, Chapter 1, and verse 29), and after the flood of Noah, Yahweh gave man meat to eat, also vegetables of the field. This statement can also be found in (Genesis, Chapter 9, and verse 3). The vegetables Yahweh gave man to eat was free from all these kinds of chemicals, that many of the Gentile European people use to grow the food to make them grow much faster, to make more money. Although the Gentile people has messed up everything from the way Yahweh made things to be, they are now telling their television viewers of the United States they must eat more vegetables, and less red meat. There is nothing wrong with the meat or the food Yahweh gave us to eat, the only problem is this, they the Gentile people of Europe keep on messing around with everything, and they do not leave things alone, as the way Yahweh made thing to be. This is because of their greed, to bring in more wheat into their system, that will causes many people to have all kinds of health-related problems, and sickness, from eating their manufacture fast and greasy food every day. Many Hamite's people of the United States, who mostly eat these different kind of fast-food, has cost many of them to become very big and fat, with legs almost as big an elephant. The Gentile European people of the United States, tell their television viewers that the reason why many people of the United States are so big and fat, it is because they are obese, or eat too much. The real problem is not because many of them eat too much, but it is because of the kinds of food many Hamite's people of the United States mostly eat. Which has caused many of them to become so big, and fat and out of shape. There are many Hamite's people of Jamaica who eat three meals per day, along with a snacks and homemade drinks that are made from fruits, and vegetables. Along with a weed that comes from out of the sea that is known as Sea Moss, and many people of Jamaica do not get big and fat like many Hamite's people of the United States do. Many of them just remain trim, and lean and it is not because they go to the gyms to work out, like so many people of the United States do, but it is the kind of food they eat. The reason for this is, because many Hamite's people of Jamaica, and in many other Caribbean Islands, where our ancestors were taken as slaves, mostly eat their ancestors 'kind of food, which is grown from the ground, or from trees, and fishes.

Also, living in a warmer climate helps to sweat off some of the excessive fat that may build up in one's body. I have come to the knowledge that many Hamite's people of Jamaica have now adapted themselves to the Gentile European American fast-food system. That is now established in many of the islands of the Caribbean, and in the land of Ham itself. Many Hamite's people of Jamaica have no idea of the kind of food they are adopting themselves to, which will only make many of them to become very big and fat, that will eventually lead to sickness like that of many Hamite's people of the United States who mostly eat the Gentile European fast and greasy food every day. Many of whom are suffering from high blood pressure, heart problem, and other health-related problems from eating this kind of Gentile fast junk and greasy food every day. Many Hamite's people of the island of Jamaica, need to realize that the mindset, and philosophy of the Gentile people who have many of these fast-food franchises in Jamaica, and also in other Caribbean islands, and in the land of Ham itself. They are only there to make money for these people, and to get richer from many people dying from eating too much of their fast and greasy junk food every day. Another reason for many of the Gentile fast-food franchises that are there in many of the Caribbean islands and in the land of Ham itself. Apart from making money, it is because the Gentile people like to push off their cultural food, by way of advertisement. Also their ways of life on many of us Hamite's people who are there, and who do not know any better. Unfortunately, many Hamite's people love to always want to run away from what they have, and to adopt themselves to the ways, and culture of the Gentile people of Europe, that many of the time are no good for us. But it seems to always fascinate many Hamite's people to always want to run away from what they have, rather than to accept what we have. The reason for this is, it is because many Hamite's people around the world, are suffering from slavery mentality, ignorance, stupidity, colonial mentality and inferiority complex of not knowing who they are, and where they are coming from. But many of the time they always trying to run away from themselves, to be like that of the Gentile people of Europe, who many of them see as the master race of the human family that many of them want to be a part of.

Many Hamite's people in Jamaica should be very thankful to Yahweh that many of us in the islands were fortunate to hold on to many of our ancestors' cultural food, and some of their ways of life. Although I would not want to embrace all my ancestors 'culture, because many of them were idol worshippers, and witchcraft workers that I would not want to be a part of. Now that I have come to a better knowledge of understanding, from reading the Scriptures of the things Yahweh hates. But I am very glad, and thankful to Yahweh for the good parts of my ancestors 'culture, that many people of the island of Jamaica still have. There are other islands where many of our ancestors were taken, and their descendants were able to hold on to some of their ancestors cultural food, who did not completely last it to the Gentile European people influence that they were exposed to. Like that of many Hamite's people of the United States, who mostly eat the Gentile European people food, as their cultural food. While living in the United States I have been to many mixed breed people restaurants, that come from different former Spanish slave colonies of the Americas, and the West Indies. The food many of these people mostly eat and sell, they classified it to be Spanish food, because they do not have any knowledge of the history of the food they are eating, and selling, and where it originated from. Their problem is because they speak the Spanish language, and they see themselves as a part of the people of the land of Tarshish, who are now known today as the Spain, and the Portugal people. This is because they have no historical knowledge of who they are, and where they and their ancestors is coming from as a people. Many of them do not know that the food they are eating, and selling, and call as Spanish food, came from the slaves who were taken to various parts of the Gentiles' European New World, of the West Indies, South and Central American coast. I am pretty sure that the people of Spain, and their cultural food have nothing to do with the cooking, and the eating of yam, that some of their former slave's people from these places eat, and call as yame. This Hamite's food also consists of green banana, plantains that many tribes in the land of Ham use to eat. This was way before many of them were taken out as slave, that was introduce into the so-call New World of the Gentile people of Europe. Also, this Hamite's food consist of yam, sweet potatoes, breadfruit, corn, and many other things that the people of Ham, in Jamaica eat today.

Although the Gentile people of Europe have been teaching us their many captives, that corn that the natives call as Maize come from the native of their New World of the Americas. This teaching of theirs is a totally false teaching, and a lies that has no truth in it. My reason for saying this is, (Genesis Chapter 41, and verse 49) clearly explained that corn was grown in the land of Mizraim, known today as Egypt for food. This was also, among many of the Canaanites people thousands of years before what became known as the New World was captured by Columbus and Americus Vespucci, who was working for the Spanish. This was also way before other Gentile people left from their Gentile land of Europe to come, and take away many of the captured lands of the New World from the Spanish as their colonies of positions.

Many Hamite's people who were taken from the land of Ham as slaves to the various colonies in what is now known as the West Indies, South and Central America, and what is now known as North America. Some of their slave masters did allow some of the food that the slaves eat to be taking from their native land to be brought along with them to sustain them to do their work. According to volume 2 of the Encyclopaedia, breadfruit was first introduced into the New World by the suggestion of Captain James Cook, to Captain William Bligh, because it was a part of the slaves 'staple diet from their homeland. It was Captain Cook who was a Gentile European man, who for the first time in his life saw breadfruit in the islands of the Pacific, and he recommended that it would be a good food for the Negro slaves of the West Indies to eat. According to the Encyclopaedia, breadfruit was also grown in what is now called as tropical Africa, and was eaten by the various natives who are there. This is the reason, why in many of the islands of the Caribbean, and some of the South American countries, they grow plenty of breadfruit, that was brought over for the slaves to eat as a part of their staple diet. This type of food was not known to many of the Arawak's and Caribs people, who were the natives of what is known as the West Indies. Also, of what became known as the Caribbean, and in various parts of the South American countries. In comparison to many Hamite's people of the United States who mostly eat the Gentile European food that were introduced to them as their type of food. According to volume 1 of the Encyclopaedia, akee which is also spelled as Ackee, was known as Blighia sapida tree, and was widely cultivated in what became known as West Africa. This food was brought to Jamaica, and other islands of the West Indies for the slaves to eat.

Along with yam, green bananas and so on, which was a part of the staple deity of various tribe who were taken to the West Indies, which became a national dish of the island of Jamaica. This food is still grown in some parts of the land of Ham, and eaten by many of the natives who are there, and it is now widely eaten in various parts of the Caribbean where our ancestors were taken as slaves. I must also point out that when I was living in London of Britain, when many British people saw yam for the first time, that is sell in their various local market places. Where many people of the Caribbean would go to these places to buy their food to eat, that they the British people called this food as wood roots, because they did not know what it was. Now I came to the understanding that many of the British people are now buying and eating yam, that they did called as wood roots. Also sweet potatoes that are eaten by many people of the Caribbean as a part of their staple food. So in many ways they have copy allot of things from us Hamite's people, without even acknowledging it. The Gentiles European people of what is now known as the United States, have been showing to their viewers of their television programs how to make drinks out of fruits. What many of their viewers do not know and realize, that we the Hamite's people of Jamaica have been making drinks out of fruits way before these Gentiles people came to the knowledge about these things. They now show on their television program, as if to say that they were the ones who started the making of drinks out of fruits. Many of the time they would give the impression to their viewers that they had the knowledge of these things before, which they did not, because many fruits and vegetables that they now make as drinks out of, do not grow in Europe, but mostly grown in tropical countries. So, it is due to their conquest of the world of people and their lands, by the people of Europe, this is the reason why they have come to the knowledge about these things that they show many times show on their television, that they are the masters of the making of these things out of fruits and vegetables. It also amasses me to see how much these Gentile people of Europe have control of the various fruits, and nuts that is grown in many of the tropical countries of the world. That they did not know anything about, while they were living in Europe, because many of these things do not grow in Europe. But now they have control over these things they sell in their various supermarket, and make allot of money from the selling of these things, because of their conquest of the world, of people and their lands that came under their control. Now they are teaching many people who came under their captivity, about the eating, and growing of these things, which they did not have any knowledge about these things before. But it is because of the prophecy of the Scripture, about the time of the Gentile rain, or domination over the earth, this is the reason why they are now in control of all these things.

Although many British people who had forth against many of us their x slaves people, who were coming into Britain, to work as cheap labors, to do their dirty works, many of them did not want to do. Also, to pay taxes to the British system, so as to build up the economy of the British system, yet it was a good thing they did open up their doors, and let some of us in, because they have learned allot of things from many of us, their captives' people who were living among them.

Although many Hamite's people who had left from the Caribbean to go to Europe to live and work, it did help to corrupt many of their offspring's who were born and raze in various countries of Europe. To adopt to the European culture, and their ways of life that were foreign to their mothers, and fathers who went to live in these places to live and work. They are still many of us Hamite's people who are living in Britain who have help the economy of Britain, and also who as help many of the British people to come to know about many different kinds of food, they did not know anythings of, before the coming of many Hamite's people from the Caribbean. I also saw on the television that watermelon that is now grown in many parts of the Gentile European people New World, was taken from a part of the land of Ham that is now known as West Africa. This is the reason why there is allot of watermelon grown in these United States, that as brought allot of wealth to the economy of the United States every watermelon season of the year. There are many Hamite's people of what became known as Ghana who eat the same kinds of food like that of many Hamite's people of the island of Jamaica, such as yam, green banana, and sweet potato and so on. According to A Short History of the West Indies, the Spanish got their knowledge, and skills of growing oranges from the Moors of North Africa, who had ruled Spain at one time. The Carthaginian people of Carthage also had ruled Spain at one time, and this was way before the Moors, and the Romans came on the seen. Who came to power, after the people of Carthage, and destroyed the power of the people of Carthage, and also the power of Greece. The people of Spain, and what became known as Portugal, got their knowledge of growing bananas, oranges, and sugar cane from the Hamite's people of the Canary Island. Also from the Madeira island, that the Spanish, and the Portuguese people had conquered, that became their subjects, who were a Berber tribe community of what became known as North Africa.

I also came to the knowledge from reading A Short History of the West Indies, that mango that is now grown in many parts of the West Indies, Mexico, and what became known as Central, and South America, was taken from India, and from the land of Ham. This was to grow in this part of the world by the Spanish and Portuguese, as well as the Dutch, and other Gentiles European people. So, in reality the Gentile people of Europe did not know anything about the growing of grapefruit, tangerine, bananas and many other fruits that became a part of their commercial industries of today. Which had brought great wealth to many of the Gentile people of what became known as Europeans, of their conquered world.

Chapter 57 - Drinking of Herbs Tea That Is Good For Many Hamite's of The United States

Many Hamite's people of the United States should try to drink more herb tea, that we Hamite's people of Jamaica call as bush tea. Rather than the drinking of the commercial coffee, and tea that was setup by the Gentile European people of the United States, as a standard way for people to drink tea. Or coffee every morning, or whenever they feel like it. Many Hamite's people of today, do not know that some of the main commodities that slavery was established upon, to make money from slave labor, was tobacco, rum, coffee, sugarcane, cotton, and tea from India and China. Including rice from the Carolinas, indigo with other spices that were taken from India to grow in the West Indies, and the Americas. So, slavery was established on many of these things I have mentioned above, that the Gentile European family did established to make themselves to be come rich people from the growing of these things to sell among themselves. Who has taken many people from their homelands, as slaves, and cheap labor to work on their plantations of their New World to become rich people. Due to their greed and the might of their guns, they have also taken many people from the land of Ham, India, China, and various parts of Asia as their captives of slave, and cheap labor people to gain wealth. This was first by the Portuguese in 1400, with other Gentile European people who came after, and it became a big business for them all to make money, and to become rich people from slave laborers, and cheap labors to work on their plantations.

Slavery was built upon the reaping, and the shipping of these various commodities, to send to Europe to sell among themselves to make big profits. also to sell in their New World amongst themselves that they had called as the slave trade business. I do not want anyone to misunderstand what I am trying to say about the drinking of coffee and tea, because there is nothing wrong with the drinking of coffee or tea. But I am mainly trying to establish the commercial aspect from where tea, coffee, sugar, rum, cotton, and tobacco came from. Which was established by slave labor to make money, by these Gentile European people, and to become rich people from their many conquered people, to buy, and drink these products to bring in big profits from their coffee and tea factories.

When I was growing up in Jamaica back in the fifties, I was told by the older ones, that the drinking too much coffee every day that come straight from the tree, without being processed commercially was not good for one's heart, and it can cause one to have weak heart. This can happen when one drinks coffee straight from the tree without adding any form of chemicals, and preservatives that many of the Gentile European companies use in these things to keep them from going bad. Jamaica does not grow as much coffee as Brazil, which was setup by the Portuguese for their many plantation owners to make big money from their Hamite's slave labors. Of their plantations owners to grow coffee, but we do grow some coffee too. I want to point out that according to what I have learned from watching the internet, coffee was first grown in what became known as Ethiopia, and was taken to many parts of the European people New World.

I would also like to point out to many of my Hamite's people of the United States, and in many other places where our ancestors were taken as slaves and leave us behind, that according to a writer by the name of Severin Carrell, who did research on the Coca Cola, and Pepsi Cola soft drinks. He discovered that these "soft drinks" was made from the coca plant, which is the same source from where the cocaine drug came from. According to volume 3 of the Encyclopaedia, the Coca Cola Company was first started in 1886, by a Gentile European man from Atlanta, who was a pharmacist, by the name of John S. Pemberton. My reason for bringing out this little information about Coca Cola, and the Pepsi Cola, it is because many Hamite's people of the United States, and elsewhere buy and drink these drinks, without knowing where the source of these drinks is coming from. As I have mentioned before that the Gentile people of Europe, are only interested in making money, in anyway they can do so, even if it is drugs that will harm many people in the long run. Because when it comes down to many of the Gentile European people mind set, it is all about the love of making of money, in any form they can do so to get rich. It is also because it is a part of their culture of greed, wealth, power, and control, of selfishness to get rich. So next time when a Hamite's person buys Coca Cola, or Pepsi Cola as a soft drink, they must remember that the Coca Cola, or the Pepsi Cola they are drinking, it is from the cocaine drug plant, that came from the coca leaf. I also want to point out to many of my Hamite's readers who might read a copy of this book, that drinking of sodas every day with its sugar contents, and absorbing allot of sugar, and chemicals in one body every day is not good for their system of the body, and can cast various problem as one get older. As I have explained before that the Gentile people is all about the love of making of money, to get rich, that they cannot take with them to the grave yard. But it is a part of their greed, and their culture for wealth, this is the reason why they did established slavery to get rich. Sugar cane continue producing wealth in our today's time for many of the Gentile family of Europe to get rich. This is in their various run manufactories, and in their supermarket's where many of us go to buy these things to satisfy our sugar needs.

The Gentile people of what became known as the European people of Japheth, who have set themselves up on a high pinnacle of life, and who also deceived themselves by thinking that they are a superior set of people to us Hamite's people, and the White people of planet earth. When there were no such a people from the beginning of the human family as the White race of people, as they Called it. Also, that the way they see it, when Yahweh was making this earth, He only had them in mine, so all of the other people of planet earth are foreigners of their Yahweh giving earth, that was made for them only, so they think. The way they see it, everyone else are an intruder of their Yahweh given earth, that was made for them only. Without any prejudice in mind, because we are all the people of planet earth, who came from Noah, and his three sons. Also, from their wives, and from, Adam and Eve, who were the first human couple Yahweh had made, and put here on planet earth. I must say that if there are any people who are more superior to the other, it would have to be the darker skin people of Ham. My reason for making this kind of statement is this, when it comes down to physical strength, the Hamite's people of Ham are far stronger people than many of their Gentile European cousins of Europe. Even stronger than many of their Asiatic cousins of the people of Shem of the East.

This is the reason why the Portuguese, Spanish, with other Gentile European people, who did replace the native's slaves of the Americas and the West Indies with that of the people of Ham, who they named as Negros, Black people, and African people. Because in their eyes they saw that the people of Ham were a stronger set of people more than many of the Asiatic natives people, who they did named as the Indian people, and who they had in bondage of slavery. Also, many of the giant tribes of people that are mentioned in the Old Covenant part of the Scripture, were referring to the people of Ham, of what became known as the Middle East, and what became known as North Aprica by the conquest of the Romans. Also of what became known as Africa, by the Angles and Saxon Germanic barbarian people of Europe, who were given the privilege to be able to read and write for themselves by the Romans, and the Roman Catholic Church. That they did not know anything of before, because they were an illiterate people, who could not read and write for themselves. They the Hamite's people were the natives, of the land of Canaan, who the Gentile European people name as the Middle East, and the Middle Eastern people.

This was way before the coming of the children of Jacob, who later became known as the children of Israel, after Jacob name was change to Isreal, by an angel of Yahweh. This is also true for the Ishmaelite people of Ishmael, of what became known as the Saudi Arabian people, of the so-call Middle East, of the land of Raamah, and Raamah who was the fourth son of Cush. This is also true for the Gentile European people of Japheth, who also came along later, of the land area they name as the Middle East, and the Middle Eastern people. So, whether it was the Canaanite people, who came from Canaan, or from the other three sons of Ham, who were the natives of the land of the ancient world. This including the Philistim people, who became known as the Philistines people, who originally came from out of the family of Mizraim that is today known as the Egyptians people, who were living in the Garza strip, of what is now known as the Middle East by the Gentile people of Europe, who name the land area as the Middle East. (Genesis Chapter 10 and verse 14) clearly explained that the Philistim people who became known as the Philistines people, was a tribe that came from out of the people of Mizraim, and Mizraim was the second son of Ham. There were many giant people of Ham, that is mentioned in the book of Deuteronomy, that Yahweh destroyed, because of the children of Israel, and also for the descendants of Esau, who was the brother of Jacob, who became known as the Edomites tribe of Esau, and for other Abrahamic seeds.

Many of these Hamite's giant tribes of people, was also destroyed for the descendants of Lot's two sons, who were known as the Moabites and the Ammonites. Furthermore, many dark skin people of Ham do not break out in sores, and acne of the face, as often as I have seen on many of the faces of the Gentile people. Also that of many other brown skin people, who have allot of the Gentile European man blood flowing true their veins. A dark skin Hamite's person can stand the heat of the sun far better than many of their Gentile cousins of the people of Japheth, who became known as the European people of Europe. The darker skin people do not change their complexion because of the heat of the sun, like I have seen with so many of the Gentile people of Europe do. The darker skin Hamite's people do not have to put on skin lotion whenever they come in contact with the heat rays of the sun, like I have seen many of the Gentile people of Europe have to do, because they are afraid of getting sunburn and peeling of the skin. I have even seen many Gentile people of Europe, with sores on their heads, hands, and maybe other parts of their bodies. But from I had been lived in the island of Jamaica, until the age of fifteen, and went to live in London, among many Hamite's people of the Caribbean, I have never seen any Hamite's people with sores all over their bodies, like I have seen on many of the Gentile people of European back ground. Weather it is here in the United States, or in the land of Europe itself. Unless, of course, those Hamite's people who have sores all over their bodies, are suffering from some skin diseases. A good looking dark skin Hamite's woman is a far better-looking woman to look at, in comparison to many good looking Gentile European women, who are of a lighter shade of pink skin, or red skin complexion. My reasons for making this kind of statement, it is because a beautiful dark skin woman shows up her natural beauty much more than many beautiful Gentile European woman do. This is without any of their false vain make, I have seen on the faces of many Gentile European women. As if to say that they were not make up properly by Yahweh, when they came into this world by His power, and by His might. So, from their vain corrupted minds set, they have invented these false make up, deceiving themselves that these make up their women put on their faces, to make themselves look more beautiful, can advance their beauty. But they are only deceiving themselves, because no one can add beauty to themselves, it's either they are beautiful, or they ugly, or attractive. Sad to say that as the saying goes, monkey see, and monkey do. My reason for making this kind of statement, it is because, I have seen many of our Hamite's women put on their faces this kind of make up. Especially in what became known as the United States, who were born and raze among these Gentile people of the United States.

They have copy these false vain make up, from these Gentile European people, that they have brought out to put on the faces of their women, fooling themselves thinking they are looking beautiful, with these false vain make up, of the people of Europe, fashion world of today. I have even seen many of our Hamite's sisters of the United States, and elsewhere, put on these false face makes up, that make many of them buy to put on their faces, that make many of them to look much more uglier, than they would normally look. But as the saying goes, one fool makes many more fools, and this is the case that have taken whole on many of our Hamite's sisters minds of today.

Especially in what became known as the United States, and also in the land of Ham, that became known as Africa. This is because of the European colonial, slavery mentality, that came down from the Gentile people of Europe, of their conquests, that many of our Hamite's women as been expose to. A dark skin Hamite's woman displays her natural beauty, much more than the average beautiful European woman do, and this is without any form of their false vain makeup, I have seen on so many of the Gentile European women faces. Who use these chemical makeups to make themselves look beautiful. Most Hamite's women have a far better-looking shape to look at, with allot of curves, that would catch the eyes of any man, in comparison to that of many Gentile European women, who mostly have flat shapes like most men. I have even seen in many of the Gentile fashion store windows, female mannequins with similar shape, and figures like that of many Hamite's women. Many Hamite's women who have children, quite often still look very good to look at, in comparison to many Gentile European women, who have children, and who start to age much faster, than many Hamite's women who has children's. A beautiful dark skin woman keeps her natural beauty for a longer period of time, than the average beautiful Gentile European women do, and this is a fact. Even when a beautiful dark skin Hamite's woman reaches the age of sixty, she still looks beautiful to look at, in comparison to that of many beautiful Gentile European women, who start to wrinkle, and age faster at the age of forty, than that of most dark skin Hamite's women do, and other dark skin Indian women of Shem.

The Hamite's people of the world with other darker skin people of Shem, have a lot of Yahweh given qualities to be thankful for, that many Gentile people of Europe wish they had these things within themselves. Although many of our Hamite's people do not realize it, but always trying to run away from themselves, to look like that of the people Europe, because of their slavery mentality, and stupidity that many of them are suffering from. The people of Ham have a lot to give Yahweh thanks for, although they do not know of it, but who instead, are always trying to run away from themselves, of who they are, and want to look like that of the Gentile European people of Japheth. They should be more appreciative of themselves of who they are, rather than they always trying to run away from themselves, and trying to look like that of the Gentile European people, who many of them idolize, and want to be a part of.

It is a natural fact that the Gentiles European people of Japheth, is a farer wickeder, violent, and a more warlike people, who love to shed blood, and make wars, and to conquer other people lands, in comparison to their Hamite's cousins, who are a far more a peace-loving people than they are. Many of the wars, and world wars that were started, it was started by the Gentile European people of Japheth, fighting among themselves for colonial conquest of wealth of the world, and their greed, that many of the time lead into world wars, that many other people get cart up into their war of greed, for wealth and power. Because many of the people of the world are controlled by the Gentile families, because of their colonial quest of the world of people and their lands to get rich. The people of Ham were given one of the richest lands on the face of all the earth, a land that was full of gold, diamonds, with oil and all sort of wild animals lives to admire. But unfortunately, we the people of Ham have lost most of our rich inherited lands to various colonial conquerors. Who came up and raped the land of all its riches and its people. They have taken many of the wealth of the land of Ham to their countries of Europe, and to many of their overseas colonies. They are still holding on to some of our land, such as the place they the Gentile people of Europe named as South West Africa, and what they name as the Middle East. They have scraped up the wealth of the land, and left many Hamite's people there biting the dust, and begging them for bread. Many Hamite's people of the United States have a tendency of using this word, by saying that it is because I am a Black person, this is the reason why I cannot get this job, or this apartment, and this is the reason why I have been harassed, and brutalize by their Gentile European police force system, feeling sorry for themselves of who they are.

What many of these foolish Hamite's people fail to realize and understand, that when they make this kind of statement, what they are actually saying, is that the Gentile European people of Japheth, who they call as the White people, are a better people than themselves. Because they have a lighter pink skin, or a red skin completion, and they have all the wealth of the world they have stolen from many of us, their captives people, and they are not a harass, and oppress as we are as a people of today. So, this kind of saying that many of our Hamite's people make, against themselves, it is of a slavery mentality, and of stupidity, because this is what the Gentile people have been teaching us their many captives, to see them as the White race of people of planet earth. I must mention that the only reason why they the Gentile people of Europe can put so much pressure on us their many captives, and their free slave people of today, it is because of the prophecy of the Scripture, about the time of the Gentile reign, and domineering over the earth, that is mention in (Luke Chapter 21, and verse 24). Until the time of the Gentile European people powers come to their end. It will be Just like how the Medes people of Japheth came to their end, also the people of Greece, the Romans, the Angles, and Saxon people, with that of the Vikings, and other various Gentiles European warrior's powers came to their end. These Gentiles European powers of today, will also come to their end eventually, because the prophecy of the Scripture cannot lie, and it must come to pass, because it is the Word, and the power of Yahweh. I would also like to let this fact to be known that the lighter skin people, who see themselves as the White race of people, come from out of the darker skin people. Also out of the brown skin people, who in turn came from out of the blood of the darker skin people. This is a fact, and a reality of life, weather one knows it or not, or like it or not. The only different is that they the Gentile people of Europe are in control of the world affair of today, and many of the time they make life become very hard, and difficult for other people, who came under their captivity of ruler ship to survive. In their established colonial world of, today, because they want to keep many of us their captive people down. Especially we the Hamite's people who they name as the Negros, Black people, and the African people. In reality many people of the would would want to be identified with that of the Gentile people of Japheth, because they are in control of the wealth of the world, that they have stolen from many other people. Plus many people have to go to them to look for employment, to be able to survive, and to put food on their table, and to live and edgiest in their system they had established true colonialism and slavery.

According to the Webster Third International Dictionary, the word "white" that is pertains to the people of Europe, came from the dialect of the Angles and Saxon people, that was spelled as "hwit," which when this word later came into Middle English, it became known as white, and the White people. This word white were also taken from the Goths dialect of Germany, that was also taken from the Sanskrit writing that came from the people of Persia, which is known today as the people of Iran. The dictionary also explained that, when this word white applied to a human beings, it is related to a light pigmentation of skin, and hair, and eyes with light complexion that is also called as blond, that was taken from the word albinoThis word white or albino, also came from down from the Latin word Blanco, which means white. The Gentile European people of Japheth have been deceived the world of people who came under their captivity to see them as the White people of Europe. When in reality there are no such a people as the White people, that is mentioned in the writing of the Scriptures of truth. Which bare records of all the people who are on planet earth of today. To give one a good example of how the Gentile European family of Japheth have been deceiving the world of people, who came under their captivity, with false teaching and lies, to see them as the White race of people. According to the Webster's Collegiate Dictionary, there it explain that the White people, is of the Caucasian race who became known as the European people of Europe. This statement the dictionary gave, it is totally a false definition, and a false statement, and a lie because there are no White races of people on planet earth of Europe, according to the definition the dictionary gave. As I have mention before that all the people who are on planet earth of today, came from Noah and his three sons, and there wives, and the Scripture did not mention anything about any White race of people during the time of Noah and his three sons. They the Gentile family of Europe, can easily deceived many people of today, because they write the dictionaries, the Encyclopaedias, and they control the school system many people go to these places to be educated by them. This is to get a good paying job in their system they have established true colonialism, and slavery to get rich. So, this is the reason why they did established what became known as the curriculum, in the school system. This was for the teacher to their student what they wanted them to teach their students, according to what is written in the curriculum. This is for their many student, to see themselves as the educated people, of their establishment of their colonialism, and slavery teaching.

According the Webster Colligate Dictionary, there the dictionary mention that the word curriculum, were taken from the Latin word kurikulum, that meant running a course. So, later this word kurikulum came down to the French people, who got their education from the Roman, and the Roman Catholic Church, as currere, that meant to run. So, this word kurikulum, that became known as curriculum in the Gentile European school system of today, mean to run a course of study, as in a collage, or in an educational institution. So, the meaning I get from this word curriculum, is to run things according to their colonial braining washing false teaching, that they has taught to many of us, their many captives, who later became their citizens, for them to see things according to what they were thought, and what they want them to know. So, if a teacher of the schooling system of the American society, knows different from what is written in the curriculum, for them to teach their students. They would not be able to teach it, because that would be going against what was lay down for them to teach their student what is lay down in the curriculum. Many of these teachers would simply lose their job, and go to prison for going against the system that was set up by the colonial masters. (Exodus Chapter 4 and verse 6,) there Yahweh said to Moses that he must put his hand into his bosom, and when Moses put his hand into his bosom, and when he takes out his hand from his bosom, his hand became "leprous as white as snow." (Verse 7 of Exodus Chapter 4), went on to say, and Yahweh told Moses to put back his hand into his bosom again, and when Moses did so, and take out his hand from his bosom, it came back to the original color of his hands, before his hand became leprous, as white as snow. So, from this Scripture that was mentioned, one can see that apart from the word righteousness, that is mentioned in the Scripture, as white and clean, and pure, that stands for a person's lifestyle, that is clean and righteous before Yahweh. This word white in the Scripture also means leprosy, which means a sore, or raw flesh that affects a person in their life by way of diseases of the body. But there are no white raw flesh of sore in a person body of diseases, as how it is express in the Scripture, that became known as the Bible, by the people of Greece. But this expression came down from the translation of the people of Europe, because they see themselves as the White race of people.

So, the word righteousness that is mention in the Scripture, mean right doing, to please Yahweh, in our day to day lives, while He allow us to keep on living from day to day here on planet earth. To show further that the word white also means leprosy, at (Leviticus Chapter 13, starting from verse 1), there Yahweh went on to say to Moses, and Aaron his brother." when a man shall have in the skin of his flesh a rising or a bright spot, and it be in the skin of his flesh like the plague of leprosy". Then he shall be brought unto Aaron the priest, or unto one of his sons who has the position of the priest.The priest shall look on the plague in the skin, of his flesh, and when the hair that is in the skin has turned white, and the plague in sight is deeper than the skin, and the hair is not turned white; then the priest shall shut him up who has the plague for seven days more." Verse 5 went on to say that the priest shall look on him again after the 7th days are full field, and behold if the plague in the sight of the priest stay and spread no further in the skin, then the priest shall have him who have the sign of this plague to be shut up for seven more days. Verse 6 went on to say, the priest shall look on him again after the seven days are expired, but if the plague be somewhat dark in his skin, and the plague spread no further in the skin, then the priest shall pronounce him clean, because it is but a scab of his flesh and he shall wash his clothes and be clean. Verse 7, and verse 8 went on to say, but if the scab spread much abroad in his skin, after he was pronounce clean, and seen by the priest, he shall be seen by the priest again, and if the priest see that the scab spread further in his skin, then the priest shall pronounce him unclean, for it is a sign of leprosy. Verse 9 and verse 10 went on to explained that, when the plague of leprosy is in the man, then he shall be brought back to the priest again, and when the priest see him, and if the rising be white in his skin of his flesh, and if the hair turn white, and there be no sign of raw flesh in the rising of his scab it is leprosy. Verse 11 of the same Chapter went on say that the priest shall pronounce him unclean, and he shall not shut him up for he is unclean. Verse 12 and 13 went on to say, if leprosy breaks out abroad, and cover over all his skin, who has the plague, from his head even to his foot, wheresoever the priest looks on him, who has the plague, and all of his flesh is turn white, he is clean.

Verse 14 went on to say, but when any raw flesh appeared in him who has the plague, he shall be unclean. Verse 15 went on to say, and the priest shall see the raw flesh and pronounce him unclean, because it is leprosy. Verse 16 went on to say, but if the raw flesh turns again, and be changed into white, then he shall come to the priest, and the priest shall see him, and behold if the plague be turn into white, then the priest shall pronounce him clean, who has the plague, he is clean. So, again, the word white in a man skin is speaking about leprosy of raw flesh that is turn white, or a scab of a sore in a person flesh. Also (Numbers Chapter 12 and verse 10), there the Scripture spoke about Moses sister, whose name was known as Miriam, she became leprous as white as snow, because she and Aaron spoke against Moses, and Yahweh was not please of their saying against him.

At (2 (Kings Chapter 5, starting from verse 1 to verse 27), there the Scripture explained that Naaman who was from the land of Sidon that is now known as Syria, by the Greek conquest. So, this Naaman who may have been of a Greek descendant, who were living in the land of Zidon that became known as the land of Syria by virtue of the Greek conquest. Was sent by his master the king, to the king of Israel to be healed of his leprosy. The king of Israel in turn sent Naaman to Elisha the prophet, who was the servant of the prophet Elijah to be healed by him. Elisha became the prophet when Elijah was taken up to heaven, according to (2 Kings Chapter 2, starting from verse 9 to verse 14). Naaman who was sent by Elisha the prophet to go and bade in the River Jordan, and he would be healed of his leprosy. So, when Naaman was healed of his leprosy, he took present to give to Elisha, but Elisha would not take the present. The servant of Elisha became greedy, and went after Naaman to receive the present he was going to give to Elisha his master. When the servant of Elisha went back to his master, Elisha told him that the leprosy of Naaman shall stick to him and his seeds for ever, and he became as white as snow. So, again, one can see that the word white, according to the Scripture, means righteousness, pure, clean, and leprosy, and there is also no man on the face of planet earth who, is pure clean, and righteous, or white, that was taken from the word leprosy of diseases of the body. So, all the people who sees themselves as the White race of people, are a curse people, that come from the word leprosy. I would also like to let this fact to be known, that all the brown skin people came from out of the darker skin people, and all the lighter skin people who are lighter than the brown skin people came from out of the brown skin people, who in turn came from out of the darker skin people.

When these brown skin people have children with a person who is of a lighter shade of complexion than themselves, the eyes texture, or the color of the eyes begins to change, and the hair texture starts to change as well. When the children of these lighter brown skin people grow up, and marry and have children with other people who are lighter in skin color than themselves. Right away, the eye texture changes from brown to a lighter brown complexion, and sometimes to light greenish, and even to blue eyes as the washing out, or the melting out process continues. As the melting out process continues, the hair texture starts to get curly straighter, or even with wavy curly hair that will look straighter sometimes. Eventually, these people turn into full-blooded Gentile European people of Europe as the melting out process continues. The hair texture start to gets straighter, and sometime these people develop blue, or brown eyes. I have even seen many Gentile European people with blond curly hair, ginger curly hair, and even with dark brown curly hair, that will get straighter as the washing out process continues. I would like to let this fact be known that there are only one set of people on the face of planet earth, who have tight curly hair, or loose curly hair. Or wavy hair, that will eventually get straighter, or just stay curly and wavy as the washout trend continues, and these people come from the people of Ham. This is also a known fact to some people of the world, who may have this knowledge, that a dark skin male and female person can bring about an albino child into this world that looks very similar in skin color to that of most of the Gentile people of Europe. Sometimes these albino people, even look lighter in skin color than many people of Europe, who see themselves as the white race of people. However, no two light brown skin people, or any Gentile male and female person cannot bring about a dark skin child into this world, it will never happen, because that is not the way Yahweh made things to be. He made it that the darker skin people to bring about the lighter skin people, and not the lighter skin people to brings about the darker skin people. The proof of this true story is down below in these pictures, that is showing in this part of this book, for one to see for themselves.

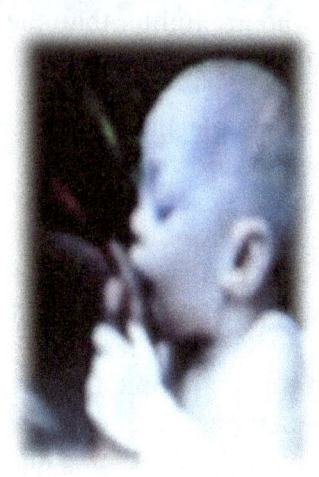

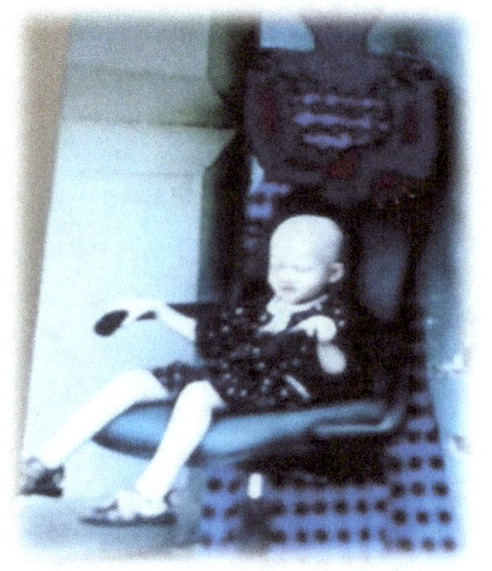

Chapter 60 - The Deception of the Gentile People, to the People on the People of Ham, and the World Over.

The Ham people of these United States, and in many of the South American countries, the Caribbean, and in the land of Ham itself, believed to themselves, that if they were to become more integrated with that of the Gentle people of Europe. This would solve their problems of oppression, and discrimination from these Gentile people of Europe, who see themselves as Yahweh's gift to the human family. Many Hamite's people who believe to themselves that if this was to take place, everyone would live happily ever after, without any problems from these Gentile people of Europe. Many of these Hamite's people who believed that if this was to take place, they would be more accepted into the European people societies, and their problems would disappear overnight. What many of these foolish Hamite's people fail to see, and to understand, that although they might feel this way, the Gentile European people would still have full control over their lives. They would continue to use us like tools, turning us against each other, for their own gain and benefit, just like how they have been doing so form the early colonial days of slavery to the present time. They would employ a few of us, while the greater number of our people will be unemployed, and at the same time, the greater numbers of their people would be employed in good paying jobs. They would be able to afford better houses, newer cars, eat, and drink much better than many Hamite's people who depend on them to put their pots on the fire, so they can have something to eat.

Those few of us who would make it into their system, would right away think to themselves, they are a superior people, to that of their many less unfortunate brothers, and sisters, who were not able to make it into the Gentile European societies of their conquered world, like they did. This is how it is in the real world of the Hamite's people of today, who were able to make it in the Gentile European colonial system, they had established by mean of slavery and colonialism. In comparison to those of us who were not able to make it into their established system of today. For a person to understand the truth of what I have explained, they only have to go to the various courthouse of the United States to see how the well to do Hamite's people treat their less unfortunately brother and sisters who come to their court house by way of the police officer. Or to go in any of the Gentile European x slavery colonial islands of their courthouses to see how much these well to do Hamite's people, treat their less unfortunate brothers and sisters who come to, their court house, by way of the policer officers.

Also, in many countries, where many of our x-slave Hamite's people were given the opportunity to become a part of the Kuru Cult Clan police Force System, of the people of Europe, that were set up for the protection of the settlers, or the colonies, as they were called in those days. This Kuru Cult Clan police Force system, were also established for the protection of the settlers from other settlers. So, for one to get a good idea, of the colonial slavery mentality of many Hamite's people, who became court officers, and judges, of the Gentile European colonial system to, see how many of these ex-slaves Hamite's people treat their own less unfortunate brother. Also, their less unfortunate sisters who come to their court system, by way of the police officers, to face whatever charges they many put against them. These Hamite's police court officers, and judges, treat their own Hamite's people who become victim of the Gentile European colonial system of oppression. With nothing but pressure, of payment and find, and disrespectfulness, all because of their position they find themselves into. In comparison to many of their less unfortunately brother, and sisters who were not able to make it into this Gentile European colonial system, they did established from the colonial slavery days to present time.

So, in other words, many of these Hamite's ex-slave people, who find themselves in high paying position of the Gentile European people colonial system, have become enforcers of the pressure they the Gentile people have set up, to bringing many revenues from their many ex-slave people of today. Who became their citizens, and subjects, and has to pay to live in their societies of the high-class people of Europe. This may sound very funny to many people, who do not have any knowledge, or experience of the many things I have mention. But for them to get a good knowledge of what I have written about, they only have to go to the various courthouses of the United States, and the prisons system. The police station, where many people would get a very good idea of what I have written pertaining to many of our Hamite's people of their European high position of their, slavery colonial system they had established. In the earlier days many of our ancestors used to work, and stick together to help their own people to survive, as many other set of people do. Otherwise many of us would not be around in today time, living under the Gentile European people system, as many of us do. Many of our children who go through the Gentile European integrated school system, will be more brainwashed, and miss-educated away from themselves, and to see things from the Gentiles European people' point of view, of what they teach them as truth, and what they want them to know.

Most of the time they would be more educated away from their own culture, and history, and they would learn more about the Gentile people of Europe history, and their ways of life, rather than their own culture and history. This is the reality living in today's societies of the Gentile people of Europe establishment, world, where many of our Hamite's people were taken as slave. They were indoctrinated to see things from the Gentiles European people perspectives'. To give one a good example of the brainwashing, and the deceptiveness of the Gentile people of Europe, toward many of us their captive people. I was working at an Auto body shop in the New Jersey area, and one day, I and an Italian man were having a conversation, and he told me that he saw in a book where it stated that Adam and Eve were White people. First, when I read the Scripture, with that of the Scripture Map, the understanding I got from it, is that the Garden of Eden were somewhere in the land of Ham, of what is now known as East Africa.

So, this Garden of Eden was nowhere in the Gentile land that became known as Europe, who see themselves as the White race of people. I cannot understand why these Gentile European people like to go around, deceiving many people of the world, to believe that Adam and Eve were some European looking people. Also for them to believe that the Garden of Eden was somewhere in Europe. The funny thing about their story, none of these European people were not around in those days, so as to give a description of what Adam and Eve look like. Due to their deceiving nature, this is the reasons why in the various translations of the Scripture, that became known as the Bible, they always show Adam and Eve looking like the people ofEurope. This is also true for their television programs, they always show various people of the Scripture looking like the Gentile people of Europe who they called as White people. This they do to deceive many people to believe that they are the special people of Yahweh, so everyone would want to look like them, and to be like them.

Many times, watching the History Channel, they even go so far as to show a picture of Yahweh, looking like a Gentile man of Europe, who no man has ever had the opportunity, and the privilege to see what Yahweh look like. Apart from Abraham and Moses the prophet, who Yahweh allow him to see His back part of his body, and His shape, and to be in His present. Yahweh made Himself very clear to Moses, when Moses ask Him to allow him to see His glory of what He look like, and Yahweh make Himself very clear to Moses that no man can see His face and live.

But He only allow Moses to see His back part of what He look like, because Moses found grace in His sight. Yahweh also said to Moses that He will have mercy on whom He will have mercy, because He is the boss of life, and that is the fact and reality of life. So, Moses and Abraham were the only two men who were able to be in Yahweh present and live. One can read (Exodus Chapter 33, and read from verse 19 to verse 23) to get a very clear picture of what Yahweh had said to Moses at Mount Sinai. This was when they the children of Israel came from out of the land of Mizraim, now known as Egypt, to go and take over the land of the Canaanites people, Yahweh gave to Abraham and his seeds after him. As I have mention that the reason why, they the Gentile people came up with these deceptiveness, it is because when many people of today read the Scripture that became known as the Bible, and see these Bible characters looking like the Gentile people Japheth. Naturally they would want to be a part of the Gentile people of Yahweh, to get some of that special blessing to rub off on them. So, my question to these deceiving European people of Japheth, how can they go around deceiving many people, by showing a picture of Yahweh who they have never seen, and also who they cannot look upon? Even

the world. Another factor is that the Gentile people of Europe, are the world's powers of today, and they have all the moneys they have stolen from us and many other people, and many people depend on them to put food on our tables. Also, for employment, and to better their standing of living. These are some of the reasons of today, why many Hamite's people do not want to be identified with their own set of people, because we as a people do not have any power or wealth, because it was all stolen from us. Also many Hamite's people worldwide, were brainwash to see the Gentile people of Europe, as the most beautiful, and intelligent people Yahweh has created and put here on planet earth. Even our lands, the land of Ham and his descendants, is now controlled by the Gentile people, and by the Mohammedans, who are known as the Saudi Arabian, and the Muslim people of Ishmael. So, quite naturally, many Hamite's people would want to be identified with that of the Gentile family of Europe, and of that of the Mohammedans, Muslim people of Saudi Arabia. Because they have all the power, and the wealth they have stolen from us Hamite's, and so our lands. Another reason for the inferiority complex in many Hamite's people mines of today, it is because they the Gentile Europe people, have been teaching the world of people who came under their captivities that we, the people of Ham, did not have any civilization in the early beginning of the history of the human family.

Also, that many of our ancestors were cannibals, and savages, so quite naturally, many of our Hamite's people would want to be identified with that of the Gentile family of Europe, who they were taught to see as the people who had started the civilization of the world. That were known in the ancient world, as craft and skills, that became known as science and technology in our modern world of the Gentile people of Europe.

Many Hamite's people, believe in the melting pot of the Gentile people of Europe, and they do not even have the sense to know and realize that by they desiring to be a part of the melting pot people of Europe, they are destroying their own set of people. This is by continuously washing out themselves into Europe looking people, and becoming a minority set of people, among the rest of the human family. Many of these foolish Hamite's people, who classified themselves to be educated people, as soon as many of them become our leaders, they seek to oppress their own people with the learning of laws, greed, and scheming they had learned from their Gentile European teachers and professors. Many of these so-call educated Hamite's people, of the European schooling system, who supposed to know better, because of their educational standard, should set examples for those other Hamite's people who do not know any better. As I have mentioned before that, although the elephants do not attend colleges, or universities and lived in the jungle. Yet they do not seek to move in to live where the tigers, and lions are living. They do not try to become a part of their family, of tigers, lions, and other animals of the jungle, but rather, they continue to stick together, and look out for the interest of their own kind of the elephant family. Also, to help each other to look out for the lions, and the tigers and other creatures who might come along to endanger their life, and well been of their elephant family. But when it comes down to many of our Hamite's people, whether here in the United States, or in many other part of the world where we happen to find ourselves, many of them would rather join with our oppressors to destroy their own people. Also, the elephant family do not try to washout, or melt themselves into half breed looking tigers, and lions, like how so many of our Hamite's people like to do, and to be a part of the melting pot people of the Gentile people of Europe.

The only time that one might see a half breed elephant, if that was even possible, it would have to be deliberately done by some human been, otherwise, it would never be so, because that is not the way Yahweh made things to be. He made each animal species to be with their own kind, although they may share the same jungle space, and live in the same land area. Yet each species sticks to their own kind, as the way He had made it to be. One of the reasons why many of the people of Ham are so divided, and cannot come together in unity, it is because majority of the people of Ham do not know who they are.

This is because we as a people were enslaved, and colonized and divided by so many different Gentile people of Europe, and also by the Mohammedans Muslim people of Ishmael, who are known as the Saudi Arabian people, who many Hamite's people speak their languages, and see themselves as a part of these people, and their religious philosophy of their ways of lives. Many Hamite's people who were born and raised in the various

Portuguese, Spanish, Dutch, French, British and the Mohammedans slave colonies of the world, see themselves as a part of these people, because they speak the language of their former slave masters. This is due to this miss-education and the indoctrination many of us their captives people had received. It have cast many Hamite's people to always want to try to run away from themselves, and want to washout themselves into the Gentile European looking people of Europe. This is also because many of us Hamite's people have no historical knowledge of themselves, and where they are coming from. I could remember when I was growing up in Jamaica in the fifties; there was a song that we sang in my school of the Kingston area that goes like this, "God save our gracious king, or queen, long live to rein over us, their slave captives people." Many Hamite's people of Jamaica grew up singing this song, feeling to themselves they had a very strong tie with the people of Britain. Also, that they the British people were destined to rule over us as our masters. Many Hamite's people of the island of Jamaica, had felt much closer in their minds and hearts toward the people of Britain, more than to the people of the land of Ham, that became known as African people. This is because they had very little knowledge of their historical past of who they are, and where they are coming from as a people.

This is the kind of slavery mentality many Hamite's people of Jamaica were made to believe in; that Britain, which is also known as England, is our mother country. I myself keep on questioning this teaching that many of the people of Jamaica did received, from our British slave masters. While I was growing up in London, I was always checking the Scripture, and the Scripture Maps to find some lead to the answer of who we are as a people. Also, where we as a people are coming from, before slavery and colonialism was imposed upon us. While growing up in Britain in the early sixties, I used to look at the various British people who are living there, and I kept on telling myself that there is no way that these British people could ever be our mother country. This is because from my observation of these British people, they do not have any resemblance to any of the people of Ham, who are living there in Jamaica, so as to associate them as our family members.

Although, in reality, all the people of planet earth are related to each other, because of Noah's and his three sons, their wives, and also because of Adam and Eve who, were the first human couple Yahweh had made, and put here on planet earth. So, we are all related to each other as the families of Yahweh. To add to the brainwashing the people of Jamaica did received from our British colonial slave masters, many people of Jamaica were told they are British people, and when many had traveled out, they were given a British passport to show that hey are British subjects. Yet according to some information on the back of a British passport I used to have, there it stated that the British people consists of the people of Briton, who became known as Britain people. Also, the people of Ireland, Scotland, Wales, the Isles of Wight, and the Isle of Man, who are really the British people. So, the other people who see themselves as British people, are mere subjects and colonies of the various British people I have mentioned above, who had conquered the various people of the world to become their subjects and prey. When I was staying in Denmark, in 1969, my money ran out and I was told by the foreign police of Denmark that I should go to the British Embassy to get help from there, because I am a British citizen, and I have a British passport. When I went to the British Embassy, they told me I must send to get help from some of my relatives who are living there in London, or from other relative who are living there in Jamaica. But for them they cannot help me, because I am not an English man. When I went back to the foreign police in Denmark, and told them what the British Embassy said to me. They told me they cannot help me neither, and they said to me, they have a steel hotel for me. So, they put me in jail, and locked me up as an undesirable alien, and finally I was deported from Denmark back to London.

When I arrived back in London Scotland Yard came to interview me, and ask me what have I done in Denmark? I explained to him about the money citation, and what the British Embassy said to me. I even show him a recommendation I did received while I was working at an Auto body shop in Amsterdam stating that I was a good worker. After this interview with Scotland Yard, I was told I am well come to come back to London. Before I was deported back to London, I asked the foreign police if they could deport me back to Jamaica, but instead, they sent me back to Britain. This is one of the reasons why many of the people of Ham throughout the world cannot come together as one, because we were given different nationalities, passports, and flags of the various islands, and slave colonies where we were born and raised in, to see as our identities of who we are.

This is of the various Gentile European families, who had control over lives, and who has give us these false documents to see ourselves belonging to them. So, we were indoctrinated by them, to see ourselves as a part of them, instead of seeing ourselves belonging to each other, as a family of the people of Ham. They do not have our interest at heart, but they only interested in using us for their own benefit and gain, when it suits their purposes to do so. Many of our Hamite's women are suffering from slavery mentality and stupidity, because many of them spent their hard-earned money to buy dye to bleach their hair blond. Ginger, brunette and red hear, just to look like some Gentile women of Europe, because they were taught to be ashamed of who they are, and to see beauty only from the eyes of the Gentile people of Europe. Many of these foolish Hamite's women of the United States, and in other places where we happen to find themselves, even tried to run away from themselves by buying wigs, just to look like that of the Gentile women of the United States, and Europe. In their eyes, they think to themselves they are looking beautiful with these Gentiles European looking wigs. This is due to their slavery mentality, and stupidity many of them are suffering from, this has made the wigs companies to become very rich, because many of our Hamite's women want to run away from themselves, of who they are, and to look like that of the Gentile women of Europe. The reason for these actions of theirs, is because there are suffering from stupidity, slavery mentality, and inferiority complex that have a great impact on their minds. Many Hamite's women of the United States spend their hard earn money to buy chemicals, to put in their hair, so that their hair can become straight like that of many Gentile women of Europe and the United States who has straight hair.

This is because of inferiority complex that many of our Hamite's sisters of the United States, and in other places are suffering from. This is the reason why the hot comb was invented, that spread throughout many parts of the Caribbean ,and in the land of Ham it self, just to look like that of the Gentile women of Europe. Many Hamite's women of the Caribbean began using the hot comb, so their hair too can look like that of the Gentile European woman of Europe. This inferiority complex of many of our Hamite's sisters of the United States, the Caribbean and the Motherland are suffering from, have cost many of them to lose their hair. By using the hot comb, and the chemicals they used in their hair, for it to become straight, wanting to run away from themselves.

Many of these foolish Hamite's women of the United States, and elsewhere, have even gone so far as to spend their hard earn money to buy hair peace, to weave into their hair to make it look longer like that of most European women of Europe. Many of them even deceived themselves, by thinking they are looking very beautiful with these hair attachments, they have paid hairdresser to weave into their hair as a part of their beauty. Many of these foolish Hamite's sisters fail to realize that no one can add beauty to themselves from the way they were born and came into this world, by the power of Yahweh. So, its either one has beauty, or they just don't have it. This inferiority complex many of our Hamite's sisters of the United States are suffering from, have also, caused many Hamite's women of the Caribbean, and the Motherland to copy their foolish ways of trying to run away from themselves. Just to look like that of the Gentile European women of Europe. Also, many of these foolish Hamite's people have even gone so far as to try to bleach out their skin color, to look like that of the Gentile people of Europe in skin complexion. Many of these foolish Hamite's women of the United States and elsewhere, have adopted themselves to put on the Gentile European women's eye shadows. False eye lashes, and other face makeup, I called as the "war paint. As if to say they were not make up properly by Yahweh when they were born, and came into this world, by His might and power." Not realizing to themselves they were given natural beauty without any form of these various chemical makeup's, many of these Gentile European people have invented, from their own vain imagination of their mind set to make money. Also, by having others of their captive's people following them in their vain madness, that they call as fashion, and beauty of their false make up. The Gentile people have a great impact on many of our Hamite's people minds, whether they are male or females, and that is the reality of what life is like today.

One of my reason for making this statement, it is the Gentile European people have invented the red lipstick, that many of their women put on their lips, to make many of them to look more beautiful as a part of their false fashion of beauty. The funny thing about this red lipstick fashion of their beauty, many of our Hamite's women have copy this form of their beauty, by putting on red lipsticks on their lips to make themselves look beautiful, with these red lipsticks, on their lips. Believing to themselves that these red lipsticks will attract the minds of other men, so they believe.

What make this situation so funny, many of our Hamite's sisters are of darker skin complexion, with these red lipsticks on their lips, thinking to themselves they are looking beautiful with these red lipstick on their lips, that make many of them looking like a clown of the circus. Deceiving themselves thinking they are looking beautiful with these red lipstick on their lips. There is an old saying that goes like this, one fool makes many more fools, and this is the kind of stupidity that has taken its toll on many of our Hamite's sisters minds of the United States and elsewhere. Many of whom have try their very best to run away from themselves, by adopting to these Gentile European people world, of their vain fashion, and false make up of their false beauty. Many Hamite's men of the United States even go so far by slicking their hair, for it to look like that of the Gentile men of the United States and Europe, who they idolize as the superior people they want to copy, and to be apart of. Many Hamite's women of the United States, and elsewhere need to realize to themselves, that many beautiful Hamite's women in the land of Ham, who are naturally beautiful women to look at. Do not need to put on these chemicals make up, that the Gentile women of Europe invented to make themselves look beautiful. Many beautiful women in the land of Hm were given natural beauty by Yahweh, when they were born, and came into the world of mankind, and that is the reality. Many Hamite's people are not proud of themselves, and are not thankful to Yahweh for who they are, and of the complexion He has gave to us as a people of the tropical sun countries. Because we as a people were made for the sun climate, this is the reason why we were given dark skin complexion, by Yahweh, to per teach us from the heat rays of the sun.

I must say that our Hamite's women are naturally beautiful to look at, although many of them do not realize it, but all of the time trying to run away from themselves, because the world, along with many Hamite's people were indoctrinated by the Gentile people of Europe, to see beauty from their point of view only. The way they see it, this beautiful woman must have blond, ginger, or brown hair, with blue eyes, and pink skin, or with a light brown skin complexion before she can be qualified as a beautiful woman to look at. This is the reason why whenever there is a beauty contest show that is shown on the television, or in the movies, they always pick a Gentile European woman as the winner, or a light brown skin woman as the winner of the beauty contest show, who look more like the people of Europe. Their reason for doing so, it is because a light brown skin woman is closer in skin complexion to that of many Gentile people of Europe, who most of the time is the organizers of these shows.

Due to their psychology, and strategy, they have been teaching to the people who came under their captivity, to see them as the most beautiful people Yahweh has created and put here on planet earth. It has created an inferiority complex in many of their captured people's minds to want to run away from themselves to look like the people of Europe. This psychology of inferiority complex has penetrated the minds and hearts of many of our Hamite's people throughout the world, that even when a Hamite person is having a beauty contest show amongst their own people, they always seem to want to pick a light brown skin Hamite sister. Or some half breed Hamite sister of a lighter skin complexion as the winner. I would like to point out to many of our Hamite's people, that if a person do not know their past history, then it is very hard for them to understand the present, because the past history guide the future history of today. This mean that whatever happened two or five hundred years ago, it still has its effect on our world, and lives of today. Because yesterday doings guide today's doing, and today's doings guide tomorrow doing. So, the trend of life would continue on this way, unless of course Yahweh change the course of life from the way it has been. But for the most part life would continue on from the way it has been from whatever conqueror came on the scene, and set up their own system of conquest over other people, and their lands. Furthermore, without our children receiving the proper knowledge of their past history, it would make it very difficult for them to understand the reason why things are the way it is in our world of today.

So, without the knowledge of our past history to guide us from making the same mistakes over and over again, we as a people would be always trusting the same people who has seek to destroy us, as a set of people for centuries. This is the reality of life in todays world with many of the people of Ham worldwide, putting their trust in the Gentile European family of Japheth. Who has seek to destroyed us a a people of Ham, and to used us to suite their own purposes, to gain wheat and power. This is the same mistake many of the people of Ham have been making since the time of slavery until present time. We have been putting our trust and hopes in these Gentiles people of Europe, looking to these same people, and the Mohammedans Muslim people, of Saudi Arabia for help, who have enslaved us, and have taken away all our belongings, and our lands for themselves.

Many of the Mohammedan Muslim people of Saudi Arabia, has helped to destroy many of the early civilizations of the people of Ham, but many Hamite's people of today in the land of Ham do not have any knowledge of these history of these facts, I have written about. Many Hamite's people of today are only going by the lies and the false history, and the false identities that were given to us as a people to go by. This was by our conquerors, and our slave masters for us to see ourselves in whatever identity's they give to us to go by. The people of Ham keep on looking to the Gentile people of Europe and the Mohammedans Muslim people of Saudi Arabia to better their standard of living, to create jobs and educational opportunities for us as a people. These were the same people who have caused our downfalls of yesterday and today. So, iIn my opinion, going to these Gentile people of Europe, and that of the Mohammedans Muslim people of Saudi Arabia for help, is like going to the jungle of the land of Ham and going there to the lions, tigers, and the snakes for guidance and help. This is the mistake many Hamite's people have been making over the centuries, simple because many of them, and our so-call leaders, of the land of Ham, do not have any knowledge, or memory of our historical past of yesterday. So, many Hamite's people, of today, just brush it aside as past history, that their ancestors of yesterday went through, and do not try to educate their children about their past history. If we were a people like many others people, who keep on teaching their children about their past history their ancestors before them went true, at least this education they would have received from their parents would serve as a guideline, which would pass on down the line to next generations that is to come.

The Gentile European people of Japheth, make sure they keep up with their pass history, and past events, and they teach these things to their children that the average young Gentile children of the United States, Canada, South Africa, Australia, and Europe will be very knowledgeable about their ancestors past history, that cast them to be. The Gentile people of Europe, teach their children of the various things they and their ancestors of yesterday have done to us Hamite's people. Also, to other native people who they had enslaved, killed and take away their lands that as brought about the wealth to their descendants of today, for them to benefit from. Due to the various doings of their ancestors of yesterday, that they have done to many people of the world, it has put their offspring of today, in the position to reap the harvest of their ancestor's doings of yesterday.

Many Gentile people of Europe, and their descendants of today, know more about the Hamate's people history, more than what most Hamite's people know about their own history. To give one a good idea of how one history is very important to a set of people. If one should read the Scripture book of (Joshua Chapter 4, and verse 2, to verse 7), there one would see that when the children of Israel were about to crossover the River Jordan. When they came from out of the land of Mizraim, to go and take over the land of Canaan, known today as Israel and the so-call Middle East. There Yahweh command Joshua that he must command the children of Israel to take out of the Jordan River twelve stones. These stones that were to be taken from out of the River Jordan, should be kept as a historical record of memory forever. This was done, so that the future children of Israel who were to come along later, would know that the River Jordan was cut off before the Ark of the Covenant of Yahweh. Also, that the children of Israel cross over on dry land to go and take over the land of the Canaanites people. This little history just goes to show to many of our foolish Hamite's people of today, who believed to themselves that their historical past is not important in today's times, because it is past history. Even the Gentile people of what became known as the United States of America, have several history channels on their various television stations, this is to teach their many captive's people of today historical things they do not know about. Also, to show their captive citizens things they themselves have done to many people, during their colonial conquest of the world, of people and their lands to become rich people. The Gentile people of Europe, know that the Hamite's people are coming from a great past, and they also know that if they were to give us Hamite's people too many changes in life, we as a people might become strong, and treat them in the same way they and their ancestors have treated us as a set of people.

I must point out that our survival as a set of people is not left up to the Gentile people of Europe, or that of the Mohammedans Muslim people of Saudi Arabia of Ishmael. Who have tried their very best to destroy us Hamite's people who did came under their colonial conquest. By mean of slavery, and colonialism, and who also have take away our lands for themselves, and called it the land of the Saudi Arabian people. Our survival and progress as a set of people of Ham, is based upon the mercy, and the kindness of the Great Yahweh, who have spare the Hamite's people who are around today from total destruction, from the Gentile people of Europe, and also that of the Mohammedans Muslim conquest of our lands and its people.

It is Yahweh Himself who has brought out all these many histories I have written about in this book, about the great civilization of the people of Ham that I, and many people of today do not have any knowledge of these histories I have written about in this book. Due to the fact that many of these histories was hidden from many of us Hamite's people at large. It is also Yahweh Himself, with His great mercy, and kindness, who have brought out this great past history of the people of Ham, that they the Gentiles European people, and that of the Mohammedan people of Ishmael have tried their very best to hide from us, the people of Ham, and from the world of other people. If it was left up to the Gentile European people, and the Mohammedans Muslim people alone, we the people of Ham of today would still be in slavery. They are many Hamite's people of today who are still in an economical, and a mental form of slavery, because of how it was design by the Gentile people of Europe, and that of the Mohammedans Muslim people of Ishmael of yesterday, to be the way it is of today. So, in my opinion, the Hamite's people are a far more a Yahweh loving fearing kind people. Who is full of forgiveness, and love of Yahweh in their hearts and minds toward the Gentile family of Japheth, and also of that of the Saudi Arabian people of Ishmael, than what they have shown toward us as Hamite's people. In which in their eyes, they see this love of the Hamite's people toward them as stupidity, and ignorance. To give one a good idea of the love many Hamite's people of the United States have toward their Gentile slave masters. Reading up from Slavery by Booker T. Washington, he mentions that during his time of slavery, whenever the slave master was beating his sons, or his daughters as a form of discipline. There were sorrows in many of the slave quarters dwelling for the master's sons, and for his daughters.

Also, whenever any of the slave master's sons got wounded in any of the conflict of wars, some of the slaves would beg their slave masters for the privilege of setting up late at night, to take care of these wounded sons of his. Booker T. Washington also mentioned that during the Civil War, many Hamite's people even went as far as taking care of their former slave masters, and his mistresses, when for some unknown reasons they became very poor, and could not sustain themselves. Many of their former slaves would work, and supply their former slave masters with food, and money to prevent them from suffering for food and wants. Booker T. Washington even mentioned that there was a time in the Southern part of the United States, that he knew of, where a slave master's son became very poor, because of his drinking habits.

So, many of their x slaves would go, and supply their former slave master's son with food for his survival. I must point out that this would never be the case with any of the Gentile people of Europe, if they were our x-slave, and we were their former masters, and became poor and in needs. We would literally die before they would come and give us food, and water to save our lives. This little story just goes to show the mine set of many Hamite's people, and the difference between them, and their Gentile European cousins of the people of Japheth. When it comes down to the Hamite's people, whether it is in the United States, or in many other places where many of us happen to find ourself, and call our homeland. They would rather seek to destroy each other, and to become jealous of their own people, rather than try to help their own people. What I have come to notice with many Hamite's people of the United States, Jamaica, and in many other countries, whenever they see the Gentiles European people, the Chinese's, or the Indian people making money from their business support, they don't seem to become jealous of these people, in any kind of way. The way it seems to me, is that many Hamite's people feel it is all right for other people to make money, and get rich from their business support, and

who thought to themselves, that these islands of the Caribbean were in the location off the Canary Islands, that they thought was in Asia of India and China.

 In reality the Canary Islands is now ruled and control by the Spanish, and it is in the area of what is now known as Morocco, of the land of Ham, when looking at the Atlas of the world, showing the Canary Islands that is off the cost of Morocco. The Portuguese captured the islands of Azores in 1427, and the island of Madeira in 1420, that is off the cost of the Canary Island, and Morocco from the natives, when reading from the Encyclopaedia, and it became their province, and colonies of their conquered people. From what I also came to understand, many of these islands were control by the Phoenician Canaanites, and the people of Carthage during Greek, and Roman time. This was before Carthage was destroyed by the Romans, who became powerful after the Greeks. The Etruscans way before the coming of the Romans, the Spanish and the Portuguese came on the scene, they had it in their intention to spread their colonial control to the area of Gibraltar, so as to conquer the rich island of Madeira and the Canaries Islands that is off the cost of Morocco. But, this plan of theirs was block by the people of Carthage, who were in opposition to their plan, because the people of Carthage, and the Etruscans were allies against the Greeks before the coming of the Romans. From what I have learn from reading volume 7 of the Encyclopaedia, the island of Madeira was captured by a Portuguese man, by the name of Joao, Goncalves Zarco in 1418, while he was on his way to what became known as the West Africa course, and after that the island became a Portuguese colony. According to the History of the West Indian People, when these Europeans sailors crossed the Atlantic Ocean they grouped these islands of the Caribbean to be that of the Antilles. As a youth, Columbus would always go by the dockside, and talk to with sailors of their various sea voyages, and when he was fourteen years old he made his first sailing voyage. Eventually, like many sailors of his day, he went to live in Portugal, where he studied various maps, and read copies of old Greek books, in which it was stated that the world was round like a ball, and it was not flat, as how many of his Gentile European people of his days, had taught to believe.

To many Greeks and Romans of their time, their belief was that there were islands of fortune lay far out in the sea, west of their Gentile land that became known as Europe, and these islands were sometimes called Antilia. Columbus had spoken to various sailors who had made the voyages to the Canary Islands, and Madeira, and from what they told him, he felt sure that there were lands on the other side of the Atlantic, away from Portugal. So, in the mind set of Columbus, these lands must be a part of the Indies of what became known as Asia. These men of Columbus became very unruly, and they was always finding some new fault to complain about, because they did not like Columbus, because he was not from Spain, and this trip of his, had seemed crazy in their eyes. As the ships was sailing along, the men notice that the compass needle was behaving very strangely. So, right away they thought to themselves the reason why the compass was acting this way, because in their minds they thought they were near the edge of the world, and they would soon fall over into space. So, while they were sailing along the wind was blowing the ships, and the men of Columbus started to feel to themselves, their chances of getting back to Spain alive was getting very slim, because the wind was against them. While they were sailing along they came across a big floating seaweed they had never seen before. Many of the men cried out to throw Columbus overboard, and some of them cried out they should hang him, and let them return back to Spain before they all perished. But Columbus was able to use his charm and diplomacy in getting the men around to sail along with him, to what seemed to be an endless ocean in their minds. Two months passed since the ships of Columbus left from the port of Palos, and his men were becoming very difficult to deal with. But Columbus was able to make an agreement with them, that if within three days if he did not see any lands, he would return back to Spain. Columbus also offered them large reward for any man who sees the first land in sight. Three days passed by without seeing any land, but Columbus did not give up hope, and while he was sailing along he notice birds flying around the ships, he had never seen this far out at sea. He also noticed there were weeds that were floating by, and a piece of bush with some fruits on it.

One of the crew also pulled up a piece of log that was floating in the water that had the imprint, that it was worked on by someone who had the knowledge and skills of a sculptor. While they were traveling through the moonlight, it appeared that they had seen lands, so the ships were hankered until the morning light appear.

When it was morning, they noticed a beautiful shore of a green island, and Columbus and his men went ashore. While he was at shore, he kneeled down and gave thanks to the Trinity gods of the Roman Catholic Church, for bringing him and his men safely over the ocean. Columbus and his men went to check out the islands, and he wasted no time, in taking possession of the islands, in the name of King Ferdinand and Queen Isabella of Spain.

Columbus named the island he first saw as San Salvador, which is a Spanish word, that meant Holy Savior, that came from the belief of Roman Catholicism of the Catholic Church. While Columbus was taking ownership of the island, the Arawak's natives were watching him from a distance, within the trees and bushes. Columbus also went to one of the islands that became known as the Bahamas, but he thought in his mind, that he had reached the island off the Eastern part of Asia, of the Indies that he was seeking to go to. So, from then on, before Columbus returned back to Spain, he called the islands of the Caribbean as the Indies, and the Arawak's and the Caribs people, he named them as Indians. According to volume 29 of the Encyclopaedia, the name Bahamas came from a Spanish word, that were known as the Bajamar, which eventually became known as the Bahamas, in the Angles and Saxon dialect, that became known as the English language. One of these islands that were visited by Columbus, was called as the Wailing Island, which is in the Bahamas, and Columbus noticed that the people were very friendly to him, and his crew. Some of them even swam out to his ships, and some of them brought various commodities to exchange. Columbus also, wrote of the friendliness of these Bahamians Arawak's, who he called as the Lucayans. From what I have read about these Bahamians Arawak's, they were so friendly, that they carried no weapons. Columbus also, mention that he found the Arawak's people willing to show him and his men where they could find water, and many of them even brought water to fill the water vessels of Columbus. It is also mentioned in the book of History of the West Indian People, that the various natives, were also receptive and willing to give Columbus and his men pleasure.

So, I assume this pleasure that was mentioned, to be sexual pleasure that they had received from the Arawak's women, or men, if they were homosexual, as many of the men of Europe has the sodomite tendency, that is now known as homosexual. Also, what they named, as gay rights, by the Gentile European people, of what became known as the United States of the Americas. The men of Columbus mentioned that when they went to shore, the report they brought back was that the Arawak's kept their houses swept and very clean. On Columbus first visit to the islands, he notices that there were plenty of birds and fish could be caught in great numbers. The Arawak's peopled also hunted with their dogs, an animal that they had called agouti, which became known as the guinea pigs, in the Anglo-Saxon dialect of the Germany people.

According to A Short History of the West Indian People, it was the Spanish settlers who first brought cattle, goats, sheep, pigs, and domesticated fowls to the islands of the West Indies. As far as this statement goes, I am not sure if this statement is a true statement, or a lie, because many of the Gentile people of Europe are liars, whose words cannot be trusted very much, because they teach allot of false history, as truth. According to History of the West Indian People, during Columbus second visit to the islands of the West Indies, he brought along horses that were first seen by the natives, and many of them were frightening to see men riding on horse backs. From what I have read from the History of the West Indian People, it was the Spanish settlers who brought sugar cane, oranges, and many other plants to what became known as the West Indies. However, I really do not know for sure if this statement of theirs is of a true statement, or a false statement. My reason for saying this is, what caught my attention about this story is this, if this statement is true that it was the Spanish who were the ones that had brought these things to the West Indies. Where did the Spanish get these things from, to bring to the West Indies? Because oranges, sugar cane, and bananas do not grow in Europe. So, the Spanish themselves could not have had the knowledge how to grow these things, because as I had mention that these products, only grow in tropical climate, and not in the climate of Europe where there is cold weather. So, they must have gotten these things from other tropical climate places that came under their colonial control. Such as the Canary Island, Madeira, and Cape Verde Island of the people of Ham, that came under the colonial control of the Portuguese and the Spanish.

Due to the colonial conquest of the world by the Gentile people of what became known as the Europeans people, they have copy many things that were foreign to them, that they have gotten, and learned from many of their conquered people, who came under their captivity of ruler ship. Columbus also noticed that many of the Arawak's wore ornament of gold, and he was told by sign language that toward south-west of the land area where he was, the king had much gold. Columbus visit another island that the Arawak's people called Cuba, that meant to the Arawaks people, land of water. Columbus also visited another island of the Arawak's people that did reminded him very much like Spain, so he named the island as Hispaniola, which, meant to him little Spain. Before Columbus named the island as Hispaniola, the Arawak's people did named the island as Haiti, which meant to them land of water, as well.

In which they were speaking of the whole land area of what is now known as Haiti and Santo Domingo, which is the same land area of the conquest of the Spanish and the French. Columbus also took possession of the island of Hispaniola, and he established it as the first Spanish settlement in the so-call West Indies. Columbus went back to Spain, and left thirty-eight of his men to guard the settlement, while he returned to Spain. Columbus also take along some parrots, and other colorful birds, and also six of the Arawak's people, to show to the king and queen of Spain, the type of people who was living there on the island. After a rough voyage back to Spain, Columbus entered the Spanish port of Palos, which he sailed from seven months earlier, and he was warmly welcomed by the King Ferdinand and Queen Isabella. Who ordered a large fleet of ships to be built for Columbus, for him to sail further in his new venture of the New World. In the latter part of September of 1493, a year later, Columbus left from the port of Cadiz in Spain for his second journey to what he still had it in his mind to be that of Asia, of the West Indies. In Columbus second trip to the West Indics, he thought was Asia, he take along with him, 1500 more men, who were enthusiastically full of excitement, to grab some of the wealth of this new captured land of the Gentile people of Europe. There was a fleet of seventeen ships that carried stores of things that was needed to setup a colony, and these ships of Columbus sailed on a southward course, because Columbus was hoping to find other islands that was full of gold. One of the islands he vested he named as Dominica, which is a Spanish name for the Lord's Day. This Lord Day that Columbus had in mind, was a Sunday, because he first saw this island on a Sunday. From what I have read from the History of the West Indian people, the island that became known as Dominica, was a part of the group of islands that the Gentile people of Europe did called as the Leeward Islands, of the West Indies.

According to the History of the West Indian Peoples, the name Windward and Leeward Islands, came about during those days of these Gentile European men, sailing their ships looking for conquests, and plunder. So, the term windward meant to these sailors of those days, the side of the ships that was exposed to the wind, and the term Leeward meant the side of the ships that was sheltered from the winds. The reason why they used the term as the windward, was to describe these islands that lay in the track of the winds, that blow from the north-east during the twelve months of the year. What these Gentile European men named as the Leeward Islands, was Antigua, St Kitts, Nevis, Anguilla, Montserrat, and what became known as the Virgin Islands.

Also, what they did considered to be the Windward Islands, is what became known as Dominica, Grenada, St Lucia, St Vincent, Trinidad, and Tobago. Columbus did not find any good place to dock his fleet of ships in Dominica, so he sailed on to another island that became known as Guadeloupe. There, for the first time, the Spanish saw what the Arawak's and the Caribs people did called as anana, which became known as pineapple, in the Angles, and Saxon dialect, that became known as the English language. From what I have read from the History of the West Indian People, it was the Arawak's people who first started the growing of cotton, in the New World to make close. They the Arawak's people, also grow tobacco for smoking, that they, the Gentile European people, later copped, and it became a part of their industries, to sell in Europe, and also among themselves in their New World, of their conquest. This was to make big profits from the selling of Tabasco, that became known as cigarettes and cigars. From what I came to understand, by reading History of the West Indian People, and the Encyclopaedia, it was Sir Walter Raleigh who made the smoking of cigarettes fashionable in Europe. These Arawak's people was also skillful in embroidery work, and they also played a game that became known as football and soccer, which the Gentile European people had copied from these people. So, the Gentile

European people have copped many things from these people, that they made fashionable in their conquered world of today, without even given credit to these people. According to volume 29 of the Encyclopaedia, the name Guadeloupe came from Our Lady of Guadeloupe of Estremadura of Spain. I am not quite sure if it was Columbus who named this island as Guadeloupe, but what I came to understand from the Encyclopaedia, is that this island was known as Karukera of Beautiful Waters, by the Caribs people, who had pushed out the Arawak's from this island, and take it over for themselves.

According to the History of the West Indian People, the island of Guadeloupe was in the hands of the Caribs when Columbus and his men visited the island. When Columbus returned from checking out Cuba and Xaymaca, that later became known as Jamaica, and various other islands, he found out that the Spanish base he had established on Hispaniola, a year earlier was destroyed, and the men he left to guard the base was no longer there. Columbus learned later that some of the men died, and others were killed in quarrels amongst themselves, fighting over gold and many of them were slain by the Arawaks for the demand of their food and for their women.Columbus became enraged, and turned on the Arawak's, and hunted them through the bushes with men that was armed and vicious dogs. Those who was captured, Columbus imposed on them a tax of gold, that they had to pay to him, and many of whom were captured, was viciously enslaved by Columbus and many of them died. Some of these people was also sent to Spain as slaves by Columbus, in which many of them died, and many who was left alive was eventually sent back to the West Indies by Queen Isabella. So, the early enslavement of these Hispaniola natives brought the people of Spain no profits. After these events, Columbus went and established another location for his second European base on the island of Hispaniola, that he had called Isabella. In the spring of 1496, Columbus sailed for Spain to face with complaints that was brought against him by some of his men, who did not like him, because they felt he wanted to make himself king of Hispaniola. In the absence of Columbus, and with his approval, his brother who was known as Bartholomew Columbus, who he had left in charge of the colony of Isabella. Removed the settlement from Isabella and went and established a new settlement on the south side of Hispaniola that became known as Santo Domingo. This was in 1496-1497, which became the capital of the first Spanish settlement in the West Indies. According to what I have learn from the Webster Third International Dictionary, the word Santo came from the Spanish Roman Catholic believers, For the word Saint, and the word Domingo is a Latin Spanish word for Sunday. According to the Webster Third International Dictionary, the word Domingo came from the word de Guzman, who in 1221, was a Spanish Roman Catholic priest. While Columbus was in Cuba, he thought to himself that the island of Cuba was a part of Asia, which he was seeking to go to, and the Arawak's people of Cuba told him of another island toward the south where he could find plenty of gold. From Cuba, Columbus sailed to the island of Xaymaca in 1494, that became known as Jamaica, but he did not find any gold there, and Columbus's named the island of Xaymaca as Saint Jago.

When the Spanish take over the island of Xaymaca in 1509, as the official ruler, they just slaughtered off many of the Arawak's and those who did not get slaughtered off, were enslaved to death. After the Spanish slaughtered off the Arawak's from Xaymaca, many Hamite's slaves was brought over to replace the Arawak's as the new slaves of Xaymaca. According to what I have come to learn from reading History of the West Indian People, in 1655, Oliver Cromwell who at the time was Prime Minster of the country of Britain, who was at war with the Dutch and the Spanish. So, Oliver Cromwell sent out Admiral Penn and General Venables to go and attack the Spanish in the West Indies, and to steal some of their islands. Admiral Penn and General Venables sailed to the island of Hispaniola to steal the island from the ruler ship of the Spanish, but before they went to Hispaniola, he went to the British Island of Barbados to recruit 4,000 British men from there. He also sail to Saint Kitts, and take 1,000 men from there, and also from the island of Nevis to make the attack on Hispaniola. While they were waiting around in the bushes to make their attack on Hispaniola, they heard noises in the bushes. The British men started to fire their guns, thinking the noise they heard was that of Spanish soldiers coming to attack them, when it was the noise of soldier crabs in the bushes. So, their location was exposed to the Spanish, and the Spanish was able to chase off the British back to their ships. When Admiral Penn and Venables and their men went back to their ships, to return back to Britain, they made the decision they cannot report back to Cromwell empty handed. So, on their way back to Britain, they stop off at the island of Xaymaca to have a try at taking this island away from the Spanish, that was not heavily guarded with Spanish soldiers. The British was able to land soldiers on the island of Xaymaca, who was expecting a stiff resistance from the Spanish settlers who was there. But they were able to march their men toward the capital that was known as Saint Jago, that became known as Spanish Town, without too much resistance from the Spanish settlers who was there. While the invasion of the British was taking place, the Spanish gave their Hamite's slaves guns to fight on their behalf. But these Hamite's slaves was so smart, that when they received the guns, they take off running to the cockpit mountain leaving these two Gentile brothers, to fight among themselves, and they were given the name by the Spanish as the Maroons. According to the Webster Colligate Dictionary, the word maroon was taken from the Spanish word Cimarron, and from the French word Marmot, which mean to them runaway slaves. So, these Hamite's slaves who had ran away from the Spanish, became known as the Maroons of Jamaica, in the dialect of the Angles and Saxon people of Germany, that became known as the English language of what is now known as Jamaica.

When the Spanish realized they could not defeat the British with the little amount of men they had, they finally decided to surrender the island of Xaymaca to the British, without the British having to fire a single shot. When the British take over the island of Xaymaca in 1655, from the Spanish. They named the island as Jamaica, as it is now called, that take its name from the Arawak's name of Xaymaca, which meant to the Awaraks people, land of water. When the British take over the island from the Spanish, the island was full of wild horses and cattle, but within four months the British soldiers killed off 20. 000 of these animals for food. Many of the new British settlers were lazy, and they refused to do any kind of digging, or planting to grow their own food. So, many of them were prepared to starve, but in 1660 the British Government recruited new British settlers from the Leeward Island, to establish this new British colony of Jamaica and to make it a successful colony for the British. In 1657, the Spanish tried to take back the island of Jamaica from the British, but they were chased off by the British, and their settlers. The Maroon population of the cockpit mountain of Jamaica of runaway slaves started to grow in vast numbers, and these Maroons gave the British settlers of Jamaica a very hard time, that British government had to spent two hundred and forty thousand pounds, trying to destroy these Hamite's people from the cockpit mountain. These Maroons was such an aggravation to the settlers of Jamaica, because they would often raid their plantations, so the British and the Maroons fourth two wars, until the British made peace with the Maroons 'leader, whose name was known as Captain Cudjoe. The British and the Maroons was at peace for a long time, until 1795, war broke out again between the British and the Maroon, because some of the Maroons was dissatisfied with the way things were going for them.

This time the British won the war against the Maroons, and those Maroons who had taken part in the war, was shipped off to Nova Scotia, which is a part of what became known today as Canada. From Canada they were shipped off to the colony of Sierra Leone that became known as a free town of the return of free slaves. This land area is a part of the land of Ham, that became known as Sierra Leone, and it was established, and set up for the return of free slaves from the European conquered New World to what became known as West Africa.

I must point out that I did not cover the full story about the Hamite's people who became known as the Maroons of the island that became known as Jamaican. From what I have read from a magazine that is call the American Legacy, it mentioned that there were run away Hamite's slaves from the Southern part of what became known as the United States. Many of whom later became known as the Maroons, because many of them escaped to the wilderness, and joined with the natives who became known as the Indians people of the United States, and formed their own communities there. According to this magazine, there was also evidence that they were Maroon settlement with the Gullah people, who was living among the natives of the rice and indigo plantation of South Carolina. From what I have gathered, there was also Maroon communities in Louisiana, Georgia and Florida, many of whom were runaway slave, who went and joined with the natives of Florida. So, after Columbus left from checking out the island of Xaymaca, and found no gold there, he went back to check out the island of Cuba some, where he reaching to the western end of the island. At this time the ship of Columbus developed leaks, and his men were not the type of men who had any discipline, or behavior, and Columbus himself finally fell sick. Columbus finally return to the colony of Isabella and was greeted with more bad news about many of the colonists, who was disappointed, because they did not fine much gold there to become rich men over night, without having to do any kind of hard work. Some of these men went back to Spain on ships that were sent out to the colony of Isabella, and some of them gave false reports against Columbus, because they did not like him, because he was not from Spain. Finally, Columbus decided he would return to Spain and explain the truth of the matter before the king and queen. King Ferdinand and Queen Isabella felt very sorry for Columbus, and two years later they decided to give him some more ships for him to make his third sailing voyage to the New World. On Columbus third voyage he sailed further and came across an Arawak's Island he named as Trinidad in 1498. According to volume 9 of the Encyclopaedia, the island of Trinidad was inhabited by the Arawak's people, and the island of what is now known as Tobago was under the control of the warlike Caribs people.

History of the West Indian People explained that when Columbus made his third voyage across the Atlantic, he sailed further south in the West Indies, and the heat of the sun was so hot that the tar they used to seal the joints of the ship started to melt. Columbus and his men started to feel sick, because of the heat they was not accustomed to, like that of the cold weather of the Gentile land of Europe. He sailed northward, and made a vow to the Holy Trinity gods of the Roman Catholic Church, that the next land he come a cross, he was going to name it in honor of the Holy Trinity. This Holy Trinity gods that Columbus was speaking about, is Father, Son and Holy Spirit of Yahweh that were translated as the Holy Ghost. This is what is taught in the various churches of today, as three gods in one person of that of Yashua, better known as Jesus Christ, which is totally a false teaching, of what became known as Christianity. My reason for making this kind of statement, it is because, there is nowhere in the writing of the Holy Scripture that became known as the Bible, where Yashua mention that he was a God, or any part of any trinity, that came down from the Roman Catholic Church of their false teaching. While Yashua was here on earth, he points all worship to his Father and his God, who had sent him to the Yehudahites and the Benjamites who were left there in the land of Canaan that became known as Israel. Furthermore at (Isaiah Chapter 45, and verse 5), there Yahweh make it very clear, that I am the Lord, and there is no one else, there is no God beside me. (Verse 6 of Isaiah Chapter 45) went on to say that they may know from the rising of the sun from the west that there is no God beside me. Also (Matthew Chapter 6) there Yeshua said that when one pray, they must enter into their closet, or their room and pray to their Father who see in secret, and your Father who sees in secret will reward you openly, so Yashua never said in the Scripture that anyone should pray to him as a god. So, while Columbus was sailing along, he noticed three mountain tops of an island peak, which he believed to be the answer to his prayer. So, he named the island as Trinidad, in the honor of the Holy Trinity gods of the Roman Catholic Church. From the island of Trinidad, Columbus saw the mainland, that became known as South America, but he thought the land mass he had seen, was that of another big island, that he named Isla Sancta, which meant to Columbus Holy Isle. From Columbus observation, he noticed that the Arawak's on the island of Trinidad were of a lighter shade of skin color, than many of the other Arawak's he had seen elsewhere in the West Indies. When Columbus returned back to the colony of Isabella, he was met with more bad news that instead of the settlers working on the lands, or of the various mines, they decided to rob the natives, and fight amongst themselves for gold. Columbus tried his best to restore order and harmony among his colonists of his settlers. But many of the men sent false reports to Spain against him, saying he was trying to make himself king of the island of Hispaniola.

When Ferdinand received this message, he sent an officer to take charge of the colony of Hispaniola as the new governor of the island, but this new governor, who was now in charge of the island, gave the order to put Columbus in chains and sent him back to Spain. While Columbus was on the ship going back to Spain, the captain who was in charge of the ship offered to take off the chains. But Columbus replied by saying that by royal order he was put in chains, and he was willing to wear them until his king and queen ordered them from him. Columbus also made the statement that when the king and queen removed the chains from him, he would keep them for his services. When Isabella saw Columbus, whose hair was now turning gray, in chains, kneeling down at her feet, she burst into tears, so she and Ferdinand was very upset when they learned of the way he had been treated. They ordered at once that he must be set free from these chains. Columbus did not reach his destination of Asia as he had it in his mind set to reach Asia, so, Ferdinand and Isabella gave him four more small ships for him to make a fourth trip of his desire of what he did still think was Asia of the West Indies. Columbus sailed from the port of Cadiz in Spain to go to what he still think to be Asia of the West Indies. But due to the citation with the colony of Hispaniola, and the men who were against him, he was told not to go there. Columbus sailed to another island he named as St Lucia, and after leaving there he reached another Caribs island that became known as Martinique. According to volume 7 of the Encyclopaedia, Columbus went to the island that became known as Martinique in 1502, during his fourth visit to what he still thought was West of India. This island of Martinique was inhabited by the Caribs, who had pushed out the Arawak's. The first European settlers after Columbus, was in 1635, when a French man by the name of Pierre Belain de Esnambuc established the island as a French colony.

From this island of Martinique, Columbus sailed to what became known as Central America, to Honduras, but he found the people not too friendly. According to volume 6 of the Encyclopaedia, what became known as Honduras was a part of the land area of the Mayan people, who were originated from what became known as Mexico, by the Spanish conquest. Columbus landed in Honduras in 1502, and it became a European settlement in 1522. Eventually the population of these Mayan people decreased, because of slavery, and the predatory presence of these Gentile people of Europe. Columbus ships developed leaks, and he was badly in need of help, and he tried to reach the island of Hispaniola, but he was able to reach as far as the island of Jamaica, where he was forced to abandon his ship at Saint Ann's Bay.

Message was sent by Columbus to the colony of Hispaniola, begging the governor for help, because he was stranded, but for several months the governor made no reply to Columbus and his needs. The Spanish citizens of Hispaniola had to beg the governor desperately to act on Columbus behalf. Finally the governor gave in to the people demands of Hispaniola and sent ships to bring Columbus to Hispaniola. Columbus stayed in Hispaniola for one month, and then sailed for Spain. Unfortunately, when Columbus reached Spain Isabella had died, and Columbus found himself broke without any friends. Columbus made the statement that after twenty years of toiling, and laying the foundation for these Spanish colonies, in his world of conquest, he didn't even own a house in Spain for him to have some where to rest his head. Columbus died May of 1506, a broke man, without even realizing he had opened the way to a new continent for his fellow Gentile people of Europe, that became known as their New World of their conquest from the various natives people. It was several years after the death of Columbus, before these Gentile European people came to the realization that there was this great big land mass, that lay between Western Europe and Asia, that is now known as the Americas and the West Indies.

Chapter 62 - Americus Vespucci

According to History of the West Indian people book 2, after the death of Columbus, Americus Vespucci take up the sailing voyage, and went to work for the government of Spain. Vespucci also sailed further south along the coast of the West Indies, and what became known as the South American coast, much further than Columbus did. Vespucci also came from what is now known as Italy, and he was living in Spain when he take up the sailing voyage for the Spanish. He also made maps of the various places he had traveled, and sent these maps, with letters to his friends, describing these places he had visited. In the writing of Vespucci to many of his friends, he mentioned that it was right to call this part of the world as the New World, because many of his people of Europe had no knowledge about this part of the world. One of the reasons why Vespucci made this statement, it is because it was the belief of many of his people of Europe, that there were no land south of the equator. But the various voyages of Vespucci proved them to be wrong. Vespucci went on to explained to many of his friends in his letters," that I have found a country that is more inhabited, with many people and animals, much more than his land of Europe. According to volume 12 of the Encyclopaedia, Amerigo Vespucci was born in 1454, in the city of Florence of Italy, and he died 1512 of Seville of Spain. Vespucci took part in the early sailing voyages of the so-called New World in 1499, and in 1500 to 1502. When Vespucci was a boy, he was given some education by his uncle who was known as Giorgio Antonio. In 1491, Vespucci went to Seville Spain where he had a business meeting with Giannotto Berardi, who it seems to have been in the business of putting together ships.

Vespucci was also present when Columbus returned from his first venture of the New World, because Berardi did also assisted in making some of the ships Columbus did sail in. While Vespucci was with Berardi he helped in the preparation of putting ships together for Columbus second and third trips to the New World. Eventually Vespucci and Columbus got to know each other, and when Berardi died in 1495, Vespucci became manager of an agency in Seville. In 1505, Vespucci was invited to the court of Spain, to work for the Commercial House of the West Indies, that was established there two years earlier at Seville, in 1508. This company gave him the position to be Chief Navigator, a position that was of great responsibility, and he was also responsible for ship masters license for sailing.

Vespucci was also giving the position to prepare official maps for the newly captured colonies of the New World, and the directions to go to these colonies, and he also became a citizen of Spain. Vespucci trips take him to Venezuela, Surinam, better known as Dutch Guyana. Also Ecuador, Peru, Brazil, Bolivia, Paraguay, Argentina, Chile, Uruguay, Equator, British Guyana and French Guyana. The reason why the Spanish Government did allow the Portuguese to have a share of their colonies of their New World, it is because they were of the same tribe and family of the land of Tarshish that became known as Spain and Portugal. The Portuguese take possession of the land area they named as Brazil, they did take away from the Arawak's, which was a part of the land of the Guianas, that eventually became known as the Guyana's, Brazil, of the South American countries. According to volume 15 of the Encyclopedia, when the Portuguese take over Brazil from the natives, they organized hunting parties to hunt down these people to put them to work as slaves. The raids, and massacre and the enslavement of these people reduced their population from millions to just a few thousand tribes, that were scattered around the area of what became known as Brazil.

Due to the massacre and the enslavement of these natives, and the increasing demand for slave labor, the Portuguese geared their attention to bring slaves from the land of Ham, to replace that of the natives by the millions. Because of the actions the Portuguese had taken, in bringing Hamite's slaves to Brazil, the land of Brazil has the largest Hamite's population, outside of the land of Ham itself. The Dutch, French, and the British, as a combine team of pirates, fought against the Spanish to take away some of their territories that became their colonies of their New World. The British who were the champion of the pirate's ring, even had captured Cuba from the Spanish, but later after the various peace treaties they had form between themselves, Cuba was return back to Span, including some other territory they the British gave back to the Spanish.

After the Spanish fought many wars against the various pirate's invaders of their New World, when the smokes of the guns was clear away, the Spanish had no choice but to open the door to let her fellow Gentile European brothers in, to shear the wealth of their pie of their New World. So, in reality these Gentile European people of Europe are a predator type of people, who has been praying up on the human family, because of their greed to get wealth and power, to become rich people.

Traveling further south in the New World, Vespucci believed to himself that he had found the beginning of the Amazon River, and on his way back he reached the island of Trinidad and came across the Orinoco River. Then he sailed toward the island of Haiti that Columbus name as Hispaniola. In the mind set of Vespucci, he also thought he was in Asia, and he was looking for a market place there that was known as Cattigara. As soon as Vespucci returned to Spain he restocked his ship with the intentions of reaching the Indian Ocean, and the Gulf of the Ganges, now known as Bay of Bengal. Also, the island of Sri Lanka, because he really thought he was in the area of Asia, where like Columbus he had it in his intention to go there, but fund himself in the place he name as the West Indies.

However, the Spanish government did not support Vespucci in his findings, so at the end of the 1500, Vespucci went to work for the government of Portugal. Working for the government of Portugal, Vespucci set off for his second journey from Lisbon, in May 13, of 1501, and he made a stop at the Cape Verde Island, that is in the land of Ham, that is now known as Africa and then he traveled toward Brazil. I must mention I did not covered the full story about Vespucci and his ventures before his death from volume 12 of the Encyclopaedia, but I just take a few abstracts from the account.

The French pirates invade and captured a part of the island of Hispaniola from the Spanish and made it their settlement in 1644. This part of the island they had captured from the Spanish, they named it as Saint Dominigue, but the island did receive back it original Arawak's name, as the land of Haiti. The other part of the island of Haiti that was still under the ruler ship of the Spanish, was known as Santo Domingo. The name Santo Domingo came from Columbus brother, who was known as Bartholomew Columbus. The part of the island that were still under Spanish ruler ship, became known today as Dominican Republic. According to volume 22 of the Encyclopaedia, the French pirates had their base on the island that was known as Tortuga, and this island of Tortuga later became known as the Cayman Islands, that is near to the island Columbus did named as Hispaniola. This western part of the island that was under the French parties control of Haiti, they did also called as Port de Paix, that was control by the French West India Company, and later they changed the name to Saint Dominigue. After Saint Dominigue was established as a French colony, a French governor was put in charge of the island affair, in the interest of France. The French of Saint Dominigue brought over 500,000 Hamite's slaves who did all the hard work of the cultivation of tobacco, but later the French settlers learned from the Portuguese, that the growing of sugar cane was far more profitable business to make big money from slave labor, than that of tobacco. Tobacco was grown in different parts of the Gentile people New World, they had shipped to Europe, to sell amongst themselves, and also in what became known as the New World. So, there was too much competition in the growing of tobacco to make big profit from. For this reason, many small tobacco cultivators 'lands were taken over by large sugarcane plantation owners, to grow sugarcane to make more profit from sugar, because sugar cane growing became the big money-making market of those day, to make money from slave labor.

From what I have read from History of the West Indian People, many European settlers who use to grow cane to make sugar from slave labor, got the knowledge from the Portuguese, who had cane plantation in the West African course. They the Portuguese had learn from the Hamite's people of what became known as the Cape Verde Island, and also in what became known as North Africa. So, many of the French plantations owners become very rich men, from their slave labors, of the growing of sugarcane and tobacco, to sell in Europe and in their New World.

According to History of the West Indian people book II, there it explained, that because of the wealth that many French settlers made from the sugarcane market, many of them were able to build big fancy houses, and live luxurious lifestyles from the sweat, and tears of their many slave laborers they had in their position. During the planting of sugarcane, many of the slaves was over work, and badly treated. Also, many of the half bread people, who were known as the Mulatto people, who later became known as the colored people, and the Hispanic and the Latino people. Were not allowed to vote, and to have the same rights as their Gentile European counterparts of the island. In France at the time, many poor French people were treated unfairly, and they had to work very hard to pay heavy taxes that many of them could hardly afford to pay to their French governmental system, of their predator ness to get rich. Due to this heavy taxation that was impose on many of the poor people of France, many of them became very unhappy of their state of lives, and in 1789, many of them rebelled against the king of France. According to this historical story, that is told by History of the West Indian People, the king of France was captured by the rebellious poor people, and was put in prison, and later he was beheaded by the guillotine. Later the country of France became a republic, that was ruled by a National Assembly. So, when the news of the revolution reached the island of Saint Dominic, the slaves and the Mulattos people, felt they too should receive a better treatment from the new government of France. Than what they had been receiving from the old government, who was in power. They also felt that the slaves should be set free by this new government of France. So, when their expectation did not materialize there was bitter resentment among the slaves, and among Mulattos people of Saint Dominigue against their French government, and against their French slave masters. From this bitter resentment of these Hamite's slave people, gave birth to a Hamite freedom fighter by the name of Toussaint L'Overture, or Francois Dominique who was owned by a French man by the name of Mr. Breda.

Toussaint was a descendant from a chief of the land of Ham, and Toussaint was a very intelligent man, that his master put him in charge over the other slaves. His father were given the chance to learn to read and write in the French language, by a Jesuit priest, who were not able to buy Toussaint father out of slavery, but he did his best to teach him how to read and write in the French language. According to the Webster's Colligate Dictionary of the Fifth Edition, the name Jesuit is the name for Jesus, in the dialect of the Germanic French and Dutch people of what became known as the Netherlands, France, and the Netherland is also known as Holland. The dictionary explained that this Christian religious group of the Jesuits people, existed in the time of 1534, in different part of the West Indies of their New World. History of the West Indian People went on to explained that Toussaint father taught him how to read and write in the French language, but he did not have the money to purchase his son freedom from out of slavery, and his long dream and desire was for him to live long enough to see the days when the slaves would be set free. Toussaint spent much of his free time studying books, that was lent to him by his slave master, who was very nice to him. Toussaint ability to learn to read and write, in the French language, gave him the hope and wish for the day when all the slaves on the French part of the island will be set free. This dream and wish of Toussaint, and his father came true in August of 1791, when the slaves of Saint Domingue rose up in rebellion against their slave masters. Before the uprising take place, Toussaint master went on some business venture in a part of Saint Domingue known as Le Cap, and leave Toussaint to take care of things while he was a way. But before his master went on his business venture, he did asked Toussaint to protect his wife, should incase there were any kind of trouble from the other slaves. So, for a good while Toussaint kept his fellow Hamite's slaves from burning his master plantation, and his house, but after a while he decided that it was time for him to support his fellow Hamite's slaves in their fight for freedom from their slave masters. Toussaint help his master wife to pack up a few of her things, and send her to meet up with her husband on Le Cap, of Saint Domingue, where he was, and where she would be safe.

After he take the step to protecting his master wife, he also take his wife and children to the other side of the island that were still under Spanish ruler ship of Santo Domingo, where there were no slave up rising was taken place. After these events, Toussaint was put in charge of taking care of the wounded, but many of his fellow Hamate's freedom fighters felt he would make a better solder, than a doctor. So, Toussaint was put in charge of the command of his fellow Hamate's freedom fighters, and he had the ability of breaking true the barrio of the enemy, that earned him the name of L Ouverture, which mean a gap.

Toussaint was also a peace-loving person, and many times during his command of the uprising, he would use his authority to protect many of his Gentile French slave masters from unnecessary cruelty from his fellow Hamate's freedom fighters. While the fighting against the French slave masters was taking place, the Spanish of Santo Domingo thought the slave uprising in Saint Domingue was the right time for them to invade that part of the island to bring it back under Spanish ruler ship. Toussaint and other freedom fighters went and join the Spanish army to carrying on the fighting against their French plantation owners, and in doing so he was made a corneal in the Spanish army. When many of the French plantation owners whose houses and farm was burn, when they learn of the Spanish intention to invade their part of the island, with that of the French freedom fighters. Many of them came to the conclusion that it was best for them to pack up, and leave the island of Saint Domingue, and some of them fled to Britain for safety. While the uprising was taking place in Saint Domingue, many of the French settlers who went to Britain, asked the British Government to invade Saint Domingue to restore order as the way thing was under French rule. But before the British could take action to invade the island of Saint Domingue on the behalf of the French plantation owners, the new French Republican Government of France declared freedom for the slaves of Saint Domingue. Although the Republican Government of France declared freedom for the slaves, the British still had it in their intention to invade Saint Domingue, to bring things back under French ruler ship, as the way it was before. Due to Toussaint wisdom and skills, within two years he was made commanding chief of the army of Saint Domingue, and by the time of 1793-1800, he was able to defeat the British army that was sent out to Saint Domingue, to restore back power to the French plantation owners. The army of Toussaint also was able to occupy Santo Domingo, that was still under Spanish ruler ship. Toussaint became so powerful with all section of the community, that they had to abide by his rules.

Also, when the French government sent out representatives to Saint Domingue, they had to abide by his wishes and rules, and eventually, Toussaint became master of the whole island of Hispaniola, and gave freedom to all the slaves who were on the Spanish side of the island. Toussaint formed a governing body of assembles to govern the island that becames a republic of the ordinary people, having share in the governmental affair.

He also encourages his fellow Hamate's people to go back and worked the various plantations for their own benefit and good, but not as slaves as how it was before. He made laws and established taxies, and built school and support the churches. As well as hospital for the well been of his people, and in 1801 the island became an independent republic. Unfortunately for Toussaint, a new ruler came to power in France by the name of Napoleon Bonaparte, and Bonaparte decided that Saint Domingue was too important for France to let the island go without a fight, and that it should remain a colony of France. Napoleon put together a large army of 25,000 men and 70 warships, and he put his brother-in-law whose name was known as General Leclerc as commandeering chief, to win back the island of Saint Domingue, and to restore slavery as how it was. When the army of Napoleon arrived on the island of Haiti, in 1802, Toussaint fought bravely to keep their liberty of freedom, but he was abandoned by many of his generals, and in 1802, he sort to established peace with the French to avoided further bloodshed. Unfortunately for Toussaint, he made a very foolish mistake, by going to the French officer home to discuss peace term with him, when he was invited by him to do so. Sad to say that Toussaint had the mentality like many of our Hamite's people of today, who love to put their trust, hope and belief in the Gentile European family of Japheth, who became known as the European people. Many of whom have set out themselves to destroy us, as a people of Ham, for many centuries, and many Ham people believe to themselves that these Gentile European people have our best interest at heart. Also, that they are going to solve our problem, and we and them will live happily ever after.

So, when Toussaint went to the French officer home to talk peace term with him, he was taken by surprise, and arrested, and he was hustled away in a carriage, and was shipped off to France. When he arrived in France he was put into a dark prison cell. Toussaint wrote letters after letters to asked to speak with Napoleon, but he got no response from him. So, on one morning of April 1803, the prison guard found Toussaint dead in a chair, with his head leaning against the prison wall. History of the West Indian People explained that although Toussaint died, his death was not in vain, because the army Napoleon sent out to regain control of Saint Domingue, was almost wiped out by a disease that was known as yellow fever.

According to volume 4 of the Encyclopaedia Britannica, Jean Jacques Dessalines was born in what became known as West Africa, and he was taken as a slave to the French part of the island of Haiti in 1791. He later joined the slave rebellion army against the French slave plantation owners of Haiti, and Dessalines take over the leadership of the slave rebellion army after the death of Toussaint. First he submitted himself to what was left of the army that was sent out by Napoleon, but when he came to the knowledge of Napoleon intentions to return the island into slavery, he was no longer willing to abide by the freedom treaty that was established in 1803, by the new Republic of France. He and another mulatto leader, with the help of the British, were able to return blow for blow with the remainder of the French army that was sent out to regain back control of the island. The French was driven out of Saint Domingue in January of 1804, and the island became an independent Republic, with the original Arawak's name of the island as Haiti. The other part of the island that was still under Spanish rule ship remain as Santo Domingo, but in September of 1805, Jacques gave himself the title of Emperor Jacques I of Haiti, and under his ruler ship he takes away many of the French people lands. He also prevents many of the French settlers who was left there, from owning any lands. Christophe served under the leadership of Toussaint during the slave revolt against their French slave masters, and he also helped Jean Jacques Dessalines to drive the French out of their part of the island of Haiti. Dessalines was killed in 1806, while trying to put down a revolt of the army that was led by P'etion Alexandre Sab'es, who was a mulatto leader.

After the death of Jacques Dessalines, the ruler ship of Haiti was now between P'etion Alexander Sab'es, and Henri Christophe, who was born a slave in the island of Saint Kitts. Christophe served under the leadership of Toussaint during the slave revolt against their French slave masters, and he also helped Jean Jacques Dessalines to drive the French out of their part of the island of Haiti. According to the History of the West Indian People, after the death of Jean Jacques in 1806, a civil war broke out between Henri Christophe and P'etion Alexandre Sab'es for the control of the ruler ship of the island of Haiti. According to volume 9 of the Encyclopaedia, Alexandre Sab'es was born April 2, 1770, in Port-au Prince Haiti, and he died in March 29, of 1818. Sab'es was the son of a wealthy French colonist, who served in the French Colonial Army before the French Revolution of France, and he later joined up with the slaved freedom fighter's army of Toussaint. While he was in the army of Toussaint, he left and joined up with a mulatto general by the name of Andr'e Rigaud, who set up a mulatto state, in the southern part of the Island of Haiti for him and his fellow mulatto people like himself. P'etion returned to Haiti in 1802, with the French army that was sent out by Napoleon Bonaparte to take back Haiti from Toussaint and his freedom fighters. History of the West Indian People explained that Henri Christophe and P'etion had a civil war that cost the French part of the island of Haiti to be divided into two separate governments. Christophe ruling over the northern part of the island, and P'etion ruling over the southern part of the island. Christophe had many qualities like that of Toussaint, who encouraged his citizens living under his ruler ship to work hard to build up their standard of living of the northern part of the island. Eventually, the northern part of the island under the ruler ship of Christophe became very prosperous, and he also built schools and established a printing press in 1811. After a while of his ruler ship, he made himself king of the northern path of the island of Haiti he was ruling over. He also built himself a beautiful palace, with beautiful furniture, and he had water flowing from the mountain to pass under his marble floor, so as to cool off the tempter of his living quarters. He also had the fear in his mind that Napoleon might plan another invasion to take back the island, so for this reason, he built for himself a great big and strong wall of defense to protect his place from any invasion from the French. History of the West Indian People explained that the place of La Ferriere stood on a mountain peak that was about 3,000 feet high in the heart of the northern bush of Haiti. This wall of defense that Christophe had built was 130 feet high, and 30 feet thick, and inside the wall area he had 365 cannon guns. History of the West Indian People, explain that the revolts Christophe was mindful of, began to take shape, when many of his citizens who was under his ruler ship revolted against his government.

He sent out soldiers to restore order, but instead, many of the solders of his army, went to join forces with the rebels, who were fighting against his ruler ship. When he saw that his power was slipping away, rather than he fall into the hands of his enemies, he decided to take his own life. According to History of the West Indian People, he gave the part of Haiti he was ruling over, prosperity and peace, and in the eyes of the Gentile European people of Haiti, he was a great man, who started life as a slave, and ended up as a king ruling over the northern part of Haiti. The eastern part of the island of Haiti that became known as Santo Domingo, was a separate republic that did remains that way under Spanish ruler ship, except for four years later in 1861 to 1862, when the Spanish Government try to take back Santo Domingo as their possession. But they were forced to withdraw from Santo Domingo, and eventually Santo Domingo became known as Dominican Republic of today. According to volume 9 of the Encyclopaedia Britannica, P'etion Alexandre Sab'es was elected president of the southern part of Haiti for life in 1816, and he divided large plantations into small lots, and gave one portion to each his soldiers of his army. These lots that were given to each of his soldiers was free from the burden of producing too much, and many of his men and their families, only produced enough for their own needs. The Encyclopaedia explained that because of the restriction actions taken by Sab'es, to produce what his men needed, for their family, it led to a slowdown in the economy, and a rapid increase of the price of things in his part of the island he was ruling over. His government was in continual conflict of struggles with what was left of the government of Henry Christophe of the north part of the island of Haiti, and also with other generals of his own community that was under his ruler ship.

Creole dialect that became the main communication of many Hamite's people of Haiti, as their own language. But many these Hamite's people of Haiti who speak Creole as their language, have no knowledge from where this dialect came from, that many of them embrace as their own language. According to volume 3 of the Encyclopaedia, there it explained that the word Creole came from the Spanish word Criollo, and also from the French word creole. This word was used in the 16th and 18th century, to describe various so-call White people, who were born in Spanish America, to that of Spanish parents, so as to distinguished them different from other Spanish people who were born in Spain of Europe. The Encyclopaedia went on to explained that the term Creole has since been used with various meanings, often conflicting by different region of the Gentile European colonial world of different places. According to the Encyclopaedia in Spanish colonial America, Creoles Spanish people were generally excluded from high office position, in both church and state. Although legally Spanish Creoles people are from the same people of Spain, who became conquerors of their New World, from the various natives. There were also some discrimination that came from the Spanish crown of Spain, that gave favored position to Spanish subjects, who hold honorable colonial position, in their various colonies of their New World of the Americas and the West Indies. As time went on many of the Hamite's slaves of Haiti adopted to this dialect that they speak as the Creoles language, that is 90 percent French, mix-up with many Spanish words.

Also, various roots words that were taken from their mother tong, from the part of the land of Ham they were taken from. This Creole dialect, or language is to many Hamite's people of the French part of the island of Haiti, but many of them do not know where the root of this language, or dialect came from.

Chapter 66 - The Pirates in The Island That Became Known As The Bahamas.

According to History of the West Indian People Book II, the Islands that became known as the Bahamas, was the first sets of islands Columbus saw when he crossed the Atlantic Ocean, to come to the so-call New World of the Gentile people Europe, of their captured lands of 1492. According to History of the West Indian People, Columbus call the islands of the Bahamas as the Lucayos, but History of the West Indian People explained that the Islands that became known as the Bahamas was inhabited by the peaceful Arawak's people. Also, that the name Bahamas was not known of, until thirty years later, when the name Bahamas came into ingestion, and its origin is unknown. History of the West Indian People also explain that many of the names of the Bahamas came from the early 16 century from the Spanish conquest. From what I have gathered from reading various volume of the Encyclopaedia Britannica, when the British came to take away the various Islands of the Bahamas from the power of the Spanish, the islands was uninhabited by the native Arawak's people. So, what the Encyclopaedia is explaining, is that the Spanish enslaved the Arawak's people of the islands that became known as the Bahamas to death. Also many of these people who did not enslave to death, were just slater off the island by the Spanish. From what I have read from the book, the first island Columbus landed on, the Arawak's people call the island as Guanahani, but Columbus later name the island as San Salvador. But during the 1800, this island became known as Walling's Island, and this Walling's island take it name from famous pirate, who had settle there, who made his men to keep the Sabbath Day Holy, and he himself did like wise.

According to History of The West Indian People in October of 1629, King Charles I of Britain gave Sir Robert Heath various territories of the Americas, which did included the islands of the Bahamas as well. Although Sir Robert Heath himself never visited any of the island of the Bahamas, but a British settlement was made on the Bahamas, in an area that was known as New Providence in 1629. Also another British settlement where made on the island of the Bahamas, who had left from the island of Bermuda, and went and established a settlement on the Bahamas, in an area that was known as Eleuthera, in 1647. I came to the understanding that this place of what was name as Eleuthera is near the Florida course, of what became known as the United States of America. From what I have read, the Spanish usually attack the islands of the Bahamas to drive off these British settlers from their islands. Although they themselves did not take any interest in settle down on any of the islands of the Bahamas, but they did not like the idea of any other European colonials settling on any of their conquered islands of the Bahamas. So, in 1633, the French Government granted certain islands of the Bahamas to a French aristocrat, but no French colonies was established there in the Bahamas at that time. According to the Encyclopaedia, the word Bahamas may have come from, when the Arawak's people were living there on the islands. According to History of the West Indian People, the Spanish did not find any gold in the Bahamas, so they did not take any interest to settle on any of the various islands of the Bahamas. Apart from taking the Arawak's people as slaves to work in their various mines, and plantations of Cuba. Also in other islands of the West Indies, and what became known as the Americas. In 1670 King Charles II of Britain put a landowners of the colony of the Carolina of the United State in charge of the islands of the Bahamas, and this British ruler was of a town of the area that the British name as Albermarle, in what became known as the Carolinas of what is now known as the United States. This ruler of Albermarle did not do a good job in taking care of the islands of the Bahamas, and because of that, the islands of the Bahamas became a breading ground for pirates, of the British, French and the Dutch. One of the most famous of these pirates was a Welshman by the name of Edward Teach, and he also was known as Blackbeard, because of his long black beard he plaited and tied with a ribbons, and put behind his ears. Blackbeard dressing was always dressed in a purple velvet coat, and he carries two pistols, and two long daggers with him all the times. According to History of the West Indian people, Blackbeard headquarters was located on the island of New Providence of the Bahamas, near to what became known as Nassau, and Blackbeard was killed in a hand to hand fight in 1717.

According to History of the West Indian People, in the next year, King George I of Britain sent out Woodes Rogers to restore law and order in the Bahamas, and this action of Woodes Rogers put an end to the pirates ring of the Bahamas, in which he was quite successful in doing so. After Woods Rogers put an end to the pirates of the Bahamas, he established a council of twelve men as judges, and this was with other officials of the islands of the Bahamas to oversee law and order. Which 200 of these council men were former pirates, who had surrendered themselves to be under the Government of King George I of Britain. Due to Woodes Rogers action, in putting an end to the sea robbers action of the Bahamas, the last strong hold of the pirates of the American course came to it end. Volume 1 of the Encyclopaedia explained that Woodes Rogers who was able to put an end to the pirates ring of the Bahamas, did so at his own expense without any monetary, and military support from Britain. The Spanish take away the Island of the Bahamas from the Arawak's in 1684, and they tried to take back the islands of the Bahamas from the British settlers in 1719- 1720, but the Spanish were unsuccessful in doing so. They the Spanish did also try to capture Nassau from the settlers, which is the capital of the Bahamas, but they were unsuccessful in doing so. There was a rumors in 1741 that the Spanish was planning an attack on the island of the Bahamas. So, the House of the Assembly of Nassau order a new fort to be built, to resist any attack from the Spanish, but the Spanish did not made the attack on Fort Montague at the time of their planning. But in 1776 at the beginning of the American War of Independence from Britain, the Spanish joined themselves with other various European settlers to fight against the British, of what became known as the United States of America. This was to attack Fort Montagu of the Bahamas, but they were only able to carry off some of the cannons guns, and other things from the Bahamas, without causing too much a problem to the everyday life of the Bahamas. In 1782, the Spanish who were helping various European settlers of what became known as the United States, to fight against the British, were able to capture the island of the Bahamas from the British settlers who were there. But after the Spanish captured the island of the Bahamas from the British, settlers, a treaty was drawn up between the British and the Spanish.

But before the news of the signing of the treaty could reach across the Atlantic, the Spanish was driven out of New Providence of the Bahamas, and this was done by Colonel Deveaux, who had less than 250 men in his army. So, Corneal Deveaux was able to push out the Spanish from New Providence of the Bahamas, by using different strategies, and diplomacy, to fool the Spanish in thinking he had a large army of men, when he only had two hundred and fifty men in his army. The Spanish Governor was shipped off back to Spain, and what was left of his army, was sent back to the island of Cuba. Due to the lock of support from Britain, the islands of the Bahamas remained poor and was open to Spanish attack, and after this citation, that was the last of the Spanish trying to take back the island of the Bahamas from the British settlers of the Bahamas, who had settled there. This is the end of the history of the Islands of the Bahamas that was taken from History of the West Indian People, and also from volume 1 of the Encyclopaedia Britannica.

Chapter 67 - The British And The French Pirates Who Became Known As The Buccaneers Of 1635-1688

The French and British pirates who became known as the Buccaneers who were formed during the 1600, in what became known as the West Indies. where they had their headquarters for robbing and stealing at high seas, of their pirates ring. According to History of the West Indian People, during the early days of the pirates Buccaneers, who were a band of British and French pirates, who had settled on the island History of the West Indian People called as Tortuga. This island of Tortuga according to a map showing in History of the West Indian People, was not too far away from the island Columbus named as Hispaniola, which is the island of Haiti, and what became known as Dominican Republic. This information about island of Tortuga is from a map of the Encyclopaedia Britannica, showing the island of Tortuga, that became known as the Cayman Island. The Cayman Island is also located near the island of Cuba. According to History of the West Indian People, the Arawak's were the true natives of the Cayman Island, who taught the French and British pirates who had settled on their island how to cure meat. By cutting the meat in pieces and smoking it on dry frame of green wood and slow fire, that the Arawak people named as boucan. So, this is how the pirates of the Cayman Island got their name as the Buccaneers, because of this craft of the Arawak's people curing meat they had called as the boucan. According to History of the West Indian People many wild cattle's and wild pigs were on the Cayman Island that did belong to the Spanish who had brought these animals there.

The Spanish try their very best to get rid of the pirates Buccaneers who were station on the Cayman Island, by killing many of the wild cattle's and pigs that were there on the Island, that was a part of the Buccaneer business of making money. In 1635, the Spanish attacked the Cayman Island killing as many Buccaneers as possible they could find on the island. According to History of the West Indian People, a new Buccaneer leader by the name of Willis returned to the Cayman Island, and made a promise to have a continual fight with their enemy the Spanish. The French Government also take the action of chasing away many of the Buccaneers from the Cayman Island.

But some of the Buccaneers who was under the leadership of Willis went and settled in what became known as Central America, speaking of what is now known as British Honduras. While the Buccaneers were in British Honduras, they became allies to the governor of the island of Jamaica, against the Spanish, and they were also allies to the French colony of Haiti against the Spanish. One of the most outstanding of these Buccaneers pirate was known as Henry Morgan, who was the son of a Welsh farmer, and his uncle was lieutenant Governor of the island of Jamaica at the time of Morgan. History of the West Indian People explain that when Morgan was a young man he became a seaman, and later he sailed with Admiral Penn and general Venables, these two British men who was responsible for the capturing of the island that became known as Jamaica, from the Spanish in 1655. Morgan also became the captain of these disperses Buccaneers. In 1668, the Governor of Jamaica was informed that the Spanish were planning to attack Jamaica, so the Governor sent out Morgan to Cuba to find out if the report he heard was of a true report, or just a false rumor. Morgan sailed from Jamaica with ten ships, and five hundred men, and he sailed toward the island of Cuba. But when he went to Cuba, he found out that Havana which is the capital, was too strong for him to attack. So, he take his men to Porto Principle, which is a town of Cuba. Morgan and his men robbed the town and carried off 500 cows the Spanish settlers paid him as a ransom for peace to leave them alone. Morgan returns to his ships, and notifies the Governor of Jamaica of what he had learn pertaining to the Spanish plan to attack the Island of Jamaica.

Morgan told his Buccaneer pirates he was going to attack what was known as Porto Bello, which was one of the strongest Spanish settlements at the time. According to a map in History of the West Indian People, showing the area that was known as Porto Bello of that time. This place is now known as Panama, Guatemala, and Belize, that is near the land area that is known today as Mexico. This information I came to, is by compare this map of History of the West Indian people with that of the world map of today. Morgan sailed to the mainland that became known as South America, leaving his men some distance downstream, while he takes twenty-three canoes loaded with his men, to make the attack on the Spanish settlement of Porto Bello. While Morgan and his men were on their way going toward Porto Bello; they met up with an escaped prisoner who became their guide to lead them to the attack on Porto Bello.

Morgan and his men overpowered the Spanish guard before he could give any alarm to the rest of his Spanish settlers, and he seized three districts of the area leading to the city. The second settlement was more difficult more than the first attack, so Morgan and his men was able to take the second settlement when he and his men climb over a ladder, and the governor who was defending the city was killed. While Morgan and his men captured the third town, the Governor of Panama came out with 300 men. But the Buccaneers was able to defeat the Governor of Panama, and his men and forced the settlers to pay him a ransom of 100,000 Spanish coins in 1668, that is known as pieces. The action of Morgan causes much alarm in Europe, and Britain and Spain sign a peace treaty of friendship, with each other, that did applied to all their subjects, and colonies of their New World. But before the news of the peace treaty could reached the Americas and the West Indies, Morgan went and attacked a city of Venezuela that was called Maracaibo. After the Buccaneers rob the city, the Buccaneers came to realize that the Spanish repair the fort, and had their cannon guns ready to prevent them from escaping. The Spanish general with three ships was waiting for Morgan and his men to try to escape, but Morgan turns a small ship into a fireball that he was able to get long side of the general ship and cause it to sink. Another Spanish ship ran a shore and was set on fire by the ship crew, and the third ship was captured by Morgan and his men.

Morgan and his men was able to escape from the Spanish, and sail back to the island of Jamaica. When he arrived back in the island of Jamaica, he was reproved by the Governor of Jamaica for doing more harm to the Spanish settlers than it was necessary to do. The Spanish were checking around in the of coast of Jamaica, and the Governor of Jamaica became aware of it, and he hurriedly appointed Morgan to be the chief commander of all war ships of Jamaica, and to deal with the Spanish according to his will. In 1671, Morgan with his Buccaneers pirates attacked the city of Panama and set it on fire, so a second peace treaty was signed between Britain and Spain, to establish a more soiled friendship, between the two colonial powers. This treaty of friendship was to prevent the British pirates Buccaneers from attacking the colonies of Spain. The British Government take a drastic step to stop Morgan from attacking the Spanish settlement in the West Indies and in the Americas.

 The British Government also set laws, and made decrees for Morgan and his Buccaneers pirates to followers. This was also, for other British settlers of the West Indies, and the Americas to follow, in keeping the peace with the Spanish of their New World. Morgan was taken prisoner and was sent back to Britain, and while he was jailed in the tower of London, King Charles II of Britain released Morgan from his jail, and sent him back to Jamaica, and gave him the title of Lieutenant Governor of Jamaica. While Morgan held the office as Lieutenant Governor of Jamaica, he tried his very best to take action against the Buccaneers of the West Indies, and that of the Americas that he was a part of. The British Government even take a stronger action to put an end to the pirates of the West Indies, and the Americas, this was by giving Morgan a few small speed boats to patrol the water ways between the island of Hispaniola and Cuba. In 1668, Sir Robert Homes of Britain arrived in the West Indies with a powerful army, also a fleet of ships to further clear the waters of the Americas and the West Indies of any remaining pirates who might have escaped the attention of Morgan, and Morgan died in 1688. The French Government also take the same steps to remove any remaining Buccaneers that might have left in the Cayman Island. The French also take a drastic step in the French part of the island of Hispaniola, they did name as Saint Domingue, to remove any remaining pirates that was left there. Before the Buccaneers were driven out from the Cayman Island, and the island of Haiti, they made themselves masters of these islands of the West Indies. According to History of the West Indian People, many of the Buccaneers pirates move away to the South Seas, and they prey upon the East Indian shipping company of the Madagascar area, by robbing them quite often. The island of Madagascar that is mentioned, is in the area of the world that the Gentile people of Europe named as Africa. Other Buccaneers went and joined with the logwood cutters, and set up a small settlement along the rivers of Central America. The Buccaneers of Central America were called Bay men by the Spanish settlers of the area, who had many fights with the Buccaneers, because they often attack the Spanish camps on a regular scale. In 1798, the Spanish was defeated by the British, and the Bay men, or the Buccaneers of Central America were left alone. The Spanish settlement of Honduras later became known as British Honduras, after the British defeated the Spanish. There were low class pirates who used to lurked around the area of the world that became known as the Bahamas for another fifty years.

Chapter 68 - The British and Their Pirates Seeking To Steal Colony In The New World Of The Spanish, Of Their Conquest

One of the early colony seekers for his country of Britain, was known as Sir Walter Raleigh, who was seeking to steal colonies in the New World of the Spanish and the Portuguese that became known as the West Indies, and the Americas. Sir Walter Raleigh was born in 1554, and he was also known as Hayes Barton. He was born in Salterton Devon of Britain, and died October 29, 1618. According to volume 9 of the Encyclopaedia, Raleigh who were a writer, and a favorite of Queen Elizabeth I of Britain, who gave him the title of a Knight in 1585, because of his good service in Ireland fighting against the Irish. He was rewarded by the queen and was given a large estate in the city of Munster in Britain. Queen Elizabeth also gave Raleigh the opportunity to lease a part of Durham House that was in Strand of London. After the various opportunities that were given to him by Queen Elizabeth, he later became the captain of the Queen's guards. Volume 9 of the Encyclopaedia went on to explained that Raleigh wanted to settle down and have a family, so he takes Queen Elizabeth daughter to be his wife. This daughter of the Queen Elizabeth, was for a man by the name of Sir Nicholas Throckmorton who was born in 1588. The Encyclopaedia explained that Raleigh marriage to the queen daughter had to be kept as a secret, because of the jealousy of Queen Elizabeth. From the reading of the Encyclopaedia, it seems to me that Sir Walter Raleigh was having a sexual relationship with Queen Elizabeth I of Britain, before he decided to get married to the queen daughter.

So, the birth of his first son in 1592, cause the secret of his marriage to come to light, and because of the jealously of the queen, Raleigh and his wife was put in prison in the Tower of London. According to this same volume 9 of the Encyclopaedia, Raleigh who had invested in the privateer business of the pirates, was able to buy his release from prison of the Tower of London, with the profits he had received from his investment, but he had lost his position and prestige at the queen's court. The first son of Raleigh by his wife did not live, but he had two more sons by his wife, and the name of his second son was known as Walter, and the third was known as Carew.

Volume 9 of the Encyclopaedia explained that in the year of 1584-1589, Raleigh tried to establish a British colony in the New World of what is now known as the Americas. He sent Philip Amada and Arthur Barlowe to find a location to set up this colony. This colony was set up near the Roanoke Island that is presently known as North Carolina, which Raleigh named as Virginia. According to History of the West Indian People Book II, this colony Raleigh had set up, and called as Virginia, this colony was a total failure, because the settlers, or colonists as they were called in those days, were slain by the natives, who the Gentile people of Europe called as Red Indians. Later during the reign of King James, I of Britain, another attempt was made to establish the colony of Virginia. But after many mistakes, and much hardship, the colony of Virginia began to prosper as a British colony. According to volume 9 of the Encyclopaedia, although Raleigh named the colony Virginia, he never went to the colony of Virginia. So, in 1595 Raleigh led an expedition to Guyana in what became known as South America, to set up another colony for his native country of Britain. Raleigh and his men sailed up the Orinoco River, along the mainstream of the Spanish Empire of their New World. The Encyclopaedia explained that Raleigh described his expedition in his book that was called the Discovery of the country of Guyana in 1595-1617. This information came from Spanish documents, and stories that they the Spanish had gathered from the natives, and Raleigh became knowledge of this golden city of El Dorado. History of the West Indian People explained that this city of El Dorado was a legendary city of the Inca people, that was in the land of Guiana, that became known as the Guyana, by the conquest of these Gentile people of what became known as Europeans. History of the West Indian People explained that the name Guiana came from the Arawak's people, that meant to them, land watery, or land of water.

The land area of Guiana was divided up among the various Genital colonial powers of Europe, and became known as Dutch Guyana, which is now known as Surinam. French Guyana, British Guyana, Peru, Ecuador, Colombia, Venezuela, Brazil, Bolivia, Paraguay, and Argentina. These names that was mentioned are colonial names that were given to the land area of Guiana, from where it was said, about the city of El Dorado, that was in the land area of Guiana, that had roof and walls of gold, and precious stones.

History of the West Indian people explained that Dutch Guyana was also known as Demerara, which had changed hands of ownership several times during the Napoleonic wars of 1793-1801, and also in 1803, and in 1815 the Dutch were defeated by France, and they the Dutch was made a vassal of France. According to the Webster Collegiate Dictionary of the Fifth Edition, the word vassals came from Old French, Middle Latin, and Late Latin, which is another word for a slave, a servant, or a bondman. So, in other words the Dutch kingdom of Holland was made a slave for France, or they at one time was controlled by France, during Napoleonic wars of Europe. History of the West Indian people explained that the British made several attempts to establish a colony in Guyana, but without success. It was not until after the treaty with Paris in 1884, that the British colony of Guyana came into existence. Volume 9 of the Encyclopaedia explained that in 1595, Raleigh went with Robert Devereux, who was known as Earl of Essex, to on an unsuccessful expedition to the city of Cadiz, and to the city of Azores, to steal these cities from the Spanish. The Encyclopedia explained that Raleigh's aggressive polices against various Spanish colonies of the New World did not gave him a very good standing with King James the six of Scotland, who later became known as King James I of Britain. Volume 9 of the Encyclopaedia explained that the enemies of Raleigh worked to bring about his ruin, in 1603.

Raleigh and others of his associates was accused of plotting to overthrow King James I of Britain, and Raleigh was convicted on written evidence of Henry Brook, and Lord Chobham, and after a last-minute reprieve from the death sentence, he was put in prison in the Tower of London. In 1616, he was release from prison, but he was not pardoned by the king. In the mind of Raleigh, he was still hoping to top the wealth of Guyana, by explaining to the king's men of authority, that the country of Guyana was in fact a British colony, and he wanted to turn it over to Britain, with the native chief of the country of Guyana, which he had it in his intention to do so, in 1595. So, with the king's permission Raleigh was able to finance, and lead a second expedition to Guyana, promising to open a gold mine there without offending the Spanish settlers of the various colonies of the area.

While Raleigh was in the land of Guyana, he became sick with a fever, and did not take his men to the location in Guyana that he had in mind. Volume 9 explained that one of Raleigh's lieutenants by the name of Lawrence Kenny's burned a Spanish settlement in Guyana and did not find any gold. Also, one of Raleigh son who was known as Walter, was also killed in the attack on the Spanish settlement. King James cancelled Raleigh's suspended death sentence of 1603, and when Raleigh went back to Britain, he was put in prison in 1618, and after he had written many letters in his defense to the king of his action, and his innocent, he was finally put to death. This is the end of the history of Raleigh and Guyana, that was taken from volume 9 of the Encyclopaedia. Also from History of the West Indian People, about Raleigh, trying to steal colonies from the Spanish.

According to volume 10 of the Encyclopaedia, the island Columbus named as Saint Christopher became known as Saint Kitts, by Thomas Warner, and his associates. Who was Another British colony seeker for his country of Britain. Who came after Sir Walter Raleigh, and Thomas Warner, was born in Suffolk of Britain. Warner like Sir Walter Raleigh, who also wanted to get on the bandwagon of greed, and the scheme to colonizing people and their lands, so as to get the riches from the land, and to get rich quickly, from the blood, sweats tears, and lives of their many victims. This was by robbing, stealing, and enslaving many of their conquered people to become rich from slave labor. According to History of the West Indian People Book II, Warner who was among the bodyguards of King James I of Britain, who wanted to venture out in the New World of the Spanish and the Portuguese, to set up a British colony in Guyana. But the colony that Warner tried to set up in Guyana, was a total failure. One of the members of Warner party, who was known as Thomas Painter, who was an experience seaman, told Warner it would be a much wiser decision for him to try to set up a colony on one of the West Indian islands. Rather than on the mainland that became known as South America, and the North America course. Speaking of what is now known as Canada and the United States as North America, that take it's name from Americus Vespucci, who came from what is now known as Italy.

History of the West Indian People went on to explained that while Warner was on his way back to Britain from the country of Guyana, he visited some of the islands of the West Indies, and he decided that the island that Columbus named Saint Christopher was the most suitable island to set up a British colony. When Warner reached Britain in 1623, he sought to get help at once for his plan to set up the colony on the Island of Saint Christopher. Merrifield who was a British merchant agree to buy a suitable size ship, and load it with foods, also with tools and other necessary things to make life easy for the colonist. Captain Jefferson was willing to sail the ship across the Atlantic Ocean, told Warner he should gather some more British colonists from the British colony of Virginia, and take them to the Island of Saint Kitts, to help to establish the island as a British colony.

History of the West Indian People explained that when the news reach Britain that the colonists arrived safely on the Island of Saint Kitts, Jefferson sailed from Britain to join up with the rest of the British colonists, who was already there on the Island of Saint Kitts. According to History of the West Indian People, the British colonist arrived on Saint Kitts in 1624, and they were kindly received by the native Caribs people who were living there on the island. When the British colonist, or settlers arrived on the Island of Saint Kitts, they started to build huts at once, and also clear the land to plant corn for food that they did received from the natives Caribs people. They also planted tobacco to export to Europe, to make big money from the selling of tobacco, that they had learn from the Arawak's and the Caribs people. I must point out that these British settlers who went to their New World of the West Indies, did not know anything about the growing of corn for food, that they had gotten the knowledge of growing corn for food from the Caribs, and the Arawak's people. History of the West Indian People explained that the European settlers, and their pirates who went to the New World got the knowledge of smoking tobacco from the Arawak's of people. According to History of the West Indian People, Sir Walter Raleigh, where the city of Rally North Carolina got it's name from, was one of the early European people to make the smoking of tobacco that became known as cigarette, and cigar fashionable in Europe. The various Hamite's slaves the Gentile European people brought over from the land of Ham, followed them in the habit of smoking cigarette, they had learned from their Gentile European slave masters, who had made the habit of smoking of tobacco fashionable to make big money.

According to History of the West Indian People, the first crops of corn, and tobacco for Warner and his British colonists, or settlers on the Island of Saint Kitts, was destroyed by a hurricane, along with their various huts. Warner and the other colonists got together and repaired their damage huts that were damage by the hurricane. Jefferson arrived from Britain to the Island of Saint Kitts in 1625, and the first crop of tobacco was ready to ship to Britain. Thomas Warner wanted more British colonist to join him on the Island of saint Kitts, to grow more crops. He also wanted more wealthy British merchants to take part in his venture of the Island of Saint Kitts, and he also wanted more protection from the king of Britain, for his British colonists who had settled on the Island of Saint Kitts.

History of the West Indian People explained that Warner went to Britain to seek help, from the British Government, but when he arrived in Britain, King James I had died, and his son Charles I was made king after death of his father. Charles welcomes Warner at his place, and made him Governor of the Island of Saint Kitts. While Warner was in Britain there was no difficulty for him getting young British farmers from the eastern part of Britain to migrate to the British colony of Saint Kitts. When Warner and his new recruits return to the Island of Saint Kitts, along with some Frenchmen who also came to the Island of Saint Kitts. These French men sailed from France, hoping to establish a French colony somewhere in the West Indies, but their ships were attacked by Spanish war ships, and many of their ships were badly damaged. Also, some of their men were killed, and some were wounded by the Spanish attack. The British settlers and the native Caribs of the Island of Saint Kitts felt very sorry for these Frenchmen, so they let them settle down on the Island of Saint Kitts, to form a little French community. History of the West Indian People explained that so for the native Caribs had been very friendly, and cooperative with their Gentile European invaders of their island. But the Caribs people were watching the number of European settlers growing, and getting larger and larger on their island and they became nervous about it. Moreover, the Crib priest told his people that these European invaders were their enemies, and in time to come they would drive them away from their island. History of the West Indian People explained that all the Caribs on the island of Saint Kitts got together with other Caribs from other islands. The planned was to have a surprise attack that was to take place by night, on the Island of Saint Kitts, against their Gentile European invaders of their island.

This plan of the Caribs was that all the Caribs from other Caribbean islands nearby, was to arrive in their canoes boats, and all the Gentile European invaders on the Island of Saint Kitts were to be killed. According to History of the West Indian People, there was a Caribs lady who was very friendly with many of the Gentile European settlers on the Island of Saint Kitts. So, she went and told the plan of the Caribs to the European settlers. On the night of the attack, when the Caribs men thought everything was going well for them, according to their plan. They came rushing over for a decisive victory, but they were driven back, leaving behind many of their fellow Caribs men killed in action. Many of the Gentile European settlers of the Island of Saint Kitts, who were struck by the poison arrows, used by the Caribs during the attack, died from their wounds.

Warner with their French settlers decided they should increase the number of European present on the Island of Saint Kitts, so Warner went back to Britain and brought back another four hundred new British settlers to the Island of Saint Kitts. The French settlers also went back to France and brought two hundred more new French settlers to the Island of Saint Kitts. This was to increase the number of British and French present on the Island of Saint Kitts. History of the west Indian People explained that in 1629, Warner went back to Britain and was given the title of a Knight by King Charles I. According to the Oxford Dictionary, a man who was given the title of a Knight, was a young man who take up arms for his country, and for this reason, the title of Sir was added to their names. Such was the case of Sir Walter Raleigh, Sir Thomas Warner, and Sir Henry Morgan, because they went out to steal and kill people to get their lands. Or whatsoever they could steal to set up as colonies for their home land of Britain. When Warner return to the Island of Saint Kitts, he found out that Saint Kitts was attack and destroyed by the Spanish. History of the West Indian People explained that the Spanish did not want to make any settlement on the various small islands of the West Indies. But they did not want any other European colonist to have control over their islands. On this attack by the Spanish, they were able to take away 600 British settlers as captive, and some of these British settlers were able to escape in their ships, and others fled to the mountain. Warner encouraged many of his British settlers who had fled to the mountain to return, and rebuild their damage homes and to plant new crops. While Warner was in Britain, he came to realize that the tobacco market was no longer a hot selling item as before, so he encourages his settlers to plant more sugar cane, as well as tobacco crops. According to History of the West Indian People, sugar was selling for a good price in Europe, and eventually Saint Kitts became the riches West Indian island for the British.

The riches of Saint Kitts came from the blood, sweats, and tears and lives of their many Hamite's captives who were brought over from the land of Ham, to the Island of Saint Kitts, to work on their tobacco and sugarcane plantations. History of the West Indian People explained that the next disaster to strike the island of Saint Kitts, came two years later, when the island was hit by a hurricane that destroyed houses, plantations and ships that were in the harbor. Some of these ships that were destroyed by the hurricane, was fully loaded with tobacco to ship to Europe.

So, because of the damages to these ships, cause the water to be poisoned by the tobacco that fell in the water, and many fish died from the poisoned tobacco water. Due to the encouragement from Warner to his British colonists, or settlers of Saint Kitts, the colony survived and became a very rich colony. The Island of Saint Kitts became fully under British controlled in 1713. History of the West Indian People explained that Warner died in 1649, but his sons and many of his descendants take over from where he left off and carry on the ruler ship of the island. The British eventually drove off the French, and they the French went and established the island colonies of Martinique and Guadeloupe as their own colonies of position, and enslave and drove off many of the native from their Yahweh given land. They the natives did not even have any rights to walk on their own lands, and were treated like insignificant creatures they the Gentile people had detested, and wanted to get rid of. According to volume 10 of the Encyclopaedia, slavery was abolished on the Island of Saint Kitts in 1838. But many of the Hamite's people of Saint Kitts had very little opportunity to better themselves, and many of them rely on the sugar plantation owners for their well bean.

Many of whom are descendants of their x slavers masters who own most of the lands of Saint Kitts for employment and for somewhere to live. In my opinion it is just like going to the Devil begging him for help, and the only help one will received from the Devil is pressure, punishment and misery. According to this same volume 10 of the Encyclopaedia, the British setters on the island of Saint Kitts, and the French had a rivalry that did developed between them that lasted for more than 100 years. After the British victory over the French, concerning the Island of Saint Kitts, the Island of saint Kitts became a sole British colony in 1783. Also, the island that became known as Nevis was taken over by the British that the French people had tried to control. This is the end of the history and story about the Island of Saint Kitts, that were taken from History of the West Indian People, and from the Encyclopadia Britannia.

Chapter 70 - After The Rivalries

After the rivalries of wars between the Dutch, French and the British fighting against the Spanish to take away some of their colonial territories of their New World for themselves. The Britain and the French established some kind of peace treaty with that of the Spanish in their New World of conquest. This was to keep the peace with the various warring factors, and to share a piece of their pie of the New World of conquest with the British and the French. The French decided to take over control of what was named as Acadia in what is now known as Canada in 1604, and they also established what became known as Quebec in 1608, and the land was shared between the British and the French as the ruling powers. Volume 12 of the Encyclopaedia explained that the British captured what they name as Virginia, in 1607, which was their first American colony, and they also established a settlement there that became known as Jamestown in 1607, and they began to plant tobacco in 1612-1619, as a part of their trade of business. According to this same volume 12 of the Encyclopaedia, by the time of 1831, the agriculture farming business of Virginia started to decline, and it became an established place for slave breeding, as a part of their business. Later, some of these British colonists established Cape Cod, and they later established the city of Plymouth in 1622. They the British colonists went on to captured Barbados in 1624, and the island of Nevis in 1628, and Massachusetts Bay in 1629, and Antigua, Montserrat and Maryland in 1632. New York was first called as New Amsterdam by the Dutch settlers of Holland, who had this part of the land as their colony, until the British take away the land area from the Dutch, and named it as New York. These British settlers also take over a part of the land area from the Spanish and the Dutch, and the French. Later the British settlement was shared with other various European people, who left from Europe to come and share the British conquest of what became known as North America. Many people of today have no knowledge of the history of how these countries and islands came about that many of us embrace and called as our homeland.

The European Ku Klux Klan police force system of today how did it come about? The European police force system of today as we know it as, came down from the army that was established during the early colonial days. This was to serve as a protection for the settlers, or the colonists as they were call in those days, from their many conquered captive people. During those days, it was the pirates of the Dutch, French and the British who were the criminal, fighting, robbing and killing the Spanish to get some of their various territories of their so-call New World. They the Spanish had taken away from the various natives, because of Columbus, and later by Americus Vespucci, who was also working for Spanish interest. This police force system came down from the pirates when the British sent out Wood Rogers to the Bahamas to get rid of the pirates from the Bahamas, and to establish law and order among the various British settlers, who were there in the Bahamas. Also, this police force system came about when the British gave Henry Morgan Lieutenant Governor over the island of Jamaica, to remove and clean up the Buccaneers pirates from the West Indies and the Americas, that he was a part of. Also, this police force system came about in 1668, when the British sent out Sir Robert Homes with a powerful army, and a fleet of war ships to further clear the water ways of the Americas and the West Indies of any remaining Buccaneers pirates who might had escaped the attention of Morgan. This police force system later came down to the Cow Boys days of the 1800, that became known as the Sheriff Marshal, of what became known as the United States of America. This Sheriff Marshal police force system was also established as a protection for the settlers, or the colonists against many of their captive people. Also, as a protection for other European settlers, who used to rob, steal and kill many of their own European people, to get what they had, so as to become rich people from what other European people had. In those days of the While West of the 1800, in order for a European person to keep their wealth, money and their lives, they had to haired many fast gun slingers to stay around them, as a protection to keep what they had.

These European crooks were known before as the pirates, that later came down to the gangsters of the Rowing Twenties of the United States. Many of these pirates used to hang around the island of the Bahamas, the Cayman Island, and Port Royal of the island that became known as Jamaica, which was a breeding ground for Dutch pirates, French pirates and British pirates.

My reason for going so deep into the pirate story of the Gentile people of Europe, it is to show that before the coming of the Gentile people of Europe to their captured so-call New World from the various natives, there were no crime rate among the various natives. It was the European people who came to their captured New World were the criminals of robbing, stealing and killing each other to get rich. Before the coming of the people of Europe to their New World as they had called it, there were no homeless people living on the Street, eating from out of garbage cans, and sleeping under various bridges as their home. Because they cannot afford to pay the high rent of the European people system to get rich. There was also, no drug addicts, no alcoholic, no winos, and no male prostitute, or any form of prostitution and homosexual people among the various natives, who were in this part of the world, before the coming of the people of Europe. There were also no rent and tax paying people, among the various natives, before the coming of the Gentile people of Europe, who came and set up their system of rent and tax paying people to get rich from their many captives people. Who became their citizens, so as to live under their system for them to get rich from their many conquered people. All the various natives used to live together as a family unity, living off the land as how Yahweh made things to be. The European people came and established their system of corruption, and violence to bring in much revenue in their system, from their many conquered people who later became their citizens of their world. So, the pirates and the gangsters of the European society became the police officers, Judges, probation officers, and prison officers of the European law system, that many of their captive's people fall into, because they have copied the ways and life, style of the people of Europe.

Technically speaking, the police force system of the European people that came down from the Sheriff Marshall of the Cow Boy area, was made for their many captives to fall into. As well as other European people who became criminals against other European people of their system. So, this is the reason why the prison system of the United States is full up with many Hamite's people, who they named as Negroes, Niggers and the Black people. Due to the fact that the prison system was built for their many captives people, and it is also is a big business for the court system to make money, the lawyers, probation officers, police officer, prison officers to be well paid for their services of the European law system.

This is also the case in Australia, New Zealand, South West Africa, and wheresoever the European people went and set up their colonial system, as, their police force system as a protection for the settlers, and many of the native's people became their victims of the European police force system. The funny thing about this story, many Hamite's men and women joined the European Ku Klux Klan police force system, after slavery was abolish by the British, because it is a good paying job, with many fringes benefits that a police officer can benefit from. Many of these Hamite's policers officers used their European police badge as a sign of authority, to brutalize and take advantage of their many Hamite's brothers and sisters of their community. This is to show how good a police officer they are, of the European police force system that was established for the protection of the European settlers. The reason why many of our Hamite's police officers behave this way toward their own struggling and oppress people, it is because they are suffering from slavery and colonial mentality and stupidity. They do not have any knowledge of how the European police force system came about, that take on different names, and different branches as a governmental body around the world. One only has to go to the local police station, or the European court system, to see how many Hamite's police officers, and various Hamite's judges treat their own Hamite's people, who come to their court house. By way of the police officers, without any kindness and respect and dignity, because of their European police badge, and their guns that was given to them, as a sign of authority over their fellow Hamite's people.

This also apply to various Hamite's judges, because of their high position, and their financial wealth of the European law system, and because they are now living the good life of the European colonial system. So, many of these well to do Hamite's people forget where they and their ancestors is coming from, because they are no longer strugglers as how many of us are. It was the same way during the colonial slavery days, certain Hamite men were given the position, as a foreman slave, over their fellow Hamite's people, as a sign of authority to keep their own people in check. The Belgium people of the Congo did the same thing, they would use many Hamite's men as solders to shoot and kill and burn down many of their own people houses. This was just to show their loyalty to the Belgium colonial invaders, who had rulership over there land of the Congo. Many of these foolish and studied Hamite's solders of the Congo were also used by the Belgium colonial rulers, to cut off children, women and men hands and foot to force them to send more rubber product to Belgium, to make King Leo Pole into a rich man of Belgium, and they did it with joy to please their colonial masters. The same is true for the Ishmaelite people of Saudi Arabia, who used foolish stupid Hamite's people, like Boko Aram of Nigeria to shoot, kill and burn down many of their own people homes, so as to send fair in the heart and mind of their own people. This was to set up a Muslim Government in Nigeria, to benefit the Muslim people of Saudi Arabia. They did it with joy because they are a very stupid and foolish people, who have no knowledge of themselves as a people. If one was to go to Australia, New Zealand, Canada, and South West Africa, they would see that the police force system was design and set up for the protection of the settlers of these places. It was not set up for the protection of the various natives of these places. This is the reason why many European settlers of Australia, and South West Africa, United States, and wheresoever can commit all sort of crime, and get away with it, because the law system was design and built for them. The same is true in what became known as South Africa, many Hamite's police officers beat and brutalize many of their own people, all in the name of the European colonial law police force system. While many European settlers of South Africa get away with all sort of crime and wickedness that many Hamite's police officers have no authority and control over.

Due to the fact that these Hamite's police officers were employed by the European settlers of South Africa, who did establish their law system of South Africa to south themselves. So, many of these Hamite's police men of South Africa were employed by these European people who are there, to keep things under their control. So, it is just like the Al Capone days of Chicago, and other gangsters who had their own police men under their control to carry out their laws, and order of their system that they had control over. This is the end of the history, and the stupidity of many Hamite's people of today, who have no knowledge of themselves of who they are, and where they are coming from.